## Praise for *Criminal Procedure, Fifth Edition*

"Criminal procedure is an extremely varied and complicated area within the broader subject of criminal law and is therefore a challenge for any writer to explain. In his fifth edition of *Criminal Procedure*, Steve Coughlan once again has provided a clear, concise, and accurate enunciation of this very complex field. Students and practitioners alike will find this book to be a valuable resource."

Tim Quigley, Professor Emeritus, College of Law, University of Saskatchewan

"Canadian criminal procedure is famously (and some would say: unnecessarily) complex, featuring multiple sources, a complicated jurisdictional landscape and a high volume of jurisprudence and legislative amendments. Prof. Coughlan's 5th edition of Criminal Procedure could not be more welcome, incorporating as it does the significant legislative changes introduced in 2019, and providing an impeccably researched, principled and doctrinally reliable analysis of important case law since the 4th edition. It will help students and practitioners understand the current state of law; more importantly, it will guide the development of this important area of the law for years to come."

Jula Hughes, Professor, Bora Laskin Faculty of Law, Lakehead University and President, Canadian Association for Legal Ethics.

# CRIMINAL PROCEDURE

FIFTH EDITION

Other Books in the *Essentials of Canadian Law* Series

International Trade Law

Administrative Law

The Law of Sentencing

Computer Law 2/e

International Human Rights Law

Franchise Law

Legal Ethics and Professional Responsibility 2/e

Public International Law 2/e

Individual Employment Law 2/e

Canadian Telecommunications Law

Intellectual Property Law 2/e

Animals and the Law

Income Tax Law 2/e

Youth Criminal Justice Law 3/e

Bank and Customer Law in Canada 2/e

The Law of Equitable Remedies 2/e

Remedies: The Law of Damages 3/e

The Law of Trusts 3/e

Ethics and Criminal Law 2/e

Insurance Law 2/e

Immigration Law 2/e

Canadian Maritime Law 2/e

Public Lands and Resources in Canada

Statutory Interpretation 3/e

Constitutional Law 5/e

Land-Use Planning

Refugee Law 2/e

Religious Institutions and the Law 4/e

Environmental Law 5/e

Fundamental Justice 2/e

International and Transnational Criminal Law 3/e

The Law of Torts 6/e

Criminal Procedure 4/e

Mergers, Acquisitions, and Other Changes of Corporate Control 3/e

Securities Law 2/e

Information and Privacy Law in Canada

The Law of Evidence 8/e

The Law of Contracts 3/e

National Security Law 2/e

The Law of Property

Pension Law 3/e

Personal Property Security Law 3/e

Criminal Law 8/e

Securities Law 3/e

The Law of Equitable Remedies 3/e

Search and Seizure

Detention and Arrest 3/e

Freedom of Conscience and Religion 2/e

Conflict of Laws 3/e

Canadian Competition Law and Policy, Updated 1/e

Bankruptcy and Insolvency Law 3/e

Civil Litigation, 2e

The Charter of Rights and Freedoms 8/e

The Law of Partnerships and Corporations 5/e

Cruel and Unusual: Section 12 of the Canadian Charter of Rights and Freedoms

Legal Research and Writing 5/e

ESSENTIALS OF
CANADIAN LAW

# CRIMINAL PROCEDURE

FIFTH EDITION

STEVE COUGHLAN

UNIVERSITY OF TORONTO PRESS
Toronto Buffalo London

Criminal Procedure, Fifth Edition

Irwin Law
An imprint of University of Toronto Press
Toronto Buffalo London
utppublishing.com
Printed and bound by CPI Group (UK) Ltd, Croydon, CR0 4YY

ISBN (paper) 978-1-0498-0162-9    ISBN (EPUB) 978-1-0498-0164-3
ISBN (PDF) 978-1-0498-0163-6

Essentials of Canadian Law



**Library and Archives Canada Cataloguing in Publication**

Title: Criminal procedure / Steve Coughlan.
Names: Coughlan, Stephen Gerard, 1957- author
Series: Essentials of Canadian law.
Description: Fifth edition. | Series statement: Essentials of Canadian law | Includes bibliographical references and index.
Identifiers: Canadiana (print) 20260143421 | Canadiana (ebook) 20260143448 | ISBN 9781049801629 (paper) | ISBN 9781049801636 (PDF) | ISBN 9781049801643 (EPUB)
Subjects: LCSH: Criminal procedure—Canada.
Classification: LCC KE9260 .C69 2026 | LCC KF9620.ZA2 C69 2026 kfmod | DDC 345.71/05—dc23

Cover design: Ashley Bernicky

The manufacturer's authorized representative in the European Union for product safety is Mare Nostrum Group B.V., Doelen 72, 4831 GR Breda, The Netherlands. Email: gpsr@mare-nostrum.co.uk

We welcome comments and suggestions regarding any aspect of our publications – please feel free to contact us at news@utorontopress.com or visit us at utppublishing.com.



We wish to acknowledge the land on which the University of Toronto Press operates. This land is the traditional territory of the Wendat, the Anishnaabeg, the Haudenosaunee, the Métis, and the Mississaugas of the Credit First Nation.

University of Toronto Press acknowledges the financial support of the Government of Canada and the Ontario Arts Council, an agency of the Government of Ontario, for its publishing activities.

ONTARIO ARTS COUNCIL
CONSEIL DES ARTS DE L'ONTARIO
an Ontario government agency
un organisme du gouvernement de l'Ontario

Funded by the Government of Canada    Financé par le gouvernement du Canada

Canada

# SUMMARY TABLE OF CONTENTS

# DETAILED TABLE OF CONTENTS

# FOREWORD

When I was called to the bar in 1979, the subject of criminal procedure was concerned mostly with technical rules about jurisdiction and court processes with some consideration of powers of arrest and search. That changed dramatically in 1982 when the legal rights guaranteed by the *Charter* transformed criminal procedure into the field in which the endless and crucially important tension between individual rights and the powers of the state is assessed and resolved in the courts, day in and day out.

This dramatic evolution of criminal procedure spawned a new genre of criminal procedure scholarship, one that engaged with the fundamental rights at stake at virtually every step in the criminal process.

Professor Coughlan's work is an important contribution to this genre. He masterfully navigates the almost overwhelming accumulation of jurisprudence, making sure that the main themes and key principles are not lost in the morass of details. Lawyers and judges need a guide to keep them focused on the basic structure and animating principles of a fair criminal process. This is precisely what Professor Coughlan has provided.

Short books about complicated subjects are rare because they are so difficult to write. Professor Coughlan has risen to this challenge admirably. While this book is one of basic principles, it addresses the leading cases so as to strike the right balance between concepts and details. There is no better evidence of the value of this work than the fact that it is now in its fifth edition.

Professor Coughlan's work goes from strength to strength. Let us hope there are many more editions to come.

Thomas A. Cromwell
Ottawa, February 11, 2026

# PREFACE

The five years since the publication of the fourth edition of this book have seen significant developments in the law of criminal procedure. In part this has come because of the extensive changes made in 2019 with the enactment of Bill C-75, *An Act to amend the Criminal Code, the Youth Criminal Justice Act and other Acts and to make consequential amendments to other Acts*. That Bill effected large-scale changes across the *Criminal Code* on a scale that had not been seen in many decades, and those changes are now beginning to be felt within the system. Most notable in the wake of that is the Supreme Court's decision in *R v Chouhan*, 2021 SCC 26 upholding the abolition of peremptory challenges but in doing so signalling a new and broader approach to dealing with potential bias in the jury selection process.

Even more dramatic than that have been developments arising from Supreme Court of Canada decisions, including significant decisions around search and seizure, powers of arrest, the right to counsel, jury selection, and other areas. Perhaps no decision is more noteworthy than *R v Carignan*, 2025 SCC 43, the very last case to be decided before this edition was completed, which overturns fifty years of caselaw around the requirements for a lawful arrest. These decisions are pursued in the appropriate chapters. The discussion of caselaw is current to December 2025.

Note as well that what can be regarded as a companion volume to this text is available: *The Anatomy of Criminal Procedure: A Visual Guide to the Law*, 2nd ed (Toronto: University of Toronto Press, 2026). That book, co-authored with Alex Gorlewski, presents much of the same material as this book, but in the form of annotated flowcharts, making it easier to see the various steps involved in applying the rules discussed here. Cross-references to the appropriate charts have been made in the footnotes to this book.

# ACKNOWLEDGEMENTS

In addition to those thanked in previous editions, I would like to add my appreciation to the Schulich School of Law for providing research funding and to Pascale Legault for her excellent research assistance for this volume. In addition, my appreciation goes to Josephine Mo and others at University of Toronto Press, who have taken over the reins for this book, which was formerly published through Irwin Law. In that regard, it seems only appropriate to thank Jeff Miller of Irwin Law, with whom I greatly enjoyed interacting for several decades over various books until his well-earned retirement in 2024.

CHAPTER 1

# INTRODUCTION

In this book, "criminal procedure" refers to the body of rules and principles that govern the investigation, prosecution, and adjudication of any offence enacted by Parliament for which an accused person would have a criminal record if found guilty by a court exercising jurisdiction under the *Criminal Code*.[1] In other words, criminal procedure governs the procedural aspects relating to indictable and summary conviction offences enacted by Parliament pursuant to its legislative authority in matters of criminal law.

This definition of the subject excludes many procedural aspects of penal law. For example, it does not include law that is enacted for

---

1 Unless otherwise indicated, all statutory references in this book are to the *Criminal Code* of Canada, RSC 1985, c C-46 [*Code*]. All references to sections of the *Canadian Charter of Rights and Freedoms*, Part I of the *Constitution Act, 1982*, being Schedule B to the *Canada Act 1982* (UK), 1982, c 11 [*Charter*] will be preceded by "*Charter*." See *Criminal Records Act*, RSC 1985, c C-47, s 3, which refers to a conviction of an offence under an Act of Parliament or a regulation made under an Act of Parliament. The procedure prescribed in the *Code* applies to all indictable offences and all offences punishable on summary conviction that have been enacted by Parliament. Notwithstanding the broad definition of this book's scope, the criminal jurisdiction of the Canadian military is excluded from consideration here, but it should be noted that this includes a distinctive body of procedural and evidentiary law. Also excluded from consideration is criminal procedure as it applies to young persons under the *Youth Criminal Justice Act*, SC 2002, c 1. For discussion of the latter issue, see Nicholas Bala & Sanjeev Anand, *Youth Criminal Justice Law*, 3d ed (Toronto: Irwin Law, 2012).

the enforcement of offences that are created by provincial or territorial legislatures and within their constitutional competence.[2] Nor does criminal procedure govern all offences enacted by Parliament. The *Contraventions Act*[3] was created to provide a non-criminal mechanism for the enforcement of some regulatory offences. Further, there are many penal matters that are largely administrative, such as disciplinary offences within the Canadian Armed Forces or the Royal Canadian Mounted Police, and procedural law for the enforcement of those offences is properly considered part of administrative law.[4] Similarly, although correctional law is related to the administration of criminal justice, its substantive content has more to do with administrative law than with criminal procedure.[5]

Criminal procedure consists of an enormous array of rules and principles in the administration of criminal justice. Many are highly technical and have narrow application. Others, such as "due process," raise fundamental issues of principle and influence virtually all aspects of procedural law. It would be foolhardy to suggest that all of these rules and principles have resulted in a clear and rational system that expresses agreed-upon values.[6] But it would be foolish not to recognize that both the most picayune rules and the grandest principles are important. For instance, what do we mean by "justice"? Hundreds of years of history attempt to offer an answer of one sort, but section 2 of the *Criminal Code* offers an answer of an entirely different kind. Taken together, these fiddly details and these fundamental values express the standard of justice in Canadian criminal procedure.

What, then, is criminal procedure about? Martin Friedland opened his study of double jeopardy with this claim: "The history of the rule against double jeopardy is the history of criminal procedure. No other

2 See, for example, *Provincial Offences Act*, RSO 1990, c P.33; *Code of Penal Procedure*, CQLR c C-25.1. In every province or territory, there is analogous legislation.

3 SC 1992, c 47. Among other features, liability for a contravention does not entail a criminal record: s 63.

4 *National Defence Act*, RSC 1985, c N-5, Part III; *Royal Canadian Mounted Police Act*, RSC 1985, c R-10, Part IV.

5 *Corrections and Conditional Release Act*, SC 1992, c 20.

6 For a sustained critique of the lack of clarity and the complexity in the law, see David Rose, *Quigley's Criminal Procedure in Canada* (Toronto: Thomson Reuters, 2021) (loose-leaf). This point was often made in working papers and reports of the Law Reform Commission of Canada. See, for example, *Our Criminal Procedure* (Ottawa: Law Reform Commission of Canada, 1988), and *Recodifying Criminal Procedure* (Ottawa: Law Reform Commission of Canada, 1991).

doctrine is more fundamental or all-pervasive."[7] The same claim could likely be made, in the same terms, for many other principles of the criminal law, such as *habeas corpus*, the presumption of innocence, or protection against self-incrimination. It matters little whether such a claim could be made for any one principle because what connects them all, as well as all of the technical rules, is another idea. The history of criminal procedure is the history of rules and principles that constrain or affirm the state's power to place a person in jeopardy of investigation, prosecution, and punishment for the commission of a criminal offence. No concept is more fundamental or pervasive in criminal procedure than jeopardy in this broad sense.

The interests of individuals can come into conflict with those of the state in many ways. Restricting discussion solely to the criminal realm, there are issues around the circumstances of a person who is suspected, accused, or found guilty of criminal wrongdoing. A person is in jeopardy of being detained, arrested, or searched, even if guilty of no offence, if the bases for the exercise of those powers has been met. A person is in jeopardy of prosecution if an investigation produces reasonable grounds to believe that an offence has been committed and the evidence is sufficient to proceed. A person on trial is in jeopardy of conviction and a criminal record if found guilty. A person found guilty is in jeopardy of a sentence, and that sentence might involve not only a criminal record, but also a loss of liberty. In this sense, jeopardy exists whenever the state invokes the power of the criminal law against a person suspected or accused of wrongdoing, and it describes the risk of lawful intrusion or deprivation that such a person faces.

It is not possible to think about jeopardy in the manner just described without also thinking of broader principles of legality, legitimacy, and fairness. If the state is entitled to use its power to enforce the criminal law, and if an individual person might be subject to the intrusion implied by investigation, prosecution, and conviction, a fuller notion of jeopardy requires attention to rules and principles that define the legitimate use of the state's power and, at the same time, the value of individual liberty and security of the person. These concerns are not exclusive to the criminal law, obviously, but they are the central concerns of criminal procedure. Indeed, the negotiation and renegotiation of due process are constant themes of criminal procedure. There is a constant tension between the interest of the state to ensure the collective security of its subjects and the interest of those subjects in liberty and privacy.

7 Martin Friedland, *Double Jeopardy* (Oxford: Clarendon Press, 1969) at 3.

Jeopardy and due process are not subjects of general agreement. The law governing criminal procedure, to borrow a phrase from the late Brian Dickson J, as he then was, not only lies in "a field of conflicting values"[8] it *is* a field of conflicting values. In the years preceding the *Charter*, it was argued by many that the law did not accord sufficient protection to persons in jeopardy.[9] Certainly, the *Charter* has forced everyone involved in the administration of criminal justice to reconsider the relation between the power of the state to enforce the law and the protection of persons who might be put in jeopardy.[10] Since 1982 there has been no more powerful engine of law reform than the *Charter* and, as a result, there have been profound changes in the law relating to criminal procedure. This development has occurred as the courts have given meaning to specific provisions of the *Charter*. The guarantee against unreasonable search and seizure in section 8, the right to counsel in section 10(b), and the right to trial within a reasonable time in section 11(b) have significantly altered the manner in which the police conduct their work, the manner in which prosecutors present their case in court, and the manner in which judges decide cases. The right of the accused to make full answer and defence to the prosecution case has also led to important changes in the handling of criminal cases, not least of which is the right of the accused generally to have disclosure of the prosecution case before trial.

Interpretation of the *Charter* is not the sole or direct cause of all recent developments in criminal procedure. Important developments have been influenced by the *Charter* in a somewhat more indirect manner. For some time before 1982, and for some time thereafter, notions of jeopardy and due process were typically thought to concern a conflict between the interests of the state and the interests of the accused. Comparatively little attention was given to the notion that third parties, who might not share the interests of the state or those of the accused, deserved recognition and enforcement of their interests within the law on criminal procedure.

---

8 *R v Sault Ste Marie*, [1978] 2 SCR 1299 at 1310.

9 See, for example, Stanley A Cohen, *Due Process of Law* (Toronto: Carswell, 1977); Ed Ratushny, *Self-Incrimination in the Canadian Criminal Process* (Toronto: Carswell, 1979); Walter Tarnopolsky, *The Canadian Bill of Rights*, 2d ed (Toronto: McClelland & Stewart, 1975). Since its creation in 1964, the Canadian Civil Liberties Association has been a vigilant advocate of such protection.

10 The literature is vast, but see, for example, David Paciocco, *Getting Away with Murder* (Toronto: Irwin Law, 1999); Kent Roach, *Due Process and Victims' Rights* (Toronto: University of Toronto Press, 1999); Kent Roach, *The Supreme Court on Trial*, 2d ed (Toronto: Irwin Law, 2016); and Don Stuart, *Charter Justice in Canadian Criminal Law*, 7th ed (Toronto: Thomson Reuters, 2018).

Most notable among these are the victims and alleged victims of crime.[11] Their interests in privacy and equality have been specifically invoked as the courts and Parliament have redefined important areas of procedure, such as disclosure by the prosecution or the production of evidence. Other parties, including the public, have also intervened to ensure that the administration of criminal justice is conducted in a manner that respects interests such as the freedom of expression.[12]

If it is accurate to state that the rules and principles of criminal procedure are a field of conflicting values, then it is also accurate that there is no dominant set of values within it. Kent Roach has argued that, in addition to concerns for effective crime control and for due process, there may be seen in recent Canadian law a more pronounced concern for the alleged victims of crime and for other third parties than was previously the case.[13] He has argued that this increased concern for victims is sometimes expressed in a manner that favours the values of efficient crime control and, on some occasions, in a manner that favours other values.

In the field of conflicting values that is criminal procedure there are broad areas for both consensus and conflict. In the development of constitutional principles, the adjudication of cases, and the formulation of measures for law reform, there is also frequent reference to the metaphorical idea that the resolution of conflict may be found in "balance." In the law, and most conspicuously the criminal law, if there is balance, it is always artificial and always delicate. The state of the law at any given point should reflect deliberate and authoritative choices by people about the appropriate distribution of weight to be made among recognized values. A claim to balance is only a claim that a given distribution is acceptable for the moment: there is no claim to balance that can eliminate the conflict of values and the eventual need for redistribution among them.

The purpose of this book is to provide an introduction to the principal features of Canadian criminal procedure. Some topics are treated in elaborate detail and some, such as the provisions dealing with terrorism, are not addressed in any detail. This book should provide a survey of the structure and the architecture of criminal procedure. Within these formal categories and, indeed, in almost every aspect of the subject, the reader will be reminded that there are important questions of

---

11 See, for example, *R v Seaboyer*, [1991] 2 SCR 577; *R v O'Connor*, [1995] 4 SCR 411; and *R v Darrach*, [2000] 2 SCR 443.

12 See, for example, *Dagenais v Canadian Broadcasting Corporation*, [1994] 3 SCR 835; and *R v Mentuck*, [2001] 3 SCR 442.

13 See Roach, *Due Process and Victims' Rights*, above note 10.

principle and value that suffuse the law. These questions invite debate, even though debate and argument are not the main themes of the text.

Nevertheless, reconsider the quotation from Professor Friedland above. Double jeopardy refers generally to the idea that a person may not be prosecuted or convicted *twice* for the same offence. Jeopardy on its own, then, refers to the proposition that no person should be investigated, prosecuted, convicted, or sentenced even *once* by the state, except in accordance with rules and principles that express values of legality, legitimacy, and fairness. Those values have changed profoundly between the time when modern criminal procedure began to take shape and today. And, of course, those values continue to evolve today with changes both small and great. This book endeavours, in a modest way, to show the past, the present, and the possible future.

## FURTHER READINGS


BALA, NICHOLAS, & SANJEEV ANAND. *Youth Criminal Justice Law*, 3d ed (Toronto: Irwin Law, 2012).

COHEN, STANLEY A. *Due Process of Law* (Toronto: Carswell, 1977).

FRIEDLAND, MARTIN. *Double Jeopardy* (Oxford: Clarendon Press, 1969).

LAW REFORM COMMISSION OF CANADA. *Our Criminal Procedure* (Ottawa: Law Reform Commission of Canada, 1988).

———. *Recodifying Criminal Procedure*, Report 33 (Ottawa: Law Reform Commission of Canada, 1991).

PACIOCCO, DAVID. *Getting Away with Murder* (Toronto: Irwin Law, 1999).

RATUSHNY, ED. *Self-Incrimination in the Canadian Criminal Process* (Toronto: Carswell, 1979).

ROACH, KENT. *Due Process and Victims' Rights* (Toronto: University of Toronto Press, 1999). http://doi.org/10.3138/9781442674127.

———. *The Supreme Court on Trial*, 2d ed (Toronto: Irwin Law, 2016).

ROSE, DAVID. *Quigley's Criminal Procedure in Canada* (Toronto: Thomson Reuters, 2021) (loose-leaf).

STUART, DON. *Charter Justice in Canadian Criminal Law*, 7th ed (Toronto: Thomson Carswell, 2018).

TARNOPOLSKY, WALTER. *The Canadian Bill of Rights*, 2d ed (Toronto: McClelland & Stewart, 1978).

CHAPTER 2

# SOURCES OF CRIMINAL PROCEDURE

Broadly speaking, the sources for criminal procedure, as for criminal law more generally, are derived from the constitution, statutes, and common law. However, it is useful to discuss each of those areas in more depth, and to do so it is convenient to distinguish between the sources of police investigative powers on the one hand and the sources of the rules of pre-trial and trial procedure on the other.

## A. SOURCES OF POLICE POWER

Deciding the amount of power to be granted to police in a society is a difficult challenge. Police power is one of the most obvious and potentially most intrusive means by which government interferes with the lives of individuals. A society in which police have excessive power risks suppression. However, a society in which police have insufficient ability to investigate and prevent crime risks lawlessness. Both extremes are to be avoided, but there is a broad range between them, with scope for reasonable disagreement over exactly where the right balance lies.

There is a fundamental principle which should be stated at the start and borne in mind throughout, which is more generally about the nature of a liberal democracy than it is about police powers specifically. The point is this:

> Absent a law to the contrary, individuals are free to do as they please. By contrast, the police (and more broadly, the state) may act only to the extent that they are empowered to do so by law. The vibrancy of a democracy is apparent by how wisely it navigates through those critical junctures where state action intersects with, and threatens to impinge upon, individual liberties.[1]

This means that the term "lawful" has two different senses, depending upon whether we are speaking of individuals or of state actors. Put simply, an individual is acting lawfully if there is no law saying they *cannot* do what they are doing. In the case of police, however, an action will be lawful *only* if the officer can point to some power authorizing them to act in that particular way.

Police powers generally are created either by a statute or the common law, though sometimes police effectively have powers based on the consent of a person being investigated. Those three possible sources are exhaustive, in the sense that if the police officer, or the state more generally, is not exercising a power authorized by statute, common law, or consent, then the action in question is not lawful.

## 1) Constitution

Any discussion of constitutional law in Canada must consider the question of division of powers under the *Constitution Act, 1867*[2] as well as the impact of the *Canadian Charter of Rights and Freedoms*, introduced as part of the *Constitution Act 1982*.[3] The former issue has relatively little direct impact on the question of police powers. Both Parliament and the provincial legislatures have the jurisdiction to create police forces, and both levels of government have done so. In addition, though, many provinces have contracted with the Royal Canadian Mounted Police (RCMP), the federal police force, to provide policing services within the province. Even in such cases, however, the RCMP remains under federal legislative jurisdiction, so that, for example, a complaint would have to be brought to the appropriate federal body rather than a provincial police complaints board.[4]

---

1 *R v Mann*, 2004 SCC 52 at para 15.

2 (UK), 30 & 31 Vict, c 3, reprinted in RSC 1985, App II, No 5.

3 Being Schedule B to the *Canada Act 1982* (UK), 1982, c 11. Sections 1–34 of the *Constitution Act, 1982* are referred to as the *Canadian Charter of Rights and Freedoms* or, more commonly, as the *Charter*.

4 See, for example, *Alberta (Attorney General) v Putnam*, [1981] 2 SCR 267.

Whatever the constitutional basis for the existence of a particular police force, however, those police will rely primarily on rules of criminal procedure set out in the *Criminal Code* in enforcing the criminal law. That matter lies squarely within Parliament's jurisdiction, thanks to section 91(27) of the *Constitution Act, 1867*, which assigns authority over "the Procedure in Criminal Matters" to the federal government. Police in various provinces can have additional powers conferred by provincial statutes. Further, the duties assigned to police by their governing legislation, whether federal or provincial, can sometimes be relevant.[5] Nonetheless, in the vast majority of situations, section 91(27) means that it is federal legislation that will determine the extent of police investigative powers.

A much more relevant constitutional law question in this context is the role of the *Charter*. Its importance is twofold. First, any law concerning criminal procedure that is inconsistent with the *Charter* can be struck down unless it can be justified as a reasonable limitation upon guaranteed rights by reference to section 1.[6] Second, the investigation and prosecution of crime in each case must be conducted in a manner that is consistent with rights guaranteed by the *Charter*. Failure to do so can give rise to a remedy under section 24.

The *Charter*, especially the rights in sections 7 to 14 under the heading "Legal Rights," affects all aspects of criminal procedure from police conduct through to bail, trial procedure, and sentencing. Sections 8 to 10, dealing with search, detention, and arrest, are all directly concerned with investigative powers, and they will be discussed at much greater length below. Further, in the absence of more precise guarantees, section 7 may be invoked as a source of "principles of fundamental justice." Although this section has had a greater impact on issues of substantive criminal law than on investigative powers, it guarantees the right to remain silent and the right to full answer and defence, and it is a source of constitutional protection against abuse of process.[7]

The *Charter* has enhanced the protection of civil liberties in Canada, and the extent of these effects will be reviewed in subsequent chapters. Paradoxically, the *Charter* has also been a direct and indirect cause of the expansion of police powers. It has been a direct cause of

---

5 See, for example, *R v Godoy*, [1999] 1 SCR 311 [*Godoy*], where the Court looked to the duties of police as set out in s 42 of the *Police Services Act*, RSO 1990, c P.15, in order to help determine whether the *Waterfield* test was met. The *Waterfield* test is discussed in greater detail at Section A(3)(b), below in this chapter.

6 *Constitution Act, 1982*, above note 3, s 52.

7 See, for example, *R v O'Connor*, [1995] 4 SCR 411 [*O'Connor*], or *R v Babos*, 2014 SCC 16.

this expansion when judicial interpretation of a right in the *Charter* has created a power that did not previously exist in law. This has occurred in the interpretation of section 8, which protects against unreasonable search and seizure, and in the interpretation of section 9, which protects against arbitrary detention.[8] In essence, what has happened is that *Charter* analysis has dictated that a lawful search will not be unreasonable, and a lawful detention will not be arbitrary. In some situations in which an accused has been searched or detained in the absence of any statutory authority, courts have been faced with a choice between finding a *Charter* violation or finding a new common law power authorizing the police action. As will be discussed below, where once courts were quite reticent about creating police powers, they became for a time much more willing to do so.[9]

The *Charter* has also been an indirect cause of the expansion of police powers when courts have found particular police action objectionable, but have suggested powers that would still be consistent with guaranteed rights. This type of judicial interpretation has sometimes given Parliament guidance for legislative expansion of police powers. This would appear to be most evident in relation to matters of search and seizure.[10]

## 2) Statute

The primary source of police powers is the *Criminal Code*. It creates powers for police to directly enforce the law, as well as a great number of powers aimed at investigating crime, such as search warrants and wiretap provisions.

Sections 494 to 528 of the *Code*, for example, create a statutory scheme allowing police officers (and others) to arrest an accused or compel an accused's appearance in court by some other means.[11] Police arrest powers are quite broad, creating a power of arrest in almost every situation a peace officer might encounter; virtually the only circumstance in which there is no arrest power is where the police officer does not find the accused committing the offence and the offence is

8 See the discussion in chapters 4 and 5.

9 See Section A(3)(b), below in this chapter.

10 See, for example, *R v Wong*, [1990] 3 SCR 36; *R v Wise*, [1992] 1 SCR 527. See also the discussion in Michal Fairburn, "Twenty-Five Years in Search of a Reasonable Approach" in Jamie Cameron & James Stribopoulos, eds, *The Charter and Criminal Justice: Twenty-Five Years Later* (Toronto: LexisNexis Butterworths, 2008).

11 See the discussion in chapters 6 and 7.

only a summary conviction one. Sections 25 to 33 create related powers, allowing the use of force to execute powers authorized by law, to prevent the commission of some offences, or to prevent a breach of the peace. In some circumstances, even the use of deadly force is authorized.

Other provisions in the *Code* create extensive powers for police to search.[12] Section 487 creates the generic search warrant provision in the *Code*, allowing a justice to issue a warrant authorizing the search of a "building, receptacle or place" and the seizure of evidence found there. Warrants under section 487 are typically issued when a justice is satisfied that the search will produce evidence with respect to the commission of an offence. However, the provision also allows a warrant to be issued where there are reasonable grounds to believe that the search will find (1) something in respect of which an offence has been committed; (2) the whereabouts of a person believed to have committed an offence; (3) property intended to be used to commit an offence; or (4) offence-related property. *Code* provisions also authorize the seizure of the material searched for, as well as material in addition to that specified in the warrant.[13] Further, the *Code* contains a general power to seize without a warrant anything that an officer reasonably believes was obtained by the commission of an offence, has been used in the commission of an offence, or will afford evidence in respect of an offence, provided the officer was lawfully present.[14]

In addition to the section 487 search warrant provision, a great number of individual police investigative powers have been incorporated into the *Code*. These include authorizations to:

1) use a tracking device to monitor the location of a person or object;[15]
2) obtain transmission data concerning electronic communications;[16]
3) perform video surveillance on a location;[17]
4) install a wiretap device to monitor telecommunications or private communications;[18]

---

12 See the discussion in Chapter 4.

13 Section 489(1).

14 The *Code* also creates a few isolated powers to search and seize without warrant; among them are s 199, which deals with common gaming houses (which also creates what amounts to a power of arrest of those found in the common gaming house), and s 462(2), which deals with counterfeit money.

15 Sections 492.1(1) and (2).

16 Section 492.2.

17 Section 487.01(4).

18 See Part VI of the *Code*.

5) obtain blood samples;[19]
6) obtain handprints, fingerprints, footprints, or impressions of teeth or other parts of the body;[20] and
7) obtain DNA samples.[21]

Some of these provisions, such as the wiretap and DNA sample items, are part of comprehensive schemes set out within the *Code*, while other powers are defined in a single section.

Beyond these specific warrant provisions, the *Code* also includes section 487.01, which allows a peace officer to apply for a warrant to "use any device or investigative technique or procedure or do any thing" that would be an unreasonable search and seizure if it were not done under a warrant.[22] Further, section 487.11 of the *Code* provides that a peace officer may "exercise any of the powers described in subsection 487(1) [search warrants] or 492.1(1) [tracking devices] without a warrant if the conditions for obtaining a warrant exist but by reason of exigent circumstances it would be impracticable to obtain a warrant."

Supporting these various warrant provisions is section 487.1, which allows officers to apply for any of a wide variety of orders or warrants by telephone. That provision has been made applicable in other circumstances outside the *Criminal Code*, to obtain a search warrant under the *Controlled Drugs and Substances Act*.[23] Other investigative techniques are also authorized by statute, such as breathalyzer demands and approved screening device tests to investigate impaired drivers.[24]

Sometimes, statutes other than the *Code* also create investigative techniques. Provincial legislation has authorized random stops of vehicles, which are used to check for both mechanical fitness and impaired drivers.[25] Other legislation, both federal and provincial, creates other investigative techniques. Legislation in British Columbia, for example,

---

19 For many years such a power existed in s 256, in connection with impaired driving offences. In December 2018 *An Act to amend the Criminal Code (offences relating to conveyances)*, SC 2018, c 21 came into force, repealing and replacing the old impaired driving provisions. The blood sample warrant provisions are now found in s 320.29.

20 Section 487.091. See also the *Identification of Criminals Act*, RSC 1985, c I-1.

21 Section 487.05.

22 See the discussion in Chapter 5, Section B.

23 SC 1996, c 19, s 11(2).

24 *An Act to amend the Criminal Code (offences relating to conveyances)* repealed and replaced these provisions, which since December 2018 are now found in ss 302.27–320.28.

25 See *R v Ladouceur*, [1990] 1 SCR 1257, considering the application of the *Highway Traffic Act*, RSO 1980, c 198, s 189(a)(1).

creates an obligation for a motorist involved in an accident to report the accident to the police.[26] The Ontario *Coroners Act*[27] authorizes taking samples of bodily fluids in the investigation of deaths.[28] The *Customs Act*[29] authorizes searches of people crossing the border to enter Canada.[30] The *Firearms Act*[31] authorizes inspectors without a warrant to enter premises, including dwelling houses, to search for prohibited firearms on reasonable grounds. Although not strictly a police power, various administrative schemes create a power to compel a person to testify, potentially giving self-incriminatory evidence.[32] There are limits placed on the extent to which evidence gained in these administrative manners can be later obtained by the police via a search warrant.[33]

A very broad police power is contained in section 25.1 of the *Criminal Code*. It permits police officers, under various circumstances, to perform acts that would, for any other person, constitute a crime; in other words, it permits the police to sometimes break the law in the course of their investigations.

Generally speaking, a statue must explicitly authorize particular action if it is to be found lawful. However, it is possible for a court to find that a particular power arises by "necessary implication" from the terms of a statute. Arguably the Court has become more willing to find police action authorized on this basis than it was in the past, though it is difficult to generalize.[34]

---

26 See *R v White*, [1999] 2 SCR 417, considering the application of the *Motor Vehicle Act*, RSBC 1979, c 288, s 61.

27 RSO 1990, c C.37.

28 *R v Colarusso*, [1994] 1 SCR 20.

29 RSC 1985 (2d Supp), c 1, s 1.

30 *R v Simmons*, [1988] 2 SCR 495; *R v Monney*, [1999] 1 SCR 652.

31 SC 1995, c 39, ss 102 and 104. There is an obligation to give reasonable notice in the case of a dwelling house.

32 See, for example, *Thomson Newspapers Ltd v Canada (Director of Investigation and Research, Restrictive Trade Practices Commission)*, [1990] 1 SCR 425, dealing with s 17 of the former *Combines Investigation Act*, RSC 1970, c C-23.

33 See the discussion in *R v Jarvis*, [2002] 3 SCR 757; *R v Ling*, 2002 SCC 74; and *Re Application under s 83.28 of the Criminal Code (Re)*, 2004 SCC 42. Complicating matters, however, see *R v Nolet*, 2010 SCC 24.

34 In *Colet v The Queen*, [1981] 1 SCR 2, police entered the accused's home and seized his firearms. The *Code* provided for a warrant to seize firearms but did not explicitly authorize searching for them, and the Court there rejected the view that a power to search was necessarily implied by a power to seize. Subsequently, however, the Court has found a power to search to be necessarily implied from a school vice-principal's duty to maintain proper order and discipline (*R v M(MR)*, [1998] 3 SCR 393) and a power to not inform an accused of their *Charter* right to counsel to be necessarily implied from a power to perform sobriety tests on a driver (*R v Orbanski*, 2005 SCC 37).

Considering the broad nature of powers given to police statutorily, it is not surprising that, on more than one occasion, the Supreme Court has sounded a note of caution about allowing police to have non-statutory powers too readily. In *R v Kokesch*, for example, it was stated that "this Court consistently has held that the common law rights of the property holder to be free of police intrusion can be restricted only by powers granted in clear statutory language."[35] Choosing the balance between protection of individual liberty and the need for public security, and the appropriate power to be given to the police in order to satisfy the latter concern without unduly sacrificing the former, is a process best undertaken in the legislative realm, where there is at least the potential for public debate. Despite expressing this concern on a number of occasions, however, the Supreme Court has not, in fact, consistently shown restraint in extending common law police powers. To that topic we now turn.

## 3) Common Law

Although the caselaw does not formally make these distinctions, there are three senses in which police can be said to have common law powers. First, there are some powers that were historically given to police and which have continued to exist despite the codification of most police powers. In essence, these powers are "found" in the way that any other pieces of common law are, by examining precedents. Second, the Supreme Court has confirmed the existence of the "ancillary powers doctrine," which allows courts to create new police powers. These first two senses are not entirely distinct from one another: a power might have historically existed but be expanded further through the ancillary powers doctrine. Finally, there is a sense in which the police have the common law power to do anything that has no negative consequences for the officer concerned and which results in evidence being admitted at a trial. Although this latter "default" sense is not usually spoken of as a common law power, it is a phenomenon that needs to be acknowledged.

### a) Historical Common Law Powers

Historical common law powers include the power of the police to search incident to an arrest or to enter a private dwelling in "hot pursuit" of a person fleeing arrest. Both powers are interesting illustrations of common law powers, in particular because of the flexibility of such

35 [1990] 3 SCR 3 at 17. See also *R v Colet*, [1981] 1 SCR 2.

powers. This feature can be both an advantage and a disadvantage in a system where predictability is a virtue.

The power to search incident to arrest was confirmed in Canadian law by the Supreme Court in *Cloutier v Langlois*.[36] Relying on British cases dating to 1829, American cases back to 1848, and Canadian cases from as early as 1895, the Court decided that there already existed in Canada, through the common law, a power for police officers to search a person who had been arrested. This power, the Court said,

> holds that the police have a power to search a lawfully arrested person and to seize anything in his or her possession or immediate surroundings to guarantee the safety of the police and the accused, prevent the prisoner's escape or provide evidence against him.[37]

Therefore, even though the *Criminal Code* did not specify such a search power, the police nonetheless had the power to search an arrested person for one of these three purposes.

A feature of the common law, however, is its ability to evolve — sometimes in desirable directions, sometimes not. In the case of search incident to arrest, the scope of the power has gradually shifted without the kind of public debate that would characterize an equivalent change to a statutory power. The original rationale for allowing the police to search for evidence incident to arrest was to prevent the destruction of any evidence that might be in the immediate control of the accused. However, the actual wording of *Cloutier* does not preclude wider searches for evidence, and within a short time other courts were interpreting the search power to allow recovery, without a warrant, of any evidence relevant to the guilt or innocence of the accused, whether at risk of destruction or not. In *R v Speid*, for example, the Ontario Court of Appeal held that a search of a vehicle that was still in the vicinity of the arrest was validly incidental to the arrest, even though it did not take place at the time of the arrest, and despite the fact that a warrant had been refused.[38]

In *R v Stillman*, the Supreme Court noted that two lines of authority had developed, suggesting that a broader search incident to arrest power applied in the case of searching a vehicle.[39] In the context of searches of the person, the Court said that search incident to arrest did not extend beyond discovering evidence that might go out of existence.[40]

36 [1990] 1 SCR 158 [*Cloutier*].
37 *Ibid* at para 49.
38 [1991] OJ No 1558.
39 [1997] 1 SCR 607 [*Stillman*].
40 *Ibid* at para 41.

However, by the time they decided *R v Caslake*, the Court had rewritten the allowed purposes for search incident to arrest to "ensur[e] the safety of the police and public, the protection of evidence from destruction at the hands of the arrestee or others, and the discovery of evidence which can be used at the arrestee's trial."[41] In *Caslake*, the Court did not acknowledge that this greater emphasis on gathering evidence was a change to the underlying purposes that were said to authorize the power in *Cloutier*.[42]

Subsequently, the Court returned to the power to search incident to arrest to determine whether the power includes the authority to conduct strip searches. In *R v Golden*,[43] the Court acknowledged that the scope of search incident to arrest had not been fully delineated and, in particular, that whether it contained the power to conduct strip searches had never been settled. In that context, the Court decided further restrictions needed to be imposed. Reasonable and probable grounds are not generally a requirement of search incident to arrest; that is precisely why the separate "incidental" power has arisen, to allow a search flowing from nothing more than the fact of an arrest. However, to do more than conduct a "frisk" search, the Court held, police must have reasonable and probable grounds to believe that a strip search is necessary in the particular circumstances of the arrest.[44] Further, the Court held, such searches must be conducted at a police station unless the police have reasonable and probable grounds to believe that the search cannot be postponed. These additional requirements were imposed by the Court to reflect the greater intrusiveness of strip searches and to attempt to maintain the appropriate balance between individual privacy rights and the needs of law enforcement. They are an explicit effort to have the common law develop in accordance with *Charter* principles.[45] In a similar way, because of the enhanced privacy interests involved the Court later articulated special rules governing search incident to arrest in regard to cellphones,[46] for strip searches involving a penile swab,[47] and for search incident to arrest inside a dwelling.[48] Performing an arrest within a private dwelling house provides another illustration of the common law's ability to evolve, but it also illuminates

41 [1998] 1 SCR 51 at para 19 [*Caslake*].

42 *Ibid*.

43 2001 SCC 83 [*Golden*].

44 *Ibid* at para 98.

45 *Ibid* at para 86.

46 *R v Fearon*, 2014 SCC 77. See the further discussion of search incident to arrest in Chapter 4.

47 *R v Saeed*, 2016 SCC 24.

48 *R v Stairs*, 2022 SCC 11.

the difficulty of determining exactly what common law powers the police have. In *Eccles v Bourque*,[49] for example, the Court confirmed that the police have the power at common law to arrest within a private dwelling and laid down rules for entering the dwelling without the permission of the owner. As noted in *R v Landry*, "the Court was simply reaffirming common law principles of some considerable antiquity."[50] That case dealt with a situation in which a warrant did exist but was technically invalid, and so it was felt for a time that the rules created might cover only that situation. In *Landry*, however, the Court held that the rules applied to any warrantless arrest, not just to the civil context of *Eccles v Bourque*.[51] Subsequently in *R v Macooh*[52] the Court also held that, at least in cases of hot pursuit, this right extended beyond indictable offences to cover provincial offences, as well.

In *R v Feeney*,[53] however, the Court further decided that the common law rules that had developed in a pre-*Charter* context[54] needed to be re-examined. Although the common law had held that a dwelling house was entitled to particular protection since *Semayne's Case*,[55] those privacy interests had become even more important with the passage of the *Charter*. Warrantless entry into a dwelling, the Court held, should, like a warrantless search, be *prima facie* unreasonable. An exception was allowed for hot pursuit, and the issue of whether an exception should be allowed for exigent circumstances was discussed but not settled. Otherwise, warrantless entries to arrest would *prima facie* violate the *Charter*. To deal with the situation, the Court read a warrant provision into the *Code*, a step that has since been undertaken more formally by Parliament.[56]

### b) New Common Law Powers — The "Ancillary Powers" Doctrine

A further feature of common law powers is that the boundaries are never closed: it is always possible for new common law police powers to be created. Sometimes, this issue arises in the context of a charge against an accused for assaulting or obstructing an officer in the execution of duty when that officer has not been acting under statutory authority. The question therefore becomes whether the officer had any power at

49 [1975] 2 SCR 739.

50 [1986] 1 SCR 145 at para 19 [*Landry*].

51 *Ibid.*

52 [1993] 2 SCR 13.

53 [1997] 2 SCR 13.

54 Although *Landry*, above note 50, was decided in 1986, the facts predate the *Charter*.

55 (1604), 5 Co Rep 91a, 77 ER 194 (KB).

56 Sections 529.1–529.5.

common law. The question can also arise when an accused claims a violation of a *Charter* right, such as that in section 9, the right not to be arbitrarily detained. An accused who has been legally detained has not been arbitrarily detained, caselaw has held, and so, in the absence of any statutory authority, the question becomes whether the detention was lawful due to a common law power. Equally, the issue can arise in the civil context, where a person sues a police officer claiming they have acted outside their powers.

Canadian caselaw has adopted a test from the British decision in *R v Waterfield* to determine this question. *Waterfield* did not itself concern the creation of a *new* power, and so referring to the "ancillary powers doctrine" to describe this situation is more accurate, though in fact the "*Waterfield* test" is the name that has often been used.[57] The *Waterfield* test asks two questions: "first, does the conduct fall within the general scope of any duty imposed by statute or recognized at common law; and second, does the conduct, albeit within the general scope of such a duty, involve an unjustifiable use of powers associated with the duty."[58]

The Supreme Court has relied on this test to support police powers to protect foreign dignitaries,[59] to enter premises without a warrant or reasonable grounds to investigate a shooting,[60] to stop cars randomly to check for impaired drivers,[61] to set up roadblocks,[62] to forcibly enter an apartment to investigate a disconnected 911 call,[63] to detain individuals for investigative purposes, and, in some circumstances, to conduct searches of those individuals.[64]

The use of *Waterfield* in this way was relatively uncommon until 1999, but the Supreme Court decision in *R v Godoy* seemed to "kick-start" greater reliance on it.[65] Prior to *Godoy*, the Court had not relied on *Waterfield* since the 1985 decision in *Dedman*, but since *Godoy* has used it to create a number of other common law powers. The explanation for that shift is uncertain, but one possibility is, ironically, the enacting of the *Charter*. Prior to the *Charter* there was less scope for demanding a determination as to whether police had or had not acted within

---

57 *Fleming v Ontario*, 2019 SCC 45 [*Fleming*] at para 43.

58 [1963] 3 All ER 659 (CA) [*Waterfield*].

59 *R v Knowlton*, [1974] SCR 443.

60 *R v Stenning*, [1970] SCR 631 [*Stenning*].

61 *R v Dedman*, [1985] 2 SCR 2 [*Dedman*].

62 *R v Clayton*, 2007 SCC 32 [*Clayton*].

63 *Godoy*, above note 5.

64 *Mann*, above note 1.

65 A search on Westlaw, for example, shows approximately fifty mentions of *Waterfield* by courts in the ten years prior to *Godoy*, but 175 in the ten years after.

their powers, and less likelihood of consequences if they had not. Post-1999 *Charter* jurisprudence, especially around section 8 (unreasonable search and seizure) and section 9 (arbitrary detention), was well enough developed that being able to point to the lawful authority for individual police action had become much more important.[66] It seems likely that that resulted in greater reliance on *Waterfield* as a way of saying that lawful authority did exist. A further irony, therefore, is that *Godoy* itself was only finding that the "in the execution of duty" element of an offence was made out: it was not a *Charter* case at all, though it has ended up having a significant impact on *Charter* rights.

Many authors have argued that great caution ought to be shown before relying on the common law in this way.[67] First, *Waterfield* itself was not intended to allow the creation of new common law powers; rather, it was intended as a way of understanding the limits on existing police powers. In *Waterfield*, the police had attempted to prevent the accused from driving away in a car they wished to examine. The accused drove the car at a constable who was physically blocking his path, and he was therefore charged with assaulting an officer in the execution of duty. He was found not guilty on the basis that, although an officer's duty might include preserving evidence, the constable was not *authorized* to prevent removal of the car. After setting out what has become known as the "*Waterfield* test," Ashworth J immediately distinguishes between police duties and police powers, pointing to the limits on the latter. He refers approvingly to *Davis v Lisle*, noting that

> even if a police officer had a right to enter a garage to make inquiries, he became a trespasser after the appellant had told him to leave the premises, and that he was not, therefore, acting thenceforward in the execution of his duty, with the result that the appellant could not be convicted of assaulting or obstructing him in the execution of his duty.[68]

---

66 See generally the discussion in Steve Coughlan, "*Charter* Protection Against Unlawful Police Action: Less Black and White Than It Seems" in Benjamin L Berger & James Stribopoulos, *Unsettled Legacy: Thirty Years of Criminal Justice Under the Charter* (Markham, ON: LexisNexis, 2012) ["Black and White"].

67 See, for example, Steve Coughlan, "Police Detention for Questioning: A Proposal — Part I" (1985) 28 *Criminal Law Quarterly* 64; Patrick Healy, "Investigative Detention in Canada" (2005) *Criminal Law Review* 98; James Stribopoulos, "In Search of Dialogue: The Supreme Court, Police Powers and the *Charter*" (2005) 31 *Queen's Law Journal* 1; and Steve Coughlan, "Common Law Police Powers and the Rule of Law" (2007) 47 *Criminal Reports* (6th) 266.

68 *Waterfield*, above note 58 at 662.

That Canadian law has not been consistent with the original intent of *Waterfield* is most clear from *R v Stenning*.[69] The facts of *Stenning* are very similar to *Davis v Lisle*: an officer entered premises without any statutory authority to do so and was assaulted by a person inside. The *Waterfield* test was applied in *Stenning*, finding that, although the officer might have been a trespasser, he, nonetheless, was in the execution of duty because he was investigating, and therefore the accused *was* guilty of assaulting an officer in the execution of duty.

Further, the actual terms of the *Waterfield* test are broad enough to potentially justify, *post facto*, a broad range of police behaviour, therefore injecting undesirable uncertainty into the law. The Court noted in *R v Dedman* that the common law duties of the police include the "preservation of the peace, the prevention of crime, and the protection of life and property."[70] In other words, the police have very broad duties, so it is unlikely that the first branch of the *Waterfield* test will fail to be met in any given case. The second branch of the test, the Court observed in *Godoy*,

> depends on a number of factors including the duty being performed, the extent to which some interference with individual liberty is necessitated in order to perform that duty, the importance of the performance of that duty to the public good, the liberty interfered with, and the nature and extent of the interference.[71]

While these factors could fail to be satisfied in some cases, as interpreted *Waterfield* nonetheless creates a test with the ability to authorize at common law an extremely wide range of police behaviour that has not been statutorily authorized. In the detention context, for example, the *Waterfield* test has been taken to allow police to make any detention which is reasonably necessary in the totality of the circumstances.[72] That test is so broadly framed as to provide virtually no advance guidance, something that is particularly troublesome when one considers the after-the-fact nature of common law powers. When arising in the context of a charge of resisting an officer in the execution of duty, the recognition of a new common law power has the effect of making the accused criminally liable for behaviour that they could not have

---

69 *Stenning*, above note 60.

70 *Dedman*, above note 61 at para 14.

71 *Godoy*, above note 5 at para 18, quoting from *R v Simpson* (1993), 79 CCC (3d) 482 (Ont CA).

72 *R v Aucoin*, 2012 SCC 66, describing the decision in *Clayton*, above note 62.

known in advance to be illegal.[73] Equally, when police try to act to pursue some legitimate goal, it is not possible for them to know in advance whether they are acting within their powers or not.[74] Neither of those is a desirable result.

Further, although the Court has held that common law powers must provide clear guidance to police once created, they do not always do so.[75] Common law powers tend to be articulated over the course of one or more judicial decisions, as opposed to being set out in a single provision of a statute. In such circumstances there are almost certainly some differences in how it is phrased in different parts of the judgment, creating scope for disagreement over which passages should be seen as controlling,[76] In consequence, the exact nature of any given power is less knowable and less certain, with the Supreme Court itself sometimes unclear about what it has earlier decided.[77] In other cases this can lead to disagreement among courts of appeal as to the requirements for individual common law powers.[78]

---

73 Further on this issue, see the range of opinions on the Court's approach in *Godoy*, above note 5, in Graeme G Mitchell, "*R. v. Godoy*: Constitutional Accommodation of Public Service Programs" (1999) 21 *Criminal Reports* (5th) 217; Don Stuart, "*Godoy*: The Supreme Court Reverts to the Ancillary Powers Doctrine to Fill a Gap in Police Power" (1999) 21 *Criminal Reports* (5th) 225; and Heather Pringle, "The Smoke and Mirrors of *Godoy*: Creating Common Law Authority While Making *Feeney* Disappear" (1999) 21 *Criminal Reports* (5th) 227.

74 See, for example, *Figueiras v Toronto Police Services Board*, 2015 ONCA 208 and *Fleming*, above note 57, both cases in which police were successfully sued for taking actions which they (unsuccessfully) argued had been authorized by the *Waterfield* test. Note, for example, that the actions in question in *Fleming* were taken in 2009, and it was not decided until 2019 that the police had not had the authority to act in that way. In the interim, police had continued to purport to use the common law power of arrest which ultimately was found not to exist.

75 *Fleming*, above note 57 at para 52: "It is important for the courts to give officers the clearest possible guidance as to what common law powers are available to them within the general scope of their duties. The police will then be able to apply these guidelines to their day-to-day operations."

76 See, for example, the discussion of psychological detention in Chapter 5, Section C(2), and the point that the very same case will sometimes refer to a requirement for the detainee to have submitted to the detention but at other times treat that as not required, leaving the actual state of the law uncertain.

77 For example, the Court created the power of search incident to investigative detention in *Mann*, above note 1. Ten years later in *R v MacDonald*, 2014 SCC 3, the Court split four to three over whether *Mann* had created a search power based on reasonable grounds to believe, or on reasonable suspicion. See the discussion in Chapter 4, Section C(1)(a)(ii).

78 For example, *MacDonald*, *ibid*, created a "safety search" power. The Courts of Appeal in Alberta and Ontario understand that power to require an *imminent* threat to safety (see *R v Del Corro*, 2019 ABCA 156 and *R v McGuffie*, 2016

Further, when a power is fully created at one time by legislation, Parliament can weigh the competing interests and craft a law which is designed to balance those interests. In the case of a common law power, however, courts are less able to anticipate all the eventualities or to have access to background research, and so the decision tends to be more about whether the police behaviour in that case should be authorized, based on the particular facts at hand.[79] As a result powers developed at common law are less likely to form a cohesive whole: why is the taking of detailed notes merely recommended for strip searches but a requirement for searching a cell phone, for example.

An additional problem is that there is often a certain amount of "creep" in the extent of common law powers, which makes them not only unknowable, but also less likely to achieve an adequate balance between individual rights and state interests. Since the rule is largely based on the facts of a case, it is easy for a judge in a later case to find that the new set of facts is not different enough from the previous one to say the police have acted without authorization, which means that new decision becomes the standard. Further sets of facts depart more from that new standard, but again not greatly, with the result that the police action is again given approval, and there is a constantly receding horizon of police powers.

For example, one common law power is that of search incident to investigative detention.[80] When the power was first created, the Supreme Court held that it only extended to conducting a pat-down of the detainee.[81] Lower court decisions subsequently held first that if the police could pat down the detainee then they ought to be able to search the passenger area of a car that had been within reach when the person

---

ONCA 365) while the British Columbia Court of Appeal has concluded that the Supreme Court did not include such a requirement (*R v Dhillon*, 2023 BCCA 38).

79 See, for example, the dissenting judgment in *R v Kang-Brown*, 2008 SCC 18 [*Kang-Brown*] at para 13:

> given the critical nature of the privacy interests at stake and the weakness of the factual foundation in this appeal and in the companion appeal of *A.M.*, the constitutional role of the Court suggests that the creation of a new and more intrusive power of search and seizure, as is being proposed in some of the opinions in this appeal, should be left to Parliament to set up and justify under a proper statutory framework.

See also para 15:

> The Court would create a new common law rule on the basis of little more than unverified and, for us in this appeal, unverifiable assumptions.

80 See the discussion of this power in Chapter 4, Section C(1)(a)(ii).

81 *Mann*, above note 1.

was detained,[82] and second that if they can search the passenger area of the car they should also be able to search the trunk.[83] As the dissenting judge in that latter case pointed out, however, that amounted to creating at common law exactly a power that Parliament had decided *not* to make available.[84]

Given the wide range of powers pre-authorized by statute or available to police by warrant provisions in the *Code* and the ability to apply for a telewarrant, along with the proliferation of communications technology in society, it seems as though police should very frequently be able to obtain judicial pre-authorization for their investigations. Given that, and also given the existence of the general warrant provisions (discussed in Chapter 5), which were consciously designed by Parliament to fill gaps in police investigative powers, the need for broad common law powers should be quite small. Although the Court seems to feel some conflict over these powers, *Waterfield* has been used frequently. Members of the Supreme Court have acknowledged that "*Waterfield* is an odd godfather for common law police powers" but nonetheless have favoured using it on the basis that "[b]uilding a composite picture of police common law powers by way of narrow precedents is not a quick fix but in the absence of Parliamentary action it is the least worst solution."[85] On the other hand, other members of the Court have argued that this developing practice of relying on *Waterfield* does not mean that "the Court should always expand common law rules, in order to address perceived gaps in police powers or apprehended inaction by Parliament."[86] In its most recent consideration of the ancillary powers doctrine the Court observed that "it does not sit well for the courts, as the protectors of our fundamental rights, to widen the possibility of

82 *R v Plummer*, 2011 ONCA 350. See also *R v Webber*, 2019 BCCA 208, allowing a search of the centre console of a vehicle while the detainee was not in the vehicle.

83 *R v Lee*, 2017 ONCA 654 [*Lee*].

84 *Lee*, *ibid* at para 112. The point was that the police were purporting to search a vehicle for a weapon in exigent circumstances, that s 117.02 of the *Code* sets out the requirements to be met for such a search, and that all parties conceded those requirements were not met. Nonetheless the majority found the search to be authorized by the common law.

85 *Clayton*, above note 62 at paras 75 and 76, Binnie J concurring in the result.

86 *Kang-Brown*, above note 79 at para 6. This statement was made by LeBel J on behalf of four judges. Justice Binnie, in response, held that it was too late to hold back from expanding common law powers, saying "[w]e have crossed the Rubicon," at para 22.

encroachments on these personal liberties."[87] There appears to be less reliance on the doctrine in recent years.[88]

### c) "Default" Common Law Powers

Courts do not talk about police officers having the power to do anything that will not result in some remedy being granted to an accused, but, nonetheless, a proper understanding of the ability of the police to interfere with the liberty of individuals requires recognition of this phenomenon. It results from a combination of *Charter* and pre-*Charter* law.[89]

Prior to the *Charter*, there was effectively no basis to exclude relevant evidence in Canada. As long as evidence was reliable, the means by which it had been obtained virtually did not matter.[90] Since the *Charter*, section 24(2) allows, in some cases, for the exclusion of evidence. However, section 24(2) depends upon the accused establishing the breach of a *Charter* right: where no *Charter* violation is found, the pre-*Charter* position on evidence still applies. In such circumstances, the evidence will be admitted.

This means that, as it delimits various *Charter* rights and concludes that certain activities by the police do not constitute a *Charter* breach, the Court is effectively authorizing the police to engage in those activities despite the absence of any statutory power. The clearest example concerns the section 8 right to be secure against unreasonable search and seizure. The Court has held that an accused has a section 8 right only if they have a reasonable expectation of privacy. The Court has also defined various circumstances in which an accused does *not* have such an expectation. There is no reasonable expectation of privacy in

---

87 *Fleming*, above note 57 at para 4, quoting *R v Wong*, [1990] 3 SCR 36 at 57.

88 See, for example, *R v McColman*, 2021 ONCA 382, relying on *Fleming*, above note 57, for the notion that it ought to "tread lightly" in the area of common law powers and declining to create an expanded vehicle stop power. Beyond that, although mentions of the *Waterfield* test or the ancillary powers doctrine in caselaw is at best a rough guide, that does give some suggestion of how frequently the issue arises. According to LexisNexis, in the twenty years prior to *Godoy* in 1999, above note 5, the power was discussed in 202 cases, but in the twenty years after it arose 882 times. However, since *Fleming* in 2019, above note 57, there seems to be a decrease: 234 mentions in the five years prior to *Fleming* but only 158 in the five years after.

89 On this issue generally, see "Black and White," above note 66.

90 *R v Wray*, [1971] SCR 272. A small residual power to exclude extremely prejudicial evidence of little probative value was articulated in that case. Subsequently, the Court began to speak about this non-*Charter* exclusionary power in a way that suggests it might have greater vigour than appeared at the time: see, for example, *R v Buhay*, 2003 SCC 30 at para 40.

electricity consumption records, for example.[91] In most cases, a warrantless search is *prima facie* illegal and will violate section 8 of the *Charter* if not justified in some way. But obtaining an accused's electricity consumption records does not bring into play any reasonable expectation of privacy, and so section 8 is not invoked. Therefore, there are no consequences for police acting without statutory or common law authority: no stay will be issued and no evidence will be excluded, since no *Charter* breach occurred. Although the Court does not describe this as "giving the police the power to obtain electricity consumption records without a warrant," this is a distinction without a difference. Similarly the Court has determined that there is no violation of a reasonable expectation of privacy when police fly over a residence to detect its heat signature with a Forward Looking Infra-Red camera (FLIR): in practical terms, this amounts to authorizing the police to do so, since there remains no basis to object to them doing so.[92]

Other cases have found that a guest in an apartment generally has no reasonable expectation of privacy engaged by a search of that apartment,[93] and passengers do not normally have an expectation of privacy in a motor vehicle.[94] These decisions effectively reflect that the police have the power to search apartments and vehicles as long as they are seeking evidence to incriminate a guest or passenger, rather than the tenant or driver. Although no explicit statutory power exists, and no pre-existing or ancillary common law power will be invoked, the evidence will be admitted just as though the police were acting with authority.

A similar phenomenon has developed with regard to the issue of detention. The Court concluded in *R v Suberu* that a person subject to an investigative detention has the right to counsel.[95] As a result, in ambiguous cases where no right to counsel has been given, trial judges are "forced to choose between finding that there was a detention and associated violations of ss. 9 and 10(b) and finding that there was no detention and no *Charter* violation."[96] In *Suberu* itself, a police officer engaged the accused in questioning for a short time, but the Court concluded that this was merely exploratory and did not result in the

91 *R v Plant*, [1993] 3 SCR 281.

92 *R v Tessling*, 2004 SCC 67.

93 *R v Edwards*, [1996] 1 SCR 128.

94 *R v Belnavis*, [1997] 3 SCR 341.

95 2009 SCC 33 [*Suberu*].

96 Hamish Stewart, "The *Grant* Trilogy and the Right Against Self-Incrimination" (2009) 66 *Criminal Reports* (6th) 97 at 100. On this issue, see also Steve Coughlan, "Great Strides in Section 9 Jurisprudence" (2009) 66 *Criminal Reports* (6th) 75.

accused being detained. Since there will be no arbitrary detention and no right to counsel if there is no detention, this decision has, in effect, created a power of "exploratory questioning" for police.[97]

More recently in *R v Le* the Court divided over a case where police had, without invitation, entered a backyard and questioned the young men standing there, one of whom was the accused.[98] It was agreed that *at some point* the accused became psychologically detained, and the issue was at exactly what point that occurred: was it when the police first entered the backyard, or was it not until they began asking the accused focused questions? The dissent took the position that it was the focused questioning that constituted the detention, which is an easy position to understand, but nonetheless it is fortunate that the majority opted for the earlier time. Had they not, effectively police would have been given the power to enter backyards uninvited so long as they did not, once there, engage in questioning that constituted a psychological detention.

What are being referred to here as "default common law powers" mean that, on a *de facto* basis, police *can* engage in particular types of behaviour without the possibility of anyone objecting. However, it is important to distinguish that situation from real statutory or common law powers. The question of whether police were authorized by law to act as they did can arise in many contexts: for example, a search without lawful authority will violate section 8 of the *Charter*, while a detention without lawful authority will violate section 9. In this context a default power should not be regarded as "lawful authority."

This point was made by the Court in *R v Spencer*, where the police obtained the accused's IP address from his internet service provider without a warrant, something that would normally be an unreasonable search.[99] Some provincial courts of appeal had found that this was lawful due to the combined effect of two provisions: a section in the *Personal Information Protection and Electronic Documents Act*, which permitted businesses to disclose information to a government agency which identified its "lawful authority,"[100] and a provision in the *Criminal Code*, which stated, in essence, that police could ask someone to voluntarily provide information.[101] The Court held that the combination of

97 See the discussion of this issue in Chapter 5, Section C(1).

98 *R v Le*, 2019 SCC 34.

99 2014 SCC 43 [*Spencer*].

100 SC 2000, c 5, s 7(3).

101 At the time *Spencer* was decided, s 487.014 of the *Code* reads:

> For greater certainty, no production order is necessary for a peace officer or public officer enforcing or administering this or any other Act of Parliament

these two provisions could not combine to create a search power. The *Code* provision was "a declaratory provision that confirms the existing common law powers of police officers to make enquiries," but "lawful authority" had to mean something more than just the ability to make a bare request.[102]

Finally, it is worth noting that the application of section 24(2), in considering whether to exclude evidence following a proven *Charter* breach, also carries the hazard of acting as an implied licence, but courts are generally on guard against that risk. That is, if there were a pattern that a particular type of police behaviour was always found to violate some right, but that violation was never found to be serious enough to result in a remedy being granted, then there would be effectively nothing preventing the police from regularly engaging in that behaviour in the future. Courts have long stressed, however, that the long-term impact on the justice system must be considered in making any decision about whether to exclude, which is a way of guarding against this danger.[103]

## 4) Consent

Cooperation by a suspect is effectively another source of police powers. As Martin J noted:

> Although a police officer is entitled to question any person in order to obtain information with respect to a suspected offence, he, as a general rule, has no power to compel the person questioned to answer. . . . If, however, the suspect chooses to answer questions put to him by the police, his answers are admissible if the prosecution establishes that his statements were voluntary.[104]

This principle, that police need no statutory or common law authority to obtain evidence by making a request of a suspect, can arise in many contexts. It arises, for example, in considering whether an accused has voluntarily chosen to speak to police, to allow a search, to provide DNA samples, to stop a vehicle, and so on.

---

to ask a person to voluntarily provide to the officer documents, data or information that the person is not prohibited by law from disclosing.

102 *Spencer*, above note 99 at paras 71–73.

103 See, for example, *R v Kokesch*, [1990] 3 SCR 3 at para 61: "This Court must not be seen to condone deliberate unlawful conduct designed to subvert both the legal and constitutional limits of police power to intrude on individual privacy."

104 *R v Esposito* (1985), 49 CR (3d) 193 (Ont CA), quoted in *R v Hicks* (1988), 64 CR (3d) 68 (Ont CA), aff'd [1990] 1 SCR 120.

As a result, it is important to be able to determine whether there truly has been consent to whatever activity the police have carried out. Mere compliance does not constitute consent: it is simply a failure to object. Consent requires actual agreement and cooperation.[105] Most people are not aware of the limits of police power, the Court has noted, and are frequently unaware that they could refuse to comply with a request. Therefore, in those circumstances, it cannot be said that the accused has really consented. Thus, pulling a car over to the side of the road when directed to,[106] emptying the contents of a sports bag,[107] or complying with a breathalyzer demand without first calling counsel,[108] for example, cannot automatically be considered a consensual action. A person will not be held to have consented in the absence of sufficient information about the right they are giving up: choosing requires not just preferring one option over another, but also having sufficient available information to make that preference meaningful.[109] A frequently relied on authority has held that, in addition to the requirement that any consent be voluntary, the giver of the consent must be aware of the nature of the police conduct to which they are being asked to give consent, that they are aware of the right to refuse, and that they are aware of the potential consequences of giving the consent.[110] Mere acquiescence to a search is not enough.[111]

Further, the Court has so far rejected the notion of "third-party consent," finding that a right can only be waived by the person to whom it belongs. If a person has a privacy interest in the contents of a computer, for example, the consent of some other person who also has a property or privacy interest in that computer will not be sufficient authority for the police to search.[112] The Court has left open, however, the question

105 *R v Knox*, [1996] 3 SCR 199 at para 10.

106 *Dedman*, above note 61.

107 *R v Mellenthin*, [1992] 3 SCR 615.

108 *R v Therens*, [1985] 1 SCR 613.

109 *R v Borden*, [1994] 3 SCR 145 at para 34 [*Borden*].

110 *R v Wills* (1992), 12 CR (4th) 58 (Ont CA). See also *R v McMahon*, 2018 SKCA 26.

111 *R v Davidson*, 2017 ONCA 257.

112 *R v Cole*, 2012 scc 53; *R v Reeves*, 2018 SCC 56 [*Reeves*]. Note, however, that this situation can be made more complicated by questions other than consent. If one person hands over to the police a computer over which they have shared possession with the accused, there will be a violation of the s 8 rights of the accused. However, if that person instead *copies the data* from the computer and hands that over or simply describes the contents of the computer to the police, there will be no s 8 violation, because the actions of the private individual who obtained the data were not subject to the *Charter* at all. See, for example, *R v King*, 2021 ABCA 271 or *R v Lambert*, 2023 ONCA 689.

of whether the consent of one person is sufficient authority for police to enter a shared home.[113]

Issues also arise around the limits of an accused's consent. For example, the Supreme Court has held that to take a DNA sample provided for the investigation of one offence and use it for purposes other than those consented to violates the guarantee against unreasonable search and seizure, specifically in the investigation of another offence.[114] On the other hand, they have also held that, if an accused does consensually provide DNA samples without attaching limits to their potential use, then the accused no longer has a reasonable expectation of privacy in the sample and the police are free to use it in any way they wish.[115]

Finally, it is worth noting that consent, even if given initially, can be revoked. In *R v Thomas*, for example, police entered a house where a noisy party was taking place, eventually leading to a confrontation in which they arrested the owner of the house for assaulting a peace officer in the execution of duty. The Court held that the only basis on which the police were in the house was by the consent of the owner, and that consent had been withdrawn before the confrontation arose. Accordingly, the police were not acting in the execution of duty and the accused was acquitted.[116]

## B. SOURCES OF PRE-TRIAL AND TRIAL PROCEDURE

### 1) Constitution

#### a) Division of Powers

As noted above, section 91(27) of the *Constitution Act, 1867* reserves the power to make laws in relation to "the Criminal Law, except the Constitution of Courts of Criminal Jurisdiction, but including the Procedure in Criminal Matters," to the exclusive legislative jurisdiction of Parliament. Although the effect of this division of power is to make decisions of Parliament by far the most important to criminal proced ure, provincial jurisdiction also has a significant impact. For example, the provinces are competent to create superior and provincial courts

113 *Reeves*, above note 112.

114 *Borden*, above note 109.

115 *R v Arp*, [1998] 3 SCR 339. See the discussion below in Chapter 4.

116 *R v Thomas*, [1993] 1 SCR 835.

with jurisdiction within their territorial limits.[117] Judges of the former are appointed by the Governor General, pursuant to section 96 of the *Constitution Act, 1867*, while judges of the latter are appointed by the appropriate Lieutenant Governor. Both of these federally or provincially appointed judges can hear criminal matters, even though the subject matter of criminal law is in federal jurisdiction. Further, while Parliament has exclusive authority to establish penitentiaries,[118] in which sentences of two years or more are served, the provinces maintain jails for shorter terms of imprisonment.[119] And while Parliament has the authority to make laws that define police powers in criminal matters, including powers of arrest and search, the provision of police services is a matter that forms part of the administration of justice within a province or territory.[120] The allocation of jurisdiction over criminal procedure to Parliament reflects a deliberate policy at Confederation that the criminal law should be national in scope.[121] This objective is more easily achieved in statutory law than in judicial decisions, which leave open the possibility of inconsistency among provinces and even within provinces. It might be noted, however, that statutory law relating to criminal procedure is not uniform in all parts of Canada. For example, the structure of the courts is not the same in all jurisdictions,

---

117 *Constitution Act, 1867*, above note 2, s 92(14). See also Jim Philips, Philip Girard & R Blake Brown, *A History of Law in Canada. Volume Two: Law for the New Dominion, 1867-1914* (Toronto: University of Toronto Press, 2018) at pp 77–78:

> New courts were established when Alberta and Saskatchewan were made provinces in 1905. Initially the NWTSC continued as the Superior Court in each jurisdiction, but in 1907 the provincial legislatures created the Supreme Courts of Alberta and Saskatchewan, and the NWTSC was abolished.

See also the *King's Bench Act*, SS 2023, c 28, continuing what had been the Saskatchewan Court of Queen's Bench as the Court of King's Bench, the superior court for the province.

118 *Constitution Act, 1867*, above note 2, s 91(28).

119 *Ibid*, s 92(6). On the division of penal institutions between federal and provincial authority and, in particular, the division at sentences of two years, see Mary Campbell, *"A Most Vexatious Burden": Jurisdiction in Canadian Correctional Law* (LLM thesis, McGill University, 1997) [unpublished]. See also Martin Friedland, *A Century of Criminal Justice* (Toronto: Carswell, 1984) at 61–62; and HG Needham, "Historical Perspectives on the Federal–Provincial Split in Jurisdiction in Corrections" (1980) 22 *Canadian Journal of Criminology* 298.

120 Section 92(14). See Peter Hogg, *Constitutional Law of Canada*, 5th ed (Toronto: Carswell, 2007) (loose-leaf) ch 19.

121 See Friedland, above note 119 at 47–49. See also the opening words of s 8 of the *Criminal Code*.

nor is the allocation of jurisdiction to those courts.[122] The courts have also held that some aspects of criminal procedure may be applied differentially across Canadian jurisdictions. That is, the constitution of Canada does not require uniform application of the law in all parts of the country.[123] There have been challenges to the validity of provincial legislation on the grounds that it trespasses upon Parliament's exclusive jurisdiction over matters of criminal law.[124] There have also been challenges to federal legislation that created criminal offences on the basis that the particular law reached into the provincial sphere, rather than being a proper exercise of power under section 91(27) of the *Constitution Act, 1867*.[125] In addition, there have been challenges suggesting that some aspects of criminal procedure were not within Parliament's legislative competence according to the division of powers.[126]

One particular division-of-powers issue that, in the words of the Court, "seems to have 'boiled up' rather late in our constitutional jurisprudence" was the question of whether the constitutional authority to prosecute criminal offences rests with the federal or the provincial government.[127] As a matter of fact, prosecutions were, at the time of Confederation and for a considerable period thereafter, conducted exclusively by the provinces (other than private prosecutions, discussed below). About 100 years after Confederation, Parliament created federal legislation, some of it constitutionally justified as criminal law under section 91(27), which was to be prosecuted by federally appointed prosecutors. For the most part, these consisted then, as they do today, of narcotics offences, now found in the *Controlled Drugs and Substances Act*.[128] This development led to a series of constitutional challenges to determine

122 Québec and Nunavut, in particular, have different structures than most provinces and territories. Nunavut, because of the great distances and scattered population, has created a unified criminal court rather than maintaining separate inferior and superior courts.

123 See, for example, *R v Turpin*, [1989] 1 SCR 1296; *R v S(S)*, [1990] 2 SCR 254; and *R v Furtney*, [1991] 3 SCR 89.

124 See, for example, *Johnson v Alberta (Attorney General)*, [1954] SCR 127; *R v Westendorp*, [1983] 1 SCR 43; and *R v Morgentaler*, [1993] 3 SCR 463.

125 See, for example, *Canada (AG) v PHS Community Services Society*, 2011 SCC 44; *Reference re Firearms Act (Canada)*, [2000] 1 SCR 783; *Reference re Validity of Section 5(a) of the Dairy Industry Act*, [1949] SCR 1; and *Proprietary Articles Trade Association v Attorney-General for Canada*, [1931] AC 310 (JCPC).

126 See *MacMillan Bloedel Ltd v Simpson Inc*, [1995] 4 SCR 725; *R v Romanowicz* (1999), 138 CCC (3d) 225 (Ont CA).

127 *Canada (Attorney General) v Canadian National Transportation Ltd; Canada (Attorney General) v Canadian Pacific Transport Co*, [1983] 2 SCR 206 at 235 [*AG (Canada)*].

128 Above note 23.

whether appointing prosecutors was constitutionally a matter of criminal procedure under section 91(27) (and therefore federal) or a matter of administration of justice in the province under section 92(14) (and therefore provincial).

Incrementally, the cases worked their way to a conclusion and eventually reached the final decision that the authority to decide who will prosecute criminal offences has always rested with the federal government and that the fact that provinces had conducted virtually all prosecutions was simply a practical accommodation resting on the abstention of the federal government from appointing prosecutors.[129] As a result, federal legislation that appointed federal prosecutors in the case of some offences did not violate the division of powers.

It is important to recognize, though, that these decisions did not purport to remove any ability for the provinces to appoint prosecutors. Parliament had created a few exceptions to the practice of provincially appointed prosecutors, and those exceptions were constitutional. Parliament had not opted to take over the task of criminal prosecutions generally (though seemingly the decisions mean that it could), with the result that, as a matter of practice, the great bulk of criminal law offences are prosecuted by provincial authorities. This reality is reflected in the definition of "Attorney General" in section 2 of the *Code*, which generally defines the term to mean the attorney general of the province where the proceedings are taken. This approach is subject to a few exceptions, such as terrorism offences, where the federal attorney general is also included: all of those exception are listed in section 2.3 of the *Code*.[130] Similarly, there are a few provisions, such as section 579.1, which give the federal attorney general a power to intervene in some prosecutions, which is roughly parallel to the power to intervene given to provincial attorneys general in section 579.

A similar issue arises around the establishment of courts. Many aspects of criminal procedure are assigned to "superior courts," which have authority pursuant to section 96 of the *Constitution Act, 1867*. As a matter of constitutional law, exclusive jurisdiction over powers that are integral to the operation of a superior court and, therefore, part of their

---

129 See *AG (Canada)*, above note 127. See also *R v Hauser*, [1979] 1 SCR 984; and *R v Wetmore (County Court Judge)*, [1983] 2 SCR 284.

130 This particular provision was introduced in Bill C-75, *An Act to amend the Criminal Code, the Youth Criminal Justice Act and other Acts and to make consequential amendments to other Acts*, Royal Assent June 21, 2019. It did not make any change to the particular offences for which the federal attorney general had authority to prosecute, but for the sake of convenience listed them all in a single section.

core functions cannot be assigned to some other court or body, whether that body is federally or provincially created.[131]

### b) The Canadian Charter of Rights and Freedoms

The impact of the *Charter* on investigative powers was noted above. In fact, it has also had considerable significance on rules of pre-trial and trial procedure. Some of the *Charter*'s "Legal Rights" provisions are aimed directly at such issues: for example, section 14 guarantees the right to an interpreter and section 13 protects against having self-incriminating testimony used. Other rights, though somewhat less specific, also have a direct bearing on these types of procedural issues: the section 11(b) right to a trial within a reasonable time or the section 11(e) right not to be denied reasonable bail without just cause, for example. Further, the guarantee in section 7 of procedures that are in accordance with the principles of fundamental justice has been held to guarantee the right to make full answer and defence[132] and the right to silence.[133] It is also the basis upon which the Supreme Court developed principles relating to pre-trial disclosure by the prosecution.[134]

Another effect of the *Charter* has been a reconsideration of the personal and public interests involved in criminal procedure. Until comparatively recently, criminal procedure was typically conceived as a matter involving the interests of the state and the accused. Civil liberties were understood to refer to the rights of the persons suspected or accused of wrongdoing. Interpretation of the *Charter* has brought an important change to these views. The courts have recognized that complainants, witnesses, and other third parties might have constitutional rights under the *Charter* that could be invoked and enforced in the course of criminal proceedings. Thus, for example, the right to a

---

131 *R v Ahmad*, 2011 SCC 6 [*Ahmad*]. In *Ahmad*, the issue was that, under the *Canada Evidence Act*, RSC 1985, c C-5, the Federal Court is given authority to decide whether a claim of national security privilege exists, which would therefore prevent disclosure of certain information to an accused in a criminal trial. The Court found that there was no constitutional problem. What was essential was that the superior court retained the ability to ensure that an accused would receive a fair trial. Since the superior court retained the ability to decide what remedy the accused would receive in light of any non-disclosure, which might include a stay of proceedings, the constitutional requirements were met.

132 See, for example, *R v Chambers*, [1990] 2 SCR 1293; *R v Rose*, [1998] 3 SCR 262; *R v Mills*, [1999] 3 SCR 668 [*Mills*]; and *R v McClure*, 2001 SCC 14.

133 See *R v Hebert*, [1990] 2 SCR 151; and *R v Liew*, [1999] 3 SCR 227. See also the Court's discussion of this right in *R v Singh*, 2007 SCC 48.

134 See, for example, *R v Stinchcombe*, [1991] 3 SCR 326; and *R v Dixon*, [1998] 1 SCR 244. See also the discussion in Chapter 8.

reasonable expectation of privacy has been identified as a reason not to disclose the personal records of complainants in the prosecution of sexual offences,[135] as helping to define the interests of a complainant in a voyeurism offence,[136] and even to be relevant to litigation over employment.[137] Similarly, freedom of expression has been invoked as a reason to allow a broadcaster the right to publish an account of some proceedings.[138]

The extent to which a person other than the accused may claim and enforce a right under the *Charter* during proceedings against the accused remains to be developed, though the interests of third parties are taken into account in regard to many issues. In deciding the reasonableness of a search against a suspect, for example, the extent to which that search will also invade the privacy of others is taken into consideration.[139] Similarly, concern for the rights and interests of third parties has had a powerful influence on the development of legislation in criminal procedure.[140] In addition, the Supreme Court has become more open to public interest standing, allowing constitutional challenges to be brought more readily outside the context of a prosecution.[141]

## 2) Statute

The essential elements of criminal procedure are found in the *Criminal Code*. The *Code* is not the sole statutory source of rules and principles of criminal procedure, however, because there are many additional elements scattered throughout federal legislation.[142] Specific police

135 *O'Connor*, above note 7, and *Mills*, above note 132.

136 *R v Jarvis*, 2019 SCC 10.

137 *York Region District School Board v Elementary Teachers' Federation of Ontario*, 2024 SCC 22.

138 See, for example, *Dagenais v Canadian Broadcasting Corp*, [1994] 3 SCR 835; *Canadian Broadcasting Corp v New Brunswick (Attorney General)*, [1996] 3 SCR 480; *R v Mentuck*, [2001] 3 SCR 442; and *Vancouver Sun (Re)*, [2004] 2 SCR 332.

139 See, for example, *R v Rogers Communications Partnership*, 2014 ONSC 3853, where the police sought a warrant to obtain records of all calls routed through a cellphone tower in order to try to trace the accused, but the judge took into account that such a warrant would also result in the disclosure to the police of the personal information of at least 9,000 individuals.

140 See the discussion of this issue in Kent Roach, *Due Process and Victims' Rights* (Toronto: University of Toronto Press, 1999).

141 See the discussion in Lisa Kerr & Elin Sigurdson, "'They Want In': Sex Workers and Legitimacy Debates in the Law of Public Interest Standing" (2017) 80 SCLR (2d) 145.

142 See, for example, *Controlled Drugs and Substances Act*, above note 23; *Customs Act*, above note 29; *Firearms Act*, above note 31; *Fisheries Act*, RSC 1985, c F-14;

powers, for example, can be found in dozens of statutes dealing with different matters within federal jurisdiction. These are especially clear in relation to search and seizure. Many statutes also contain specific provisions that affect procedural aspects of the enforcement of criminal offences. There are also statutes that stand apart from the *Code* but contain important elements of criminal procedure, for example, the *Identification of Criminals Act*[143] and the *Criminal Records Act*.[144] In addition, although they are not strictly matters of criminal procedure, all provinces have statutes which govern the prosecution of provincial, as opposed to criminal, offences. In some cases, these provincial statutes largely adopt the summary conviction procedures from the *Code*,[145] but in others entirely separate regimes have been established.[146] Provided a court has jurisdiction under each statute, a judge can exercise jurisdiction under each simultaneously.[147]

The presentation of the rules and principles of criminal procedure in the *Code* has become increasingly complex with successive amendments.[148] There are important features in the introductory part, including some definitions applicable throughout (though other definitions are also found within particular parts) and provisions concerning the liability of persons who exercise powers under the *Code*. There are also important aspects of procedure that are found among parts of the *Code* that comprise substantive offences. Illustrations of this include the provisions on electronic surveillance,[149] the application for disclosure of personal records,[150] and the procedure for taking breath or blood samples in suspected cases of impaired driving.[151]

---

*Competition Act*, RSC 1985, c C-34; *Food and Drugs Act*, RSC 1985, c F-27; *Income Tax Act*, RSC 1985 (5th Supp), c 1; *Proceeds of Crime (Money Laundering) and Terrorist Financing Act*, SC 2000, c 17; *Security of Information Act*, RSC 1985, c O-5; *Crimes Against Humanity and War Crimes Act*, SC 2000, c 24; *Youth Criminal Justice Act*, SC 2002, c 1; *Excise Act*, RSC 1985, c E-14; *Bankruptcy and Insolvency Act*, RSC 1985, c B-3.

143 Above note 20.

144 RSC 1985, c C-47.

145 See, for example, the *Summary Proceedings Act*, RSNS 1989, c 450, s 7.

146 As an instance of the latter, see the *Provincial Offences Act*, RSO 1990, c P.33.

147 *R v Sciascia*, 2017 SCC 57.

148 For an attempt to impose a logic on the various provisions in the *Criminal Code* and to make the underlying structure and connections more apparent, see Steve Coughlan & Alex Gorlewski, *The Anatomy of Criminal Procedure: A Visual Guide to the Law*, 2nd ed (Toronto: University of Toronto Press, 2026).

149 Section 184.

150 Section 278.1ff.

151 Section 320.27ff.

The *Criminal Code* contains twenty-eight Parts, and most of the provisions concerning procedure are found beginning in Part XIV. The general organizing principle is the chronological sequence of a criminal prosecution. This organizing principle is more approximate than rigorous, but it remains the only discernible principle for the order of these Parts of the *Code*. Each individual Part comprises clusters of provisions that are thematically linked, although the thematic coherence of some Parts is less apparent than in others. The major procedural themes in Part XIV and the following are jurisdiction, search and seizure, compelling appearance, preliminary inquiry, trial procedure for summary conviction offences, and for indictable offences tried with or without a jury, sentencing, judicial review, and appeal.

It should also be noted that there are many cross-references among the various Parts, with the result that the rules governing one set of procedures are found in whole or in part in an entirely different place. Somewhat oddly, much of Canadian criminal trial procedure derives from procedure in jury trials, the rules for which are found in Part XX of the *Code*. As a matter of fact, few criminal trials are conducted with a jury, and, indeed, most occur in provincial courts, which cannot have juries. However, the rules in Part XX are incorporated by reference in other Parts, and they therefore have general application.[152]

## 3) Common Law

The *Criminal Code* is not, strictly speaking, a code. It is not a single, comprehensive statement of Canadian criminal law because, as already noted, there are many other statutes that deal with aspects of criminal law in Canada. The *Code* prohibits the prosecution of common law offences, with the exception of criminal contempt, but it expressly preserves the power of the courts to develop new common law defences. It contains no complete general part.[153] Hence, the *Code* is more accurately defined as a consolidation of the principal elements of Canadian criminal law.[154]

---

152 Sections 572 and 795.

153 A general part would specify the blameworthy states of mind for each offence. Its absence has been identified as a shortcoming for which "[l]egislative intervention is sorely needed": *R v Tatton*, 2015 SCC 33 at para 25.

154 For further discussion, see Alan Mewett, "The Criminal Law, 1867–1967" (1967) 45 *Canadian Bar Review* 726; Josiah Wood & Richard Peck, eds, *One Hundred Years of the Criminal Code in Canada* (Ottawa: Canadian Bar Association, 1993).

See also Gerry Ferguson, "From Jeremy Bentham to Anne McLellan: Lessons on Criminal Law Codification" in Don Stuart, Ronald J Delisle, & Allan Manson,

This description is particularly apt as regards procedure. The *Code* establishes the architectural elements of criminal procedure and provides, in addition, many of the details, but it is not a comprehensive statement of positive rules. To fill in the gaps, two sources may be called in aid. The first is the judicial interpretation of statutory provisions; this is not truly the common law at work because it is just interpretation of what the legislature has said. Nevertheless, the common law is often useful in this exercise because it is an important historical source of analogies and other guidance.

The second source is the common law itself. In some instances, where the *Code* is incomplete, the common law might provide a source for the resolution of ambiguity. Indeed, the *Code* occasionally makes reference to principles of the common law without any further development or elaboration. For example, the *Code* expressly recognizes the power of the courts to punish for contempt (this is, substantively, the only common law crime that still exists in Canada, preserved in section 9). However, because it is a common law crime, there is no definition of the offence and no procedure for such cases. In effect, therefore, the *Code* incorporates the common law by reference, as it relates to contempt for a substantive definition and for procedure.[155]

Similarly, in instances where the *Code* is silent, the common law might afford a solution of its own. Many illustrations might be given, but two will suffice. The doctrine of abuse of process leading to a stay of proceedings is a creation of the courts in Canada and, accordingly, until it was partly merged with the principles of fundamental justice in section 7 of the *Charter*, it was a creature of the common law.[156] The rule against multiple convictions is also a development of the courts at common law that extends the principle of protection against double jeopardy.[157]

---

*Towards a Clear and Just Criminal Law* (Toronto: Carswell, 1999) 192 or Jula Hughes, "Making Amendability a Priority in Criminal Code Reform" in Julie Desrosiers, Margarida Garcia & Marie-Ève Sylvestre (dir), *Réformer le droit criminel au Canada: défis et possibilités / Criminal Law Reform in Canada: Challenges and Possibilities* (Cowansville: Éditions Yvon Blais, 2017).

155 See *United Nurses of Alberta v Alberta (Attorney General)*, [1992] 1 SCR 901; and *R v Arradi*, 2003 SCC 23. To similar effect, see *R v DLW*, 2016 SCC 22. That case considered s 160 of the *Code*, which makes bestiality an offence but does not define the term. The Court concluded that "bestiality" had a well-understood common law legal meaning at the time the offence was put in the *Code*, and therefore that meaning had to be used.

156 See, for example, *R v Jewitt*, [1985] 2 SCR 128; and *O'Connor*, above note 7.

157 See *R v Kienapple*, [1975] 1 SCR 729; and *R v Prince*, [1986] 2 SCR 480.

## 4) Rules of Court

Section 482 of the *Criminal Code* allows for the creation of rules of court by the various courts of criminal jurisdiction. These rules and practice directions are administrative in nature, and their purpose is the effective and efficient administration of the criminal law within the jurisdiction to which they apply. Rules of court cannot alter the rights and liabilities of any party as they stand within the Constitution, statute, or common law: that is, they cannot be inconsistent with the law.[158] Nonetheless, rules of court can have a major impact: bans on broadcasting judicial proceedings are established by rules of court, for example. Such a ban violates the section 2(b) *Charter* guarantee of freedom of expression, but can be saved under section 1.[159]

Of growing importance in the administration of the courts, especially in large urban areas where, consequently, the courts have a large volume of cases, are procedures for the management of cases. Section 482.1 provides that trial and appellate courts can make rules for this purpose. The courts have discretion to determine whether there should be such rules and, if so, what the purpose and content should be. Once made, however, they are mandatory.

Further, section 551.1 allows for the appointment of a case management judge on the application of the prosecutor, the accused, or a supervising judge.[160] A case management judge can be appointed where that is necessary for the proper administration of justice. The legislation was intended to respond to the problems that arise in so-called mega-trials, though now it is looked to more generally as a way to reduce delay in the system. The case management judge (who might or might not be the trial judge) is empowered to take steps aimed at making the process more efficient, such as assisting the parties to identify the witnesses to be heard, encouraging the parties to make admissions and reach agreements, or adjudicating matters before trial, such as questions of disclosure, the admissibility of evidence, *Charter* motions, change of venue applications, and so on.[161] In addition, the case management judge can adjudicate

---

158 See, for example, *R v Purdy*, 2010 BCCA 413, holding that the court cannot rely on the power to make rules of court as a means of creating appeal rights not already set out in the *Code*.

159 *Canadian Broadcasting Corp v Canada (Attorney General)*, 2011 SCC 2.

160 Section 551.1 allows the Chief Justice, the Chief Judge of the court before which the trial will be held, or some judge designated to make the decision or order a case management judge on their own motion.

161 Section 551.3.

issues during trial referred by the trial judge, potentially in a joint hearing which will affect more than one related trial.[162]

## 5) Judicial Independence

Although judicial independence is not strictly a separate source of criminal procedure, the Supreme Court has described it as the "lifeblood of constitutionalism in democratic societies."[163] This principle is referred to in sections 96 to 100 of the *Constitution Act, 1867* and in section 11(d) of the *Charter*, but it also extends beyond the limited situations covered by those provisions.

Judicial independence requires both individual independence (that of individual judges) and institutional independence (that of the court of which the judge is a member). It depends on objective guarantees of the judiciary's freedom from influence or any interference by others in security of tenure, financial security, and administrative independence. The historic rationale for judicial independence was to ensure that judges were able to decide individual cases without governmental interference. More recently, it has also come to be seen as important to the courts' role of ensuring protection of the rule of law and of acting as a shield against unwarranted deprivations by the state of the rights and freedoms of individuals. It includes a core administrative component extending to administrative decisions that bear on the exercise of the judicial function such as assignment of judges, sittings of the court, and direction of the administrative staff engaged in carrying out these functions.[164]

Concerns about judicial independence led provinces to amend their processes for appointing justices of the peace to ensure that these officials will be capable of acting in a proper judicial manner when dealing with applications by police to obtain warrants, lay charges, and so on.[165]

# FURTHER READINGS

Campbell, Mary. "A Most Vexatious Burden": Jurisdiction in Canadian Correctional Law (LLM thesis, McGill University, 1997) [unpublished].

162 Sections 551.6 and 551.7. See the discussion of case management judges and other issues related to "mega-trials" in Christine Mainville, "Report on the CIAJ's Complex Criminal Trials Roundtable" (2015) 62 *Criminal Law Quarterly* 339.

163 *R v Beauregard*, [1986] 2 SCR 56 at 70.

164 *Ontario v Criminal Lawyers' Association of Ontario*, 2013 SCC 43.

165 *Ell v Alberta*, [2003] 1 SCR 857.

Coughlan, Steve. "Police Detention for Questioning: A Proposal — Part I" (1985) 28 *Criminal Law Quarterly* 64.

———. "Common Law Police Powers and the Rule of Law" (2007) 47 *Criminal Reports* (6th) 266.

———. "Great Strides in Section 9 Jurisprudence" (2009) 66 *Criminal Reports* (6th) 75.

——— & Alex Gorlewski. *The Anatomy of Criminal Procedure: A Visual Guide to the Law*, 2nd ed (Toronto: University of Toronto Press, 2026).

Fairburn, Michal. "Twenty-Five Years in Search of a Reasonable Approach" in Jamie Cameron & James Stribopoulos, eds, *The Charter and Criminal Justice: Twenty-Five Years Later* (Toronto: LexisNexis Butterworths, 2008).

Ferguson, Gerry. "From Jeremy Bentham to Anne McLellan: Lessons on Criminal Law Codification" in Don Stuart, Ronald J Delisle, & Allan Manson, *Towards a Clear and Just Criminal Law* (Toronto: Carswell, 1999) 192–218.

Friedland, Martin. *A Century of Criminal Justice* (Toronto: Carswell, 1984).

Healy, Patrick. "Investigative Detention in Canada" (2005) *Criminal Law Review* 98.

Hoggy, Peter. *Constitutional Law of Canada*, 5th ed (Toronto: Carswell, 2007) (loose-leaf) ch 19.

Hughes, Jula. "Making Amendability a Priority in Criminal Code Reform" in Julie Desrosiers, Margarida Garcia & Marie-Ève Sylvestre (dir), *Réformer le droit criminel au Canada: défis et possibilités /Criminal Law Reform in Canada: Challenges and Possibilities* (Cowansville: Éditions Yvon Blais, 2017).

Kerr, Lisa, & Elin Sigurdson. "'They Want In': Sex Workers and Legitimacy Debates in the Law of Public Interest Standing" (2017) 80 *Supreme Court Law Review* (2d) 145.

Mainville, Christine. "Report on the CIAJ's Complex Criminal Trials Roundtable" (2015) 62 *Criminal Law Quarterly* 339.

Mewett, Alan. "The Criminal Law, 1867–1967" (1967) 45 *Canadian Bar Review* 726.

Mitchell, Graeme G. "R v Godoy: Constitutional Accommodation of Public Service Programs" (1999) 21 *Criminal Reports* (5th) 217.

Needham, HG. "Historical Perspectives on the Federal–Provincial Split in Jurisdiction in Corrections" (1980) 22 *Canadian Journal of Criminology* 298.

Philips, Jim, Philip Girard & R. Blake Brown, *A History of Law in Canada. Volume Two: Law for the New Dominion*, 1867–1914 (Toronto, Ontario: University of Toronto Press, 2018)

Pringle, Heather. "The Smoke and Mirrors of Godoy: Creating Common Law Authority While Making Feeney Disappear" (1999) 21 *Criminal Reports* (5th) 227.

Roach, Kent. *Due Process and Victims' Rights* (Toronto: University of Toronto Press, 1999).

Steward, Hamish. "The Grant Trilogy and the Right Against Self-Incrimination" (2009) 66 *Criminal Reports* (6th) 97.

Stribopoulos, James. "In Search of Dialogue: The Supreme Court, Police Powers and the Charter" (2005) 31 *Queen's Law Journal* 1.

Stuart, Don. "Godoy: The Supreme Court Reverts to the Ancillary Powers Doctrine to Fill a Gap in Police Power" (1999) 21 *Criminal Reports* (5th) 225.

Wood, Josiah, & Richard Peck, eds. *One Hundred Years of the Criminal Code in Canada* (Ottawa: Canadian Bar Association, 1993).

CHAPTER 3

# ELEMENTS OF CRIMINAL PROCEDURE

## A. CLASSIFICATION OF OFFENCES AND MODE OF TRIAL

### 1) Introduction

Over a number of years, and with increasing amendments to the *Criminal Code*,[1] the procedures for deciding the mode of trial have become needlessly complex. The current scheme is "based more on the accidents of history than on any rational plan."[2] As a practical matter, it is easiest to understand the current system first by imagining the very simple system that, at least conceptually, underlies it and then by looking at the variety of exceptions that serve to effectively conceal that model.

Imagine a system of prosecuting crimes that has only two types of offences and two methods of prosecution: less serious offences that are prosecuted in lower courts, and more serious offences that are prosecuted in superior courts. That seems to be the underlying theory of our classification and mode of trial system, but it is subject

1 For an explanation of this issue in chart form, see Steve Coughlan & Alex Gorlewski, *The Anatomy of Criminal Procedure: A Visual Guide to the Law*, 2nd ed (Toronto: University of Toronto Press, 2026) [*Anatomy of Criminal Procedure*], Chart 2.4(a), "Determining the Mode of Trial."

2 Law Reform Commission of Canada, *Classification of Offences* (Ottawa: Law Reform Commission of Canada, 1986) at 1 [*Classification of Offences*].

to amendments, exceptions, and sub-exceptions relating to the number of types of offences, the number of modes of trial, and the provision to the accused of a choice of mode of trial in some cases and then the removal of that choice in others. We shall pursue each of these issues in more detail below, but an overview of how these exceptions overlay the simple model will be a useful starting point.

First, in one sense, our system has only two types of offences: summary conviction offences and indictable offences. However, the model is made more complex because the *Code* provides for a great number of offences that can be prosecuted in either fashion: these are referred to as "hybrid offences." In addition, there are offences under provincial acts which are not crimes but which nonetheless are tried in the same courts as summary conviction offences.[3]

Second, there are not really only two modes of trial, but three. One mode of trial is in front of the "court of criminal jurisdiction," (often referred to as an "inferior court") and the other mode of trial is in front of the "superior court of criminal jurisdiction." However, the superior court can hear matters in two ways: either without a jury (a judge-alone trial) or with a jury.

Third, we do not automatically send all less serious offences to the lower court and all more serious matters to the superior court. For summary conviction offences that equation does hold, and the only mode of trial for them is in the court of criminal jurisdiction. In the case of indictable offences, however, the accused is not forced to choose the top-of-the-line mode of trial and can instead choose whether to have a trial by superior court judge and jury, by superior court judge alone, or by provincial court judge. This choice is referred to as an "election."

Fourth, having given that election to the accused, the *Code* then takes it away again in a number of situations. For example, section 469 lists a series of offences that must be tried by a judge and jury, so the accused is given no election. Further, section 553 lists a number of offences that will be tried in provincial court, and so again the accused is given no election. In principle, the rationale for these two lists relates to the relative seriousness of the offences on them. Section 469 contains serious enough offences — for example, murder — that the public interest demands a jury trial.[4] In contrast, section 553 lists offences that

3 Additional confusion is avoided here by the Supreme Court's finding that a judge with jurisdiction over both summary conviction and provincial offences can try both sets of charges jointly: *R v Sciascia*, 2017 SCC 57.

4 This is the rationale for the particular list of offences, but one could easily disagree as to whether that goal has been achieved. For example, s 469 long included the offence of "Alarming Her Majesty," until that offence was removed

are less serious than most indictable offences (though not so much less serious as to be summary conviction offences, it seems), and so there is no justification to offer the accused any choice beyond provincial court.

Fifth, if the trial will eventually take place in a superior court (either a judge alone, or a judge and jury) and is for an offence with a punishment of fourteen years or more imprisonment, the matter does not go immediately to trial, but can first be referred to a preliminary inquiry in front of the provincial court.[5] Only if this proceeding concludes that there is sufficient evidence will a trial actually take place. However, there is an exception to that rule, in that the Crown has the ability to prefer a "direct indictment," sending the accused to trial without a preliminary inquiry or even despite a discharge at the preliminary inquiry.[6]

Finally, there are various other exceptions to exceptions, such as the ability of the Crown, in some cases, to compel a jury trial regardless of the accused's election,[7] or the ability of the accused to re-elect having made one election,[8] and so on.

One might also note that the way in which the *Code* is drafted does not contribute to an easy understanding of this structure. Section 471, for example, states that trial by jury is compulsory for all indictable offences, unless some other *Code* provision creates an exception to that requirement. Other *Code* provisions then create exceptions for literally *every* offence. One could easily gain the impression that trial by jury is the norm when, in fact, it is a rarity.

We shall pursue each of these issues individually in greater detail. Before doing so, however, it is worth adding a word about the impact of the division of powers between the federal government and provincial governments set out in the *Constitution Act 1867*, essentially just to note that in practice it does *not* create difficulties which might have existed. Jurisdiction over virtually all aspects of the criminal justice

---

from the *Criminal Code* entirely: see *An Act to amend the Criminal Code and the Department of Justice Act and to make consequential amendments to another Act*, SC 2018, c 29.

5 Section 535.

6 Section 577. It is worth being aware of some ambiguity in terminology. The action of laying an information in the ordinary course of proceedings is referred to as "preferring" an indictment: s 574. The use of a "direct indictment" in s 577 is an extraordinary step. However, as a matter of common usage a "direct indictment" is also often referred to as a "preferred indictment." This can create ambiguity over whether it is the ordinary or extraordinary step being referred to.

7 See ss 568 and 577.

8 See s 561.

system is divided between both levels of government. Criminal law and procedure is assigned to the federal government. However, both levels of government have the jurisdiction to create courts and to appoint prosecutors, and as a matter of fact the great majority of criminal prosecutions are conducted by provincially-appointed prosecutors in front of provincially-appointed judges. See the discussion of division of powers in Chapter 2.

## 2) Types of Offences

Criminal offences are classified as indictable or as offences punishable on summary conviction. These are the only two classifications in Canadian criminal procedure. In every statutory provision that creates an offence, Parliament designates the offence by one classification or the other.[9] However, for many offences, Parliament has applied a hybrid classification to give the prosecutor discretion as to whether to proceed by the indictable offence procedure or the summary conviction procedure. That is, the offence is designated to fall into either category. Offences thus designated are commonly called hybrid, or "dual procedure," offences, though that term does not appear in the *Criminal Code*.[10] These are not a third category of offence: they are offences where the Crown has a choice whether to proceed summarily or indictably.[11]

---

9 The *Contraventions Act*, SC 1992, c 47, creates another category of offence called a "contravention," which means, according to s 2, "an offence that is created by an enactment and is designated as a contravention by regulation." Section 8 prohibits the designation of an indictable offence. Section 4 states that the purposes of the Act are to provide a procedure for the prosecution that distinguishes between criminal and regulatory offences and to abolish the legal consequences of conviction. Section 63 specifically provides that there shall be no criminal record upon conviction. In sum, a contravention is not properly classified as a criminal offence, even though Parliament might have originally enacted the offence under the authority of s 91(27) of the *Constitution Act, 1867* (UK), 30 & 31 Vict, c 3.

10 The Supreme Court has described them as existing "nowhere — and everywhere — on the landscape of Canadian criminal procedure": *R v Dudley*, 2009 SCC 58 at para 13 [*Dudley*].

11 If the Crown fails to elect a mode of procedure and the accused then enters a plea before a summary conviction court, the Crown will be deemed to have elected to proceed summarily: *Dudley*, above note 11 at para 3. However, the *Interpretation Act*, RSC 1985, c I-21, s 34, provides that an offence which can be prosecuted by indictment is an indictable offence, which means hybrid offences are treated as indictable offences in some other contexts, such as the exercise of police powers: see, for example, *Collins v Brantford Police Services Board* (2001), 158 CCC (3d) 405 (Ont CA).

Once that election is made, the procedure for that type of offence will be followed.

In broad terms, indictable offences are more serious than summary conviction offences but, unfortunately, the classification of the offence is not always a reliable indication of its relative seriousness. It is certainly true that indictable offences carry a higher maximum penalty than summary conviction offences (and this is uniformly true for hybrid offences, where the penalty will vary depending on the Crown election) but this, by itself, is not a sound or sophisticated gauge of the seriousness of crimes. Indeed, the existence of hybrid offences, and the growing numbers of them, seems only to prove that the classification of offences is not something that can be rationalized by reference only to their seriousness. For example, changes made to the *Code* in 2019 by Bill C-75 have turned almost all indictable offences that are punishable by a maximum penalty of ten years or less into hybrid offences, but did not make that change in every case, leaving a number of weapons offences as purely indictable.[12] Similarly, other changes in that Bill now mean that some hybrid offences carry a maximum penalty of two years when prosecuted by indictment but two years less a day when prosecuted summarily, a very fine distinction.[13]

Nevertheless, the classification of offences is one of the most important organizing principles in the law of criminal procedure. The most obvious is perhaps the jurisdiction of the courts over offences, but some other ramifications of the classification might be noted briefly. The scope of police powers is affected by the classification of offences. The power of the police to arrest, for example, is defined differently for summary conviction and indictable offences.[14] Procedures for compelling appearance and interim release, whether by authority of the police or a judge, are also affected by the classification of the offence with which the accused will be charged or already has been charged.[15]

The classification of offences, of course, also has a profound effect on the manner in which proceedings are conducted in court. Another major difference between summary conviction and indictable offences is that there is no "statute of limitations" for the latter, but there is

12 Bill C-75, *An Act to amend the Criminal Code, the Youth Criminal Justice Act and other Acts and to make consequential amendments to other Acts* [Bill C-75], Royal Assent June 21, 2019.

13 See, for example, s 129. There is the practical difference for an accused that a sentence of two years or more is served in a federal institution while one of less than two years is served in a provincial one.

14 Section 495.

15 See Part XVI.

for the former. Summary conviction offences are usually time-barred twelve months after the completion of the offence.[16] In a case where the only available charge is a summary conviction offence, the classification might therefore determine whether there can be any proceedings at all. If a hybrid offence could be charged in relation to conduct that was completed more than twelve months previously, the prosecutor is not generally time-barred against proceeding by way of indictment.[17] However, doing so might be an abuse of process if the Crown had initially elected to proceed summarily and re-elects only to avoid the limitation period.[18]

The classification of offences has important consequences with regard to the mode of procedure and the jurisdiction of the courts. Virtually all prosecutions begin with a charge document that is called an "information."[19] In all summary conviction matters, and some indictable matters, the information remains the document of charge throughout the proceedings. In such cases the proceedings at trial are conducted in the provincial court.[20] For indictable offences where the trial will take place in superior court, however, the *Code* sometimes allows an accused to begin with a preliminary inquiry on the information before a provincial court judge (preliminary inquiries will be the subject of Chapter 9).[21] The inquiry provides an opportunity for the parties to test the evidence of selected witnesses on specific issues. If there is a preliminary inquiry and the accused is committed for trial, the prosecutor can thereafter file a new charge document, called the "indictment," in the court where the accused will be tried.

---

16 Section 786(2). Until Bill C-75, above note 12, this limitation period was only six months. The limit was raised because many offences that had previously been purely indictable were made hybrid, meaning that the set of offences potentially dealt with summarily now includes more serious offences than it used to.

Note that s 786(2) allows summary proceedings outside this time limit if both the Crown and the accused consent. An accused might choose to waive the protection of this limitation period if the alternative would be that the Crown would instead proceed by way of indictment, raising the risk of a higher penalty.

17 *R v Phelps* (1993), 79 CCC (3d) 550 (Ont CA).

18 *R c Quinn* (1989), 54 CCC (3d) 157 (Que CA).

19 Part XXVIII, Form 2.

20 By virtue of s 553 of the *Code*, offences within the absolute jurisdiction of the provincial court are classified as indictable, but they are tried on an information.

21 Bill C-75, above note 12, has limited preliminary inquiries to offences punishable by imprisonment for fourteen years or more, rather than being available for all indictable offences tried in superior court, as had been the law.

That indictment can be for the charge upon which the person was ordered to stand trial or for "any charge founded on the facts disclosed by the evidence taken on the preliminary inquiry."[22] If there was no preliminary inquiry, either because the accused did not request one or was not entitled to request one, then after the accused has elected the prosecutor can prefer an indictment on any charge (or included charge) in the information.[23] In most provinces the trial court will be the superior court: the exceptions are Québec, where the provincial court has jurisdiction to try all offences except those in which there is trial by judge and jury, and Nunavut, which has a unified federal–provincial criminal court.[24] Thus, the classification of the offence as a summary conviction matter or as an indictable matter has a controlling effect on most elementary matters of jurisdiction.

Another important aspect of whether an offence is classified as summary conviction or indictable concerns sentencing. Indictable offences are typically defined to allow a maximum term of imprisonment that exceeds two years. This definition does not mean, of course, that all indictable offences are in fact punished with imprisonment exceeding two years. Nonetheless, the point is significant because summary conviction offences allow a maximum of two years less a day imprisonment or a maximum fine of five thousand dollars, or both, unless the *Code* prescribes a different punishment.[25] In other words, a convicted accused is likely to receive a lighter sentence if the Crown has elected to proceed summarily rather than indictably on a hybrid offence. However, it is significant that until 2019, the ordinary maximum term of imprisonment for summary conviction offences was only six months: Bill C-75 increased the maximum potential penalty when it swept a large number of relatively more serious offences into the "hybrid" category, meaning they might be dealt with summarily. It is possible that this higher ceiling could lead to an inflation in sentences for summary conviction offences generally. On the other hand, the Court has previously made clear that a sentence should not be "scaled down" or "scaled

---

22 Section 574(1).

23 Section 574(1.1).

24 Section 552.

25 Bill C-75, above note 12, increased the "default" maximum penalty for summary conviction offences to two years less a day imprisonment. This is a reflection of another change in that Bill, which is to hybridize a number of more serious offences which until then could only be prosecuted by indictment: that is, the summary conviction procedure will, because of Bill C-75, be used for more serious offences than in the past.

up" simply by reason of the Crown's election, but should be a fit one,[26] so perhaps there will be no change in practice.[27]

One particular oddity is worth noting here, simply as an illustration of the way in which competing goals and successive amendments can have anomalous results. Until Bill C-75 in 2019, the *Code* singled out a few particular summary conviction offences for eighteen-month maximum sentences, rather than the norm of six months: this was meant to reflect that those offences were more serious than most other summary conviction offences. One of those offences, not surprisingly, was sexual assault when prosecuted summarily. With the changes in Bill C-75 now almost all summary conviction offences had their potential penalty increased to two years less a day. However, no changes were made to the sentences for offences which included a mandatory minimum sentence, because a broader review of those sentences was being undertaken.[28] Sexual assault was one of those offences, and so it was left at the time with a sentence of only eighteen months rather than two years less a day. Since that time the review of mandatory sentences has been completed and a number of changes were made to them.[29] Seemingly as an oversight, however, those changes did not include any change to the *ordinary* sentence for sexual assault when prosecuted summarily. The result is that that more serious offence now has a lesser, rather than greater, sentence than summary conviction offences generally.

As previously noted, offenders sentenced to terms of less than two years are incarcerated in provincial jails, whereas offenders sentenced to

---

26 *R v Solowan*, 2008 SCC 62.

27 The data to date are difficult to interpret. According to Statistics Canada, in the four years after Bill C-75 the percentage of sentences shorter than six months seemed to decrease significantly. In 2015–19 sentences of less than six months made up 81.72%, 70.06%, 68.17%, and 66.63% respectively. In the four years after, those percentages were 43.96%, 49.43%, 47.72%, and 43.61%. There was relatively little change in the percentages of sentences between six months and two years or of over two years, though the former was down slightly and the latter up slightly. However, the largest increase was in the "unknown sentence length" category, which makes it difficult to draw any firm conclusions. See Statistics Canada, *Adult Sentenced Custody Admissions to Correctional Services by Sex and Sentence Length Ordered,* (table), No 35-10-0018-01 (formerly CANSIM 251-0024) (Ottawa: Statistics Canada, 2024).

28 See the letter from the minister of justice to the Standing Senate Committee on Legal and Constitutional Affairs, 10 May 2019, online: https://sencanada.ca/content/sen/committee/421/LCJC/Briefs/2019-05-10-LCJC-MinisterJustice_e.pdf.

29 *An Act to amend the Criminal Code and the Controlled Drugs and Substances Act*, SC 2022, c 15. It is proposed to remedy that omission in Bill C-16, *An Act to amend certain Acts in relation to criminal and correctional matters (child protection, gender-based violence, delays and other measures)*, art. 29, introduced December 2025.

more than two years are incarcerated in federal penitentiaries. Provincial jails, therefore, house offenders serving sentences for offences that might be summary conviction or indictable, provided that the actual term in the warrant of committal is less than two years. Inmates in federal penitentiaries are necessarily there to serve sentences for indictable offences. These factors are relevant in important ways, including the prosecutor's exercise of discretion with regard to hybrid offences and plea discussions.

Finally, the *Criminal Code* provides different arrangements for appeal in summary conviction and indictable matters.[30] The former are heard by the superior court of the province and the latter are heard in the court of appeal. There are also provisions in the *Code*[31] and the *Supreme Court Act*[32] dealing with appeals to the highest court in criminal matters. These matters are further discussed in Chapter 12.

Much criticism has been made of the current classification of offences.[33] Some form of classification is obviously necessary, but the thrust of most critiques has been that the system of classification in current Canadian law is irrationally complex and no longer has any prescriptive coherence. Dividing offences into the approximate categories of "more serious" and "less serious" through the distinction between indictable and summary conviction offences has some intuitive attraction, but we now have the oddities that some indictable offences are treated as summary for all purposes but sentencing, and almost all summary conviction offences are now much closer to indictable offences for the purpose of sentencing. The distinctions are becoming so porous that it is difficult to see principle operating at a very strong level. Instead, the system reflects the anomalous accretion of particular rules and practices as Canadian law emerged from its origins in English law and was progressively adapted to accommodate Canadian needs. The Law Reform Commission of Canada and others have argued that the current classification of offences is a profound impediment to needed reform of Canadian criminal procedure in all areas, but especially as regards the jurisdiction of the courts over offences.[34]

---

30 Sections 675 and 813.

31 See, in particular, s 677 and ss 691–96.

32 RSC 1985, c S-26.

33 See, for example, David Rose, *Quigley's Criminal Procedure in Canada* (Toronto: Thomson Reuters, 2021) (loose-leaf), ch 3. See also *Classification of Offences*, above note 2.

34 Law Reform Commission of Canada, *Our Criminal Procedure* (Ottawa: Law Reform Commission of Canada, 1988).

## 3) Mode of Trial

The *Constitution Act, 1867* gives provinces the authority to establish courts within their territorial jurisdiction.[35] In the *Criminal Code*, Parliament allocates jurisdiction over offences to the courts thus created by the provinces.[36] This section looks at some of the devices Parliament uses in defining the jurisdiction of the courts for trial, appeal, and other purposes.

For trial, the *Code* allocates jurisdiction over summary conviction offences to the provincial court. Indictable offences, on the other hand, may be tried either in a "superior court of criminal jurisdiction" or a "court of criminal jurisdiction." According to section 468, the superior court of the province is competent to try any indictable offence, but, in practice, the allocation of jurisdiction is more complex. Section 468 is broad, but it must be seen in the light of section 469, which provides that a court of criminal jurisdiction is also competent to try all indictable offences except for the few offences listed there. For practical purposes, then, the "court of criminal jurisdiction" has general competence to try indictable offences other than those offences that are specifically enumerated as being within the "exclusive jurisdiction" of the superior court. For further complexity, however, section 553 of the *Code* reserves to the provincial court the "absolute jurisdiction" to try a variety of offences listed there, almost all of them property offences. The "exclusive" jurisdiction of a court means that an offence can be prosecuted in that court alone and that no other court, even in principle, will have jurisdiction. Thus, any offence listed in section 469 can be tried only in the superior court. By virtue of section 468, jurisdiction over all other indictable offences is concurrent between the provincial and superior court, subject only to the definition of a "court of criminal jurisdiction" in section 552. Offences listed in section 553 are in the "absolute jurisdiction" of the provincial court in the sense that their jurisdiction does not depend upon the election of the accused.[37] In other words, the provincial court is the only court that *will* exercise jurisdiction with regard to the offences listed in that section, not that the superior court has no jurisdiction.[38]

35 Above note 9, s 92(15).

36 See Patrick Healy, "Constitutional Limits on the Allocation of Trial Jurisdiction to the Superior or Provincial Court in Criminal Matters" (2003) 48 *Criminal Law Quarterly* 31.

37 *R v Tucker* (2006), 213 CCC (3d) 89 (Ont CA). See also *R v Beaudry*, [1967] 1 CCC 272 (BCCA).

38 In some circumstances, an absolute jurisdiction offence might end up in a superior court, for example, because when the evidence is presented at trial in

There is little difficulty in identifying the superior court of criminal jurisdiction or the provincial court, but it is not as simple to identify the "court of criminal jurisdiction" that has general competence to try indictable offences not reserved to those other two courts. A partial definition is provided in section 2 of the *Code*, but a more useful guide to practice is the definition of "judge" in section 552. When read with others, this provision states that in all provinces, except Québec, a judge of the superior court has jurisdiction to try any indictable offence except those reserved to the exclusive jurisdiction of the superior court or those reserved to the provincial court by section 553. The Cour du Québec has jurisdiction to try all indictable cases except those reserved to the superior court of criminal jurisdiction.[39]

The terms "superior court of criminal jurisdiction" and "court of criminal jurisdiction" are neither clear nor essential. To minimize the difficulty it is advisable to bear two points in mind with regard to indictable offences. The exclusive jurisdiction of the superior court is defined in section 469. The absolute jurisdiction of the provincial court is defined in section 553. For the rest, the court of criminal jurisdiction as defined in section 2 is (at least in theory) the court of trial, and for practical purposes, the court is identified in section 552.

As noted above, however, there is yet another qualification. For all indictable offences, except those in the exclusive jurisdiction of the superior court or the absolute jurisdiction of the provincial court, the accused has a right of election as to the mode of trial: that is, a right to choose among trial by jury, trial by judge alone, or trial by a judge of the provincial court.[40] Thus, although the *Code* stipulates that all of these offences may be tried by a court of criminal jurisdiction, the right of election allows the accused a choice of jurisdictions. As a matter of fact, the vast majority of criminal trials take place in provincial court.

---

superior court, it becomes apparent that the value involved was low enough that the offence falls within s 553. In such a case, the superior court has jurisdiction to continue the trial nonetheless: *R v Holliday* (1973), 26 CRNS 279 (Alta SCAD). Similarly, s 555(1) permits a trial judge in some circumstances to convert a trial into a preliminary inquiry and send the trial to the superior court: this power could be used in the case of an absolute jurisdiction offence: *R v Turton* (1988), 44 CCC (3d) 49 (Alta CA). Note, however, that *Turton* predates the changes to preliminary inquiries restricting them to offences punishable by fourteen years or more imprisonment: those changes would mean that the trial could not continue as a preliminary inquiry, but nothing in the language of the amended s 555(1.1) ought to change that the matter could be sent to superior court.

39 That is, the Cour du Québec will not hear trials of offences listed in s 469 or of any offence where the accused elects trial by jury.

40 Section 536.

In addition to the right of election, the accused may be entitled to a re-election under certain conditions.[41] In some circumstances the accused can re-elect as of right, but in other cases the consent of the prosecutor is needed. In broad terms, it is easier to re-elect "down" from trial in superior court to trial by provincial court. It is also easier to re-elect the earlier the decision is made. For example, an accused who elects trial by provincial court judge can re-elect "up" as of right until sixty days before trial, but only with the prosecutor's consent thereafter.[42]

The right to re-elect is by no means absolute, however, and is considerably narrowed if the prosecutor refuses consent. The election of the accused may also be pre-empted by the prosecution if the attorney general uses its power to require trial by judge and jury for an offence punishable by more than five years,[43] or prefers a direct indictment.[44] Section 565(2) says that if the Crown has preferred a direct indictment, the accused is deemed to have elected trial by judge and jury. However, it also says that the accused "may re-elect to be tried by a judge without a jury":[45] on its face that wording gives the accused a right to re-elect without the Crown's consent that would not be available otherwise, though it seems unlikely that such a right would be upheld.[46]

Apart from appeal and trial, the allocation of jurisdiction is important for a wide variety of functions, including the issuance of forms of process and the conduct of hearings, such as bail applications and preliminary inquiries. Many of these functions are identified and discussed throughout this text. Here, it is important to note a broader point. Only superior courts have general and inherent jurisdiction, which means, among other things, that the superior court is the court of first instance for any justiciable issue not otherwise allocated by statute.[47] Provincial courts only have the powers that are expressly given to them by legislation. This means, in principle, that they are subject to review by way of a prerogative writ unless such relief is specifically excluded by law. The most common among these is the writ of *certiorari*, which may be issued by a superior court to quash a decision of a judge in a lower court who has acted without jurisdiction.

41 Section 561ff.
42 Section 561(2).
43 Section 568.
44 Section 577.
45 Section 565(2).
46 See *R v Skibicki*, 2024 MBKB 11 at para 59, noting that s 568 gives the Attorney General the power to compel a jury trial even if an accused re-elects under s 565(2).
47 *MacMillan Bloedel Ltd v Simpson Inc*, [1995] 4 SCR 725.

# B. JURISDICTION

"Jurisdiction" is a word used variously to mean power, authority, competence, or geographical space. It is used to describe the functions of police officers, judges, courts, legislative bodies, and others. It is also used to describe limitations upon them. In criminal procedure, all of these various meanings are used in different contexts and, given the importance attached to several, this chapter introduces elementary notions of jurisdiction in criminal procedure.

## 1) Jurisdiction to Prosecute

Almost all criminal cases in Canada are public prosecutions conducted by agents of the attorney general. In principle, however, anyone may commence a prosecution by laying an information. If the information is sworn, a private prosecution may proceed unless the case is taken over by the attorney general.

### a) Public Prosecutions

The attorney general is the principal law officer of the Crown, which means that they are the chief barrister and solicitor for the government.[48] There is an attorney general in the federal government and in each of the provincial governments. As noted in Chapter 2, public prosecutions are, as a general rule, conducted by provincial authorities: the federal government has constitutional jurisdiction to conduct those prosecutions if it chooses to, but has only asserted that jurisdiction with regard to a few offences.[49]

Prosecutions are almost never conducted personally by the attorney general, but by persons who are legally authorized to act in their name.[50] Section 2 of the *Code* specifies that the attorney general may be represented by their deputy.[51] With regard to public prosecutions, the definition of "prosecutor" in section 2 includes counsel appearing for the attorney general with regard to indictable offences. Some provinces have adopted a model in which routine responsibility for the

---

48 See John Edwards, *The Law Officers of the Crown* (London: Sweet & Maxwell, 1964); and John Edwards, *The Attorney General, Politics and the Public Interest* (London: Sweet & Maxwell, 1984).

49 See the list of offences in s 2.3 of the *Code*.

50 *R v Harrison*, [1977] 1 SCR 238. Unless the personal intervention of the attorney general is required by law, the agent may exercise the powers of the attorney general: see, for example, *R v Light* (1993), 78 CCC (3d) 221 at 253 (BCCA).

51 Section 2. See also *Interpretation Act*, above note 11, s 24.

conduct of criminal prosecutions is confided to a senior person called the "director of public prosecutions." This model does not change the constitutional position of the attorney general as chief law officer of the Crown, but it does ensure a measure of professional independence for purposes of prosecution. It also helps guarantee greater openness and accountability around decisions to lay or withdraw charges, at least where the attorney general is directly involved. Counsel can include not only professional prosecutors but also private counsel who are appointed *ad hoc* to act on behalf of the attorney general.[52] With regard to summary conviction matters, the definition of "prosecutor" in section 785 allows prosecution by the attorney general, counsel appearing for the attorney general, or an "agent." In some instances, a summary conviction prosecution may also be conducted by a peace officer.[53]

Apart from general principles governing the authority to prosecute, Parliament occasionally imposes a requirement that a prosecution cannot proceed without the consent of the attorney general. This requirement is found in section 7 of the *Code* in the case of some offences over which Canada exerts extraterritorial jurisdiction or in the provision that creates the offence in other cases.[54] In most instances where consent is required, it refers to the attorney general of the province, but there are numerous exceptions where the consent of the attorney general of Canada is required.[55] There are also instances where either attorney general can provide the necessary consent.[56] In most cases, proof of consent need not be established unless the issue of jurisdiction to prosecute on this ground is raised by the accused; some exceptions apply, however.[57] Where this requirement exists, it virtually guarantees that a private prosecution could not be commenced because the

52 *R v Moscuzza* (2003), 63 OR (3d) 636 (CA).

53 See the definition of "prosecutor" in s 785, which includes an agent. However, an agent may not prosecute an indictable offence, even if the trial is in provincial court: see *R v Edmunds*, [1981] 1 SCR 233.

54 See, for example, s 136 (giving contradictory evidence), s 319(6) (wilful promotion of hatred), or s 251(3) (unseaworthy vessel).

55 Sections 7(4.3), 83.24, 136, 166, 172, 318, 319, 754, and 803 for the former, and ss 7(2.33), 7(7), 54, 119, and 477.2 for the latter.

56 See the offences listed under (f) and (g) of the definition of "Attorney General" in s 2.

57 See *Minot v Canada (Attorney General)*, 2011 NLCA 7 [*Minot*] or *R v Sunila* (1987), 35 CCC (3d) 289 (NSSCAD), for the former point. Section 477.2(4) of the *Code* specifically requires that the consent of the attorney general must be filed with the clerk of the court: most provisions requiring consent do not contain a provision parallel to this.

likelihood that the attorney general would give consent in such a case is theoretically real but practically nil.

The requirement for the consent of the attorney general is presumably intended to ensure a critical examination of cases before charges are laid. It arguably exists in relation to offences that are likely to be highly sensitive to the public or that otherwise require rigorous consideration of the public interest in prosecution. However, the Law Reform Commission of Canada suggests that there is no obvious unifying factor among offences where consent is required.[58] The Commission was also critical of the non-public nature of the decision and the fact that an attorney general was not required to give reasons for either granting or refusing consent to a prosecution: in their view no offences should have a consent requirement.[59]

There are several ways in which the requirement for consent is expressed in the *Criminal Code* and other statutes.[60] Despite these variations, the essential distinction to retain is between cases in which the *personal* consent of the attorney general is required[61] and the majority of instances in which the statute demands only the "consent of the attorney general." In the latter case, there is some scope for ambiguity as to precisely what is required. The *Interpretation Act* sets out who may act on behalf of a Minister, which includes not only the Minister and their deputy, but also "a person appointed to serve … in a capacity appropriate to the doing of the act or thing."[62] Something less than the personal consent of the attorney general would be sufficient, but anything less than the consent of prosecuting counsel in the particular case might be inadequate. Accordingly, such authorization might be sought from senior prosecuting counsel within the territorial jurisdiction in which the case arises: broadly speaking, the consent should be given by someone senior enough to be commensurate with the seriousness of the prosecution.[63] This person might be senior counsel responsible

58 Law Reform Commission of Canada, *Controlling Criminal Prosecutions: The Attorney General and the Crown Prosecutor* (Ottawa: Law Reform Commission of Canada, 1990) at 67 [*Controlling Criminal Prosecutions*]. Offences which require such consent include terrorism offences (s 83.24) and public nudity (s 174).

59 *Controlling Criminal Prosecutions*, *ibid* at 68.

60 See, for example, ss 7, 54, 119, 174, and 385.

61 For example, s 485.1.

62 *Interpretation Act*, above note 11, s 24(2).

63 *Minot*, note 51 at paras 31–37. In that case, the Acting Chief Federal Prosecutor, Atlantic Regional office consented to the prosecution of the accused, and her consent was found to be sufficient. On the other hand, see *R v Ross*, 2017 MBCA 77, where the Director/General Counsel at the Criminal Conviction Review Group in the Department of Justice was not authorized under s 24(2) of the

for the direction of prosecutions in a province or region. In any case, where some form of consent is required, it should be given in writing and placed before the court.

The attorney general and their agents have a large measure of discretion in the conduct of prosecutions beyond the requirement of consent to some offences. The prosecutor exercises various statutory powers, such as deciding whether an accused must have a jury trial, whether to proceed by direct indictment, or whether to enter a stay of proceedings.[64] In addition, what is termed "prosecutorial discretion" covers a wide range of prosecutorial decision-making. It includes whether to pursue a charge laid by police, stay proceedings, accept a guilty plea to a lesser charge, withdraw from criminal proceedings altogether, or take control of a private prosecution.[65] It also includes the decision to repudiate a plea agreement, pursue a dangerous offender application, charge multiple offences, negotiate a plea, proceed summarily or by indictment, or initiate an appeal.[66] In some provinces, the prosecution has input into whether to lay charges at all and, if so, what charges.[67] Prosecutors also have discretion over whether to stay private prosecutions.[68] Prosecutors also have no specific legal duties to the police in the way they conduct prosecutions.[69]

Prosecutorial discretion is seen as a necessary part of a properly functioning criminal justice system, which advances the public interest by enabling prosecutors to make discretionary decisions without fear of judicial or political interference, thus fulfilling their *quasi-judicial* role as "ministers of justice."[70] However, that does not mean that decisions made by Crown prosecutors are immune from review. To the contrary, all such decisions can potentially be overridden by a

*Interpretation Act* to expand the scope of a Ministerial Review under Part XXI.1 of the *Code*.

64 Sections 568, 577, and 579.

65 *Krieger v Law Society of Alberta*, 2002 SCC 65 at para 46 [*Krieger*].

66 *R v Anderson*, 2014 SCC 41 [*Anderson*].

67 *R v Lafrance*, [1975] 2 SCR 201. See the discussion in *R v Regan*, 2002 SCC 12, of the ways in which the institutional arrangements between police and the Crown differ from province to province with regard to authority over charging decisions.

68 See the discussion below of private prosecutions and cases such as *Pereira v British Columbia (Attorney General)*, 2023 BCCA 31 [*Pereira*] or *R v Mivasair*, 2025 ONCA 179 [*Mivasair*].

69 See *Ontario (Attorney General) v Clark*, 2021 SCC 18, where police officers attempted to sue a Crown prosecutor who had not contested claims that officers had assaulted an accused. The Supreme Court held that prosecutorial independence would be threatened if such suits were allowed.

70 *Anderson*, above note 66 at para 37; *Miazga v Kvello Estate*, 2009 SCC 51.

court, though there is some ambiguity as to when and on what basis. Courts have inherent jurisdiction to control their own processes, and that power gives a judge the ability to review prosecutorial decisions which are classified as simply part of a Crown prosecutor's "tactics or conduct" on a relatively low standard.[71] However, the exact standard for reviewing these decisions will vary depending on the circumstances, the nature of the Crown conduct, the presence or absence of statutory authority, the impact on trial fairness, and any other relevant interest.[72] Some decisions by Crown prosecutors, however, are immune from review by a court unless the accused can show an abuse of process.[73] In *Krieger* the Court spoke about this abuse of process standard as applying to decisions made as a part of "core" prosecutorial discretion. Twelve years later in *Anderson* the court held that the use of the word "core" had led to a narrow definition, confusion regarding the standard of review by which particular Crown decisions were to be assessed, and an "unsatisfactory state of the law."[74] *Anderson* described prosecutorial discretion as an expansive term covering all decisions regarding the nature and extent of the prosecution and the Attorney General's participation in it and took the abuse of process standard to apply to exercises of prosecutorial discretion generally.[75] Eleven years after *Anderson* in *Varennes*, the Court returned to the "core versus non-core" distinction and found that the abuse of process standard applied only to the former.[76] Core prosecutorial discretion decisions are those that impact the "nature and extent" of the criminal proceedings but not those that only impact how the proceedings will be conducted.[77] In *Varennes* itself, they concluded that this meant it would be open to a trial judge to override a Crown prosecutor's refusal to consent to a judge-alone trial for a section 469 offence without needing to show an abuse of process.

Muddying the water, though, is that until *Varennes* it had seemed clear that there were only two categories of prosecutorial decisions: on the one hand those insulated by the abuse of process standard (whether

71 *Krieger*, above note 65 at para 47; *Anderson*, above note 66 at para 36. See also the further discussion of this issue in Chapter 11, Section F(1).

72 *R v Varennes*, 2025 SCC 22 at para 57 [*Varennes*].

73 *Anderson*, above note 66; *Krieger*, above note 65; *R v Nixon*, 2011 SCC 34; *Varennes*, above note 72.

74 *Anderson*, above note 66 at paras 41 and 43.

75 *Anderson*, above note 66 at para 44.

76 *Varennes*, above note 72 at para 57: "courts may review or override non-core prosecutorial discretion on a less demanding standard than an abuse of process."

77 *Varennes*, above note 72 at para 48.

that category was *called* "prosecutorial discretion" or "core prosecutorial discretion) and on the other hand tactics and conduct, which could be supervised by the court's power to control its own process. *Varennes* speaks of *three* categories: core prosecutorial discretion (to which the abuse of process standard applies), tactics and conduct (supervised by the power to control the process), and then a middle ground of "non-core" prosecutorial discretion with a variable standard for supervision. The majority says that:

> [57] ... courts may review or override non-core prosecutorial discretion on a less demanding standard than an abuse of process ... Because these non-core decisions cover a broad range — from the everyday issues that form part of a litigant's conduct of a trial to decisions authorized under statute — the standard for a judge to override a Crown decision will vary with the circumstances. The precise standard in a given case will depend on the nature of the Crown conduct, the presence or absence of statutory authority, the impact on trial fairness, and any other relevant interest.

In the end, arguably the *rule* is relatively simple to state: core prosecutorial discretion decisions are only reviewable on an abuse of process standard, but other decisions are reviewable based on the power of a court to control its own processes. However, deciding whether a particular decision is part of "core" prosecutorial discretion could be challenging, as could be determining the exact standard for review of a decision which is not in that category.

### b) Private Prosecutions

The concept of a private prosecution is ancient in the common law, and it reflects the right of every person subject to the sovereign to invoke the protection of the law by making a complaint of a breach of the King's Peace. Indeed, the *Code* provision dealing with laying an information to commence a criminal prosecution simply states that "any one" may do so: as a matter of fact that is almost exclusively done by peace officers or other Crown agents, but there is no legal requirement that that be so.[78] In modern terms, a private prosecutor is any prosecutor under the *Code* who is not an agent of the attorney general. A private prosecution of alleged crime is not, however, in any way a private action between the parties. The private prosecutor is not a plaintiff but is allowed under the criminal law to prosecute in the place of the attorney general.

---

78 Section 504.

Although the right to commence a private prosecution is ancient, the growth and development of the role of the attorney general as the public prosecutor has diminished the frequency and the significance of private prosecutions. Indeed, virtually the only reason that motivates people today to commence a private prosecution is that a public prosecutor has decided not to proceed, either because there is insufficient evidence to sustain the case or because prosecution of the alleged offence is otherwise not in the public interest. Thus, private prosecutions now tend to occur only when the Crown has refused to lay charges. For precisely that reason, the current rules reflect a certain amount of skepticism about the legitimacy of any individual private prosecution: although they are still possible, various barriers exist making it unlikely that they will occur often. That is, although anyone can lay an information, since 2002 different sets of procedures apply thereafter depending on whether it is a public or private prosecution.

In all cases, indictable or summary, the attorney general may intervene in a private prosecution for the purpose of assuming the carriage of the prosecution or for the purpose of entering a stay of proceedings. This power to enter a stay can be exercised at any time, including before the hearing and before a justice (called a "pre-enquete") has taken place, in which case no hearing would take place at all.[79] In addition, section 579.01 gives the attorney general the ability to intervene without either staying or conducting the proceeding, in order to call witnesses, examine and cross-examine witnesses, present evidence, or make submissions.

With respect to indictable offences, the power to stay the proceedings is recognized expressly in section 579 of the *Code*. A similar power is given in section 579.1 to the attorney general of Canada, with respect to private prosecutions concerning federal offences outside the *Code* in which no provincial attorney general has intervened. With respect to summary conviction offences, the definition of "prosecutor" refers to instances in which the attorney general has not intervened, but there is no express provision in Part XXVII of the *Code* that is comparable to section 579 or 579.1. Even without these statutory provisions, a Crown prosecutor has the power at common law to withdraw charges, though that power only arises once process has issued.[80] As with issues of prosecutorial discretion generally, a decision to stay a private prosecution

---

79 *R v Ackerman*, 2018 MBCA 75; *Klippenstein v R*, 2019 MBCA 13.

80 *McHale v Ontario (Attorney General)*, 2010 ONCA 361 [*McHale*]; *Pereira*, above note 68.

can only be overturned if it is shown to be an abuse of process, which is a high standard to meet.[81]

Further, the *Criminal Code* imposes procedural steps at the commencement of a private prosecution that do not exist for a public prosecution. Section 507.1 requires that any information laid under section 504 by a private informant must be referred to a judge of the provincial court or, in Québec, a judge of the Cour du Québec. It is also possible to refer the matter to a justice designated specifically for this purpose if there is one in the jurisdiction. This judicial officer will decide whether a charge will be laid and whether to compel the appearance of the accused to answer that charge by summons or by arrest warrant. No such decision can be made unless the judge or designated justice has heard and considered the allegations of the informant and the evidence of any witnesses. Further, the justice must be satisfied that the attorney general has already received a copy of the information, with reasonable notice of the date for hearing the informant and witnesses, and been given the opportunity to appear at the hearing to cross-examine witnesses and call any other relevant evidence. The standard to be met by the private prosecutor is to establish a *prima facie* case.[82] Finally, even if all these requirements are met, the court has a limited discretion to decline to issue process in the clearest of cases.[83]

These various barriers are meant to guard against the use of private prosecutions for spurious, vexatious, or frivolous claims, and generally to filter out dubious claims.[84] Primarily for that reason, the pre-enquete is held *in camera*, though unlike the pre-enquete for a public prosecution, the relevant section does not require an *ex parte* hearing, and indeed the attorney general is entitled to appear.[85] It has been held that there is no bar to the attorney general contacting the named accused.[86]

In the relatively uncommon event that the prosecution continues as a private one, the formal procedure for commencement is the same whether the offence alleged is indictable or summary, but the position

---

81 See, for example, *Jackson v Ontario*, 2017 ONCA 812. The application must be brought through a *certiorari* application: *Mivasair*, above note 68.

82 *R v Ambrosi*, 2014 BCCA 123 [*Ambrosi*].

83 See *Canadian Broadcasting Corp v Morrison*, 2017 MBCA 36 at para 22 quoting *R v Halik*, 2010 ONSC 125 at para 20: "the justice has a discretion not to issue process where he or she forms the opinion that the informant or his witnesses are not credible in the sense that they are mentally disordered or the charge is frivolous, vexatious or abusive."

84 *McHale*, above note 80; *Duarte v British Columbia (Attorney General)*, 2012 BCCA 6; *Ambrosi*, above note 82.

85 See s 507(1)(a) and 507.1(4).

86 *Ambrosi*, above note 82 at para 32.

is not the same for purposes of trial. Assuming that a judge receives and endorses the information, the informant becomes the prosecutor. The prosecutor has carriage of the case from that point and must conform to all of the obligations that prosecutors are obliged to fulfil. A private prosecutor, for example, would be no less bound by the obligation to make full disclosure to the defence than an agent of the attorney general.

A private prosecutor can appear personally or be represented by counsel.[87] If the accused is entitled to a preliminary inquiry (which is particularly unlikely in a private prosecution now that they are limited to offences punishable by fourteen years or more imprisonment), a private prosecution may proceed to the conclusion of the preliminary inquiry. At this point, however, the *Criminal Code* erects barriers to the continuation of the prosecution at trial. If the accused is ordered to stand trial after a preliminary inquiry, a private prosecutor may not prefer an indictment against that person without the written authorization of a judge in the court of trial. Similarly, in the event that there was no preliminary inquiry or there was a preliminary inquiry at which the accused was discharged, the private prosecutor may not prefer a direct indictment without the written order of a judge.[88]

If neither a summons nor a warrant is issued at the conclusion of the hearing, the presiding judge or designated justice will endorse the information to that effect. If the informant does not seek to compel the issuance of process within six months of this endorsement, the matter is closed. If such proceedings are taken but no process is issued, the information is deemed never to have been laid.

Finally, there are several provisions of the *Code* that allow for a privately laid information to be received and, if endorsed, to lead to the issuance of an order for the respondent to be bound over. Such an order is usually referred to as a "peace bond" because the central condition will be a promise to "keep the peace and be of good behaviour" for a period of time up to one year. The model is found in section 810: any person who has reason to believe that an indictable offence will be committed upon them or upon a third party may swear an information to this effect and, if it is received, seek an order for the respondent to be bound over upon conditions. There are also several similar orders that nominally can be sought by any person, though in practice they are sought by the state. These include applications based on the fear that

87 Section 785.

88 Section 577. See also *Johnson v Inglis* (1980), 52 CCC (2d) 385 (Ont HCJ); *Garton v Whelan* (1984), 14 CCC (3d) 449 (Ont HCJ), discussing the circumstances in which a judge should consent.

the respondent will commit a criminal organization, terrorism, forced marriage, sexual, or serious personal injury offence.[89] A peace bond is meant to be preventive rather than punitive, and an application for one does not amount to charging an offence, but a failure to abide by the conditions of a peace bond is an offence.[90] Even though the peace bond process does not involve charging the person with an offence, the arrest and bail provisions in the *Code* nonetheless apply, with necessary modifications: those modifications include that the conditions attached to the person's release cannot be allowed to become more stringent than could result from a successful peace bond application itself.[91] These forms of procedure have become increasingly important in daily practice.

## 2) Territorial Jurisdiction

### a) Extraterritoriality

Two separate issues need to be discussed with regard to extraterritoriality:[92] prescriptive jurisdiction, which deals with the issue of whether offences in the *Criminal Code* apply to behaviour that occurs outside Canadian territory; and enforcement jurisdiction, which deals with the extent to which Canadian officials can act outside Canada.

As a general rule, prescriptive jurisdiction matches up with the territory of Canada: that is, a person can be held liable under Canadian criminal law only for an offence that they commit within Canadian territorial limits. This principle of limitation is based upon the historical rationale that a violation of the criminal law is a violation of the sovereign's peace. Accordingly, the scope of the criminal law is normally co-extensive with the territorial sovereignty of the state. This principle is expressed in section 6(2) of the *Criminal Code*.

Similar to almost every rule of criminal procedure, this general principle is subject to exceptions. First, in a variety of provisions, the *Code* and other statutes explicitly create exceptions giving Canadian courts jurisdiction over offences committed outside Canadian territorial limits.[93] Generally speaking, these provisions reflect obligations or agreements contracted by Canada in treaties with other states.

---

89 Sections 810.01, 810.011, 810.02, 810.1, and 810.2.

90 Section 811. See the discussion in *R v Budreo* (2000), 32 CR (5th) 127 (Ont CA).

91 *R v Penunsi*, 2019 SCC 39.

92 For an explanation of this issue in chart form, see *Anatomy of Criminal Procedure*, above note 1, Chart 2.2(c)(ii), "Extraterritorial Jurisdiction over Offences" and Chart 2.2(c)(iii), "Extraterritorial Jurisdiction and the *Charter*."

93 See, for example, ss 7, 57, 58, 74, 75, and 465.

However, the extraterritorial jurisdiction created in the *Code* does not, in every case, map onto pre-existing international agreements. Some, though very few, reflect a deliberate decision in policy to unilaterally extend the reach of Canadian jurisdiction.[94] Second, the Supreme Court of Canada has held that, if an offence is committed abroad but has a "real and substantial" connection to Canada, it falls within the class of offences committed in Canada.[95] This test does not require that any particular elements of the offence, or that the essential elements of the offence, take place in Canada, but only that on the facts there is a sufficient connection.[96] This is not truly an exercise of extraterritorial jurisdiction, but rather extended territoriality taking into account that the offence can be partly located in Canada. Based on this rule, it has been found, for example, that courts have jurisdiction over an accused for behaviour that occurred outside of Canada's boundaries, if that behaviour was in violation of a court order issued in Canada,[97] or is aimed at removing an ordinary resident of Canada from the country in order to commit an offence outside the country.[98]

The real and substantial connection test applies as well with regard to enforcement jurisdiction. In *British Columbia (Attorney General) v Brecknell*, RCMP in British Columbia tried to obtain a production order

---

94 See, for example, ss 7(3.74) and 7(3.75), which give extraterritorial jurisdiction over terrorism offences other than those covered by treaties. For a review of the underlying theory behind extraterritoriality in criminal law, see Robert J Currie & Steve Coughlan, "Extraterritorial Criminal Jurisdiction: Bigger Picture or Smaller Frame?" (2007) 11 *Canadian Criminal Law Review* 141; and Steve Coughlan et al, *Law Beyond Borders: Extraterritorial Jurisdiction in an Age of Globalization* (Toronto: Irwin Law, 2014).

95 *Libman v The Queen*, [1985] 2 SCR 178.

96 See, for example, *R v Karigar*, 2017 ONCA 576 where a decision to pay bribes to obtain contracts was made in New York and the bribes were in fact paid in India, but nonetheless there was a sufficient connection because a Canadian businessman had proposed the scheme, most of the work under the contracts was done in Canada, and a Canadian company reaped most of the benefits.

97 See, for example, *R v Greco* (2001), 159 CCC (3d) 146 (Ont CA) (where an assault committed by the accused in Cuba was found to be a breach of his probation order), or *R v Rattray*, 2008 ONCA 74 (where the accused was proven to be in possession of a firearm in Michigan, which constituted a breach of court orders issued in Canada prohibiting him from possessing firearms).

98 In *R v Oler*, 2018 BCCA 323, the accused took steps while outside Canada to assist with removing a fifteen-year-old girl from the country so that she could be married in the United States to a religious leader. There was a sufficient connection to Canada despite the fact that the accused acted while in the United States, because the girl was an ordinary resident of Canada, she was being removed from Canada, and the underlying offence (s 273.3) anticipated extraterritorial behaviour from the marriage itself.

to be served on Craigslist, an American company with headquarters in California, and the information sought was on servers that were not in the province. Nonetheless the British Columbia Court of Appeal held that a British Columbia justice would have jurisdiction to issue the production order. One of the purposes of the production order regime was to avoid potential problems with offshore storage of data, and therefore it was only necessary that the person on whom the production order was to be served was in British Columbia. Craigslist was found to be in British Columbia not physically but virtually, through the operation of its website in the province, and therefore there was jurisdiction to issue the production order.[99] Although there has been some pushback on that result, it has generally been followed.[100]

The issue that has attracted the most judicial attention with regard to enforcement jurisdiction is the extent to which *Charter* rights apply abroad. For example, suspects are sometimes interrogated while outside Canada, most often by foreign police but sometimes by Canadians. Canadian police might also be involved in searches conducted in other countries. A question has arisen, therefore, as to the extent to which an accused can complain of a failure to comply with *Charter* standards when the alleged failure occurred outside Canada.

As a generalization, it is safe to say that the *Charter* is unlikely to have much influence on investigative techniques employed abroad. Foreign officials cannot be expected to comply with *Charter* standards and their failure to do so will not give rise to a *Charter* violation. The fact that US police do not give a warning in accordance with section 10(b) requirements, for example, cannot give rise to a section 10(b) claim. However, if the conditions in which a statement was obtained are particularly egregious, it is possible that attempting to introduce that evidence at a trial in Canada might constitute a section 7 violation.[101] Similarly, sending a person to a place where they might face significant negative consequences can give rise to *Charter* jurisdiction if the decision was made in Canada.[102] The *Charter* was also found to apply in *R v Cook*, where two Canadian police officers went to the United States and

---

99 *British Columbia (Attorney General) v Brecknell*, 2018 BCCA 5.

100 *In the Matter of an application to obtain a Production Order pursuant to section 487.014 of the Criminal Code of Canada*, 2018 CanLII 2369 (NL PC) disagreed with the approach in *Brecknell*. However, *Brecknell* has been followed in other decision: see, for example, *R v Love*, 2022 ABCA 269, (Re) Service de police de la Ville de Montréal, 2022 QCCS 3935, and *Application for a Production Order, s 487.014 of the Criminal Code (Re)*, 2024 ONCJ 627.

101 See the discussion in *R v Harrer*, [1995] 3 SCR 562; *R v Terry*, [1996] 2 SCR 207.

102 See, for example, *United States v Burns*, 2001 SCC 7, or *Boily v Canada*, 2022 FC 1243. In the latter case the applicant faced the risk of torture which would

interrogated an accused after having given him a section 10(b) warning that was clearly deficient.[103] However, *Cook*'s authority is overshadowed by the Supreme Court's later decision in *R v Hape*, which (while not calling *Cook* wrong on its own facts) concluded that the approach to extraterritorial application of the *Charter* in *Cook* was wrong.[104]

In *Hape*, Canadian police participated in several warrantless searches in the Turks and Caicos Islands that, if conducted in Canada, would have violated section 8. There was no evidence in the case as to whether the searches complied with Turks and Caicos law. The Court held, though, that the accused could not claim a *Charter* violation. The general approach laid out in that case requires courts to answer two questions. The first, for the *Charter* to have any prospect of applying, is whether section 32 is met: under this section, the *Charter* is applicable only to Canadian state actors. However, even if a Canadian state actor is involved, consideration of comity between nations will normally mean that the *Charter* does not apply to that person's activities abroad. The *Charter* will apply only if there is an exception to sovereignty, such as evidence that the foreign state consented to the application of *Charter* standards: the Court observed that "[i]n most cases, there will be no such exception and the *Charter* will not apply."[105] In that event, the second question is whether admitting evidence obtained through the foreign investigation renders the trial unfair, thus giving rise to a section 7 violation. In most cases, however, neither part of the test will be met. Thus, the *Charter* has a minimal impact on investigations conducted outside Canada.

Nonetheless, the possibility does still exist. In *Hape* the Court had held that comity did not justify Canadian participation in activities of a foreign state or its agents that were contrary to Canada's international obligations: there would be no deference where the actions complained of violated international law and fundamental human rights. In *Canada (Justice) v Khadr* the Court relied on that exception to find that the *Charter* did apply to the actions of Canadian officials who had interviewed a Canadian citizen being detained by the US government at Guantanamo Bay. The Court noted that various aspects of US government officials' behaviour at Guantanamo Bay had already been found by the US Supreme Court to violate international law. In that event

---

occur in Mexico, but there was territorial jurisdiction because the decision to extradite him was made in Canada.

103 [1998] 2 SCR 597.

104 2007 SCC 26 [*Hape*].

105 *Ibid* at para 113.

comity concerns did not justify deference to the foreign state and so the *Charter* was applicable extraterritorially.[106]

### b) Territorial Jurisdiction Within Canada

Proof that a Canadian court has jurisdiction over an offence committed within[107] or without Canada is a necessary condition of criminal liability, but it is not the end of the analysis. The court must be satisfied that it has jurisdiction over the offence, whether that offence was allegedly committed outside Canada or within its territorial limits. Having jurisdiction requires more than the offence occurring in Canada, however. In keeping with the adage that all crime is local, a criminal prosecution will typically be conducted in the judicial district within which an offence is alleged to have been committed.[108] Precisely where this is will depend upon the manner in which a province or territory has organized its courts. Further, the *Code* provides that if the offence is alleged to have occurred in an unorganized area within a province, it may be prosecuted in the nearest judicial district.[109] Offences occurring in parts of Canada that are not in any province and not in the internal waters or territorial seas of Canada can be prosecuted in any province.[110]

Not all offences are committed in a single place, of course. As a result, there can be jurisdiction in more than one country, more than one province or territory, or more than one judicial district within a province or territory.[111] While no province or territory may assert jurisdiction over an offence wholly committed in another, a prosecution may be conducted in any province or territory in which an element of the alleged offence occurred. This principle therefore allows for concurrent jurisdiction. Territorial jurisdiction in a province will be found when there is a link between the judicial district of the court and the offence in the sense that some part of the *actus reus* of the offence occurred in that district.

In *R v Bigelow*,[112] for example, the accused was charged with detaining a child with the intent to deprive the mother of lawful custody. He had picked up the child for an access visit in Ontario and then flown

106 2008 SCC 28.

107 For an explanation of this issue in chart form, see *Anatomy of Criminal Procedure*, above note 1, Chart 2.2(c)(i), "Which Province Has Jurisdiction?"

108 Where the offence occurred extraterritorially this is not possible, of course. In such cases, the *Code* typically provides that the offence can be prosecuted anywhere in Canada: see, for example, s 83.25.

109 Section 480.

110 Sections 481 and 481.1.

111 *R v L(DA)* (1996), 107 CCC (3d) 178 (BCCA).

112 (1982), 69 CCC (2d) 204 (Ont CA) [*Bigelow*].

to Alberta before the scheduled time to return the child. His argument was that the offence of "detaining" had not occurred in Ontario but in Alberta, and, therefore, that the Ontario trial court lacked jurisdiction.

The Ontario Court of Appeal acknowledged that section 478 would prevent an Ontario court from trying an offence "committed entirely in another province." However, the Court noted that offences could have elements that signify they were committed in more than one province, and identified three such grounds: (1) continuity of operation, (2) commission of an overt act, and (3) the generation of effects. These three grounds are not entirely distinct and can overlap with each other. This would be the case, for example, where a telemarketing scheme that originates in one province causes the victim to make a decision to their detriment in another province and leads to the deposit of funds to the offender's credit in a third province. In such a case, all three of the grounds identified in *Bigelow* would operate. In *Bigelow* itself the commission of the overt act of boarding a plane with the child in Ontario, as well as the facts that this act was part of a preplanned scheme and that the mother was deprived of her custody rights in Ontario because of this act, was sufficient to give Ontario courts jurisdiction.[113]

People alleged to have committed an offence do not always stay in the judicial district that would have territorial jurisdiction. For a very long time the rule was that various investigative warrants, such as search warrants, DNA warrants, or wiretap authorizations could only be executed in the province where they were issued, unless a judge of some other province endorsed the warrant for execution there. However, in 2019 those provisions were changed generally to permit warrants to be executed anywhere in Canada, as long as the person executing it has authority to act in the particular province or territory.[114] The *Code* provides that such persons may be transferred to the judicial district in which the offence is alleged to have been committed.[115]

---

113 See also *R v Trudel, ex p Horbas & Myhaluk*, [1969] 3 CCC 95 (Man CA). In contrast see *R v Webber*, 2021 NSCA 35, where in the context of a "pimping" prosecution two counts against the accused alleged sexual offences occurring in New Brunswick. The Crown argued that there was a link to Nova Scotia because of an element of exploitation occurring there, but the Nova Scotia Court of Appeal found that there could be no jurisdiction where the charge alleged *only* an offence occurring in another province.

114 See Bill C-75, above note 12, which made this change to the warrants in ss 188.1, 395, 487, 462.33, 487.01, 487.02, 487.05, 487.092, 492.1, and 492.2 of the *Code*, and to warrants in s 11 of the *Controlled Drugs and Substances Act*.

115 See, for example, s 543, permitting a justice conducting a preliminary inquiry to have the inquiry and the accused transferred to the jurisdiction where the offence is alleged to have occurred.

Following arrest, a judge may issue a warrant that, in effect, authorizes the forced removal of the accused to the jurisdiction in which the prosecution will take place.[116] Further, although a court cannot *try* an offence committed wholly in another jurisdiction, it is permitted to accept a guilty plea from an accused and impose sentence, provided the attorney general consents.[117] The *Code* does not allow the accused to be tried on the merits in the place where they are found because the evidence is not there. The consent of the attorney general ensures that a disposition of the case upon a guilty plea is consistent with the public interest.

A trial that is scheduled within the judicial district of the alleged offence may be moved to another district within the same province. Section 599 provides that a change of venue may be ordered if it is "expedient to the ends of justice."[118] This would appear to confer a broad discretion upon the court, but, in practice, a change of venue has always been exceptional. It may be sought by the prosecutor or the accused, and the applicant must show cause as to why a change of venue is necessary. Clearly, the application will be granted if there are grounds to believe that a jury in that venue could not try the accused impartially, but applications for a change of venue are not restricted to a lack of impartiality in a jury trial. Further, questions of jury partiality in a particular location, at least where they arise out of extensive pre-trial publicity, might be better resolved through the challenge for cause procedures in the *Code* rather than through a change of venue. Whether the trial is by jury or judge alone, a change of venue may be ordered if the applicant can identify a cogent reason to suggest that the trial would be unfair or prejudicial to either party if it continued where it began.[119] The potential unfairness must relate to the location of the trial: where it relates to the evidence to be heard, moving the trial to a different location will not solve matters.[120]

116 Sections 503(3) and 528.

117 Section 478(3).

118 In this context the "ends of justice" include promoting a fair and efficient trial and ensuring the safety of victims or witnesses. In addition, s 599(1)(b) permits a change of venue to be ordered if there is no jury panel in the district where the prosecution has begun. See the discussion of change of venue in Chapter 10.

119 *R v Charest* (1990), 57 CCC (3d) 312 (Que CA). See, for example, *R v Anugaa* (2018), 44 CR (7th) 186 (Nun CJ) where potential jurors had already been called four times and the accused was notorious in the community of under 900 people, and so the trial was moved elsewhere.

120 *R v Suzack* (2000), 30 CR (5th) 346 (Ont CA).

## 3) Jurisdiction over the Accused

Apart from jurisdiction over the subject-matter of an offence, no court can adjudicate in respect of a particular person unless it also has jurisdiction over the accused,[121] often also referred to as "jurisdiction over the person." The central question is whether the accused is properly before the court. Initially, a court has jurisdiction over an accused if they were arrested or in custody within its territorial jurisdiction, or were lawfully ordered to stand trial in that court.[122] However, courts can lose jurisdiction over an accused through various irregularities.

For practical purposes the question has arisen chiefly in relation to the exercise of jurisdiction by provincial courts. As their authority to adjudicate is statutory, courts can lose their jurisdiction over the accused by an error or omission relating to the process by which the accused is required to appear in court, such as appearances, adjournments, or the conduct of proceedings in the absence of the accused.[123] The primary effect of a loss of jurisdiction over the person is relatively minor: an accused who failed to appear in court following some flawed process could not be charged with the separate offence of failure to appear, but nothing is likely to prevent the Crown from regaining jurisdiction over the accused and continuing the proceedings on the original charge. At one point these issues caused some concern,[124] but there are fewer such difficulties today. First, some of the rules that potentially caused a loss of jurisdiction over the person have been removed from the *Code*. Second, section 485 now excuses most errors relating to the appearance of the accused. Because of that section, jurisdiction over an offence is not lost simply because a judge fails to exercise jurisdiction at any particular time or fails to comply with any of the *Code* provisions respecting adjournments or remands. Generally speaking, jurisdiction

---

121 For an explanation of this issue in chart form, see *Anatomy of Criminal Procedure*, above note 1, Chart 2.2(a), "Jurisdiction over the Person."

122 Section 470. See also s 798 with regard to summary conviction offences.

123 For example, ss 505 and 508 of the *Code* lay out two steps in the process of compelling an accused person to appear in front of a court: s 505 deals with laying an information before a justice after an appearance notice has been issued, and s 508 deals with the justice deciding whether to act on that information (see the discussion in Chapter 6, Section C(1)). A defect in the process at either stage would mean that the court has lost jurisdiction over the person; however, the defect would not affect the underlying information, and so jurisdiction over the offence would not be lost: see *R v Markovic* (2005), 200 CCC (3d) 449 (Ont CA); and *R v Ladouceur*, 2013 ONCA 328.

124 See the discussion of the history of some such problems in *R v Millar*, 2012 ONSC 1809.

over an accused is not lost because of non-appearance.[125] Finally, the courts have broad authority to issue process, such as a bench warrant for arrest, which allows jurisdiction over the person to be regained in the event that it is lost.[126] Indeed, some authorities suggest that a court obtains jurisdiction over the person so long as the person is present in court, no matter what process has brought that person there.[127]

Perhaps the most common situation today in which there is a loss of jurisdiction over the accused occurs in the case of non-compliance with section 650, which gives the accused the right to be present at the whole of their trial. Occasionally, accused are, because no one adverts to the impact of that rule, absent for small portions of trial such as a chambers meeting or discussion carried on in the absence of a jury. At one time such errors caused difficulty because, even if the impact on the accused's interests was minimal, the error would necessarily result in a successful appeal: section 686(1)(b)(iii) allows an appeal to be dismissed where an error of law is harmless, but this was found not to apply to jurisdictional errors.[128] Subsequently, section 686(1)(b)(iv) was added to the appeal provisions, allowing appeals to be dismissed despite a jurisdictional error as long as the trial court had jurisdiction over the class of the offence and the accused suffered no prejudice.[129]

Apart from the possibility of losing jurisdiction, there are some persons over whom the courts have no jurisdiction. These include persons under the age of twelve, who are presumed by section 13 of the *Code* to be incapable of crime and persons who are immune from prosecution for reasons of policy. The most obvious example of immunity is that extended to diplomats, but there was also an ancient principle that the Crown is immune from liability, based on the fiction that the sovereign can do no wrong.[130] It is noteworthy, though, that various amendments to the *Code*, intended to expand the circumstances in which organizations can be held criminally liable, include "public

---

125 Section 485(1.1) provides that jurisdiction is not lost "so long as the provisions of this Act or a rule made under s 482 or 482.1 permitting the accused not to appear personally apply."

126 Section 485(2).

127 *R v Lindsay* (2006), 207 CCC (3d) 296 (BCCA).

128 *R v Meunier*, [1966] SCR 399.

129 Section 686(1)(b)(iv). This provision covers loss of jurisdiction due to a failure to comply with s 650: see *R v Khan*, 2001 SCC 86, adopting the reasoning from *R v Cloutier* (1988), 43 CCC (3d) 35 (Ont CA). See the discussion of this provision in Chapter 12.

130 See *Interpretation Act*, above note 11, s 17; and *R v Eldorado Nuclear Ltd; Uranium Canada Ltd*, [1983] 2 SCR 551.

body" in the definition of "organization."[131] This could have the effect, in some cases, of extending the liability of the Crown.

## 4) Jurisdiction in Time

Indictable offences are generally not barred by a period of limitation or prescription.[132] In other words, offences committed many years previously might still be prosecuted, subject, of course, to considerations about the quality of evidence.[133] Summary conviction matters, however, are barred twelve months following the completion of the offence.[134] These matters will influence the decision of prosecutors as to whether to proceed by indictment in the prosecution of hybrid offences.[135] Some difficulty can arise in determining when the time limit for prosecuting an alleged summary conviction offence has passed.[136]

Where the Crown elects to proceed summarily, a hybrid offence is treated in all respects as a summary conviction offence. Equally, where the Crown has not expressly elected but the trial has proceeded before a summary conviction court, it will be presumed that the Crown elected to proceed summarily.[137] If it subsequently transpires that the proceedings were time-barred because they were instituted after the limitation period for commencing summary conviction procedures,[138] there are several possibilities. The first is that the proceedings might still take place because the Crown and the accused agree.[139] If there is no such agreement and the trial has not been completed, a mistrial should be declared. If the trial has been completed and the

131 Section 2, and *An Act to Amend the Criminal Code (Criminal Liability of Organizations)*, SC 2003, c 21.

132 For an explanation of this issue in chart form, see *Anatomy of Criminal Procedure*, above note 1, Chart 2.2(b), "Temporal Limits on Jurisdiction."

133 The most common instances of this are the prosecutions of what are known widely as "historical sexual offences."

134 Section 786(2). Until Bill C-75, above note 12, the limitation period was six months.

135 *R v Belair* (1988), 41 CCC (3d) 329 (Ont CA); *R v Kalkhorany* (1994), 89 CCC (3d) 184 (Ont CA).

136 *R v Belgal Holdings Ltd*, [1967] 3 CCC 34 (Ont HCJ).

137 *Dudley*, above note 10 at para 3.

138 For many years that limitation period was six months, but Bill C-75, above note 12, amended s 786(2) to raise the time limit to twelve months. This was a result of other amendments in that Bill, which changed a number of more serious offences that had previously been purely indictable to hybrid offences.

139 Section 786(2) allows for this possibility. The accused might be motivated to agree to what would otherwise be a time-barred proceeding in order to avoid the higher range of penalties available in the case of indictable offences.

accused was convicted, an appeal on the ground that the proceedings were statute-barred should be granted. If that is the only basis upon which the appeal is granted, or if a mistrial was declared, the Crown is entitled to start new proceedings by way of indictment, unless in the circumstances, to do so would be an abuse of process. However, if the accused was acquitted at trial, the Crown is not entitled to appeal on the basis that the proceedings were statute-barred: "Having elected to proceed by way of summary conviction before the right court, the Crown should not be heard to complain *after an adverse adjudication on the merits* that it neglected to obtain the consent of the accused before the accused was acquitted!"[140]

It is an elementary feature of the principle of legality that criminal offences do not have retrospective application, from which it follows that a court has no jurisdiction to try a charge of conduct that was not an offence when it occurred. This principle is confirmed in the *Criminal Code* and in section 11(g) of the *Charter*. In *R v Finta*, the Supreme Court stated that there is a partial exception to this principle for war crimes allegedly committed in Europe during the Second World War. The Court qualified the retroactive application of provisions of the *Code* concerning such crimes as a partial exception to the principle because the alleged crimes took place before they were declared offences in Canada. Nonetheless, the Court was satisfied that such offences were recognized as crimes in international law at the time of their commission, which meant the prosecution did not violate section 11(g).[141]

The rule against retrospective application is that new legislation affecting substantive rights is presumed to have only prospective effect unless there is clear legislative intent that it is to apply retrospectively, but new procedural legislation is presumed to apply to both pending and future cases. However, the point is not simply to label legislation as either "substantive" or "procedural": procedural provisions can affect substantive rights in the way they are applied, and if that is the case they will only be applied prospectively.[142] In general, a law will be classified as procedural in this analysis only if it is exclusively so and will be classified as substantive if it creates or impinges on vested rights.[143] However, there is no vested right to particular procedures, and so even

140 *Dudley*, above note 10 at para 6 [emphasis in original].

141 [1994] 1 SCR 701.

142 *R v Chouhan*, 2021 SCC 26 at para 91 [*Chouhan*]. See also *R v Dineley*, 2012 SCC 58.

143 *Application under s 83.28 of the Criminal Code (Re)*, 2004 SCC 42.

if a procedure was important or advantageous to one party that does not alone mean that a change removing it was substantive.[144]

The right to trial within a reasonable time, guaranteed by section 11(b) of the *Charter*, is not typically seen as an aspect of jurisdiction. Nevertheless, it should be mentioned because unreasonable delay can cause a *Charter* violation and the remedy for it is a stay of proceedings. When granted, the net effect is that the state has run out of the time within which it can prosecute the accused. Technically, this does not mean that there is a loss of jurisdiction arising from unreasonable delay. But the effect of the stay is a judicial order that there is no jurisdiction to proceed. See the more extensive discussion of trial within a reasonable time in Chapter 10, Section B(2)(c)(i).

## 5) Jurisdiction Under the *Charter*

Section 24 of the *Charter* allows a court of competent jurisdiction to grant an appropriate and just remedy for the breach of rights guaranteed by that part of Constitution.[145] But what is a court of competent jurisdiction? Could the accused argue at a bail hearing that they had been arbitrarily detained or that their right to counsel had been breached? Could they argue that they did not have adequate disclosure from the prosecution? Could they seek the exclusion of evidence obtained in violation of a guaranteed right? Could they seek a remedy at the preliminary inquiry?

In *R v Mills*[146] the Supreme Court decided that a court of competent jurisdiction means, for most practical purposes in criminal matters, the trial court. The majority observed that the *Charter* itself included no express allocation of jurisdiction. On this basis, then, it was appropriate to determine if a judge at a preliminary inquiry was a court of competent jurisdiction by reference to the ordinary principles of

---

144 *Chouhan*, above note 142 at para 96. *Chouhan* concerned the abolition of peremptory challenges, and the Court concluded that the changes applied retrospectively. See the discussion of other aspects of the case in Chapter 10, Section C.

145 The issue for the purposes of this section is the meaning of "court of competent jurisdiction." An "appropriate and just" remedy can include orders related to the trial process, such as adjournments or orders for disclosure, but also other remedies such as a stay of proceedings, damages, or a sentence reduction. On the range of remedies available generally, see, for example, *Doucet-Boudreau v Nova Scotia (Minister of Education)*, 2003 SCC 62; *R v Bjelland*, 2009 SCC 38; *Vancouver (City) v Ward*, 2010 SCC 27; and *Henry v British Columbia (AG)*, 2015 SCC 24.

146 [1986] 1 SCR 863 [*Mills*].

jurisdiction in criminal matters. In this regard, the *Criminal Code* did not expressly attribute jurisdiction over constitutional issues to provincial courts presiding over preliminary inquiries.

The Court's decision that a judge conducting a preliminary inquiry is not a court of competent jurisdiction to decide issues under the *Charter* was affirmed in *R v Hynes*.[147] There are arguments either way as to whether this was the right conclusion. On the one hand, this position avoids the possibility of contradictory decisions at the preliminary inquiry and trial. On the other, it avoids the likelihood of interlocutory appeals that would arise if constitutional remedies were granted at the preliminary inquiry. In short, there are arguments based upon the efficient administration of cases that support the decisions in *Mills* and *Hynes*. However, there is some awkwardness about this position, too. It effectively requires a judge to ignore a possible *Charter* breach, no matter how glaring it might be. In any event, subsequent amendments have radically trimmed the scope of preliminary inquiries and the range of offences for which they are available, and so the significance of these issues is diminished.

However, it is also possible that the "court" of competent jurisdiction will be an administrative tribunal rather than a traditional court. Some decisions within the criminal process (such as how to deal with persons found not criminally responsible by reason of mental disorder) are given to administrative bodies. The Court has concluded that such tribunals will be courts of competent jurisdiction for *Charter* purposes if they have been given the ability to decide questions of law and the ability to decide *Charter* issues has not been removed by statute. If those conditions are met, the tribunal has the ability to grant any remedy which is otherwise available to it as a *Charter* remedy. In other words, once a tribunal is found to be a court of competent jurisdiction it is presumed to have jurisdiction over any remedies not removed from it.[148]

Remedies are also available under section 52 of the *Constitution Act 1982*, which allows legislation to be struck down where it is in conflict with the *Charter* or some other part of the constitution. Formally, only superior court judges, who have inherent jurisdiction, and courts with statutory authority to do so can declare legislation unconstitutional and strike it down. However, on the basis that no one can be convicted or sentenced under an invalid law, provincial court judges are entitled

147 [2001] 3 SCR 623 [*Hynes*].

148 *R v Conway*, 2010 SCC 22. See the discussion in Steve Coughlan, "Tribunal Jurisdiction over *Charter* Remedies: Now You See It, Now You Don't" (2010) 75 *Criminal Reports* (6th) 238.

to consider the constitutionality of legislation and, if they find it to be unconstitutional, refuse to apply it in the case in front of them.[149]

## C. STATUTORY OVERVIEW OF PROCEDURE FROM CHARGING DECISION TO TRIAL

One major obstacle to getting a real sense of how criminal procedure works at the trial stage is the fact that the relevant sections are found in widely disparate parts of the *Code*. As noted above, the *Code* is arranged in a roughly chronological fashion, but there are exceptions to this rule. For example, the procedures for summary conviction offences are set out nearly at the end, in Part XXVII, but nonetheless incorporate many earlier provisions by reference. Liberal use of the *Code*'s index is necessary simply to find where to look for the right rules. Therefore, it might be useful to lay out a brief road map showing the various routes that might be followed in the case of a public prosecution, from the commencement of proceedings to an eventual trial, and the relevant *Code* sections.[150]

Under section 504, anyone can lay an information alleging the commission of an offence in front of a justice of the peace. This information will, according to section 506, be in Form 2. Under section 788, this is the document under which a summary conviction trial will take place.

The justice of the peace decides, under section 507, whether to issue a summons or a warrant in order to require the accused to attend court, where "a case for doing so is made out."[151] Note that these are two distinct steps: whether to do anything, and if so, whether to proceed by warrant or summons. Under section 507(3), the evidence is taken on oath.

Alternatively, rather than initially seeking process under section 504, a peace officer might have arrested, or been able to arrest, a person without a warrant. That person might still be in custody or might have already been released at some stage.[152] In that event, section 505 creates an obligation to present whatever process was issued to a justice of the peace. Section 508 then imposes an obligation on the justice to perform a screening process similar to that in section 507.

149 *R v Lloyd*, 2016 SCC 13.

150 See also *Anatomy of Criminal Procedure*, above note 1, which presents the rules of criminal procedure in chart form for each area of the law pulling all the disparate sections into a single place to show the connections.

151 Section 507(1)(b).

152 See the discussion in Chapter 6.

Presuming the matter goes further, the accused will be arrested or will receive the summons that was issued. If the accused was arrested, they will (under section 503) be taken in front of a justice of the peace who will decide whether to hold or release them. This bail hearing will be conducted in accordance with the procedures in section 515. Frequently, as a practical matter, bail hearings are by a judge rather than a justice of the peace.

Following any issues concerning the release of the accused will be the "arraignment"— the accused's initial appearance in court to answer the charge. If the offence is hybrid, the Crown should elect whether to proceed by indictment or summary conviction at this stage. If the matter is a summary conviction offence, automatically or by election, the accused enters a plea and will be tried on the information in Form 2. However, it is possible at this stage for that information to be withdrawn and a different information laid. The procedures in Part XXVII apply to summary conviction trials, and under section 798, a summary conviction court judge has jurisdiction. If the matter is indictable, section 471 says the trial must be by judge and jury unless some other part of the *Code* specifies otherwise. In fact, exceptions of some sort are then made for every offence, and the vast majority of criminal trials occur without a jury. Most indictable offences can be tried in any court.

Section 469 gives a superior court of criminal jurisdiction (defined in section 2 for each province) the ability to try any offence. Section 468 gives a court of criminal jurisdiction (also defined in section 2 for each province) the ability to try any offence other than those listed in section 469. Section 554 gives a provincial court the ability to try any offence other than those listed in section 469. "Provincial court" is also defined in this section of the *Code*, and in some provinces that definition overlaps with the definition of "court of criminal jurisdiction."

Although section 471 mandates jury trials as the putative norm, section 558 says that an accused can elect not to have a jury except for the offences listed in section 469, meaning that for everything except those offences an accused is automatically entitled to an election. Further, section 473 states that an accused can elect not to have a jury even for the offences listed in section 469, with the attorney general's consent. There is a limited ability to review the refusal of the attorney general to provide consent, but only where proceeding with a jury would result in an unfair trial and a violation of sections 7 and 11(d) of the *Charter*, or where the manner in which the Crown's discretion was exercised amounts to an abuse of process.[153]

153 See the discussion in *R v Millard*, 2017 ONSC 6040 or *R v Oland*, 2018 NBQB 253.

If the offence is listed as in the absolute jurisdiction of a magistrate, then the accused cannot elect and is tried in provincial court.[154] Similarly, if the offence is listed in section 469, the accused does not elect and is sent to a trial by judge and jury (subject to the attorney general's consent to dispense with the jury under section 473). In all other cases (that is, the majority), the accused is entitled to elect a mode of trial. In the past this was simply a matter of asking the accused to choose among trial by provincial court judge, by superior court judge alone, or by superior court judge with a jury: either of the superior court options automatically meant that the accused was entitled to a preliminary inquiry. However, Bill C-75 has restricted preliminary inquiries only to indictable offences punishable by fourteen years or more imprisonment, and so two different forms of election are now set out in the *Code*. If the offence is one of those for which a preliminary inquiry is available, the accused is asked to elect a mode of trial and is informed of that option; if it is not, the accused is simply asked to elect a mode of trial.[155]

If the accused refuses to elect, then according to section 565(1)(b), they will be deemed to have elected trial by judge and jury. The same is also true, under section 567, if there is more than one co-accused and they elect differently from one another (though in that case, the judge could allow the different elections and sever the trials). Further, even if the accused does not want a jury, the attorney general can compel a jury trial if the offence is punishable by more than five years, under section 568. In addition, section 577 (discussed below) allows for a "direct indictment," one consequence of which is that the accused is (under section 565(2)) deemed to have elected judge and jury and not to have elected a preliminary inquiry.

If the accused elects trial by a provincial court judge, the accused can then enter a plea and the trial can take place at any point.

If the accused elects trial by judge alone or trial by judge and jury, then under section 535, there might be a preliminary inquiry if the offence is punishable by imprisonment for fourteen years or more, and if the accused or the Crown request one. Preliminary inquiries are governed by the procedures in Part XVII of the *Code* (see Chapter 9). Note that an accused does not enter a plea at the preliminary inquiry stage: that is done in front of the court where the trial will take place.

---

154 Section 553.

155 Sections 536(2) and (2.1), respectively. This section starkly demonstrates the lack of clarity around the procedures in the *Code*: no section actually provides that the accused *has* the right to these various elections, but these subsections require that the accused must be told of these options.

Where a matter is before a provincial court judge, under section 555(1) the judge can decide "for any reason" that the charge should be prosecuted in superior court. In that event the accused will be put to an election between a judge alone or a judge and jury trial. Also in that event, if the charge is one of the few for which a preliminary inquiry is available and one of the parties so requests, the judge shall continue the proceedings on that basis. Similarly, under section 555(2), where the value of a stolen item turns out to be high enough that the offence was not one of absolute jurisdiction, the accused is offered an election as to mode of trial under section 536(2.1): if the accused elects superior court, the proceedings stop and the matter is sent there, but if the accused elects provincial court, the trial continues.

The accused has various rights of re-election set out in section 561. Depending on whether the accused is re-electing up or down, and the point to which the proceedings have advanced, re-election is either as of right or requires consent from the prosecutor.

If an accused elects trial by judge and jury but then fails to appear, then, under section 598, the later trial will not be in front of a judge and jury unless the accused shows a legitimate excuse.

Following the preliminary inquiry, if there is one, the judge will either discharge the accused or order the accused to stand trial on some offence in respect of the transaction charged. These powers are set out in section 548(1), but neither result is quite what it sounds like. First, "ordering the accused to stand trial" has no independent effect. It is simply a precondition to further action, normally by the Crown. For an indictable offence trial to take place, a new document, an "indictment" (hence "indictable offence") must be "preferred" (that is, laid in front of the trial court to commence trial). According to section 566, the indictment may be in Form 4 (also found in section 849). Section 576 dictates that an indictment can be preferred only on a basis set out in the *Criminal Code*. Some of those bases are set out in section 574, which permits an indictment to be preferred (1) on a charge for which the preliminary inquiry judge ordered the person to stand trial, or (2) on any charge founded on the facts disclosed at the preliminary inquiry. This latter provision means that the indictment may charge a different offence from the one charged in the information.

Where no preliminary inquiry is requested or was available, section 574(1.1) permits an indictment to be preferred on any charge set out in an information after the accused has made an election on it.

Normally, these powers to prefer an indictment would be relied upon by a Crown prosecutor, but section 574(3) permits a private prosecutor to prefer an indictment with leave of the intended trial court.

Note that discharging the accused does not guarantee that the accused will not stand trial. Under section 577, an indictment can also be preferred where no preliminary inquiry was held, a preliminary inquiry was commenced but not concluded or, most notably, a preliminary inquiry was held and *the accused was discharged.* An indictment under these circumstances, usually referred to as a "direct indictment," requires the written consent of the attorney general, or, in the case of a private prosecution, an order of a judge of the court where the information is preferred.

The various discretionary powers of the Crown prosecutor mentioned above do not violate the *Charter*, provided they are not used abusively. The Crown also has other powers, including staying the proceedings with the ability to recommence them within one year, under section 579, and intervening to take over a private prosecution, under sections 579.01 and 579.1.

## FURTHER READINGS

Coughlan, Steve. "Tribunal Jurisdiction over *Charter* Remedies: Now You See It, Now You Don't" (2010) 75 *Criminal Reports* (6th) 238.

——— et al. *Law Beyond Borders: Extraterritorial Jurisdiction in an Age of Globalization* (Toronto: Irwin Law, 2014).

——— & Alex Gorlewski. *The Anatomy of Criminal Procedure: A Visual Guide to the Law*, 2nd ed (Toronto: University of Toronto Press, 2026).

Currie, Robert J, & Steve Coughlan. "Extraterritorial Criminal Jurisdiction: Bigger Picture or Smaller Frame?" (2007) 11 *Canadian Criminal Law Review* 141.

Edwards, John. *The Law Officers of the Crown* (London: Sweet & Maxwell, 1964).

———. *The Attorney General, Politics and the Public Interest* (London: Sweet & Maxwell, 1984).

Healy, Patrick. "Constitutional Limits on the Allocation of Trial Jurisdiction to the Superior or Provincial Court in Criminal Matters" (2003) 48 *Criminal Law Quarterly* 31.

Law Reform Commison of Canada. *Classification of Offences* (Ottawa: Law Reform Commission of Canada, 1986).

———. *Our Criminal Procedure* (Ottawa: Law Reform Commission of Canada, 1988).

———. *Controlling Criminal Prosecutions: The Attorney General and the Crown Prosecutor* (Ottawa: Law Reform Commission of Canada, 1990).

Rose, David. *Quigley's Criminal Procedure in Canada* (Toronto: Thomson Reuters, 2021) (loose-leaf).

CHAPTER 4

# SEARCH AND SEIZURE

## A. INTRODUCTION

Other than in powers of arrest, the ability of police to interfere with the liberty of individuals is most evident in powers of search and seizure. Powers to search exist within the *Criminal Code* and other statutes and are also found at common law. Powers to seize are typically associated with search powers, though there are occasional exceptions to that rule.

The study of the law of search and seizure is made simpler by early decisions concerning section 8 of the *Canadian Charter of Rights and Freedoms*, which protects against "unreasonable search and seizure." The Court decided that, for purposes of section 8, a search which was not authorized by law was unreasonable.[1] The effect of that decision is to make the law of search and seizure and the *Charter* rules around search and seizure essentially co-extensive: broadly speaking, what is not authorized by law violates the *Charter*, but what is authorized by law does not. Accordingly, to understand the law of search and seizure, one needs to focus on the section 8 right.

One immediate consequence of this fact is that for section 8 to apply, as with any other *Charter* right, there must be state action involved.[2]

---

1 *R v Collins*, [1987] 1 SCR 265 [*Collins*].

2 In *Schreiber v Canada (Attorney General)*, [1998] 1 SCR 841, for example, the applicant objected to the gathering of information about his financial records in

Typically in the criminal law context this will be the case, such as when a search is conducted by police or other investigative arms of the state. In some circumstances, other people, such as school officials, can constitute state actors.[3] Further, an individual can become an agent of the state in certain circumstances, if they conduct themselves differently in an interaction because of their relationship to police or other state officials.[4] Without that sort of relationship, however, a private individual such as a security guard is not a state actor, and so *Charter* rights do not arise.[5]

Considering whether there has been an unreasonable search requires looking at two questions: was what occurred a search, and if so, was the search unreasonable? All section 8 cases, no matter what the context, follow the same basic structure. First, it is necessary to decide whether the police investigative technique constituted a "search": that question is answered by determining whether the person had a "reasonable expectation of privacy."[6] If the answer to that question is no, then whatever occurred was not a "search" at all, and section 8 could not have been violated. On the other hand, if the answer is yes, then there was a search, and the second question must be asked: was the search unreasonable? That second question is answered by applying the three-part *Collins* test: (1) was the search authorized by law; (2) was the law itself reasonable; and (3) was the manner in which the search

---

Switzerland. The Court held that the only action to which the applicant could object under the *Charter* was that taken by Canadian state officials, which was limited to sending a letter of request to Swiss officials. Sending that letter of request did not by itself violate his *Charter* rights.

3 *R v M(MR)*, [1998] 3 SCR 393 [*M(MR)*]. Note that this can be true, and s 8 can therefore apply, even outside the criminal law context: see *York Region District School Board v Elementary Teachers' Federation of Ontario*, 2024 SCC 22.

4 *R v Broyles*, [1991] 3 SCR 595; *R v Buhay*, 2003 SCC 30 [*Buhay*].

5 *Buhay*, *ibid*; *R v Jacobs*, 2014 ABCA 172. See also the discussion in Chapter 3, Section B(5).

6 In *Hunter v Southam Inc*, [1984] 2 SCR 145 [*Hunter*], the Supreme Court specifically rejected the notion that the intent of s 8 was to protect property rights and, instead, said that the important issue was privacy. The Court also observed that the s 8 right "might protect interests beyond the right of privacy" (*ibid* at 159). David Stratas, "*R v B(SA)* and the Right against Self-Incrimination: A Confusing Change of Direction" (2003) 14 *Criminal Reports* (6th) 227 [Stratas] observes that "while the Court opened the door to s 8 covering interests other than privacy back in *Hunter v Southam* in 1984, it has never gone through that door in any later case." In *R v SAB*, 2003 SCC 60 [*SAB*], the Court considered the extent to which s 8 protected an accused against self-incrimination, and that is to date still the only case that has considered anything other than privacy concerns when dealing with s 8.

was carried out reasonable?[7] It will often be the case that the answer to one of those questions is not in dispute on the particular facts of a case: for example, no one would argue that a person subject to a strip search did not have a reasonable expectation of privacy, and typically in a search authorized by warrant no one would argue that section 487 of the *Criminal Code* is an unreasonable law. Even when there is no explicit discussion of a particular question, however, it has implicitly been considered and answered.

This chapter will follow that structure, looking first at reasonable expectation of privacy and then at the *Collins* test.[8] However, there are additional foundational rules and principles that need to be recognized at the start.

An important rule was established in one of the earliest *Charter* decisions, *Hunter v Southam Inc*: a warrantless search is *prima facie* unreasonable. That particular rule is a consequence of the more general principle that the purpose of section 8 is "*preventing* unjustified searches before they happen, not simply of determining, after the fact, whether they ought to have occurred in the first place."[9] The effect of this rule is to create a practical distinction between warrantless searches and searches with a warrant. In the former case, the burden shifts to the Crown to demonstrate that, despite the absence of a warrant, the search was nonetheless authorized by law.[10] There are, in fact, warrantless search powers, for the most part created at common law, and therefore typically less well defined than statutory powers. As a result, section 8 cases concerning warrantless searches tend to focus on the first step in the *Collins* test: Was the search authorized by law? On the other hand, in cases where a warrant provision exists and a warrant has been issued, that first step tends not to be controversial: instead, argument is more likely to focus on the second and third steps, whether the law itself is reasonable, and whether the manner of search was reasonable. Similarly, discussion of whether there was a reasonable expectation of privacy tends not to arise in cases of searches with a warrant: the very fact that the police obtained a warrant makes it hard to deny that there *was* such an expectation. Thus, although the same

7 *Collins*, above note 1 at para 23.

8 For an explanation of this issue in chart form, see Steve Coughlan and Alex Gorlewski, *The Anatomy of Criminal Procedure: A Visual Guide to the Law*, 2nd ed (Toronto: University of Toronto Press, 2026) [*Anatomy of Criminal Procedure*], Chart 1.1(b)(i), "Is There a Section 8 Violation?"

9 *Hunter*, above note 6 at 160 [emphasis in original].

10 *Ibid* at 161: s 8 "require[s] the party seeking to justify a warrantless search to rebut this presumption of unreasonableness."

test applies in both situations, there are practical differences in application between searches with a warrant and searches without a warrant. Accordingly, this chapter will discuss those two situations separately.

One final overarching governing principle about searches must be noted. Rules relating to search and seizure (like all rules of criminal procedure) try to balance two competing interests: "that of the individual to be free of intrusions of the state and that of the state to intrude on the privacy of the individual for the purpose of law enforcement."[11] *Hunter* noted that the question was "whether in a particular situation the public's interest in being left alone by government must give way to the government's interest in intruding on the individual's privacy in order to advance its goals, notably those of law enforcement."[12] In general, "[t]he state's interest in detecting and preventing crime begins to prevail over the individual's interest in being left alone at the point where credibly-based probability replaces suspicion."[13]

That standard creates a kind of benchmark against which all search powers can be measured. In essence *Hunter* establishes that, where there is the "normal" expectation of privacy and the "normal" state interest, a search cannot be justified based on anything less than reasonable grounds. Sometimes, however, a person will have a reduced expectation of privacy, while in other circumstances, it will be enhanced, and this will affect the proper balance. An olfactory search of luggage by means of a sniffer dog is relatively unintrusive and therefore can be permitted relatively readily, for example, while a body cavity search is a significant intrusion and therefore should not occur without a correspondingly greater justification.[14] This change in the nature of the individual interest can shift the balance. Equally, the nature of the state interest can shift the balance. Search incident to arrest, for example,[15] is justified not because a person arrested has a lesser expectation of privacy, but because the immediate interest of the state in protecting the security of the arresting officer and others increases at the point of

---

11 *Baron v Canada*, [1993] 1 SCR 416 at para 24 [*Baron*]. See also *SAB*, above note 6 at para 43, where the Court noted that the issue in considering search powers is the balance between "the truth-seeking interests of law enforcement and the equally essential respect for individual rights."

12 *Hunter*, above note 6 at 159.

13 *Ibid* at 167.

14 On the reduced expectation of privacy in a vehicle generally, see *R v Wise*, [1992] 1 SCR 527 [*Wise*]; *R v Belnavis*, [1997] 3 SCR 341 [*Belnavis*]; and *R v Fliss*, [2002] 1 SCR 535 [*Fliss*]. On the intrusive nature of body cavity searches, see *R v Simmons*, [1988] 2 SCR 495 [*Simmons*].

15 See discussion at Section C(1)(a)(ii)(b), below in this chapter.

arrest.[16] The state's interest in DNA evidence is significant, since it is a particularly powerful tool either to show an accused's guilt or prevent wrongful convictions.[17] Searches are more readily permitted at border crossings, due as much to the enhanced state interest in preventing the entry of undesirable persons and prohibited goods as to the reduced expectation of privacy of individuals in that setting.[18] The result of changing the nature of the competing interests in this way means that sometimes it is appropriate either to allow searches more readily or make them more difficult to authorize.

In essence, the preconditions to be met before a search is allowed should be a reflection of the protection offered to the person being searched, and that protection should accurately reflect the strength of the individual interest and the strength of the state interest. As the Court has held, "[i]n interpreting s 8, courts seek to strike an acceptable balance, in a free and democratic society, between sometimes conflicting interests in the privacy necessary for personal dignity and autonomy and the need for a secure and safe society."[19]

These considerations are true of both warrantless searches and searches with a warrant, and we will see departures from the *Hunter* benchmark both upward and downward.[20] In some cases, searches will be allowed based on mere "reasonable suspicion" that an offence has been committed, as opposed to "reasonable grounds to believe."[21] In other cases, "reasonable grounds to believe" alone will not be sufficient, and it will be necessary for the Crown to meet other conditions as well, such as proving that issuing a particular warrant is in the best interests of the administration of justice.[22]

---

16 *R v Caslake*, [1998] 1 SCR 51 at para 17 [*Caslake*].

17 *SAB*, above note 6 at para 51.

18 *Simmons*, above note 14.

19 *R v Mills*, 2019 SCC 22 at para 38 [*Mills*].

20 Departures from the norm can also be justified based on a change in the state interest being protected. For example, searches are more readily permitted at border crossings, due as much to the enhanced state interest in preventing the entry of undesirable persons and prohibited goods as to the reduced expectation of privacy: *Simmons*, above note 14.

21 As will be noted below, a warrantless search using a sniffer dog is permitted based on reasonable suspicion, and a warrant to attach a device which will track the location of a vehicle (but not of a person) is allowed on reasonable suspicion.

22 As will be noted below, electronic surveillance of communications without the consent of the parties requires showing not only reasonable grounds but also "investigative necessity," which amounts to showing that other evidence-gathering methods are unlikely to succeed. The common law power of conducting a strip search incident to arrest, as opposed to a pat-down search, requires not

The Supreme Court has summarized these points:

> If, in the first instance, a reasonable expectation of privacy is determined to exist, a search intruding upon that interest will engage s 8 of the *Charter*. Because the *Charter* protects only against unreasonable searches, the next step after a reasonable expectation of privacy has been established is to inquire whether the search is reasonable. A search involving a *Charter*-protected privacy interest will be reasonable if the police are authorized by law to conduct the search, if the law authorizing the search is reasonable, and if the search is conducted in a reasonable manner (*R v Collins*, [1987] 1 SCR 265, at p 278). In most cases, this requires obtention of a search warrant requiring police to satisfy a judicial authority that there are reasonable and probable grounds to believe that a search will reveal evidence of an offence (see, e.g., *Criminal Code*, RSC 1985, c C-46, s 487). In certain situations where only a lowered expectation of privacy is recognized, police must instead have a reasonable suspicion that a search will uncover evidence of an offence before they may undertake it (see, e.g., *Kang-Brown*). Where no reasonable expectation of privacy is established, no threshold justification is required because the search does not trigger *Charter* protection (see, e.g., *Patrick*).[23]

With this overview established, we turn to the first question, that of reasonable expectation of privacy.

## B. WAS THERE A SEARCH? REASONABLE EXPECTATION OF PRIVACY

Over the course of a number of decisions, the Supreme Court has developed a test for determining whether a person has a reasonable expectation of privacy, often referred to as the "totality of the circumstances" test. It has evolved over time, but has now settled into a reasonably stable structure which involves addressing four considerations: the subject matter of the search, whether the accused has a direct interest in that subject matter, whether the accused has a subjective expectation of privacy in that subject matter, and whether an expectation of privacy

---

only reasonable grounds to think that an offence has been committed, but also reasonable grounds to believe that the person searched has a weapon and is a danger to the police or others: *R v Golden*, 2001 SCC 83 [*Golden*].

23 *R v Gomboc*, 2010 SCC 55 at para 20 [*Gomboc*]. There is no single majority opinion in *Gomboc*, but this passage from the judgment of Deschamps J (subscribed to directly by four of the nine judges) is not controversial.

is objectively reasonable. Below we will explore that test in detail, but some observations about the concept of reasonable expectation of privacy should first be made.

## 1) The Roles Played by Reasonable Expectation of Privacy: A Threshold and a Scale

Reasonable expectation of privacy plays two distinct roles in a search and seizure analysis. A section 8 analysis involves asking the two questions of whether there was a search and if so whether it was unreasonable, and reasonable expectation of privacy figures in both. As already noted, it is what defines whether the police investigative technique is or is not a search: if the technique does not infringe a reasonable expectation of privacy, then it is not a search.[24] This principle applies equally to seizures.[25] Second, it helps define whether a particular search power is or is not "reasonable": simply put, if a person has a reduced expectation of privacy, then a lesser justification is needed before infringing on it, and if that person has an enhanced expectation of privacy, then a greater justification is needed.[26]

Courts tend only to engage in a single reasonable expectation of privacy analysis, but it is important to keep clearly in mind the difference between these two roles. At the first stage, the analysis is asking a purely binary question: is there or is there not a reasonable expectation of privacy? As the Court has observed, "[a] reasonable though diminished expectation of privacy is nonetheless a reasonable expectation

---

24 See, for example, *R v Bykovets*, 2024 SCC 6 [*Bykovets*] at para 31: "A search occurs where the state invades a reasonable expectation of privacy."

25 *R v Cole*, 2012 SCC 53 [*Cole*] at para 34: "An inspection is a search, and a taking is a seizure, where a person has a reasonable privacy interest in the object or subject matter of the state action and the information to which it gives access."

26 It is also frequently relevant in a third way: to help determine whether, if a person's s 8 right has been violated, the person is likely to receive a remedy; that is, the Court has established a test for exclusion of evidence, one consideration in which is the impact on the accused's *Charter*-protected interests: *R v Grant*, 2009 SCC 32 [*Grant*]. In that analysis, therefore, evidence is more likely to be excluded if the accused had a high expectation of privacy and less likely to be excluded in the case of a reduced expectation. An illegal search of a vehicle in which there is said to be a reduced expectation of privacy is a less serious violation, for example, than an unlawful body cavity search: see, for example, *Belnavis*, above note 14; *Fliss*, above note 14; and *Wise*, above note 14. More generally, the Court held in *Grant*, above in this note at para 78 that "[a]n unreasonable search that intrudes on an area in which the individual reasonably enjoys a high expectation of privacy, or that demeans his or her dignity, is more serious than one that does not."

of privacy."[27] If there is, then the investigation constituted a search. It is not actually necessary, in determining this threshold question, to ask *where* on a scale of privacy expectations the accused's interest falls. At the second stage, however, of deciding whether the search that occurred was reasonable, a sliding scale is used.[28]

At the first stage, many things have been found to cross the threshold and therefore to be classified as a search. Frisking suspects, having them turn out their pockets, and so on are searches, but so is the passive technique of conducting a "bedpan vigil."[29] Both the physical act of installing a tracking device in a car and the subsequent electronic monitoring of that car's movements constitute searches.[30] An inspection of a workplace is a search.[31] A wiretap is a search,[32] as is video surveillance and all existing or future technology allowing the state to intrude electronically on privacy.[33] Using an IP address to find out the name associated with an internet account is a search,[34] as indeed is finding that IP address in the first place.[35] Police engage in a search when they obtain the contents of a computer, even if given the computer by a person who

---

27 *Cole*, above note 25 at para 9. See also *R v Le*, 2019 SCC 34 [*Le*] at para 136: "it is possible for an individual to have a diminished or qualified reasonable expectation of privacy while still retaining the benefit of s. 8 protection."

28 *R v Plant*, [1993] 3 SCR 281 [*Plant*], illustrates the wisdom of keeping a clear distinction between these two possible approaches. Police relied on the accused's electricity consumption records to seek a warrant to search his residence for marijuana, but they initially obtained those records without a warrant. The Court suggests at times that Plant had "no reasonable expectation of privacy with respect to the computerized electricity records" (at 295), at other times that he "cannot be said to have held a reasonable expectation of privacy in relation to the computerized electricity records *which outweighs* the state interest in enforcing the laws relating to narcotics offences" (at 296) [emphasis added]. If the latter characterization is the correct one, the Court really ought to have engaged in more analysis concerning the reasonableness of the search, not just Plant's expectation of privacy.

See also Lisa M Austin, "Is Consent the Foundation of Fair Information Practices? Canada's Experience under *PIPEDA*" (2006) 56 *University of Toronto Law Journal* 181, noting that "[a]lthough the threshold question and the balancing question are distinct, the jurisprudence is replete with examples where the two have been conflated." She suggests that this results in a kind of "double counting" against individual privacy interests, which inappropriately minimizes otherwise reasonable expectations of privacy.

29 *R v Monney*, [1999] 1 SCR 652. See also *R v Poirier*, 2016 ONCA 582 [*Poirier*].

30 *Wise*, above note 14.

31 *Amax Potash Ltd v Saskatchewan*, [1977] 2 SCR 576 [*Potash*].

32 *R v Duarte*, [1990] 1 SCR 30 [*Duarte*].

33 *R v Wong*, [1990] 3 SCR 36 at 43–44 [*Wong*].

34 *R v Spencer*, 2014 SCC 43 at para 18 [*Spencer*].

35 *Bykovets*, above note 24.

shares it with another person.[36] Using a drug-sniffer dog to smell a person's belongings or vehicle is a search.[37] Executing a search warrant on the interior of a building is, of course, a search, but so is inspecting the perimeter of the building.[38] Indeed, since it intrudes on a person's reasonable expectation of privacy, it is also a search when the police knock on a door to see whether they will be able to smell marijuana when it is opened.[39] To be clear, this does not mean the police cannot engage in any of these activities: it simply means they will need lawful authority to do so: as the Court has put it, "in the age of telewarrants and around-the-clock access to justices of the peace, this burden is not onerous."[40]

The same approach applies to deciding whether a "seizure" has occurred. The issue is not whether some measure of compulsion or deprivation was involved, but whether the accused's reasonable expectation of privacy was infringed. Thus, for example, making copies of a company's documents constitutes a seizure.[41] Further, even if a doctor willingly hands over a blood sample to the police, this will still be considered a seizure if the doctor was authorized to have the blood sample only for limited purposes.[42] There is some suggestion that there is a distinction between evidence that is "seized" and evidence that is merely "found." It has been suggested that if the police take a sample of blood from a car seat at the scene of an accident, such action will not infringe the accused's reasonable expectation of privacy because the blood was abandoned, and so it will not be a seizure.[43]

Because it does not matter *to what extent* a reasonable expectation of privacy exists at the threshold stage, this test ought to be easy to meet: as noted earlier, this is a purely binary yes/no question. At a policy level, that also ought to be the case. To say that there is no reasonable expectation of privacy is to remove the police conduct from any possible scrutiny under section 8: if there was no reasonable expectation of privacy, then what occurred was not a search, and so no court will ever be entitled to assess whether what the state did was "unreasonable"

---

36 *R v Reeves*, 2018 SCC 56 [*Reeves*].

37 *R v Kang-Brown*, 2008 SCC 18 [*Kang-Brown*]; *R v AM*, 2008 SCC 19 [*AM*]; *R v Chehil*, 2013 SCC 49 [*Chehil*]; *R v MacKenzie*, 2013 SCC 50 [*MacKenzie*].

38 *R v Kokesch*, [1990] 3 SCR 3 [*Kokesch*].

39 *R v Evans*, [1996] 1 SCR 8 [*Evans*]. The Court reaffirmed in *R v Patrick*, 2009 SCC 17 at para 52 [*Patrick*], the correctness of the rulings in *Kokesch*, above note 38 and *Evans*.

40 *Bykovets*, above note 24 at para 86.

41 *Potash*, above note 31.

42 *R v Dyment*, [1988] 2 SCR 417 [*Dyment*]. See also *R v Culotta*, 2018 SCC 57 [*Culotta*].

43 *R v Leblanc* (1981), 64 CCC (2d) 31 (NBCA), cited in *Dyment*, above note 42.

or not.[44] The whole point of section 8 is to balance competing interests,[45] but to find no reasonable expectation of privacy is to remove any possibility of balancing. Put starkly, if some police investigative technique is found not to infringe a reasonable expectation of privacy, that can amount to saying that the police can use the technique any time, against anyone, anywhere, without the possibility of advance oversight or after-the-fact review. In contrast, to say that the technique *does* infringe a person's reasonable expectation of privacy is not to say that that person should be immune from search: merely that the search power must be a reasonable one.

It is worth drawing a distinction here, however. Most of the time the analysis functions as noted above, and a "no reasonable expectation of privacy" finding amounts to the conclusion that *no one* could be seen to have a reasonable expectation of privacy. For example, in *R v Tessling* the Court concluded that the use of a Forward Looking Infra-Red scanner (FLIR), which detects the pattern of heat emanating from a building, does not gather information in which there could be a reasonable expectation of privacy.[46] The effect of that decision is to say that police can use a FLIR at any time without judicial authorization.[47] That amounts to a broad grant of police power, and the Court has recognized concerns over that effect.[48]

However, in some cases the reasonable expectation of privacy analysis functions instead as a finding about the individual accused, and is presented as a question of the standing of that person to raise a *Charter* argument. In *R v Edwards*, for example, police took items from a closet in an apartment rented by the accused's girlfriend. One could not plausibly claim that examining and physically removing items from the closet did not constitute a search *at all*. However, the Court concluded that the accused could only object to this search under the *Charter* if it was a violation of *his* section 8 right, rather than a violation of someone else's rights. That is, unless the accused

44 See, for example, *M(MR)*, above note 3 at para 31: "[I]f there is no reasonable expectation of privacy held by an accused with respect to the relevant place, there *can be no* violation of s 8" [emphasis added].

45 *Baron*, above note 11.

46 *R v Tessling*, [2004] 3 SCR 432 at para 42 [*Tessling*].

47 See the discussion of "default" common law powers in Chapter 2, Section A(3)(c).

48 See, for example, *Bykovets*, above note 24 at para 65:

> Without the protection of s 8, nothing prevents the state from preemptively collecting IP addresses and comparing that user's IP address against their database. Further, and significantly, the scope of information that an IP address can reveal is enormous if correlated against information held by a third party.

*personally* had a reasonable expectation of privacy in his girlfriend's apartment, *he* was not searched. Put another way, although it might in the abstract have been a search, it would not be a search of the accused, and so he would not have standing to make a section 8 claim. In fact, the Court found in *Edwards* that, based on the totality of the circumstances, he was only a "privileged guest" in the apartment, rather than a person who had a reasonable expectation of privacy in it.[49] Similarly in *R v Belnavis*, this same reasoning led to the conclusion that the passenger in a vehicle — at least on the facts of that case — had no reasonable expectation of privacy.[50] Once again, that meant that the accused had no section 8 claim, despite a warrantless search that the trial judge found to have taken place without reasonable and probable grounds.

One can envision these cases as ruling that the accused was not searched at all and therefore could not have been unreasonably searched. However, the result is also sometimes phrased as a matter of standing: that an accused does not have standing to object to the violation of someone else's section 8 right. *Belnavis* adopts the former description, while *Edwards* uses the latter. Both *Edwards* and *Belnavis* saw vigorous dissenting judgments from LaForest J, decrying the dilution of section 8 protection that was inherent in the decisions. They were also criticized, for example, for giving police an improper motive to conduct searches they know to be unreasonable.[51]

---

49 *R v Edwards*, [1996] 1 SCR 128 [*Edwards*]

50 *Belnavis*, above note 14. *Belnavis* is not meant to establish that a passenger *never* has a reasonable expectation of privacy in a vehicle; the decision is always to be made based on the totality of the circumstances. See, for example, *R v Dreyer*, 2008 BCCA 89, where the Court of Appeal concluded that the passenger in a vehicle who was being driven, as he often was, by his sister "had the same expectation of privacy of his property in the car as would a passenger with a shopping bag in a taxi" (para 13). In contrast, see *R v Plummer*, 2011 ONCA 350 [*Plummer*], which does deny standing to raise s 8 to a person sitting in a car, but which has been criticized for being too formulaic in its reasoning: see Paul Calarco, "*R v Plummer*: Standing to Challenge Searches" (2011) 85 *Criminal Reports* (6th) 62.

51 Steven Penney, "Unreasonable Search and Seizure and Section 8 of the *Charter*: Cost-Benefit Analysis in Constitutional Interpretation" (2013) 62 *Supreme Court Law Review* (2d) 101 at para 44, observes:

> Consider the following scenario: police suspect (without objective grounds) that a group of young Aboriginal or African-Canadian men are drug traffickers and collectively use a particular car or apartment for their business. If police search either place without grounds or a warrant, they will undoubtedly violate the s 8 rights of the owner or driver of the car as well as the residents of the apartment. Any evidence obtained would likely be excluded

More recently, the Court seems to be less willing, on the basis of standing, to deny a chance of considering section 8. For example, a similar issue arose in the context of text messaging in *R v Marakah*.[52] The accused Marakah and another person, Winchester, had exchanged text messages about illegal transactions in firearms. Both were arrested and the police searched Winchester's cellphone, finding the text messages from Marakah. The trial judge concluded that although the search of Winchester's cellphone had been unlawful, Marakah had no standing to object to that unlawful search. The Ontario Court of Appeal upheld that result, but the Supreme Court of Canada reversed it, finding Marakah did in fact have standing to raise a section 8 claim. In this case, the conclusion was largely dictated by what the Court understood the subject matter of the search to be: not the physical item "Winchester's cellphone," but rather the content of the text message conversation between the two of them.[53] The later decision in *Campbell* not only follows this approach but expands it, finding the accused to have a reasonable expectation of privacy in a text message conversation he had using a borrowed phone.[54]

Similarly, in *Le*, police entered a backyard of a residence uninvited and asked questions of the guests there. The dissent suggested that, on the basis of *Edwards* and *Belnavis*, the accused likely did not have standing to complain of the police trespassing on the property of his host. The majority, however, made clear that they did not accept that position, holding that "a case can be made that invited guests can, in some circumstances, have reasonable expectations of privacy in their host's property."[55]

A further aspect of the "reasonable expectation of privacy" analysis worth discussing is that it is not an all-or-nothing issue. It is possible to give up the interest for some purposes while retaining it in other ways. For example, the reasonable expectation of privacy in one's

---

in any prosecution of these individuals. But it is unlikely that any other person found in the car or apartment could make a s 8 claim. Knowing this, police have an incentive to search illegally, since not searching will uncover no evidence, but searching could reveal evidence admissible against those without sufficient possessory interests.

52 *R v Marakah*, 2017 SCC 59 [*Marakah*].

53 See the further discussion of this issue below, in looking at the subject matter of the search.

54 *R v Campbell*, 2024 SCC 42 [*Campbell*] at para 67: the accused "did not lose the protection of s. 8 of the *Charter* simply by sharing private information with the other party to his text message conversation or by using the phone of an acquaintance."

55 *Le*, above note 27 at para 137.

home might be given up to the extent that visitors are given an implied licence to knock on the door to communicate with the resident: however, that implied licence does not give police the right to knock on the door if their real purpose is to conduct a warrantless "olfactory search."[56] Indeed, the police lose any benefit of the implied licence doctrine and become trespassers if they enter property with the subsidiary purpose of carrying out an investigation.[57] Implied consent allowing a doctor to take a blood sample for medical purposes does not eliminate the reasonable expectation that the sample will not be used for other purposes.[58] A person speaking in the presence of others has accepted the risk of being seen and heard by those present, but that does not imply any agreement to a permanent electronic record of the remarks being made.[59]

For the most part, the threshold stage has not been used as a barrier to section 8 protection, but that is not universally the case. Part of the difficulty arises from the *post facto* nature of the determination and from the unintended consequence of the combination of two rules: "if there is no reasonable expectation of privacy there was no search" and "a warrantless search is *prima facie* unreasonable." If one were building a set of search powers from the ground up, one might look at a situation and conclude "the accused has a much reduced expectation of privacy but it is not non-existent, so the police should be required to obtain a warrant but that warrant should be relatively easy to obtain." In fact, though, courts typically are not confronted with such situations until after the fact, and in cases where as a matter of fact the police did not obtain a warrant; otherwise there would be no *Charter* claim. In such cases, a court is faced with an all-or-nothing situation: a finding that what the police did constituted a search will inevitably result in the finding that it was an unreasonable one. In close cases, therefore, it cannot be surprising that the option of concluding that what the police did was not a "search" after all is sometimes an attractive way to avoid the conclusion that there was a *Charter* violation.[60]

---

56 *Evans*, above note 39. See also *R v Singer*, 2023 SKCA 123 [*Singer*], leave to appeal to the SCC granted 2024 CanLII 58467, applying the same reasoning to police officers who, for investigative purposes, walked up the accused's driveway, knocked on the window of his truck, and opened the truck door.

57 *Le*, above note 27 at paras 126–28.

58 *Dyment*, above note 42, and *Culotta*, above note 42.

59 *Wong*, above note 33 at para 22; *Duarte*, above note 32; *Fliss*, above note 14, and *Campbell*, above note 54.

60 Although courts do sometimes seem to feel this pressure, it is an unnecessary one because another option exists. A violation of s 8 does not automatically lead to the exclusion of the evidence. Evidence would be excluded under s 24(2) only

As a final point about the threshold stage, note the potentially harmful long-term consequence to finding that a person had no reasonable expectation of privacy in close cases: it encourages police to push the envelope. If police are faced with a situation in which they know that they have no search power, they have a choice between not searching or searching on the chance that a judge will later decide that the accused had no reasonable expectation of privacy. From a principled constitutional perspective, we would like police to adopt the first choice: the purpose of section 8 is, after all, "*preventing* unjustified searches before they happen."[61] It is therefore unfortunate when courts adopt an approach which encourages police to adopt the second.

## 2) The Normative Approach

It is crucial to recognize that "reasonable" in the context of "reasonable expectation of privacy" is intended to be an assessment of *entitlement* to privacy, not a measure of whether a person, as a matter of fact, *has* privacy. The Court has reiterated again and again that reasonable expectation of privacy "is not a purely factual inquiry. The reasonable expectation of privacy standard is normative rather than simply descriptive,"[62] and that "the inquiry is always driven by the question of whether a privacy claim ought to 'be recognized as beyond state intrusion absent constitutional justification if Canadian society is to remain a free, democratic and open society'."[63] The assessment is "laden with value judgments which are made from the independent perspective of the reasonable and informed person who is concerned about the long-term consequences of government action for the protection of privacy."[64]

Further — and this point is often overlooked but is absolutely fundamental — the issue is not one of an expectation of privacy in general, but of an expectation of privacy *against the state*.[65] To say that

---

following an analysis based on the factors set out in *Grant*, above note 26. One of those factors takes into account the accused's *Charter*-protected interests, and so if there was only a minimal reasonable expectation of privacy, it is much less likely that the evidence would be excluded.

61 *Hunter*, above note 6 at 160 [emphasis in original].

62 *Spencer*, above note 34 at para 18.

63 *Le*, above note 27 at para 136, quoting *Reeves*, above note 36 at para 28.

64 *Patrick*, above note 39. See also *Tessling*, above note 46 at para 42.

65 See, for example, *Campbell*, above note 54 at para 68: "The relevant question under s. 8 is not whether the individual reasonably expected the subject matter of the search to remain private from just anybody; what matters is whether they reasonably expected it would remain private from *state intrusion*."

a person has no reasonable expectation of privacy is to say that they have no protection under section 8 of the *Charter*: that the state can, at will, gather that information. We often expect that our activity or statements will not remain private from *everyone*, but a recognition that someone will know sometimes cannot be allowed to translate into the result that the state has a complete entitlement to that information at all times. In *R v Duarte*, for example, the Court dealt with "consent interceptions," which are wiretaps where one party to the conversation consents to having it recorded. The Court rejected the suggestion that this was simply analogous to the risk that a person with whom we have a conversation might later disclose the contents of that conversation: "the regulation of electronic surveillance protects us from a risk of a different order, i.e., not the risk that someone will repeat our words but the much more insidious danger inherent in allowing the state, in its unfettered discretion, to record and transmit our words."[66] Similarly in *Reeves* the Court held that "I cannot accept that, by choosing to share our computers with friends and family, we are required to give up our *Charter* protection from state interference in our private lives."[67]

There was briefly some cause to question the Court's commitment to this approach, but it has been reaffirmed. In *Mills*, the accused had engaged in an electronic conversation with someone he believed to be an underage girl but whom was in fact an undercover police officer. There was no clear majority set of reasons in finding that the accused did not have a reasonable expectation of privacy, but one cohort of judges held that it was because "it is not reasonable to expect that your messages will be kept private from the intended recipient (even if the intended recipient is an undercover officer)."[68] Subsequently in *Campbell*, another case involving an electronic conversation between an accused and a police officer, the Crown relied on that argument, but the Supreme Court rejected it, adopting the same approach as the dissent in *Mills*, that this approach was inconsistent with *Duarte*: "speaking with a caller on a telephone is constitutionally different from creating a permanent electronic record of the communication through a surreptitious sound recording or by using the medium of text messaging."[69]

66 *Duarte*, above note 32 at para 23.

67 *Reeves*, above note 35 at para 44. See also *R v Villaroman*, 2018 ABCA 220, noting that a person who takes a computer in to be repaired accepts that the technician will see the files on it, but that is not a waiver of privacy against third parties such as the police.

68 *Mills*, above note 19 at para 36.

69 *Campbell*, above note 54 at para 70.

There is a certain danger inherent in section 8 rights, and of course *Charter* rights in general, being limited to state action, which is the danger that privacy breaches will be carried out by non-state actors. For example in *Buhay*, bus station security guards opened a bus locker without lawful authority, while in *Cole* illicit material was found on a teacher's laptop by a school board technician: neither of those actions themselves constituted *Charter* breaches.[70] But even in such cases, the analysis does act to preserve a person's reasonable expectation of privacy once state action enters the picture. In each of *Buhay* and *Cole*, there was found to be a section 8 violation when the police obtained that same material or information through the private actors without first obtaining a warrant.

Indeed, in *Bykovets* the Court relied heavily on the potential role of non-state actors in order to find that a reasonable expectation of privacy existed. It had previously been determined that using an IP address to seek identifying information such as a subscriber name and address from an internet service provider engaged a person's reasonable expectation of privacy.[71] *Bykovets* concluded that there was also a reasonable expectation of privacy in the IP address itself. This conclusion was based on how readily information about a person could be obtained simply through use of the IP address, given that "the largest social media companies in the world use IP addresses to, for example, personalize the advertisements their users see, identify their users' preferences, and infer even more information about their users, such as their age, their gender, and their interests."[72] The core of the reasoning was that, given that private corporations could gather such vast information without *Charter* constraint, there needed to be a chance for judicial oversight before it was handed over to the state.

Another way to think about that point is to say that a reasonable expectation of privacy should *not* be judged based on a risk analysis. Speaking in the particular context of video surveillance, the Court noted that "we can only be sure of being free from surveillance today if we retire to our basements, cloak our windows, turn out the lights and remain absolutely quiet."[73] The correct question is to ask about "the standards of privacy that persons can *expect* to enjoy in a free and democratic society."[74] Thus, for example, a person whose property is stolen still has a reasonable expectation of privacy in that property,

70 See *Buhay*, above note 4 and *Cole*, above note 25.

71 See *Spencer*, above note 36.

72 *Bykovets*, above note 24 at para 77.

73 *Wong*, above note 33 at para 11.

74 *Ibid* at para 46 [emphasis added].

despite the obvious fact that the thief has, at least temporarily, rendered that interest ineffective in any practical sense.[75]

That a risk analysis is not the proper approach is unambiguous. Unfortunately, courts do sometimes slip into looking at the ease with which things *can* be searched and take that to determine the reasonable expectation of privacy analysis. In part, this might be the case because, although there is a structured test for analyzing privacy, asking about the normative entitlement to privacy is not explicitly one of the steps: that principle is meant to govern the overarching approach rather than be inquired into independently. Beyond that, of course, it is easier to go about assessing whether privacy *can* be intruded on in a particular situation and harder to assess whether it *should* be intruded upon, and so there can be a tendency to fall into the easier but incorrect approach.[76]

Further, the totality of the circumstances test itself, especially the "objective reasonableness" portion, can unintentionally act to steer the analysis *away* from the normative question. This portion of the test will be discussed at greater length below, but the Court has tended to identify a number of questions that should be asked about the situation, such as whether the accused had possession or control of the property or place searched, whether the accused had the ability to regulate access, whether the subject matter of the search was in plain view, whether the accused was present at the time of the search, and so on. Those questions are fundamentally factual ones, even though the conclusion to be reached is *not* meant to be a purely factual one. It is only by, in addition, reaching conclusions about what possession or presence or any of the other considerations ought to *imply* about entitlement that we can reach a normative assessment, but that is not explicit in the test.

---

75 *R v Law*, [2002] 1 SCR 227 [*Law*].

76 See, for example, *R v Boersma*, [1994] 2 SCR 488, aff'g [1993] BCJ No 2748 at para 11 (CA), where the Court upheld a British Columbia Court of Appeal decision that an accused growing marijuana on Crown land had no reasonable expectation of privacy based on the question of "whether they were susceptible to being seen by other people." See the discussion of this issue in James Stribopoulos, "Reasonable Expectation of Privacy and 'Open Fields' — Taking the American 'Risk Analysis' Head On" (1999) 25 *Criminal Reports* (5th) 351. In *R v Kwiatkowski*, 2010 BCCA 124, it was found that an accused had no reasonable expectation of privacy in the contents of greenhouses located in a wooded and difficult-to-access portion of a remote rural property, on the basis that a police officer flying over neighbouring property 1000 feet away and using a telephoto lens on one occasion saw a plant he thought was marijuana through an open door. See also the discussion in Steve Coughlan, "*Kwiatkowski*: Privacy Protection and Risk Analysis: Losing the Forest in the Telephoto Shots of the Trees" (2010) 73 *Criminal Reports* (6th) 260. See also Austin, above note 28.

The Supreme Court is now careful to keep the normative approach front and centre. Recent cases dealing with electronic communications, for example, have created debate over whether a person can reasonably expect privacy in data which is necessarily held by a third party, the service provider, and have concluded that such a reasonable expectation of privacy does exist. Although the accused has little to no ability to control the data, that is not the question: rather, "as a normative matter, it is reasonable to expect a service provider to keep information private where its receipt and retention of such information is incidental to its role of delivering private communications to the intended recipient."[77] In *Bykovets*, in finding that there was a reasonable expectation of privacy in an IP address, the majority rejected the view that the analysis should look at the information actually revealed about the particular accused, because the "normative standard demands we take a broad, functional approach to the subject matter of the search and that we focus on its *potential* to reveal personal or biographical core information."[78] Similarly in *Campbell* the Court observed "[i]n determining whether a subjective expectation of privacy is objectively reasonable, courts must employ an approach that is both normative and content-neutral. Several interveners urge this Court to affirm these basic postulates of the s. 8 analysis. I agree that it is useful to do so."[79]

## 3) The Totality of the Circumstances Test

Over a number of years, the Court has created a test for determining whether a person has a reasonable expectation of privacy, usually referred to as the "totality of the circumstances" test.[80] In a series of cases, the Court identified various factors to be taken into account, gradually adapting the test as different relevant considerations came to light. As it is applied now, these factors are considered under four headings: (1) the subject matter of the alleged search; (2) whether the claimant has a direct interest in the subject matter; (3) the claimant's subjective expectation of privacy in the subject matter; and (4) whether a subjective expectation of privacy is objectively reasonable, having

---

77 *R v Jones*, 2017 SCC 60 [*Jones*] at para 44. See also *Jones* at para 45: "Canadians are not required to become digital recluses in order to maintain some semblance of privacy in their lives."

78 *R v Bykovets*, 2024 SCC 6 at para 7.

79 *Campbell*, above note 54 at para 47.

80 *Edwards*, above note 49 at para 31.

regard to the totality of the circumstances.[81] Many different considerations can arise, especially under the last heading, and exactly what factors will be taken into account in any given case depends on which are most relevant. In principle, no single factor is controlling; it is a matter of weighing the considerations and coming to a conclusion. In practice, there is a good argument that the first factor, the subject matter of the search, has come to be the crucial consideration: we shall first consider each factor individually, then return to that point.

The "subject matter of the alleged search" is sometimes obvious, but not necessarily. The real subject matter needs to be identified precisely because, for example, a person with no privacy interest in a place might nonetheless have a reasonable expectation of privacy with regard to an item found in that place.[82] Most importantly, other factors in the test might apply differently depending on how the subject matter is identified: garbage bags might be in public view although their contents are not, for example.[83]

This subject matter of the search is to be assessed not "narrowly in terms of the physical acts involved or the physical space invaded, but rather by reference to the nature of the privacy interests potentially compromised by the state action."[84] More simply, the question is "what the police were really after."[85] So, for example, in *R v Kang-Brown* the police used a sniffer dog on the accused's luggage, and it was argued that the subject matter of the search was the air around the bag: physically, that was what was being searched. The Court rejected that argument, holding that the subject matter was the contents of the bag, an inference about which could be made from the dog's reactions.[86]

Similarly, in *R v Patrick* the police took a garbage bag from the accused's property, and the Crown argued that the subject matter of the search should be considered only that: garbage. The Court held

---

81 *Spencer*, above note 36 at para 18. See also *Tessling*, above note 46 at para 42, *Patrick*, above note 39 at para 27, *Reeves*, above note 35 at para 28, or *Mills*, above note 19 at para 13.

82 *Edwards*, above note 49; *Belnavis*, above note 14, and *Plant*, above note 28, all raise this possibility, though, in fact, none of the accused succeeded with the claim. In *Belnavis*, for example, the Court allowed the possibility that a passenger who had no reasonable expectation of privacy in the vehicle in which she was found might, nonetheless, have had a reasonable expectation of privacy in the bags next to her, making a search of those bags unreasonable.

83 *Patrick*, above note 39 at para 53.

84 *Spencer*, above note 36 at para 31, quoting *R v Ward*, 2012 ONCA 660 at para 65 [*Ward*].

85 *Marakah*, above note 52 at para 15, quoting *Ward*, *ibid*.

86 *Kang-Brown*, above note 37.

that that argument "assumes away" the point in issue and that the subject matter of the search should be considered in light of the reason the police seized the bag: because it was "a bag of 'information' whose contents, viewed in their entirety, paint a fairly accurate and complete picture of the householder's activities and lifestyle."[87] In *R v Spencer* the police knew that a particular IP address had downloaded child pornography and obtained the accused's name and address from the service provider. The Court held there that the subject matter of the search was not merely the accused's name and address, which would not attract much privacy protection, but instead "the identity of a subscriber whose Internet connection is linked to particular, monitored Internet activity."[88] In *R v Marakah* the police searched a third party's cellphone and found text messages from the accused: the subject matter of the search was not the physical device, but the electronic conversation.[89]

Although this portion of the test is often framed as "what the police were really after," this does not mean that it should be understood as limited to the stated intended use by the police: rather, it is about the tendency of what is sought to support inferences in relation to other information. In *Bykovets*, for example, the police obtained an IP address for the purpose of applying for a warrant to determine the subscriber information associated with it. But, the majority concluded many other things *could* be done with an IP address, and it was on that broader basis that the subject matter had to be evaluated. Importantly, this also means that the subject matter must be understood not just based on what the information can reveal *on its own* but also what it can reveal in combination with other information.[90]

The second factor, the claimant's interest in the subject matter, is not normally an obstacle to a privacy claim. Where a person's house, vehicle, pocket, or body cavity is searched, it is obvious that they had a direct interest. The accused's interest need not be proprietary or even necessarily a possessory one to attract privacy protection.[91] In *Spencer*, for example, the fact that the accused used an internet connection with permission of the subscriber was sufficient to give him an interest capable of attracting privacy protection in that internet activity. As we will see below in *Jones*, the Crown's theory that the accused was

87 *Patrick*, above note 39 at para 30.

88 *Spencer*, above note 36 at para 33.

89 *Marakah*, above note 52 at para 17.

90 *Bykovets*, above note 24 at para 28: "To find that s. 8 does not extend to an IP address because police collected it only to obtain a *Spencer* warrant ignores the information it *can* reveal without a warrant."

91 See, for example, *Plant*, above note 28 at 291.

the author of text messages was by itself sufficient to establish a direct interest, without evidence that the accused genuinely was the author.

A noteworthy point about the accused's interest is that whether the activity is illegal or not should not be taken into account: this is a reflection of the normative approach to privacy, which is meant to protect overarching interests. In *R v Wong*, for example, the police had placed a hidden camera in a hotel room. The Ontario Court of Appeal had concluded that a person who rents a hotel room in order to conduct illegal gambling has no reasonable expectation of privacy, but the Supreme Court held that this was the wrong way to frame the issue. The question that had to be asked was whether someone renting a hotel room had a reasonable expectation of privacy — the nature of the activity carried on within it was not relevant.[92] Similarly, in *Patrick* the Alberta Court of Appeal had reasoned that the accused had no privacy interest in evidence (found in garbage bags) that he was involved in manufacturing drugs because that information was not part of the core biographical details to which privacy protection ought to be extended. The Supreme Court rejected that approach, holding: "The issue is not whether the appellant had a legitimate privacy interest in the concealment of drug paraphernalia, but whether people generally have a privacy interest in the concealed contents of an opaque and sealed 'bag of information.'"[93]

Equally, in *Spencer* the issue was whether people generally have a privacy interest in their internet activity. In that case, the Court concluded that the fact that the accused's particular activity was to download child pornography did not change the question.[94] Similarly in *Campbell* the police had, through subterfuge, taken part in a text message conversation with the accused about the sale of drugs: the Court found that both levels of court below "erred by focussing on the actual contents of the text messages at issue" rather than the proper question, "the potential or tendency to reveal private information about the claimant, whatever the actual contents of the conversation may be."[95]

---

92 *Wong*, above note 33 at para 19.

93 *Patrick*, above note 39 at para 32. There, the Court also said: "The issue ought to be framed in terms of the privacy of the area or thing being searched and the potential impact of the search on the person being searched, not the nature or identity of the concealed items."

94 *Spencer*, above note 36 at para 36: "the issue is not whether Mr. Spencer had a legitimate privacy interest in concealing his use of the Internet for the purpose of accessing child pornography, but whether people generally have a privacy interest in subscriber information with respect to computers which they use in their home for private purposes."

95 *Campbell*, above note 54 at para 60.

Also notable in *Campbell* was its treatment of their own earlier decision in *Mills* where a cohort of three judges, in the context of an online child-luring sting, had held that an adult could not have a reasonable expectation of privacy in their online communications with a child they did not know. While not explicitly rejecting this "non-content neutral" argument, the Court made clear that it was unsympathetic to that approach.[96]

The third general heading for reasonable expectation of privacy claims is the claimant's subjective expectation of privacy in the subject matter. The Court has observed that the subjective expectation portion of the analysis is "not a high hurdle," that testimony from the accused about their subjective expectation is not a necessary requirement, and that a subjective expectation of privacy in activities associated with the home is to be presumed.[97] In *R v Cole* the accused's subjective expectation of privacy in the informational content of his laptop was inferred simply from the facts that he used it to browse the internet and stored personal information on the hard drive.[98]

Further, the Court has warned against allowing the subjective issue to settle matters:

> The *subjective* expectation of privacy is important but its absence should not be used too quickly to undermine the protection afforded by s 8 to the values of a free and democratic society. In an age of expanding means for snooping readily available on the retail market, ordinary people may come to fear (with or without justification) that their telephones are wiretapped or their private correspondence is being read . . . . Suggestions that a diminished *subjective* expectation of privacy should automatically result in a lowering of constitutional protection should therefore be opposed. It is one thing to say that a person who puts out the garbage has no reasonable expectation of privacy in it. It is quite another to say that someone who fears their telephone is bugged no longer has a subjective expectation of privacy and thereby forfeits the protection of s 8. Expectation of privacy is a normative rather than a descriptive standard.[99]

---

96 See Steve Coughlan, "*R. v. Campbell*: Reaffirmed Privacy but Relaxed Exigency" (2025) 99 *Criminal Reports* (7th) 346.

97 *Patrick*, above note 39 at para 37.

98 *Cole*, above note 25 at para 43.

99 *Tessling*, above note 46 at para 42 [emphasis in original]. See also *Patrick*, above note 39 at para 14: "A government that increases its snooping on the lives of citizens, and thereby makes them suspicious and reduces their expectation of privacy, will not thereby succeed in unilaterally reducing their constitutional entitlement to privacy protection."

Despite this clear statement that a subjective expectation of privacy is not a *sine qua non*, there is a lurking ambiguity over the point. In describing the privacy analysis in *Patrick* the Court asked whether the accused subjectively had a reasonable expectation of privacy and "if so" whether that expectation was reasonable.[100] The phrase "if so" could imply that a failure at the subjective stage relieves the judge of the need to go any further. The subsequent formulation of the test in *Spencer* frames the fourth heading in the test as "whether *this* subjective expectation of privacy was objectively reasonable" (emphasis added), which again could imply that there must be a subjective expectation of privacy: that wording has generally been used since.[101] Although the Court has never explicitly said that a subjective expectation of privacy is now an absolute requirement, some lower courts have taken that to be the rule, though others have rejected that position.[102]

It seems unlikely that the Court intended to signal a reverse of its previous unambiguous position that a subjective expectation of privacy is not essential in such an oblique and stealthy fashion: more plausibly the Court has not turned its mind to the potential implication of saying "this subjective expectation" rather than "a subjective expectation," because in none of those cases has the issue mattered to the result. It would also not make sense for a single factor to be determinative in what is always referred to as the "*totality* of the circumstances" test. Nonetheless, it is not an impossible reading. This assessment matters especially because accused persons often choose not to testify, even on a *voir dire*, and so there might be no direct evidence about that person's subjective expectation.

---

100 *Patrick*, *ibid* at para 27.

101 *Spencer*, above note 36 at para 18. For use of essentially this general phrasing, which seems to have become standard, see *Marakah*, above note 52, *Jones*, above note 77, *Reeves*, above note 35, *Mills*, above note 19, *Campbell*, above note 54, or *Bykovets*, above note 24.

102 One the one side, see *R v Grunwald*, 2010 BCCA 288 at para 50: "A subjective expectation of privacy need not be reasonable: *Patrick* at para. 37. However, it must exist." Similarly, in *R v Beairsto*, 2018 ABCA 118 the reasonable expectation of privacy analysis is a single paragraph noting the absence of evidence of a subjective expectation. Also in *R v Walton*, 2022 ABCA 276, a reasonable expectation of privacy claim failed simply on the failure to prove the subjective portion. On the other hand, see *R v Orlandis-Habsburgo*, 2017 ONCA 649 [*Orlandis-Habsburgo*] at para 44: "A subjective expectation of privacy cannot, however, be a prerequisite to a finding of a reasonable expectation of privacy. Otherwise, the protection afforded to personal privacy by s. 8 would shrink in direct correlation to the pervasiveness and notoriety of state intrusions upon personal privacy." See also *R v Chehil*, 2009 NSCA 111 [*Chehil* NSCA], noting this ambiguity.

However, there is a factor that might reduce the significance of this ambiguity: the decision of the Court in *R v Jones*. In that case, the police had obtained a number of text messages by means of a production order, and therefore knew the subscriber account that those text messages were associated with and were of the view that the text messages had been authored by the accused. On the one hand the accused wanted to challenge the lawfulness of the search which obtained those text messages: on the other hand, he had not conceded that he was the author of those texts at all. It was agreed that *if* the accused were the author of the texts then he had a direct interest in them as well as a subjective expectation of privacy, but the Crown argued that those conclusions could not be reached unless the accused actually acknowledged authorship. The Court disagreed, holding that the accused was entitled to rely on the Crown's *theory* that he was the author in order to establish a subjective expectation of privacy. Any other approach would create a catch-22 for the accused, because admitting authorship amounted to conceding identity and the *actus reus* of the offences: that is, the accused would be forced to choose between challenging the search or defending himself on the charge, but would not be able effectively to do both.

Indeed, in *Jones* the court reiterated the point from *Tessling*, above, that the absence of a subjective expectation should not too quickly be taken to remove section 8 protection: "a *Charter* claimant's subjective belief that Big Brother is watching should not, through the workings of s. 8, be permitted to become a self-fulfilling prophecy."[103] Further, the argument in *Jones* might nearly *always* be available to establish the subjective expectation: if the Crown did not have the theory that whatever has been found through the search was associated with the accused, it seems unlikely that they would be presenting it as evidence. The argument has been found to apply to territorial privacy, not just informational privacy as in *Jones*, for example.[104] It has also been found to apply to possession of items.[105] There is some disagreement, however,

103 *Jones*, above note 77 at para 21.

104 See *R v Labelle*, 2019 ONCA 557 [*Labelle*]. See also, *R v Okemow*, 2019 MBCA 37, where the accused was allowed to rely on the Crown's theory that he was connected to a particular residence with regard to the subjective portion of the test.

105 See *R v Ahmed*, 2022 ONCA 640 [*Ahmed*]. A gun was found in a vehicle in which one accused, the passenger, had been sitting. Although the passenger did not have a reasonable expectation of privacy in the *vehicle*, he "was permitted to rely on the Crown's theory to establish a direct interest and subjective expectation of privacy in the item seized (i.e., the gun), pursuant to *R. v. Jones*, 2017 SCC 60, [2017] 2 S.C.R. 696" (para 51).

over whether an accused's decision to lead contrary evidence at the *voir dire*, as opposed to simply rely on the Crown's position, makes a difference.[106]

Ultimately, it has been made easy if not automatic for the accused to establish a subjective expectation of privacy, and so the cases where that aspect of the test cannot be met should be few. Still, it would be useful to know whether that aspect of the test *must* be met. One hopes this point will be clarified at some near opportunity.

The fourth heading is whether an expectation of privacy would be objectively reasonable. In some ways this step is where it is most important to keep the normative nature of the test in mind, and that the goal is to protect "a biographical core of personal information which individuals in a free and democratic society would wish to maintain and control from dissemination to the state."[107] This means that the issue to be considered in any given case is what *could* be revealed, rather than what is in fact revealed in the case at hand.[108] It is important to keep these guiding principles in mind because, as noted above, the approach generally taken is to identify a number of factual considerations and discuss them, often without conscious consideration of the normative

---

106 *Labelle*, above note 104, and *R v Mohamed*, 2024 ONCA 691 present quite similar facts. In each the police obtained a search warrant for a residence and charged the accused with possession of material found there, in each the accused wanted to rely on the Crown's assertion in the ITO that they lived at the residence as the basis for their standing claim, and in each the accused led evidence through another person that they did not in fact live at the residence. In *Labelle* the Ontario Court of Appeal found that *Jones* meant the accused *did* have standing. In *Mohamad* a different panel of the Ontario Court of Appeal reached the conclusion that the accused did *not* have standing because he contested the Crown's claim that he lived at the residence. In the latter case the Ontario Court of Appeal held that the accused was not in the same "catch-22" dilemma as in *Jones* of being forced to choose between proving standing or maintaining a substantive defence. Steve Coughlan, "*R v Mohamed*, Case Comment" (2024) 98 *Criminal Reports* (7th) 91 points out that the dilemma in *Jones* and *Mohamad* is exactly the same one, and that the only difference is the choice made by the accused as to how to deal with it.

107 *Bykovets*, above note 24 at para 51, quoting *Plant*, above note 28. *Bykovets* adds that: "The 'biographical core' is not limited to identity, but 'include[s] information which tends to reveal intimate details of the lifestyle and personal choices of the individual.'"

108 See, for example, *Bykovets*, above note 24 at para 57:

> The police's specific intention to restrict the use of information in a particular case — no matter how well-intentioned — is thus irrelevant to s. 8. The "reasonable expectation of privacy" analysis revolves around the *potential* of a particular subject matter to reveal an individual's biographical core to the state, not whether the IP addresses revealed information about the appellant *on these facts*.

point *behind* whether, the accused, for example, has a proprietary interest in the object searched or whether the information was in public view.

This heading is subject to the most variation in application from case to case, and, indeed, the Court has noted that "there is no definitive list of factors that must be considered in answering this question."[109] For example, in *Edwards*, a number of factors were said to be relevant: presence at the time of the search; possession or control of the property or place searched; ownership of the property or place; historical use of the property or item; and the ability to regulate access, including the right to admit or exclude others from the place.[110] In *Patrick*, a long and different list of considerations was used: the place where the alleged "search" occurred and whether the police trespassed; whether the informational content of the subject matter was in public view; whether the informational content of the subject matter had been abandoned; whether the information was already in the hands of third parties and if so whether it was subject to an obligation of confidentiality; whether the police technique was intrusive in relation to the privacy interest; whether the use of the evidence-gathering technique was itself objectively unreasonable; and whether the informational content exposed any intimate details of the appellant's lifestyle or information of a biographical nature.[111] In *Spencer*, in contrast, the objective reasonableness question was determined almost exclusively by considering the contractual and statutory framework governing the accused's internet usage.[112] In *Campbell* the court listed nine factors potentially going to objective reasonableness but discussed only three of them.[113]

There is a good reason for this wide variation from case to case, which relates to a growing understanding of the nature of "privacy." A reasonable expectation of privacy includes at least three separate types of interest that ought to be distinguished: (1) personal privacy, (2) territorial privacy, and (3) informational privacy.[114] Personal

---

109 *Cole*, above note 25 at para 45.

110 *Edwards*, above note 49 at para 45.

111 *Patrick*, above note 39 at para 27.

112 *Spencer*, above note 36 at para 52ff.

113 *Campbell*, above note 54 at para 54: "The parties focussed their submissions before this Court on three factors: (1) the private nature of the subject matter; (2) the intrusiveness of the police technique in relation to the privacy interest; and (3) the level of control over the information."

114 *Tessling*, above note 46 at para 20. See also *SAB*, above note 6 at para 40, relying on *Dyment*, above note 42: "privacy may include territorial or spacial aspects, aspects related to the person, and aspects that arise in the informational context."

privacy relates essentially to the body, though it covers a range of situations: whether one can be frisked, strip-searched, or subject to a body cavity search, for example. Territorial privacy relates to searches of places and is contingent on the particular place being searched (a person typically has the greatest degree of privacy in a home, less in a motor vehicle, and less still in a prison, for example). Informational privacy protects "a biographical core of personal information which individuals in a free and democratic society would wish to maintain and control from dissemination to the state" as well as "information which tends to reveal intimate details of the lifestyle and personal choices of the individual."[115]

It is largely because "privacy" does not have a single meaning that the list of relevant factors in the objective assessment can vary so widely. In listing relevant factors in *Edwards*, the Court had territorial privacy in mind, and so the considerations are relevant to that issue. Whether the accused was present or not at the time of the search could affect how reasonable the search of an apartment might be, for example, and so is a useful territorial privacy consideration. However, it is a factor which could not fail to be satisfied in the context of a body cavity search but which will never be satisfied when police obtain information from an internet service provider, and so it is difficult to see how it is even worth considering in the case of either personal or informational privacy.[116] Therefore, depending on the type of privacy claim at issue, different factors will be taken into account.

Cases need not be rigidly fitted into one of the three types of privacy: those are merely analytical guides, and a claim can assert overlapping interests.[117] In *Tessling*, for example, police trained a Forward Looking Infrared camera (FLIR) on the accused's home following a tip that he was conducting a marijuana grow operation, in order to determine the pattern and amount of heat being emitted: that was found to be a partly territorial claim, since the police were interested in what

---

115 *Tessling*, above note 46 at para 25 [emphasis omitted], quoting *Plant*, above note 28.

116 See, for example, *Bykovets*, above note 24 at para 49:

> Nor is the place where the search occurred detrimental to a reasonable expectation of privacy here. This factor was largely developed in the context of territorial privacy, and digital subject matter "does not fit easily within the strictures set out by the jurisprudence" (*Marakah*, at para 27). As this Court recently remarked, "online spaces are *qualitatively* different" from physical spaces (*R v Ramelson*, 2022 SCC 44 at para. 49 (emphasis in original)).

117 *Patrick*, above note 39 at para 26.

was going on inside the house, but primarily an informational privacy interest.[118]

At one point there appeared to be some danger of informational privacy becoming the "weak sister" of privacy claims. Personal privacy, raising issues of body cavity or strip searches and the autonomy of the person, has been seen as particularly important.[119] Similarly, territorial privacy has long been recognized as very important: in the maxim that a home is a person's castle, for example.[120] In *Plant*, *Tessling*, and *Patrick*, in contrast, claims that might have been seen as being about the home were cast as informational privacy claims, and in each case the accused was found to have no reasonable expectation.[121] For a time, lower courts held that observations such as how an accused behaved while in an ambulance, or the undetectable-by humans odours coming from belongings, to be mere information.[122] In particular, it was often

---

118 *Tessling*, above note 46 at para 24. Similarly in *Gomboc*, above note 23 at para 22, police attached a Digital Readout Ammeter (DRA) to power lines entering the accused's home, in order to detect the pattern of electrical usage. This was treated as straddling informational and territorial privacy.

119 See also *Golden*, above note 22, or *Dyment*, above note 42.

120 Among other cases referring to the notion, see *Tessling*, above note 46, *R v Silveira*, [1995] 2 SCR 297 [*Silveira*], or *R v Feeney*, [1997] 2 SCR 13 [*Feeney*].

121 *Plant*, above note 28, permitted police to obtain electrical consumption records about the accused's home from a power company without a warrant. *Tessling*, above note 46, as noted, concerned the use of a FLIR to detect heat patterns in the home, and *Patrick*, above note 39, involved reaching across the accused's property line to take garbage bags.

In *Tessling* the Court held that the FLIR information did not attract informational privacy because on its own it was "meaningless." Stuart criticized this reasoning, pointing out that if the records reveal no personal information, the Court should not have concluded that they helped give reasonable grounds for issuing a search warrant: Don Stuart, *Charter Justice in Canadian Criminal Law*, 5th ed (Toronto: Thomson Carswell, 2010) at 268. See also Renée Pomerance, "Shedding Light on the Nature of Heat: Defining Privacy in the Wake of *R v Tessling*" (2005) 23 *Criminal Reports* (6th) 229; James A Stringham, "Reasonable Expectations Reconsidered: A Return to the Search for a Normative Core for Section 8?" (2005) 23 *Criminal Reports* (6th) 245; and Steve Coughlan & Marc S Gorbet, "Nothing Plus Nothing Equals . . . Something?: A Proposal for FLIR Warrants on Reasonable Suspicion" (2005) 23 *Criminal Reports* (6th) 239.

122 See, for example, *R v LaChappelle*, 2007 ONCA 655; *R v Taylor*, 2006 NLCA 41; *R v Brown*, 2006 ABCA 199 [*Brown* 2006]. *Brown* 2006 has since been reversed by the Supreme Court of Canada: *Kang-Brown*, above note 37. The decision is complex because there are four opinions and no clear majority on any single approach. However, all nine judges agreed that there was a reasonable expectation of privacy and that the dog sniff was a search. Indeed, only one judgment even discusses that question, with the other seven judges taking it as simply unquestioned that the dog sniff was a search. In the companion case, *AM*, above

observed that the information in question was not part of the accused's "biographical core of personal information" and so was not protected by the *Charter.* In each case the result was that the Court found the accused to have no reasonable expectation of privacy, and therefore no search in the meaning of section 8 had occurred: consequently, there was no section 8 violation. These cases were the subject of critical comment.[123]

Fortunately, informational privacy has ultimately come into its own and is recognized as "particularly critical."[124] In *R v Morelli*, for example, where the accused was subject to a search warrant which resulted in his home computer being searched, it was held that it was difficult to imagine a search which could be more intrusive, extensive, or invasive of privacy.[125] Similarly, in *Spencer* the Court re-emphasized that informational privacy protects not *just* "biographical core" material, but also "information which tends to reveal intimate details of the lifestyle and personal choices of the individual."[126] This was reiterated in *Bykovets*.[127]

---

note 37, Binnie J did suggest that a dog sniff was "through the wall" technology, and that, unlike a FLIR, it permitted precise inferences about the concealed interior.

123 See Don Stuart, "Police Use of Sniffer Dogs Ought to Be Subject to *Charter* Standards: Dangers of *Tessling* Come to Roost" (2005) 31 *Criminal Reports* (6th) 255; Steve Coughlan, "Privacy Goes to the Dogs" (2006) 40 *Criminal Reports* (6th) 31; Jonathan Shapiro, "Narcotics Dogs and the Search for Illegality: American Law in Canadian Courts" (2007) 43 *Criminal Reports* (6th) 299.

124 *Bykovets*, above note 24 at para 8. The decision adds that is it also "particularly challenging."

125 2010 SCC 8 at para 2 [*Morelli*]. The Court also held at para 105:

> As I mentioned at the outset, it is difficult to imagine a more intrusive invasion of privacy than the search of one's home and personal computer. Computers often contain our most intimate correspondence. They contain the details of our financial, medical, and personal situations. They even reveal our specific interests, likes, and propensities, recording in the browsing history and cache files the information we seek out and read, watch, or listen to on the Internet.

See also *Cole*, above note 25, finding a teacher to have a reasonable expectation of privacy in the contents of a laptop which was issued to him by the school board for which he worked.

126 *Spencer*, above note 36 at para 27. See also the discussion of "biographical core" information in Penney, above note 51.

127 *Bykovets*, above note 24 at para 74:

> Even "information that may at first blush appear mundane and outside of the biographical core may be profoundly revealing when situated in context with other data points" (N. Hasan et al., *Search and Seizure* (2021), at p. 59).

Indeed, *Spencer* goes further, elaborating and expanding on the meaning of "informational privacy." That concept includes at least three conceptually distinct but overlapping concepts: privacy as secrecy, privacy as control, and privacy as anonymity.[128] Privacy as secrecy is reflected in many areas of the law and is primarily concerned with confidentiality. This is related to privacy as control, which is the claim to determine for oneself when, how, and to what extent personal information is communicated to others. Privacy as anonymity matters when pieces of information are already known, but are not yet connected to any individual: for example, when an accused knows that there *is* a police informant but does not know who that informant is. In such cases, the privacy "is not simply the individual's name, but the link between the identified individual and the personal information provided anonymously."[129]

Privacy as anonymity is particularly important in the context of internet usage. People can reasonably wish, for example, to present ideas publicly without being associated with them. Further, the internet gathers a great deal of information about individuals without their knowledge or control, but guarding the link between the information and the identity of the person to whom it relates assures the user that the activity remains private. Accordingly, the identity of a person linked to his or her use of the internet gives rise to a privacy interest beyond that inherent in the person's name, address, and telephone number found in the subscriber information. In *Spencer* itself, this meant that the police request to the internet service provider for subscriber information corresponding to specifically observed, anonymous internet activity engaged a high level of informational privacy.[130]

In the end, the strength of privacy protection to which a person is entitled does not vary in any noticeable way depending on whether that privacy is identified as territorial, personal, or informational. As a result, although categorizing the claim as falling under one or the other can be a useful guide to thinking, nothing fundamental turns on that classification: the same four factors in the totality of the circumstances test are considered in any event.

It was suggested above that the first of those factors, the subject matter of the search, has arguably become the most important consideration: it is time to return to that point, to see how it might be true. The argument is most easily understood by looking at the facts in

128 *Spencer*, above note 36 at para 38.
129 *Ibid* at para 42.
130 *Ibid* at para 51.

*Marakah*.[131] It will be recalled that in *Marakah*, the police had unlawfully searched the cellphone of Marakah's co-conspirator Winchester, and the question was whether the Crown could use the text messages from Marakah found on Winchester's cellphone. One could quite plausibly argue that the subject matter of the search was "Winchester's cellphone," and if that were the case, Marakah's claim to a reasonable expectation of privacy would be unpersuasive: his situation would seem akin to Edward's unsuccessful claim to privacy in an apartment belonging to someone else, or Belnavis' unsuccessful claim to privacy in a vehicle belonging to someone else.

However, that was not how the Court identified the subject matter of the search. They specifically rejected the notion that the search was about the cellphone, finding instead that "the subject matter of the search was Mr. Marakah's 'electronic conversation' with Mr. Winchester."[132] Once the subject matter of the search is understood to be "the conversation" rather than "Winchester's cell phone," the entire analysis changes.

Marakah had no direct interest in Winchester's cell phone, for example, which will be true of most people engaged in a text message conversation: they *will*, however, have a direct interest in that inherently private conversation itself, virtually all the time. Similarly, most people are unlikely even to have considered the nature of their privacy interest in another person's cell phone, and so could hardly be said to have a subjective expectation of privacy in it. When the question is whether a person subjectively expected privacy in the text message conversation, however, again the answer will nearly uniformly be "yes." And, of course, the objective test will be approached differently on this basis, particularly when one takes into account the fundamentally *normative* nature of that question. Is a person entitled to expect privacy in the physical device of another person's cell phone? Very probably not. Is a person entitled to expect privacy in their inherently private conversation with another person, by whatever means it happened to take place? Almost certainly yes.[133]

---

131 *Marakah*, above note 52.

132 *Ibid* at para 17.

133 For a period, there was seen to be some difficulty reconciling *Marakah* on this point with the later decision in *Mills*, above note 19. *Marakah* found that there was a reasonable expectation of privacy in electronic conversations, but in *Mills* the accused was found to have no reasonable expectation of privacy in his electronic conversation with an undercover officer whom he believed to be an underage girl. One view, from the Ontario Court of Appeal in *R v Campbell*, 2022 ONCA 666 was that "*Mills* carved out an exception in circumstances where the electronic communications themselves constitute a crime against

A similar result can be seen in *Reeves*, where police entered a home with the consent of the accused's common law spouse and seized a computer that was in a common area. Ultimately the police obtained a warrant before examining the contents of the computer, and so the section 8 question concerned only the initial seizure. The Ontario Court of Appeal had found that the subject matter was the physical item of the computer itself, and had found that the accused had no reasonable expectation of privacy. The majority in the Supreme Court rejected that ultimate conclusion, and did so largely because of their categorization of the subject matter of the search. It was not, they held, the physical device that the police were after in seizing it: it was the data it contained, specifically the accused's data. Once the subject matter was "the accused's data" rather than "the physical device," then direct interest, subjective expectation, and objective reasonableness all ended up favouring the existence of a privacy claim.

The point to recognize is that defining the subject matter of the search is a key step, and the rest of the argument might be won or lost by how that first point is settled.

## 4) Unsettled Issues

To conclude this discussion, we should look at two particular considerations in the totality of the circumstances test that remain something of a problem: the role of abandonment and the impact of private contracts or public regulatory schemes.

Abandonment was the central issue in *Patrick*. The police reached across the accused's back fence to take garbage bags that he had left for collection in an open container, still on his property but within easy reach of anyone walking by. The accused's section 8 claim failed because he was found to have no reasonable expectation of privacy in the bags. This was so not because it was physically possible for others to reach the garbage bags, or because the police had not literally "set foot" on the property: the Court stressed it was not concluding that

---

the recipient — in that case, the victimization of children." Whether this was correct or not arose on appeal to the Supreme Court in *Campbell*, above note 54, with intervenors arguing that allowing this exception would be an unwise dilution of the content-neutral approach. Ultimately the Court found that they did not have to answer the question, but in doing so they stressed that *Mills* was a decision with no majority judgment and that "*Marakah* remains the governing authority on when a text message conversation attracts a reasonable expectation of privacy under s. 8" (para 78). In effect, *Campbell* removes any real precedential value of *Mills*.

police could take garbage bags left on a porch, in a garage, or within the immediate vicinity of the dwelling house, or rent a cherry picker to take items from parts of the property not within reach.[134] Rather, Patrick no longer had a reasonable expectation of privacy because he "had done everything required of him to commit his rubbish to the municipal collection system."[135]

Abandonment is a powerful doctrine capable of defeating an otherwise strong privacy claim. All other factors favoured Patrick's privacy claim, but it failed because he had abandoned the bags.[136] As a result, there is a tendency for the Crown to argue abandonment any time an accused has parted company in some way with an object or information, sometimes successfully. It has been suggested that when an accused who is being pursued or otherwise interacting with the police throws away a backpack, tosses a gun out a window, pulls the battery from a BlackBerry and throws it to the ground, runs away leaving behind a jacket, or even hands over a document on request, they should be found to have abandoned any privacy interest in the item.[137] A number of cases have looked at the issue of whether a person running away from a vehicle has abandoned that vehicle.[138] The same argument has been made around the deletion of computer files[139] the

134 *Patrick*, above note 39 at paras 62 and 44.

135 *Ibid* at para 55.

136 *Ibid* at para 40.

137 See, respectively, *R v Nesbeth*, 2008 ONCA 579 [*Nesbeth*] or *R v Wilkinson*, 2023 BCCA 3; *R v Stevens*, 2012 ONCA 307 [*Stevens*], leave to appeal to SCC refused [2012] SCCA No 23; *R v Tsekouras*, 2014 ONSC 2420 [*Tsekouras*]; *R v Reddy*, 2010 BCCA 11; and *R v Leong*, 2014 BCPC 99. See also *Plummer*, above note 50, where the accused was found both to have no reasonable expectation of privacy in a handgun he had left behind when fleeing the scene, but also to have sufficient control over it to be guilty of possession. Criticizing that decision, see Calarco, above note 50.

138 See *R v Gambilla*, 2015 ABQB 40 for a case where the accused was found to have no reasonable expectation of privacy in the vehicle by reason of abandoning it. In addition, see *R v Ellis*, 2016 ONCA 598 [*Ellis*] and *R v Cuff*, 2018 ONCA 276 [*Cuff*] for cases in which the accused was found to have abandoned a vehicle, but where abandonment played a different role in the analysis. In those two cases, the fact of abandonment led to a provincial traffic power to impound the vehicle, which in turn led to an ability to conduct an inventory search. The cases do not consider the point, but implicitly finding it necessary to have an authorization for the search would be a concession that there *was* a reasonable expectation of privacy. See also *Morrison v R*, 2024 NBCA 35, where an accused was found to have possessed a vehicle at an earlier point but to have abandoned it when he denied ownership to a police officer and left in a taxi.

139 *R v McNeice*, 2013 BCCA 98 [*McNeice*].

failure to password-protect a cell phone,[140] or failing to pay rent for and returning the keys to a rental property.[141] Sometimes, these claims have succeeded, with the result that the accused has no entitlement to section 8 protection.[142] It is therefore important that some careful limits be set on the concept of abandonment, and that it be thought through fully.

Three issues are worth thinking about in this analysis. One relates to the greater need to think about an accused's intention when considering abandonment. An equally plausible claim is often that the accused is *asserting*, rather than renouncing, a privacy interest by taking such action. For example, in *Tsekouras*, upon being confronted by police, the accused took the batteries out of his Blackberry and threw it to the ground. Although the accused had literally discarded the device, the trial judge rejected the argument that he had abandoned it: rather, his action was "an assertion of his privacy interest," not an abandonment of it.[143] Similarly in *McNeice*, the Crown argued abandonment because the accused had deleted files from his computer, but the trial judge concluded that "deletion of the files is more consistent with an intention on the part of the user to destroy the information, or at least to conceal it from view by anyone else, including himself."[144] Contrast that reasoning to that in *Plummer*, where an accused was found to have abandoned a gun because he "hid it in his girlfriend's bag": one might think that implicit in the very word "hid" is that one still feels some kind of possessory claim.[145]

Another way to think about this issue is as one of identifying the subject matter of the search. Recall that in *Spencer*, where the police had obtained subscriber information from an ISP, the Court held that the subject matter of the search was not simply a name and address, but the link between a name and address and particular online activity.

140 In *R v Fearon*, 2014 SCC 77 at para 53 [*Fearon*], the Court held that "[a]n individual's decision not to password protect his or her cell phone does not indicate any sort of abandonment of the significant privacy interests one generally will have in the contents of the phone."

141 *R v Herntier*, 2020 MBCA 95.

142 *Nesbeth*, above note 137, *Stevens*, above note 137, and *R v Gambilla*, 2015 ABQB 40 were all cases where the accused was found to have no remaining privacy interest. See also *R v LB*, 2007 ONCA 596, where the accused was asked who owned a satchel sitting near him and replied "I don't know," when as a matter of fact it was his: he was found to be precluded from putting forward a s 8 claim because he had renounced his privacy interest.

143 *Tsekouras*, above note 137 at para 115.

144 *McNeice*, above note 139 at para 52.

145 *Plummer*, above note 50 at para 42. The Ontario Court of Appeal also took into account that the accused then ran away, making it "double abandonment."

One aspect of privacy, they concluded there, was privacy as anonymity, where what is protected is the link between the accused and particular information, not the particular information itself. In many cases what is being claimed to be abandonment might be better understood as an attempt to assert and protect anonymity. In those kinds of cases, the accused's actions ought not to weaken, let alone eliminate, a reasonable expectation of privacy claim.[146]

A second abandonment issue is another aspect of this point of identifying the subject matter of the search, particularly in the context of DNA evidence. It is easiest to see this point by starting with the *Stillman* decision, though it does not squarely address the issue. In *Stillman* the police had the accused in custody, and he declined to provide a DNA sample.[147] However, while he was detained he blew his nose and threw the tissue in a wastebasket, and the police seized that tissue in order to conduct DNA testing. The Court rejected the notion that the accused had abandoned his DNA and therefore had no reasonable expectation of privacy in it. The key to their reasoning, however, arguably gave more weight to the fact that the accused was in custody at the time than to the nature of DNA evidence.[148] In *obiter* they suggested that police *could* conduct DNA sampling on discarded items in the case of an accused not in custody.[149]

In the more than twenty years since *Stillman*, the reasonable expectation of privacy analysis has developed significantly, especially around the issue of identifying the subject matter of the search. The subject matter is now understood to be "what the police were really after."[150] When police pick up a cigarette butt or piece of gum discarded by a suspect, they are not after that physical item, but the information which can be obtained from DNA testing. The situation can be seen as analogous to *Reeves*, where in seizing a computer the police were considered to be seizing the data on it merely by taking possession of the

---

146 For further discussion of abandonment, see the discussion in Penney, above note 51, and Steve Coughlan, "On Abandonment and Flight" (2014) 10 *Criminal Reports* (7th) 322.

147 *R v Stillman*, [1997] 1 SCR 607 at para 62 [*Stillman*].

148 The Court held at para 59 that the accused had no effective choice about "abandoning" his DNA: "He would be required to destroy every tissue he used, to hide every spoon he ate from, to keep cigarette butts, chewed gum or any other potentially incriminating evidence on his person at all times in order to prevent the police from 'retrieving' this 'potentially useful waste'."

149 *Stillman*, above note 147 at para 62: "Thus, where an accused who is not in custody discards a kleenex or cigarette butt, the police may ordinarily collect and test these items without any concern about consent."

150 *Marakah*, above note 52.

item, even though they did not examine the data until after obtaining a warrant.[151] If that information is the subject matter of the search, it is not clear that "abandonment" is really made out when a person discards a piece of gum: they have clearly abandoned the item, but there is more room to argue over whether they abandoned their DNA profile.[152]

This is still a challenging area for courts. The difficulties are illustrated nicely by the Quebec Court of Appeal decision in *R v D'Amico*. In that case the police had wanted to obtain a DNA sample from the accused, and had followed him around public locations trying to retrieve a discarded item without success. As a result they set up a sting, creating a ruse whereby an undercover officer arranged a false business meeting with the accused in a café, and then collected the coffee cup he had used. As no authority for this ruse had been obtained (such as a general warrant) the only potential argument against a section 8 violation was that the accused did not have a reasonable expectation of privacy. The three Court of Appeal judges all reasoned differently about the situation. In the view of one judge, the accused had abandoned the coffee cup, and that was sufficient: he had thereby also abandoned any confidential information in it.[153] In the view of a second judge, the dissenting judge, "[w]hat needed to be determined was if the appellant's DNA information had been abandoned, not the coffee cup."[154] That judge questioned whether the distinction in *Stillman* between an accused in custody and one not in custody should be maintained, and further concluded that at a minimum, in these circumstances where the police had engineered the abandonment of the cup, the accused had not lost his reasonable expectation of privacy. The third judge agreed about the abandonment point with the dissenting judge. He noted that earlier decisions had failed to distinguish between abandonment of the item on which the DNA was found and the DNA itself, and concluded that "it is simply impossible to imagine that individuals implicitly abandon any protection to their genetic data through the natural loss of bodily

151 *Reeves*, above note 35.

152 See, for example, *R v Nguyen*, (2002), 48 CR (5th) 338 (Ont CA) [*Nguyen*], where police officers offered an accused a piece of gum while transporting him from detention to court, knowing that he would need to discard the gum before he entered the courtroom. The Crown conceded that this behavior had violated s 8 and the Ontario Court of Appeal accepted that concession, rejecting the finding at trial that abandonment applied. However, it is not clear whether this is because it was the accused's DNA at stake, or simply because the accused was in custody.

153 *D'Amico c R*, 2019 QCCA 77 at para 314 [*D'Amico*]. The judge analogizes to *Patrick*, above note 39.

154 *D'Amico*, above note 153 at para 93.

substances in public."[155] Nonetheless the third judge found for other reasons that the accused had no reasonable expectation of privacy and therefore that there was no section 8 violation.[156]

This is very much an area where guidance from the Supreme Court would be valuable.[157]

The second unsettled issue relates to the impact of private contracts or public regulatory schemes on a reasonable expectation of privacy. There have been many cases where police have obtained information from an internet service provider, electrical company, or other business without a warrant. A question which has arisen on such occasions is whether the accused had a reasonable expectation of privacy in the information.[158] In such cases, a controlling factor has frequently been either the terms of the contract between the company and the customer, or the terms of the *Personal Information Protection and Electronic Documents Act*, often known as *PIPEDA*.[159]

In *R v Godbout*, for example, a clause in a contract with a courier company said "governmental authorities . . . may also open and inspect any shipment and its contents at any time." The British Columbia Court of Appeal found "that that clause negated any objectively reasonable expectation of privacy."[160] In other cases, some courts have reasoned roughly along the lines that since *PIPEDA* or the individual contract envisions the possibility of information being provided to the police in *some* circumstances, the accused cannot reasonably expect privacy: in

---

155 *Ibid* at para 352.

156 See *ibid* at paras 370–82.

157 In *D'Amico* itself, the Supreme Court concluded that the accused did not have an appeal as of right (2019 SCC 23) and dismissed the application for leave to appeal.

158 See *Chehil* NSCA, above note 102, dealing with an airline passenger manifest. For pre-*Spencer* cases considering whether a person has a privacy interest in the name and address associated with a particular IP address, see *R v Ward*, 2008 ONCJ 355; *R v Friers*, 2008 ONCJ 740; *R v Trapp*, 2009 SKPC 5; and *R v Wilson*, [2009] OJ No 1067 (SCJ), for decisions where an accused was found not to have a reasonable expectation of privacy, and *R v Kwok*, [2008] OJ No 2414 (Ct J), and *R v Cuttell*, 2009 ONCJ 471, for cases reaching the opposite conclusion. *Spencer*, above note 36, concluded that a reasonable expectation of privacy did exist. See also *R v Telfer*, 2021 MBCA 38, finding an accused not to have a reasonable expectation of privacy in information obtained from a car rental agency, based in part on the terms of the contract and provincial legislation.

159 SC 2000, c 5 [*PIPEDA*].

160 *R v Godbout*, 2014 BCCA 319 at para 27. Note that this decision adopts a risk analysis rather than a normative-based approach to privacy: see Steve Coughlan, "Signing Away Rights: Should Private Contracts Trump the *Charter*?" (2014) 13 *Criminal Reports* (7th) 124.

that event, obtaining the information is not a "search" and so no warrant is necessary. Ironically, this approach results in the protection of privacy act diminishing privacy protection.

This issue was directly before the Court in *Spencer*, where the question was whether the accused had a reasonable expectation of privacy in the ISP records linking him to the IP address that had downloaded child pornography. The Crown argued the accused had no such expectation, relying both on the terms of the contract and on *PIPEDA*. The Court concluded that Spencer was, in fact, entitled to section 8 protection and that "the contractual and statutory framework may be relevant to, but not necessarily determinative of, whether there is a reasonable expectation of privacy."[161] In that case, the contract was confusing and equivocal, but supported the existence of a reasonable expectation of privacy since it narrowly circumscribed the internet service provider's right to disclose the personal information of subscribers. Similarly, the existence of some possibility of disclosure of information under *PIPEDA* did not have the consequence that no reasonable expectation of privacy existed.[162] This is a reflection of a point discussed earlier, that the issue must be a reasonable expectation of privacy *against the state*: knowing that someone sometimes might see the information is not a forfeiture of all right to freedom from government intrusion.

*Spencer* was a very positive development with regard to the issue of private contracts. It stressed a normative approach, which is the important issue. In principle, internet service providers could include a clause in their privacy policies which says "we will hand over any information about you to anyone we want any time we want," which would mean that as *a matter of fact* contractual schemes would remove all privacy protection from everyone. But it would not be reasonable as a matter of the kind of privacy we are entitled to *expect* — that is, on a normative analysis — for internet service providers to adopt such a policy, and ought not to lead to the normative conclusion that a reasonable expectation of privacy had disappeared. Subscriber agreements are private arrangements and typically are contracts of adhesion negotiated between parties without equal bargaining power, and in *Gomboc* a plurality of the Court warned of the need to "proceed with caution" in

161 *Spencer*, above note 36 at para 54. To similar effect, see *R v El-Azrak*, 2023 ONCA 440, where an accused's reasonable expectation of privacy was reduced but not eliminated because she was subject to regulation as a pharmacist.

162 *Ibid* at para 62: "*PIPEDA* thus cannot be used as a factor to weigh against the existence of a reasonable expectation of privacy since the proper interpretation of the relevant provision itself depends on whether such a reasonable expectation of privacy exists."

considering the impact of such contracts on privacy rights.[163] Access to the internet or, indeed, to anything else should not be made to depend upon contracting away one's constitutional rights, and *Spencer* is a strong step in that direction.

The Court has discussed this issue further, with its decision in *R v Jones*. In that case the issue was whether the accused retained a privacy interest in text messages that were in the hands of Telus. The Court concluded that the accused did still have such an expectation. Unlike in *Spencer*, there was no need — or indeed, ability — to look at the contract, because in *Jones* the text messages were obtained from the account of a third party, not from the account used by Jones. The real focus of the reasoning therefore related to the issue of control, and the Court concluded that "as a normative matter, it is reasonable to expect a service provider to keep information private where its receipt and retention of such information is incidental to its role of delivering private communications to the intended recipient."[164]

Although the terms of a contract were not relevant, the Court did consider the significance of the absence of such a relationship: specifically that the accused had no confidentiality agreement with Telus, from whom the text messages were obtained. That fact made no difference: in both *Spencer* and *Gomboc*, the presence of an agreement allowing disclosure "could not singularly defeat the claimants' reasonable expectations of privacy" and therefore "the *absence* of any such agreement here does not defeat Mr. Jones' reasonable expectation of privacy.[165]

What is most noteworthy about the reasoning in *Jones*, compared to either *Gomboc* or *Spencer*, is the willingness to reach a conclusion about the accused's privacy interest without getting into the intricacies of the contractual relationship.[166] That was of course a reflection of the facts, and the absence of such a relationship, but nonetheless the Court was willing to engage directly with, and decide the case based on, normative expectations about how a corporation should behave with regard to data, independent of either contractual or statutory obligations. That is a positive sign suggesting that private contracts and regulatory schemes very likely will not be used to undermine *Charter* rights, or

163 *Gomboc*, above note 23 at para 33.

164 *Jones*, above note 77 at para 44.

165 *Ibid* at paras 50–51.

166 See *Orlandis-Habsburgo*, above note 102, for a case which both acknowledges the fundamentally normative nature of the privacy analysis, but nonetheless also engages in a detailed examination of the contractual and regulatory scheme governing the relationship between the accused and his electrical provider. See, in particular, paras 83–111.

at a minimum cannot be determinative on their own. However, this remains an area where greater clarification would be of benefit.

## C. WAS THE SEARCH UNREASONABLE? THE COLLINS TEST

As noted in the introduction to this chapter, whether a search is reasonable is in all cases governed by the three-part *Collins* test: Was the search authorized by law? Was the law itself reasonable? And was the manner of search reasonable? A failure at any stage will mean that the search is unreasonable and, therefore, violates section 8.

We will consider those three steps in turn, dealing separately with warrantless searches and searches with a warrant within the first two steps. Although in principle the same questions are being asked in each situation, different considerations tend to arise.

### 1) Was the Search Authorized by Law?

A fundamental point must first be made about the nature of police powers. The Supreme Court held in *R v Mann* that "Absent a law to the contrary, individuals are free to do as they please. By contrast, the police (and more broadly, the state) may act only to the extent that they are empowered to do so by law."[167] The key thing to recognize from that is that "lawful" means something different, depending on whether we are talking about private citizens or police officers. In the case of individuals, behaviour is lawful if no law *forbids* it. In the case of the police, however, behaviour will not be lawful unless it is possible to point to some particular source *permitting* it. To show that a search is authorized by law, therefore, it is necessary to point to the source of authority for the activity.

#### a) Warrantless Searches

It was noted previously that[168] the police can only derive authority from one of three sources: statute, common law, and consent.[169] All three sources are relevant to determining whether a warrantless search

167 *R v Mann*, 2004 SCC 52 at para 15 [*Mann*].

168 For an explanation of the relationship between various warrantless search powers presented in chart form, see *Anatomy of Criminal Procedure*, above note 8, Chart 1.1(a)(i), "Which Warrantless Search Power is Appropriate?"

169 See Chapter 2.

is reasonable. First, various statutory provisions, some of which are contained in the *Code* but most in other statutes, allow warrantless searches in certain circumstances. Second, some existing common law rules allow for warrantless searches, such as search incident to arrest and search incident to investigative detention. In principle, the ancillary powers doctrine allows the creation of new, common law, warrantless search powers. But, also in principle, that ought to be unlikely. *Hunter* points out that the role of the *Charter* is to determine the limits on police power, not to create new search powers.[170] On a number of occasions, the Court has observed that it is Parliament's role, not that of the Court, to determine whether new search powers are necessary:

> it does not sit well for the courts, as the protectors of our fundamental rights, to widen the possibility of encroachments on these personal liberties. It falls to Parliament to make incursions on fundamental rights if it is of the view that they are needed for the protection of the public in a properly balanced system of criminal justice.[171]

Indeed, the Court has held that the common law should not be interpreted to allow searches in situations where there is a statutory scheme that applies to determine whether searches are permitted.[172] However, the possibility of creating new common law search powers remains open, and indeed, despite the ringing words in *Hunter* about the role of courts under the *Charter*, the Court has since then created at common law a power for police to enter the home in some limited circumstances, the power of search incident to investigative detention, safety searches, and sniffer dog searches.[173] Finally, there are also circumstances in which warrantless searches have been permitted because the accused were taken to have consented to them.

---

170 *Hunter*, above note 6 at 156: the *Charter* "is intended to constrain governmental action inconsistent with those rights and freedoms; it is not in itself an authorization for governmental action."

171 *Wong*, above note 33 at para 35. See also *R v Landry*, [1986] 1 SCR 145 at 187, and *R v Bernard*, [1988] 2 SCR 833 at 891.

172 *Evans*, above note 39 at para 24. Note, as well, that only existing common law powers and the ancillary doctrine are relevant sources of authority in this context. It was noted in Chapter 2 that police effectively have the power to adopt any practice that will not result in the exclusion of evidence. Although that point remains true, it is clear that it is not what the Court has in mind when speaking of a search being "authorized by law." Although many violations do not lead to the exclusion of evidence, they may still be s 8 violations.

173 See the discussion of these powers at Section C(1)(a)(ii), below in this chapter.

### i) *Authorization by Statute*

#### a. Warrantless Searches

Warrantless searches are provided for in the criminal law context and in various administrative schemes. In the criminal law context, warrantless powers to search can be found in both the *Code* and the *Controlled Drugs and Substances Act*.[174] Each of these powers has been amended to conform to *Charter* decisions concerning predecessor sections. The need for this step was not surprising, since warrantless searches are *prima facie* unreasonable. Therefore, these statutory powers depend on the existence of some fact that creates an out-of-the-ordinary situation. In each case, there is an attempt to limit the warrantless power to circumstances where it can be said that the state interest takes priority over individual privacy interests.

Section 11 of the *CDSA*[175] allows a peace officer to obtain a warrant to search a place for a controlled substance, for anything in which a controlled substance is concealed, for offence-related property, or for evidence in respect of an offence under the *CDSA*. While executing that search warrant, however, under section 11(5), a peace officer is entitled to search any person found in the place, if the officer has reasonable grounds to believe that the person has the controlled substance or thing set out in the warrant. This power is broader than the normal search warrant provision in section 487 of the *Code*, which does not permit searches of the person; it is, however, more limited than the predecessor provision in the *Narcotic Control Act*.[176] That provision permitted police officers to search any person found in a place being searched for narcotics, based on nothing more than their presence in the location. In *R v Debot*, the Ontario Court of Appeal held that a similar provision in the *Food and Drugs Act*[177] would not be reasonable and read it down to situations where the officer also had reasonable grounds to search the person.[178] Section 11(5) involves a slight broadening of police power, since the *NCA* search power was limited to a search for narcotics, while the *CDSA* warrant allows a search for other things, such as evidence of an offence, as well. This difference is unlikely to lead any court to conclude that the appropriate balance found in *Debot* has been upset.[179]

---

174 SC 1996, c 19 [*CDSA*].

175 *Ibid*, s 11(2).

176 RSC 1985, c N-1, repealed 1996, c 19, s 94 [*NCA*].

177 RSC 1985, c F-27.

178 [1989] 2 SCR 1140, aff'g (1986), 30 CCC (3d) 207 (Ont CA) [*Debot*].

179 This change in wording also resolves another difficulty that had confronted the Crown in *R v Grant*, [1993] 3 SCR 223 [*Grant* 1993]. In that case, police had conducted a warrantless perimeter search of the accused's property, looking for

A warrantless statutory search power sometimes exists when there are exigent circumstances. It is important to recognize, in this context, that exigent circumstances do not function as the justification for the search itself, but merely as justification for conducting the search without the delay involved in obtaining a warrant: that is, grounds for the search other than the exigent circumstances themselves must exist independently. The role of exigent circumstances is to justify not risking the delay involved in getting judicial pre-authorization, not to justify the search itself.

The Court first adopted this approach to statutory warrantless searches on *Charter* grounds. The *NCA*[180] allowed police officers to search a place other than a dwelling house if they had reasonable grounds to believe narcotics were present. It was held that to comply with section 8, this and similar provisions needed to be read down to allow a warrantless search only where exigent circumstances made it impracticable to obtain a warrant.[181] Subsequent legislative change has enacted this principle for some search powers.[182]

The concept of "exigent circumstances" in the search and seizure context[183] has been defined in a manner consistent with its role: "an

---

information based upon which they could obtain a search warrant. The Court noted that under the statutory provision in question, police could conduct warrantless searches only when looking for a narcotic. Therefore, the warrantless perimeter search could fall under the power granted by the statute only if the police thought they would find narcotics in the perimeter, which, of course, was not their expectation. By allowing searches for evidence of an offence as well as for controlled substances, s 11(7) of the *CDSA*, above note 174, removes that difficulty.

A superficially similar power, found in s 199(2) of the *Code*, permits an officer to take any person into custody and to seize any evidence found while in a common gaming house; however, the provision does not explicitly confer a power to search the persons found and amounts to an arrest power. Although a power to search incident to arrest may thereby arise, it is not a statutory power.

180 Above note 176.

181 *Grant* 1993, above note 179; *R v Wiley*, [1993] 3 SCR 263 [*Wiley*]; *R v Rao* (1984), 40 CR (3d) 1 (Ont CA) [*Rao*]; *R v D(ID)* (1987), 61 CR (3d) 292 (Sask CA) [*D(ID)*].

182 See s 487.11 of the *Code*, and s 11(7) of the *CDSA*, above note 174. To similar effect, see also ss 117.02 and 117.04(2) of the *Code*, dealing with warrantless seizures of weapons.

183 In addition to justifying the failure to obtain a warrant for a search, exigent circumstances can be relevant in other ways. In *Golden*, for example, the Court held that strip searches should ordinarily be held at a police station and could take place in the field only in exigent circumstances. In that context, such circumstances would include an urgency to search for weapons that might pose an immediate threat making it unsafe to wait and conduct the strip search at the

imminent danger of the loss, removal, destruction or disappearance of the evidence if the search or seizure is delayed."[184] For a search power to be justified on this ground, two requirements must be met: first, the existence of exigent circumstances, which "denotes not merely convenience, propitiousness or economy, but rather *urgency*, arising from circumstances calling for immediate police action to preserve evidence, officer safety or public safety," and secondly impracticability, which means that it must "be impossible in practice or unmanageable to obtain a warrant."[185] Further, the exigency must be the cause of the impracticability.[186] The decision is to be made on a case-by-case basis. It had, for example, been argued that a warrantless search exemption for vehicles should exist, on the basis that they are mobile and can quickly leave the scene.[187] The Court rejected this argument, holding that "[w]hile the fact that the evidence sought is believed to be present on a motor vehicle, water vessel, aircraft or other fast moving vehicle will often create exigent circumstances, no blanket exception exists for such conveyances."[188]

In addition, where warrant provisions allow warrantless circumstances in the case of exigent circumstances, the existence of exigent circumstances alone is not sufficient: they must also make it "impracticable" to obtain a warrant.[189] The "impracticability" standard is a high one: it is not enough that it would be inconvenient or impractical to proceed in another way.[190] Further, that it is impracticable to obtain a warrant cannot itself be the foundation for a claim of exigent

---

police station: *Golden*, above note 22. Similarly, exigent circumstances can be relevant to the exclusion of evidence. A court might find that, although a search was illegal, exigent circumstances made the violation less serious, thus affecting the analysis under s 24(2) of the *Charter*: *Silveira*, above note 120; *R v Klimchuk* (1991), 67 CCC (3d) 385 (BCCA) [*Klimchuk*].

184 *Grant* 1993, above note 179.

185 *R v Paterson*, 2017 SCC 15 at para 33 and 36. See also *Campbell*, above note 54 at para 112.

186 *Paterson*, above note 185 at para 34; *Campbell*, above note 54 at para 112.

187 *D(ID)*, above note 181; *Grant* 1993, above note 179; *Klimchuk*, above note 183.

188 *Grant* 1993, above note 179 at para 32.

189 "Impracticable" is the language in s 11(7) of the *CDSA*, above note 174, but equivalent language is found in other provisions.

190 See *R v Paterson*, above note 185, where police entered premises without a warrant to seize some marijuana "roaches" the accused had told them were inside. The police had decided not to arrest the accused, merely to take and dispose of the controlled substance, but the Supreme Court found that their entry was not authorized by s 11(7): "If, as the Crown says, the situation was not serious enough to arrest and apply for a warrant, then it cannot have been serious enough to intrude into a private residence without a warrant."

circumstances. This is similar to the point noted above, that the exigent circumstances themselves cannot be the justification for conducting a search in the first place.[191] Further, the police are not permitted to deliberately create exigent circumstances and then rely on them as a justification.[192]

Arguably some ambiguity over the exigent circumstances standard was created in *Campbell*, a decision with four judgments among nine judges. While the police were arresting a drug dealer, text messages arrived on his phone from Campbell offering to sell heroin laced with fentanyl; the officers used the phone to arrange to have Campbell deliver the drugs and then arrested him when he arrived. The Court found, by a clear majority, that this action satisfied the "exigent circumstances" requirement of section 11(7) of the *CDSA* because the police needed to act immediately to prevent the drugs from being trafficked in the community imminently.[193] Three judges, however, felt that these facts did not meet the "imminence" requirement: there was no evidence of another buyer, just a fear that the accused might at some point sell the drugs to someone, and a "generalized, societal safety concern" is not sufficient.[194] The majority did not address this argument, but one judge writing alone argued that this approach looked at the wrong question: the issue was the limited window of opportunity available to the police, not whether another sale was in the wings.[195] In essence, three judges give more weight to the requirement for exigency while one gives more weight to impracticability, and the majority does not weigh in on the issue.

In addition, a great variety of individual provisions in various federal and provincial statutes allow for investigative techniques that meet the definition of a search. Various cases have dealt with provisions of the *Food and Drugs Act*,[196] the *Customs Act*,[197] the Nova Scotia *Education*

---

191 The Ontario Court of Appeal in *R v Fountain*, 2015 ONCA 354 [*Fountain*], could be read as permitting a search based only on the existence of exigent circumstances, but since then that view has been rejected: see *R v Squires*, 2016 NLCA 54 [*Squires*].

192 *Campbell*, above note 54 at para 125: "the police cannot devise an investigative strategy to create circumstances of exigency in order to proceed without a warrant." See also *R v Phoummasak*, 2016 ONCA 46.

193 *Campbell*, above note 54 at para 124. This judgment was written by Jamal J and endorsed by Wagner CJ, Rowe, Kasirer, and O'Bonsawin JJ.

194 *Campbell*, above note 54 at para 324. This judgment was written by Martin J and Moreau J, with Karakatsanis J concurring.

195 *Campbell*, above note 54 at paras 161-163. Rowe J endorsed Jamal J's reasons but wrote his own reasons responding to the exigent circumstances argument.

196 *Debot*, above note 178.

197 *Simmons*, above note 14.

*Act*,[198] and various administrative schemes.[199] Indeed, the leading case, *Hunter*, was itself based on a provision in the *Combines Investigation Act*.[200] Finally, there are occasional warrantless seizure powers in the *Code*, such as those authorizing the seizure of a weapon from a person who cannot produce a licence for it,[201] of cocks from a cockpit,[202] or of counterfeit money.[203]

An important instance of a search power *not* being created by law was established by the Court in *Spencer*, dealing with a situation which had arisen in many cases and had been subject to conflicting decisions: obtaining subscriber information from an internet service provider.[204] Some courts had taken the view that the "lawful authority" for obtaining such information could, in essence, be created through circular reasoning. *PIPEDA*, a federal statute intended to protect privacy rights, allows disclosure to a police officer who has identified her "lawful authority to obtain the information."[205] This was combined with a provision in the *Code* stating that nothing took away the ability of a peace officer "to ask a person to voluntarily provide to the officer documents, data or information that the person is not prohibited by law from disclosing."[206] Combining these two provisions, it was sometimes held that the ability to ask an internet service provider to voluntarily provide the documents *was* the police officer's "lawful authority" under *PIPEDA* and, therefore, that this was a method by which police could obtain information without needing to seek a warrant.

*Spencer* authoritatively rejected that position:

> 487.014(1) is a declaratory provision that confirms the existing common law powers of police officers to make enquiries, as indicated by the fact that the section begins with the phrase "[f]or greater certainty": see *Ward*, at para. 49. *PIPEDA* is a statute whose purpose, as

198 *M(MR)*, above note 3.

199 *Rao*, above note 181, for example, attaches an appendix listing twelve statutes outside the criminal law sphere containing warrantless search powers. See the separate discussion of administrative searches at Section C(2)(b)(ii)(a), below in this chapter.

200 *Hunter*, above note 6. That Act has since been replaced with the *Competition Act*, RSC 1985, c C-34.

201 Section 117.03.

202 Section 447(3).

203 Section 462(2).

204 *Spencer*, above note 36.

205 *PIPEDA*, above note 159, s 7(3)(c.1).

206 At the time of *Spencer*, above note 36, this was the wording of s 487.014 of the *Code*. The relevant sections have since been changed, but a similar provision is now found at s 487.0195.

> set out in s. 3, is to increase the protection of personal information. Since in the circumstances of this case the police do not have the power to conduct a search for subscriber information in the absence of exigent circumstances or a reasonable law, I do not see how they could gain a new search power through the combination of a declaratory provision and a provision enacted to promote the protection of personal information.[207]

In this context, however, it is worth noting proposed legislation in Bill C-2, omnibus legislation dealing with many different matters, which is still before Parliament at the time of this writing. Among the new powers proposed there is an "information demand," which would allow a peace officer or public officer to make a demand for various information to a person who provides services to the public. No judicial authorization is required for such a demand, though the officer would have to have reasonable suspicion that there had been an offence and that the information would assist in the investigation.[208] If passed as is, this provision would largely reverse the result in *Spencer.*

b. Warrantless Seizures

Section 489 of the *Code* creates two separate warrantless seizure powers, which very largely overlap. Both allow for a seizure of what the person authorized to seize believes on reasonable grounds to be evidence.[209] Subsections (1) and (2) differ from one another by the initial prerequisite which must be met before such a seizure can occur.

---

207 *Spencer*, above note 32 at para 73. *R v TELUS Communications Co*, 2015 ONSC 3964 at para 18 [*TELUS* 2015], observes:

> I do note that TELUS has, in the past, willingly provided to the police, without any court order or other authorization, the name and address of its customers, on a simple request being made by a police service advising that such information was needed for an ongoing police investigation. TELUS says that it has changed that practice as a result of the decision of the Supreme Court of Canada in *R v Spencer*, [2014] 2 SCR 212.

In *Orlandis-Habsburgo*, above note 102, it was found that neither *PIPEDA* nor the *Municipal Freedom of Information and Protection of Privacy Act*, RSO 1990, c M.56 create search powers.

208 See Bill C-2, "An Act respecting certain measures relating to the security of the border between Canada and the United States and respecting other related security measures" and in particular the new proposed s 487.0121.

209 Sections 489(1) and (2) both allow for the seizure of any thing the person believes on reasonable grounds:

> (a) has been obtained by the commission of an offence against this or any other Act of Parliament;

Subsection 489(1) is specific to the execution of a warrant. Warrants must be specific about what they authorize the person executing it to seize: in general terms, a warrant does not say "go see what you find," but rather "go to this location and seize these particular things." That need for specificity is a way of balancing the privacy interests of individuals against the investigative needs of the state, and is meant to guarantee that searches are not allowed too readily.[210] However, in some circumstances that approach could tip the balance too far from legitimate state interests: if an officer executing a search warrant to seize unlawful firearms sees illegal narcotics sitting on the table next to them, it seems difficult to justify insisting that the officer take the guns but leave the drugs. Accordingly, section 489(1) permits a person who executes a warrant to seize other evidence in addition to the things mentioned in the warrant.

Section 489(2), as noted, is almost identical, but with a different triggering condition. Rather than applying while executing a warrant, this subsection gives a seizure power to a peace officer or public officer "who is lawfully present in a place pursuant to a warrant or otherwise in the execution of duties." Questions of interpretation arise around both of these powers, some common to both and some not.

One particular question is whether section 489 is meant to be a codification of the common law plain view doctrine or not. The Supreme Court of Canada has not considered this issue, and courts of appeal have disagreed.[211] That question is made more difficult by the fact that

---

(b) has been used in the commission of an offence against this or any other Act of Parliament; or

(c) will afford evidence in respect of an offence against this or any other Act of Parliament.

210 See the discussion below in Section C(1)(b)(i), "Searching Places for Things: Section 487."

211 The plain view doctrine, in essence, is meant to apply to unanticipated evidence, but it is not clear s 489 contains any such requirement. See also *R v Frieburg*, 2013 MBCA 40 at para 65:

> In *R. v. Le* (T.D.), 2011 MBCA 83, 270 Man.R. (2d) 82, this court found that s. 489(1) (which is similar to s. 489(2) except that it applies to items that are not specified in a search warrant but that are seized while executing a search warrant) and the plain view doctrine are not coextensive. The Courts of Appeal of Alberta and Ontario have both come to this conclusion regarding s. 489(2). (See *R. v. Makhmudov (R.) et al.*, 2007 ABCA 248 at para. 19, 417 A.R. 228, *R. v. Bottineau (E.) et al.*, 2011 ONCA 194 at paras. 75–77, 276 O.A.C. 173, leave to appeal to S.C.C. denied, [2011] S.C.C.A. No. 455, and *Jones* at para. 58.) The Court of Appeal of Québec has come to the contrary conclusion. (See *R. v. Boudreau-Fontaine*, 2010 QCCA 1108 at para. 50, and *L'Espérance v. R.*, 2011 QCCA 237 at para. 36.)

the plain view doctrine itself has not been as authoritatively developed as it might be. Most recently the Court has held that "two requirements must be satisfied for the plain view doctrine to apply: (1) the police officers must have a legitimate 'prior justification for the intrusion into the place where the "plain view" seizure occurred' ... and (2) the incriminating evidence must be in plain view in that it is 'immediately obvious' and '"discovered inadvertently' by the police," though that decision also finds it "unnecessary to express a settled opinion on the limits of the doctrine."[212]

It is clear that section 489 is only a seizure power, not a search power. In *R v Clarke*, for example, the police found firearms by looking through a pile of items covered by a tarp. The British Columbia Court of Appeal found that section 489(2) did not authorize that police action: it did not give them the authority to conduct the search of the pile that resulted in the seizure.[213] Rather, the type of situation envisioned by section 489 is as in *R v Warren*, where police responded to a domestic call from the accused's spouse, who reported that the accused was in their house with their children and with a number of firearms. The accused was eventually arrested outside the home, and an officer then entered to check the welfare of the children (which meant the officer was "lawfully present ... otherwise in the execution of duties"): as he walked in the door he immediately saw firearms and ammunition, which section 489(2) authorized him to seize.[214]

---

212 *R v McGregor*, 2023 SCC 4 at para 37. A source frequently cited as setting out the doctrine is *R v Jones*, 2011 ONCA 632 at para 56 [*Jones* ONCA]:

> The "plain view" doctrine operates when a police or peace officer is in the process of executing a warrant or an otherwise lawfully authorized search with respect to one crime and evidence of another crime falls into plain view. Resort to this common law power is subject to the following restraints, however:
>
> (i) The officer must be lawfully in the place where the search is being conducted ("lawfully positioned", in the language of the authorities); (ii) the nature of the evidence must be immediately apparent as constituting a criminal offence; (iii) the evidence must have been discovered inadvertently; (iv) the plain view doctrine confers a seizure power not a search power; it is limited to those items that are visible and does not permit an exploratory search to find other evidence of other crimes.

213 *R v Clarke*, 2017 BCCA 453. See also *R v Bottineau*, 2011 ONCA 194.

214 *R v Warren*, 2017 MBCA 106. Note that the officer was of course not surprised to see firearms, since that had been part of why he was at the scene, but his purpose in entering was to check the welfare of the children. If the plain view doctrine *does* include an inadvertence requirement, this would be an interpretation that makes s 489 depart from that common law rule.

The exact dividing line between "search" and "seizure" could be ambiguous in some cases, however. In *R v Frieburg*, police used a sniffer dog to check for narcotics in the trunk of the accused's car, getting a positive indication. Noting that the requirement in section 489(2) was that the police officer "believes on reasonable grounds" that there was evidence, and that the sniffer dog created such reasonable grounds, the Manitoba Court of Appeal found the physical search of the trunk to be authorized by the subsection.[215]

The use of section 489 is also challenging when police are searching electronic devices, and there are issues which will need to be authoritatively settled. When searching a computer, for example, although police are required to only search for evidence of the offence named in the warrant, there is a very good chance that if there is other illicit material it will turn up. Search protocols are not generally imposed because files can be given deceptive names, so that for instance an image file might be placed within a Word document.[216] Not uncommonly a forensic examination is made of a computer, which involves producing a duplicate of its contents to be forensically examined:[217] this amounts to seizing every file on the computer and can mean that all of them are examined in some degree or other. It could be argued that the material is not in "plain view" or "immediately obvious," but that argument has not succeeded to date.[218] On the one hand the police would need a warrant if they wanted to continue to search for more instances of the newly-discovered illicit material, but they should have no difficulty in obtaining one. It is arguable that the intended balance — not ignoring inadvertently-discovered material but not expanding the scope of a warrant unreasonably — is not met in this context.

There is also an issue, unique to section 489(2), in particular to its requirement that the officer is "lawfully present in a place ... in the execution of duties." As noted in the introduction to this broader discussion, "lawfully" in the execution of duties in that section ought to mean that some authority can be pointed to, specifically saying that the police are permitted to do what they are doing: the mere fact that no law *forbids* them from being in the place should not be sufficient.

---

215 *R v Frieburg*, above note 211. The decision could also be read as finding that the sniffer dog result itself created a warrantless search power, but it is not apparent what that power would be, without, for example, arresting the accused and searching him incident to that.

216 See *R v Vu*, 2013 SCC 60 at para 57.

217 See, for example, the description of the EnCase program in *R v Cox*, 2003 ABQB 212.

218 See *Jones* ONCA, above note 212.

Relatively little attention has been paid to how to interpret this requirement, and it is not clear that the proper approach is being taken. In *Frieburg*, for example, the "lawfully present" criterion was found to be met when police seized something from a vehicle on the grounds that it was parked on a public street and the police were not required to trespass on private property to reach it.[219] In both *R v Fedan* and *R v Attard* equipment from vehicles which had been in an accident was seized, and this was found to have been authorized by section 489(2).[220] Neither of those cases explicitly consider whether "lawfulness" in this context requires a source of authority rather than merely the absence of anything forbidding the action: they do not consider the criterion *at all*. *Attard* quoted section 489(2) and underlined some passages for consideration, but not the "lawfully present" one. *Fedan* omitted mention of the "lawfully present" requirement entirely. In fact, courts should insist on finding that the police are acting under some defined authority before permitting the use of section 489: that is, after all, the point of the section. As noted, it was intended to avoid an unintended consequence in the course of executing a search warrant: that if obvious evidence of an offence was found, it should be possible to seize it even though it had not been specifically listed in the search warrant. Two of the three circumstances in which section 489 applies — executing a search warrant or being in a place pursuant to some other warrant — require that the police have received particular judicial pre-authorization for the very behaviour they are engaged in at the time. To interpret "lawfully present in a place" simply to mean there is nothing which *forbids* the police presence would be entirely out of step with the rest of the section.

To the extent that there is guidance from the Supreme Court, it suggests that specific authority permitting the presence is required, rather than the mere absence of anything make the presence unlawful. In *Reeves*, police had entered the home the accused shared with his spouse and seized a computer that was present there. One possible source of authority for the seizure was section 489(2), and the issue that the parties argued about was whether the consent of the spouse to the police entry was sufficient to mean that they were "lawfully present." In fact the Court found that section 489(2) did not apply because on the facts, the requirement that there be reasonable grounds to believe the computer contained evidence was not satisfied.[221] The Court therefore left aside the question of whether the consent of the spouse was sufficient

219 *Frieburg*, above note 211.

220 *R v Fedan*, 2016 BCCA 26; *R v Attard*, 2024 ONCA 616.

221 *Reeves*, above note 35 at para 21.

authority or not. The important point in the section 489(2) context, however, is that the Court thought it *necessary* to find authority for the entry. That issue would not have arisen unless "lawfully present" was being interpreted to require that the police justify the source of their power to be there.

### ii) *Authorization by Common Law*

#### a. Entry into the Home

A person's home has long been recognized at law as attracting a very high degree of privacy and, generally speaking, can only be searched with a warrant. However, the common law does permit a limited entry into the home and consequent search in at least one context, dealing with emergencies. This example can be seen as the most fundamental common law power, in the sense that it was recognized by the Court in *R v Godoy*, and the decision in *Godoy* is the one that made reliance on common law powers commonplace in Canadian law.[222]

In *Godoy*, police received a 911 call that was disconnected before they could get any information. These calls are treated as high priority calls, and so the police went to the apartment unit which had been the source. The accused answered the door, said there was no problem, and attempted to shut the door. The police instead forced their way in, which led to an altercation and charges being laid against the accused: whether those charges were made out largely depended on whether the police were acting in the execution of their duty. The question therefore became whether they had the power to enter the apartment: if they did not, the accused was not guilty.

The Supreme Court concluded that, based on the *Waterfield* test, the police had been acting lawfully. The *Waterfield* test sets out two requirements for an interference with liberty to be lawful: that the police were acting in the course of their duty, and that their conduct did not involve an unjustifiable use of powers in the circumstances.[223] Responding to an emergency call easily satisfied the first requirement, and the second was also met, because the police had no realistic alternative to entering the apartment in order to ascertain whether there was an emergency.

However, the Court also recognized the significant privacy interest in the home: although this did not prevent the police entry entirely, it did act to limit it. The Court concluded that:

---

222 *R v Godoy*, [1999] 1 SCR 311 [*Godoy*]. See the discussion in Chapter Two, Section A(3)(b), "New Common Law Powers — the 'Ancillary Powers' Doctrine."

223 See the discussion of *Waterfield* in *ibid*, Chapter Two.

> the intrusion must be limited to the protection of life and safety. The police have authority to investigate the 911 call and, in particular, to locate the caller and determine his or her reasons for making the call and provide such assistance as may be required. The police authority for being on private property in response to a 911 call ends there. They do not have further permission to search premises or otherwise intrude on a resident's privacy or property.[224]

Generally speaking, lower courts have continued to respect the high privacy interest in the home and therefore kept this police power of entry limited. The police have been found not to be acting within this common law power when, for example, the person said to be in danger was the one who answered the door, and the police could have asked that person to step outside rather than enter themselves.[225] Similarly where the person said to be in danger — a child — was already outside the residence and in his mother's arms, any purported emergency could be handled without entering the home.[226] Although the entry power is not necessarily limited to 911 calls, the police must have reasonable grounds to believe that there is a real public safety concern inside the home, and that belief must also be subjectively held.[227]

The power to enter in response to an emergency is, strictly speaking, not the only common law rule allowing entry into a home. The common law had long contained a "knock and announce" rule governing police entry into a home in order to effect an arrest, but those common law powers were eventually found to be unconstitutional, in *R v Feeney*.[228] In the short term the Court created different common law rules, but Parliament has since legislated in that area.[229] In addition, the common law power of search incident to arrest now includes a limited power to enter a home in some circumstances: see the discussion in the section immediately below.

Finally, note that the question of whether one occupant's consent to enter a home is sufficient authority against the privacy interest of all occupants has been raised but not authoritatively settled.[230]

---

224 *Godoy*, above note 222 at para 22.

225 *R v Timmons*, 2011 NSCA 39.

226 *R v Davidson*, 2017 ONCA 257 [*Davidson*]. See also *R v Okemow*, above note 104.

227 *Davidson*, above note 226, and *R v McMahon*, 2018 SKCA 26 at para 100.

228 *Feeney*, above note 120.

229 See ss 529–529.5 and the discussion in Chapter 7, Section D.

230 See *Reeves*, above note 35.

### b. Search Incident to Arrest

The goal of search and seizure law is to protect a reasonable expectation of privacy, primarily by preventing unreasonable searches before they take place. Generally, greater privacy should be expected with regard to one's person rather than to a place. Therefore, it is ironic that although searches of a place generally require a warrant, searches of the person are most often authorized on a common law and warrantless basis. With few exceptions (such as a warrant to obtain a blood or DNA sample), searches of the person are as a matter of fact not authorized by warrant provisions, and so they are not typically subject to judicial oversight beforehand, but instead are assessed for validity after the fact. The most important of these common law powers to discuss is search incident to arrest.[231]

Search incident to arrest is the search where the common law has been most active. As the law has developed, there is now an "ordinary" power of search incident to arrest and a method for deciding whether that ordinary power needs to be modified when dealing with particular situations. We shall first consider the ordinary power and then turn to look at the circumstances in which it has been modified.

When the police have validly arrested a person they are entitled, within some limits, to search that person. A form of this rule has existed for centuries, and in 1990, with *Cloutier v Langlois*,[232] the Court decided that a properly delimited power was consistent with *Charter* protections. Deciding what counts as proper delimitation has not, however, been so straightforward in the years since this rule with "nebulous parameters"[233] was upheld. Nonetheless, making this evaluation is particularly important. Although, in principle, warrantless searches are intended to be the exception rather than the rule, searches incident to arrest are generally taken to constitute the majority of searches conducted by police.[234] Therefore the limits on this power need to be clear and accepted.[235]

Although there was some early variation in how the test was articulated, the current standard for search incident to arrest is well established: that (1) the individual searched has been lawfully arrested; (2) the search is truly incidental to the arrest in the sense that it is for

231 For an explanation of this issue in chart form, see *Anatomy of Criminal Procedure*, above note 8, Chart 1.1(a)(ii), "Search Incident to Arrest."

232 [1990] 1 SCR 158 [*Cloutier*].

233 *Golden*, above note 22 at para 23.

234 *Ibid* at para 84; Stanley A Cohen, "Search Incident to Arrest: How Broad an Exception to the Warrant Requirement?" (1988) 63 *Criminal Reports* (3d) 182.

235 *Stillman*, above note 127 at 27.

a valid law enforcement purpose connected to the arrest; and (3) the search is conducted reasonably.[236] Of these, it is the second factor that is in dispute most frequently and is the most important limit,[237] though each can be an issue.[238]

The usual starting point for analyzing whether a search was truly incidental to the arrest is *R v Caslake*. The Court held there that:

> the search must be truly incidental to the arrest. This means that the police must be able to explain, within the purposes articulated in *Cloutier*, *supra* (protecting the police, protecting the evidence, discovering evidence), or by reference to some other valid purpose, why they searched. They do not need reasonable and probable grounds. However, they must have had some reason related to the arrest for conducting the search at the time the search was carried out, and that reason must be objectively reasonable.[239]

That is, although search incident to arrest simply flows from the fact that the accused has been arrested,[240] nonetheless there must be some sort of legitimate or logical connection between the arrest and the purpose for the search. Put another way, there must be some *purpose* to the search beyond the simple fact that the accused was arrested. To be "truly incidental" the search must be for a valid law enforcement purpose, three of which have been identified: (a) police and public safety; (b) preventing the destruction of evidence; and (c) discovering

---

236 *R v Stairs*, 2022 SCC 11 [*Stairs*] at para 35. In *Cloutier*, above note 232, the three factors listed by the Court were (1) the power did not impose a duty; (2) the search must be for a valid objective; and (3) the search must not be conducted in an abusive fashion. The stipulation that the power does not impose a duty is not really a limit (it would be difficult for an accused to object to the fact that the police exercised their discretion to search unless there were also facts showing the search was not for a valid objective), though whether the arrest was lawful can function as a limit.

237 *Caslake*, above note 16 at para 25.

238 See, for example, *Klimchuk*, above note 183, or *R v Gerson-Foster*, 2019 ONCA 405, where the search was not lawful as a search incident to arrest because the arrest was not lawful. Note as well that the third requirement, that the search be conducted in a reasonable manner, is in any event a requirement of the *Collins* test for any search to be a reasonable one. This makes the issue either redundant as part of the search incident to arrest test, or alternatively means that if the "was the search authorized by law" step is met because of search incident to arrest, then of necessity the "was the search conducted in a reasonable manner" step has been satisfied.

239 *Caslake*, above note 16 at para 25.

240 *Debot*, above note 178 at para 3 (SCC); *Caslake*, above note 16 at para 20.

evidence that may be used at trial.[241] In principle, other purposes *could* be found in the future, but as a practical matter analyses of search incident to arrest simply look at whether one of these three purposes justified the search.[242]

Further, the officer must subjectively be searching for one of those three purposes, and that belief must be objectively reasonable. In this context, the objective standard does not require reasonable and probable grounds. It simply means that the officer must have "some reasonable basis" to do what they did, which is a much lower standard.[243]

In the case of a search for evidence, this standard means that "there must be some reasonable prospect of finding evidence of the offence for which the accused is being arrested."[244] Two things are important in that statement. First, it must be plausible that relevant evidence would be found at all. If an accused is arrested for a traffic offence, there is no sensible basis to think that relevant evidence would be in the trunk, and so a search of the vehicle would not be authorized incident to arrest. If the accused were arrested for a narcotics offence while in a vehicle, however, it would be plausible that evidence might be in the trunk and so such a search would be authorized.[245] Second, it must be plausible not merely that evidence of some sort could be found, but that evidence of the offence *for which the accused was arrested* could be found.[246] So, for example, an accused who is known to have a history of drug offences cannot be searched for drugs if the actual arrest is for a traffic violation.[247] If the police begin to investigate the accused for a different offence after the arrest, they cannot rely on the search incident to arrest power to obtain evidence relating to that other offence.[248]

---

241 *Stairs*, above note 236 at para 36.

242 Although it has not yet arisen in caselaw, there is arguably a lingering ambiguity over this list, which is discussed below.

243 *Stairs*, above note 236.

244 *Fearon*, above note 140 at para 22.

245 See *Caslake*, above note 16 at para 18. See also *Ellis*, above note 138 (arrest for careless driving and no trunk search permitted) as opposed to *R v Pearson*, 2017 ONCA 389 (arrest for driving while impaired by drugs and trunk search permitted) on the other. Note that in *Pearson* the police searched not only the trunk but also a knapsack found in the trunk, but this was still held to be incident to the arrest.

246 This rule is stated in both *Caslake*, above note 16, and *Fearon*, above note 140.

247 *Golden*, above note 22 at para 92.

248 See *R v Balendra*, 2019 ONCA 68 [*Balendra*], where the accused was arrested because he was carelessly driving a stolen vehicle. A USB key was found in his pocket and police examined it some hours after the arrest: since their purpose

Similarly, a search incident to arrest cannot be undertaken to obtain evidence about someone other than the arrestee.[249]

The same rule applies to searches which are said to be based on safety concerns: no reasonable grounds are required to believe that there is such a risk, but there must be some logical basis for asserting it. A search incident to arrest based on safety grounds would be permitted if the accused has already had a weapon taken from them, for example, or has been arrested for a violent offence.[250] However, where an accused is arrested some distance from a vehicle and then handcuffed before being taken back to it, a search based on safety concerns cannot be justified.[251]

A search incident to arrest can extend to the surrounding area, and so often includes searching the vehicle in which the accused is arrested. Courts have found it relatively easy to approve of vehicle searches, looking in appropriate cases in the trunk or glove compartment, or even removing a loose door panel as part of a search incident to an arrest.[252] However, much depends on the particular circumstances of the case. For example, the police cannot contrive to arrest a person in a particular location as a pretext for performing a warrantless search of that location.[253] Searches of the home, in contrast, raise greater privacy issues for the accused, and special rules modifying the ordinary power of search incident to arrest have been created for that situation: see the discussion below.

The Court has been reluctant to impose strict temporal limits on search incident to arrest. A search can be incidental to an arrest even if it precedes the formal arrest. However, the grounds for the arrest must have already existed — evidence found during the search cannot then help justify the arrest.[254] There is also no strict time limit on how long after the arrest a search can take place. For example, a search of a vehicle six hours later could still be incidental to the arrest depending

for that search did not relate to either careless driving or possession of stolen property, it was not lawful.

249 See *Campbell*, above note 54 at para 107, where the police arrested one person, Gammie, but then used his phone to carry on a conversation about the sale of drugs with the accused, Campbell. That search of Gammie's phone was not about Gammie nor about the offence for which he had been arrested and so was not permitted incident to that arrest.

250 See, respectively, *R v Land*, 2018 MBCA 132 and *R v Aviles*, 2017 ONCA 629.

251 *Ellis*, above note 138.

252 *R v Smellie*, [1994] BCJ No 2850 at para 49 (CA) [*Smellie*]. See also the discussion contrasting searches of vehicles to searches of the person.

253 *R v Lim (No 2)* (1990), 1 CRR (2d) 136 (Ont HCJ), as cited in *Smellie*, *ibid*.

254 *R v Polashek* (1999), 25 CR (5th) 183 (Ont CA); *Debot*, above note 178 (Ont CA).

on the factors affecting the timing. The further in time from the arrest, the less likely the inference that the search is incidental to that arrest, but there is no absolute rule. What matters is the actual purpose motivating the search.[255]

Indeed, the police officer's motives and purposes for the search can be taken into account in other ways. If the search was done to intimidate or put pressure on the accused, for example, then it was not incidental.[256] Further, if a search is conducted because of a policy to search everyone arrested, that will not be sufficiently incidental. Rather, the Court has held, the search must be incidental on both objective and subjective criteria.[257] Not only must a valid purpose objectively exist, but subjectively, the officer must have made an individualized decision to conduct the search for that purpose. Thus, in *Cloutier*, for example, although the police force in question maintained a general directive to search everyone arrested, the Court noted that the officers in the case had exercised their discretion in choosing to search the accused.[258] In *R v Caslake*, though, the officer testified that he conducted the search only because of an RCMP (Royal Canadian Mounted Police) policy to inventory the contents of an impounded car.[259] Thus, although objectively a search incident to the accused's arrest would have been justifiable, the actual search conducted was not incidental to the arrest. The Court has adopted this approach to be more consistent with the goal of preventing the occurrence of unjustified searches, rather than remedying them after the fact.[260]

Note as well that the search is justified not because of a reduced expectation of privacy on the part of the arrested person nor because of exigent circumstances, but rather because the police have an increased need to gain control of things or information following an arrest, which outweighs the individual's interest in privacy.[261] Accordingly, although the accused has been arrested or detained and so is entitled to be told

---

255 *Caslake*, above note 16 at para 18. See also *R v Nolet*, 2010 SCC 24 at para 50 [*Nolet*]. In addition, see *Balendra*, above note 248, where the search (although unlawful for other reasons) was not barred because it did not occur until seven hours after the arrest.

256 *Cloutier*, above note 232, and *Caslake*, above note 16.

257 *Caslake*, *ibid*.

258 *Cloutier*, above note 232.

259 *Caslake*, above note 16.

260 *Ibid* at para 27. See also *R v Golub* (1997), 9 CR (5th) 98 (Ont CA) where the Ontario Court of Appeal makes note that the search of the accused's house was not based on a pre-set protocol, but on a decision made at the scene by the officer in charge based on the available information.

261 *Caslake*, above note 16 at para 17. See also *Fearon*, above note 140 at para 25.

of the right to counsel, the search does need to wait on the accused exercising that right.[262]

As mentioned above, there is a lingering ambiguity around the acceptable purposes, and it is to that issue that we now turn. Recall that two of the three purposes are protecting evidence from destruction, and discovering evidence to use at trial. In effect, those amount to "finding evidence which might cease to exist" and "finding any evidence at all," but when they are put that way, the former purpose becomes redundant: if finding *any* evidence is an acceptable purpose, there is no need to specify that finding evidence which might cease to exist is an acceptable purpose.

The explanation for this oddity comes from the way the common law power developed.[263] The original purposes of this search power were related only to short-term goals: to find items that might allow the arrested person to harm the officer or to escape and to prevent evidence under the control of the arrestee from being destroyed. In *Stillman*, the Court noted that after *Cloutier*, some courts of appeal had extended the search power beyond just preventing evidence from being destroyed, and had added the third broader purpose of finding evidence relevant to the guilt or innocence of the accused. They also noted that those cases had concerned searches of vehicles, not of a person.[264] The Court rejected that broader goal on the facts of *Stillman*, which concerned taking various bodily samples from the accused (including scalp and pubic hair, as well as dental impressions) because there was "no likelihood that the appellant's teeth impressions would change, nor that his hair follicles would present a different DNA profile with the passage of time."[265] Therefore, the search could not be justified as an incident of the arrest. Similarly, in *R v Golden*, dealing with the more intrusive issue of strip searches, the Court focused on the risk of disposal of evidence in assessing the reasonableness of the search power.[266]

However, in *Stillman*, the Court specifically expressed no opinion about whether the broader purpose might be acceptable when the search involved a vehicle rather than the accused's person. In *Caslake*, a case actually dealing with a vehicle, it adopted a broader formulation of the type of evidence for which police can search. The Court listed both preventing the destruction of evidence and finding evidence that could

262 *Debot*, above note 178 at para 3 (SCC).

263 *Caslake*, above note 16. See the discussion of this issue in Stephen G Coughlan, "Developments in Criminal Procedure: The 1997–98 Term" (1999) 10 *Supreme Court Law Review* 273 at 319.

264 *Stillman*, above note 127 at para 39.

265 *Ibid* at para 49.

266 *Golden*, above note 22 at para 93.

be used at the accused's trial as legitimate purposes for the search.[267] Thus, the Court followed the line of authorities that expanded the search incident to arrest power in the case of vehicles. However, the Court did not explicitly acknowledge that it was now deciding a point it had previously left open. More importantly, it did not suggest that the broader third purpose was *limited* to vehicle searches. As a result, cases now routinely cite all three purposes, including "obtaining evidence to use at trial," as one of the purposes that can make a search genuinely incidental to the arrest. However, as we shall see in a moment in discussing the special cases, thinking about whether evidence is in danger of going out of existence or not has not disappeared entirely from consideration.

Those are the rules governing the power of search incident to arrest in its basic form. Those rules are premised on what we can think of as the ordinary privacy and state interests, but there are circumstances where additional considerations arise. Accordingly, sometimes the standard has been modified in order to balance the nature and extent of the privacy interests implicated and the importance of the police's law enforcement objectives. As a result, there is "a spectrum of standards, with some contexts requiring a higher threshold for a search incident to arrest than others."[268] The Court has so far identified what can be thought of as five "special cases" where additional criteria must be met beyond the ordinary search incident to arrest rules. In principle further special cases could be identified and requirements created depending on where the particular search is seen as falling on the spectrum.

The most stringent special case was just discussed and arises from *Stillman*: bodily samples cannot be seized at all through a search incident to arrest. That rule is based on the heightened expectation of privacy in a person's body and the fact that evidence such as an accused's DNA is not in danger of being destroyed or altered.[269] This special case actually forbids the use of the search incident to arrest power for the purpose of gathering that particular sort of evidence. The other special cases relate to heightened privacy interests on the part of the accused which are not sufficient to mean that search incident to arrest cannot

267 *Caslake*, above note 16 at para 19.

268 *Stairs*, above note 236 at para 40.

269 *Stillman*, above note 127 at para 42: "the invasive nature of body searches demands higher standards of justification." This rule is consistent generally with the Court's view, for example, in *Simmons*, above note 14, that the greater the intrusion, the greater the need for justification for the search.

be used at all, but are sufficient to mean that additional requirements and limitations must be imposed on the power.[270]

The next most stringent special case deals with strip searches: that is, "the removal or rearrangement of some or all of the clothing of a person so as to permit a visual inspection of a person's private areas, namely genitals, buttocks, breasts (in the case of a female), or undergarments."[271] Most searches incident to arrest are justified because the police have a heightened interest in searching the accused that outweighs the accused's reasonable expectation of privacy. However, the accused's expectation of privacy becomes higher in the case of a strip search and so, in addition to the ordinary requirements for a search, other limitations are imposed. Most notably, where usually the search power is simply an incident to a lawful arrest, in the case of a strip search the police must be able to point to *reasonable grounds to believe* that a strip search, rather than the more usual pat-down, is required in the particular circumstances.[272] Further, strip searches can only be used for two of the three usual purposes: safety and preventing the disposal of evidence.[273] In addition, the Court set out a number of guidelines for how the strip search should be conducted, including that it should be done by officers of the same gender as the accused, with the minimum of force, and conducted in such a way that the accused is not at any point completely undressed.[274] The exact status of these guidelines is a source of some disagreement in lower courts, with varying views on whether compliance with them, or all of them, is required or merely advisable.[275]

---

270 This is an illustration of the "balance" point referred to above, that where an accused's privacy interests are greater, the correspondingly greater protections of that interest must be incorporated into the search power.

271 *Golden*, above note 22 at para 47.

272 *Ibid*. See, for example, *R v Gonzales*, 2017 ONCA 543, where the accused was arrested because in the back of his vehicle police found an industrial sized garbage bag filled with large vacuum-sealed Ziploc bags of bulk marijuana. Noting that a strip search was aimed at finding items which had been secreted and might be disposed of, and that these large Ziploc bags were "[n]ot apparently capable of secretion" (para 144), the Ontario Court of Appeal found the strip search unlawful.

273 *Golden*, above note 22 at paras 93–94. The decision does not explicitly *say* that the power is not available for the purpose of searching for evidence generally, but only talks about these two purposes in discussing when the power is available.

274 *Ibid* at para 101.

275 See, for example, among the many cases considering strip searches, *R v M(S)*, 2013 ONCJ 219; *R v Lozano*, 2013 ONSC 1871; *R v Muller*, 2011 ONCA 78; *R v Rezaei*, 2017 BCSC 1639; or *R v Lee*, 2018 ONCA 1067.

A separate emerging issue relates to the video-recording of strip searches, which was not addressed in the *Golden* guidelines. On the one hand, video-recording seems obviously to make the invasion of privacy more serious and the experience more traumatic, factors which led to the more stringent rules in the first place. On the other hand, the existence of a video-recording has sometimes been crucial evidence demonstrating that the manner of a strip search was unreasonable.[276]

A strip search must also be carried out at the police station, unless there are exigent circumstances requiring that it be conducted in the field. In that event the power is even more stringent: exigent circumstances exist only where "there is a demonstrated necessity and urgency to search for weapons or objects that could be used to threaten the safety of the accused, the arresting officers or other individuals."[277]

Although they created the common law power relating to strip searches, the Court suggested that legislative intervention would be valuable;[278] Parliament, however, has not acted on that suggestion. The Court also identified body cavity searches as a type of search even more intrusive than strip searches. Although the Court has yet to decide the point, the reasoning in *Golden* seems to clearly indicate that a body cavity search could not proceed without a higher degree of justification and greater constraints as to the manner in which it could be reasonably performed.[279]

As a final observation on strip searches, it should be noted that serious concerns have been raised about police compliance with these procedures. A report of Ontario's Office of the Independent Police Review Director in 2019 concluded that there were serious problems with police training around the law on strip searches and with compliance with the *Golden* decision,[280] and cases have referred to systemic ignorance of its rules.[281] It seems reasonable to think that similar concerns could be raised in other provinces.

---

276 See, for example, *R v S(B)*, 2010 ONCJ 561.

277 *Golden*, above note 22 at para 102. See also *R v Pilon*, 2018 ONCA 959, which argues that the Court in *Golden* might not have absolutely ruled out strip searches in the field for the purpose of preserving evidence, but also acknowledged at para 26 that there is not "any case from an appellate or trial court that explicitly found that concerns over the need to preserve evidence constituted exigent circumstances that justified a field strip search."

278 *Golden*, above note 22 at para 103.

279 *Ibid* at para 87.

280 Ontario, Office of the independent Police Review Director, *Breaking the Golden Rule: A Review of Police Strip Searches in Ontario* (Toronto: Office of the Independent Police Review Director, March 2019).

281 See *R v Foster*, 2018 ONCA 53 at para 115.

An equally stringent special case deals with penile swabs incident to arrest; that is, the situation where the police swab the accused's penis with the goal of determining whether the DNA of the complainant in a sexual assault case can be found on it. In *R v Saeed*, the Court rejected the argument that this type of search should be seen as equivalent to a bodily sample search (as in *Stillman*) and therefore banned entirely (at least as a search incident to arrest).[282] Rather, the majority concluded that a penile swab was less invasive than taking a dental impression or removing hair from a person's body, because it is in general "quick and painless."[283] In addition, they noted that the technique would gather information about the *complainant's* DNA, not that of the accused, and was therefore less intrusive on privacy than a bodily sample search. Further they noted that the DNA sought would be in danger of disappearing, unlike the accused's own DNA. Accordingly, they concluded that such searches could be permitted as long as additional limitations to protect the accused's interests were imposed.

The Court analogized penile swabs to strip searches, and therefore imposed a "reasonable grounds" requirement similar to that in *Golden*. Just as strip searches cannot be carried out routinely, so too are penile swabs limited: the police can only take a penile swab incident to arrest "if they have reasonable grounds to believe the swab will reveal and preserve evidence of the offence, and if the search is carried out in accordance with guidelines that are designed to respect the accused's privacy interests and interfere with them as little as possible."[284]

The Court elaborated on those guidelines, which include that: the penile swab should be conducted at the police station (though it was imaginable that a hospital could in some cases be an appropriate location); a supervisory officer should authorize the swab; the accused should be offered the opportunity to do the swabbing himself, failing which an officer of the same gender should do it with the minimum of force and number of officers present; it should be done in a private area and as quickly as possible; and a proper record should be kept.[285]

In addition, a special evidentiary rule was created. The Court rejected the analogy to bodily samples on the grounds that a penile swab would be seeking the complainant's DNA, but as a practical matter such a swab might in fact obtain the accused's DNA as well. In that

282 *R v Saeed*, 2016 SCC 24 [*Saeed*].
283 *Ibid* at para 49.
284 *Ibid* at para 42.
285 *Ibid* at para 78.

event, the *Stillman* rules around bodily sample searches would still govern and "the accused's DNA cannot be used for any purpose."[286]

The fourth special case in terms of stringency, but the most-recently created chronologically, relates to searches inside the home, dealt with in *Stairs*. A search incident to arrest inside the home raises special privacy concerns, because it has long been established that a person's home attracts a high expectation of privacy. However, the Court concluded, searches of the home do not invariably infringe dignity and bodily integrity in the way that taking a bodily sample, conducting a strip search, or performing a penile swab would. Further, searches in the home are more likely than those types of searches to raise other legitimate police objectives, such as locating potential victims needing help or aggressors posing a safety risk. Accordingly, the additional protection necessary did not need to be as high as the absolute prohibition on taking bodily samples or the incorporation of a reasonable and probable grounds standard as with strip searches incident to arrest or penile swabs.

Warrantless searches of the home are *prima facie* unreasonable, and *Stairs* created only a limited exception to that rule. To properly understand the rule created there, it is important to see that it in effect distinguishes three areas which can be thought of as concentric circles: the area in the physical control of the accused, the surrounding area not in the physical control of but "sufficiently proximate" to the accused, and the portion of the house not sufficiently proximate. In the innermost ring, the area in the accused's physical control, there is no special case and the ordinary search incident to arrest rules apply. In the outermost ring there is also no special rule: the ordinary rule that a warrantless search of the home is not permitted continues to apply. It is only for the middle ring that the Court created a new rule.

There is no easy test for deciding which portions of the surrounding area are "sufficiently proximate." The Court described this as a "contextual and case-specific inquiry" which asks whether there is a "link between the location and purpose of the search and the grounds for the arrest" and held that "the determination must be made using a purposive approach to ensure that the police can adequately respond to the wide variety of factual situations that may arise."[287]

Where the search does relate to that sufficiently proximate area, two additional requirements beyond the ordinary search incident to arrest rules are imposed: 1) the police must have reasonable suspicion

286 *Ibid* at para 67.

287 *Stairs*, above note 236 at para 60.

that there is a safety risk to the police, the accused, or the public which would be addressed by the search; and 2) the search must be conducted in a reasonable manner tailored to the heightened privacy interests in a home. Note that this standard is less stringent than those for strip searches or penile swabs in that only reasonable *suspicion*, as opposed to reasonable grounds, is required.

To establish reasonable suspicion, the police must subjectively have a safety concern and must point to a constellation of objectively discernible facts assessed against the totality of the circumstances giving rise to the suspicion of the risk. In addition, the police must have reason to suspect that the search will address the risk. Relevant considerations include (a) the need for a search, (b) the nature of the apprehended risk, (c) the potential consequences of not taking protective measures, (d) the availability of alternative measures, and (e) the likelihood that the contemplated risk actually exists.[288]

To establish that a search was conducted in a reasonable manner, the police must show that it was tailored to its specific purpose, to the circumstances of the arrest, and to the nature of the offence. As a general rule, the police cannot use the search incident to arrest power to justify searching every nook and cranny of the house: the search should be no more intrusive than is necessary to resolve the police's reasonable suspicion. It would be good practice for the police to take detailed notes, and insufficient notes could lead a trial judge to make adverse findings impacting the reasonableness of the search.

The fifth special case, and one with the least stringent additional requirements, relates to the search of cell phones incident to arrest. Cell phones raise particularly acute privacy concerns, because they

> may have immense storage capacity, may generate information about intimate details of the user's interests, habits and identity without the knowledge or intent of the user, may retain information even after the user thinks that it has been destroyed, and may provide access to information that is in no meaningful sense "at" the location of the search.[289]

A cell phone search, however, is less intrusive than either a bodily sample or strip search because those searches "*invariably* and *inherently*" constitute very great invasions of privacy, while cell phone searches have only the potential to do so.[290] As a result, the Court rejected the

---

288 *Stairs*, above note 236 at para 69.

289 *Fearon*, above note 140 at para 51.

290 *Ibid* at para 55. Note in this regard that the Court chose not to distinguish, in the rule it created, between "smart" and "dumb" phones, holding that the same rules would apply to all.

suggestions that there should be a categorical prohibition on search incident to arrest of cell phones, that there should be a reasonable and probable grounds requirement, or that such searches should be limited to exigent circumstances.

Instead, cell phone searches are subject to three additional requirements, which are aimed at limiting their intrusiveness and keeping them within the truly "incidental" range. First, such searches can be undertaken only if the investigation will be significantly hampered without the ability to promptly search the cell phone incident to arrest. This requirement is similar to the question of whether evidence is in danger of going out of existence: cell phone searches are permitted only where there is thought to be another suspect still at large, stolen property that could be immediately recovered, firearms unaccounted for, or something similar. In the absence of such circumstances, "it is hard to see how police could show that the prompt search of a suspect's cell phone could be considered truly incidental to the arrest as it serves no immediate investigative purpose."[291] Second, police cannot engage in an open-ended search of the contents of the cell phone: in general, they will be only able to examine things such as recently sent or drafted emails, texts, photos, and the call log, since those are the only sorts of items likely to have a link to the need for prompt examination. Any search more extensive than that would require the police to obtain a warrant. This requirement is meant to balance individual and state interests, in the sense that the amount of intrusion on privacy allowed will be limited to that which is justified given the seriousness of the offence: indeed, for a minor offence a cell phone search will generally not be justified at all.[292] Finally, police are required to take detailed notes of what they have examined on the device and how it was searched.[293] This requirement is meant both to focus the officers on searching only for those things that are truly incidental and to facilitate after-the-fact review, since prior authorization has not taken place.[294]

*Fearon* was specific to cell phones, but declined to distinguish between relatively unsophisticated devices and those which are the equivalent of a computer.[295] It has been held that the logic which applies to increased restrictions on cell phone searches applies similarly in the

291 *Ibid* at para 80.

292 *Ibid* at para 79. On a related point, see *R v Kossick*, 2018 SKCA 55, holding that the plain view doctrine does not apply to messages which appear on an unlocked cell phone's screen while it is in the possession of the police.

293 *Fearon*, above note 140 at para 83.

294 *Ibid* at para 82.

295 *Ibid* at para 52.

case of other items, such as a USB key, which are therefore entitled to the same protection.[296] Exactly when such extra protection might apply remains to be authoritatively determined.[297]

c. Search Incident to Investigative Detention

In *R v Mann*, the Court created a common law power of search incident to investigative detention.[298] While superficially similar to search incident to arrest, this search power has some noteworthy differences. Arguably, it ought not to be called search "incident to" investigative detention, since the authority for it does not flow directly from the fact that an investigative detention has occurred. That is, when a suspect has been *arrested*, no independent reasonable grounds for a search need to exist because the arrest itself would have been illegal without such grounds. An investigative detention, however, typically occurs when there are no reasonable grounds for an arrest. As a result, the Court has held that a search cannot automatically be conducted in such circumstances. Rather, there must be independent reasonable grounds specifically justifying the search.

Also, the scope of a search incident to investigative detention is more limited than a search incident to arrest because it is limited to concerns of officer or public safety. A search incident to *arrest* can be conducted on those grounds, or to protect evidence from destruction at the hands of the arrestee or others, and to discover evidence to be used at trial, but those latter purposes are not permitted when only an investigative detention is justified.[299]

Further, the Court notes that, in accordance with *R v Collins*, the search must be conducted in a reasonable manner. In this context, the Court held that that meant the search must be limited to a pat-down of the accused. Only if that pat-down gives rise to reasonable grounds to believe that a more intrusive search is necessary will an officer be enabled to proceed further and, for example, reach into a suspect's pocket. In addition, the search must be both objectively and subjectively justified. Ultimately, the Court concluded:

---

296 *Balendra*, above note 248.

297 See, for example, the pre-*Fearon* decision in *R v Caron*, 2011 BCCA 56, holding at para 60 that "a digital camera may serve as an electronic journal or diary."

298 *Mann*, above note 167. In *Mann*, the Court also first approved the existence of a police power to detain for investigative purposes. See the discussion of that power in Chapter 7. For an explanation of this issue in chart form, see *Anatomy of Criminal Procedure*, above note 8, Chart 1.1(a)(iii), "Search Incident to Investigative Detention."

299 *Caslake*, above note 16.

where a police officer has reasonable grounds to believe that his or her safety or that of others is at risk, the officer may engage in a protective pat-down search of the detained individual. Both the detention and the pat-down search must be conducted in a reasonable manner.[300]

On the facts of *Mann*, the Court concluded that the initial pat-down search was justified (Mann had been stopped in connection with a break and enter and so may have had tools that could be used as weapons, and was stopped after midnight in an area with no other people around).[301] However, there was no justification for going beyond the initial pat-down. On the initial pat-down the officer felt something soft in the accused's pocket, but that did not reasonably give rise to safety concerns, and so the officer was not justified in then reaching into the pocket to see what was there. Therefore, the search violated section 8. Indeed, the Court found the violation to be serious enough to justify the exclusion of the evidence under section 24(2).

As is frequently the case with the common law, there has been some slippage around this search power, resulting in its expansion.[302] The Supreme Court was specific that the power was merely one "to conduct a pat-down search" incident to an investigative detention.[303] However, it has been held that the search might also include questioning the accused, though only if those questions relate specifically to safety concerns.[304] In addition, some lower court decisions have expanded the scope of the pat-down to include looking in items carried by the accused, like a fanny pack or purse, still provided the search is done for safety purposes.[305] Other decisions have expanded the search

300 *Mann*, above note 167 at para 45.

301 *Ibid* at para 47. The absence of other people is a curious rationale. The only purpose for which such searches are permitted is to protect the safety of the officer *or others*. That would suggest that the presence of other people would increase the justification for a search, which, in turn, suggests that their absence would reduce the need. The presence of others and their absence cannot both add to the justification for the search.

302 See Scott Latimer, "The Expanded Scope of Search Incident to Investigative Detention" (2007) 48 *Criminal Reports* (6th) 201.

303 *Mann*, above note 167 at para 40.

304 *R v Patrick*, 2017 BCCA 57 at para 102: "questioning a detainee about to be frisk searched as to whether they are in possession of anything that might cause the searching officer injury is minimally intrusive … narrowly tailored questions of this kind motivated *solely* by safety concerns are permissible." (emphasis in original)

305 See, for example, *R v Thibodeau*, 2007 BCCA 489 and *R v Sheck*, 2015 BCCA 471 [*Sheck*]. See also *R v McKenzie*, 2022 MBCA 3 [*McKenzie*] at para 49, rejecting the argument "that *Mann* stands for the proposition that a search incident to a

power to the area of a car in which the accused had been sitting when detained,[306] to other portions of the interior of a vehicle,[307] or even to the trunk of such a vehicle, although that last result should be seen as questionable.[308]

There is also a curious confusion around the standard for using this power. *Mann* was very specific that "the officer must *believe on reasonable grounds* that his or her own safety, or the safety of others, is at risk."[309] Shortly afterward, the Court was asked to reconsider this particular aspect of their decision, on the basis that if there were only reasonable grounds to *suspect* that the detainee was connected to an offence at all (which is all that the investigative detention power requires), then there were not likely to be reasonable grounds to *believe* that that detainee presented a safety risk. Alternatively, if there were reasonable grounds to believe the accused presented a safety risk, then grounds for arrest likely existed. However, the Court declined this request for a rehearing.[310] Subsequently, when creating the safety search power in *R v MacDonald* (discussed immediately below), the Court returned to an explicit discussion of this standard.[311] The majority quoted the statement from *Mann* above, and relied on that in deciding that the standard for a freestanding safety search was also reasonable grounds, *not* reasonable suspicion.

However, despite what seem like these quite clear repeated pronouncements, some lower courts had, prior to *MacDonald*, decided that search incident to investigative detention required only reasonable suspicion rather than reasonable grounds, generally because of what is seen as the impracticality of the "reasonable grounds" standard. That was also the view of the minority in *MacDonald* as to what the safety

---

detention must follow a rigid sequence of a pat-down search first, before a bag or pocket may be opened or otherwise searched,"

306 *Plummer*, above note 50 or *R v Webber*, 2019 BCCA 208 [*Webber*].

307 See *Ahmed*, above note 105 at para 61: "A pat-down alone would be pointless if the occupants could simply return to the car and arm themselves with a gun left in easy reach."

308 *R v Lee*, 2017 ONCA 654 [*Lee* 2017]. As the dissenting judge points out, the majority decision amounts to creating at common law a power which Parliament had decided against creating. The search was made to look for a firearm in a vehicle in exigent circumstances: s 117.02 of the *Code* creates a power governing that situation, and all parties agreed that the requirements of that section were not met.

309 *Mann*, above note 167 at para 40 (emphasis added).

310 See James Stribopoulos, "The Limits of Judicially Created Police Powers: Investigative Detention after *Mann*," 2006 52 299 at n 44 and n 45.

311 *R v MacDonald*, 2014 SCC 3.

search standard ought to be, by analogy to *Mann*.[312] The decision in *MacDonald* has therefore led some lower courts to question whether the standard for search incident to investigative detention has now been *raised* — or "recalibrated," as it has sometimes been put — to be reasonable grounds rather than reasonable suspicion. In most cases those decisions have not found it necessary to answer the question, typically because the result on the facts of the particular case would be the same either way, but it has also been found that the standard is "still" that of reasonable suspicion.[313] On the other hand there are also cases which simply use the "reasonable grounds" standard without adverting to the question of whether it was ever lower or not.[314]

It might be that in some circumstances there is no conflict between having a higher standard for the search than for the detention. In *Tim*, for example, the accused was found to have been unlawfully arrested on the basis that the reasonable grounds standard was not met, but he was at the same time subject to a lawful investigative detention in relation to a traffic accident. He had been searched (unlawfully at first) which had turned up bullets on his person. The officer then saw him walking oddly as though he had something hidden in his pants and saw two more bullets fall from the accused's pant leg: in those circumstances the officer had reasonable grounds to believe there was a safety concern.[315] Similarly in *Buakasa*, based on information about a possible firearm police officers conducted a safety search of a vehicle even though they were not arresting the driver of that vehicle. The trial judge found that the information in the hands of the police gave them reasonable grounds to have a safety concern related to a possible

---

312 The minority argument is complex, but in part rests on the view that reasonable grounds to believe there is a "risk," as opposed to reasonable grounds to believe there is a certainty, amounts to reasonable suspicion. The minority also point to a footnote in *Chehil*, above note 37, describing *Mann* as creating a search power based on reasonable suspicion, though it should be noted that that same footnote also describes — incorrectly — *M(MR)*, above note 3, as creating a reasonable suspicion search power.

313 For cases raising but not settling the point see *R v Ahmed-Kadir*, 2015 BCCA 346, *R v Peterkin*, 2015 ONCA 8, *Sheck*, above note 305, *R v Patrick*, 2017 BCCA 57, *R v Del Corro*, 2019 ABCA 156, or *McKenzie*, above note 305. See also *Webber*, above note 306 at para 65, concluding that "the Supreme Court of Canada did not recalibrate the test for lawful police safety searches from the traditional 'reasonable suspicion' standard."

314 See, for example, *Lee* 2017, above note 277. See also the discussion in *Labreche-Meyer c R*, 2025 QCCQ 1715.

315 *R v Tim*, 2022 SCC 12.

firearm in the *vehicle*, even if it did not give them reasonable grounds to connect that firearm to the accused.[316]

However, that will not always be the case, which leaves the law in an unusual situation. The Supreme Court of Canada was quite clear initially, and on re-examination, that the standard for a search incident to investigative detention is reasonable grounds to believe. It has continued to describe the standard for the initial detention and for the search differently much more recently, as though there is no controversy over the issue in lower courts.[317] However, few cases reach the Supreme Court. On the other hand, courts of appeal in two of the most populous provinces seem inclined to the reasonable suspicion standard, and it is probably fair to say that that seems to be the prevailing opinion. As a practical matter it might not matter whether the reasonable suspicion standard is "wrong" unless the accused in question is willing and able to take the matter to the Supreme Court.

#### d. Safety Searches

The Supreme Court's 2014 decision in *R v MacDonald* introduced another common law search power to Canadian law.[318] Both search incident to arrest and search incident to investigative detention had brought along with them the power for police to search a person for safety purposes: that is, to see whether the person had a weapon which could be a threat to the officer or others. In the case of an arrest, reasonable grounds to believe that the person had already committed an offence needed to be made out; in the case of a detention, reasonable grounds to believe that the person had a weapon were needed. In *MacDonald*, the Court turned that into a freestanding power which could be exercised in any circumstance where the requirements were made out, without needing to be "incident" to something else.

---

316 *R v Buakasa*, 2023 ONCA 383. At issue in the case was a safety search (discussed immediately below) rather than a search incident to investigative detention, but the reasoning could apply in either context.

317 See, for example, *Tim*, above note 315 at para 53:

> This Court in *Mann* recognized that the police have a common law power to search incident to investigative detention under certain circumstances. Speaking for the majority, Iacobucci J. stated that "police officers may detain an individual for investigative purposes if there are reasonable grounds to suspect in all the circumstances that the individual is connected to a particular crime and that such a detention is necessary" (para. 45). He added that a police officer "may engage in a protective pat-down search of the detained individual" when the officer "has reasonable grounds to believe that his or her safety or that of others is at risk" (para. 45).

318 *MacDonald*, above note 318.

A police officer had attended at MacDonald's condominium in response to a noise complaint and knocked on the door. MacDonald opened the door only partway and did not answer when the officer asked what he was holding in his hand, hidden behind his leg. Thinking that the object might be a knife, the officer pushed the door open further, saw that the object, in fact, was a gun, and forced her way into the apartment. The Court concluded that the officer was authorized by the common law to act as she had. Specifically, they applied the *Waterfield* test as it has been developed in Canada to allow for the creation of new common law powers.[319] That test requires first that the officer was acting within the general scope of her duties, which was satisfied because the police have a common law duty to protect life and safety. The second question was whether what the officer did was a justifiable exercise of powers associated with the duty, or as it has come to be phrased in the jurisprudence on this test, whether the police action was *reasonably necessary* for the carrying out of the particular duty in light of all the circumstances.[320] In considering whether this test is made out in any particular situation, the Court held that three sets of factors must be considered: (1) the importance of the performance of the duty to the public good; (2) the necessity of the interference with individual liberty for the performance of the duty; and (3) the extent of the interference with individual liberty. Where weighing these factors leads to the conclusion that a search should be allowed, that search is authorized by law.[321]

Some structure has been imposed on this otherwise situation-specific test. First, such a search will be authorized by law only if the police officer believes on reasonable grounds that their safety or that of the public is at stake and that, as a result, it is necessary to conduct a search. Second, the infringement on individual liberty will be justified only to the extent that it is necessary to search for weapons. In that event, although the way in which a safety search is carried out will vary from case to case, the authority for the search runs out at the point at which the search for weapons is finished.[322]

There has been some disagreement over one aspect of implementing this power. In the case of both search incident to arrest and search incident to investigative detention, the search will be unlawful if the

---

319 See the discussion of *R v Waterfield*, [1963] 3 All ER 659 (CA), in Chapter 2, Section A(3)(b).

320 See, for the development of this test in Canada, the discussion in Chapter 5, Section C.

321 *MacDonald*, above note 318 at para 37.

322 *Ibid* at para 39.

prior arrest or detention was not lawful. Where the safety search is not tied to any prior power, there is room for dispute about whether any equivalent rule applies. The prevailing — and preferable — view is that while there need not be some separate lawful power the police were exercising beforehand, it does not follow that they can have been acting unlawfully: "*MacDonald* does not extend to permitting a safety search as incident to an arbitrary (*i.e. otherwise unlawful*) detention."[323] The Supreme Court has not explicitly endorsed this view, but they do seem to act in accordance with it. In *Tim*, the accused was searched four separate times over the course of an encounter, the first two being unlawful because his arrest on drug charges was unlawful. The third search was potentially incident to an investigative detention, but the Court found that an investigative detention based on the drug charges would not have been lawful: however, they also found that he was simultaneously subject to a lawful investigative detention on a traffic-related issue. The important point is that the Court saw it as *necessary* to find the officer to have been lawfully detaining the accused as a prerequisite to the legality of the search. If that were not a requirement, they could have simply considered the free-standing safety search power.[324] It has also been held that police cannot manipulate the circumstances in order to create the need for a safety search.[325]

Another issue which has arisen with regard to safety searches is whether the threat to safety must be imminent. It is surprising that this should be a question. In creating the power in *MacDonald*, the Court said "the principles laid down in *Mann* and reaffirmed in *Clayton* require the existence of circumstances establishing the necessity of safety searches, reasonably and objectively considered, to address an *imminent* threat to the safety of the public or the police"[326] and "it is only when police officers have reasonable grounds to believe that there is an *imminent* threat to their safety that it will be reasonably necessary to conduct such a search"[327] (emphasis added). Nonetheless the British Columbia Court of Appeal has concluded that the threat need not be imminent, though this view does not seem to have taken root in any other province to date.[328]

323 *Squires*, above note 191 at para 9 (emphasis in the original).

324 *Tim*, above note 315 at paras 51–64.

325 See also *R v McGuffie*, 2016 ONCA 365 at para 54: "the police cannot, through unlawful conduct, create a circumstance said to justify a safety search of an individual." For the contrary view, however, see *Fountain*, above note 167.

326 *MacDonald*, above note 318 at para 41.

327 *MacDonald*, above note 318 at para 43.

328 See *R v Dhillon*, 2023 BCCA 38. The reasoning hearkens back to the same question around the standard for the search. In essence, the Court of Appeal argues

It is arguable that the law in this area is not yet fully developed. In fact, *MacDonald* saw a 4:3 split over the exact standard for the safety search power. The majority held that, as noted, the power existed only when the police had reasonable grounds to believe that a threat to safety was present. The three judge minority, in contrast, would have held that the power should be permitted on the lower standard of "reasonable suspicion" (see the more detailed discussion of reasonable grounds versus reasonable suspicion later in this chapter, in Section C(2)). This had been a question of some disagreement earlier in the Court,[329] and given that there is not yet a decision with a five-judge majority on the point, it is possible that the standard could change. (See also the discussion above concerning the impact of this finding on the separate power of search incident to investigative detention.)

e. Sniffer Dog Searches

Sniffer dog searches — that is, the use of trained dogs to detect the smell of marijuana or other narcotics — can be thought of as having meandered their way into existence in Canadian law. Police began using sniffer dogs on backpacks, at airports or bus stations, or while inspecting vehicles, without any kind of authorization. This use was challenged as violating section 8 on the basis that it was a warrantless search. Most of the early caselaw focused on the question of whether the use of a sniffer dog was a search *at all*: that is, the Crown argued with some success that a person had no reasonable expectation of privacy in the smells coming from their belongings, especially smells that were not detectable by human senses. This argument succeeded at times, for example in *Kang-Brown*, where the Alberta Court of Appeal concluded that the accused whose bag was sniffed by a dog at a bus station had not been subject to a search and therefore had no section 8 claim.[330]

The Supreme Court of Canada reversed that particular finding, but in an odd way. Nine judges rendered four separate decisions in *Kang-Brown*, and there is no set of reasoning that can be considered the majority. However, none of the nine judges directly address the

---

that *Mann* did not articulate an imminence requirement, that *MacDonald* did not clearly change *Mann*, and therefore that there is no imminence requirement.

329 In *R v Aucoin*, 2012 SCC 66 [*Aucoin*], a search was found to be unreasonable by both the majority and the minority. In *Aucoin*, the minority would have held that all searches for safety purposes required reasonable grounds; the majority held that the particular search in that case required reasonable grounds but refused to commit to the more general proposition. Justice Moldaver wrote the majority decision in *Aucoin* and was the author of the dissent in *MacDonald*, above note 318.

330 *Brown* 2006, above note 122.

reasoning in the court below concerning reasonable expectation of privacy, and indeed only three judges address the issue at all.[331] All nine judges concluded that the use of a sniffer dog was a search and where they disagreed was over whether that search was authorized by law. Four judges — the largest single group of judges but the dissent in the end — would have held that there was no authority for the search and, therefore, there was a section 8 violation. Two different cohorts of two judges each subscribed to decisions saying that police had a common law power to use a sniffer dog where they had reasonable suspicion about the particular accused. Finally, one judge would have held that police had the power to use a sniffer dog based on "generalized suspicion": that is, since there is reason in general to be suspicious of things arriving at airports, for example, police could use sniffer dogs in situations like that.[332]

The result left some uncertainty, but police took the decision to amount to an endorsement of a reasonable suspicion common law sniffer dog power, presumably on the theory that four judges had adopted that view and one judge had allowed for an even broader power. That was where the matter stood for four years, until the matter returned to the Supreme Court in *Chehil* and *MacKenzie*, when the existence of a reasonable suspicion sniffer dog search power was authoritatively confirmed: "In *Kang-Brown*, a majority of the Court found that the decision to deploy a sniffer dog meets the *Collins* test where the police have a reasonable suspicion based on objective, ascertainable facts that evidence of an offence will be discovered."[333]

Specifically, in order to deploy a drug-sniffing dog, the police must be able to point to a constellation of facts that reasonably support the suspicion of drug-related activity that the dog deployed is trained to detect. Doing this does not require the police to point to a specific ongoing crime or to identify the precise illegal substance being searched for, but it must be linked to the possession, traffic, or production of drugs or other drug-related contraband.[334] The Court also elaborated in *Chehil* on the meaning of "reasonable suspicion": this aspect of the case

---

331 Justice Deschamps for herself and Rothstein J applies the totality of the circumstances test while Bastarache J for himself devotes just a paragraph to the issue.

332 On the same day it decided *Kang-Brown*, above note 37, the Court also handed down *AM*, above note 37, concerning the use of sniffer dogs without reasonable suspicion or reasonable grounds at a school. The judges split in exactly the same 4:2:2:1 fashion in *AM* as in *Kang-Brown*.

333 *Chehil*, above note 37 at para 19.

334 *Ibid* at paras 36 and 37.

will be discussed in Section C(2)(a), below in this chapter, when the reasonableness of warrantless search laws is considered.

f. Inventory Searches

It must be made clear at the start that this subsection is not meant to describe a police power called an "inventory search": it is to suggest there is *not*, in fact, such a power. The Supreme Court has held that there is no inventory search power, but police continue to behave as though there is, and some courts have been persuaded to agree with them.

In *R v Caslake*, police arrested the accused, towed his car to a garage, and six hours later searched it. The central issue at trial was whether that search was authorized by law, and the primary argument in favour of the claim that it was so authorized would have been that the search was made incident to arrest. The Court rejected that argument, for the central reason that the officer was not subjectively conducting a search incident to arrest: his purpose in conducting the search was to comply with "an RCMP policy which required that the interior of impounded vehicles be inventoried."[335]

The Crown's secondary argument that the search should be seen as authorized by law was therefore that the Court should create an "inventory search exception" to section 8. That argument did not succeed either. Strictly the majority said in *Caslake* that it was not necessary to decide whether such an exception existed, although in that case their reasoning clearly excluded the argument that taking an inventory itself counts as "authorization" for purposes of the *Collins* test. They noted that "[t]he respondent was unable to find either statutory or common-law authority for inventory searches," which meant that it was not authorized by law.[336] And in any event the Court returned to the issue in *Nolet*, finding without caveat that "*Caslake* ruled that 'an inventory search *per se* does not serve a "valid objective in pursuit of the ends of criminal justice"' because its purposes 'relate to concerns extraneous to the criminal law.'"[337]

It is important to recognize a distinction here. The issue is not whether police are allowed to make an inventory of the contents of vehicles they search: they are. The issue is whether making an inventory counts as "authorization by law" to conduct a search for the purposes of section 8. To talk about an "inventory search" is to conflate

335 *Caslake*, above note 16 at para 42. See the discussion above under "Search Incident to Arrest."

336 *Ibid* at para 30.

337 *Nolet*, above note 255 at para 53.

those two issues. Indeed, the phrase "inventory search" is itself misleading and contributes to the conflation. To make a record of all the items in a location is to conduct an inventory: it is quite unnatural to refer to it as a "search" at all. The two things are quite distinct. This distinction is the core of the Court's reasoning in *Caslake*, where they held "If the police feel the need to inventory a car in their possession for their own purposes, that is one thing. However, if they wish to tender the fruits of that inventory search into evidence at a criminal trial, the search must be conducted under some lawful authority."[338]

Nonetheless Courts of Appeal have regularly acceded to the Crown's argument that particular inventory searches conducted by police constituted authorization by law for section 8 purposes, seemingly because they miss this crucial distinction. Typically they have done so by distinguishing the Supreme Court authorities on the basis of a provincial highway traffic act power.[339] However, in each of those cases, the statutory provision in question did not create a search power, but rather gave the police the power to impound a vehicle in certain circumstances: the officers in question then took an inventory of the impounded vehicles. Factually that situation is identical to that in *Nolet*, where there was a statutory power to seize the vehicle and police then conducted an inventory search. The Supreme Court found that to be a section 8 violation, and so the later cases cannot properly be distinguished on that basis.[340]

In any case, the approach in these Court of Appeal cases ignores the distinction which was crucial to the reasoning in *Caslake*. *Caslake* did not hold that police were not permitted to take an inventory of a vehicle they had seized: it held that the authority to do *that* did not constitute "authorization by law" for purposes of claiming that evidence had been found through a lawful search. Even if it is accepted that the power to impound a vehicle creates a statutory ability to take an inventory of

---

338 *Ibid*.

339 See, for example, *R v Nicolosi* (1998), 127 CCC (3d) 176 (Ont CA); *Ellis*, above note 138; *R v Dunkley*, 2016 ONCA 597 (which does not find the power to be made out on the facts of the case); *Cuff*, above note 138; or *R v Russell*, 2018 BCCA 330. In contrast, see *R v Harflett*, 2016 ONCA 248, which did not find an inventory search power. See also *R v Ahmed*, 2019 SKCA 47 at paras 18 and 19, noting the cases on both sides of this issue.

340 See the discussion in Steve Coughlan, "*R v Harflett*: Case Comment" (2016) 28 CR (7th) 54. Note as well that there is an inconsistency in the highway traffic act argument. Frequently, the power to impound has been found to exist on the basis that the vehicle has been abandoned. However, if the vehicle were truly abandoned there would be an argument that the accused no longer had a reasonable expectation of privacy, and so no search power would be needed.

that vehicle, it does not follow that there is no section 8 violation in attempting to use whatever was found in a criminal prosecution.

There is an argument which does not seem to have been made but which might be relevant here. Section 489(2) of the *Criminal Code* allows an officer who is "lawfully present in a place … in the execution of duties" to seize evidence of criminal offences found in that place. As noted above, under "*Warrantless Seizures*," the limits on section 489(2) are not entirely clear: it is meant only to be a seizure power, not a search power, and the meaning of "lawfully present" has not been developed. However, it is certainly possible that some seizures which courts have found to be authorized as inventory searches could instead have been found lawful under s 489(2).

It will be useful if the Supreme Court has occasion to return to this issue at some point.

*iii) Authorization by Consent*

The final fashion in which a warrantless search can be authorized is if the suspect consents to the search: "valid consent acts as a waiver of the claimant's section 8 rights."[341] The central questions to be asked in such cases concern whether the consent was valid and the extent of the consent.

The Court has recognized that an apparent consent must be taken with a grain of salt. In *R v Dedman*, dealing with a random stop by police officers of a vehicle, it observed:

> because of the intimidating nature of police action and uncertainty as to the extent of police powers, compliance in such circumstances cannot be regarded as voluntary in any meaningful sense . . . . A person should not be penalized for compliance with a signal to stop by having it treated as a waiver or renunciation of rights, or as supplying a want of authority for the stop.[342]

As the Ontario Court of Appeal has noted, "acquiescence and compliance signal only a failure to object; they do not constitute consent."[343] Therefore, a certain balance must be struck in considering consent. On the one hand, it is reasonable in some situations for police officers to

341 *Reeves*, above note 35 at para 13.

342 [1985] 2 SCR 2 at para 59 [*Dedman*].

343 *R v Wills* (1992), 12 CR (4th) 58 at para 44 (Ont CA) [*Wills*]. Similarly see *Davidson*, above note 226, where the police entered the accused's home but were found to have acted unlawfully: the evidence showed that the accused "acquiesced to the police's inevitable intrusion into his home, but not that he consented" (para 34).

ask a person, in the absence of reasonable grounds, whether they will consent to a search. On the other hand, such a search will be warrantless and therefore *prima facie* unreasonable. Further, the consent will have acted as a waiver of *Charter* rights, and the standard for finding waiver has appropriately been set high.[344]

In some circumstances, police with suspicions but without reasonable grounds will try to create a situation in which they can obtain the suspect's consent to a search.[345] Such a search may be permissible, but sometimes a suspect will feel no option but to consent to the search. It is important, therefore, to determine when consent is valid. The Court has noted that a valid waiver requires that the accused have at least "sufficient available information to make the preference meaningful."[346] The Ontario Court of Appeal in *R v Wills* held that several conditions need to be satisfied:

> In order for consent to operate as a waiver of section 8 rights, the Crown must establish on balance that i) there was a consent, express or implied; ii) the giver of the consent had the authority to give the consent in question; iii) the consent was voluntary and was not the product of police oppression, coercion or other external conduct which negated the freedom to choose whether to not to allow the police to pursue the course of conduct requested; iv) the giver of the consent was aware of the nature of the police conduct to which he or she was being asked to give consent; v) the giver of the consent was aware of his or her right to refuse to permit the police to engage in the conduct requested, and; vi) the giver of the consent was aware of the potential consequences of giving the consent.[347]

Therefore, although there is no constitutional obligation to inform a suspect of the right to refuse a search, failure to do so will likely result in the search being found involuntary.[348]

There is not always an obligation to inform an accused of the right to counsel prior to a consensual search.[349] In some circumstances, the accused will have been detained prior to the search and so is entitled to be informed under section 10(b). In that event, the failure to inform the accused of the right to counsel could lead to violations under both

---

344 *R v Clarkson*, [1986] 1 SCR 383.

345 See, for example, *R v Truong*, 2002 BCCA 315; and *R v Jones*, 2002 NSSC 101.

346 *R v Borden*, [1994] 3 SCR 145 at para 34 [*Borden*], quoting *Wills*, above note 343.

347 *Wills*, *ibid*.

348 *R v Lewis* (1998), 38 OR 3d 540 (CA) [*Lewis*].

349 *Wills*, above note 343.

section 10(b) and section 8.[350] Further, when the search is nominally conducted with the suspect's consent, the police are required to suspend the search until the suspect has had the opportunity to consult with counsel.[351] However, if there is no *Charter* right to counsel, the important question is whether the suspect's consent was informed, a standard that can be achieved without access to counsel.

A further issue arises around the actual scope of consent given by a suspect. In some situations, evidence that is obtained from an accused can be used only for limited purposes.[352] Further, an accused can sometimes attach limits to the extent of the consent given.[353] It can be difficult in practice, however, to tell whether this has occurred or what limits apply.

In *Borden*,[354] police were investigating an accused in connection with two sexual assaults. A DNA sample was left at the scene of the first offence, but not the second. The accused was arrested for the second assault, and as part of their investigation the police asked him whether he would supply hair samples and a blood sample. Their primary motive was to see whether the sample would connect Borden to the first offence. They did not specifically disclose that fact to him, though the consent form he signed was deliberately worded to use the plural: "investigations."

The Court held that Borden had not consented to the use of his bodily samples in connection with the first investigation. Since there was also no statutory or common law authority allowing police to use them, the seizure was not authorized by law and his section 8 right was violated. It concluded:

> It was incumbent on the police, at a minimum, to make it clear to the respondent that they were treating his consent as a blanket consent to the use of the sample in relation to other offences in which he might be a suspect . . . it will not be necessary for the accused to have a detailed comprehension of every possible outcome of his or her consent. However, his or her understanding should include the fact that the police are also planning to use the product of the seizure in a different investigation from the one for which he or she is detained.[355]

350 *R v France*, 2002 NWTSC 32.

351 *Debot*, above note 178.

352 See *Dyment*, above note 42, where the Court held that blood samples taken by a doctor for medical purposes cannot simply be handed over to the police for use in a criminal investigation.

353 *R v Colarusso*, [1994] 1 SCR 20 at para 70 [*Colarusso*].

354 *Borden*, above note 346.

355 *Ibid* at paras 39–40.

This broad proposition has been narrowed by the Court's later decision in *R v Arp*.[356] The police must disclose any specific uses they intend at the time they take the sample. However, if further possible uses arise later, there is no bar to using the sample. In *Arp*, the accused had consented to provide hair samples in connection with a murder investigation. He was informed that any evidence arising from the samples would be used against him. In fact, he was discharged at the preliminary inquiry for that offence, but three years after providing the hair samples he was investigated for a second murder. Police used a warrant to obtain the hair samples, and DNA testing linked him to the second murder. Relying on *Borden*, the accused objected to use of the sample provided for one investigation in a different investigation, but the Court dismissed his appeal. The Court re-affirmed that any consent must be an informed one, but also held that

> if neither the police nor the consenting person limit the use which may be made of the evidence then, as a general rule no limitation or restriction should be placed on the use of that evidence . . . the obligation imposed on the police in obtaining a valid consent extends only to the disclosure of those anticipated purposes known to the police at the time the consent was given.[357]

On the facts of *Arp*, the Court held that the original seizure by consent was valid because the police did not know that Arp would later be the suspect in another homicide, and they did inform him that any evidence gathered would be used in court. In the absence of a specific limitation to his consent, the Court held that the accused had given up any expectation of privacy in the hair sample. Accordingly, his section 8 right was not violated.

Even where consent is not valid, it can still have some relevance. In deciding under section 24(2) whether evidence should be excluded, some courts have held that an officer's mistaken belief that the accused had consented to the search made the section 8 breach less serious.[358]

Finally, note that consent can be given only by the person with the privacy interest: that is, there is no doctrine of "third party consent." In *Cole* the police had conducted a warrantless search of a laptop used by a teacher which had been issued to him by a school board. The search was conducted because the school board had turned the laptop over to the police, reporting it to contain nude photographs of a student. The Court rejected the argument that the search had been conducted with

356 [1998] 3 SCR 339 [*Arp*].

357 *Ibid* at paras 87–88. See also *R v Colson*, 2008 ONCA 21.

358 See *Lewis*, above note 348; *R v Daley*, 2001 ABCA 155.

the consent of the school board. Although the accused had a diminished reasonable expectation of privacy, it was still *his* expectation, and to say that a third party could waive it would be inconsistent with the rules requiring such a consent to be fully informed and voluntary. The Court noted that although third party consent was an accepted doctrine in the United States, the privacy analysis there was based on the risk analysis approach which has been rejected in Canada.[359] This rejection of third party consent can carry over to shared items. In *Reeves*, a computer which the accused shared with his spouse was seized by the police, with his spouse's consent: however, the subject matter of the search was found to be the accused's data on the computer, and the spouse's consent to the seizure was not permitted to nullify the accused's privacy interest in that data.[360]

An unsettled issue in the law is the interrelationship between third party consent and entry into shared premises. In *Reeves*, the police entered into common areas in the home the accused shared with his spouse: they did so without his knowledge but with her consent. The majority noted that whether police entry into a shared home with the consent of one resident violated the *Charter* raised complex questions, and left it to be decided in a later case.[361]

### b) Searches with a Warrant

One foundational principle of section 8 law is that a warrantless search[362] is *prima facie* unreasonable.[363] The creation of this rule has had an observable effect on the state of the law. Specifically, in a number of early *Charter* cases, police undertook particular forms of investigation and did so without a warrant because no warrant provision existed that would have authorized the investigation in question existed. The Court therefore found the search to violate the *Charter*, and in response Parliament created a new warrant provision.

*Wong* is a seminal example of this approach. The police wanted to investigate illegal gambling in a hotel room, and to do so installed a hidden camera to visually record the activity. Had they been planning to audiotape, they could have obtained an electronic surveillance authorization under Part VI of the *Code*, but those provisions did not

359 *Cole*, above note 25 at paras 74–79.

360 *Reeves*, above note 35 at para 47.

361 *Ibid* at paras 23–26.

362 For an explanation in chart form of the relationship between various warrants provisions, see *Anatomy of Criminal Procedure*, above note 8, Chart 1.1(b)(ii), "Which Warrant is Appropriate?"

363 *Hunter*, above note 6.

deal with videotaping. The search warrant provisions in section 487 of the *Code*, the only real alternative that existed at the time, were limited to obtaining warrants to search for physical items: the images captured by a video camera would not fall within that category. As a result, no warrant *could* have authorized the police action, and so they proceeded without a warrant. The Crown argued, in essence, that in the absence of a scheme imposing limits on police investigative techniques, it was open to the police to proceed as they had; the Court concluded that this approach "wholly misunderstands" the way section 8 works.[364] Rather, they held, the police were allowed to use an investigative technique *only if* some law specifically authorized them to do so. In addition, the Court held that any such authorizations should not be created at common law, but instead should come from Parliament:

> it does not sit well for the courts, as the protectors of our fundamental rights, to widen the possibility of encroachments on these personal liberties. It falls to Parliament to make incursions on fundamental rights if it is of the view that they are needed for the protection of the public in a properly balanced system of criminal justice.[365]

As a result, many changes have been made to the *Code* in the years since *Wong* either to add powers in situations where a search was found unconstitutional in the absence of one or to avoid any such finding in the first place. Where once the search warrant provision in section 487 of the *Code* was followed immediately by section 488, there are now more than forty other provisions in between.[366] Warrant provisions now not only authorize searches of places for things with search warrants, but also obtaining data from financial organizations,[367] using devices to

---

364 *Wong*, above note 33 at para 28.

365 *Ibid* at para 35. They held as well at para 36:

> It is for Parliament, and Parliament alone, to set out the conditions under which law enforcement agencies may employ video surveillance technology in their fight against crime. Moreover, the same holds true for any other technology which the progress of science places at the disposal of the state in the years to come. Until such time as Parliament, in its wisdom, specifically provides for a code of conduct for a particular invasive technology, the courts should forebear from crafting procedures authorizing the deployment of the technology in question.

366 Further on this, see the discussion in Michal Fairburn, "Twenty-Five Years in Search of a Reasonable Approach" (2008) 40 *Supreme Court Law Review* (2d) 55. Note that because of successive amendments to the same powers, the *Code* contains sections with such remarkable numbers as s 487.055(1)(c.1).

367 Section 487.018.

track the movements of persons or vehicles,[368] obtaining records identifying who has transmitted a particular message,[369] obtaining DNA from a suspect,[370] video surveillance,[371] and more. Indeed, the general warrant provision in section 487.01 of the *Code* literally has the potential to authorize the police to "do any thing." That particular provision is so broad in its impact as to go beyond merely being a search power, and so it is not discussed here, but instead is discussed in Chapter 5.

*i) Searching Places for Things: Section 487*

The search warrant provision, found in section 487 of the *Criminal Code*,[372] raises a number of issues worthy of note. Broadly, section 487 is a way to authorize searches of physical locations for physical objects. That is not absolutely true, since it is, for example, possible to obtain a warrant to get data from a computer, but it is the general thrust of the provision. In fact, that is more limiting than it might appear at first glance, and a good deal of the proliferation of other warrant provisions can be traced to the fact that often the police want to obtain evidence which is not a "thing."

Section 487 allows the issuance of a warrant for the search of a "building, receptacle or place" if a justice is satisfied on oath of reasonable grounds that evidence falling into one of four categories will be found. Each element, which reflects various aspects of the need for restraint in the use of investigative powers, is worth considering in turn.

A warrant must be issued by a justice: this requirement of the *Code* means that section 487 complies with one of the minimum constitutional prerequisites laid down in *Hunter*.[373] That justice must be sure that some particular person is charged with responsibility for the search. This does not require that only one officer be named, that no one not named in the warrant can participate in the search, or that everyone named in the warrant must participate; however, "there must

---

368 Section 487.017. See also s 492.1.

369 Section 487.015. See also s 492.2.

370 Section 487.04ff.

371 Section 487.01(4).

372 Section 11(1) of the *CDSA*, above note 174, though not identical in wording, is closely modelled on s 487 of the *Code*, and any analysis of the latter is likely to apply equally to the former. For an explanation of this issue in chart form, see *Anatomy of Criminal Procedure*, above note 8, Chart 1.1(b)(iv), "Section 487 Search Warrants."

373 *Hunter*, above note 6 at 162. See the further discussion of these requirements in Section C(2), below in this chapter.

be some person responsible for the way the search is carried out."[374] This issue of accountability is a reflection of the need for restraint in the use of state power. In the context of warrants issued under the previous *Narcotic Control Act*,[375] the Court characterized a warrant that did not describe the officer who was to conduct the search, limit the times during which the search could be conducted, or list the items being searched for as "a fishing license, not a search warrant."[376]

In addition, a person executing a search warrant has a duty to have it with them where feasible and to produce it on request.[377] That person is also required to give a copy of the warrant and a notice with the address of the court to which anything seized will be taken to any person who is present and in control of the place to be searched or if no such person is present, to affix the copy and the notice in a prominent location within the place.[378] Where a team of people execute a warrant it is sufficient for one of them to have a copy, and even in the case of a search by forced entry, the better practice would be for that person to be among the first group of officers in the door. However, the duty will still be complied with so long as the person in charge of the search has a copy and is immediately at hand.[379] A search warrant can be executed anywhere in Canada, provided that the person executing it is a peace officer or public office with authority to act in that capacity in the place where the warrant is executed.[380]

---

374 *R v Strachan*, [1988] 2 SCR 980 at para 28. The Court observes at para 30 that "the warrant should make it clear who is in charge of, and responsible for, the search . . . . Listing an entire drug squad by name in a warrant may undermine the effectiveness of the naming requirement just as much as a failure to name anyone at all."

375 Above note 176, s 94.

376 *R v Genest*, [1989] 1 SCR 59 [*Genest*].

377 Section 29.

378 Section 487.093(1). Section 487.093(2) provides that "subsection (1) does not apply if the warrant authorizes the search of anything that is detained under this Act after it has been lawfully seized."

379 *R v Cornell*, 2010 SCC 31 [*Cornell*].

380 Section 487(2). Until changes made in Bill C-75, *An Act to amend the Criminal Code, the Youth Criminal Justice Act and other Acts and to make consequential amendments to other Acts*, Royal Assent June 21, 2019, a warrant could not be executed outside of the territorial division where it was issued, unless it was endorsed by a justice in that other territorial division. Bill C-75 eliminated that requirement for s 487 warrants, and the similar requirement for wiretap authorizations (s 188.1), general warrants (s 487.01), assistance orders (s 487.02), DNA warrants (s 487.05), bodily impression warrants (s 487.092), tracking device warrants (s 492.1), transmission data recorder warrants (s 492.2), and *Controlled Drugs and Substances Act* warrants (s 11 of the *Controlled Drugs and Substances Act*). All of these powers are discussed elsewhere in this book.

The power to search is limited to a "building, receptacle or place." This authority does not allow a warrant to be issued to search a person[381] or to take hair samples.[382] This latter finding has become of less importance since the passage of section 487.05 of the *Code*, which allows for warrants to take bodily samples in order to obtain DNA. "Place" includes the area surrounding a building, which has two main consequences. First, it means that a warrant is available to search the exterior of buildings and the surrounding area. This leads to the result that, since it would be possible to obtain a warrant to search the area around a house in principle, a search of that area without a warrant is *prima facie* unreasonable, in accordance with the rule laid down in *Hunter*.[383] Second, when coupled with the need for specificity in warrants, this also means that a warrant to search the area around a house (the curtilage) does not include the ability to seize items found inside the house, while a warrant to search a house might not include the ability to search the area around the house or other buildings on the property.[384]

The justice must be satisfied of more than the possibility that evidence will be found; otherwise, intrusions based only on suspicion would be too readily permitted.[385] Further, the justice must be given facts allowing them personally to form the necessary reasonable and probable grounds and not simply be satisfied that the police officer has such a belief.[386] The Court has noted that the affidavit supporting a warrant need not be

> as lengthy as *À la recherche du temps perdu*, as lively as the *Kama Sutra*, or as detailed as an automotive repair manual. All that it must do is set out the facts fully and frankly for the authorizing judge in order that he or she can make an assessment of whether these rise to the standard required in the legal test for the authorization. Ideally, an affidavit should be not only full and frank but also clear and concise.[387]

---

381 *Laporte v Laganière* (1972), 8 CCC (2d) 343 (Que Ct QB) [*Laporte*].

382 *R v Légère*, [1998] NBJ No 712 (CA).

383 *Debot*, above note 178; *Kokesch*, above note 38; *Plant*, above note 28. However, see *Grant* 1993, above note 179, where the Court held that although the power in s 10 of the *NCA*, above note 176, to conduct warrantless searches of a place other than a dwelling house violated s 8, the section did not need to be struck down completely, but rather could be read down to apply only in exigent circumstances.

384 See, for example, *R v Chuhaniuk*, 2010 BCCA 403.

385 *Hunter*, above note 6 at 167.

386 *R v Pastro* (1988), 42 CCC (3d) 485 at 511 (Sask CA).

387 *R v Araujo*, [2000] 2 SCR 992 at para 46 [*Araujo*].

In this context, the Court has discouraged the use of "boiler plate" language in applications, on the basis that it adds little and can imply meaning which is not there. The Court has also recommended using affidavits directly from those with firsthand knowledge of the facts therein, such as the officers conducting the investigation.[388]

Beyond that, the requirement that the justice be satisfied on oath of reasonable grounds is interesting primarily for the issues of what will constitute reasonable grounds and how they may be obtained. For entirely understandable reasons, warrants are issued on an *ex parte* basis: the need for effective law enforcement certainly justifies not informing a suspect in advance of a search that will take place.[389] However, in accordance with the principle of restraint, it is open to an accused to argue after the fact that, even though the warrant was issued by an independent decision-maker based on sworn information, the warrant ought not to have been issued.[390]

Cases have held that the information justifying the issuing of a warrant can be hearsay and need not be admissible in court. Similarly, the information might be privileged, because the police obtained the information from a confidential informer, for example. The Court has held that the identity of an informer need not be disclosed, either on an application to quash or at trial, unless the accused shows that disclosure of the identity of the informer "is necessary to establish the innocence of the accused" (known as the "innocence at stake" exception).[391] In any other circumstance, the legitimate needs of law enforcement to protect the identity of informers outweigh the interests of the accused to openness and disclosure. This can, however, lead to issues in defending the warrant later: see the discussion in Section C(1)(b)(v), below in this chapter.

There are some limits on the type of information that can justify a warrant. In particular, the information must have been legally gathered;

---

388 *Ibid* at para 48.

389 See the discussion of this issue in *R v SAB*, 2001 ABCA 235 [*SAB* CA], holding that *ex parte* applications for warrants generally do not violate the *Charter*, whether the *Code* provision specifies that approach or not. In particular, the Alberta Court of Appeal held in *SAB* CA that *ex parte* applications for DNA warrants are acceptable because, although a suspect's DNA cannot be changed despite notice of the application, the suspect might flee if given notice. The Supreme Court of Canada upheld this result (*SAB*, above note 6) without making specific reference to the possibility of flight. The Court also noted that s 487.05(1) does not prevent a judge from requiring that an application be *inter partes* in particular cases: see para 56.

390 See the discussion at Section C(1)(b)(v), below in this chapter.

391 *R v Leipert*, [1997] 1 SCR 281.

therefore, a warrant which depends on information gained through a *Charter* violation in order to meet the reasonable grounds standard will be quashed. In *Kokesch*,[392] for example, the police conducted a search of the exterior of the accused's residence. They found a metal vent covered with plywood, heard machines humming inside, and smelled marijuana from the edge of the plywood. Based on this information, the police obtained a search warrant for the premises, but it was subsequently quashed. Since the officers had no reasonable grounds to inspect the perimeter of the accused's residence initially, and since that inspection was itself a search, their observations — and therefore the evidence that was the foundation for the search warrant — violated the *Charter*.[393] Accordingly, those observations could not be used as a basis for the warrant, meaning the warrant ought not to have been issued and the search was therefore not authorized by law, and the evidence obtained through use of the warrant itself was excluded.[394]

The Court has also upheld the individual right to privacy in less clear circumstances, such as where police knock on a suspect's door in order to gain reasonable grounds for a search by, for example, trying

392 *Kokesch*, above note 38.

393 See, in contrast, *Wiley*, above note 181 where, although the police relied on evidence obtained from a perimeter search to obtain a search warrant, there was still enough information to justify the warrant even without those observations, and the warrant was allowed to stand.

394 Of course, it is not the case that evidence obtained in violation of s 8 or any other section of the *Charter* will be immediately excluded. Rather, that is a question that must be decided under s 24(2) of the *Charter*. It had been suggested that, in drug cases, the Court was generally quite reluctant to exclude drugs found as a result of an unconstitutional search: see Don Stuart, "Eight Plus Twenty-Four Two Equals Zero" (1998) 13 *Criminal Reports* (5th) 50. See also Nathan JS Gorham, "Eight Plus Twenty-Four Two Equals Zero-Point-Five" (2003) 6 *Criminal Reports* (6th) 257. However, those analyses were based on the test for exclusion of evidence in *Stillman*, above note 127. In *Grant*, above note 26, the Court created a new analytical scheme for the exclusion of evidence, leading to the formation of new patterns: see Michael Madden, "Empirical Data on Section 24(2) under *R. v. Grant*" (2010) 78 *Criminal Reports* (6th) 278; Thierry Nadon, "Le paragraphe 24(2) de la Charte au Québec depuis *Grant* : si la tendance se maintient!" (2011) 86 *Criminal Reports* (6th) 33; Ariane Asselin, "Trends for Exclusion of Evidence in 2012" (2013) 1 *Criminal Reports* (7th) 74; Justin Milne, "Exclusion of Evidence Trends Post *Grant*: Are Appeal Courts Deferring to Trial Judges?" (2015) 19 *Canadian Criminal Law Review* 373; Richard Jochelson, Debao Huang, and Melanie Murchison, "Empiricizing Exclusionary Remedies: A Cross Canada Study of Exclusion of Evidence under s. 24(2) of the *Charter*, Five Years after *Grant*" (2016) 16 *Criminal Law Quarterly* 206.

to smell marijuana inside.[395] Although homeowners can sometimes be taken to have issued an implied invitation to anyone to knock on the door, that invitation is for limited purposes. When the police who approach a residence also have a subsidiary purpose, that vitiates any implied license they had to approach, and their behaviour constitutes a warrantless search.[396] On the other hand, if the police approach for legitimate reasons but then discover evidence giving them reasonable grounds to search, there will be no *Charter* violation.[397]

In addition, the types of things for which search warrants may be issued must be noted. The *Code* sets out four categories: (1) anything on or in respect of which an offence has been committed; (2) anything that will provide evidence regarding an offence or the location of a person suspected of committing an offence; (3) anything reasonably believed to be intended to be used to commit an offence for which the person could be arrested without warrant; or (4) offence related property.[398] "Offence related property" is defined in section 2 of the *Code* to mean, essentially, property that has been or will be used in committing an indictable offence.

These purposes for a search are broad, but they are not unlimited. They allow warrants to search not just for evidence of an offence, but also for evidence allowing the Crown to determine whether an accused will be able to put forward a successful defence, such as due diligence.[399] The Court has noted:

---

395 *Evans*, above note 39.

396 *Le*, above note 27 at para 127. See also *Singer*, above note 56 at para 27:

> The implied licence to knock is a subset of the implied licence to enter private property *on legitimate business*. It authorizes the person who has entered the property only to approach the door and knock. A person approaching the door to "case" the residence, whether by looking for useful information or by asking the occupant questions, is not there on legitimate business. They are a trespasser. The same is true of a police officer who approaches the door for the purpose of gathering evidence against the occupant.

397 See, for example, *R v Duong* (2002), 49 CR (5th) 165 (BCCA), leave to appeal to SCC refused [2002] SCCA No 112, where the police approached the accused's door while looking for witnesses to a home invasion in the area, but then formed reasonable and probable grounds to believe he was committing a narcotics offence, which authorized an arrest and a search incident to that. See also *R v Roy*, 2010 BCCA 448, where undercover officers purporting to sell marijuana were invited into the accused's home to see marijuana of the quality the accused wished to buy. The Court of Appeal concluded that the police had never acted outside the scope of the express invitation to them, and so they had not infringed the accused's reasonable expectation of privacy.

398 Sections 487(1)(a)–(c.1).

399 See *CanadianOxy Chemicals Ltd v Canada (AG)*, [1999] 1 SCR 743.

> The words "in respect of" are, in my opinion, words of the widest possible scope. They import such meanings as "in relation to", "with reference to" or "in connection with." The phrase "in respect of" is probably the widest of any expression intended to convey some connection between two related subject matters.[400]

However, although the purpose for the search is broad, there are some limits. In particular, the purposes have been interpreted as limiting the power to a search for physical items and therefore do not allow the seizure of the contents of a bank account.[401]

Special limits have been imposed by the Supreme Court to govern situations where a computer is found in the location for which a search warrant has been obtained. The Court noted in *R v Vu* that "[c]omputers differ in important ways from the receptacles governed by the traditional framework and computer searches give rise to particular privacy concerns."[402] Computers store immense amounts of information in comparison to other receptacles such as filing cabinets, create some information whether the user wants it created or not, and retain information even after the user has tried to delete it. Further, a search of a computer connected to a network or the internet is no longer really a search of the location for which the warrant was issued. Because these are unusual and special privacy considerations, the Court held, it will not be clear that a justice of the peace issuing a search warrant took them into account — unless, that is, the ability to search such a computer was specifically mentioned in the warrant. Accordingly, that special rule has been created: if police want to be able to search a computer found at the scene, they must satisfy the justice in advance that the type of material they are seeking could reasonably be expected to be on a computer, and the warrant must specifically authorize the search of the computer. If that has not occurred but the police find a computer which might reasonably be thought to obtain the type of material sought, the

---

400 *Ibid* at para 16, quoting from *Nowegijick v the Queen*, [1983] 1 SCR 29 at 39.

401 See *Re Banque Royale du Canada and the Queen* (1985), 44 CR 3d 387 at 389 (Que CA). The Court quotes with approval the Law Reform Commission of Canada:

> 196. Another anachronism is the restriction of most search and seizure powers to "things", particularly in the case of those powers concerned with the recovery of the fruits of crime. The original common law search warrant developed by Hale was for stolen "goods." This focus on tangible objects was carried into subsequent provisions for search and seizure covering crimes of theft, including the present subs 443(1) [now s 487] of the *Criminal Code*. This focus, however, excludes from coverage forms of property such as funds in financial accounts, or information from computers, which may also represent the fruits of a crime.

402 2013 SCC 60 at para 2 [*Vu*].

police are limited to seizing that computer and then seeking a warrant to search it.

Important as a limit on the search warrant power is the need for specificity in advance. It is not sufficient for police simply to show that they believe some sort of evidence will be found if a search occurs. Rather, they must inform the issuing justice, with some reasonable degree of precision, *what* evidence will be found. At a policy level this is a reflection of the difference between warrantless searches and those conducted with a warrant: in the latter case, the power to search rests in the warrant itself, and the officer should simply be seen as carrying out the instructions in it. Thus, for example, an application for a warrant that specified one publication by name but otherwise only indicated that "other obscene materials" would be found was quashed with respect to all but the one named magazine, because it left too much to the discretion of the officers.[403] Nonetheless, the degree of specificity required varies with the type of offence: it will be more difficult for investigators to specify in advance precisely what evidence they will find of tax evasion or fraud, for example, and so more latitude must be shown in such cases.[404] In addition, a further reason for making the warrant specific is so that the person whose property is searched is sufficiently informed of the reason for that search.[405]

Once again what is reflected here is the balancing of the legitimate interests of the individual and the state. The purpose of prior authorization, whether considering the search as a possible *Charter* violation or not, is to prevent a search from occurring unless it is genuinely shown to be necessary. Where the police cannot say, in advance and with some degree of precision, what evidence they think will be found, the warrant begins to look more like "a fishing license."[406]

However, the legitimate interests of law enforcement are not sacrificed. The *Code* also contains section 489(1), which allows the police who are searching under a warrant to seize items not mentioned in the warrant if they believe on reasonable grounds that they were obtained by, were used in, or afford evidence concerning an offence. In other words, as long as the warrant was validly issued, then the intrusion on the suspect's privacy has been justified. If, in the course of that search, different evidence is found, then new considerations arise,

403 *R v Times Square Book Store* (1985), 48 CR (3d) 132 (Ont CA) [*Times Square*].
404 *R v Church of Scientology (No 6)* (1986), 27 CCC (3d) 193 (Ont HCJ).
405 *Alder v Alberta (Attorney General)* (1977), 37 CCC (2d) 234 (Alta SCTD).
406 *Genest*, above note 376.

justifying the seizure of that unanticipated material.[407] Provided that the reviewing courts are vigilant not to engage in *post facto* justification of warrants simply because evidence was found, rather than judging them based on the information provided to the issuing justice, this is a workable compromise.

*ii) Electronic Surveillance*

The provisions in Part VI of the *Criminal Code* are long-standing sections dealing with wiretaps and other forms of intercepting communications,[408] which are referred to as "interceptions."[409] Rather than speaking of a warrant in this context, the provisions refer to "authorizations," though the concept is the same. These provisions are very detailed, and only a general overview will be provided here.[410]

These provisions deal specifically with intercepting private communications by means of devices: that is, they do not deal with every conceivable situation in which one person overhears a conversation of another. Each of those key terms has been defined in section 183 of the *Code*.

A "private communication" means an oral communication or telecommunication "that is made under circumstances in which it is reasonable for the originator to expect that it will not be intercepted by any person other than the person intended by the originator to receive it." To "intercept" means to listen to, record, or acquire the substance of a communication, and the devices in question are "any device or apparatus that is used or is capable of being used to intercept a private communication" other than a hearing aid.

Intercepting private communications engages a particularly strong privacy interest, which is demonstrated by the fact that it is an offence to intercept absent an authorization, by virtue of section 184 of the

---

407 It is an open question as to whether the additional material must literally be "unanticipated" as opposed to merely not mentioned in the warrant: see the more complete discussion of s 489 above under Section A(1)(i)(b), "Warrantless Seizures."

408 For an explanation in chart form of the relationship between the various electronic surveillance powers, see *Anatomy of Criminal Procedure*, above note 8, Chart 1.1(c)(i), "Which Wiretap Authorization is Appropriate?"

409 Sections 183–196.1.

410 For a more complete discussion, see Robert W Hubbard, Peter M Brauti, & Scott K Fenton, *Wiretapping and Other Electronic Surveillance: Law and Procedure* (Toronto: Thomson Carswell, 2000) (loose-leaf) [Hubbard], or James G Carr & Patricia L Bellia, *The Law of Electronic Surveillance* (Eagan, MN: West, 2011).

*Code.*[411] As a result, authorizations are more difficult to obtain than other warrants. Many rules are parallel to those for search warrants: authorizations can be issued only by a person acting judicially who has a reasonable belief that an offence has been (or will be, in this case) committed and that information will be obtained through the authorization.[412] However, other additional requirements are imposed as well.

The provisions distinguish between consent and non-consent interceptions: in the former, one party to the conversation has agreed to it being intercepted, while in the latter no one has consented.[413] Non-consent electronic surveillance (whether audio or video)[414] is available only in the case of offences listed in section 183.[415] That is an ever-expanding list, but it is to date still something less than all offences.

---

411 This offence is subject to a number of other exceptions in which the interception is not criminal, most notably in s 184(2)(a) in the case of "a person who has the consent to intercept, express or implied, of the originator of the private communication or of the person intended by the originator thereof to receive it."

412 Strictly, this is the language of s 184.2(3)(c), dealing with consent authorizations, while s 185(1)(e), dealing with non-consent authorizations, asks whether there are reasonable grounds to believe that intercepting the communications may assist the investigation of the offence.

413 For an explanation of these two powers in chart form, see *Anatomy of Criminal Procedure*, above note 8, Charts 1.1(c)(ii), "Consent Audio or Video Surveillance" and 1.1(c)(iii) "Non-consent Audio or Video Surveillance."

414 Provisions for video surveillance were added as an adjunct to the general warrant provisions in s 487.01 and adopt the rules governing audio surveillance.

415 It is accepted that this list limits only non-consent interceptions and does not apply to consent interceptions, but that is curious. Section 183 defines the word "offence" for all of Part VI. Section 184.2(2) deals with authorizations for consent interceptions, and that section refers to the need to show reasonable grounds to believe that "an offence" has been or will be committed. Consent interceptions ought therefore to be available only for those offences listed in s 183. Nonetheless the limited number of offences is routinely taken to be a difference between the two types of interceptions. See, for example, Hubbard, above note 410, ch 2.2.5 at 2–19: "While s. 186 authorizations are restricted to investigating only the more serious offences set out in s. 183, s. 184.2 authorizations can be used to investigate any offence contrary to federal legislation."

It is likely that this anomaly is a result of the history of the provisions. When first drafted, non-consent interceptions required an authorization but consent interceptions did not, and so it was true that the limitation created by the definition in s 183 applied to one but not the other. Eventually the Court in *Duarte*, above note 32, concluded that consent interceptions also required authorization. In all likelihood, when drafting s 184.2(2) to create such authorizations, no one adverted to this particular issue around the definition of "offence."

Consent and non-consent interceptions both require evidence on oath creating reasonable grounds, but they vary as to who must act judicially in this regard. Consent authorization applications can be made to a provincial court or superior court judge:[416] non-consent applications can be made only to a superior court.[417] In either case, the application cannot be made to a justice of the peace in the way that search warrant applications can be.

Further, interceptions have special provision as to *who* can make the application. In the case of consent interceptions, peace officers and public officers are allowed to apply for the authorization, while in the case of non-consent interceptions, the list of eligible applicants is much smaller: the attorney general, the minister of Public Safety, or a specially designated agent.[418]

Consent interceptions contain the rule that the issuing judge can attach conditions in the public interest.[419] Non-consent applications, however, are subject to stricter requirements: the judge must be satisfied that the authorization would be in the best interests of the administration of justice[420] and that the "investigative necessity" requirement is met. The "best interests" requirement "imports as a minimum requirement that the issuing judge must be satisfied that there are reasonable and probable grounds to believe that an offence has been, or is being, committed and that the authorization sought will afford evidence of that offence."[421] These requirements are not otherwise explicit in the section and are required to render the section constitutional. "Investigative necessity" encompasses three possibilities: that other methods have been tried and have failed, that as a practical matter no other method of investigation is likely to succeed, or that because of the

416 *Criminal Code*, s 184.2(2).

417 *Ibid*, s 186(2).

418 *Ibid*, s 185(1).

419 *Ibid*, s 184.2(4)(d).

420 There is a slight incongruity here. Consent interceptions are not subject to this requirement if they deal only with audio surveillance. However, all video surveillance, including consent interceptions, must be authorized under the general warrant provisions, and all general warrants are subject to the "best interests" requirement: s 487.01(1)(b). It is hard not to see this as happenstance rather than a deliberate policy choice. See also *R v Li*, 2013 ONCA 81, noting the ambiguity created by the fact that provincial court judges have jurisdiction to issue general warrants but not non-consent authorizations, and therefore that it is unclear whether they can issue general warrants for non-consent video surveillance.

421 *Duarte*, above note 32 at para 24.

urgency of the matter other methods would be impractical.[422] However, the investigative necessity requirement does not apply to investigations for criminal organization or terrorism offences.[423] Non-consent authorizations cannot intercept communications at the office or residence of a solicitor, unless there are reasonable grounds to believe that that solicitor has been or is about to become a party to an offence.[424]

A controversial issue is whether Part VI has a broader application to the interception of electronic communications than has been understood until now. Resolving this rests on two related questions. First, can text messages, Facebook posts, and other messages sent electronically or by social media constitute "private communications"? Second, does "interception" have a temporal component: that is, must the state acquire the substance of the communication *as it occurs* for Part VI to be triggered, or is it still considered an interception if it is acquired after the fact? In *R v TELUS Communications Co*, the police obtained a general warrant requiring TELUS to deliver, each day for the next two weeks, the text messages sent between two telephone numbers in the previous twenty-four hours. Five of the seven members of the Court deciding the case found that that was not a valid general warrant.[425] Justice Abella for three deciding judges concluded that what the police were trying to do required them to be authorized under Part VI: the text messages were "private communications," TELUS's computer system was a "device," and obtaining them after the fact constituted "intercepting" them. No majority opinion on the point arose, since the other two judges concurring in the result expressed no view on that point, and the two dissenting judges specifically reject the position. Justice Cromwell for the dissent noted that Abella J's approach would cause Part VI to be applicable to many situations, such as copying emails from a seized BlackBerry, seizing copies of internet chats from a computer, and so on, where, in the past, ordinary search warrants or production orders have been seen as sufficient.

In the wake of *TELUS*, courts were in fact required to determine whether it, and in particular Abella J's approach, caused Part VI to have wider application. Shortly afterward trial courts decided, based on Abella J's reasoning, that Part VI applies to chats on a Facebook

422 See s 186(1)(b), and *Araujo*, above note 387. The third branch is referred to in *Araujo* as dealing with emergency situations.

423 Section 186(1.1). This has been challenged but upheld: *R v Lucas*, 2014 ONCA 561.

424 Section 186(2).

425 2013 SCC 16 [*TELUS*]. See the further discussion of *TELUS* in Chapter 5, Section B.

wall, to past (as opposed to prospective) text messages stored by an internet service provider, or to surveillance camera footage showing an accused's BlackBerry screen.[426] Two of those three results have now been directly contradicted by the Supreme Court, and so the likelihood is that that portion of the reasoning will not have a very great impact.

The most direct potential application of it arose in *R v Jones*, with facts which parallel a portion of those in *TELUS*.[427] In *TELUS*, police had actually sought text messages over a four-week period: two weeks before the application and two weeks after. That decision only challenged the procedures used to obtain the prospective text messages, not the historical ones, which had been obtained through a production order. However, Abella J's reasoning in *TELUS* had effectively removed the temporal requirement from the concept of "interception," meaning that obtaining the text messages after the fact should still invoke Part VI. That was indeed Abella J's position in *Jones*, but she was writing only for herself in dissent. The majority concluded that there was a difference between disclosing information and intercepting communications (which had been one of Cromwell J's points in dissent in *TELUS*), that "intercepting" implied gathering the information at the time it was communicated, and therefore that providing historical text messages did not constitute an interception. As a result, although a production order could not be used for messages "that are either not yet in existence or are still capable of delivery at the time the order is issued," otherwise it was an acceptable method.[428]

Justice Rowe, in a concurring opinion, noted that the anomalous result of the combination of *TELUS* and *Jones* was that if police applied an hour before a text was sent they were required to meet the high standards of Part VI, but if they applied an hour after a simple production order would do. In effect, therefore, the police could avoid the greater strictures simply by waiting a short time. However, this would only be true for texts sent through TELUS, rather than Bell or Rogers, because the latter two do not retain copies of sent text messages.

Justice Abella's approach in *TELUS* also turned out to have relatively little impact in *Mills*. In that case, the police had created a fictitious Facebook profile for a teenage girl as a way of investigating child luring: the accused had a number of conversations with "Leann" through Facebook and email. The trial judge concluded — based on *TELUS* — that this action on the part of the police constituted an

426 See, respectively, *R v Mills* (2013), 7 CR (7th) 268 (NLPC); *R v Croft*, 2013 ABQB 640 and *R v Hoelscher*, 2016 ABQB 44; and *R v Ley*, 2014 BCSC 2108.

427 *Jones*, above note 77.

428 *Ibid* at para 80.

interception of private communications which required authorization under Part VI. The Supreme Court of Canada rejected that conclusion, though in a very divided decision.

Three judges (including, interestingly, Abella J) held that it was not an interception of private communications because there was no "private communication" in the first place. This conclusion was based on that cohort's conclusion that the accused, an adult, could not have a reasonable expectation of privacy in an online conversation with a child they did not know.[429]

A second cohort of two judges concluded that no interception was taking place: the interaction between the officer and the accused happened to be via a medium which created a permanent electronic record, but creating that record was the action of the individual, not the state.[430] The dissenting judge rejected the significance of the fact that the accused personally created the record, holding that the issue was whether the state was *acquiring* permanent electronic recordings, whomever had made them.

Subsequently in *Campbell*, however, the Court by a clear majority rejected the argument that there was no privacy claim because the accused had created the record and adopted the same reasoning as the dissent in *Mills*, that what matters is the state action in acquiring the record.[431]

However, *Campbell* leans away from an expansionist reading of Abella J's approach in a different way. The police had seized the phone of a drug dealer and received text messages about the sale of drugs, leading them to engage in a text message conversation which resulted in the arrest of Campbell. The accused argued that the police action of engaging in the conversation was itself an interception, but the majority rejected this argument. They held that in talking about the use of a "device," the *Code* intended something *other than* the device which was being used to make the communications in the first place, some separate technological means which intercepted the communications. In that event, no Part VI authorization had been required.

429 See *Mills*, above note 19 at para 33, and the discussion above under "The Normative Approach." See also the discussion at note 66 as to whether this decision constitutes the majority reasoning.

430 *Mills*, above note 19 at para 48. Again, this relates to that cohort's conclusion about reasonable expectation of privacy: that one cannot expect privacy against the person with whom one is communicating.

431 *Campbell*, above note 54 at paras 70–71.

It is always possible that tendencies will swing in the other direction, but at present it seems that the expansive reading of the application of Part VI proposed by Abella J is not likely to gain favour.

A few more features of interceptions should be noted. Time limits are imposed on the length of any interception. Non-consent interceptions can last at most sixty days, though renewals (of up to sixty days each) are available.[432] Consent authorizations are also limited to sixty days.[433] No provision specifically envisions a renewal of a non-consent authorization, but further applications for a new authorization are possible.[434] When the offences being investigated relate to organized crime or terrorism, however, all these time limits increase to one year.[435]

Finally, note that the *Code* also contains some "abbreviated" versions of the powers. Section 188 allows a thirty-six-hour authorization for non-consent authorizations if the judge "is satisfied that the urgency of the situation requires that interception of private communications commence before an authorization could, with reasonable diligence, be obtained under section 186." The notion behind this temporary authorization seems to be that the applicant will use the thirty-six hours in order to bring a proper application under section 185.

Beyond that, interceptions are sometimes available without an authorization. Section 184.1 permits an agent of the state to intercept a private communication if three conditions are met: (1) one of the parties to the communication consents to the interception; (2) the stage agent believes on reasonable grounds that there is a risk of bodily harm to the person who consented; and (3) the purpose of the interception is to prevent the bodily harm. These interceptions, however, are limited to protective purposes: that is, any private communications intercepted are not admissible as evidence and must be destroyed as soon as practicable.[436] Similarly, section 184.4 creates an exigent circumstances

---

432 Sections 186(4)(e) and 186(7).

433 Section 184.2(4)(e).

434 Section 184.2(2)(e). The existence and particulars of a previous authorization must be disclosed. It is also possible to seek a new authorization rather than a renewal for a non-consent authorization. This course of action is appropriate if the old authorization has expired, or if the terms are to be changed by adding new parties or new locations: *R v Thompson*, [1990] 2 SCR 1111 [*Thompson*].

435 Section 186.1.

436 Sections 184.1(2) and (3). The exception is that the evidence is admissible in proceedings relating to actual, attempted, or threatened bodily harm. Evidence based on s 184.1 is generally inadmissible because the conditions triggering it would usually be met in undercover police operations, which would allow interceptions in virtually all of those cases. This would be inconsistent with

exception specific to non-consent interceptions. The situation must be so urgent that not even a temporary authorization is available, the interception must be "immediately necessary to prevent an offence that would cause serious harm to any person or to property," and one party to the communication must be either the person who would cause the harm or the intended victim. If those conditions are met, then a police officer (that is, a narrower range than an "agent of the state" under section 184.1) can intercept private communications without any judicial authorization. The Supreme Court upheld the constitutionality of this section, as long as provision for after-the-fact notice of the interception was incorporated.[437]

*iii) Search of the Person: DNA Warrants and others*

In their 1997 decision in *Stillman*, the Supreme Court noted that section 487 warrants "did not authorize the search of a person, nor the seizure of parts of the body."[438] Since there was also no common law authority for the actions in that case, where the police had taken hair and buccal samples as well as having dental impressions made against the accused's will, the absence of lawful authority meant that the accused's section 8 rights had been violated. In order to provide authority for such searches, the *Code* now contains warrant provisions that allow the police to obtain hair, buccal swabs, or blood samples from a suspect, as well as dental or other bodily impressions. This section will focus on the DNA warrant provisions, but will also consider blood sample warrants related to impaired driving and bodily impression warrants.

In a general outline, the rules surrounding DNA warrants[439] are similar to those surrounding search warrants. As is appropriate, however, the greater intrusiveness of allowing a search directly affecting bodily integrity is balanced by greater protections for privacy (see the further discussion of this point below in Section C(2)). The Court has held that these provisions do not violate section 8 of the *Charter*.[440]

The basic requirements for a DNA warrant necessitate that a provincial court judge be satisfied by information on oath that a bodily

---

the "protection of privacy" theory behind interceptions: *R v Riley* (2008), 60 CR (6th) 105 (Ont SCJ).

437 *R v Tse*, 2012 SCC 16 [*Tse*]. Such provisions are now found in ss 195 and 196.1.

438 *Stillman*, above note 127 at para 26.

439 For an explanation of this issue in chart form, see *Anatomy of Criminal Procedure*, above note 8, Chart 1.1(b)(vii), "DNA Warrants."

440 *SAB*, above note 6.

substance connected with an offence[441] has been found, that a person was a party to the offence, and that DNA analysis of the substance will provide evidence about whether the bodily substance was from that person. These conditions more or less parallel the corresponding requirements for a search warrant, though note that the application cannot be made to a justice of the peace. There is also an explicit statement of the rule, implicit for search warrants, that conditions can be imposed to make the taking of the sample reasonable in the circumstances.[442]

Other requirements act to limit the availability of DNA warrants. They are available only in the case of "designated offences," for example, which consist of lists of offences in section 487.04. (The section divides offences into the two categories of "primary" and "secondary" designated offences, but the distinction is only relevant to DNA databank orders, discussed below, not to DNA warrants.) When the provisions were first introduced, these lists consisted predominantly of sexual offences and offences causing death or bodily harm: they have since grown longer (as did the similar list relating to electronic surveillance). In addition, the judge is required to believe that issuing the warrant is in "the best interests of the administration of justice."[443] Issuing a DNA warrant that is unnecessary will not be in the public interest, though this is not the equivalent of the "investigative necessity" requirement for non-consent authorizations.[444] The Ontario Court of Appeal has held that the presence of a *Charter* violation in the course of obtaining grounds for a DNA warrant is not alone sufficient to prevent the warrant being issued, though the court reserved judgment on whether a "pattern of wilful and flagrant misconduct on the part of the police could lead a judge to deny a DNA warrant on the ground that it would be contrary to the best interests of justice to do so."[445] Section 487.05(2) also requires the judge to have regard to "all relevant matters," which will include the nature of the offence, the circumstances of its commission, and whether a qualified peace officer or other person is available to take the sample.

---

441 The *Code* specifies that the substance could have been found at the place the offence was committed, on or within the body of the victim, on anything worn or carried by the victim, or on or within the body of any person or thing "at any place associated with the commission of the offence": s 487.01(4)(b).

442 Section 487.06(2).

443 Section 487.05(1).

444 *SAB*, above note 6 at para 54.

445 *Nguyen*, above note 152.

Other provisions also aim at counterbalancing the intrusiveness of DNA warrants. A peace officer executing the warrant is required to inform the suspect of its contents, the nature of the procedures for taking samples, the purpose for taking them, and the police officer's authorization to use force.[446] In taking the sample, the officer is also required to respect the accused's privacy in a manner that is reasonable under the circumstances. Further, the *Code* requires that the samples taken and the results of analysis should not be used for any other purpose than the investigation of a designated offence meeting the warrant requirements.[447] Failure to comply with this obligation is actually an offence.[448] In addition, in many circumstances there is an obligation to destroy the samples taken and the results obtained. This is the case where the analysis shows that the sample does not come from the person, the person is acquitted, or (unless new proceedings are commenced) one year has passed after a discharge at a preliminary inquiry, a withdrawal of charges, or a stay of proceedings.

In addition to these requirements, additional rules exist when the DNA warrant concerns a young person. In that event, the young person is to be informed of the right to a reasonable opportunity to consult with and have the warrant executed in the presence of counsel, a parent, or other adult.[449] This requirement is similar to the rules concerning statements by young persons.[450]

The Court found the DNA warrant provisions to survive *Charter* scrutiny in *SAB*. In particular, it was argued that the provisions were unconstitutional on the grounds that such searches should be available only as a last resort (similar to investigative necessity for interceptions), that a higher standard than reasonable grounds should be required for such a warrant, and that a DNA warrant should not be issued *ex parte*. The Court rejected these arguments, holding, in essence, that the differences between DNA warrants and search warrants did not justify these particular higher standards. The Court noted that, although DNA warrants are quite intrusive in an informational sense, they are also more focused than wiretaps and would not intrude on the privacy of third parties. The state's interest in the evidence was also quite high, since it could be virtually conclusive either to prove an accused's guilt or to prevent a wrongful conviction. A judge issuing a DNA warrant would

446 Section 487.07(1).
447 Sections 487.08(1) and (2).
448 Section 487.08(3).
449 Section 487.07(4).
450 *Youth Criminal Justice Act*, SC 2002, c 1, ss 146(2)(c) and (d).

consider whether it was necessary in the interests of justice, which might act as a type of "last resort" rule where necessary, and would permit a judge to allow an *inter partes* application where appropriate.[451]

The Court also considered whether the principle against self-incrimination was violated by the provisions, but held that, given the absence of reliability concerns about DNA evidence and the additional safeguards built into the DNA warrant application process, this principle was not violated.[452]

A further aspect of DNA warrants that should be noted is the portion of the *Code* creating a DNA databank.[453] Those provisions allow the gathering of DNA samples at the time of a finding of guilt[454] not for the purpose of investigating a particular crime, but rather to create a bank of information (similar to mugshots or fingerprints) to be used in the future. The offences for which DNA warrants are available are divided into "primary designated offences" (nearly all of which involve sexual assault or homicide) and "secondary designated offences." In addition, the scheme divides the primary designated offences into two groups: those in subsection 487.04(a) and (c.02) (primarily sexual or violent offences) and the other primary designated offences (primarily what might be thought of as security-related offences such as hijacking or various terrorism offences, and predecessor versions of the offences in subsection (a)). The scheme operates slightly differently with regard to each of those three categories.

Where an accused is convicted of a primary designated offence in subsection 487.04(a) or (c.02), the court simply "shall make an order" authorizing a DNA sample to be taken for the DNA databank.[455] These offences are primarily current statutory versions of sexual offences. If the accused is convicted of one of the other primary designated offences (a broader range of current offences and historical versions of various sexual offences), the court again shall make an order, but the accused has the opportunity to persuade the court otherwise. Specifically, there is no obligation to make an order if the accused satisfies the court that the impact of the order on their privacy would be grossly

---

451 *SAB*, above note 6 at paras 44–56.

452 See the discussion of this aspect of the case, which is more directly relevant to potential s 7 claims, in Stratas, above note 6 and Don Stuart, "*R. v. B. (S.A.)*: Annotation" (2003) 14 *Criminal Reports* (6th) 208.

453 For an explanation of this issue in chart form, see *Anatomy of Criminal Procedure*, above note 8, Chart 1.1(b)(viii), "DNA Databank Orders."

454 Section 487.051(1).

455 Section 487.051(1).

disproportionate to the public interest in the protection of society and proper administration of justice.[456] It will be rare for such a challenge to succeed.[457] The convicted person will be required to prove that the circumstances depart markedly from the cases Parliament is likely to have had in mind in drafting the provisions[458] and that no terms or conditions could adequately restore the proper balance.

In the case of a conviction for a secondary designated offence, the court may make an order on the application of the prosecutor if satisfied it is in the best interests of the administration of justice to do so. This same standard applies if the accused, rather than being convicted, is found not criminally responsible for *any* designated offence.[459] The "best interests" standard is to be judged taking into account the person's criminal record, whether the person was previously found not criminally responsible on account of mental disorder for a designated offence, the nature of the offence, the circumstances surrounding its commission, and the impact such an order would have on the person's privacy and security of the person. As a practical matter, the convicted person is held to have a minimal privacy interest.[460] On the other hand, the state interest is quite significant and includes deterring potential repeat offenders, promoting the safety of the community, detecting when a serial offender is at work, assisting in the solving of cold crimes, streamlining investigations, and assisting the innocent through early exclusion from suspicion or by exonerating the wrongfully convicted.[461] The result is that such orders are granted in most cases.[462]

It is also possible to make retroactive orders in some cases; that is, beyond making orders for historical offences if the conviction occurs in the present, the scheme also permits some orders to be made with regard to offenders convicted before the DNA databank provisions were enacted. These retroactive provisions are limited to a relatively narrow range, including dangerous offenders, those convicted of murder, and

---

456 Section 487.051(2).

457 *R v RC*, 2005 SCC 61 at para 65, citing *R v Jordan*, 2002 NSCA 11 [*Jordan*].

458 *Jordan*, *ibid*, adopted in *R v May*, 2009 BCCA 161, and *R v BR*, 2011 NLCA 23.

459 Section 487.051(3).

460 *R v Durham*, 2007 BCCA 190 at para 12 [*Durham*].

461 *R v Briggs* (2001), 157 CCC (3d) 38 at para 22 (Ont CA), relied on in many other cases, such as *Durham*, above note 460, or *R v Bacon*, 2013 BCCA 397 [*Bacon*]. See also *R v PRF* (2001), 48 CR (5th) 310 (Ont CA).

462 See *Durham*, above note 460 at para 12, or *R v Awasis*, 2009 BCCA 134 at para 59. Nonetheless, the trial judge does have the discretion to decline to make an order: see, for example, *Bacon*, above note 461.

those still serving sentences for certain sexual offences at the time of the application.[463]

The DNA databank provisions have been upheld by the Court, though it is worth observing that the scheme has been made applicable to an increased number of offences and offenders since then.[464] In rejecting challenges to the legislation, based on both section 8 and section 11 of the *Charter*, the Court held:

> Society's interest in using this powerful new technology to assist law enforcement agencies in the identification of offenders is beyond dispute. The resulting impact on the physical integrity of the targeted offenders is minimal. The potential invasive impact on the right to privacy has carefully been circumscribed by legislative safeguards that restrict the use of the DNA data bank as an identification tool only. As convicted offenders still under sentence, the persons targeted by s. 487.055 have a much reduced expectation of privacy. Further, by reason of their crimes, they have lost any reasonable expectation that their identity will remain secret from law enforcement authorities. Having regard to the interests at stake and the procedural safeguards afforded by the legislative scheme, I have also concluded that the *ex parte* nature of the proceedings meets the dictates of procedural fairness afforded under s. 7 of the *Charter*. Finally, ss. 11(h) and 11(i) of the *Charter* are inapplicable. The taking of DNA samples does not constitute a punishment within the meaning of s. 11 anymore than the taking of fingerprints or other identification measures.[465]

An emerging issue is an investigative practice by police which relies on DNA but not on DNA warrants or on the DNA database. With the rise of widespread submission of DNA samples for genealogical purposes, large DNA databases have begun to exist in private hands. In turn, private companies now exist which will test, for police, samples of DNA from crime scenes. That testing can determine the likely genetic background of the source of the sample or potentially likely close family members.[466] From that information, police then identify

463 Section 487.055.

464 *R v Rodgers*, [2006] 1 SCR 554.

465 *Ibid* at para 5.

466 See, for example, *R v Ali*, 2023 BCSC 2438, where sampling originally suggested that the DNA sample came from someone of Kurdish origin, leading the police to obtain voluntary samples from members of the local Kurdish community. That in turn led to the conclusion that the sample at the crime scene had likely come from a brother of a particular person who provided a sample. See, as well,

suspects for further investigation. Challenges have been made to this practice but to date none have succeeded, though the legality of the practice has not yet reached a court of appeal.

Independent of the DNA provisions, there are also blood sample warrants available in the context of impaired driving. In a sense the primary response there is to allow a peace officer to make a warrantless demand for a blood sample, if they have reasonable grounds to believe that a driver has operated a conveyance while impaired by alcohol or drugs.[467] However, in some circumstances a warrant is available and indeed required as a practical matter. Specifically, where there are reasonable grounds to believe that the person has operated a conveyance that was involved in an accident that resulted in bodily harm to themselves or another person or in the death of another person within the preceding eight hours, there are reasonable grounds to suspect that the person has alcohol or a drug in their body; and a qualified medical practitioner believes that the person is unable to consent to the taking of samples because of a physical or mental condition *and* taking the samples will not endanger the person's health, then a justice is able to issue a warrant for the taking of the blood samples.[468]

Finally, the *Code* also contains a provision creating an "impression warrant" that allows a peace officer to obtain a handprint, footprint, tooth impression, or impression of any part of the body.[469] Seemingly, Parliament's assumption is that such procedures will necessarily be less invasive of a person's bodily integrity and privacy than obtaining DNA samples, since few limitations surround such warrants, other than a requirement that issuing the warrant be in the best interests of the administration of justice. There is room to question this assumption: an impression of "any part of the body" has the potential to invade privacy quite significantly. Further, in *Stillman* the Court described taking dental impressions as "a lengthy and highly intrusive process" that, in the particular context of that case, amounted to "the abusive exercise of raw physical authority by the police."[470]

---

*R v Wright*, 2020 ONSC 6021 and *R v Cochrane*, 2023 ABKB 160, where suspects were identified and targeted for further investigation after DNA samples were submitted to a private company.

467 Section 320.28. Where the impairment is believed to be solely due to alcohol, there is the additional requirement that the officer believes the person may be incapable of providing a sample of breath or that it would be impracticable to take one: s 328(1)(a)(ii).

468 Section 320.29.

469 Section 487.092.

470 *Stillman*, above note 127 at para 46.

Impression warrants may be issued by a justice in respect of any offence, based on reasonable grounds to believe that the print will provide information concerning the offence. This wording does not seem to require that the person from whom the impression is taken be a suspect. Conditions that make the search and seizure reasonable in the circumstances can be imposed to ensure that the warrant is in the best interests of the administration of justice.

*iv) Other Statutory Search Warrant Provisions*

Other warrant provisions allow for the gathering of particular kinds of evidence that could not be obtained under a search warrant, which is restricted to tangible "things." Section 492.1 allows for tracking warrants, which authorize police to attach a device which will track the location of a thing or person. Notably, the section treats these two situations separately: tracking the location of a person requires reasonable grounds to *believe* that an offence has been or will be committed and that tracking the person will assist in the investigation of the offence. Where it is only a thing, such as a vehicle, which is to be tracked, the warrant can be issued on the lower standard of reasonable *suspicion*.[471] Either warrant is limited to a maximum of sixty days, or one year in the case of organized crime or terrorism offences.[472]

The *Code* also contains section 492.2, allowing for "transmission data" warrants, which, in 2015, replaced what had been called "number recorder" warrants, which were aimed at telephones. The expanded power is primarily aimed at capturing the same kind of information about communications in addition to those through telephones. These warrants are aimed at tracking information about communications other than the contents of those communications: in essence, anything that will indicate which devices communicated with one another, for

---

471 Sections 492.1(1) and (2). The Court in *Wise*, above note 14, found a *Charter* violation where the police used a tracking device without a warrant. However, they observed that a device which determines only the location of the item to which it is attached is a minimal intrusion on privacy and could be justified based on reasonable suspicion. A predecessor version of s 492.1 was introduced in response to that decision and used the reasonable suspicion standard. The current version of the section was introduced in 2015 as part of the *Protecting Canadians from Online Crime Act*, SC 2014, c 31; it notes the distinction between tracking things and tracking people. See the further discussion of reasonable suspicion in Section C(2), below in this chapter.

472 Sections 492.1(4) and (5).

how long, from where, how large a file was exchanged, and so on.[473] The warrants are available on the reasonable suspicion standard and are limited to a maximum of sixty days, or one year in the case of organized crime or terrorism offences.[474] The reasonable suspicion standard has been challenged but upheld in this section.[475]

Outside the *Code*, the *CDSA* creates a search warrant provision which is quite similar to section 487: the application is made to a justice, is made on oath, and must satisfy the justice on reasonable grounds.[476] Since the particular offence in question will relate to controlled substances, the requirement that there be evidence of an offence is specific to that context: the justice must be persuaded that drugs, something containing drugs, offence related property, or evidence of a *CDSA* offence will be found. However, there are some unique features of drug warrants. First, only a peace officer (not a public officer) can be empowered to search under the warrant. Second, although section 487 warrants require special authorization to be executed at night,[477] drug warrants are executable at night as a matter of course. Third, the power to search persons differs between the two. Search warrants authorize the search of a location but not of persons found at that location. Drug warrants, on the other hand, do authorize such personal searches, if the executing officer has reasonable grounds to believe that the person has the things set out in the warrant on their person. This difference is accounted for by the nature of the offence and the simplicity with which drugs could be hidden on the person.

---

473 *TELUS* 2015, above note 207 at para 15:

> The function of a transmission data recorder warrant ("TDRW") is to provide the police with information regarding the activity on a cellular telephone. More specifically, it can be used to reveal communications made to and from the phone, that is, calls made to and from the phone and text messages sent to and from the phone. If so configured, it may permit other communications, such as email messages or social media contacts, to be tracked. Whichever communications are being tracked, however, the TDRW does not reveal the content of any of those communications. In other words, the TDRW reveals the fact of a communication between phones but not the actual communication.

See s 492.2(6), for the precise definition.

474 Sections 492.2(4) and (5).

475 See *R v Otto*, 2019 ONSC 2473, where the application judge decided that on the record before him, the reasonable suspicion standard was sufficient but left open the possibility that further evidence could show that transmission data warrants obtained evidence which should not be available on that basis.

476 Above note 174, s 11.

477 Section 488.

In addition to these warrants, other statutory provisions contain more specific search powers. Most notably, a number of sections of the *Code* contain what are known as "production orders."[478] The purpose of a production order, as opposed to a warrant, is to employ it with regard to bodies that are likely to have relevant information but that can be expected to cooperate with the police: banks, telephone companies, internet service providers, and so on. Indeed, the relevant provisions specify that they cannot be served on the person who is under investigation.[479] When cooperation can be expected, it is easier for both the police and the body whose records are sought if the information is assembled by the people who already have control of the records. There are several production orders, paralleling various warrant provisions in the *Code*. The general production order is found in section 487.014. This section allows a judge to order a person other than the target of the investigation to produce or prepare documents or data. The grounds upon which these production orders can issue are functionally equivalent to those for search warrants: reasonable grounds to believe that an offence has been (or will be, in this case) committed and that the person has documents or data that will provide evidence respecting that offence. There will, of course, be costs caused by complying with production orders, but no compensation is necessarily available to the parties required to produce documents.[480] However, it is possible for an entity served with a production order to challenge that order, and a judge can revoke or vary the order if satisfied that it is unreasonable in the circumstances to require the applicant to prepare or produce the document or that production of the document would disclose information that is privileged or otherwise protected from disclosure by law.[481] Where the cost of compliance is unreasonable, an application to vary or revoke the order could be made.[482]

Other specific production orders can be issued with regard to transmission data and tracking data, therefore being equivalent to those warrant provisions. Two separate production orders relating to transmission data exist: one to be used when police know that a

478 For an explanation in chart form of the relationship between the various production orders, see *Anatomy of Criminal Procedure*, above note 8, Chart 1.1(b)(ix), "Which Production Order is Appropriate?"

479 See ss 487.014(4), 487.015(5), 487.016(4), 487.017(4), and 487.018(5).

480 *Tele-Mobile Co v Ontario*, 2008 SCC 12 [*Tele-Mobile*].

481 Section 487.0193.

482 In *Tele-Mobile*, above note 480, the Court noted this possibility based on the exemption section in force at the time. There are some differences in wording between the former s 487.015(4)(b) and the current s 487.0193, but they are relatively minor and so it seems this possibility should still exist.

communication was made but do not know who has the transmission data (for example, they do not know which carrier handled the cell-phone call) and the other when the police know that a particular entity has the information sought.[483] Like tracking and transmission data warrants, these production orders are available on the lower standard of reasonable suspicion. Further, a production order relating to limited financial information — for example, the name of a person associated with a particular account, or the number of the account that goes with a particular name — can also be issued on reasonable suspicion.[484]

In addition to these warrants and production orders, the *Protecting Canadians from Online Crime Act* in 2015 added to the *Code* preservation demands and preservation orders, whose primary purpose is to assist with production orders. Either a preservation demand or order requires a person who is in possession or control of computer data not to destroy it: the goal is to give a peace officer enough time to seek a production order or warrant. A preservation demand can be made by a peace officer personally and expires after twenty-one days; no new demand can be made.[485] A preservation order is issued by a justice or judge and lasts at most ninety days.[486] Both of these powers are based on reasonable suspicion, and like production orders cannot be served on the person under investigation.[487]

Finally, there are a number of other quite specific warrant provisions in the *Code*. Some of these warrant provisions are for purely investigative purposes, but others are in whole or in part motivated by the nature of the item searched for. That is, the goal of the seizure is not simply to obtain evidence concerning a crime but also has a preventive aspect. This motive seems to help explain the separate warrant provisions dealing with common gaming and betting houses,[488] hate propaganda,[489] valuable minerals,[490] the search power in section 11 of the *Controlled Drugs and Substances Act*,[491] and the power to seize

483 Sections 487.015 and 487.016.

484 Section 487.018.

485 Sections 487.012(4) and (6). The demand does not expire for ninety days if it is made in relation to an offence committed under the law of a foreign state.

486 Section 487.013(6).

487 Sections 487.012(3) and 487.013(5).

488 Section 199. That section also authorizes taking into custody anyone found in the common gaming house or common betting house.

489 Sections 320 and 320.1.

490 Section 395.

491 Above note 174.

explosives.[492] Although it does not explicitly create a search power, this also appears to be the motive behind section 164, which permits a justice to issue a warrant for the seizure of voyeuristic recordings, intimate images, obscene publications, crime comics, child pornography, or advertisements for sexual services.[493] Indeed, the preventive concern can be dominant over the investigative one. For example, section 117.04 allows the police to seek a warrant to search for and seize a weapon on the grounds that it is not in the interests of safety for the person to have it.[494] Similar forfeiture concerns motivate provisions that allow warrants to search for property that can be forfeited under proceeds of crime legislation.[495] It is worth noting that the Ontario Court of Appeal struck down an earlier version of section 117.04 for failing to comply with the standards in *Hunter*.[496] Although the section required the justice to be satisfied that it was not desirable for a named person to possess a firearm or other weapon, it did not require the justice to be satisfied that the person was in possession of such an item. The court found that, without that requirement, the provision permitted too sweeping a search power, which could not be saved under section 1 of the *Charter*. The section has since been amended to include that requirement.

*v) Supporting Provisions*

Normally a person applying for a warrant must do so in person. However, section 487.1 allows for "telewarrants": that is, a warrant issued after the application is made "by a means of telecommunication."[497] Until 2023 telewarrants were available for section 487 warrants and a few others, but legislation prompted by the COVID-19 pandemic broadened

---

492 Section 492.

493 Some of these provisions are long-standing, while others have been added later. For example, the seizure power dealing with advertisements for sexual services was added in the *Protection of Communities and Exploited Persons Act*, SC 2014, c 25, which made various changes to the law around prostitution, while the seizure power concerning intimate images was added in the *Protecting Canadians from Online Crime Act*, SC 2014, c 31.

494 This section, unlike the others discussed here, does not explicitly require that the information be provided on oath. In *R v Hurrell* (2002), 4 CR (6th) 169 (Ont CA) [*Hurrell*], the Ontario Court of Appeal held that the word "application" in the section should be read as a term of art, requiring that it be under oath.

495 Section 462.32(1).

496 *Hurrell*, above note 494.

497 Section 487.1. In addition s 11(7) of the *Controlled Drugs and Substances Act* adopts s 487.1 "with such modifications as the circumstances require" for warrants issued under that Act.

their availability significantly.[498] It did this not only by expanding the list of warrants available through the telewarrant procedure but also by simplifying the application procedure. Prior to that new legislation, additional requirements were imposed on all telewarrants, most notably that the application was required to include "a statement of the circumstances that make it impracticable for the peace officer to appear personally before a justice."[499] Now, section 487.1 draws a distinction between telewarrant applications that "produce a writing" and those that "do not produce a writing." Telewarrant applications which do produce a writing are, in essence, simply subject to the same rules as any other warrant application.[500] Where the application is submitted by a means which does not produce a writing, however, there is an obligation to show that "it would be impracticable in the circumstances to submit the application by a means of telecommunication that produces a writing."[501]

This distinction is also reflected in the availability of some warrants. Authorizations for interceptions of private communications are not specifically included in section 487.1, though they are dealt with separately. Section 184.3 permits authorizations for consent or non-consent interceptions and some related applications to be sought by telewarrant but only "by a means of telecommunication that produces a writing." Perhaps limiting telewarrants even further, general warrants (discussed in Chapter 5) can be sought by telewarrant but only if they do "not authorize the observation of a person by means of a television camera or other similar electronic device."[502] On the face of it that makes the telewarrant provisions unavailable entirely for video-surveillance warrants. However, section 487.01(5) makes section 184.3 and other interception of private communications provisions applicable to video-surveillance warrants, and so presumably the same

---

498 See *An Act to amend the Criminal Code and the Identification of Criminals Act and to make related amendments to other Acts (COVID-19 response and other measures)*, SC 2022, c 17.

499 Former s 487.1(4)(a), since repealed.

500 Section 487.1(1) requires that the applicant can seek one of the warrants on the list "if they are permitted to apply for any of the following," which reflects the different availability of some warrants. As a minor difference in procedure, see s 487.1(2), providing that the applicant can "instead of swearing the oath, make a statement in writing stating that all matters submitted in support of the application are true to their knowledge and belief, and the statement is deemed to be a statement made under oath."

501 See s 487.1(5)–(9). To date there is no caselaw considering these new subsections.

502 Section 487.1(1)(m).

rule, that telewarrant applications by a means that produces a writing are available, will apply.

Another relevant provision is the possibility of an "assistance order" under section 487.02. That section allows a judge or justice who issues a warrant or authorization to also "order a person to provide assistance, if the person's assistance may reasonably be considered to be required to give effect to the authorization or warrant." Where the warrant is issued by telewarrant, the assistance order can also be issued in that way.[503] What these provisions most obviously have in mind is that when some type of physical intrusion is necessary as part of a search — a door needs to be unlocked, a tracking device needs to be placed, a listening device needs to be installed — a landlord, garage mechanic, or telecommunications company employee might need to be involved, and a judge or justice can order that involvement.[504] In *R v National Post*, the editor of a newspaper was ordered to have a journalist working for that paper bring in an envelope which the journalist had placed in a secret location.[505] Many uses of assistance orders are uncontroversial, but that is not true of all uses.

In *Re: section 487.02 of the Criminal Code*, RCMP had sought a transmission data recorder (TDR) warrant in order to discover which telephone numbers were communicating with the particular cell phone that was associated with an investigation.[506] In addition, they sought an assistance order requiring the telecommunications service providers to provide the subscriber information associated with those other telephone numbers. The judge to whom they applied declined, holding that that fell outside the scope of an assistance order, and that decision was upheld at the first level of judicial review: the reviewing judge concluded that the point of an assistance order in the context of a TDR warrant could only be to assist in obtaining transmission data, and that "subscriber information is not transmission data."[507] However, the majority of the Newfoundland and Labrador Court of Appeal held that section 487.02 could in fact be used in that way.

The essence of the majority's reasoning was that the other telephone numbers by themselves were of very little use, and the goal of

503 Section 487.02(2).

504 See, for example, *R v Pham* (1997), 122 CCC (3d) 90, where an assistance order for the "installation, maintenance, monitoring and removal of devices" to effect a wiretap was issued.

505 *R v National Post*, 2010 SCC 16 [*National Post*].

506 *Re: section 487.02 of the Criminal Code*, 2019 NLCA 6 [*Re: section 487.02*].

507 *Ibid* at para 5.

the RCMP in seeking the transmission data was to determine *who* those numbers were associated with. They held that:

> an assistance order under section 487.02 is available to realize the objective of a section 492.2 warrant. To make a TDR warrant effective — or useful — its objective must be realized. Its objective is to obtain transmission data that will assist in an investigation.[508]

Therefore, rather than require the police to take some further step such as apply for a production order, the majority allowed an assistance order to be used for the task of obtaining the additional information. However, that reasoning ignores the significance of the fact that a TDR warrant is available based on the low standard of reasonable *suspicion*, rather than the more demanding standard of reasonable grounds to believe. If an assistance order can be used in that way, then subscriber information would become routinely available on that lower standard: that would conflict with the Supreme Court of Canada's view that obtaining the name and address of a subscriber is significant enough to require the police to meet the "reasonable grounds" standard.[509] The limits of the assistance order provisions therefore need to be sorted out.

Another issue relating to assistance orders is whether they can be directed at the person who is the subject of the search. Some sections explicitly preclude powers from being used in that way, but section 487.02 does not, and so it appears that there is no absolute bar to doing so. However, some uses of an assistance order, such as requiring an accused to disclose the password to an electronic device, would violate the *Charter*.[510]

The *Criminal Code* contains other provisions which are relevant to warrants but are not themselves authorizations to search. For example, section 488 of the *Code* requires that a section 487 warrant shall be executed by day unless reasonable grounds for executing it by night are provided to the issuing justice, and the warrant itself authorizes its execution by night. However, no similar limitation is imposed on search warrants issued under the *CDSA*. The policy behind that rule is to limit the state intrusion on privacy: a potentially forceful entry onto property is already quite intrusive, but especially so if it occurs at night. That issue does not arise, of course, with regard to many other

---

508 *Ibid* at para 49.

509 See *Spencer*, above note 36.

510 See *R v Shergill*, 2019 ONCJ 54 or *R v Talbot*, 2017 ONCJ 814. See ss 487.012(3), 487.013(5), or 487.014(4) as some instances of the use of a power being explicitly prohibited against the person who is under investigation for the offence.

warrants, such as interceptions or tracking warrants, which do not involve any physical intrusion.

See also the discussion above of exigent circumstances, which permits many searches which normally require prior judicial authorization to be conducted if the prerequisites for obtaining such authorization exist but it is, more or less, too much of an emergency to wait to go through that process.[511]

The *Code* also contains provisions setting out how police should deal with property after they have seized it: these rules apply to searches with a warrant, but also to searches conducted without a warrant due to exigent circumstances, as well as to items seized pursuant to section 487.11, section 489, or otherwise in execution of duty. There is more than one possibility, but in any event the officer must report the result to the justice who issued the warrant or some other justice.

If what was seized is no longer required and the person entitled to possession is not in dispute, the officer can return the item to that person, obtain a receipt, and then report that to the justice. In any other case, the officer either brings the thing seized to the justice, or reports to the justice that they have seized the item and are detaining it to be dealt with under section 490.[512] Under that latter section, the justice can either return the item or order it still detained for a period of no more than three months, though more than one such order can be issued. However, nothing can be detained for longer than twelve months unless either a superior court judge so orders or proceedings are instituted at which the property detained may be required.[513] If these provisions are not complied with, it means that the continued seizure of the item is not authorized by law, which in turns means that the seizure violates section 8.[514]

Finally, the *Code* contains provisions relating to the sealing of a warrant and the application. The public can have an interest in seeing the information used by police to obtain search warrants or the search warrants themselves, but the police might see an ongoing need to keep that information confidential. Section 487.3 of the *Code* therefore

511 See the discussion above under Warrantless Searches, Authorization by Statute, Section C(1)(a)(i)(a).

512 Section 489.1(1)(a). Section 489.1(1)(b) provides only the latter option for any person who is not a peace officer but who has seized items in the execution of duty: that is, such a person does not have the option of returning the item to the person entitled to it.

513 Section 490(3). The section also contains provisions allowing for applications to have things returned, or for their disposal.

514 *R v Garcia-Machado*, 2015 ONCA 569; *R v Craig*, 2016 BCCA 154.

permits an application, at the time of the application for the warrant (or other order such as a production order) itself, for an order prohibiting access to or disclosure of any information relating to the warrant. Sealing an application is the exception rather than the rule: the Court has held that the appropriate balance of interests in this situation favours openness and that "[o]nce a search warrant is executed, the warrant and the information upon which it is issued must be made available to the public unless an applicant seeking a sealing order can demonstrate that public access would subvert the ends of justice."[515] In reaching this conclusion, the Court applied the same standard that it created in the case of publication bans to search warrants.[516]

*vi) Reviewing Warrants*

The whole purpose of requiring a warrant for a search is so that there is judicial oversight in advance of the search. However, that does not mean that there is no scope for after-the-fact review[517] as well. To fully understand searches with a warrant, then, it is necessary to consider the rules governing their review. These rules also apply to reviews of production orders, unless that order was initially issued by a superior court.[518]

The *Code* contains no provisions that allow for an appeal from the decision to issue a warrant, and in the absence of such a statutory provision, there is no right of appeal.[519] This is true even if there is an issue as to whether the search violated section 8 of the *Charter*, because the *Charter* does not create new appeal procedures.[520] It is possible to challenge the issuance of a warrant through *certiorari*, but this approach has been called an "idle exercise" since it does not result in either the return of the items seized or their exclusion as evidence.[521] For this rea-

515 *Toronto Star Newspapers Ltd v Ontario*, 2005 SCC 41, relying on *Attorney General of Nova Scotia v MacIntyre*, [1982] 1 SCR 175. This language is in s 487.3, but is also the test at common law, which applied in that particular case because the warrant there was not issued under the *Criminal Code*.

516 See *Dagenais v Canadian Broadcasting Corp*, [1994] 3 SCR 835, as well as *Vancouver Sun (Re)*, [2004] 2 SCR 332. See also *Ottawa Citizen Group Inc v Ontario* (2005), 31 CR (6th) 144 (Ont CA), concerning the search warrants in the Maher Arar case. See also the discussion of publication bans in Chapter 11, Section F(2).

517 For an explanation of this issue in chart form, see *Anatomy of Criminal Procedure*, above note 8, Chart 1.1(b)(x), "Review of Warrants."

518 *R v Vice Media Inc*, 2018 SCC 53 [*Vice Media*] at paras 68–70.

519 *Knox Contracting Ltd v Canada*, [1990] 2 SCR 338; *Kourtessis v MNR*, [1993] 2 SCR 53.

520 *R v Meltzer*, [1989] 1 SCR 1764.

521 *R v Zevallos* (1987), 59 CR (3d) 153 at 158 (Ont CA) [*Zevallos*].

son challenges to a warrant are usually left to the trial stage. If a warrant is quashed, then the search was warrantless, which means that it was *prima facie* unreasonable and in violation of section 8. However, it will still need to be determined whether the evidence should be excluded under section 24(2), a determination that depends on considerations broader than just those that relate to the warrant. As a result, that decision can be made only at trial, when the overlapping questions of violation and remedy can be dealt with together.[522] A pre-trial challenge to a warrant is possible, but is appropriate only where issues such as preventing a search arise.[523]

The central issue in reviewing a warrant is whether the requirements for its issuance under the *Code* have been met. Thus, for example, if the warrant fails to adequately describe the premises to be searched or the offence under investigation, the warrant can be quashed.[524] More commonly, however, the issue is whether there is a problem with the "Information to Obtain" (ITO) which was presented to the justice in the application for the warrant. Challenges can be made on the basis that even on its face the material presented was not sufficient to justify the warrant (a "facial" challenge) or on the basis that for one of several reasons the material used to obtain the warrant was not reliable or acceptable (a "sub-facial" challenge).

For example, it is open to an accused to argue that the evidence in an ITO would not be sufficient to show that the things sought would still be in the location to be searched a week later[525] or that reasonable grounds to believe that information would be found specifically on electronic devices in the location had been established.[526] "The record examined on a facial review is fixed: it is the ITO, not an amplified or enlarged record."[527]

In contrast, a sub-facial challenge goes behind the form of the ITO to impeach the reliability of its content.[528] For example, the informant must present all material facts, whether favourable or not, and is not permitted to choose those that make it most likely that the warrant will be issued. If relevant facts are omitted or unrelated facts are

---

522 *Ibid*; *R v Tunner* (1989), 46 CCC (3d) 513 (Alta CA); *R v Williams* (1987), 38 CCC (3d) 319 (YTCA).

523 *Zevallos*, above note 521. See also the discussion below of searches of journalists and the provisions in the *Code* allowing for a particular challenge to the warrant in those circumstances.

524 *Bergeron v Deschamps*, [1978] 1 SCR 243.

525 *R v Donovan*, 2025 BCCA 30.

526 *R v McNeill*, 2020 ONCA 313.

527 *R v Sadikov*, 2014 ONCA 72 at para 37 [*Sadikov*].

528 *Araujo*, above note 387 at para 50. See also *Sadikov*, above note 527 at para 38.

presented in a way to suggest a connection between them, then the ITO might be misleading: it need not be intentionally misleading for it to be quashed.[529]

Cross-examination on an ITO to perform a sub-facial challenge is not automatically available. Some early cases suggested that the applicant must show on a *prima facie* basis that there was deliberate falsehood, omission, or a reckless disregard for the truth by the person swearing the affidavit before cross-examination would be permitted.[530] In *Garofoli*, however, the Court held that, although cross-examination should not be the general rule and that leave of the reviewing judge was required, the standard of a *prima facie* case was too high. Rather, all that is necessary is a basis for the view that "the cross-examination will elicit testimony tending to discredit the existence of one of the preconditions to the authorization, as for example the existence of reasonable and probable grounds."[531] Put another way, it is only necessary to show "a reasonable likelihood that cross-examination of the affiant will elicit testimony of probative value to the issue for consideration by the reviewing judge."[532] That does not, however, mean that it is easy to obtain leave to cross-examine: that is still a narrow window, because the basis upon which a warrant can be quashed is itself narrow.[533] For that same reason, cross-examination should normally be limited to questions aimed at showing there was no basis for issuing the warrant.[534] One consequence of this is that simply showing that some of the information relied on by the affiant was false is not, by itself, useful. The relevant question is whether the affiant had reasonable and probable grounds for their belief, and so it would also be necessary to show a basis to infer that the affiant knew or ought to have known that the information was false.[535]

One particular issue that arises in this context is when a warrant has been issued based on an ITO containing information from a

---

529 *Morelli*, above note 125.

530 *R v Collins* (1989), 69 CR (3d) 235 (Ont CA).

531 *R v Garofoli*, [1990] 2 SCR 1421 at 1452 [*Garofoli*] at 1465.

532 *R v Pires, R v Lising*, [2005] 3 SCR 343 [*Pires*] at para 3.

533 See *Pires*, above note 522 at para 40:

> the *Garofoli* leave requirement is simply a means of weeding out unnecessary proceedings on the basis that they are unlikely to assist in the determination of the relevant issues. The reason that the test will generally leave just a narrow window for cross-examination is not because the test is onerous — it is because there is just a narrow basis upon which an authorization can be set aside.

534 *Garofoli*, above note 531 at 1465.

535 *Pires*, above note 522 at para 41.

confidential informant. Informer privilege is broad and strongly protected: "any information — even the smallest detail — that may lead directly or indirectly to the identification of the informer must be kept confidential."[536] As a result, before being disclosed to the accused and filed in court, an ITO must be edited to remove any information that might identify an informant.[537] A difficulty that can arise, however, is that such an ITO on its redacted face might no longer contain enough material for the reviewing judge to say that the warrant could have been issued; in that event, the warrant will be quashed. In essence, the Crown is faced with a dilemma: they can either preserve the confidentiality promised to the informant or show that the warrant was properly issued, but they cannot do both.

To address this problem, the Supreme Court suggested in *R v Garofoli* a procedure that could be used in such situations, which is usually referred to as "step six in *Garofoli*":

> 6. If, however, the editing renders the authorization insupportable, then the Crown may apply to have the trial judge consider so much of the excised material as is necessary to support the authorization. The trial judge should accede to such a request only if satisfied that the accused is sufficiently aware of the nature of the excised material to challenge it in argument or by evidence. In this regard, a judicial summary of the excised material should be provided if it will fulfill that function. It goes without saying that if the Crown is dissatisfied with the extent of disclosure and is of the view that the public interest will be prejudiced, it can withdraw tender of the wiretap evidence.[538]

For a long time, Crown prosecutors seemed to be reluctant to use this option. There were suggestions from courts that it ought to be employed more frequently, so that jurisprudence about how to apply it could be developed.[539] In fact it is now used much more often, and some

536 *Canadian Broadcasting Corp v Named Person*, 2024 SCC 21 at para 44.

537 See also s 487.3, permitting an order prohibiting access to or disclosure of any information relating to the warrant, for purposes as not compromising the nature and extent of an ongoing investigation, not injuring international relations, national defence or national security, or not prejudicing the interests of an innocent person.

538 *Garofoli*, above note 531 at 1461.

539 See *R v Rocha*, 2012 ONCA 707, citing *R v Learning*, 2010 ONSC 3816, and arguing that prosecutors ought to try more frequently to rely on step six, See also David Tice, "Into the Black: Litigating Search Warrants and Wiretaps under the Sixth Step of *Garofoli*" (2014) 61 *Criminal Law Quarterly* 102; and Chris De Sa, "*Garofoli* Step 6: Getting Behind the Black" (2014) 61 *Criminal Law Quarterly* 418.

principles around it have been developed, particularly by the Ontario Court of Appeal.

That court has offered a number of observations about the step six procedure, and in particular about how informer privilege can be protected while still protecting the accused's right to a fair trial. First, a challenge to the basis upon which the warrant is issued is not part of the actual trial on the merits, but merely a pretrial hearing about the admissibility of particular evidence (though as a practical matter the result of that hearing will often settle matters). Further, the accused will have material beyond what is in the judicial summary to use in challenging the warrant, because of the Crown's disclosure obligations. In addition, the issue being addressed is not whether the informer's tips were ultimately true, but whether the affiant knew or should have known they were false: the issue being addressed is whether the affiant had reasonable grounds for seeking the warrant, and so any review is directed towards that issue.[540] This does not mean that the right to full answer and defence has been attenuated, but does mean that it is to be understood in context.[541]

The summary given to the accused need only make the accused aware of the nature of the redacted details, not the details themselves, but it must be sufficient to allow the accused to make both a facial and a sub-facial challenge. Exactly how the accused might do the latter will be fact-dependent, but might include things such as whether the authorizing justice was informed of an informer's criminal record and motivation for speaking to police, or whether the accused had an alibi of which the police should have been aware for dates noted only approximately in the summary.[542]

The Ontario Court of Appeal also offered guidance to judges for preparing the judicial summary, noting that it needs to include sufficient information for the accused to evaluate whether the preconditions for issuing the warrant were met. In particular, it will need to include information that relates to the criteria for assessing the evidence of confidential informers: whether the information was compelling and corroborated, and whether the informer was credible.[543] They also suggested a very long list of matters that might be included in the summary, such as whether the information is first-hand or hearsay, the informer's relationship with the accused, whether the informer has previously provided information to police and if so whether that has

540 *R v Crevier*, 2015 ONCA 619 [*Crevier*] at paras 63–65.

541 *Ibid* at para 101.

542 *Ibid* at paras 78–79.

543 *Ibid* at para 84.

led to arrests, seizures, or convictions, the degree of detail and recency or timing of the information provided, and any discrepancies, inaccuracies, or information that was contradicted by investigation, among other things.[544] In addition, "the judicial summary should inform the accused not only of what was redacted but also where in the ITO the redacted information is contained. The judicial summary should also say if the nature of a redaction in a specific paragraph of the ITO cannot be summarized."[545]

Ultimately, the reviewing judge does not decide whether the warrant *should* have been issued or whether they *would* have issued it. Rather, the question is whether there was evidence upon which the issuing judge or justice *could* have decided to issue the warrant.[546] The actual result of the search is not relevant on review.[547]

On review, evidence that was used in support of the warrant may be excised from the application. Information that was misleading[548] or that the police should have known was not true[549] may be removed from the material that potentially justified the issuance of the warrant. Equally, if evidence used to justify the warrant was obtained through a *Charter* breach, that evidence will also be excluded.[550] If relevant evidence ought to have been included in the ITO but was omitted, that material can be taken into account on review.[551] The question then becomes whether the remaining evidence could have been sufficient to justify issuing the warrant.

However, it might be possible for the Crown to "amplify" the grounds that justified the issuance of the warrant if evidence is excised at the review hearing. This possibility exists only where the error leading to the excision occurred despite good faith on the part of the police.[552] In *Plant*, for example, the ITO stated that an anonymous informant had reported marijuana being grown at a particular address: in fact the informant had given a general location and described the house, and the police had then gone there and determined the address.

---

544 *Ibid.*

545 *Ibid* at para 85.

546 *Garofoli*, above note 531. *Garofoli* concerns a wiretap authorization, but the same standard is applicable to search warrants: see *R v Breton* (1994), 93 CCC (3d) 171 (Ont CA). See, for example, the application of this standard in *R v Knapp*, 2020 ABCA 406 or *R v Arendt*, 2024 SKCA 89 [*Arendt*].

547 *Descoteaux v Mierzwinski*, [1982] 1 SCR 860.

548 *R v Sismey* (1990), 55 CCC (3d) 281 (BCCA).

549 *Garofoli*, above note 531.

550 *Evans*, above note 39; *Grant* 1993, above note 179; *Wiley*, above note 181.

551 *Morelli*, above note 125 at para 60.

552 *Araujo*, above note 387 at para 58.

This was a good faith error made in an attempt to state the grounds concisely, and so the Crown was permitted to amplify the record by providing the more complete and accurate account.[553] The Court has noted that amplification requires a delicate balance. To never permit it would sometimes lead to a warrant being overturned due to some technical error, even if the police had valid grounds to obtain that warrant. Conversely, if amplification were too readily allowed, it could circumvent the *Charter* requirement of prior authorization for the warrant.[554]

Some earlier cases suggested that the basis upon which evidence was excised was of little importance in the reviewing process. In *R v Bisson*, for example, the Court held that "errors in the information presented to the authorizing judge, whether advertent or even fraudulent, are only factors to be considered in deciding to set aside the authorization and do not by themselves lead to automatic vitiation of the wiretap authorization."[555] The issue, the Court suggested, was whether, after the fraudulent information had been removed, the remaining information was sufficient to justify issuance of the warrant. Subsequently, however, in *Araujo* the Court recognized a basis for review beyond whether sufficient evidence remains. Although in agreement that fraud does not automatically lead to quashing a warrant, the Court held that

> [t]his does not mean that errors, particularly deliberate ones, are irrelevant in the review process. While not leading to automatic vitiation of the warrant, there remains the need to protect the prior authorization process. The cases just referred to do not foreclose a reviewing judge, in appropriate circumstances, from concluding on *the totality of the circumstances* that the conduct of the police in seeking prior authorization was so subversive of that process that the resulting warrant must be set aside to protect the process and the preventive function it serves.[556]

This passage seems to make it clear that reviewing courts can quash a warrant based either on the inadequacy of the material remaining after some information is excised, or based on behaviour of the police that intentionally misled or otherwise subverted the process of prior

553 *Plant*, above note 28. Similarly see *Crevier*, above note 540 at para 75, suggesting that amplification might be used to correct a good faith mistake about the date events occurred.

554 *Ibid* at para 59.

555 [1994] 3 SCR 1097 at para 2.

556 *Araujo*, above note 387 at para 54, cited from *R v Morris* (1998), 134 CCC (3d) 539 at para 43 (NSCA) [emphasis added by Supreme Court].

authorization.[557] However, not all courts of appeal have taken the point as settled. The Ontario Court of Appeal, for example, expressed doubt about whether *Araujo* had actually adopted the position quoted above, but nonetheless concluded for itself that a residual discretion to quash for "deliberate non-disclosure, bad faith, deliberate deception, fraudulent misrepresentation or the like" did exist, though with a high standard to be met to invoke that discretion.[558] The British Columbia Court of Appeal decision has indicated that it "has yet to decide whether such discretion exists."[559]

A further issue which arises in reviewing warrants is the role of the justice who issued it. There has been some level of controversy over what level of interaction is permissible between the applicant for the warrant and the justice. It clearly is possible for the justice to become involved in a way that causes real concerns about impartiality and independence.[560] Some courts have held that there should be no interaction at all: that the justice should make a decision to issue or not, but that is the extent of it.[561] However, it seems that the correct view is that interaction which does not impair judicial independence does not invalidate a warrant.

---

557 See generally Robert W Hubbard & Scott K Fenton, "Supreme Court of Canada Wiretap Update — February 2001" (delivered at Search and Seizure Law in Canada, the Professional Development Program, Osgoode Hall Law School, Toronto, 3 November 2001).

558 *R v Paryniuk*, 2017 ONCA 87 at para 69. *Arendt*, above note 546 at paras 16–19, seems to approve this approach from *Paryniuk*, as does *R v Payne*, 2025 NSCA 10 at para 18. In both cases the decision under appeal had relied on *Paryniuk*, and there is no suggestion in the Court of Appeal that doing so was an error of law.

559 *R v Montgomery*, 2016 BCCA 379 at para 100. See also *R v Beaumont*, 2018 BCCA 342 at para 43.

560 See, for example, *R v Gray* (1993), 81 CCC (3d) 174 (Man CA) at para 11:

> Evidence disclosed that in many instances the information to obtain would, after its initial preparation by the appropriate police officer, be reviewed, while still unexecuted and in draft form, with the magistrate. If the unexecuted information to obtain was not acceptable to the magistrate, advice would then be sought and given on how to satisfactorily word the document to enable the warrant to be issued. Sometimes the magistrate would dictate the wording so as to ensure a document that was acceptable to her/him. One witness indicated that the magistrate would on occasion type the information to obtain for him. Attestation of the document would only occur after all the suggested additions had been made to the satisfaction of the issuing magistrate.

561 See *R v Gordon* (1999), 139 CCC (3d) 239 (Man CA) at para 50: "there should be no interaction between the affiant and the authorizing justice."

In *Clark*, an officer applied for a telewarrant in the early morning hours: the justice to whom the application was submitted asked the officer why the application could not be submitted in person during normal hours and then told the officer to include that explanation in the application.[562] This only amounted to advising the officer to fully set out the reasons for making a telewarrant application: it did not prejudge whether those reasons were sufficient to grant the application and so was an acceptable interaction. Indeed, in *Araujo*, speaking in the specific context of wiretaps, the Court said that a judge "should not be reluctant to ask questions from the applicant, to discuss or to require more information or to narrow down the authorization requested if it seems too wide or too vague."[563] The real issue is not whether there was interaction, but whether it was of a type to suggest that something improper occurred.

## 2) Was the Law Itself Reasonable?

### a) The General Approach to Assessing Reasonableness

The central purpose of section 8 of the *Charter*, and in particular the question of whether a particular search power is reasonable or not, has from the start been to assess "whether in a particular situation the public's interest in being left alone by government must give way to the government's interest in intruding on the individual's privacy in order to advance its goals, notably those of law enforcement."[564] A law will be reasonable if it properly balances the individual and state interests at stake: however, those interests are not the same in every situation. Individual interests will vary according to the importance of the privacy interest at stake: searching the trunk of a vehicle invades privacy less than a body cavity search does, for example. Similarly, state interests can vary: investigating terrorism offences or controlling the border are generally seen as having greater importance than the investigation of most crime.

The "baseline" for reasonableness was established very early with *Hunter v Southam*.[565] That case held that a warrantless search is *prima facie* unreasonable. In addition, it set out the normal requirements for a warrant provision:

562 *R v Clark*, 2015 BCCA 488. As noted above, the Supreme Court decision "substantially" adopts the reasoning of the British Columbia Court of Appeal.

563 *Araujo*, above note 387 at para 29.

564 *Hunter*, above note 6 at 160.

565 *Hunter*, above note 6.

> reasonable and probable grounds, established upon oath, to believe that an offence has been committed and that there is evidence to be found at the place of the search, constitutes the minimum standard, consistent with s 8 of the *Charter*, for authorizing search and seizure.[566]

*Hunter* found that in the ordinary case the standards for a warrant include four factors. First, the warrant must have been issued by someone who is capable of acting judicially. Second, that person must be satisfied of the necessary factors on a "reasonable grounds to believe" standard. Third, the evidence must have been given on oath, and fourth and finally, it must give the person issuing the warrant reasonable grounds to believe (as opposed to suspect) that an offence has been committed and that evidence will (rather than might) be found by the search. It has also been found that a warrant provision that does not leave any residual discretion with the issuing judge will violate section 8.[567] In fact, these requirements are satisfied by section 487, which allows those search warrants to be seen as representative of the benchmark.[568]

In the rest of this section we will look at the ways in which particular search powers either relax those requirements (for example by dispensing with the need for a warrant) or restrict them further (for example by adding additional requirements beyond those in *Hunter*). Before turning to those individual examples, however, two things are worth discussing: the distinction between reasonable grounds to believe and reasonable suspicion and the framework for assessing statutory search powers.

The distinction between "reasonable suspicion" and "reasonable grounds to believe" is relevant in many contexts, but the Court has primarily articulated the distinction in cases involving common law powers. Reasonable suspicion searches are an illustration that, where the impact of a search on a person's privacy interests is seen as relatively minimal, the standard for being allowed to search is lower.[569] This is the rationale behind allowing sniffer dog searches on reasonable suspicion, for example: merely having a dog with the ability to detect

566 *Hunter*, above note 6 at 168.

567 *Baron*, above note 11 at para 24.

568 The Supreme Court has not explicitly approved s 487, though it was found by the Ontario Court of Appeal to be in compliance with the requirements of *Hunter*, above note 6: see *Times Square*, above note 403.

569 See criticism of the reasonable suspicion standard in Peter Sankoff & Stéphane Perrault, "Suspicious Searches: What's So Reasonable about Them?" (1999) 24 *Criminal Reports* (5th) 123.

one thing — narcotics — smell the air around a piece of luggage is less intrusive than opening that bag and going through all of its contents. As the Court held in *Chehil*:

> In *Hunter*, this Court also recognized that this balancing of interests can justify searches on a lower standard where privacy interests are reduced, or where state objectives of public importance are predominant (p. 168). Thus, the Court has found reasonable suspicion to be a sufficient threshold in certain investigative contexts, and Parliament has employed this standard when authorizing certain searches in legislation.[570]
>
> In the case of sniff searches, the use of the reasonable suspicion standard reflects, in part, the minimal intrusion of a dog sniff. For a physical search of luggage incident to arrest, which will be more intrusive, the more exacting reasonable and probable grounds standard is engaged, as the arrest must be justified.[571]

The Court spent some time in *Chehil* elaborating on the "reasonable suspicion" standard. Because it is lower than "reasonable belief" it deals only with the possibility of crime, not its probability, which "necessarily means that in some cases the police will reasonably suspect that innocent people are involved in crime."[572] But although the standard is lower, it must still be based on objectively reasonable facts and must amount to more than a generalized suspicion that something is going on.[573] Reasonable suspicion must be based on a totality of the circumstances, which means that both the inculpatory and exculpatory information must be taken into account. Some individual factors might be incriminating all on their own, but this need not be the case: ambiguous factors that are capable of innocent explanation can, nonetheless, when taken with other considerations, contribute to reasonable suspicion. As the Court says:

> The same is true of factors that may "go both ways", such as an individual's making or failing to make eye contact. On their own, such factors cannot support reasonable suspicion; however, this does not preclude reasonable suspicion arising when the same factor is simply one part of a constellation of factors.[574]

---

570 *Chehil*, above note 37 at para 23.

571 *Ibid* at paras 23–24 [footnotes omitted].

572 *Ibid* at para 28.

573 *Ibid* at paras 27 and 30.

574 *Ibid* at para 31.

Criminal behaviour need not be the only inference available for a suspicion to be reasonable.[575] Beyond that, police have no duty to investigate further to eliminate possible innocent explanations before conducting a search, and the reasonableness of the search should be assessed based on the circumstances the police were aware of at the time of the execution of the search.[576] Finally, officer training and experience can enter into the objective test for reasonableness, but such claims ought not to be accepted uncritically: "[e]vidence as to the specific nature and extent of such experience and training is required so that the court may make an objective assessment of the probative link between the constellation of factors relied on by the police and criminality."[577]

As a final observation about the reasonable suspicion standard, it is particularly important in the case of common law searches to recall that that standard can only justify an intrusion on privacy that is lesser than those which reasonable grounds would justify. As noted above in the discussion of search incident to investigative detention, there is a tendency for "slippage" in common law powers, permitting greater and greater intrusion to be allowed in successive cases: "there is an understandable tendency to expand a narrow rule to endorse the police conduct being challenged, since the case before the court will always be one where the search actually yielded a weapon or some other valuable evidence."[578] It is important for courts to be certain that the ability to intrude on privacy granted by reasonable suspicion does not extend beyond what that relatively low state interest justifies.[579]

---

575 *Ibid* at para 32.

576 *Ibid* at para 34.

577 *Ibid* at para 47. See also the companion decision handed down the same day in *MacKenzie*, above note 37. In *Chehil* all nine justices agreed that the reasonable suspicion standard was met. In *MacKenzie* there was a 5:4 split, with the dissent warning against the creation of broad categories of suspicious behaviour into which almost anyone could fall, which would risk transforming the standard of reasonable suspicion into a generalized suspicion standard, which had earlier been rejected by the Court. For discussion of officer training and experience, see Steve Coughlan, "Learning from Experience about Learning from Experience: Modifying the Objective Test for Arrest and Detention" (2013) 4 *Criminal Reports* (7th) 245.

578 *Plummer*, above note 50 at para 76.

579 See, for example, the discussion of assistance orders and *Re: section 487.02*, above note 506. By way of analogy, see *R v Barclay*, 2018 ONCA 114, where police made the accused wait nearly two hours until a sniffer dog could be brought to the scene. Speaking of the detention rather than the search and finding it to be a *Charter* violation, the court held at para 28 that "[t]he relatively

That observation raises a more general point about the reasonableness of common law powers: as a matter of fact, there tends to be little separate discussion of the second step in the *Collins* test in the case of search powers created at common law. In those cases, deciding that the common law power exists at all requires a court to decide its extent. Since the common law is to be developed in a way that is consistent with the *Charter*, the result is likely to be to settle the question of whether the law is reasonable. Common law powers are created by application of the ancillary powers test, but that test, like the *Collins* test, asks about reasonableness, and so the two tests overlap.[580] The effect of this approach tends to render redundant, for searches based on common law powers, the separate step of asking "is the law itself reasonable?" This is so not because the question is unimportant but because it will already have been answered.

The Court has noted that this is so in the particular context of the common law power of search incident to arrest, observing that establishing the bounds of that power must be done in light of the *Charter*:

> This Court has enunciated a two-part analytical approach for determining whether the common law standard for search incident to arrest should be modified to comply with s. 8 of the *Charter* (see *Stillman*, *Golden*, *Fearon*, and *Saeed*):
>
> (1) Stage One: Determine whether the search satisfies the common law standard for search incident to arrest.
> (2) Stage Two: If so, determine whether the standard must be modified to comply with s. 8 of the *Charter*, given the particular privacy interests and law enforcement objectives at stake.[581]

In that particular decision the Court placed the various search incident to arrest powers on a spectrum from most intrusive (infringing

---

low 'reasonable suspicion' standard cannot constitutionally sustain a detention that is not 'brief.'"

580 *Mann*, above note 167 at para 44. The most extreme example of this approach is in *R v Clayton*, 2007 SCC 32, where (as the minority noted) the creation of the common law power is substituted entirely for the *Charter* analysis: see paras 58–63. However, it is a power to detain, not a search power, which is the central issue in that case.

581 *Stairs*, above note 236 at para 32. Note that it is in principle possible to separate the steps of creating a common law power and deciding whether it is *Charter*-compliant. In each *R v Hufsky*, [1988] 1 SCR 621, and *R v Ladouceur*, [1990] 1 SCR 1257, in the context of s 9 of the *Charter*, the Court created common law powers of detention but then found that those powers were arbitrary (and then saved them under s 1). See the discussion in Chapter 5.

bodily integrity) to least intrusive (searching a vehicle) and then situated the power in issue (searching a portion of the home incident to arrest) on that spectrum, deciding the appropriate additional limits accordingly.

This leads to the second preliminary point to discuss, which is that in the context of statutory search powers, lower courts have recently more consciously relied on a framework first articulated by the Supreme Court in *Goodwin v British Columbia (Superintendent of Motor Vehicles)*. The Court there observed that they had "generally declined to set out a 'hard and fast' test of reasonableness" and that "this flexible approach remains compelling."[582] Nonetheless, they identified factors that are helpful in the reasonableness analysis: the nature and the purpose of the legislative scheme, the mechanism employed and the degree of its potential intrusiveness, and the availability of judicial supervision. Decisions sometimes refer to this as the "*Goodwin* framework," though various decisions treat these as three, four, or five different factors. Courts have used these factors to assess a variety of statutory search powers, including testing of drivers,[583] random drug tests for worker in the nuclear industry,[584] obtaining health records in a child protection context,[585] searches of electronic devices at the border,[586] and others.[587]

A major factor in considering the nature and purpose of the scheme is whether the search is a criminal or regulatory one: "[w]here an impugned law's purpose is regulatory and not criminal, it may be subject to less stringent standards."[588] The relative importance of the purpose will also matter: increasing the ability to detect impaired drivers, for example, is an important purpose, making a law more likely to be found reasonable.[589] A similar result has been found with respect to the

---

582 *Goodwin v British Columbia (Superintendent of Motor Vehicles)*, 2015 SCC 46 at para 57 [*Goodwin*].

583 See *Goodwin* itself, above note 582, as well as *Legault c R*, 2024 QCCA 1136 and *R v Wright*, 2025 SKCA 52 [*Wright*].

584 *Power Workers' Union v Canada (Attorney General)*, 2024 FCA 182 [*Power Workers' Union*].

585 *TL v British Columbia (Attorney General)*, 2023 BCCA 167.

586 *R v Pike*, 2024 ONCA 608.

587 See, for example, *R v Thomas*, 2022 ONCJ 623 [*Thomas*] considering a challenge to the provisions in the *Cannabis Control Act, 2017*, SO 2017, c 26.

588 *Goodwin*, above note 582 at para 60. See also Thomas, above note 587 at para 25:

> However, I am of the view that the *Cannabis Control Act* leans more toward being a regulatory statute than a criminal statute. Section 12(3) exists at the junction of two highly regulated activities: motor vehicle operation and the consumption and use of cannabis.

589 *Wright*, above note 583.

highly regulated nuclear power industry, one with particularly high risks.[590]

In looking at the mechanism employed and the potential intrusiveness, several factors can arise. The likelihood that innocent people will or will not be captured by the provision enters into deciding the reasonableness of a search power. A power which is available in more limited circumstances, and therefore to have fewer people subject to it, is more likely to be reasonable.[591] A search which physically interferes with the bodily integrity or dignity of the subject, or which delves into particularly personal information, will require a higher justification.[592] Further, the accuracy of the information obtained can be relevant: where it is highly reliable it is easier to justify obtaining the information than when the result of the search might or might not be useful: "[t]he reliability of a search or seizure mechanism is directly relevant to the reasonableness of the search or seizure itself."[593] Similarly, overly discretionary powers which might in application result in racial profiling will be less likely to be reasonable.[594]

Finally, whether judicial oversight is available is an important factor: indeed, in *Goodwin* itself "the absence of meaningful review" was the primary factor leading to the law being found unreasonable.[595] This

---

590 *Power Workers' Union*, above note 484.

591 See *Wright*, above note 583 at para 64, holding that contributing to the reasonableness of a law were features that "limit the circumstances under which a screening demand can be made, the duration of a roadside detention, and the type of search that can be conducted."

592 See, for example, *TL*, above note 585, where the warrantless ability to demand health records "interferes with and compromises informational privacy by giving the state broad and essentially untrammeled access to highly intimate information without the individual's knowledge or consent, or any ability on their part to control the disclosure" (para 197).

593 *Goodwin*, above note 582 at para 67. See also, for example, *Legault*, where the Quebec Court of Appeal pointed to the high degree of reliability of roadside screening devices in upholding the law. In contrast, in *Pike*, above note 586 at para 64, a factor entering into finding the warrantless power to search electronic devices at the border to be unreasonable was that:

> the searches the law authorizes mostly miss the mark due to its low threshold. Approximately 62% of the 31,579 digital device searches the Agency conducted between 2017 and 2020 found no evidence of any border law violations. This significant invasion of the privacy of many innocent travellers is a strong sign that the law is unreasonable.

594 *Pike*, above note 586 at para 65: "Linked to these reliability concerns is the risk that border officers will, consciously or unconsciously, target travellers based on their race or racial stereotypes."

595 *Goodwin*, above note 582 at para 75. To similar effect see *Tse*, above note 437 at para 11: "[Section] 184.4 falls down on the matter of accountability because the

issue assumes greater importance in the case of warrantless searches, where there will have been no prior authorization mechanism.[596] Judicial oversight is meant to ensure meaningful review of the use of a search power and to mitigate the potential for indiscriminate and discriminatory uses of it.[597] This factor can compound with others, in the sense that oversight is even more important when the search technique is unreliable, gathers unnecessary information, or is too discretionary.

With those preliminary points out of the way, we shall turn to consider how, in practice, the point that the standard varies according to how privacy and state interests differ from the norm is reflected in the requirements of various statutory search powers. Note, for example, that the requirements for the issuance of a general production order, which engages exactly the same individual and state interests as a search warrant but simply provides practical convenience in gathering the evidence, are the same as those for a search warrant. On the other hand, some production orders are seen as gathering less intrusive information: for instance, the name of a bank account holder.[598] For the most part, this sort of information will only allow the police to go and seek further authorization, in that case to now seek a search warrant because they have identified the person to investigate. Alternatively, production orders are available to obtain "transmission data," but this is explicitly defined as information that "does not reveal the substance, meaning or purpose of the communication."[599] These production orders and others infringe on privacy less than other searches, and so are available on reasonable suspicion.

Similarly, note that tracking warrants are divided into two categories: those that track the location of items, which can be issued on reasonable suspicion, and those that track the location of people, which require reasonable grounds. This difference reflects that tracking a person's location is more intrusive than tracking property. The important point is that a warrant power which authorizes a search too readily will be an unreasonable law and will therefore violate section 8.[600]

---

legislative scheme does not provide any mechanism to permit oversight of the police use of this power."

596 *Goodwin*, above note 582 at para 71; *Pike*, above note 586 at para 75.

597 *Goodwin*, above note 582 at para 70; *TL*, above note 585 at para 170.

598 Section 487.018.

599 Section 487.011.

600 See, for example, *R v Grandison*, 2016 BCSC 1712, dealing with a since-replaced production order, which permitted police to gain the contents of text messages if there were reasonable grounds to believe that an offence had been or "is suspected to have been" committed. The court found at para 96 that the provision was unconstitutional because it used the lower standard to permit obtaining

Further, the addition of greater protection can also easily be seen in the requirements of other warrant provisions. For example, additional requirements are imposed in the case of electronic surveillance and DNA warrants, both of which engage particularly high privacy interests. First, DNA warrants and authorizations are not available for all offences: in each case, they are available only to investigate particularly serious offences, where a higher state interest is at play.[601] Further, both of those sets of provisions have the minimum *Hunter* requirements, but in addition impose other conditions before a warrant can be issued. For example, *Hunter* requires only that the warrant be issued by someone capable of acting judicially, and for the most part, warrants are available from a justice of the peace. Consent authorizations and DNA warrants, on the other hand, cannot be obtained from a justice: only a provincial or superior court judge has the authority. Non-consent authorizations are even more restricted and can be obtained only from a superior court judge. In addition, even after the minimum *Hunter* standards are met, non-consent authorizations and DNA warrants can be issued only if the judge is also satisfied that issuing the warrant is in the best interests of the administration of justice.[602] Beyond that, non-consent authorizations also require that investigative necessity be met.[603]

Essentially, the thing to be recognized is that for a law to be reasonable, it must properly balance the individual and state interests. *Hunter* and section 487 of the *Code* provide a benchmark against which to measure that balance: a law which permits a search relatively easily cannot be allowed to apply when a more serious privacy interest is at stake. This issue is central to the Court's reasoning in *TELUS*, a case discussed in Chapter 5 when considering general warrants.[604]

---

"the kind of information that must be supported by information on oath upon the higher standard of reasonable and probable grounds to believe."

601 See the definition of "offence" in s 183 and the lists of designated offences in s 487.04.

602 Sections 186(1)(a) and 487.05(1), respectively. This is also true of general warrants: s 487.01(1)(b).

603 Section 186(1)(b).

604 *TELUS*, above note 425. Justice Moldaver in that case observes at para 71, for example, that

> [i]f the police sought a general warrant, they would have to meet the requirements of s. 487.01 which are deliberately stricter than those for a conventional warrant. For example, the requirements that a general warrant can only be issued by a judge, not a justice of the peace, and that issuance must be in the best interests of justice themselves serve to ensure that the general warrant remains a rearguard warrant of limited resort.

The primary way in which the question of the reasonableness of a law arises in the search with a warrant context is by variations in the actual requirements of the provisions. However, it is not the only way in which that consideration is reflected. In addition, there are special cases in which the Court has held that the way in which a particular statutory power is to be interpreted or applied should vary depending on the context. We shall consider five such situations: (1) regulatory searches, (2) searches by school officials, (3) searches of media offices, (4) searches of lawyers' offices, and (5) border searches of electronic devices.[605]

### b) Special Cases

#### i) *Regulatory Searches*

The Court has held on many occasions that *Charter* rights must be interpreted in a way consistent with the context in which they arise. This is equally true in the case of section 8, where the Court has held that the approach to section 8 rights as described in *Hunter* does not apply outside the criminal law context. On some occasions, the state's primary interest in conducting a search will not be to prosecute a criminal offence, but rather to enforce the rules of some regulated activity. In that event, the state may well have an interest in "the restaurateur's compliance with public health regulations, the employer's compliance with employment standards and safety legislation . . . the developer's or homeowner's compliance with building codes or zoning regulations [or] compliance with minimum wage, employment equity and human rights legislation."[606] Effective regulation of these areas may require surprise inspections or the examination of records, and, therefore, the Court has held that people engaged in these activities have a lower expectation of privacy in relation to those activities. Accordingly, searches and seizures that do not comply with the *Hunter* standards might nonetheless be reasonable under section 8: "[w]here an

---

605 One might note as well in this context the decision in *Laporte*, above note 381. The police were seeking a search warrant to authorize surgery to remove a bullet from a suspect's shoulder. The Crown argued that the suspect's shoulder fell within s 487 as a "building, receptacle or place," but the judge refused to read the section in a way which would allow for the warrant. He concluded that the interest of the accused in the physical integrity of his body was a much more important interest than that intended to be covered by s 487 and, therefore, outweighed the state's interest in investigation.

606 *Thomson Newspapers Ltd v Canada (Director of Investigation and Research, Restrictive Trade Practices Commission)*, [1990] 1 SCR 425.

impugned law's purpose is regulatory and not criminal, it may be subject to less stringent standards."[607]

On this basis, the Court has concluded that compelling a person to testify regarding predatory pricing procedures under the *Combines Investigation Act*,[608] or to produce various documents under the *Income Tax Act*[609] or the British Columbia *Securities Act*[610] does not constitute unreasonable search or seizure. Although possible prosecution could follow from engaging in the behaviour being investigated, the investigations and the offences are not criminal offences. Accordingly, a search can sometimes be reasonable, even if the *Hunter* protections are not in place.[611]

The Court has at times recognized the importance of keeping this exception in its proper, limited place, so that it does not undermine the *Hunter* standards, or mean that a search will automatically be constitutional if it can be characterized as for a regulatory purpose. In *Colarusso*,[612] for example, the coroner seized blood samples after a fatal traffic accident under provisions of the Ontario *Coroners Act*.[613] No judicial pre-authorization was needed for such a seizure. On the facts, it was clear that the seizure was just as much for the purposes of the police investigation into criminal charges as it was for the legitimate purpose of an inquest (the police transported the samples to the analyst, gave up their previous efforts to obtain a sample from the accused, and so on). The Court held that the evidence was not admissible in the criminal proceedings. Although no difficulty would arise in using the evidence in the context of an inquest "once the evidence has been appropriated by the criminal law enforcement arm of the state for use in criminal proceedings, there is no foundation on which to argue that the coroner's seizure continues to be reasonable."[614]

607 *Goodwin*, above note 582 at para 60.

608 *Ibid*.

609 *R v McKinlay Transport Ltd*, [1990] 1 SCR 627; *R v Jarvis*, [2002] 3 SCR 757 [*Jarvis*]; *R v Ling*, 2002 SCC 74.

610 *British Columbia Securities Commission v Branch*, [1995] 2 SCR 3. See also *Comité paritaire de l'industrie de la chemise v Potash; Comité paritaire de l'industrie de la chemise c Sélection Milton*, [1994] 2 SCR 406, regarding inspection of documents relating to work arrangements.

611 See, for example, *Ontario (Attorney General) v Bogaerts*, 2019 ONCA 876, where a warrantless search power in the context of provincial animal welfare legislation was found to be reasonable. See also *R v Thomas*, 2022 ONCJ 623, dealing with a search power in the *Cannabis Control Act, 2017*, SO 2017, c 26.

612 *Colarusso*, above note 353.

613 RSO 1990, c C.37.

614 *Colarusso*, above note 353. See the similar point in *R v White*, [1999] 2 SCR 417, where an accused was obliged under the British Columbia *Motor Vehicle Act*,

Similarly, in *Goodwin v British Columbia (Superintendent of Motor vehicles)*, the Court struck down a breath-testing scheme which was found to be *intra vires* the province, and therefore regulatory, but which nonetheless departed too greatly from the required levels of protection. For example, under the *Criminal Code* breath-testing scheme which existed at the time, the police needed reasonable suspicion to administer a roadside breath test which would produce a "pass/fail" result, but the only criminal consequence of a "fail" would be that the officer would then have reasonable grounds to make a breathalyzer demand. Under the provincial scheme, however, the accused's license would immediately be suspended for ninety days and their car would be impounded for thirty days. Based on that and other concerns, the Court concluded that the scheme "fails to strike a reasonable balance between the interests of the state against those of individual motorists" and struck it down.[615]

In *R v Jarvis*, the Court attempted to distinguish more clearly when the different levels of *Charter* protection apply. In that case the accused was required to produce various pieces of information under the *Income Tax Act*, a statute that the Court notes depends on self-reporting and, therefore, is especially dependent on the honesty of taxpayers. As a result, broad inspection and audit powers are necessary to maintain the integrity of the tax system. At a certain point, however, investigation as to whether a taxpayer has remitted sufficient funds to the government can become an investigation into whether that taxpayer should be prosecuted for an offence. Accordingly, the Court said, differing levels of *Charter* protection might be found within the same statute. As a general guideline, administrative officials must cease to use their broader investigative powers, such as mandatory inspection or production of documents, "where the predominant purpose of a particular inquiry is the determination of penal liability," or, put another way, where there has been a "crystallization of the adversarial relationship."[616] Determining when officials have "crossed the Rubicon," as the Court puts it, depends on consideration of various factors, none

RSBC 1996, c 318, to report an accident to the police. Although that provision did not violate the principle against self-incrimination inherent in s 7 if the statement was confined to the context in which it was taken, it would violate s 7 to let the statement be used in criminal proceedings.

615 *Goodwin*, above note 582 at para 77. See also *R v Gorman*, 2022 NLSC 67, finding a search power in s 41 of the *Canada Post Corporation Act*, RSC 1985, c C-10 (the *CPCA*) to violate s 8 on the basis that the law provided insufficient protection to the privacy rights at stake.

616 *Jarvis*, above note 609 at paras 88 and 102, respectively.

of which is conclusive on its own. These include, in the income tax context, whether there are reasonable grounds to lay charges, whether the general conduct of the authorities was consistent with a criminal investigation, whether an auditor's files have been transferred to investigators, whether an auditor effectively acted as an agent for investigators and whether the investigators intended that to happen, whether the evidence concerns liability to taxation or prosecution, and other circumstances.[617]

The general justification for departing from the *Hunter* standards in regulatory contexts is the principle that *Charter* rights must be interpreted in context.[618] That principle is well established, but its application does create a potential slippery slope around section 8 protection. In *Jarvis*, for example, the Court specifically notes that nothing prevents an auditor from passing files to investigators or stops investigators from using that evidence. This stance seems inconsistent with the approach in *Colarusso*.[619] Further, there is surely some irony in the fact that *Hunter*, the case that first delineated the high standards to which searches are generally to be held under section 8, itself concerned a search in a regulatory context. The Court suggests in *Jarvis* that the search in *Hunter* was a greater violation of privacy expectations because it authorized entry onto private premises.[620] Still, it must be said that, despite the steps taken in *Jarvis* to help clarify when different levels of *Charter* protection apply, there remains considerable scope for difference of opinion. Therefore, in many cases, the decision as to whether a search was reasonable will be made only after the fact. That is a departure from the goal of section 8, which is to prevent unreasonable searches from occurring.

The situation is further muddied by the decision in *R v Nolet*. In that case the police stopped a tractor trailer driving through Saskatchewan, relying on regulatory powers to stop and search from provincial motor vehicle legislation. At some point while examining the truck the officer became suspicious of criminal activity, and eventually he found a large sum of cash inside a duffel bag in the cab. A further search

---

617 *Ibid* at para 94.

618 See, for example, *Law Society of Alberta v Sidhu*, 2017 ABCA 224 at para 17, upholding a search made into a lawyer's conduct by the Law Society: "What is unreasonable in a criminal investigation may well be reasonable in a regulatory investigation."

619 *Colarusso*, above note 353. See also David Stratas, "'Crossing the Rubicon': The Supreme Court and Regulatory Investigations" (2003) 6 *Criminal Reports* (6th) 74.

620 *Jarvis*, above note 609 at para 61.

turned up drugs in a hidden compartment. The trial judge had found the initial search of the cab to violate section 8: although the officer had tried still to use regulatory powers to conduct the search, his predominant purpose by that time was the investigation of a criminal offence. The Supreme Court of Canada, however, held that that was incorrect reasoning.[621]

The Court concluded that as long as the officer still had a continuing regulatory purpose upon which to justify the search, it did not matter what the officer's predominant purpose was.[622] Indeed, they held that reliance on *Jarvis* in this context was misplaced. *Jarvis* had concerned using powers relating to a civil dispute for purposes of a penal proceeding, they held: in *Nolet* the context was always penal.[623]

This approach creates the danger of a real expansion of what amount to criminal law powers, so long as *some* criminal law purpose can still be found. What the Court seemed to have in mind in *Nolet* was "fluid" factual situations, where police have either no particular suspicion or an undefined one at the start, which at some point crystallizes into an opinion about criminal activity. What they were trying to avoid was having the interaction between the police and the accused suddenly become subject to section 8 criminal standards and unexpectedly, almost retroactively, become unconstitutional. The difficulty is that the test they have articulated to accomplish that creates the real risk of police *starting* with criminal concerns but being able to make use of non-criminal powers to investigate them, which is exactly what *Jarvis* was aiming to avoid. It permits police to be primarily motivated by a criminal law interest in a person but to rely on powers that would not be available and would be unconstitutional if used for that purpose, provided the trial judge will accept that *some* regulatory purpose was also in the officer's mind.[624] That is an approach which encourages police to push the limits, which is an undesirable result.

---

621 *Nolet*, above note 255.

622 *Ibid* at para 41.

623 See the discussion in Steve Coughlan, "Stopping Vehicles on a Downhill Slope: *R v Nolet*" (2010) 76 *Criminal Reports* (6th) 24.

624 See, for example, *R v Ali*, 2016 ABCA 261, where officers saw Fearon, a person known to be involved in criminal activity, as a passenger in a vehicle driven by the accused, who was unknown to them. There was nothing remarkable about the way in which the vehicle was being driven and a CPIC check of the vehicle raised no concerns, but nonetheless the police stopped the vehicle to "see what Mr. Fearon was up to": this eventually led to the accused being searched and narcotics being found. The Alberta Court of Appeal upheld the search, on the basis that the trial judge's finding of fact that the police *also* had the traffic act regulatory purpose of checking ownership of the vehicle was entitled to

Nonetheless, it is clear that the Court has not intended to abandon the notion that powers created for one context with less severe consequences than a criminal proceeding cannot be used for criminal prosecution purposes. In *Cole*, for example, a teacher was discovered by a school technician to have nude and semi-nude photographs of a student stored on his laptop. The school board was entitled, because of its statutory obligation to maintain a safe environment for students, to examine the teacher's laptop and was authorized to make a CD of the material found. However, when the board then handed that CD to the police without a warrant, the accused's section 8 rights were violated. Although the school board had acquired lawful possession of the laptop for administrative purposes, that did not give the police a power to search: "[w]here a lower constitutional standard is applicable in an administrative context, as in this case, the police cannot invoke that standard to evade the prior judicial authorization that is normally required for searches or seizures in the context of criminal investigations."[625]

Exactly when regulatory search powers can or cannot be used is now less clear than it might have been.

### ii) *Searches by School Officials*

Most statutory search powers are given to peace officers or at least to public officers such as customs officers.[626] In *R v M(MR)*, however, the Court decided that, in some circumstances, school officials such as a vice-principal can have statutory search powers.[627] These powers might even arise off the school grounds, in the case of off-site school-sanctioned events, such as a prom.[628] Strictly the decision in *M(MR)* dealt only with the Nova Scotia *Education Act*, but subsequent cases have found the equivalent statutes in other provinces to be similar enough that the same power exists there.[629]

In *M(MR)* the accused was a student at a junior high school. Based on a tip that the accused would be selling drugs at a school dance, the vice-principal told the accused to come to his office. An RCMP officer

---

deference. On the other hand, see *R v Frederick*, 2021 ONSC 7140, where the officer's purported "dual purpose" was found, on the facts, to actually only be a concern about criminal matters.

625 *Cole*, above note 25 at para 69.

626 See the definition of "public officer" in s 2 of the *Code*.

627 *M(MR)*, above note 3.

628 *Gillies (Litigation guardian of) v Toronto District School Board*, 2015 ONSC 1038 (*Gillies*].

629 See, for example, *R v Ermine*, 2014 SKPC 162; *R v JM*, 2012 BCPC 126; or *R v SMZ*, [1998] MJ No 587 (CA).

who had been requested by the vice-principal arrived at this point and was present in the room as the vice-principal searched the accused, finding a bag of marijuana in his sock. The vice-principal gave the bag to the officer who arrested the accused. The accused argued at trial that he had been subject to an unreasonable search.

The Court agreed that the accused had a reasonable expectation of privacy: a diminished one because of the school environment, but he did have one. They also agreed that the search by the vice-principal constituted state action: *not* because the vice-principal had acted as an agent of the state (he had not, they found) but because school officials themselves for these purposes constituted state actors. In other words, what was at issue was, in essence, a regulatory search rather than a criminal search. Had this been a search by an agent of the police, the ordinary *Hunter* standards and, in particular, the need for a warrant, would have applied. Because it was a search in a non-criminal context, a different standard could apply.

The question therefore became whether the search was authorized by law, as the *Collins* test requires. In this case, there was no explicit statutory search power. Nor could the *Waterfield* test be applied to create a common law power since it was not a police officer who had searched. However, the Nova Scotia *Education Act* and regulations imposed a duty on the school officials to maintain proper order and discipline in the school, and this "by necessary implication authorizes searches of students."[630] Obviously, the exact nature of that power had to be articulated by the Court, though they noted that the reduced expectation of privacy coupled with the need to protect students meant that "a more lenient and flexible approach should be taken to searches conducted by teachers and principals than would apply to searches conducted by the police."[631]

Specifically, they concluded that searches by school officials should not be subject to the presumption of unreasonableness by reason of being warrantless. Instead, a school official can search without a warrant if they have reasonable grounds to believe that there has been a breach of school regulations or discipline and that a search of a student would reveal evidence of that breach. This is a relaxed standard but still provides protection against searches without sufficient justification.[632]

630 *M(MR)*, above note 3 at para 51.

631 *Ibid* at para 47.

632 See, for example, *Gillies*, above note 628, where a school principal wanted to require every student attending prom to take a breathalyser test as a condition of entry. Although the principal had an educated hunch that drinking was a problem at the school, he did "not possess the necessary reasonable grounds

Those reasonable grounds might arise from "information received from one student considered to be credible, information received from more than one student, a teacher's or principal's own observations, or any combination of these pieces of information which the relevant authority considers to be credible."[633]

One oddity around *M(MR)* ought to be noted, namely, that it has sometimes been mischaracterized in later decisions. The decision is unambiguous in stating that the school official "must have reasonable grounds to *believe*" that a rule was broken and evidence will be found.[634] It has been wrongly described, however, as creating a search power based on reasonable *suspicion*.[635] *M(MR)* did discuss that US caselaw on school searches was based on the reasonable suspicion standard and after that observed that a relaxing of the *Hunter* requirements was also appropriate in Canada. Nonetheless, the relaxation actually adopted was to dispense with the warrant requirement and to allow investigations for school rules rather than criminal offences: it is simply wrong to say *M(MR)* created a search power based on reasonable suspicion.

#### *iii) Searches of Media Offices*

Special concerns come into play when warrants are issued for the search of media offices, because in such cases, the guarantee of freedom of the press in section 2(b) of the *Charter* becomes relevant. For many years the Supreme Court of Canada has taken the view that these special considerations provided "a backdrop against which the reasonableness of the search may be evaluated" and meant that a justice issuing such a warrant had to give careful consideration to whether to issue the warrant or impose conditions, but nonetheless they held that there were no additional formal requirements.[636] The Court has held to this position

---

to believe that a school rule or the law is being or has been violated, and that evidence of that violation will be found in the search of a student" (para 125). The *M(MR)* power would therefore not permit a search. In contrast see *R v Calabretta*, 2020 ONCJ 435, where the trial judge concluded that "[d]espite the absence of reasonable grounds, the mandatory security search of bags at a prom is reasonable in all the circumstances." With respect, it is not clear in *Calabretta* what the actual source of authority was taken to be, other than the general "reasonableness," which ought not to be sufficient.

633 *Ibid* at para 50.

634 *Ibid* [emphasis added].

635 See the decision of Binnie J in *AM*, above note 37 at para 45, or footnote 1 in *Chehil*, above note 37, for the claim that it is based on reasonable suspicion.

636 *Canadian Broadcasting Corp v New Brunswick (Attorney General)*, [1991] 3 SCR 459 at para 32. See also *Canadian Broadcasting Corp v Lessard*, [1991] 3 SCR 421. In addition, see *National Post*, above note 505, in which the applicant unsuccessfully sought a reconsideration of those principles.

as recently as 2018.[637] However, in 2017 the *Journalistic Sources Protection Act* came into force, amending the *Criminal Code* and the *Canada Evidence Act* so that different rules apply when a warrant relates to a journalist's communications or material in the hands of a journalist.[638] The continuing common law rules will be set out below, but it appears they should have at best a residual role, and so it is the new statutory scheme that is most important.

The earlier caselaw had acknowledged the special situation involved when warrants targeted information in the hands of a journalist, but the journalist was not the target of the investigation: the media play a vital role in a democracy and they would generally be innocent third parties in relation to any criminal proceedings. Those concerns now animate the new provisions in the *Code*. They create a two-stage process, imposing special rules first around the issuance of a warrant, and then secondly around dealing with any material obtained by that warrant.

The new provisions apply when essentially any type of warrant, authorization or production order targets "a journalist's communications or an object, document or data relating to or in the possession of a journalist."[639] In that event, whatever might normally be the case for that particular warrant, the application must be made to a superior court judge. That judge can issue the order only if, in addition to whatever the ordinary requirements for it might be, the judge is satisfied that

> (a) there is no other way by which the information can reasonably be obtained; and
> (b) the public interest in the investigation and prosecution of a criminal offence outweighs the journalist's right to privacy in gathering and disseminating information.

These requirements are very similar to the considerations the Court had said should be taken into account by a justice asked to issue a warrant concerning media offices, but have now statutorily been made preconditions. That they are now threshold requirements, rather than simply relevant considerations, is a reflection of the greater protection

637 *Vice Media*, above note 518.

638 See *Journalistic Sources Protection Act*, SC 2017, c 22, adding ss 488.01 and 488.02 to the *Code*.

639 The full list in s 488.01(2) is "a warrant under section 487.01, 487.1, 492.1 or 492.2, a search warrant under this Act, notably under section 487, an authorization under section 184.2, 184.3, 186 or 188, or an order under any of sections 487.014 to 487.017."

offered by the statutory scheme.[640] A further reflection of that point is that the judge asked to issue the warrant can appoint a special advocate to present observations in the interests of freedom of the press, which is an unusual step in what is normally an *ex parte* procedure.

Those first-stage rules do not apply when the warrant is issued in relation to the commission of an offence by a journalist, but the second-stage rules described below will still apply to any material which might disclose a journalistic source.[641]

As further protection for freedom of the press, the new provisions also anticipate the situation in which the police are executing a warrant and in the course of doing so discover material that relates to a journalist's communications or an object, document or data relating to or in the possession of a journalist. In that event, they are to refrain from examining or reproducing any documents, place them in a sealed packet, and then make an application to a superior court judge for direction. That judge has a range of choices, including confirming the warrant, varying it or sealing some portion of what was found to be dealt with by the second-stage process described below, or even revoking the warrant "if the judge is of the opinion that the applicant knew or ought reasonably to have known" that these provisions should have been used initially.[642]

At the second stage, when police obtain material under these provisions, they are to place the material in a sealed packet which is to be kept in the custody of the court. An officer can only examine the material by first giving notice to the journalist or media outlet, who can apply for "an order that the document is not to be disclosed to an officer on the grounds that the document identifies or is likely to identity a journalistic source."[643] The judge, in considering whether to order disclosure, is to take into account the same special considerations applying at the first stage to issuing the warrant, and can order that it be disclosed with or without conditions, or that it be returned to the journalist or media outlet.

That sets out the statutory scheme. The 2018 decision in *R v Vice Media Inc* postdates those provisions, but the facts arose beforehand and

---

640 See the discussion of the *Journalistic Sources Protection Act* amendments in *Denis v Côté*, 2019 SCC 44. That *Act* also added provisions dealing with subpoenas issued to journalists to the *Canada Evidence Act*, RSC 1985, c C5: see s 39.1. It is those amendments, rather than the ones to the warrant provisions in the *Criminal Code*, which are at issue in *Denis v Côté*.

641 Section 488.01(5), (6).

642 Section 488.01(10).

643 Section 488.02(3).

so the Court consciously did not consider the new provisions. Given the very broad scope of the statute — any type of warrant seeking "a journalist's communications or an object, document or data relating to or in the possession of a journalist" — it seems unlikely that there can be much of even a residual role for the common law scheme in the issuing of warrants or production orders. However, the decision also sets out rules for review after the fact of such orders, and so it is worth setting out the decision.

In very large measure, *Vice Media* just reaffirmed the existing common law rules from earlier cases such as *Lessard*, but with some reorganization. The test is a four-part analysis. First, the authorizing judge decides whether to give notice to the media of the application, based on questions such as whether there is urgency, whether the judge might not otherwise have all the necessary information, and so on. Second, all the statutory preconditions for the order must be met. Third, the judge must balance the state's interest in the investigation and prosecution of crimes and the media's right to privacy in gathering and disseminating the news. The relevant circumstances to take into account may include but are not limited to:

(a) the likelihood and extent of any potential chilling effects;
(b) the scope of the materials sought and whether the order sought is narrowly tailored;
(c) the likely probative value of the materials;
(d) whether there are alternative sources from which the information may reasonably be obtained and, if so, whether the police have made all reasonable efforts to obtain the information from those sources (*Lessard* factor 5);
(e) the effect of prior partial publication, now assessed on a case-by-case basis (*Lessard* factor 6); and
(f) more broadly, the vital role that the media plays in the functioning of a democratic society and the fact that the media will generally be an innocent third party (*Lessard* factor 3).

Fourth, the authorizing judge should consider whether to impose conditions on the order to ensure that the media will not be unduly impeded in the publishing and dissemination of the news, or to order that the materials be sealed for a period pending review.[644]

*Vice Media* also noted the rules for reviewing production orders served on media organizations (which is more likely than the use of a search warrant). The Court noted that in any event there is a statutory

644 *Vice Media*, above note 518 at para 82.

right of review for all production orders.[645] In addition, they concluded that a production order not issued by a superior court judge could be reviewed by essentially the same rules as those applying to search warrants (see the discussion above), but with special rules potentially applying because of the media context:

> if the order is granted *ex parte* and is later challenged by the media, the standard of review is determined by applying the following test: if the media points to information not before the authorizing judge that, in the reviewing judge's opinion, could reasonably have affected the authorizing judge's decision to issue the order, then the media will be entitled to a *de novo* review. If, on the other hand, the media fails to meet this threshold requirement, then the traditional *Garofoli* standard will apply, meaning that the production order may be set aside only if the media can establish that — in light of the record before the authorizing judge, as amplified on review — there was no reasonable basis on which the authorizing judge could have granted the order.[646]

Note, however, that in conclusion the new statutory rules take precedence over these common law rules, which will dramatically limit the application of the latter. The Court in *Vice Media* said they were not considering the impact of the new provisions, but as a matter of fact they seem to mean that many of the common law rules in that case were already outdated. *Vice Media*, for example, limits *certiorari* applications reviewing production orders to those orders which were not issued by a superior court. The new journalistic source protection provisions, however, require that applications be brought to a superior court, which seems to mean that the common law rule could only have effect during a transitional period.

#### iv) *Searches of Lawyers' Offices*

The issue of searches of lawyers' offices first arose for the Court in *Descôteaux v Mierzwinski*,[647] where police went to a legal aid office with a search warrant, seeking evidence that a suspect had falsely represented his income in order to obtain legal aid. This highlighted the danger that the use of search warrants could on occasion come into conflict with protecting solicitor–client privilege. As a result, Parliament placed section 488.1 in the *Code*, intending that it should govern the situation. In fact, that provision was then found, in *Lavallee, Rackel & Heintz*

645 Section 487.0193.

646 *Vice Media*, above note 518 at para 83.

647 [1982] 1 SCR 860.

*v Canada (Attorney General)*, to insufficiently protect solicitor–client privilege and to violate section 8 as a result.[648] The Court chose to strike down the entire provision in order to give Parliament an opportunity to redraft it, but set out general principles that would govern such searches in the interim. As a matter of fact Parliament has never enacted replacement legislation, and so the Court's general principles about how to apply section 487 when lawyers' offices are targeted still set out the governing law.

Those principles are as follows:

1. No search warrant can be issued with regards to documents that are known to be protected by solicitor–client privilege.
2. Before searching a law office, the investigative authorities must satisfy the issuing justice that there exists no other reasonable alternative to the search.
3. When allowing a law office to be searched, the issuing justice must be rigorously demanding so to afford maximum protection of solicitor–client confidentiality.
4. Except when the warrant specifically authorizes the immediate examination, copying and seizure of an identified document, all documents in possession of a lawyer must be sealed before being examined or removed from the lawyer's possession.
5. Every effort must be made to contact the lawyer and the client at the time of the execution of the search warrant. Where the lawyer or the client cannot be contacted, a representative of the Bar should be allowed to oversee the sealing and seizure of documents.
6. The investigative officer executing the warrant should report to the justice of the peace the efforts made to contact all potential privilege holders, who should then be given a reasonable opportunity to assert a claim of privilege and, if that claim is contested, to have the issue judicially decided.

---

648 2002 SCC 61 [*Lavallee*]. The Court commented at para 36:

> Since *Hunter*, this Court has striven to strike an appropriate balance between privacy interests on the one hand and the exigencies of law enforcement on the other . . . . Sometimes, however, the traditional balancing of interests involved in a s. 8 analysis is inappropriate. As it was stated in *R v Mills*, [1999] 3 SCR 668 at para. 86, "the appropriateness of the balance is assessed according to the nature of the interests at stake in a particular context, and the place of these interests within our legal and political traditions." Where the interest at stake is solicitor–client privilege — a principle of fundamental justice and civil right of supreme importance in Canadian law — the usual balancing exercise referred to above is not particularly helpful.

7. If notification of potential privilege holders is not possible, the lawyer who had custody of the documents seized, or another lawyer appointed either by the Law Society or by the court, should examine the documents to determine whether a claim of privilege should be asserted, and should be given a reasonable opportunity to do so.
8. The Attorney General may make submissions on the issue of privilege, but should not be permitted to inspect the documents beforehand. The prosecuting authority can only inspect the documents if and when it is determined by a judge that the documents are not privileged.
9. Where sealed documents are found not to be privileged, they may be used in the normal course of the investigation.
10. Where documents are found to be privileged, they are to be returned immediately to the holder of the privilege, or to a person designated by the court.[649]

*Lavallee* was targeted specifically at searches of a lawyer's office. However, it has been held that the key consideration is that documents protected by solicitor-client privilege are the subject of the search, and documents in a lawyer's officer are presumptively protected by that. Therefore, in any case where documents protected by that privilege are targeted, wherever they might be located, special considerations apply.[650]

More recently, the Court has applied the same principles to demands by Revenue Canada on lawyers and notaries. Provisions in the *Income Tax Act* allowed tax authorities to require any person to provide information or documents for purposes related to that Act, and in fact many such requests were made to notaries in Quebec, leading to a *Charter* challenge in *Canada (Procureur General) c Chambre des notaries du Quebec*.[651] Relying in part on *Lavallee*, the Court struck down that power.

---

649 *Ibid* at para 49.

650 See *R v Douglas*, 2017 MBCA 63 at paras 59–65. See also *R v Wendt*, 2025 ONSC 812, where a lawyer had a law office in a rented room in a private residence but occasionally had documents in a common area. In that particular case a *Lavallee* warrant was issued for a search of the law office when a meth lab (alleged to be operated by the owner of the residence was found, but at trial that warrant was quashed. Only conclusory statements were offered for the claim that relevant evidence might be found in the law office, and a search of that location was not a last resort.

651 *Canada (Procureur General) c Chambre des notaries du Quebec*, 2016 SCC 20 [*Canada (Procureur General)*]. The Court concluded that no difference in analysis arose because the notices were served on notaries as opposed to lawyers: see para 43.

Interestingly, the case combines two special considerations, since although the search was of a lawyer's officer, it was also a regulatory search. The Court concluded, however, that the latter fact made no difference. In other regulatory searches the demand was made of the person subject to the regulatory scheme, but here it was made of the notary or lawyer, and so solicitor-client privilege was at stake. The lesson of *Lavallee* was that "solicitorclient privilege must remain as close to absolute as possible if it is to retain relevance," and in this case the scheme failed that standard.[652] No notice was given to clients of the demand, and the onus was placed on the notary or lawyer to assert a claim of privilege. That was not an adequate protection, because the notary or lawyer will not always make the same choice the client would, might be negligent on occasion, and is in a conflict of interest because of the possibility of being prosecuted for non-compliance.[653] In addition disclosure was not absolutely necessary, since other sources for the information might be available. The provisions were therefore found to violate section 8 and not be saved under section 1.

*v) Border Searches of Electronic Devices*

An area which has been in flux for some years, and remains in that state at this time of writing, concerns searches by border officers of electronic devices such as laptops or cellphones carried by persons entering or returning to Canada. For some time, customs officers exercised such a power, arguing that it was given to them by the *Customs Act*. That Act states that a customs officer has the power to "examine any goods that have been imported,"[654] and "goods" are taken to include documents, including electronic ones. In addition, anything which is brought into the country is being "imported," even if it belonged to the person and went with them when they left the country in the first place. On that basis, it was argued that a customs officer was authorized to examine the contents of a cellphone or laptop.[655] Border security in the abstract

652 *Canada (Procureur General)*, above note 651 at para 38, quoting *Lavallee*, above note 648 at para 36. On a similar point, see *R v Telfer*, 2019 MBQB 12, where a wiretap authorization did not allow police to live monitor calls to the subject's lawyer. The trial judge concluded that this limitation applied even to calls where the subject was only speaking with administrative staff at the lawyer's office.

653 *Canada (Procureur General)*, above note 651 at paras 55–56.

654 *Customs Act*, RSC 1985, c 1 (2nd Supp), s 99(1).

655 See, for example, *R v Leask*, 2008 ONCJ 25; *R v Whittaker*, 2010 NBPC 32; *R v Saikaley*, 2012 ONSC 6794; *R v Buss*, 2014 BCPC 16; or *R v Gibson*, 2017 BCPC 237, among others. For academic commentary see Robert J Currie, "Electronic Devices at the Border: The Next Frontier of Canadian Search and Seizure Law"

does invoke a higher state interest, and that was reflected in the standard set for such *Customs Act* searches: they did not require reasonable grounds, nor reasonable suspicion, nor indeed any individualized grounds: they were available as a matter of routine.

Many trial level courts found such searches to be lawful, but the first court of appeal level decision concerning the power, the Alberta Court of Appeal decision in *R v Canfield*, found the law itself to be unreasonable.[656] Early *Charter* caselaw had grouped border searches into three categories, the least serious of which — "routine questioning which every traveller undergoes at a port of entry, sometimes accompanied by a search of baggage and perhaps a pat or frisk of outer clothing"[657] — was seen as not attracting any *Charter* protections. However, those rules had been laid down before the proliferation of personal electronic devices, which had since become commonplace and were recognized to attract a strong privacy interest. The strong privacy interest in electronic devices meant that the standard in the *Customs Act* — that such devices could be searched without individualized grounds — was an unreasonable one. The Alberta Court of Appeal accepted that the term "goods" in the *Customs Act* did include such devices, thereby allowing such searches, and they therefore struck down that definition. They did not, however, pass judgment as to what standard would be appropriate, saying that was a matter for Parliament.[658]

Subsequently, the Ontario Court of Appeal also struck down the legislation in *R v Pike*.[659] They echoed the concern from *Canfield* about the high privacy interest in electronic devices. In addition, they noted that the absence of any real standard for the search increased the possibility that the power would be used in a discriminatory way.[660]

---

(2016) 14 *Canadian Journal of Learning and Technology* 289; Steven Penney, "'Mere Evidence'? Why Customs Searches of Digital Devices Violate Section 8 of the *Charter*" (2016) 49:2 *UBC Law Review* 485; Liam M Hayes, "Smartphone Searches: A Legal Crossroads Between Charter Rights and Law Enforcement" (2018) 66 *Criminal Law Quarterly* 196; and Robert Diab, "Protecting the Right to Privacy in Digital Devices: Reasonable Search on Arrest and at the Border" (2018) 69 *University of New Brunswick Law Journal* 96.

In addition, s 153.1 of the *Customs Act* makes it an offence for a person to hinder or prevent an officer from doing anything that the officer is authorized to do under the Act, which it was sometimes argued meant that there was an obligation for the owner to reveal the password for a device, in order to enable the search.

656 *R v Canfield*, 2020 ABCA 383 [*Canfield*].

657 *Canfield*, above note 656 at para 3, quoting from *R v Simmons*, [1988] 2 SCR 495.

658 *Canfield*, above note 656 at para 75.

659 *R v Pike*, 2024 ONCA 608 [*Pike*].

660 *Pike*, above note 659 at paras 64–66.

The Ontario Court of Appeal went further than *Canfield* had, in that they concluded that the appropriate standard for such a search power would be reasonable suspicion. That standard would prevent searches based on mere hunches, would guard against the concern of mass surveillance and would reduce the risk of the search power being used in a discriminatory way but would still account for the state's border control interests and travellers' reduced expectation of privacy at the border.

*Canfield* suspended its 2020 declaration of invalidity for one year at first, then for a further six months,[661] but declined to grant a further suspension after that.[662] *Pike* was decided in 2024, by which time *An Act to amend the Customs Act and the Preclearance Act, 2016*[663] had gone through the Senate and had first reading in the House of Commons. Pike also suspended its declaration of invalidity, but only for six months since the legislative process was already underway. That Bill would have set a reasonable suspicion standard for searches of electronic devices. However, the Bill did not proceed past first reading in the House before the federal election in April 2025, and no replacement Bill has yet been proposed.

## 3) Was the Manner of Search Reasonable?

Even if a search power exists and that power is reasonable, the *Collins* test allows a court to find that the search in question was unreasonable because of the manner in which it was conducted. In looking at this question, there is no strong reason to distinguish between searches with a warrant and those without.[664]

In *Collins*, the accused was searched for drugs by an officer who grabbed her by the throat at the first moment. The Court agreed that a search power may have existed, but noted that "without very specific information, a seizure by the throat, as in this case, would be unreasonable."[665] In general, the more intrusive the nature of the search, the

661 *R v Canfield*, 2021 ABCA 352.

662 *R v Canfield*, 2022 ABCA 145.

663 Bill S-7, *An Act to amend the Customs Act and the Preclearance Act, 2016*, 44th Parliament, 1st Session.

664 To some extent in the case of common law police powers, there can be overlap between this third stage of the *Collins* test and the *Waterfield* test; that is, the existence of the common law power depends on the officer's actions having been reasonably necessary, and so "[i]f the extent of the infringement is greater than what is required to search for weapons, the search will not be authorized by law": *MacDonald*, above note 318 at para 47.

665 *Collins*, above note 1 at para 24.

greater the constraints on the way in which the search can reasonably be performed.[666] Thus, for example, in *Golden*, beyond deciding the circumstances in which strip searches incident to arrest were permitted, the Court went on to suggest guidelines for the manner in which such searches could be conducted. These guidelines raise issues such as the number and gender of the officers conducting the search, the location of the search, how quickly the search is conducted, and so on.[667]

One context in which the question of the reasonableness of the manner of search often arises is in the case of a "hard entry" or "dynamic entry" to execute a search warrant. Most commonly, this occurs in connection with drug searches where the police believe that the inhabitants of the building might be armed or that the evidence might be quickly destroyed. The ordinary rule is that police must obey the "knock and announce" rule, by which they would give notice of their presence, identify themselves as peace officers, and show their warrant.[668] The police must also give the occupants of the place some period of time after this announcement to allow the police in, before resorting to a dynamic entry.[669] Where the police do not do so, the onus is on the police to explain why: the greater the departure, the heavier the onus.[670] The Court in *R v Cornell* laid out several governing principles for dynamic entries.

First, the dynamic entry must be justified based on the information known to the police at the time: it cannot be justified *post facto*, but equally the discovery after the fact that no weapons were in the place searched does not automatically invalidate the search. Second, the police must be allowed a certain amount of latitude in the manner in which they choose to enter premises, because they cannot be expected in advance to measure precisely the amount of force that will

---

666 *Golden*, above note 22 at para 87.

667 *Ibid* at para 101.

668 *Eccles v Bourque*, [1975] 2 SCR 739; *Genest*, above note 376. See also *Cornell*, above note 379 at para 18: "In the ordinary case, they should give: '(i) notice of presence by knocking or ringing the door bell, (ii) notice of authority, by identifying themselves as law enforcement officers and (iii) notice of purpose, by stating a lawful reason for entry'."

669 See *R v Robertson*, 2019 BCCA 116, where the police waited only four seconds after identifying their lawful basis for entry before using a battering ram on the door. This was found to be a hybrid approach which defeated the purpose of both the knock and announce rule and a hard entry, and violated s 8.

670 *Cornell*, above note 379.

be required. Finally, on review, the trial judge's assessment of the facts in these regards must be accorded substantial deference.[671]

A dynamic entry will be found to have been unreasonably conducted if the police simply follow a blanket policy to use them in all drug raids.[672] The fact that a policy exists, however, is not necessarily fatal to the validity of the manner of search if the facts of the case justified a dynamic entry.[673] Nor does the fact that police reach the same conclusion about the need for a dynamic entry in the vast majority of drug cases mean that there is a blanket policy.[674]

The manner in which a search was carried out could be found to be unreasonable for reasons other than the amount of physical force used. For example, a search of a computer might be unreasonable if it is looking for evidence of a particular offence but examines portions of the computer that could not reasonably contain evidence of that offence.[675] Similarly a physical search of a location could be broader than necessary[676] or carried out at the wrong time.[677] And although racial profiling is typically discussed in the context of detentions rather than searches, there is some authority that the practice can also invalidate a search.[678]

In addition, the manner of a search could be unreasonable because of its impact. As discussed above when looking at reasonable expectation of privacy, a *Charter* breach can be asserted only by the person whose *Charter* rights were violated.[679] Nonetheless, the *Charter* rights of others can be relevant to the manner in which a search is conducted.

---

671 *Ibid* at paras 22–25. In *Cornell* itself, the Court was divided 4:3 over whether the dynamic entry violated the *Charter*. The majority deferred to the trial judge's conclusions, while a vigorous dissent argued that there was no basis for the police to have concluded that anyone's safety was at risk. See the discussion of the case in H Archibald Kaiser, "*Cornell*: A Divided Court Accords to Much Latitude to the Police — 'Canada Is Not a Police State'" (2010) 76 *Criminal Reports* (6th) 263.

672 *R v Lau*, 2003 BCCA 337; *R v Schedel*, 2003 BCCA 364.

673 *R v DeWolfe*, 2007 NSCA 79.

674 *R v Pileggi*, 2021 ONCA 4 at para 36.

675 See, for example, *R v John*, 2018 ONCA 702, though in that case this principle was not violated.

676 See, for example, *R v Myers*, 2022 NSCA 69, where police were authorized to conduct an inventory of an impounded vehicle but in doing so opened a backpack belonging to a passenger. This was unreasonable, in part because the passenger ought to have been allowed to take his backpack with him.

677 See, for example, *R v Carstairs*, 2022 BCCA 69 where a search was found to be unreasonable because the warrant was executed at night without sufficient justification.

678 See *R v Bailey*, 2024 ONSC 2136.

679 *Edwards*, above note 49 at para 34.

In *R v Thompson*, for example, a wiretap authorization allowed the police to tap not only the accused's telephone, but also other telephones to which he might resort, including pay phones. The Court acknowledged that it was permissible for authorizations to permit tapping of public phones and that, therefore, the search was authorized by law. However, no restrictions had been placed on the wiretap, such as allowing interception only when there were reasonable grounds to believe the accused was using the public telephone in question at the time. In some cases, the police simply installed listening devices and left them activated in case the accused came along, an approach that likely resulted in the interception of hundreds of unrelated private calls. On those facts, "given the extent of the invasion of privacy authorized in this case, a total absence of any protection for the public created a potential for the carrying out of searches and seizures that were unreasonable."[680]

As *R v Thompson* makes clear, there could be some difficulty reconciling the notion that the *Charter* rights of other persons are relevant to the manner of the search when, according to the facts in *Debot*,[681] the accused's own *Charter* rights are not relevant to that determination. In any event, in *Edwards*[682] the Court appears to limit the relevance of third party rights to cases where there is a "potentially massive invasion of . . . privacy."

One such area of contention concerns so-called "tower dump" warrants, where police seek to obtain information concerning cell phone calls that have been routed through a particular tower or towers. Such warrants — or more typically, production orders — are used when, for example, police believe that the participants in several robberies communicated with one another by cell phone at the time of the robberies, and therefore finding the few particular numbers which made use of each of the relevant towers at the relevant times could be a useful way to identify suspects. However, this technique can have an impact on many people other than the targets of the investigation.[683] It has been suggested that police and justices dealing with such applications should be guided by a number of principles, including that the applica-

---

680 *Thompson*, above note 434.

681 *Debot*, above note 178.

682 *Edwards*, above note 49.

683 See, for example, *R v Rogers Communications Partnership*, 2014 ONSC 3853 at para 11, where the judge noted:

> The existing order will require TELUS to disclose the personal information of at least 9,000 individuals. Rogers estimates that it will be required to conduct 378 separate searches and retrieve approximately 200,000 records related to 34,000 subscribers.

tion should reflect things such as the principles of incrementalism and minimal intrusion, and that the application should show why all of the named locations or cell towers, and all of the requested dates and time parameters, are relevant to the investigation, as well as why all of the types of records sought are relevant. In addition, the application should include any other details or parameters which might permit the target of the production order to conduct a narrower search and produce fewer records, such as for example limiting the search to shorter calls if it is known that that was what was involved. Further, the intrusiveness of a search can be limited by requesting specified data rather than the underlying data itself: for example, where the purpose of the investigation is to identify telephone numbers that used towers proximate to multiple robbery locations, that particular data could be sought rather than the information of all subscribers to all the towers. If there is a request for the underlying data then that broader request should be justified, and the application should demonstrate that the types and amounts of data that are requested can be meaningfully reviewed.[684]

## FURTHER READINGS

Austin, Lisa M. "Is Consent the Foundation of Fair Information Practices? Canada's Experience under *PIPEDA*" (2006) 56 *University of Toronto Law Journal* 181.

Calarco, Paul. "*R* v *Plummer*: Standing to Challenge Searches" (2011) 85 *Criminal Reports* (6th) 62.

Cohen, Stanley A. "Search Incident to Arrest: How Broad an Exception to the Warrant Requirement?" (1988) 63 *Criminal Reports* (3d) 182.

———. "The Paradoxical Nature of Privacy in the Context of Criminal Law and the *Canadian Charter of Rights and Freedoms*" (2002) 7 *Canadian Criminal Law Review* 125.

Cook, Eric. "Reasonable Expectation of Privacy in Multi-Unit Dwellings: A Better Approach" (2025) 73 *Criminal Law Quarterly* 6.

Coughlan, Steve. "Privacy Goes to the Dogs" (2006) 40 *Criminal Reports* (6th) 31.

684 See *R* v *Rogers Communications Partnership*, 2016 ONSC 70 generally, and specifically at para 65.

———. "Kwiatkowski: Privacy Protection and Risk Analysis: Losing the Forest in the Telephoto Shots of the Trees" (2010) 73 *Criminal Reports* (6th) 260.

———. "Stopping Vehicles on a Downhill Slope: R v Nolet" (2010) 76 *Criminal Reports* (6th) 24.

———. "Learning from Experience about Learning from Experience: Modifying the Objective Test for Arrest and Detention" (2013) 4 *Criminal Reports* (7th) 245.

———. "Signing Away Rights: Should Private Contracts Trump the *Charter*?" (2014) 13 *Criminal Reports* (7th) 124.

———, & Marc S Gorbet. "Nothing Plus Nothing Equals . . . Something?: A Proposal for FLIR Warrants on Reasonable Suspicion" (2004) 23 *Criminal Reports* (6th) 239.

——— & Alex Gorlewski, *The Anatomy of Criminal Procedure: A Visual Guide to the Law*, 2nd ed (Toronto: University of Toronto Press, 2026).

Crookshanks, Rebecca. "Under Investigation: Revoking the Implied Licence Doctrine" (2025) 28 *Canadian Criminal Law Review* 187.

Currie, Robert J. "Electronic Devices at the Border: The Next Frontier of Canadian Search and Seizure Law" (2016) 14 *Canadian Journal of Learning and Technology* 289.

De Sa, Chris. "*Garofoli* Step 6: Getting Behind the Black" (2014) 61 *Criminal Law Quarterly* 418.

Diab, Robert. "Protecting the Right to Privacy in Digital Devices: Reasonable Search on Arrest and at the Border" (2018) 69 *University of New Brunswick Law Journal* 96.

———. "'Must the Police Refuse to Look?'" Resolving the Emerging Conflict in Search and Seizure over Civilian Disclosure of Digital Evidence" (2023) 68 *McGill Law Journal* 369.

Fairburn, Michal. "Twenty-Five Years in Search of a Reasonable Approach" (2008) 40 *Supreme Court Law Review* (2d) 55.

Fehr, Colton. "Cell Phone Searches Incident to Arrest: Revisiting *R. v. Fearon* Ten Years Later" (2025) 73 *Criminal Law Quarterly* 278.

Gorham, Nathan JS. "Eight Plus Twenty-Four Two Equals Zero-Point-Five" (2003) 6 *Criminal Reports* (6th) 257.

Hayes, Liam M. "Smartphone Searches: A Legal Crossroads Between Charter Rights and Law Enforcement" (2018) 66 *Criminal Law Quarterly* 196.

HUBBARD, ROBERT W, & SCOTT K FENTON. "Supreme Court of Canada Wiretap Update — February 2001" (delivered at Search and Seizure Law in Canada, the Professional Development Program, Osgoode Hall Law School, Toronto, 3 November 2001).

HUTCHISON, SCOTT C, & JAMES C MORTON. *Search and Seizure Law in Canada* (Toronto: Carswell, 1991) (loose-leaf).

JONES, BROCK. "Reconciling Reasonable Expectation of Privacy and Modern Technologies: US and Canadian Approaches" (2011) 83 *Criminal Reports* (6th) 28.

KAISER, H ARCHIBALD. "*Patrick*: Protecting Canadians' Privacy Interest in Garbage; 'A Step Too Far' for the Supreme Court" (2009) 64 *Criminal Reports* (6th) 30.

———. "*Cornell*: A Divided Court Accords to Much Latitude to the Police—'Canada Is Not a Police State'" (2010) 76 *Criminal Reports* (6th) 263.

———. "*Gomboc*: The Supreme Court Weakens the Search Warrant Requirement and Facilitates Police Investigations, Again" (2011) 79 *Criminal Reports* (6th) 245.

LATIMER, SCOTT. "The Expanded Scope of Search Incident to Investigative Detention" (2007) 48 *Criminal Reports* (6th) 201.

LAW REFORM COMMISSION OF CANADA. *Search and Seizure* (Ottawa: Law Reform Commission of Canada, 1984).

LUTHER, GLEN. "Consent Search and Reasonable Expectation of Privacy: Twin Barriers to the Reasonable Protection of Privacy in Canada" (2008) 41 *University of British Columbia Law Review* 1.

MACKINNON, WILLIAM. "Discarding Reasonable Expectations of Privacy: A Critique of *R v Patrick*" (2010) 47 *Alberta Law Review* 1037.

———. "Section 8 Meets the iPhone: Searching Cell Phones Incident to Arrest" (2011) 84 *Criminal Reports* (6th) 232.

MCINNES, JOHN S. "Sniffing Out a Theory of Privacy after *Kang-Brown* and *M.(A.)*" (2009) 47 *Supreme Court Law Review* (2d) 53.

PENNEY, STEVEN. "Conceptions of Privacy: A Comment on *R v Kang-Brown* and *R v A.M.*" (2008) 46 *Alberta Law Review* 203.

———. "Unreasonable Search and Seizure and Section 8 of the *Charter*: Cost-Benefit Analysis in Constitutional Interpretation" (2013) 62 *Supreme Court Law Review* (2d) 101.

———. "'Mere Evidence'? Why Customs Searches of Digital Devices Violate Section 8 of the *Charter*" (2016) 49:2 *UBC Law Review* 485.

Pomerance, Renée. "Shedding Light on the Nature of Heat: Defining Privacy in the Wake of *R v Tessling*" (2005) 23 *Criminal Reports* (6th) 229.

Pringle, Heather. "Kicking In the Castle Doors: The Evolution of Exigent Circumstances" (2000) 43 *Criminal Law Quarterly* 86.

Quigley, Tim. "The Impact of the *Charter* on the Law of Search and Seizure" (2008) 40 *Supreme Court Law Review* (2d) 117.

Robertson, Kate. "Investigative Genetic Genealogy and the Charter: Consent, the Immutability of DNA, and Canada's Arriving Future" (2025) 73 *Criminal Law Quarterly* 471.

Rose, David. *Quigley's Criminal Procedure in Canada* (Toronto: Thomson Reuters, 2021) (loose-leaf) ch 8.

Sankoff, Peter, & Stéphane Perrault. "Suspicious Searches: What's So Reasonable about Them?" (1999) 24 *Criminal Reports* (5th) 123.

Shapiro, Jonathan. "Narcotics Dogs and the Search for Illegality: American Law in Canadian Courts" (2007) 43 *Criminal Reports* (6th) 299.

Skolnik, Terry. "Policing, Technology, and the Erosion of Constitutional Rights" (2023) 49 *Queen's Law Journal* 40.

Stewart, Hamish. "Normative Foundations for Reasonable Expectations of Privacy" (2011) 54 *Supreme Court Law Review* (2d) 335.

Stratas, David. "'Crossing the Rubicon': The Supreme Court and Regulatory Investigations" (2003) 6 *Criminal Reports* (6th) 74.

———. "*R v B(SA)* and the Right against Self-Incrimination: A Confusing Change of Direction" (2003) 14 *Criminal Reports* (6th) 227.

Stribopoulos, James. "Reasonable Expectation of Privacy and 'Open Fields' — Taking the American 'Risk Analysis' Head On" (1999) 25 *Criminal Reports* (5th) 351.

Stringham, James AQ. "Reasonable Expectations Reconsidered: A Return to the Search for a Normative Core for Section 8?" (2005) 23 *CriminalReports* (6th) 245.

Stuart, Don. "Eight Plus Twenty-Four Two Equals Zero" (1998) 13 *Criminal Reports* (5th) 50.

———. "Police Use of Sniffer Dogs Ought to Be Subject to *Charter* Standards: Dangers of *Tessling* Come to Roost" (2005) 31 *Criminal Reports* (6th) 255.

———. *Charter Justice in Canadian Criminal Law*, 7th ed (Toronto: Thomson Carswell, 2018) ch 3.

TICE, DAVID. "Into the Black: Litigating Search Warrants and Wiretaps under the Sixth Step of *Garofoli*" (2014) 61 *Criminal Law Quarterly* 103.

CHAPTER 5

# OTHER INVESTIGATIVE POWERS

## A. INTRODUCTION

This chapter deals with police investigative techniques other than searches with and without a warrant, which were discussed in Chapter 4. There are a number of such techniques — indeed, as the discussion below will show, there is, in principle, no necessary limit to their number — but the discussion here will focus on three specific areas. All three areas, this discussion suggests, show a significant expansion in police powers, all postdating, and in some cases ironically due to, the *Charter.*

First, section 487.01 of the *Code*, which creates "general warrants," will be examined. Most of the principles relating to the review of the issuance of search warrants discussed in Chapter 4 apply equally to these warrants, and they also authorize techniques that infringe on a reasonable expectation of privacy. As a result, it would have been possible to discuss them in that chapter. However, general warrants can authorize techniques going well beyond anything that one would traditionally think of as a search — in the terms of the statute, they are available to authorize police to "do any thing" — and so they are worth singling out for particular discussion.

Second, police powers of detention will be considered. There are statutory powers of detention, some of which occur in the investigative process (breathalyzer tests, for example, involve a power to detain). What will be of most interest, however, are post-*Charter* developments in caselaw that expand the powers of detention given to the police at common law and, indeed, expand the notion of "common law powers" themselves.

Finally, section 25.1 of the *Code*, which authorizes designated officers to break the law, will be discussed. It is perhaps obvious without elaboration that this provision might be a cause for concern about the expansion of police powers, though there is remarkably little discussion of them in the caselaw or by commentators.

## B. GENERAL WARRANTS: SECTION 487.01

Section 487.01[1] of the *Code* contains what is normally referred to as the "general warrant provision."[2] It was introduced in the wake of a decision by the Supreme Court about warrantless searches and is intended to provide for warrants to perform investigative techniques not covered by other *Code* provisions. It is sometimes described as filling the gap left by section 487 and other warrant provisions in the *Code*, though it is a question for debate as to whether there could properly have been said to be a gap. Section 487.01 has had something of a checkered interpretive journey: for about two decades it was interpreted by lower courts in a very broad fashion creating an almost unlimited array of police powers, until in 2013 the Supreme Court gave guidance which narrowed the legitimate use of the provision. The net result is that the section quite arguably has been given an interpretation that is broader than Parliament had in mind, but where the worst excesses are probably now in check.

In *R v Wong*, the police had placed a small video camera in a hotel room to record activities within.[3] Had they wanted to audiotape the room, they would have had to comply with the *Code* provisions dealing with wiretaps. However, those provisions made no mention of video

1 For an explanation of these provisions in chart form, see Steve Coughlan & Alex Gorlewski, *The Anatomy of Criminal Procedure: A Visual Guide to the Law*, 2nd ed (Toronto: University of Toronto Press, 2026) [*Anatomy of Criminal Procedure*], Chart 1.1(b)(iv), "Section 487.01 General Warrants."

2 It is worth being aware of some ambiguity associated with this term. The *Code* contains search warrants in s 487 but also has many much more specific warrant powers (see Chapter 4, Section C(1)(b)). Because there are so many specific warrant provisions, judges sometimes refer to s 487 search warrants as the "general warrant provisions." In addition, one will occasionally see references to the common law principle that there cannot be a "general warrant": that is, a search warrant must be aimed at a particular person and particular evidence: see, for example, *R v Noble*, [1985] OJ No 809 at para 17 (CA).

3 *R v Wong*, [1990] 3 SCR 36 at para 28 [*Wong*].

cameras, so the police argued that they needed no special permission; that is, in the absence of specific limitations on their powers, they were free to use whatever investigative means they chose. That approach, the Supreme Court decided, "wholly misunderstands *Duarte*. It is the *Charter*, specifically s. 8, that protected the appellant there and it is the *Charter* that protects the present appellant . . . s. 8 was designed to provide continuing protection against unreasonable search and seizure and to keep pace with emerging technological development."[4] In other words, the Court relied on the principle that individuals are to be free from state interference unless such interference is specifically authorized. The Court noted that, in the absence of authorization, video surveillance fell into the general category of warrantless searches, which are *prima facie* unreasonable. The Court also held that it was not their role to create authorization for video surveillance — that was a decision for Parliament to make:

> Until such time as Parliament, in its wisdom, specifically provides for a code of conduct for a particular invasive technology, the courts should forebear from crafting procedures authorizing the deployment of the technology in question. The role of the courts should be limited to assessing the constitutionality of any legislation passed by Parliament which bears on the matter.[5]

One would most naturally read *Wong*, which refers to George Orwell's "classic dystopian novel" *1984*[6] in its reasoning, as a recognition of the right of individuals to be generally free from state interference: "The notion that the agencies of the state should be at liberty to train hidden cameras on members of society wherever and whenever they wish is fundamentally irreconcilable with what we perceive to be acceptable behaviour on the part of government."[7] However, Parliament appears to have read the decision as making precisely the opposite invitation. Section 487.01, although it does not quite allow agents of the state to search "wherever and whenever" they wish, verges dangerously close to that direction.[8]

---

4 *Ibid*.

5 *Ibid* at para 36.

6 *Ibid* at para 15, referring to George Orwell, *1984* (New York: Harcourt, Brace, 1947).

7 *Wong*, above note 3.

8 One would, of course, comply with the letter of the principle, "the police only have the powers explicitly given to them," if one explicitly gave the police the power to do anything, but that would clearly violate the notion of restraint that is the spirit of the principle. A similar approach can be seen in the government's approach to the rule of law reflected in s 25.1 of the *Code*, discussed in Section D, below in this chapter.

Put broadly, the problem facing the police in *Wong* was that no warrant was available for placement of a video camera, but without a warrant, the search was *prima facie* unreasonable. Parliament's response to the decision was to enact section 487.01, which is aimed at avoiding loss of evidence in cases of video surveillance, and in essentially any other case as well. Section 487.01 creates warrants to "use any device or investigative technique or procedure *or do any thing* described in the warrant that would, if not authorized, constitute an unreasonable search and seizure."[9] In other words, Parliament took a decision that relied on the assumption that there need to be limits to police investigative techniques and used it to justify a provision creating an unlimited range of potential police investigative techniques.

It is hard to reconcile this approach with the conclusion in *Hunter v Southam Inc* that "an assessment of the constitutionality of a search and seizure, or of a statute authorizing a search and seizure, must focus on its 'reasonable' or 'unreasonable' impact on the subject of the search or the seizure, and not simply on its rationality in furthering some valid government objective."[10] Section 487.01 seems to be justified only for the purpose of furthering a government objective. That is, if the *Code* had been amended to include warrants authorizing a number of predefined specific investigative techniques (video surveillance warrants, the use of sniffer dogs, facial recognition software, etc.) then one could argue that Parliament had considered the competing interests involved in each and decided that the particular *Code* provisions balanced those adequately. When the *Code* provision permits a warrant for police to "do any thing," however, it is apparent that all of the competing interests *cannot* have been considered.

In 2013 the Court handed down its decision in *R v TELUS Communications Co*, which began to rein in the very broad scope of the provision, suggesting that it should be "used sparingly as a warrant of limited resort."[11] However, that decision followed two decades of expansive use of the power, and so there are already many precedents allowing for quite broad uses of the provision.[12] As a result, there is a certain tension around exactly how to apply the provisions in some cases.

---

9 Section 487.01(1) [emphasis added].

10 *Hunter v Southam Inc*, [1984] 2 SCR 145 at 160 [*Hunter*].

11 2013 SCC 16 at para 56 [*TELUS*].

12 See Steve Coughlan, "*R. v. Ha*: Upholding General Warrants Without Asking the Right Questions" (2009) 65 *Criminal Reports* (6th) 41 [Coughlan, "*R. v. Ha*"] and Steve Coughlan, "*Telus*: Asking the Right Questions About General Warrants" (2013) 100 CR (6th) 290.

Section 487.01 can be thought of as containing two investigative techniques: (1) the very general power noted above, and (2) the power to engage in video surveillance. As video surveillance must meet all the requirements of general warrants and additional requirements as well, it is sensible to discuss the more general power first.

It is most useful to examine the general warrant in terms of the similarities and differences that arise from a comparison with section 487. Some features are common to the two provisions. A warrant in each depends on reasonable grounds being established by an information provided on oath, for example. A section 487.01 warrant also does not permit interference with bodily integrity and can be subject to conditions. Both of these requirements are specifically stated in section 487.01, though they were only implicit in section 487.[13] Like a search warrant (and other warrants), a general warrant can be executed anywhere in Canada, provided that the person executing it is a peace officer or public officer with authority to act in that capacity in the place where the warrant is executed.[14] Of the requirements that are unique to section 487.01, some make the provision wider than the standard search warrant provision, while others are intended to attach greater restrictions. This, of course, is as it should be in a provision intended to balance competing interests, though it is questionable whether the balance has been adequately achieved.

Broadly, section 487 warrants allow for a search of a "place" for a "thing," but general warrants do not have either of those limitations. The general warrant provision is not limited to a search of a building, receptacle, or place, as section 487 is, which means it can be used to obtain intangibles, like a video recording of events. Further, it is not limited to a search for physical evidence, but also allows the police to use any device, technique, or procedure, or "do any thing." The Ontario Court of Appeal has held that "do any thing" is to be read literally and broadly and is not limited to practices such as the use of devices.[15] An additional requirement in section 487.01(1)(c) is that no other statutory provision can authorize the procedure in question. The Supreme Court did eventually, in *TELUS*, interpret this requirement to mean

13 See *Re Laporte and the Queen* (1972), 29 DLR (3d) 651 (Que QB), and *Descôteaux v Mierzwinski*, [1982] 1 SCR 860.

14 Section 487.01(6). Until changes made in Bill C-75, *An Act* to *amend the Criminal Code, the Youth Criminal Justice Act and other Acts and to make consequential amendments to other Acts*, Royal Assent June 21, 2019, warrants generally could not be executed outside of the territorial division where they were issued unless they were endorsed by a justice in that other territorial division. Bill C-75 eliminated that requirement.

15 *R v Noseworthy* (1997), 33 OR (3d) 641 (CA) [*Noseworthy*].

that general warrants were to be "used sparingly as a warrant of limited resort."[16] For a significant period of time, however, lower courts interpreted the "no other provision" requirement more as though it meant that there were *no* limits on the techniques that could be authorizable. For example, courts have considered applications under section 487.01: to install a digital recording ammeter for the purpose of recording the cycling pattern of electricity usage in a residence,[17] to make electronic copies of data in a computer system,[18] to perform phallometric testing,[19] to use a forensic fluorescent light to illuminate the inside of a vehicle to look for bloodstains,[20] to record the sender and addressee information on mail delivered to a post office box,[21] to require an airline to notify the police when a particular person booked a ticket,[22] to covertly open a package to examine its contents before sending it on its way,[23] to allow a police officer to deliver a package while dressed as a postal worker and to install a trigger alarm to alert them when the package was opened,[24] or to detain a person in order to search their cell phone.[25]

In all of those instances, it is quite arguable that the existence of the general warrant provision had a beneficial effect. If the police intend to use one of those techniques, it is better for there first to be judicial scrutiny of that intention, rather than have the police simply proceed on their own. In principle one could argue that it ought to be employed more frequently, as a mechanism for restraint: as new technology develops (facial recognition software, for example) police should be bound to seek authorization under section 487.01 before using it.

Indeed, that interpretation of the "do any thing" component of section 487.01 *ought* to have led to the result that no new common law search powers would be created. Since section 487.01 is applicable in any situation where the accused had a reasonable expectation

---

16 *TELUS*, above note 11 at para 56.

17 *R v Christensen*, 2001 ABPC 227. Note that since the Court's decision in *R v Gomboc*, 2010 SCC 55, in some cases, a person will not have a reasonable expectation of privacy in the information disclosed by a digital recording ammeter, and so no warrant of any type would be needed.

18 *Keating v Nova Scotia (Attorney General)*, 2001 NSSC 85.

19 *R v Rayworth*, [1999] OJ No 5289 (SCJ), aff'd without reference to this issue [2001] OJ No 4111 (CA).

20 *Criminal Code of Canada (Re)*, 2002 SKPC 11.

21 *Canada Post Corp v Canada (Attorney General)* (1995), 95 CCC (3d) 568 (Ont Ct Gen Div).

22 *R v Baldovi*, 2016 MBQB 221. See also *R v Oliveira-Britton*, 2025 NLSC 88.

23 *R v Raqib*, 2025 MBPC 50.

24 *R v Anderson*, 2020 ONCA 780; *R v Badu*, 2022 ABCA; and *R v Feizi*, 2022 ONCA 517 (although in the last case there is no mention of a trigger alarm).

25 *R v Bhatti*, 2025 ONCA 697.

of privacy and no other statutory provision applies, it would always be available as a potential source of authority. A primary rationale for creating new common law search powers is to fill gaps left by Parliament:[26] that interpretation of "do any thing" in section 487.01 meant that, in principle, there no longer *could* be any gaps. Logically, therefore, no common law search powers should be required, since it will always have been open to the police to seek a section 487.01 warrant. The law does not always develop logically, of course, and several new common law search powers have been created in the interim nonetheless.[27]

However, that merely points to a potential benefit of general warrants which did not materialize. There are also harmful results which can come from an "open-ended" approach. One technique authorized under general warrants which might seem questionable is the "pretext theft": police in fact conduct a lawful seizure of contraband but break a window or otherwise make it look as though the subject of the seizure has been robbed.[28] One might reasonably question whether conducting a lawful seizure while making the subject believe they have been the victim of a crime is appropriate.[29] In this regard it is worth noting that the subject would eventually have to be given notice of what really occurred, but that notice could be delayed for as much as three years.[30]

General warrants have also often been issued to perform a "pretext stop": that is, to stop a drug courier's vehicle ostensibly for highway traffic reasons when the real purpose is to allow police to appear to accidentally discover the narcotics in the trunk.[31] In these kinds of cases, the purpose of the particular investigative technique is to permit the police to seize a single drug shipment without exposing the fact that an entire conspiracy was under investigation, which is an understandable motivation. Nonetheless, the "pretext stop" general warrant raises a real concern, which courts are beginning to address.

---

26 See the discussion of this issue in *R v Kang-Brown*, 2008 SCC 18.

27 See the discussion in Chapter 4.

28 See *R v Knight*, 2008 NLCA 67 [*Knight*]. See also *R v Ruthowsky*, 2024 ONCA 432 at para 45 and above note 7, discussing the use of such a general warrant.

29 *Knight*, above note 28, upheld the general warrant at issue in that case. However, the issue was whether the affiant had misled the judge issuing the warrant by not disclosing that the pretext theft would create a risk of harm to the accused from the criminal organization for whom he was transporting narcotics. The Newfoundland Court of Appeal noted at para 14 that "[t]he authority to permit the mimicked theft was not challenged."

30 Section 487.01(5.1), (5.2). Strictly s 487.01 only requires notice to be given of a overt search, which leaves slight room for argument as to whether notice must be given of a seizure.

31 See, for example, *R v HHN*, 2000 ABPC 173; *R v Whipple*, 2016 ABCA 232 [*Whipple*]; or *R v McWhirter*, 2017 BCSC 2314.

If, without a general warrant, the police stopped a vehicle in order to search for drugs but gave the detainee a different explanation for the detention — for example, the false claim that the vehicle had been speeding — then the police would be violating the detainee's section 10(a) *Charter* right to be informed of the reason for the detention. But a general warrant for a pretext stop authorizes exactly that sort of behaviour on the part of police, which creates a problem: as a matter of constitutional law, a judge ought not to be able to issue a warrant authorizing a *Charter* violation. Certainly there are many circumstances in which what would otherwise be a *Charter* violation is not one because of the existence of a warrant (a warrantless search is *prima facie* unreasonable, but one made with a warrant is not, for example), but in that case the warrant is making lawful what would otherwise not be lawful. However, that is very different from a warrant saying "violate *Charter* rights."

In *R v Whipple* the Alberta Court of Appeal found a trial judge to have erred in concluding that such a general warrant was invalid. In doing so they relied on analogies to undercover work and to dual purpose searches, suggesting that this was just a situation where the police were allowed "to not be forthcoming about the total basis for their interaction with the respondent."[32] However, it is noteworthy that in *Whipple*, although the police had been authorized to mislead the accused about the purpose for the detention, in the end they did not do so, since he did in fact commit a highway traffic violation. In addition, within minutes he had been told of the suspicion of narcotics, and so his section 10(a) right was never violated. It has been argued that *Whipple* does not stand for the view that general warrants can authorize a section 10(a) violation.[33] There are also aspects of the reasoning in *Whipple* which are otherwise problematic.[34]

In contrast, the Quebec Court of Appeal in *Woods* has clearly found that a general warrant cannot authorize a violation of section 10(a) and

32 *Whipple*, above note 31 at para 34.

33 Nader Hasan, Mable Lai, David Schermbrucker, and Randy Schwartz, *Search and Seizure*, (Toronto: Emond, 2021) at 239.

34 The Alberta Court of Appeal criticized the trial judge's s 9 analysis on the basis that "[t]he trial judge conflates 'illegal' with 'arbitrary' in this approach" (para 45). The difficulty there is that the trial judge was not "conflating" anything: he was acting in accordance with the well-established rule that "a detention not authorized by law is arbitrary" (*R v Grant*, 2009 SCC 32 [*Grant*] at para 54). It is in fact the Court of Appeal which is mistaken, because it relies on the definition of "arbitrary" developed in the context of s 7 cases, which is deliberately different from the s 9 meaning of the term: see the discussion below under "Was the Detention Arbitrary?"

will be invalid if it does so.[35] They characterize *Whipple* as assuming that a general warrant cannot authorize a section 10(a) violation but explaining why that rule was not violated on the facts. In *Woods*, on the other hand, the accused was given a fictitious reason for his arrest and only discovered the true reason for the stop months later, as part of Crown disclosure. This was a violation of his section 10(a) right. In addition, this meant that his section 10(b) right to counsel was also violated, since he could not properly obtain legal advice when he had been misled about the reason for the detention.

*Woods* points out that section 487.01(1) specifically refers to issuing warrants for actions that, "if not authorized, constitute *an unreasonable search or seizure*" (emphasis added). The general warrant power therefore explicitly contemplates that section 8 rights will be at stake. If the provision was meant to allow infringement of rights other than those in section 8, Parliament would have adopted different wording.[36] Further, in addition to not being explicit, the ability to violate section 10 was not necessarily implicit in executing a general warrant.

Further support for the view pretext stops cannot be authorized by a general warrant can be found in the Ontario Court of Appeal decision in *R v Poirier*.[37] In that case the police had obtained a general warrant allowing them to retain the accused until he excreted drugs he was (correctly) believed to have concealed in his rectum. In fact this resulted in his continuous detention at a police station for a period of forty-three hours: that is, well in excess of the maximum allowable time for a detention under section 503 of the *Code* before an arrested person must be taken before a justice of the peace. On the facts of the case, this was not accidental: the police intended to violate section 503 and to obtain a general warrant authorizing them to do so. The Ontario Court of Appeal concluded that this was not permissible: section 503 reflects an important right, and a judge is not allowed to issue a warrant authorizing a violation of it.[38] That same reasoning ought to apply even more clearly in the case of a *Charter* right: if a general warrant cannot authorize a violation of an ordinary statute, it surely cannot authorize a violation of section 10(a) of the *Charter*.

There is another, arguably more problematic, way in which an open-ended approach to the "no other provision" requirement creates

---

35 *R v Woods*, 2025 QCCA 943 [*Woods*].

36 *Woods*, above note 35 at para 56.

37 *R v Poirier*, 2016 ONCA 582 [*Poirier*].

38 *Ibid* at paras 55–57.

problems. This is most easily illustrated by considering the idea of an "anticipatory search warrant." Although section 487.01 can authorize more than just a search of a place for a thing, it *includes* that ability: section 487.01 can *also* be used to issue a warrant to search a location, as section 487 authorizes. One limitation on section 487 search warrants is that the justice must be satisfied that the evidence to be sought is already in the location for which the warrant is sought. But section 487.01 allows an application based not just on reasonable grounds to believe that an offence has been committed, but on the basis that an offence "*will be* committed."[39] Further, section 487.01 requires only that "information concerning the offence will be obtained," which does not have the temporal implications of the requirement in section 487 that the evidence already "*is* in" the place to be searched. As a result, the general warrant provision has been interpreted as creating an "anticipatory search warrant," authorizing police to search a location at a later point in time, when the thing sought is expected to be there. The fact that such a power was not available under section 487 was taken to satisfy the "no other provision" requirement.[40]

However, this points to the problem with this broad approach and to the failure to consider a distinction which ought to have been drawn. There is a difference between a technique for which no warrant provision existed because that technique had never been contemplated, and a technique for which no warrant provision existed because of a deliberate decision *not* to authorize it. This is the point referred to earlier: the question of whether general warrants fill a "gap."

In *Wong*, it was perfectly plausible to suppose that the law had simply not kept up with technology and, therefore, no provisions authorizing video surveillance had yet been put in the *Code*. It is not reasonable

---

39 Section 487.01(1)(a), emphasis added. Ordinary search warrants do have a small anticipatory component in s 487(1)(c) that permits the seizure of anything "intended to be used for the purpose of committing any offence against the person for which a person may be arrested without warrant."

40 *Noseworthy*, above note 15. Similarly, the general warrant provision has been interpreted to allow for what might be called "contingent" warrants, where the police are authorized to conduct a search on the occurrence of some triggering event. Provided that triggering event is defined precisely enough that it can still be said that the judicial officer issuing the warrant has authorized the search, rather than having delegated the decision to the police officer, such a general warrant will be valid. Such an approach is not allowed under s 487, but that is taken to be the justification for allowing it under s 487.01. See *R v Jodoin*, 2018 ONCA 638 at para 12: "a warrant to be executed in the future upon the occurrence of a specified contingency is not a procedure contemplated by the conventional search warrant."

to draw that same conclusion with regard to every investigative technique that police can think of. In *R v Ha*, for example, the Ontario Court of Appeal found that the "no other provision" requirement had been met because "there is no provision in the *Code*, the *CDSA* [*Controlled Drugs and Substances Act*], or in any other federal statute that would authorize an unlimited number of covert entries and searches on private property over a two-month period."[41] Surely it would be reasonable to at least ask whether the reason no such provision exists is that no such search power ought to exist.[42] Similarly, when in *Noseworthy* the Ontario Court of Appeal found that the general warrant provisions authorized "anticipatory warrants," surely it should have been asked whether the decision by Parliament to include in section 487 the requirement that the evidence sought "is in" the place to be searched was a conscious decision to exclude the possibility of an anticipatory warrant. In that event, if that requirement of section 487 is not met, the proper conclusion ought to be that a warrant cannot be issued at all, rather than that it should be issued under section 487.01 instead.[43]

This point was eventually addressed, though perhaps not definitively, by the Supreme Court of Canada with its decision in *TELUS*.[44] In *TELUS* the police wished to obtain text messages between two parties, covering a two-week period in the past and a two-week period in the future. They obtained a production order for the past messages, but for the prospective messages obtained a general warrant which obliged TELUS, on a daily basis, to produce the text messages sent or received within the previous twenty-four hours. The issue was whether that prospective order could be made under the general warrant provisions: the Court held that it could not, though in a divided decision which obscures the case's precedential value to a certain extent. However, on many of the key principles about how to interpret section 487.01, there was some sort of consensus.

Justice Abella, writing for three judges, concluded that what the police were doing was intercepting a private communication within the meaning of Part VI of the *Code* and, therefore, that they were obliged to seek an authorization under that part: in that event, the "no other provision" requirement for a general warrant was not met. Her decision finds that the general warrant in the case was not properly issued, but

---

41 2009 ONCA 340 [*Ha*].

42 See Coughlan, "*R. v. Ha*," above note 12.

43 See the discussion of *R v Christiansen*, 2017 ONCA 941 [*Christiansen*], below note 47.

44 Above note 11.

says little about how to interpret section 487.01 in general, other than to note that it is "residual" and should not be applied presumptively.[45]

Justice Moldaver, writing for two judges, spends more time on the general warrant requirements. In particular, he concludes that the "no other provision" requirement should include not only situations where the police are doing something that is identical to another provision (*literally* intercepting a private communication) but should also be seen as preventing the police from using a general warrant to do something that is "substantively equivalent" to what another provision would authorize. He reaches this conclusion precisely because the provision is "meant to fill gaps, not create them."[46] Most clearly, his decision demonstrates that a general warrant cannot be used as a means of engaging in an investigative technique which ought to be subject to even more stringent preconditions, such as an interception.[47] However, the decision goes beyond that and extends this same observation to other warrant provisions. Justice Moldaver holds that the purpose of the "no other provision" requirement is to see to it "that the general warrant is used sparingly as a warrant of limited resort."[48] He observes:

> in creating the general warrant, Parliament did not erase every other search authorization from the *Code* and leave it to judges to devise general warrants on an *ad hoc* basis as they deem fit. Courts must therefore be careful to fill a legislative lacuna only where Parliament has actually failed to anticipate a particular search authorization.[49]

Justice Cromwell, writing for two judges, dissents in the result and also specifically disagrees with Moldaver J's view that general warrants are to be used sparingly and that they eliminate techniques that are substantively equivalent to other provisions. At a level of principle, however, he agrees that "this does not mean that the court should authorize anything the police seek to do simply because it is not authorized elsewhere"[50] and also agrees that "[t]he section should not be approached on the assumption that Parliament intended that every investigative technique not authorized elsewhere could be authorized under s. 487.01(1)."[51] In Cromwell J's view, however, this should be

45 *Ibid* at paras 18–19.

46 *Ibid* at para 93

47 *Ibid* at para 76: a general warrant cannot be used "to avoid the rigours of a more demanding legislative authorization such as Part VI."

48 *Ibid* at para 56.

49 *Ibid* at para 78.

50 *Ibid* at para 170.

51 *Ibid* at para 190.

accomplished not through the "no other provision" requirement, but through the separate requirement in section 487.01 that the warrant must be in the best interests of the administration of justice.

Because Abella J concurs with Moldaver J's "substantively equivalent" approach (without discussing the issue at all), that is the majority result.[52] This approach to the "no other provision" requirement has the ability to rein in the use of section 487.01. In essence, until this point some courts adopted the approach of saying "the application would not *succeed* under another provision; therefore, no other provision authorizes this technique." That seems to be the basis upon which anticipatory searches were approved under *Noseworthy*, for example. That is precisely the argument that the "substantively equivalent" argument is meant to prevent. Now the proper question is this: Whether this application would succeed or fail under another section or not, is that other section the governing authority? That is the point of looking for substantive equivalence: to locate those situations where the rules have anticipated investigative techniques such as the one in question and have set out limits for their use.

Of course, it is difficult to assert with any certainty whether "tendencies" in how to use a provision have changed. However, there are some indications that general warrants are being understood in a more restricted fashion since *TELUS*. For example, an earlier view of the provision, in *R v Ford*, was that the police could use a general warrant even though a search warrant was already available: that even if they are in a position to conduct a search and seizure, the police are still entitled to obtain a general warrant to do so.[53] In that case police intended to carry out a search and seizure of marijuana at an isolated property, but they first obtained general warrants to do a number of things, which include confirming the presence of the marijuana. The accused objected that if the grounds for a search warrant already existed (as was taken to be the case) then the "no other provision" requirement meant that a general warrant could not be issued: the British Columbia Court of Appeal disagreed, holding that "there is nothing in the language of s. 487.01(1)(c) that precludes a peace officer from obtaining a general warrant solely because he or she has sufficient information to obtain a search warrant."[54] Since *TELUS*, however, that view has been challenged. In *R v*

52 *Ibid* at para 20.

53 *R v Ford*, 2008 BCCA 94 [*Ford*].

54 *Ibid* at para 50. The Court of Appeal also held at para 51: "I see nothing wrong in utilizing a general warrant to obtain information with a view to gathering additional and possibly better evidence than that which could be seized immediately through the execution of a search warrant."

*Villaroman*, for example, the trial judge had (pre-*TELUS*) relied on *Ford* to say that a general warrant had been validly issued even though a section 487 search warrant would have been available.[55] The Alberta Court of Appeal found that that conclusion was incorrect, based on the direction in *TELUS* that general warrants were to be used restrictively.[56]

Similarly, in *R v Christiansen* the police sought a general warrant for a very similar purpose to that in *Ford*: to confirm that the evidence they wished to seize with a search warrant (under the *Controlled Drugs and Substance Act* (*CDSA*)) was in the location at that time. The Ontario Court of Appeal relied on the direction in *TELUS* that general warrants were to be used "sparingly" to find that this general warrant ought not to have been issued. In particular they found that the police were acting "for the impermissible purpose of circumventing the standards" of the *CDSA* in acting as they did.[57] This is particularly noteworthy not only because it exemplifies restraint in the use of general warrants generally, but also because it concludes that a general warrant cannot be used to avoid the provisions of a *CDSA* warrant: unlike the interception of communications authorization at issue in *TELUS*, a *CDSA* warrant does not have generally stricter standards than a general warrant.

Other cases have relied on not merely Moldaver J's interpretation of the provision in *TELUS*, but his view that they should be resorted to in limited circumstances,[58] and so there is some reason to think that the tide on this point has turned.[59]

Other aspects of section 487.01 are also intended to make it more restrictive than section 487. First, the warrant can be issued only by a judge or justice, not by a justice of the peace.[60] Second, the judge can

---

55 *R v Villaroman*, 2012 ABQB 630.

56 *R v Villaroman*, 2018 ABCA 220 at para 5.

57 *Christiansen*, above note 43.

58 See, for example, *R v Bijelic, Flammia*, 2018 ONSC 6676 at para 11 or *R c Bettez*, 2018 QCCQ 7274 at para 87. See also the discussion in *R v Wise*, 2020 ONSC 7716; *R v Nguyen*, 2022 ONSC 1102; and *Durham Regional Police Service (Re)*, 2024 ONSC 1928.

59 See also *R v Tulk*, 2025 NLSC 1, where the judge found a general warrant to have been improperly issued where s 11(7) of the *Controlled Drugs and Substances Act* was potentially applicable, holding at para 310 that "the point of the substantial equivalence test in *Telus* is to locate those situations where the rules have anticipated investigative techniques such as the one in question and have set out the limits for their use by police."

60 The Court noted in *R v SAB*, 2003 SCC 60 at para 38, that the similar requirement in the case of DNA warrants showed that Parliament was attentive to the seriousness of the interests at stake. In *TELUS*, above note 11, this is said to be a factor showing that general warrants are meant to be "a rearguard warrant of limited resort" (para 71).

attach conditions "to ensure that any search or seizure authorized by the warrant is reasonable in the circumstances."[61] Finally, there is a specific requirement that the judge be satisfied that "it is in the best interests of the administration of justice to issue the warrant."[62]

Difficulties have been noted at times with the procedures used by justices of the peace in issuing warrants,[63] so requiring that a general warrant can be issued only by a judge does show a commitment to greater formality. However, *Hunter* had already required that whoever issued a warrant, whether under the *Code* or any other statute, had to be capable of acting judicially. Perhaps the terms of section 487.01 give greater grounds for confidence that this standard will consistently be met, though it is arguable that, inferentially, the heightened requirement suggests that the minimum constitutional standard is not consistently met in the case of other warrants.[64]

The ability to attach conditions has the potential to provide for sufficient balancing of individual freedom against the investigative needs of the state, but it does not guarantee such balancing. Only the conditions that "the judge considers advisable" need to be imposed, and so a great deal will depend upon which judges the police choose to approach when seeking a general warrant.

More work might be done by the separately imposed requirement that issuing the warrant is in the best interests of the administration of justice. This additional requirement holds the greatest hope of providing a reasonable limit on the search power and balancing the greater intrusiveness of the rest of the section. What do these words mean? *TELUS* holds that the "best interests" requirement is, in the abstract, meant to "ensure that the general warrant remains a rearguard warrant of limited resort," but does not give any real substance to that test.[65] In *Ha* the Ontario Court of Appeal found that the "best interests"

---

61 Section 487.01(3).

62 Section 487.01(1)(b).

63 It was noted, for example, in *Criminal Code of Canada (Re)*, above note 20 at para 11, that the relative lack of formality in having warrants issued by justices of the peace is efficient, but the JP has in many instances become involved in a manner which has raised questions about the requisite judicial neutrality . . . see, for example, *R v Gray* (1993), 22 CR (4th) 114 (Man CA); *R v Hallman*, [2001] BCJ No 1966 (SC); *R v Howe*, [1994] BCJ No 2731 (CA); *R v McCluskie*, [1995] BCJ No 1075 (SC); *R v Clarkson*, [1999] BCJ No 559 (SC); *R v Kelly*, [1995] BCJ No 1369 (CA); *R v Baker*, [1997] 7 WWR 713 (Sask QB); and *R v Paulson*, [1993] BCJ No 1944 (SC).

64 See generally the discussion of this issue and protocol for applying for s 487.01 warrants set out in *Criminal Code of Canada (Re)*, above note 20.

65 *TELUS*, above note 11 at para 71: the requirements of s 487.01 "are deliberately stricter than those for a conventional warrant. For example, the requirements

requirement meant at least that a general warrant could not be used in circumstances that would amount to a "fishing expedition." In finding the general warrant in that case to meet this prerequisite, the court looked at the nature of the offence being investigated, the need for the investigative technique, the duration of the warrant, and the existence of conditions in the warrant.[66]

The constitutionality of the general warrant provisions was not raised in *TELUS*. In *R v Lucas* the Ontario Court of Appeal concluded that there were legitimate concerns about the provisions but that interpreted properly they were constitutional, at least with regard to anticipatory search warrants.[67] They noted that section 487.01 had been taken to allow for anticipatory search warrants, which on the face of it conflicts with the requirement in *Hunter* that the application establish that an offence *has been* committed and that evidence *is* in the place to be searched: anticipatory warrants permit searches when an offence *will be* committed and evidence *will be* in a location. Relying, in part, on the conclusion in *TELUS* that general warrants were to be used sparingly, the Court of Appeal concluded that anticipatory search warrants were constitutional under section 487.01 if two main conditions were met: (1) the particular offences to be committed had to be specified and reasonable grounds established to show that those particular offences will be committed, and (2) conditions should be attached so that the warrant is executed only when there are reasonable grounds to believe that information about that specific offence will be obtained. They suggested as safeguards that

- The conditions in the anticipatory warrant must be explicit, clear, and narrowly drawn so as to avoid misunderstanding or manipulation by government agents.
- The triggering event must be ascertainable and preordained.
- The warrant should restrict the officers' discretion in detecting the occurrence of the event to almost ministerial proportions, similar to a search party's discretion in locating the place to be searched.[68]

---

that a general warrant can only be issued by a judge, not a justice of the peace, and that issuance must be in the best interests of justice themselves serve to ensure that the general warrant remains a rearguard warrant of limited resort." The dissent would have relied on the "best interests" criterion as the way to combat "the assumption that Parliament intended that every investigative technique not authorized elsewhere could be authorized under s. 487.01(1)": see para 190.

66 *Ha*, above note 41.

67 2014 ONCA 561.

68 *Ibid* at para 116.

These conditions did not need to be in the statute itself, but issuing anticipatory warrants would not violate section 8 of the *Charter* if they were understood to be implicit in the "best interests" requirement.[69]

As noted at the start, then, general warrants seem now to have a broader scope than was originally intended, but no longer an unlimited one. If the *TELUS* approach to the "no other provision" requirement had been adopted from the start, it is possible that things such as anticipatory search warrants would not have been authorized in the first place. *TELUS* means that no further relaxations of the requirements of other provisions are likely to develop, but the existing ones are not likely to cease to exist.

The last issue to discuss is the video surveillance provisions of section 487.01, which incorporate all of the other general warrant requirements and additional ones as well. Section 487.01(4) imposes the particular obligation that a warrant for video surveillance[70] in circumstances where a suspect has a reasonable expectation of privacy shall contain conditions that respect the privacy of the individual as much as possible. It is not immediately apparent how one should read this section in comparison with section 487.01(3), which simply allowed a judge issuing a general warrant to attach conditions to make the search or seizure "reasonable in the circumstances." Presumably, this should be taken as imposing an enhanced degree of concern for privacy when video surveillance is in issue, to reflect the greater potential for infringing on privacy.[71]

The real limits on video surveillance are not found directly in section 487.01(4), but rather in its incorporation of the rules concerning consent and non-consent electronic surveillance: those rules are considered in Chapter 4, Section C(1)(b)(ii). This has the effect that, unlike other procedures potentially authorized under section 487.01, non-consent videotaping can be used only when other techniques have failed or are doubtful to succeed, due to the incorporation of the

---

69 *Poirier*, above note 37, finds the particular search carried out to have violated s 8 because it was conducted unreasonably, but had earlier found that the general warrant could not have authorized that particular search in any case, so it did not consider the constitutionality of the general warrant.

70 Strictly speaking, s 487.01(4) refers only to an authorization to "observe" by means of television cameras, although it has been held to include recording by that means as well: *R v McCreery*, [1996] BCJ No 2405 (SC).

71 Note that the section does not have the result that *all* video surveillance requires a general warrant. If a person is subject to video surveillance in circumstances where they do not have a reasonable expectation of privacy, s 487.01(4) does not apply: *R v Piasecki*, 2017 ABQB 192.

"investigative necessity" requirement.[72] The requirement of presenting an annual report concerning authorizations is also incorporated.

One small anomaly exists around the video surveillance provisions, relating to which judge has jurisdiction to issue the warrant. A general warrant can be issued by either a provincial court judge or a superior court judge. However, section 487.01(4) incorporates the provisions in Part VI which limit jurisdiction to issue non-consent authorizations solely to superior court judges. As a result, there is some ambiguity over whether a provincial court judge does or does not have jurisdiction to issue a video surveillance warrant.[73] Courts seem to be leaning to the view that that particular form of general warrant can only be issued by a superior court judge, and certainly the path of caution for police would be to go to such a court rather than risk having the warrant invalidated after the fact.[74]

## C. POWERS OF DETENTION

### 1) Introduction

Today, the issues relating to powers of detention[75] can best be understood through the lens of section 9 of the *Charter*, which guarantees everyone the right to be free from arbitrary detention. In that regard, it parallels search and seizure, where effectively all the law is arranged around an analysis of section 8. The primary difference, however, is that in the case of section 8, the very earliest *Charter* cases established that approach, and so the caselaw was able to develop relatively consistently. In the case of section 9, where the two relevant questions are whether there was a detention and whether it was arbitrary, decisions about those points were put off much longer: "detention" was not fully

72 It has also been suggested that the reference to a suspect's reasonable expectation of privacy in s 487.01(4) is a "limiting feature" on the accused's right which is not present in the case of audiotaping. In other words, in some circumstances, a suspect might be protected against audiotaping but not be protected against videotaping. See *R v Pangman*, 2000 MBQB 85 at para 27.

73 See *R v Li*, 2013 ONCA 81, referring to but not settling this question.

74 See the discussion in *R v Acciaioli*, 2018 ONCJ 969 at paras 43–66. That was also the position taken in *R v Edwardsen*, 2017 BCSC 1578, where the police first went to a provincial court judge but then re-applied to a superior court judge.

75 For an explanation of this issue in chart form, see *Anatomy of Criminal Procedure*, above note 1, Chart 1.2(a), "Is There a Section 9 Violation?"

defined until *Grant* in 2009,[76] and the test for arbitrariness was not fully articulated in a single case until *Le* in 2019.[77]

The reason for this lack of development of an arbitrary detention jurisprudence can likely be traced to the early caselaw. As will be discussed below, one of the earliest cases concluded that a vehicle stop power which allowed for stops anywhere, at any time, and based on no criteria whatsoever could be saved under section 1. As a result, defence counsel were given little incentive to argue section 9, because if that sort of detention was to be allowed under the *Charter*, it seemed unlikely that section 9 was going to provide very much protection. There would be little reason to devote much time to section 9, especially because any case worth taking to court would almost certainly also involve an alleged unreasonable search or violation of the right to counsel (since the detention itself would not have produced evidence) and because there were well-developed rules around sections 8 and 10.[78]

This problem was exacerbated by a second choice on the part of the Court: for over a quarter century they deliberately left unsettled the question of whether an *unlawful* detention was thereby an *arbitrary* detention. That "unreasonable" and "unlawful" meant the same thing in section 8 was established from the very start, but in the context of detention the Court, without deciding the point, declined to eliminate the possibility that a detention could lack lawful authority but nonetheless not be arbitrary. That further decreased the incentive for defence counsel to argue section 9: proving that the police acted without authority would not guarantee success, and it was not clear what more than proving a lack of authority *would* lead to success.

On the other hand, proving that there *was* authority for a detention was sufficient to prove that it was not arbitrary. That led to the asymmetrical situation that although it was not worth defence counsel's time to argue about lawfulness, there was a direct benefit to the Crown to do so. The ironic result, as will be discussed below, was that for a time the primary impact of section 9 caselaw was the creation of new police powers of detention.

Although the Court did eventually equate arbitrariness with lack of authority, by the time it did so these new police powers were well

76 *Grant*, above note 34.

77 *R v Le*, 2019 SCC 34 [*Le*].

78 See the similar point in *R v Grant* (2006), 38 CR (6th) 58 (Ont CA) the decision under appeal in *Grant*, above note 34:

> 48 Violations of s 9 of the *Charter* rarely yield conscriptive or derivative evidence affecting the fairness of a trial. The more typical case is a violation of s 10(b) or even s 8.

entrenched and more have followed. Further, it seems that even now, well after the point was decided, not all courts have yet understood it.[79] In any event, although it was not always the case, now the sensible approach to powers of detention is to consider them in light of section 9 of the *Charter*. Therefore, just as with section 8, there are two primary questions: was there a detention at all and, if so, was it an arbitrary one?

It is to those two questions we now turn.

## 2) Was There a Detention?

Detention[80] can have more than one meaning and so could deal, for example, with long-term interferences with liberty, such as those involved in being placed in a psychiatric facility following a not criminally responsible by reason of mental disorder finding,[81] being declared a dangerous offender,,[82] or being held under an *Immigration and Refugee Protection Act* security certificate.[83] In this context, however, it is detention at the investigative stage that is relevant,: those detentions most similar to arrests in their purpose and duration. Essentially, that amounts to considering detentions where rights can arise under section 10 of the *Charter*. Section 10 gives various rights on arrest or detention, including the right to counsel, and indeed the definition of "detention" was initially developed in that context, although the same definitions apply to detention under section 9.[84] Much of the discussion of those issues is contained in Chapter 7 and will also be relevant here.

Whether a person has been detained is therefore relevant for more than one reason: in essence, it can be the threshold issue for both section 9 and section 10. That is, once it has been determined that a person was as a matter of fact detained, two *Charter* issues arise: was that detention arbitrary (in which case there was a section 9 violation) and was there a failure to inform the person of the reason for the detention and of the right to counsel (in which case there was a section 10 violation).

The section 10 issues will be pursued in Chapter 7, but it can be noted here that the primary purpose of granting *Charter* rights on detention, and in particular the right to contact counsel, is to protect

79 See the discussion below in Section C(3)(a) "Was the Detention Arbitrary?"

80 For an explanation of this issue in chart form, see *Anatomy of Criminal Procedure*, above note 1, Chart 1.2(b), "Shades of Detention."

81 *R v Owen*, 2003 SCC 33.

82 *R v Johnson*, 2003 SCC 46.

83 *Charkaoui v Canada (Citizenship and Immigration)*, 2007 SCC 9.

84 *R v Hufsky*, [1988] 1 SCR 621 at para 12 [*Hufsky*].

the detainee from possible self-incrimination.[85] The concept of "detention" is therefore designed to deal with interactions between the individual and the state, normally, though not exclusively, in the context of the investigation of a criminal offence. A demand by a school's vice-principal that a student comes to the office is not a detention in the relevant sense.[86] Similarly, routine questioning of everyone entering the country by customs officials is not a detention, though singling out a particular person for a strip search is.[87] Although there is a particular focus on the right to obtain legal advice, the Court has been resistant to arguments that the right should be reduced in situations where legal advice would have been of limited value to the accused. The fact that counsel would likely have informed a detainee of the obligation to comply with a breathalyzer demand, for example, does not affect the content of the *Charter* section 10(b) right or the likelihood of the evidence being excluded under section 24(2).[88] Similarly, the fact that there was a statutory power to conduct a search, whether the detainee consented or not, does not mean that the detainee would not have benefited from the advice of counsel.[89]

However, although whether the person was detained is important to the right to counsel, the focus of the discussion in this chapter is the section 9 issue: if there was a detention, was it arbitrary? The important first question is therefore whether the person was detained at all.

The Court has delineated three types of detention: physical detention, legal detention, and psychological detention. In *R v Thomsen*, the Court held:

> 1. In its use of the word "detention", s. 10 of the *Charter* is directed to a restraint of liberty other than arrest in which a person may reasonably require the assistance of counsel but might be prevented or impeded from retaining and instructing counsel without delay but for the constitutional guarantee.

---

85 *R v Bartle*, [1994] 3 SCR 173.

86 *R v M(MR)*, [1998] 3 SCR 393. For criticism of the Nova Scotia Court of Appeal decision to the same effect, see A Wayne MacKay, "Don't Mind Me, I'm from the R.C.M.P.: *R v M(MR)* — Another Brick in the Wall Between Students and Their Rights" (1997) 7 *Criminal Reports* (5th) 1.

87 *R v Simmons*, [1988] 2 SCR 495 [*Simmons*]. The same reasoning has been held to apply to those leaving the country through customs: *R v Nagle*, 2012 BCCA 373.

88 *R v Therens*, [1985] 1 SCR 613 [*Therens*].

89 *Simmons*, above note 75. See also *R v Strachan*, [1988] 2 SCR 980 at para 44, where the Court rejected an approach that "would result in treating violations of s. 10(b) differently depending on the role counsel could have performed and would invite idle speculation on what might have happened if the accused had exercised the right to counsel."

2. In addition to the case of deprivation of liberty by physical constraint, there is a detention within s. 10 of the *Charter*, when a police officer or other agent of the state assumes control over the movement of a person by a demand or direction which may have significant legal consequence and which prevents or impedes access to counsel.
3. The necessary element of compulsion or coercion to constitute a detention may arise from criminal liability for refusal to comply with a demand or direction, or from a reasonable belief that one does not have a choice as to whether or not to comply.
4. Section 10 of the *Charter* applies to a great variety of detentions of varying duration and is not confined to those of such duration as to make the effective use of *habeas corpus* possible.[90]

In other words, "detention" encompasses three different situations: physical constraint (where the police physically take control of the person), legal detention (where the police have a legal power to compel a person to remain), and psychological detention (in which no such power in fact exists, but the person complies with the police demand because of a reasonable belief they are required to do so).[91] There is some ambiguity in the language, since *Thomsen* treats these three situations as three categories, but in *Grant* the Court suggests that all detentions divide into "physical or psychological,"[92] and that psychological detention includes both the situation in which there is a legal power to compel the person to remain, and the situation in which there is no legal power but the person reasonably believes there is.[93] This is only a matter of labelling, in the sense that either way all three situations constitute a detention, but the latter language is to be used now.[94]

Whether a person has been physically constrained is fundamentally just a factual question and typically not a difficult one. In *R v Nesbeth*, for example, police yelled "stop, police" to the accused, who did not stop but instead ran, and who was eventually caught.[95] Whether the accused had been psychologically detained at the start of the chase could easily be a matter of some debate, but it was unambiguous that he was detained when the police tackled him. Note that this case illustrates the importance of determining the point at which a detention

---

90 [1988] 1 SCR 640 at 649 [*Thomsen*].

91 *Therens*, above note 88.

92 *Grant*, above note 34 at para 25.

93 *Ibid* at para 30.

94 The Court has continued to treat detention as always either physical or psychological: see *Le*, above note 77 at paras 25 and 28.

95 2008 ONCA 579 [*Nesbeth*].

arose: if it was at the start, the police would have needed to show that the demand for him to stop was not arbitrary, but if it was not until later, the question was whether detaining a person who had fled was arbitrary.[96]

Whether a person has been "legally detained" is also largely an unambiguous and factual question. The most common power would be an arrest (and those powers are discussed in Chapter 7). However, legal detentions also include breathalyzer demands at the side of the road, demands for breath samples for a roadside screening device,[97] or a breathalyzer demand made at an accused's home after the accused has been initially questioned by consent without being detained.[98] The laws around stops to demand breath samples were changed in December 2018,[99] but nothing about the changes should alter the fact that those stops are detentions (though the removal of the need for grounds in some circumstances is likely to lead to *Charter* challenges as to whether the law is now arbitrary).[100]

It should be noted that the only question at this threshold stage is which power the police *purport* to be using, not whether they actually have that power in the circumstances. That is, if the police say to a person "you are being detained for investigative detention" then that person is detained: if it later transpires that the police did not have the grounds to conduct an investigative detention,[101] then the detention was arbitrary, but it was still a detention. In most cases it should be apparent which power police are relying on, if for no other reason than that they have a *Charter* obligation to inform a detainee of the reason for the detention.[102] Nonetheless there are of course occasions where the interaction between the police and the individual is ambiguous:

---

96 To illustrate the same point, see *Le*, above note 77. The police entered a backyard without any authority to do so, and while in the backyard formed reasonable suspicion that the accused had a weapon. If the detention occurred when the police entered the backyard (as the majority found) then it was an arbitrary detention: if it did not occur until after the police had formed reasonable suspicion (as the dissent would have held) it would not have been arbitrary.

97 *Thomsen*, above note 78.

98 *R v Schmautz*, [1990] 1 SCR 398.

99 See Part VIII.1, Offences Relating to Conveyances.

100 The amendments added s 320.27(2), which allows a peace officer to make an immediate demand for a breath sample without reasonable suspicion as long as the officer "has in his or her possession an approved screening device." *R v Blysniuk*, 2020 ONCJ 603 found that the section violated s 9 but was saved under s 1, citing the reasoning in the vehicle stop cases, discussed below in this Section.

101 See the discussion below under "Investigative Detention."

102 See the discussion in Chapter 7 under "*Charter* Rights Arising on Arrest."

in many of those situations, it might become more useful to consider whether the accused was purely psychologically detained. However, psychological detention is the most complicated form of detention to assess, and therefore it is well to remember that it is not necessarily the starting point. In most situations it is clear that either a physical or legal detention is in issue, and in many of those cases the complications of the psychological detention analysis might simply be avoided.[103] This is not necessarily true, however, because the exact time at which a person becomes "detained" can affect the overall analysis. It might be that the facts giving grounds to make a legal detention only arise because the person felt compelled to stay, and so there would have been no legal authority for the psychological detention.[104]

It is also worth noting that the stakes tend to be higher in psychological detention cases, precisely because of the ambiguity. That is, when the police physically or legally restrain a person, it will typically be clear to everyone — especially to the police — that the person has been detained and therefore that *Charter* rights have arisen. Of course there are cases where police fail to comply with those *Charter* rights in some way, but in the vast majority of cases they do advise the person of the reason for the detention and of the right to counsel. When a person has been psychologically detained, however, frequently that fact will not be apparent to the police at the exact moment the detention crystallizes,[105] and so the police will not inform the person of their section 10 rights. Similarly, the very thing that distinguishes a psychological detention from a legal detention is that in the case of the former, there is in fact *not* a legal power to detain the person: as a result (as will be discussed further below), the detention is an arbitrary one. In practical terms, therefore, whether the accused was psychologically

103 See, for example, *R v Heppner*, 2019 BCCA 108, where the trial judge entered into an analysis of whether the accused was psychologically detained while being questioned by police, but the Court of Appeal pointed out that the accused was under arrest the entire time.

104 See, for example, the facts of *Nesbeth*, above note 95. See also *Le*, above note 77 at para 29:

> There is no dispute, whether among the courts below or the parties to this appeal, that Mr. Le was detained *at some point* in the backyard. What we must decide is when this occurred and whether it was arbitrary.

105 Justice Brown in dissent in *R v Omar*, 2018 ONCA 975 [*Omar* Ont CA] noted at para 81 that the Supreme Court "did not offer — and really could not offer — a 'bright-line' solution for the problem of telling when a psychological detention begins." The Supreme Court of Canada overturned the decision of the majority in the Ontario Court of Appeal in *Omar*, "substantially for the reasons of Brown J.A. at the Court of Appeal": 2019 SCC 32 [*Omar*].

detained will frequently be the only relevant question in determining whether there was a violation of both section 9 and section 10.[106] That is not the case for the other forms of detention, where there will be a genuine analysis of the later questions of arbitrariness and right to counsel.

Although the Court acknowledged the concept of psychological detention very early in *Charter* jurisprudence, it took quite some time before they articulated a definition of "detention" which was useful in that context.[107] Psychological detention is both harder to define and harder to judge than the other forms of detention. This is especially so in the case of encounters between police and individuals on the street, though it can also be true of more formal questioning that takes place at a police station.

A wide range of potential on-the-street interactions can arise. Police might simply be at the scene of an accident questioning everyone, witnesses and those involved, alike. In other cases, police simply question persons they meet on the street or whom they drive by, asking the person their name or purpose, or asking to see identification. Sometimes, the questioning might not be entirely random, and police might, for example, question a person who partly meets the description of a person wanted for an offence. In other cases, factors such as the time, location, or race of the person questioned may have factored into an officer's decision to ask questions. Clearly, some of these persons should be considered detained and others should not.

The difficulty in this area arises from the fact that there are competing legitimate interests. Not every conversation between a police officer and an individual should automatically be considered a detention: police interviewing the witnesses to a traffic accident should not be obliged to warn each of them of the right to counsel. The Court has, however, recognized the concept of psychological detention precisely because most people do not know whether they are compelled to comply with police requests or not, and so cooperation cannot always be seen as truly voluntary.[108]

Further, the primary justification for the section 10(b) right is that people interacting with the police are entitled to be protected from potential self-incrimination. In situations where an offence is being

---

106 However, the ambiguity of the situation and the possibility that police will have inadvertently caused a psychological detention without realizing that could be relevant to the question of remedy: see *Omar* Ont CA, above note 105.

107 For an explanation of this issue in chart form, see *Anatomy of Criminal Procedure*, above note 1, Chart 1.2(c), "Is a Person Psychologically Detained?"

108 *Therens*, above note 88.

investigated and the extent of a person's involvement is unclear, there is a benefit for police, and a corresponding detriment to the individual, to be able to characterize the individual as merely a witness, not a suspect, and therefore not advise that person of the right to counsel. The less likely it is that a situation will be classified as a detention, the greater the risk that rights will not be adequately protected. Equally, where the police are nominally "randomly" asking questions on the street, the potential that any detention would be seen as arbitrary is that much greater. If it is not a detention, however, there is no potential for courts to engage in the balancing involved in deciding whether it was arbitrary or not. Among other issues, it becomes more difficult to determine whether the detention was random, or whether it was instead based on improper motives, such as the race of the person.[109] The net effect would be a potential expansion of police power: not by design, but in result. This expansion would, based on the caselaw, often arise in exactly those situations where the person questioned would have benefited from legal advice. An accused who gives their name, which the police then run through the Canadian Police Information Centre (CPIC) while continuing to engage in conversation, might well have wanted to know that there was no obligation to remain or to answer questions, particularly when they are then arrested for violating curfew or on an outstanding warrant.[110]

It was those issues that the Court tried to resolve with the decision in *R v Grant*. They concluded that the question of whether there was a detention should be settled by an objective detainee-centred approach. In other words, the important question is not whether the person felt detained, nor whether the police intended to detain the person; rather, psychological detention was to be determined by "whether the reasonable person in the individual's circumstances would conclude that he or she had been deprived by the state of the liberty of choice" as to whether to stay or go.[111] This is not uncommonly described as whether a reasonable person would feel "free to leave," but that is not entirely accurate. A person might be in a location they had no wish

---

109 On the issue of race as a factor in these decisions, see David Tanovich, "*R. v. Griffiths*: Race and Arbitrary Detention" (2003) 11 *Criminal Reports* (6th) 149; and David Tanovich, "Using the *Charter* to Stop Racial Profiling: The Development of an Equality-Based Conception of Arbitrary Detention" (2002) 40 *Osgoode Hall Law Journal* 145 [Tanovich, "Using the *Charter*"]. See also David Tanovich, *The Colour of Justice* (Toronto: Irwin Law, 2006).

110 See, for example, *R v H(CR)*, 2003 MBCA 38 [*H(CR)*]; *R v Tammie*, 2001 BCSC 366 [*Tammie*]; *R v Powell* (2000), 35 CR (5th) 89 (Ont Ct J).

111 *Grant*, above note 28 at para 44.

to leave but still become psychologically detained by actions of the police.[112]

The Court also listed various factors that can be taken into account in determining this question. These are as follows:

(a) The circumstances giving rise to the encounter as they would reasonably be perceived by the individual: whether the police were providing general assistance; maintaining general order; making general inquiries regarding a particular occurrence; or, singling out the individual for focussed investigation.
(b) The nature of the police conduct, including the language used; the use of physical contact; the place where the interaction occurred; the presence of others; and the duration of the encounter.
(c) The particular characteristics or circumstances of the individual where relevant, including age; physical stature; minority status; level of sophistication.[113]

In *Grant* itself the Court concluded that the accused had been detained. He had been approached on the street by a police officer who stepped in his path and asked him general questions: at that stage he was not detained. However, he was then told to keep his hands in front of him, two other officers arrived and showed their badges, and pointed questions aimed at determining whether he had anything he should not were asked. The questioning was respectful but inherently intimidating, especially given the accused's age (he was eighteen) and that he was outnumbered. Accordingly, the accused had become psychologically detained. The Court reached this conclusion even though the accused did not testify, and so did not say that he felt detained. The Court noted that this was not fatal to the claim, precisely because the test is objective. Indeed, in the later case of *Le* the accused testified that he had felt free to leave, but the Court nonetheless found a psychological detention, stressing that the test was an objective one: see the discussion below.[114]

We will work through each of the three sets of factors of the *Grant* test in a moment, but first it is worth looking at some of its broader implications. The Court has made clear that the *Grant* test is the

---

112 See, for example, *Le*, above note 77, where the accused was in a backyard when police entered it, and the Court noted at para 52 that:

> In the circumstances of this appeal, *to where*, precisely, was Mr. Le expected to "walk away"? And *from what* was he being "delayed" when he was socializing at a friend's house?

113 *Ibid.*

114 *Le*, above note 77 at paras 111–21.

exclusive test for determining whether a person has been psychologically detained. Factually, the issue of psychological detention has tended to arise primarily in two situations: "on-the-street" encounters and persons who are being questioned at a police station. Pre-*Grant* the leading authority on police station psychological detentions was *R v Moran*,[115] and when that was factually the situation at hand many courts continued to rely on *Moran* or at least take its considerations as relevant, post-*Grant*.[116] The Court has more recently specified in *R v Lafrance*, however, that *Moran* should no longer be used.[117] They held that "*Grant* is comprehensive in scope, applying to every instance of alleged detention by police by addressing the full breadth of circumstances that engage the right against self-incrimination protected by s. 10 of the *Charter*."[118]

In a concurring opinion in *Grant* Binnie J argued that a wholly claimant-centred approach was inadequate and that the perceptions of the police ought also to be factored into the analysis.[119] He argued that there is a significant difference between the police saying "stay put" to the witnesses to an accident and saying it to an obvious suspect and that that ought to be reflected in the analysis. In addition, he argued that leaving the police perspective out of the analysis meant that if police can mask their true intentions a person might not be detained.

---

115 *R v Moran* (1987), 36 CCC (3d) 225 (Ont CA) [*Moran*].

116 See, for example, *R v Seagull*, 2015 BCCA 164 at para 38; *R v Tessier*, 2020 ABCA 289 at paras 66–69; *R v Eaton*, 2019 ONCA 891 at para 12; or *R v NB*, 2018 ONCA 556 at para 121.

117 *R v Lafrance*, 2022 SCC 32 [*Lafrance*] at para 27:

> Respectfully, the better view is that, as a result of *Grant*, *Moran* is no longer good law (S. Coughlan and G. Luther, *Detention and Arrest*, 2d ed (Toronto: Irwin Law, 2017), at 287), and it should no longer be applied or relied upon. In *Grant*, the test for detention was restated to direct the inquiry to the perspective of the reasonable person in the accused's shoes. In contrast, the *Moran* factors focus principally on police conduct and information that will not be readily available to the accused at the time of detention (such as the stage of the police investigation). And, while the test in *Grant* is objective, *Moran* encourages courts to consider the subjective perceptions and beliefs of the accused, thereby emphasizing considerations that play a limited (if any) role in an objective assessment (*Le*, at paras 111–17).

118 *Lafrance*, above note 117 at para 28. See also *R v Tessier*, 2022 SCC 35 [*Tessier*], a police station interview case, holding at para 105 that "[t]he psychological detention question in this case is governed by the three factors discussed in *Grant* and affirmed in *Le*."

119 See also Tim Quigley, "Was It Worth the Wait? The Supreme Court's New Approaches to Detention and Exclusion of Evidence" (2009) 66 *Criminal Reports* (6th) 88 [Quigley, "Was It Worth the Wait?"] for the same opinion.

There is some force to this suggestion. But against that, it is worth recognizing that the claim by the police that they would have let a person leave if the person had asked to do so had, pre-*Grant*, frequently resulted in a finding that the person was not detained: the person therefore had no claim to have been arbitrarily detained.[120] That amounted to the paradoxical result that the absence of any power authorizing the police to do the thing they were doing made it *less* likely there was a *Charter* violation. The majority's approach in *Grant* avoids that dilemma.[121]

Further significance of the detainee-centric approach is illustrated in *R v Le*.[122] In that case, three police officers had come to a housing cooperative looking for a specific person. Although they had been told that the person they were seeking was not in the cooperative, the officers nonetheless went to a particular townhouse that they were told was a "problem address." The accused and four other young men, all visible minorities, were in the backyard of that townhouse talking and not appearing to do anything wrong. Two of the officers entered the backyard through the opening in the fence, while the third first walked the perimeter and then stepped over the fence to enter. All the young men were asked for their identification and other questions about what they were doing. Eventually, after the accused behaved in a way that made the police suspicious, he was asked what was in his satchel, at which point he fled, was arrested, and was found to be in possession of a firearm and cocaine. The key issue in the case was *when* the accused was first psychologically detained: if it was not until he was specifically asked about the contents of his satchel, then the detention would not be arbitrary, but if the psychological detention began the moment the police entered the backyard, then it was arbitrary. The Supreme Court, in a decision which not only casts light on the significance of a focus on the detainee, but also considers the viewpoint of a *reasonable* person in the position of detainee in a society where members of visible minorities are over-policed, found the detention to have arisen at the earlier point and found the accused's section 9 right to have been violated.

One significance of focusing on the detainee is that it makes irrelevant the question of whether the police had a legitimate purpose in investigating: in the case of *Le*, in entering the backyard. The reasonable detainee might not know what the subjective police purpose is, and so

120 See, for example, *H(CR)*, above note 110; *R v LB*, 2007 ONCA 596; or *Tammie*, above note 110.

121 See the discussion in Steve Coughlan, "Great Strides in Section 9 Jurisprudence" (2009) 66 *Criminal Reports* (6th) 75 [Coughlan, "Great Strides"].

122 *Le*, above note 77.

it does not affect the issue of whether there was a psychological detention. Not knowing the police purpose could have the effect of causing a reasonable person to perceive that the motive for the police presence was them.[123] And even if the person does know that purpose — as in *Lafrance*, where the police were executing a search warrant — "this is not determinative of — and indeed is unlikely to affect — how a reasonable person perceives his or her interactions with the police."[124]. Whether there was a legitimate purpose or lawful authority will affect whether that detention was arbitrary or not, at a later stage, but it is not relevant to the threshold stage.[125]

Another important significance of focusing on the detainee, not the police, was the role that racial profiling played: specifically, that it did not matter that the trial judge had found there was no racial profiling in this case. Whether there was racial profiling was a question about the "internal mental process" of the police officers involved, and so did not affect how the situation would be viewed by a reasonable person in the position of the detainee.[126] However, the broader racial context in which this interaction took place was one in which there is "disproportionate policing of racialized and low-income communities," and that "would have had an impact on the perceptions of a reasonable person in the shoes of the accused."[127]

Further, the trial judge and Court of Appeal had both relied on evidence that the accused subjectively felt that he could leave as relevant to the question of whether he was detained, but the Supreme Court stressed that the test was an objective one: and indeed, if the accused did think he could leave, he was mistaken. They stressed that the test should be objective for three important reasons: that the objective test allows police to know when the detention has occurred in order to comply with their *Charter* obligations; that the objective standard treats everyone equally; and that some individuals will be incapable of forming subjective perceptions while interacting with the police.[128] The test is the standpoint of the reasonable person "who is imbued with the experiences that accompany the accused's particular circumstances."[129]

---

123 Le, above note 77 at para 40.
124 *Lafrance*, above note 117 at para 32.
125 *Ibid* at para 37.
126 *Ibid* at para 78. The Court carries on to note: "This means that racial profiling is primarily relevant under s. 9 when addressing whether the detention was arbitrary because a detention based on racial profiling is one that is, by definition, not based on reasonable suspicion."
127 *Ibid* at para 97.
128 *Ibid* at para 115.
129 *Ibid* at para 121.

*Le*'s focus on the reasonable person in the detainee's position, rather than the actions of the detainee personally, should also settle an inconsistency in some lower court decisions about psychological detention. Some decisions had taken the view that only an accused who actually *submitted* to a detention could claim to be psychologically detained, and that a person who fled therefore could not bring a section 9 claim.[130] At a policy level that would be an unfortunate result: a person might have fled an unlawful order to remain, but if that person could not get past the threshold stage of showing that the order created a detention, then the question of the arbitrariness of the police action could never be considered by a court.[131] *Le* makes apparent, however, that that is not the correct approach. First, the test for psychological detention cited makes no reference to actual submission (unlike the earliest cases), only to the requirement that "a reasonable person in the accused's shoes would feel obligated to comply with a police direction or demand and that they are not free to leave."[132] This is consistent with the later confirmation in *Lafrance* that "*Grant* is comprehensive in scope."[133] Second, focusing on the reasonable person, not the actual person, shows that the actions of that person are not determinative. As noted, the accused here testified that he thought he could leave but the Court concludes that he was wrong about that and was detained nonetheless: by the same token, that an accused actually *did* leave would not determine what a reasonable person would have perceived.[134]

---

130 See, for example, *Nesbeth*, above note 95, or *R v Atkins*, 2013 ONCA 586 at para 10: "if the appellant did not acquiesce or submit to any deprivation of liberty, there could be no detention." See also *R v Ratt*, 2020 SKCA 19 at para 37; *R v Julom*, 2022 ABCA 198 at para 31; and *R v Saretzky*, 2020 ABCA 421 at paras 39–40. This approach arises from the fact that *Therens*, above note 88 at para 57, had said that the test was whether the person "submits or acquiesces in the deprivation of liberty *and* reasonably believes that the choice to do otherwise does not exist" (emphasis added).

131 This approach would also treat psychological detention differently and less favourably than the other forms of detention. A person who resisted an unlawful arrest, for example, would be allowed to argue a s 9 violation based on the illegality of the police action, despite not having submitted to it.

132 *Le*, above note 77 at para 26.

133 *Lafrance*, above note 117 at para 28.

134 On this issue see *R v Rumbaki*, 2024 ONCJ 49, a case where the Crown conceded that a detention would have been arbitrary but argued there was no psychological detention because the accused fled. The trial judge concluded that *Le* did not abolish the acquiescence requirement but did diminish its role by an emphasis on the reasonable person. The decision suggests that if the police conduct or words are likely to make a reasonable person believe that they must comply, then it does not matter whether the particular accused complies or not, However, if the conduct or the words fall short of that, then some measure of acquiescence or evidence about the accused's subjective state of mind will be necessary to show a detention.

None of this is to say that whether a person did or did not leave cannot be *relevant* to deciding whether there was a psychological detention: only that leaving should not on its own be *determinative*.[135]

Having looked at those broader implications, we should now consider the three sets of factors in the *Grant* analysis, grouped under the circumstances of the encounter, the nature of the police conduct, and the relevant characteristics of the detainee. The overall assessment based on them is necessarily something of a judgment call.[136] Circumstances of the encounter looks primarily at whether the police were engaged broadly in police work (providing general assistance or making general inquiries) or on the other hand were singling out an individual for focussed investigation. In *R v Kiene* the accused was questioned by a peace officer while confined to a hospital bed following a car accident, but the nature of the encounter was an interview of the accused looking at whether the *other* driver was guilty of an offence, and so there was no psychological detention.[137] In contrast, in *R v Wong* a person had reported her car stolen and allowed police into her apartment for that purpose. However, police observed drug paraphernalia in her apartment and the interview became focused on her activity, turning it into a psychological detention.[138] In *Lafrance*, the police executed a search warrant at the accused's home, arriving while he was still in bed but not arriving to arrest him: nonetheless the Court observed "it is inconceivable that a reasonable person in Mr. Lafrance's shoes — woken and confronted by armed police officers in his home telling him to leave — would believe that they had arrived to 'provid[e] general assistance', 'maintai[n] general order' or make 'general inquiries'. The reasonable person would immediately understand that he or she is being singled out for investigation."[139]

---

135 See, for example, *R v Francois*, 2025 MBCA 93 setting out the proper approach:

> [159] In my view, it was open to the trial judge, in her analysis, to rely on the fact that the accused exercised his choice to walk away from the officers during the encounter as evidence that there was little, if any, power imbalance.
>
> [160] As noted in *Le*, nothing more can be taken from the subjective perception of an accused as "the detention analysis is principally objective in nature" (at para 114). Just because the accused did walk away from Cst. Keith is not determinative as to whether he was detained; the test is always an objective one as to what a reasonable person in the position of the accused would have perceived.

136 See *Omar*, above note 105.

137 *R v Kiene*, 2015 ABCA 326.

138 *R v Wong*, 2015 ONCA 657 [*Wong* 2015]. See also the discussions of whether there was or was not a focused interrogation in *R v Peterson*, 2013 MBCA 104; *R v Kalturnyk*, 2014 MBPC 24; or *R v Moulton*, 2015 ONSC 1047.

139 *Lafrance*, above note 117 at para 32.

One consideration which sometimes arises is whether the person is able to leave or not. If the person effectively cannot leave — because, for example, the police have the person's identification card[140] — then that is likely to mean that the person was detained. Similarly if the person is in a situation where the officer is present but the person cannot leave, due to being in a hospital bed, ambulance, or something similar, that might well indicate a detention.[141] That factor is not necessarily determinative, however because as noted above, whether the person can leave is not necessarily a relevant question. In *Le* the trial judge noted that the accused had not been delayed on his way anywhere and could have left, but the Supreme Court held that this was irrelevant: the accused was socializing at a friend's house, not stopped on the street, and was not trying to go anywhere.[142]

An examination of "the nature of the police conduct" involves looking at "the language used; the use of physical contact; the place where the interaction occurred; the presence of others; and the duration of the encounter." In *R v Koczab* (SCC), for example, the statement of the officer to the accused "I just have to go to my car for a minute" was found to be an implied direction not to leave.[143] At least as important a consideration, though, is how the police behaved otherwise. In *Grant* the officers who stood in front of the accused on the street were described as taking "tactical adversarial positions."[144] In *Le* two officers entered through an opening in the fence without an invitation, and the third officer first walked the perimeter then stepped over the fence to enter: this manner of entering was seen as communicating "an exercise of *power*" and contributing to a finding of psychological detention.[145] Further, the words the police use are very relevant,[146] but are not necessarily the end of the story. "[A]ctions speak louder than words," as the Court observed in *Le*, and "[t]he nicest of hellos could not mask the fact that the three persons entering onto this private property were uniformed police officers acting without permission, consent or legal authorization." Similarly they have held that "no single consideration, including a police statement to an individual that he or she is 'not

---

140 *R v Loewen*, 2018 SKCA 69.

141 See, for example, *R v Jackson*, 2019 NWTTC 6 or *R v Stewart*, 2018 BCCA 76.

142 *Le*, above note 77 at para 52: "such considerations have limited, if any, relevance when applied to police conduct at a private residence."

143 See *R v Koczab*, 2014 SCC 9 [*Koczab* SCC], which adopted the reasons of the dissenting judge in *R v Koczab*, 2013 MBCA 43.

144 *Grant*, above note 34 at para 49.

145 *Le*, above note 77 at para 56, emphasis in original.

146 In *Wong* 2015, above note 138, the officer said to the accused that he could arrest her. In *R v Todd*, 2019 SKCA 36, in contrast, the officer specifically told the person they were free to go.

detained' or otherwise under any obligation to cooperate or may leave, is determinative of whether a detention has occurred."[147]

Indeed, illustrating that actions speak louder than words, the Court found in *Lafrance* that despite the various assurances given to the accused — "you don't have to provide me a statement . . . that it would be completely voluntary on your point," "you don't hafta sit here and speak with me today," "you are at any time Nigel free to leave," and others — the accused was in fact detained. These words were outweighed by other aspects of the police behaviour, which included that eleven officers with firearms and bulletproof vests had arrived at his residence, ordered him to get dressed and leave the house, had driven him to the police station when he agreed to go, and then had taken him to an interview room in the back of the station that was behind two sets of locked doors. Illustrating further that it is the detainee's perspective that is important, a further factor which mattered was not that the door to the room in which he was left alone was in fact unlocked but rather that the police did not *inform* him that the door was unlocked.[148]

On the other hand in *Tessier* among the factors leading to the conclusion that the accused was not detained were that he had brought himself to the police station and that he did at one point choose to leave the interview room, to have a cigarette.

The last set of factors relate to the relevant characteristics of the accused "including age; physical stature; minority status; level of sophistication." In large measure this amounts to asking whether a reasonable person with those characteristics was likely to be intimidated and therefore to feel compelled to comply. Courts often note the young age, gender, or small stature of an accused or that they were outnumbered. In *Le*, the Court spent some time developing the significance of the "minority status" factor, observing that "various groups of people may have their own history with law enforcement and that this experience and knowledge could bear on whether and when a detention has reasonably occurred."[149] They considered evidence demonstrating the disproportionate policing of minority communities, ultimately holding that:

> it is in this larger social context that the police entry into the backyard and questioning of Mr. Le and his friends must be approached. It was another example of a common and shared experience of racialized young men: being frequently targeted, stopped, and subjected to pointed and familiar questions. The documented history of the

147 *Lafrance*, above note 117 at para 39.
148 *Lafrance*, above note 117 at para 40.
149 *Le*, above note 77 at para 73.

> relations between police and racialized communities would have had an impact on the perceptions of a reasonable person in the shoes of the accused.[150]

Note that the important point is not the subjective view of the accused but that of a reasonable person with the accused's characteristics.

The Court also rejected the argument (often successfully made in prior cases[151]) that a person who has frequently interacted with the police before will have greater familiarity with the system and therefore be less likely to feel compelled to remain. They saw the opposite as more reasonable, that frequent police contact was more likely to increase the level of psychological compulsion, holding that "[i]ndividuals who are frequently exposed to forced interactions with the police more readily submit to police demands in order to move on with their daily lives because of a sense of 'learned helplessness.'"[152]

The Court also noted that it was unlikely the police would have acted in the same way, entering a backyard without permission, in a more affluent neighbourhood. In a passage which is likely to be frequently cited, they held that

> the reputation of a particular community or the frequency of police contact with its residents does not in any way license police to enter a private residence more readily or intrusively than they would in a community with higher fences or lower rates of crime. Indeed, that a neighbourhood is policed more heavily imparts a *responsibility* on police officers to be vigilant in respecting the privacy, dignity and equality of its residents who already feel the presence and scrutiny of the state more keenly than their more affluent counterparts in other areas of the city.[153]

---

150 *Le*, above note 77 at para 97. To similar effect see *R v Francois*, above note 135 at para 131:

> In my view, a reasonable person aware of the relevant social context of mistrust and fear that many Indigenous Peoples have of police, particularly in an impoverished and crime-ridden area, would have a concern in a situation of police questioning where a suspicion is articulated (even if done professionally and civilly and in a public place) that they are "not free to choose to walk away or decline to answer questions" (*Grant* at para 41).

151 See, for example, *R v Poole*, 2015 BCCA 464 [*Poole*] at para 9.

152 *Le*, above note 77 at para 109. Despite this clear finding, the position has not been unambiguously adopted. See, for example, *R v Corner*, 2023 ONCA 509 at para 99: "Prior experience with the police in similar circumstances can cut both ways on the question of what a reasonable person in the appellant's circumstances would perceive or not perceive about his entitlement to walk away from the scene."

153 *Le*, above note 77 at para 60.

Although in principle whether a person is psychologically detained is simply determined by looking at the *Grant* criteria, it is also necessary to look at the decision in *R v Suberu*, handed down by the Court on the same day as *Grant*.[154] Suberu was in a liquor store where a person he was with was using a stolen gift card: a police officer arrived at the scene as Suberu was leaving, and Suberu said to him, "He did this, not me, so I guess I can go." The officer replied: "Wait a minute. I need to talk to you before you go anywhere." The officer followed Suberu outside, where he posed half a dozen questions and then asked Suberu for his identification and registration. Eventually, the officer received more information by radio, arrested the accused, and advised him of his right to counsel. The issue in *Suberu* was whether the officer had violated the accused's section 10(b) right to counsel by not cautioning him when he was first detained. The Ontario Court of Appeal had concluded there was no section 10(b) violation because a short delay was permissible in the context of an investigative detention. The Supreme Court of Canada rejected that view, holding that the right to counsel arises immediately upon an investigative detention. However, they upheld the result in the courts below on the basis that Suberu had not been detained *at all* until he was arrested: they concluded that the definition of detention "gives the police leeway to engage members of the public in non-coercive, exploratory questioning without necessarily triggering their *Charter* rights relating to detention."[155]

This conclusion was surprising. All the judges at every level below had concluded that there *was* a detention and disagreed over only the legal consequences of that detention. Justice Binnie argued in a dissenting judgment that this application of the test in *Grant* was mistaken and underestimated the coercive power of police commands. On the facts the accused had been leaving and had been told by an officer to wait and answer some questions. Holding that "[g]enerally speaking, the police mean what they say when they direct a citizen to stay put," he would have concluded that the accused was detained.[156]

The effect of the Supreme Court reaching the conclusion it did has been to create a kind of sorting mechanism for assessing detentions. *Suberu* is being taken to have established the notion of an "exploratory investigation" which does not amount to a detention.[157] In essence,

154 2009 SCC 33 [*Suberu*].

155 *Ibid* at para 45.

156 *Ibid* at para 50. See also the discussion in Quigley, "Was It Worth the Wait?" above note 119, and Coughlan, "Great Strides," above note 121.

157 See, for example, *R v Mihalik*, 2010 ABPC 253; *R v Johnson*, 2010 ONSC 1490; *R v Oulton*, 2011 ABQB 243; *R v Bagnato*, 2011 ONSC 2440; *R v Lyons*, 2011 ABPC 297; *R v Munro*, 2012 ONSC 43; *R v Smith*, 2012 ONCJ 116 [*Smith* 2012]; *R v Goodwin*, 2014 ABPC 170; or *R v Chui*, 2015 ONSC 552.

police have been given the power to engage in exploratory questioning to orient themselves, even if doing so results in them investigating and eventually arresting an accused.[158]

The Court observed in *Suberu* that "[t]he line between general questioning and focussed interrogation amounting to detention may be difficult to draw in particular cases."[159] As a practical matter, the decision as to whether a particular accused was detained often comes down to whether the facts are seen as more like *Grant* or more like *Suberu*.[160]

## 3) Was the Detention Arbitrary?

### a) Introduction

The test under section 9 for whether a detention is "arbitrary" is consciously parallel to the test under section 8 for whether a search is "unreasonable":

> the detention must be authorized by law; the authorizing law itself must not be arbitrary; and, the manner in which the detention is carried out must be reasonable.[161]

That is a sensible policy decision and not a surprising choice. What *is* surprising is that in the case of section 8, that approach was adopted in one of the very earliest decisions, *Collins*, in 1987:[162] the full parallel approach for section 9 was not authoritatively articulated until over three decades later in 2019, with *Le*. This had, and continues to have, an impact on the law around arbitrary detention.

For example, the discussion here will focus on the three different questions determining arbitrariness, but it is less easy in the case of section 9 than it was for section 8 to neatly separate the caselaw into those questions. There were of course many cases about arbitrary detention decided in the several decades before the analytical framework was

---

158 See the discussion of "default" common law powers in Chapter 2, Section A(3)(c).

159 *Suberu*, above note 154 at para 29.

160 *R v Peacock*, 2009 ONCJ 479 at para 28: "At its simplest, answering the question of whether the defendant was detained depends on whether the totality of circumstances renders him closer to the fact pattern presented in *Grant* or that captured by the facts in *Suberu*." Cases approaching the issue on this basis include *R v Reddy*, 2010 BCCA 11; *R v Sonne*, 2011 ONSC 6700; *R v Simpenzwe*, 2009 ABQB 579; *Smith* 2012, above note 157; *R v Guenter*, 2016 ONCA 572; *R v Reid*, 2019 ONCA 32; *R v Jacques*, 2021 ABPC 295; and *R v Qasim*, 2021 ABPC 86. Indeed, this is in essence the approach of the dissenting judgment in *Le*, above note 77. See also the discussion in *R v Francois*, above note 125.

161 *Le*, above note 77 at para 124.

162 *R v Collins*, [1987] 1 SCR 265. See the discussion of the *Collins* test in Chapter 4, Section A.

established, and it is not always easy to firmly conclude which step should be seen as at issue. Some powers of detention were created at common law by the Supreme Court: in those cases it can be difficult or impossible to separate the analysis of whether the detention was authorized by law from the question of whether the law itself was arbitrary, since the same analysis created the authorizing law and then applied it.[163] Similarly, the articulation of some common law powers of detention takes into account the way in which they were exercised, which has the potential to collapse the distinction between whether the detention was authorized by law and whether the manner of detention was reasonable.[164] And as will be pursued below, it is clear that racial profiling will make a detention arbitrary, but it is not always easy to say whether that is because the detention is not authorized by law, whether a law which leaves scope for racial profiling is arbitrary, or whether engaging in racial profiling makes the manner of detention unreasonable.

A further problem is that for several decades the Court deliberately declined to settle a key aspect of the test: whether an unlawful detention was automatically an arbitrary detention. They concluded that it was with *Grant* in 2009, but the failure to settle the point earlier had two noticeable impacts. First, as was noted above in Section C(1), it was an impetus to the creation of additional common law police powers. Second, because the point was unsettled for so long, authorities inconsistent with the current state of the law became established: despite the fact that the Court has now settled the point, those authorities continue sometimes to be relied upon. The result is that the proper analysis is sometimes not followed. It is worth elaborating on that second point here.

For some considerable time, the Court had left unsettled the question of whether a detention could be unlawful (in the sense that the police acted outside of their powers to arrest or detain) but nonetheless not be arbitrary for purposes of section 9. They held in *R v Latimer*, for example, that "[u]nlawful arrests may be inherently arbitrary . . .

---

163 See, for example, *R v Clayton*, 2007 SCC 32 [*Clayton*] at para 61, where in minority reasons Binnie J observes:

> My colleague writes:
>
> The statement that a detention which is lawful is not arbitrary should not be understood as exempting the authorizing law, whether it is common law or statutory, from *Charter* scrutiny. [para. 21]
>
> We thus agree on the need for "*Charter* scrutiny". It seems to me problematic in a case like this, however, to say the authorizing law is subject to *Charter* scrutiny without in fact subjecting the authorizing law to any recognizable *Charter* scrutiny.

164 See the discussion of *R v Aucoin*, 2012 SCC 66 [*Aucoin*], below in Section 3(d).

However, it is not necessary to address that question."[165] In the absence of binding authority, many lower courts concluded that something more than just a failure to act within the limits of a power was required. One view, for example, was that an unlawful arrest might nonetheless not be an arbitrary one.[166] The Ontario Court of Appeal, in the early decision *R v Cayer*, held that an arbitrary detention was one which was "capricious, despotic or unjustifiable."[167] This decision was followed by other courts of appeal[168] and was often used to find that there was no section 9 violation despite an arrest being unlawful. That was justifiable while the Supreme Court had left the point open.

However, *Grant* in 2009 definitively settled that unlawfulness automatically leads to a finding of arbitrariness, holding that "for a detention to be non-arbitrary, it must be authorized by a law which is itself non-arbitrary."[169] They have reiterated this point: "an unlawful arrest or detention is necessarily arbitrary and infringes s. 9 of the *Charter*."[170] It is no longer possible to argue that something *more* than illegality must be shown for a detention to be arbitrary. Nonetheless, *Cayer* continues to be cited as authority that a detention could be unlawful but not arbitrary.[171] Indeed, independent of simply relying on outdated precedents, the opposite view continues to be actively argued, seemingly in ignorance of the fact that *Grant* decided the point. In *R v Steadman*, for example, the Alberta Court of Appeal maintained that "it should not be correct in law to say that the mere fact a detention might be unlawful would automatically make the detention arbitrary for the purposes of s 9 of the *Charter*."[172]

---

165 See, for example, *R v Latimer*, [1997] 1 SCR 217 at para 26: "Unlawful arrests may be inherently arbitrary: see PW Hogg, *Constitutional Law of Canada* (3d ed 1992) at 1073. However, it is not necessary to address that question."

166 *R v Duguay* (1985), 18 CCC (3d) 289 (Ont CA): "It cannot be that every unlawful arrest necessarily falls within the words 'arbitrarily detained.'"

167 *R v Cayer* (1988), 66 CR (3d) 30 (Ont CA).

168 See *R v Sieben*, 1989 ABCA 258 or *R v Baker* (1988), 88 NSR (2d) 250 (CA).

169 *Grant*, above note 34 at para 56.

170 *R v Tim*, 2022 SCC 12 at para 22.

171 See, for example, *R v Veen*, 2020 ABQB 99, though in that case the error was noted on appeal: 2022 ABCA 350 at para 64. See also *R v Kachmarski*, 2014 SKQB 39; *R v Al-Adhami*, 2020 ONSC 6421; or *R v Osorio*, 2025 ONCJ 351. See also *R v Hassan*, 2020 ONSC 6354 at paras 24–25, where the decision in successive paragraphs states the correct rule but also insists on something more than unlawfulness.

172 *R v Steadman*, 2021 ABCA 332 at para 38. See also *R v Zolmer*, 2019 ABCA 93 at para 52, envisioning a detention which is "unlawful even if not arbitrary" or *R v Vuozzo*, 2013 ABCA 130, finding that a detention would not be arbitrary "unless on the facts it can be said that what the police did 'bears no relation or is inconsistent with' the law which founds the state action" (para 44).

This problem is exacerbated by the fact that "arbitrariness" has also developed as a principle of fundamental justice under section 7 of the *Charter*, where it means that "there is no connection between the effect and the object of the law."[173] That is *not* the question to ask under section 9 where, as noted, a detention could be found arbitrary by failing any of three steps: not being authorized by law, the law authorizing it being arbitrary, or the manner of detention being unreasonable. Nonetheless, there are cases which use the section 7 definition of arbitrariness as the test for deciding whether there has been a section 9 violation.[174]

This confusion also illustrates the hazards that arise from not having had a framework for section 9 analysis from the start. As noted, *Cayer* is sometimes still cited for the proposition that a detention needs more than just unlawfulness to be arbitrary. The context of the decision, however, was to consider a detention which *was* lawful, and the Ontario Court of Appeal observed that "[a] detention may be arbitrary within s. 9 of the *Charter* even though the arrest is lawful, when the policy underlying the statute which authorizes detention or imprisonment is itself arbitrary in the sense of being capricious, unreasonable or unjustified." That is, *Cayer* was not saying that there needed to be capriciousness *in addition* to unlawfulness: it was saying that capriciousness could make a detention arbitrary *even if* it was lawful. With a clearer framework at the time, it would have been apparent that *Cayer* was not addressing the first step in the framework, whether the detention was arbitrary, but a later stage.

A similar point could be made about the use of section 7 principles in a section 9 analysis. Early section 9 cases dealing with vehicle stops, again operating without an overall framework, found those random stops to be arbitrary detentions "because there were no criteria for the selection of the drivers."[175] Although that was in essence the complete analysis at the time, now we would understand that as going to the second stage, "was the law itself reasonable"? Arguably some-

173 *Canada (Attorney General) v Bedford*, 2013 SCC 72 at para 98.

174 As an example of this error, see the Alberta Court of Appeal decision in *Whipple*, above note 31. In assessing the arbitrariness of a traffic stop, the Court of Appeal concluded at para 49 that the traffic stop was not arbitrary "because the police action was not shown to be completely disconnected from or grossly disproportionate to the objectives of the criminal law generally or the *Criminal Code* in particular." To similar effect see *R v Vassell*, 2015 ABCA 409, applying the wrong understanding of "arbitrary" to non-compliance with s 503 of the *Code*. The result in the case was reversed by the Supreme Court of Canada (*R v Vassell*, 2016 SCC 26) but for reasons unrelated to this issue, which was not commented on.

175 See the longer discussion of these cases below in this section.

thing similar should be true of the section 7 arbitrariness principle of fundamental justice: it might be a basis for saying that a law is arbitrary, rather than being substituted for the entire section 9 test. In the absence of that clear framework for so many years, it is not surprising that ambiguity arose.

The rest of this discussion will focus on the three questions determining whether a detention is arbitrary, but it is less easy in the case of section 9 than it was for section 8 to neatly separate the caselaw into those questions. Despite the fact that there was no governing framework for section 9 until several decades after the section came into force, there nonetheless were many cases during that period of time which found particular detentions to be either arbitrary or not arbitrary. As a result, at this stage, a certain amount of "retrofitting" is necessary in order to understand those previous cases in light of the framework which has now been articulated. There are also other unique features of the section 9 context.

For example, on any occasion when the question is whether there is lawful authority for some state action, the only possible sources of that authority are statute, common law, or consent. In the case of section 9, however, as a practical matter consent is not a very relevant question. If a person is physically or legally detained (for example, by being arrested) the source of authority is not the detainee's consent. In the case of a psychological detention, it seems far more likely that any factors which might lead to the conclusion that the person consented to the detention would equally lead to the conclusion that a reasonable person would not think they were obligated to comply — which would mean that it was not a detention at all. It is not impossible to think about consent as a source of authority in the detention context: for example, it has been held that complying with a police officer's request to stop does not make the stop voluntary and therefore not a detention.[176] Similarly, consent might be relevant in considering the lawfulness of any search carried out during the detention, which will often be the bigger issue.[177] However, in considering the lawfulness of a detention itself, the more relevant issues are statutory powers of detention and common law powers of detention.

There are many statutory powers of detention. Some of these are outside the scope of the "investigative powers" focus of this chapter, such as the dangerous offender provisions in the *Code* or security certificates under the *Immigration and Refugee Protection Act*, but are

---

176 *R v Dedman*, [1985] 2 SCR 2 [*Dedman*].

177 See the discussion in Chapter 4, Section C(1)(a)(iii), "Authorization by Consent."

still detentions which could be tested against section 9.[178] Those that do relate to the focus of this chapter are, for the most part, discussed elsewhere in this book. For example, arresting a person amounts to detaining them for purposes of section 9, and so that detention would be arbitrary if the police act outside their powers of arrest (which are discussed in Chapter 7). If, having arrested a person, the police fail to comply with the provisions in the *Code* governing when and how that person should be released (discussed in Chapter 6), that too would be unlawful and violate section 9.[179]

Other powers blur the line between detention and search. For example, the *Code* has long contained powers allowing a police officer to demand breath samples, and in December 2018 the requirements to be met before a peace officer could make such a demand were significantly relaxed.[180] A detention is involved in obtaining such evidence from an accused, but the *Charter* challenges which are sure to be brought against these new provisions are far more likely to be based on section 8. However, there is typically a detention aspect to any such case: before an officer can be in a position to make a breath demand of a driver, the officer must have first stopped the vehicle, and so the question of whether that stop was an arbitrary detention arises.[181] Indeed, the earliest section 9 caselaw arose in this context, and it is useful to begin by discussing it. Because that caselaw precedes the development of an analytical framework for section 9, however, it melds together what we should now think of as the separate questions of whether the detention was authorized by law and whether the law itself is arbitrary. That series of cases also started the trend of creating new police powers at common law, which ultimately led to the creation of police powers of investigative detention short of arrest, to permit a police roadblock, and eventually to permit any detention which is reasonably necessary

178 See *R v Lyons*, [1987] 2 SCR 309 and *Re Charkaoui*, 2007 SCC 9, respectively.

179 See *Poirier*, above note 37.

180 See s 320.27. This section was upheld in *Blysniuk*, above note 100, which found that the section violated s 9 but was saved under s 1, citing the reasoning in the vehicle stop cases. *Blysniuk* was cited in *R v Korduner*, 2025 ABCA 30 and *R v Wright*, 2025 SKCA 52, neither of which found a problem with s 320.27(2) but neither addressed the section by way of a s 9 analysis.

181 See, for example, *R v Orbanski; R v Elias*, 2005 SCC 37, holding that the power to conduct roadside sobriety tests was implicit in the general power to stop vehicles in s 76.1(1) of Manitoba's *Highway Traffic Act*, SM 1985–86, c 3. In addition, note that one of the controversial features of the changed breath demand provision in s 320.27 is that in some circumstances police will be able to make a demand of a person who is not in a vehicle, if there is reasonable suspicion the person was driving within the previous three hours.

in the circumstances.[182] Therefore, we shall first discuss the "vehicle stop" cases, then turn to discuss those other common law police powers. Those cases have been foundational in the way that section 9 developed, though as we will see below there is the possibility of a significant change of course on the horizon.

In *Dedman*, the Court considered the RIDE program of randomly stopping vehicles with the goal of detecting impaired drivers.[183] No statutory authority allowed the stops, so the question became whether they were authorized at common law. The majority of the Court, relying on the *Waterfield* test for creating new police powers,[184] held that they were.

The *Waterfield* test involves asking two questions of the conduct of the police: whether "(a) such conduct falls within the general scope of any duty imposed by statute or recognized at common law and (b) whether such conduct, albeit within the general scope of such a duty, involved an unjustifiable use of powers associated with the duty."[185]

The Court held that the random stops satisfied both aspects of the test. Preventing crime and protecting life and property by controlling traffic, the goals of the RIDE program, were well within the scope of duties of the police. Given the seriousness of the problem of impaired driving, the need to deter it, the fact that driving is a licensed activity, the well-publicized nature of the program, and that the stop would be of a short duration and minimal inconvenience, the interference was deemed not unreasonable. Accordingly, the use of power was not unjustifiable, and the police were authorized to make the stops at common law.

*Dedman* determined that there was a common law power to randomly stop vehicles, but did not consider whether such random stops violated section 9 of the *Charter*. The next cases concerned a provincial statute which created the power to stop vehicles in order to perform spot checks for mechanical fitness. In decisions two years apart, the Court first concluded that stationary spot checks were permissible, and then expanded that finding to conclude that a "roving random

---

182 [1963] 3 All ER 659 [*Waterfield*]. See *R v Mann*, 2004 SCC 52 [*Mann*]; *R v Clayton*, above note 163; and *R v Aucoin*, above note 164.

183 *Dedman*, above note 176.

184 See the discussion of the *Waterfield* test in Chapter 2.

185 *Waterfield*, above note 182, quoted in *Dedman*, above note 176 at para 66. See also *R v Decorte*, [2005] 1 SCR 133, which upheld the ability of First Nations constables to conduct RIDE stops just outside a reserve, though in that case, that ability was based on a statutory power.

stop" was also permitted.[186] Translating those findings into the current framework, there are two observations to be made.

The first relates to whether those stops were "authorized by law." The statutory provision in question simply said that police had the power to stop vehicles, without mentioning the purpose behind such stops. The language of "random" stop makes it sound as though there need not be a reason, but that is true in only one sense. The officer need not have any reason to have chosen the particular car in question for the stop: however, the reason for making the stop at all must have been "related to driving a car such as checking the driver's licence and insurance, the sobriety of the driver and the mechanical fitness of the vehicle."[187] A peace officer who makes a "random stop" for some other purpose, such as to investigate an offence, will not be authorized by this power.[188]

The second issue is that, although the Court in *Hufsky* (and *Ladouceur*) found that the statute gave the power to make the stop in question, they nonetheless concluded that the detention violated section 9. They held:

> Although authorized by statute and carried out for lawful purposes, the random stop for the purposes of the spot check procedure nevertheless resulted, in my opinion, in an arbitrary detention because there were no criteria for the selection of the drivers to be stopped and subjected to the spot check procedure. The selection was in the absolute discretion of the police officer. A discretion is arbitrary if there are no criteria, express or implied, which govern its exercise.[189]

---

186 See *Hufsky*, above note 84, and *Ladouceur*, [1990] 1 SCR 1257 [*Ladouceur*], respectively.

187 *Ladouceur, ibid.*

188 There are many such cases, but see, for example, *R v Gonzales*, 2017 ONCA 543 at paras 66–71 [*Gonzales*].

189 *Hufsky*, above note 84 at para 13. Importantly, though not for this particular point, the Court went on to find that despite being an arbitrary detention, the vehicle stop could be saved under s 1. In *Hufsky*, vehicle stops at fixed checkpoints were saved unanimously under s 1, in part because such anti–drunk driving programs were well publicized. In *Ladouceur*, above note 186, a "roving random stop" power, unrelated to a program to stop drunk driving, was saved by a 5:4 margin. The majority thought the situation analogous enough to *Hufsky* that the same rationale would apply. The minority at para 8 described the situation as the "last straw," since it meant the Court was approving a power for police to "stop any vehicle at any time, in any place, without having any reason to do so," which was "a total negation of the freedom from arbitrary detention guaranteed by s. 9 of the *Charter*." The result in *Ladouceur* is probably largely responsible for the fact that it took two decades before a real s 9 jurisprudence began to develop: if that violation could be saved under s 1 there would have seemed little reason to try to establish a s 9 violation.

The most natural way to understand that conclusion in light of the framework which has now developed would be to say that the detention failed at the second stage: the law itself was arbitrary.

In principle that is not a problem, but it does leave this as a significantly underdeveloped area of the law. The Court's discussion of this step in *Hufsky* was confined to a single paragraph and is heavily influenced by the context of a vehicle stop. Nonetheless this definition of when a law will be arbitrary has been relied on many times since, in many contexts.[190] That would not be a problem if it simply meant that being based on no criteria was *one* of the ways in which a law could be arbitrary. However, all of those cases treat "being based on no criteria" as the *definition* of when a law will be arbitrary, but it is clearly inadequate: a detention based on *unreasonable* criteria is more objectionable than one based on *no* criteria and clearly ought to be within the definition.

Some instances of unreasonable criteria for stops can be found. In the Ontario Court of Appeal decision in *R v Calderon*,[191] for example, the court found a section 9 violation when the police had stopped a vehicle based on what they claimed a drug-interdiction course had taught them were indicators that the occupants were drug couriers. The "indicators" that the officers had relied upon were the presence of cellphones, a pager, a road map, some fast-food wrappers, and two duffel bags, as well as the notion that the car being driven seemed too expensive "for what the driver and the passenger looked to me."[192] The last criterion was rejected outright as an inappropriate criterion, but so ultimately were the preceding ones. All of those factors, the court held, were neutral and were unsurprising items to find in a car. Each of the officers acknowledged on cross-examination that they had stopped many cars based on these "indicators" and had never before found drugs. The stop based on these neutral and unreliable factors was therefore an arbitrary detention.[193]

---

190 See, for example, *Ladouceur*, above note 186 (traffic stops); *R v Duguay*, [1989] 1 SCR 93 (powers of arrest, by the dissent); *R v Swain*, [1991] 1 SCR 933 (consequences of s 16 verdict); *R v Pearson*, [1992] 3 SCR 665 (bail); and *R v Morales*, [1992] 3 SCR 711 (bail).

191 (2004), 23 CR (6th) 1 (Ont CA).

192 *Ibid* at para 61.

193 To similar effect, see *R v Gonzales*, above note 188. The officer in that case was patrolling a neighbourhood where there had been break-ins: on two separate days he saw two young men in a vehicle driving through the area, and on one of those occasions one of the men looked at him. The stop based on these criteria was not a reasonable one.

The Court has, in fact, elsewhere suggested a different definition of when a law is unreasonable which does look at the content of the criteria themselves. In *Charkaoui v Canada (Citizenship and Immigration)*, while considering security certificates under the *Immigration and Refugee Protection Act*, they proposed that "[d]etention is not arbitrary where there are 'standards that are rationally related to the purpose of the power of detention.'"[194] However, that definition has not been widely applied, having been mostly considered in the immigration or other "long term" detention contexts. To the extent that it has been mentioned in the context of the types of detentions at issue here, it is only where courts have mistakenly applied that standard *instead of* considering whether a detention was authorized by law, rather than using it to assess the law itself.[195]

The most obvious instance of unreasonable criteria would be stops based on racial profiling. Despite the "no criteria" test which has been articulated, it has been clear for a long time that a racially motivated stop would be an arbitrary detention,[196] so work clearly needs to be done in developing the "law itself is arbitrary" portion of the framework.

There is a developing jurisprudence on stops based on racial profiling and a recognition that it leads to a finding of a section 9 violation. Observing that racial profiling occurs "when race or racial stereotypes about offending or dangerousness are used, consciously or unconsciously, to any degree in suspect selection or subject treatment,"[197] the Court has adopted a definition of the term:

> Racial profiling is any action taken by one or more people in authority with respect to a person or group of persons, for reasons of safety, security or public order, that is based on actual or presumed membership in a group defined by race, colour, ethnic or national origin or religion, without factual grounds or reasonable suspicion, that results in the person or group being exposed to differential treatment or scrutiny.

---

194 *Charkaoui v Canada (Citizenship and Immigration)*, 2007 SCC 9 at para 89.

195 See, for example, *Steadman*, above note 172; *Veen*, above note 171; or *Vuozzo*, above note 172, all discussed above in this Section.

196 See, for example, the comments of the dissent in *Ladouceur*, above note 186: "racial considerations may be a factor too. My colleague states that in such circumstances, a *Charter* violation may be made out. If, however, no reason need be given nor is necessary, how will we ever know?" Similarly see *Le*, above note 77 at para 78: "a detention based on racial profiling is one that is, by definition, not based on reasonable suspicion."

197 *Ibid* at para 76, quoting Ottawa Police Service, *Racial Profiling* (June 27, 2011), Policy No 5.39 (online) at 2.

> Racial profiling [also] includes any action by a person in a situation of authority who applies a measure in a disproportionate way to certain segments of the population on the basis, in particular, of their racial, ethnic, national or religious background, whether actual or presumed.[198]

As a general proposition, racial profiling claims have been difficult to establish. The Court observed in *Le* that the substantial body of reliable research over many decades allowed courts to take judicial notice of the social fact that our society has "disproportionate policing of racialized and low-income communities."[199] The difficulty tends not to be showing that there *are* instances of racial profiling, but that the particular case before a court *is* one of those instances:[200] since the accused is claiming a section 9 violation, the onus is on the accused on balance of probabilities to prove the allegation. Indeed, an irony in *Le* is that although that case is the Court's most complete discussion and acknowledgement of racial profiling, it occurs in a decision where they were bound by the trial judge's conclusion that the officers in question had *not* been motivated by race in investigating those particular accused. Similarly, a common result in court of appeal cases is to find that the trial court erred in some way in concluding that there was not racial profiling but not to actually find that there *was* racial profiling.[201]

The Ontario Court of Appeal in *R v Brown* suggested that racial profiling cases are unlikely to be proven by direct evidence, and so must be inferred from the circumstances:

> where the evidence shows that the circumstances relating to a detention correspond to the phenomenon of racial profiling and provide a basis for the court to infer that the police officer is lying about why he or she singled out the accused person for attention, the record is

198 *Ibid* at para 77, quoting *Quebec (Commission des droits de la personne et des droits de la jeunesse) v Bombardier Inc (Bombardier Aerospace Training Center)*, 2015 SCC 39 at para 33, emphasis deleted in *Le*.

199 *Le*, above note 77 at para 97, and see the discussion preceding that.

200 As the Court observed in *Le*, *ibid* at para 80, "it is still open to a trial judge to determine that something that often occurs did not actually happen in the particular case before them." See, for example, *R v Kenowesequape*, 2018 ABQB 135 [*Kenowesequape*] at para 16: "It is a leap to go from taking judicial notice that Indigenous people, in particular Indigenous male youths, are disadvantaged in our society and over represented in our legal system, to the conclusion that the police must be engaging in racial profiling generally, or specifically in this case."

201 See, for example, *R v Dudhi*, 2019 ONCA 665 [*Dudhi*] at para 24 or *R v Sitladeen*, 2021 ONCA 303 [*Sitladeen*].

> then capable of supporting a finding that the stop was based on racial profiling.[202]

This is often referred to as the "correspondence test." More recently, and based on *Le*, the Ontario Court of Appeal in *R v Dudhi* put forward a test for assessing racial profiling claims:

> [54] Racial profiling has two components: (1) an attitudinal component; and (2) a causation component. As Brown and Martin JJ. explained in *R. v. Le*, 2019 SCC 34, at para. 76, for the majority of the Court:
>
> [T]he concept of racial profiling is primarily concerned with the motivation of the police. It occurs when race or racial stereotypes about offending or dangerousness are used, consciously or unconsciously, to any degree in suspect selection or subject treatment. [Citations omitted.]
>
> [55] The attitudinal component is the acceptance by a person in authority, such as a police officer, that race or racial stereotypes are relevant in identifying the propensity to offend or to be dangerous .... The causation component requires that this race-based thinking must consciously or unconsciously play a causal role.[203]

They stressed, in particular, that reliance on improper stereotypes "to any degree" was sufficient to support a racial profiling claim. They have also held that there is no need to show that police are deliberately misleading the court about their motives in order to establish a racial profiling claim.[204]

Although racial profiling has been recognized in principle, successful racial profiling claims at trial have been relatively few, though they are increasing.[205] It has been argued that trial judges are unlikely to find the attitudinal component to be met unless there is no other explanation for the stop.[206] The effect of that is that, although in principle racial profiling could invalidate an otherwise lawful detention, in practice the fact that the detention is lawful defeats the racial profiling claim.[207]

---

202 (2003), 173 CCC (3d) 23 at para 45 (Ont CA) [*Brown*].

203 *Dudhi*, above note 201.

204 *Sitladeen*, above note 201.

205 See, for example, *R v Khan* (2004), 24 CR (6th) 48 (Ont SCJ); *R v Ferguson-Cadore*, 2016 ONSC 4872; *R v Ohenhen*, 2016 ONSC 5782; *R v Thompson*, [2016] 28 CR (7th) 394; *R v Holloway*, 2021 ONSC 6136; *R v Byfield*, 2023 ONSC 4308; *R v Douglas-Hodgson*, 2023 ONSC 6769; or *R v Sparks*, 2022 NSPC 51.

206 Elizabeth Fleet, "One Step Forward, Two Steps Back: Racial Profiling Claims in the Wake of *Dudhi*" (2025), 100 CR (7th) 282.

207 See generally on this topic DM Tanovich, "Applying the Racial Profiling Correspondence Test" (2017), 64 *CLQ* 359.

However, it is possible that the phenomenon of racial profiling will have a broader impact on vehicle stop powers. In *Procureur général du Québec c Luamba*, the Quebec Court of Appeal overturned the result in *Ladouceur* allowing for roving random stops without grounds, precisely on the basis that the law itself violated section 9 of the *Charter* and could not be saved under section 1. It will be recalled that in *Ladouceur* the law was found to be arbitrary because it had no criteria. *Luamba* carries that point further, in light of the significant evidence of racial profiling in the use of the "random" vehicle stop power that had been gathered since *Ladouceur*. The Quebec Court of Appeal found that the problem was not with individual "bad apple" actors but with the law itself: although the provincial statutory power "does not expressly authorize traffic stops based on racial profiling, the evidence establishes that it has the effect of allowing racial profiling to permeate the exercise of the police discretion conferred by that provision."[208] In their view the absence of criteria was "the source of the alleged *Charter* breaches because it fosters racial profiling."[209] *Ladouceur* had also, of course, found a section 9 violation but had saved it under section 1. In *Luamba* the section 1 analysis did not save the provision, essentially because once the negative impacts of racial profiling were included in the analysis, the provision was neither minimally impairing nor proportional.[210]

Strictly *Luamba* only concerns the statutory vehicle stop power in Quebec's *Highway Safety Code*. However, the decision has been appealed to the Supreme Court, though at the time of this writing the appeal has not been heard.[211] If the decision is upheld, the same reasoning would seemingly apply to all other provincial or territorial vehicle stop powers which do not set out criteria for their use. As these are statutory powers and provincial legislation, of course, there is scope for variation from jurisdiction to jurisdiction.[212]

---

208 *Procureur général du Québec c Luamba*, 2024 QCCA 1387 at para 53 [*Luamba*].

209 *Luamba*, above note 208 at para 74.

210 *Luamba* also found the stop power to violate the equality rights guarantee in s 15 and not be saved by s 1.

211 *Attorney General of Quebec v Joseph-Christopher Luamba*, leave granted 2025-05-01, case number 41605.

212 See, for example, *R v McColman*, 2023 SCC 8. In that case the Crown argued that police in Ontario should be able to use a vehicle stop power on private property so long as they had formed the intention to make the stop while the vehicle was on a highway. That had been the conclusion of the Saskatchewan Court of Appeal about the legislation in that province: *R v Anderson*, 2014 SKCA 32. The Supreme Court rejected that argument, noting at para 31 that "Ontario's *HTA* differs in important ways from the other provincial statutes that regulate driving and drivers."

As noted above, the vehicle stop cases are relevant to more than one part of the section 9 framework. Another significance of them, perhaps the greatest significance, was the use in *Dedman* of the *Waterfield* test, which was intended to be a way to understand the limits on existing police powers, but which the Court used as a method of creating new powers.[213] As discussed in Chapter 2, the use of *Waterfield* to expand police powers is well entrenched in Canadian law. We have already seen that it was used in *Dedman* to create a vehicle stop power. More significantly, it has been used to create various common law powers of detention relating to individuals, thereby satisfying what is now the "authorized by law" portion of the framework. The rest of this part of this chapter will be devoted to looking at the impact of that approach and the particular new powers created.

In *R v Mann*, the Court relied on *Waterfield* to decide that police officers who do not have reasonable grounds to arrest a person have the power to stop that person for investigative purposes, nonetheless, if they have "reasonable grounds to detain."[214] The Court also relied on *Waterfield* in *R v Clayton*.[215] On the surface, *Clayton* creates only a police power to set up roadblocks, but as will be seen when that case is discussed, the approach taken to *Waterfield* in *Clayton* is extremely expansive. The later decision in *R v Aucoin* confirms that it created exactly the "general power of detention" that the Court warned against creating in *Mann*.[216]

It is best to begin by discussing the "investigative detention" power created in *Mann*.

### b) Investigative Detention

The first suggestion that there was a power of investigative detention in Canada came in the Ontario Court of Appeal decision in *R v Simpson*. That decision suggested that such a power existed on some occasions, though not on the facts of that case itself. There was no general power to detain, the Court noted, but they held that a person could be briefly detained for questioning "if the detaining officer has some 'articulable cause' for the detention."[217] Articulable cause — which is a consciously lower standard than the "reasonable grounds to believe" required for

---

213 See, for example, James Stribopoulos, "A Failed Experiment? Investigative Detention: Ten Years Later" (2003) 41 *Alberta Law Review* 335 at 348–52; Don Stuart, "*R. v. Dedman*: Annotation" (1985) 46 *Criminal Reports* (3d) 194 at 195. See also the discussion of *Waterfield* in Chapter 2, Section A(3)(b).

214 *Mann*, above note 182.

215 Above note 163.

216 *Aucoin*, above note 164.

217 (1993), 20 CR (4th) 1 at para 58 (Ont CA) [*Simpson*].

an arrest — was said to be a necessary but not sufficient condition for the detention, and the detention was meant to be brief. This approach was adopted by a number of other courts of appeal, though later courts largely ignored the notion that articulable cause was only the first step and turned that concept into the test for detention.[218]

Further, the notion that articulable cause should normally support only a brief detention to ask for identification was largely lost, as many courts added an automatic ability to search the person as an incident to the detention or even to use reasonable force in effecting the detention.[219]

Although investigative detention based on articulable cause proved popular with lower courts, it was unpopular with commentators, who generally saw it as an expansion of police powers and a diminution of individual liberty created with too little attention to principle.[220] However, the issue was settled by the Court's decision in *Mann*.[221] In *Mann* the Court decided that police can sometimes detain individuals for

---

218 A very incomplete list of cases that applied the doctrine includes *R v Burke* (1997), 118 CCC (3d) 59 (Nfld CA); *R v Chabot* (1993), 86 CCC (3d) 309 (NSSCAD); *R v Boudreau* (2001), 196 DLR (4th) 53 (NBCA); *R v Lewis*, (1998), 38 OR (3d) 540 (CA); *R v Lake*, (1997), 113 CCC (3d) 208 (Sask CA) [*Lake*]; *R v Dupuis* (1994), 162 AR 197 (CA); *R v Yum*, 2001 ABCA 80 [*Yum*]; *R v TAV* (2001), 48 CR (5th) 366 (Alta CA); and *R v Ferris* (1998), 16 CR (5th) 287 (BCCA), leave to appeal to SCC refused [1998] SCCA No 424 [*Ferris*].

219 For incidental search powers, see *Ferris*, *ibid*; *R v Lal* (1998), 56 CRR (2d) 243 (BCCA), leave to appeal to SCC refused [1999] SCCA No 28; *R v McAuley* (1998), 126 Man R (2d) 202 (CA); *Lake*, above note 218; and *R v Waniandy*, (1995) 162 AR 293 (CA). For the use of force, see *Yum*, above note 218.

220 See, for example, Aman S Patel, "Detention and Articulable Cause: Arbitrariness and Growing Judicial Deference to Police Judgment" (2000) 45 *Criminal Law Quarterly* 198; Peter Sankoff, "Articulable Cause Based Searches Incident to Detention — This *Cooke* May Spoil the Broth" (2002) 2 *Criminal Reports* (6th) 41; Steve Coughlan, "Search Based on Articulable Cause: Proceed with Caution or Full Stop?" (2002) 2 *Criminal Reports* (6th) 49; Lesley A McCoy, "Liberty's Last Stand? Tracing the Limits of Investigative Detention" (2002) 46 *Criminal Law Quarterly* 319; Jason A Nicol, "'Stop in the Name of the Law': Investigative Detention" (2002) 7 *Canadian Criminal Law Review* 223; Stribopoulos, above note 213; *H(CR)*, above note 110; and Steve Coughlan, "*R v Mann*: Annotation" (2003) 5 *Criminal Reports* (6th) 306.

221 Generally speaking, the decision in *Mann* was not well received by commentators either: see Benjamin L Berger, "Race and Erasure in *R. v. Mann*" (2004) 21 *Criminal Reports* (6th) 58; Eric V Gottardi, "*R. v. Mann*: Regulating State Intrusions in the Context of Investigative Detentions" (2004) 21 *Criminal Reports* (6th) 27; Tim Quigley, "*Mann*, It's a Disappointing Decision" (2004) 21 *Criminal Reports* (6th) 41; David Tanovich, "The Colourless World of *Mann*" (2004) 21 *Criminal Reports* (6th) 47; and Joseph R Marin, "*R. v. Mann*: Further Down the Slippery Slope" (2005) 42 *Alberta Law Review* 1123.

investigative detention, but the reasoning is cursory. In substance, the decision amounted to confirming that such a power *does* exist without explaining very fully *why* it should exist. The Court referred briefly to *Simpson*[222] and to one other court of appeal decision, devoted two short paragraphs to the nearly forty years of US jurisprudence on this issue, and engaged in essentially no analysis of the many arguments that commentators had raised against the power.

The investigative detention power articulated in *Mann* was quite limited. On the one hand, the Court appeared to take the question of whether an investigative detention power based on less than reasonable grounds exists at all as settled by the lower court jurisprudence, though this is not explicitly stated. On the other hand, *Mann* clearly did not adopt or confirm the broad approach to investigative detention reflected in those cases — it was a fresh starting point. Indeed, the Court specifically stated that it would not be "appropriate for this Court to recognize a general power of detention for investigative purposes."[223] The Court described the limited power it does create in this way:

> The detention must be viewed as reasonably necessary on an objective view of the totality of the circumstances, informing the officer's suspicion that there is a clear nexus between the individual to be detained and a recent or ongoing criminal offence. Reasonable grounds figures at the front end of such an assessment, underlying the officer's reasonable suspicion that the particular individual is implicated in the criminal activity under investigation. The overall reasonableness of the decision to detain, however, must further be assessed against all of the circumstances, most notably the extent to which the interference with individual liberty is necessary to perform the officer's duty, the liberty interfered with, and the nature and extent of that interference, in order to meet the second prong of the *Waterfield* test.[224]

It is clear from this requirement of a nexus to a "recent or on-going criminal offence" that police cannot detain a person because they are suspicious in some general way. Rather, they must be suspicious of a particular person because of some suspected connection to a particular crime already known to them: as the Court has reaffirmed as recently as 2019, there must be a "a recent or still unfolding crime."[225] This point is important. There is a great difference between the police stopping a

---

222 Above note 217.
223 *Mann*, above note 182 at para 17.
224 *Ibid* at para 34.
225 *Le*, above note 77 at para 131.

person who is leaving the scene of a reported break-in and the police stopping a person who is walking along the street while looking in some way "suspicious."[226]

Consistent with this approach, the Court in *Mann* specifically rejected as not relevant any consideration at this stage of whether an accused was in a "high crime area"; suspicions must be specific to the accused.[227] This is a sensible approach for a number of reasons. First, police tend to find crime where they look for it, and so the concept of a "high crime area" can be to a certain extent a self-fulfilling prophecy. Related to that, there is a risk that allowing consideration of the "neighbourhood" to enter into reasoning will be to give legitimacy to conscious or unconscious racial profiling. But even though the crime rate in a neighbourhood should not by itself be relevant, reference to this factor is nonetheless very common, particularly by police in their testimony: it seems as though the notion that it *ought* to be seen as relevant has proven difficult to dislodge.[228] The Court has in 2019 again stressed, however, that, "[e]ven though some apartment buildings in a neighbourhood may be known to the police as havens of drug activity, that does not mean that anyone who enters any apartment building in an ill-defined area or neighbourhood can objectively be suspected of criminal activity."[229] Perhaps this will help to dislodge reference to this irrelevant factor.

The reference to a "recent or on-going" criminal offence precludes using the power because of a suspicion that a person contemplated committing a criminal offence. In that event, the Canadian power of detention is more limited than its US counterpart. The US Supreme Court created their "stop and frisk" power in *Terry v Ohio*, where a police officer became suspicious that several men were planning to rob a store.[230]

---

226 See, for example, *R v Sabiston*, 2023 SKCA 105, where police stopped a known gang member because they saw him wearing a bulletproof vest. The Saskatchewan Court of Appeal found the investigative detention to be unlawful because it was not tethered to the investigation of any offence but was just a blanket or general concern of criminality. The result in *Sabiston* was overturned (2024 SCC 33) but that was based on the conclusion that the Saskatchewan Court of Appeal had wrongly decided to exclude the evidence as a result of the breach.

227 *Mann*, above note 182 at para 45.

228 Among cases which refer to this factor, though they do not generally make clear whether they accept it as relevant or not, are: *R v Mark*, 2017 ONSC 2206; *R v Walters*, 2018 ONSC 4194; *R v Robertson*, 2018 ABQB 658; and *R v Reid*, 2019 ONCA 32.

229 *Le*, above note 77 at para 132, quoting *R v NO*, 2009 ABCA 75 at para 40.

230 392 US 1, 88 S Ct (1968).

Despite the fact that *Mann* is clear on these points, they have not always been recognized or respected by lower courts. For example, in the immediate aftermath of *Mann* some lower courts seemed to take it simply to affirm *Simpson*, rather than to have articulated a new test with particular requirements. As a result, the need for a clear nexus to a recent or ongoing offence and the prohibition on using the power for anticipated offences was not always acknowledged.[231] That was not uniformly so, however: some decisions were careful to identify the particular offence to which there was a clear nexus.[232]

Some courts of appeal have consciously relaxed the standard of "recent or on-going offence." In *R v Nesbeth*, for example, the Ontario Court of Appeal held that the police need not be able to identify "with absolute precision" the particular crime of which they suspect the detainee.[233] In that case, the police pursued an accused after he ran away upon being asked what he was doing in an apartment building in which there was a smell of freshly smoked marijuana. His eventual detention after a chase was found to be lawful on the basis that the police reasonably suspected he had drugs or weapons or both.

In *R v Yeh*[234] the Saskatchewan Court of Appeal considered the issue of whether an investigative detention could be undertaken in the case of a nexus to a suspected, rather than a known, offence. In an earlier decision they had held that a *Mann* investigative detention would not be lawful if the officer merely suspected an offence.[235] In *Yeh* they reconsidered that point and reversed themselves, concluding that *Mann* should be read as authorizing investigative detentions in relation to offences that are only reasonably suspected at the time of the detention.[236] In *R v Schrenk*, the Manitoba Court of Appeal agreed, adding that reasonable suspicion of bad behaviour in general was not

231 See the discussion of this issue in Christina Skibinsky, "Regulating *Mann* in Canada" (2006) 69 *Saskatchewan Law Review* 197. Even more recently this problem has not disappeared. In *R v Wilkinson*, 2023 BCCA 3, the British Columbia Court of Appeal held of the "nexus" requirement in *Mann* that "[t]he judge interpreted the above-noted passage as requiring a specific crime investigation to be underway when the detention occurs. Subsequent decisions have clarified that is not always the case" (para 48). However, the Court of Appeal there makes a fundamental mistake, taking the description in *R v Chehil*, 2013 SCC 49 [*Chehil*], of what "reasonable suspicion" *means* to be the complete test for the investigative detention power. See the discussion in Steve Coughlan, "*Wilkinson*: Reasonable Suspicion, But About What?" (2023) 86 *Criminal Reports* (7th) 348.

232 See, for example, *R v Cooper*, 2005 NSCA 47, or *R v Scott*, 2004 NSCA 141.

233 *Nesbeth*, above note 95 at para 18.

234 2009 SKCA 112 [*Yeh*].

235 *R v Nguyen*, 2008 SKCA 160.

236 *Yeh*, above note 234 at para 85.

sufficient: "[i]t is a reasonable suspicion of specific criminal activity that gives rise to the grounds to detain."[237]

It is important to note that *Nesbeth* and *Yeh* consider two different ways of relaxing the *Mann* standard. *Nesbeth* holds that the offence need not be identified precisely. *Yeh* does not reach that conclusion (indeed, it expressly does not decide it)[238] but holds that once the offence is precisely identified, the police need only reasonably suspect that it has been committed rather than know that fact. It is necessary to be careful with that distinction.[239] In particular, there is a great danger in relaxing the *Mann* standard in both ways by failing to recognize the difference between them. Even the Saskatchewan Court of Appeal in *Yeh* stresses that police ought not to be permitted to conduct an investigative detention "to determine whether an individual is, in some broad way, 'up to no good.'"[240]

It is also worth acknowledging that many courts, without consciously adverting to the legal issue in *Yeh*, nonetheless *act* as though it is sufficient for there only to be reasonable suspicion that the offence has been committed. A very common scenario is for police to stop a vehicle as part of a random stop program but then detain the driver further to investigate some sort of contraband-related offence, such as transporting narcotics. The point to recognize is that in cases of that sort, the grounds leading the officer to think the accused is connected to an offence and the grounds to think that there is an offence at all are exactly the same grounds: if they only reach the reasonable suspicion standard on the former, they are also only reaching that standard on the latter.

On the other hand there is a strong tendency for courts in fact to identify the particular offence about which the police must be

---

237 *R v Schrenk*, 2010 MBCA 38 at para 85.

238 *Yeh*, above note 234 at para 75: "In order to justify an investigative detention, the police suspicion must be particularized, *i.e.* it must relate to specific criminal wrongdoing. Just *how* specific it must be is not an issue in this appeal" [emphasis in original].

239 See *Yeh*, *ibid* at para 74:

> There is a conceptual and practical distinction between (a) the question of how particular or specific a police suspicion must be in order to justify an investigative detention, and (b) the question of whether an investigative detention may be conducted only in respect of an offence which has been reported to the police or which the police otherwise understand has been committed. Any analysis which fails to appreciate the difference between these two notions will, of necessity, be flawed.

240 See *ibid* at para 75. See also the discussion in Tim Quigley, "Investigative Detention: Some Loose Ends Remain" (2009) 69 *Criminal Reports* (6th) 247.

reasonably suspicious,[241] or to insist that generalized suspicion is not sufficient,[242] while others reaffirm the *Mann* standard of "a particular crime" without reference to *Nesbeth*.[243] As a result it is far less clear whether that relaxation should be seen as widespread.

Subsequent to both *Yeh* and *Nesbeth* the Court, in *R v MacKenzie*, characterized *Mann* as deciding that "the police are entitled to detain a person for investigative purposes where they have reasonable grounds to suspect that the individual is connected to particular criminal activity and that such a detention is reasonably necessary in the circumstances."[244] This articulation of the test continues to require a link to "particular criminal activity," which seems to hold to the standard that *Nesbeth* relaxed, and says nothing to suggest that criminal activity need only be reasonably suspected (though the case relies on *Yeh* with regard to several other issues). However, the central issue in *MacKenzie* related to a search, not a detention, and so it would be unwise to read too much into its description of *Mann*. Explicit clarification from the Court as to whether the *Mann* standard should be relaxed in either of the ways proposed would be helpful.[245]

A further relaxation of the *Mann* standard has crept into police practice, though the Ontario Court of Appeal has tried to curb it. The Court held in *Mann* that an investigative detention "must be of brief duration."[246] The model they had in mind was that of a person briefly delayed along their way while walking down the street. In fact, however, as police have used the power there has been a tendency to increase the extent of the interference with liberty and the length of time a person

---

241 See, for example, *R v McGuffie*, 2016 ONCA 365 [*McGuffie*]; *R v Ellis*, 2016 ONCA 598; *R v Squires*, 2016 NLCA 54; *Omar* Ont CA, above note 91 (rev'd on other grounds 2019 SCC 32); or *R v Reid*, 2019 ONCA 32.

242 See, for example, *R v Dunkley*, 2016 ONCA 597 at para 31: "This was not a situation where the police stop a member of the public based on a generalized feeling that the individual is doing something wrong." See also *R v Mitchell*, 2019 ONSC 2613 at para 100: "a very generalized suspicion that Mr. Mitchell could be involved in something nefarious" was not sufficient for an investigative detention.

243 See, for example, *R v Mhlongo*, 2017 ONCA 562 at para 41; *R v Ohenhen*, 2016 ONSC 5782 at para 62; or *R v Omeasoo*, 2019 MBCA 43 at para 40.

244 2013 SCC 50 at para 35 [*MacKenzie*].

245 In *Chehil*, above note 231, handed down with *MacKenzie*, Karakatsanis J, for the Court, observed at para 35: "I do not accept that the evidence must itself consist of unlawful behaviour, or must necessarily be evidence of a specific known criminal act." She was speaking, however, about the kind of evidence necessary in general terms to satisfy the "reasonable suspicion" standard, not about the particular test for an investigative detention.

246 *Mann*, above note 182 at para 22.

is delayed. In *R v McGuffie*, for example, police had received a report of a handgun being passed around among some men in a bar, and the accused was identified to the police, as he was leaving, as one of those men. An officer stopped the accused and conducted a pat-down search. The accused was then placed, while handcuffed, in the back of a police car, left there for thirty minutes, then searched again.[247] Similarly in *R v Barclay*, police detained the accused at a train station because of reasonable suspicion (based on a tip) that he had drugs in his bag. When they could not personally smell drugs, they took the accused to the police station and made him wait for nearly two hours until a drug-sniffing dog was brought there. In each of these cases, the Ontario Court of Appeal concluded that the initial detention was justified, but that it went on too long. They observed in *Barclay* that the purpose of the investigative detention power was that police would either quickly confirm their suspicions and arrest the accused, or would not quickly be able to do so and would release the accused, but must do one of those, because "[t]he relatively low 'reasonable suspicion' standard cannot constitutionally sustain a detention that is not 'brief.'"[248] They acknowledged no precise time limit could be set out, but that the limit in each individual case would depend on consideration of a number of factors such as the intrusiveness of the detention, the nature of the suspected criminal offence, immediate public or individual safety concerns, or the immediate availability (or lack thereof) of the required investigative tools.[249] *Barclay* has been relied on in this regard in later caselaw.[250] It is also worth observing that the *Mann* test is narrower than just the test of a "clear nexus." That is, even when a clear nexus exists, the specific individual decision to detain must still be justified based on the circumstances: it must be "reasonably necessary on an objective view of the totality of the circumstances."

A further explicit change made from existing caselaw relates to terminology. Where lower courts had spoken about "articulable cause," the Supreme Court substituted the phrase "reasonable grounds to detain," holding that this phrasing would be more consistent with Canadian terminology. Justice Deschamps, in dissent, suggested that this phrasing would lead to confusion because "'[r]easonable grounds' has traditionally been employed to describe the standard which must be

---

247 *McGuffie*, above note 241.

248 *R v Barclay*, 2018 ONCA 114 at para 28 [*Barclay*].

249 *Barclay*, above note 248 at para 31.

250 See, for example, *R v McPake*, 2021 BCSC 751; *R v Enchin-Dixon*, 2022 BCSC 1342; *R v Baglee*, 2022 YKTC 13; *R v Hayatibahar*, 2022 ONSC 1281; *R v Chopra*, 2022 ONCJ 322; *Balde c R*, 2023 QCCQ 919; *R v Makortoff*, 2023 BCSC 2524; *R v Barton*, 2024 ABCA 34, or *R v Anderson*, 2025 ONCA 408.

met in order to give rise to the power to *arrest* a suspect."[251] In fact, the terminology that has come to be employed in practice is to refer to "reasonable suspicion." This development is due, in part, to the growth in other detention (and search) powers that have been made available on this lower standard.[252] Most recently the Court has even used the term "reason to suspect" interchangeably with "reasonable suspicion."[253]

Although *Mann* created this investigative detention power based on the lower reasonable suspicion standard, it did relatively little to articulate what that standard required. Subsequent to *Mann* the standard came to be more widely used in other common law powers (both of detention, as noted below, and of search), and eventually the Court did describe in some detail how reasonable suspicion and reasonable belief differ: see the discussion of warrantless searches in Chapter 4, Section C(2)(a). See also the discussion about search during an investigative detention in Chapter 4, Section C(1)(a)(ii)(c).

*Mann* left unsettled whether the section 10 right to counsel arises during an investigative detention; however, it has since been determined that the *Charter* right does arise. One view in lower courts had been that, because investigative detentions were meant to be brief, the accused's right to counsel under section 10(b) did not arise. In *Suberu* the Supreme Court rejected that view and had no difficulty concluding that issues of compelled self-incrimination and interference with liberty arise with an investigative detention as much as with any other. Accordingly, the police have the obligation to inform a detainee of the right to counsel without delay as soon as an investigative detention begins. This immediate obligation is subject only to concerns for officer or public safety or to limits under section 1 of the *Charter*.[254]

### c) Police Roadblocks

Subsequent to *Mann*, the Court relied on the *Waterfield* test to create another police power of detention. On the facts of the case the Court

251 *Mann*, above note 182 at para 64 [emphasis in original].

252 See the discussion in *MacKenzie*, above note 211 at para 74:

> Parenthetically, I note that there are several ways of describing what amounts to the same thing. Reasonable suspicion means "reasonable grounds to suspect" as distinguished from "reasonable grounds to believe" (*Kang-Brown*, at paras 21 and 25, per Binnie J., and at para 164, per Deschamps J.). To the extent one speaks of a "reasonable belief" in the context of reasonable suspicion, it is a reasonable belief that an individual *might* be connected to a particular offence, as opposed to a reasonable belief that an individual *is* connected to the offence.

253 See *R v Stairs*, 2022 SCC 11.

254 *Suberu*, above note 154 at para 2.

was simply approving the actions of the police in setting up a roadblock. However, the way in which the majority reasoned raised the possibility that other, much broader powers to detain also exist, and as we will see in *Aucoin*, that is how the test has come to be interpreted.

In *Clayton*[255] the police received a report of men with guns in a parking lot (and describing particular vehicles), and in response the police set up a roadblock. They stopped all vehicles leaving the parking lot, whether they matched the vehicle descriptions or not, and Clayton and Farmer, the occupants of one car, were both found to have handguns. A central issue was whether there was a violation of the section 9 right of both of the accused not to be arbitrarily detained. The majority held that there would have been no violation if the police had acted lawfully, and so the real issue in the case became whether the police had a power to set up the roadblock. Since they had no statutory power to do so, the only possibility was that they were authorized at common law.

There was both a majority and a minority decision in the case. All nine judges concluded that the police did have the power to act as they had, but they reached that conclusion for different reasons. It is in these different approaches that the new and potentially enormous expansion to *Waterfield* can be seen.

The minority judges held that the proper method of analysis was first to ask whether the police acted lawfully in stopping the accused, which amounted to asking whether there was a common law power permitting them to do so. The second question was whether that common law power resulted in an arbitrary detention. If so, the next step was to ask whether that law was justified under section 1 of the *Charter*. Finally, in some cases it would be necessary to ask whether the power was exercised reasonably in the totality of the circumstances. Applying that approach, the minority concluded that no previously existing common law power (such as those in *Dedman*[256] or *Mann*[257]) authorized the stop but that (using the *Waterfield* test) a new common law power should be created. Specifically, a power should be created to set up a roadblock of all vehicles in response to a report of ongoing serious firearm offences. As a result, the detention was authorized by law. That law would create an arbitrary detention (since it would permit stops in the absence of individualized suspicion) but would be saved under section 1, much like the power in *Ladouceur*.[258]

---

255 Above note 163.

256 Above note 176.

257 Above note 182.

258 Above note 186.

The majority agreed that the issue was whether the police had the power to act as they did, but did nothing further by way of *Charter* scrutiny. As the minority pointed out, the majority substituted the question of whether the *Waterfield* test was met for the *Charter* analysis. Further, their approach to *Waterfield* seems to broaden the scope of what powers police have or, alternatively, to limit when police action will be found to violate the *Charter*, which, on the majority approach, will amount to the same thing. As noted above, the *Waterfield* test depends on two criteria: (1) that the police were acting in the general course of their duties, and (2) that the actions they took were not an unjustifiable use of powers associated with those duties. The first criterion is rarely an issue, and so it is the second that really settles the point. In *Clayton*, the majority effectively reduced that question to whether, in the totality of the circumstances, "the detention of a particular individual is 'reasonably necessary'."[259] But to say that the police can detain an individual whenever it is reasonably necessary is to make that ability available to police far more frequently.

Even in *Mann* the Court noted the fundamental principle that "the police … may act only to the extent that they are empowered to do so by law."[260] That amounts to saying that the norm is for the police to be unable to interfere with individual liberty unless they have been given a specific power. The approach in *Clayton*, in contrast, amounts to saying that the police have the power to do anything that is reasonably necessary. To say that is to remove entirely the notion of predetermined and particular police powers.[261] There has been some tendency in lower courts, since then, simply to consider the justifiability of police action in the abstract, rather than look at whether it was authorized by some common law power.[262] Although it might have been unclear at the time

---

259 *Clayton*, above note 163 at para 30.

260 *Mann*, above note 182 at para 15.

261 For discussions of the hazards inherent in the *Clayton* decision, see Steve Coughlan, "Whither — or Wither — Section 9" (2008) 40 *Supreme Court Law Review* (2d) 147, and James Stribopoulos, "The Forgotten Right: Section 9 of the *Charter*, Its Purpose and Meaning" (2008) 40 *Supreme Court Law Review* (2d) 211.

262 See, for example, *R v Okemow*, 2019 MBCA 37, where police received a call about a shooting and eventually entered the building where the accused was found, without a warrant. Although the Manitoba Court of Appeal considered the point from *Clayton* that police need to act quickly when dealing with firearms, as well as the common law power to enter a building in response to a 911 call and the common law safety search power (both considered in Chapter 6), it made no attempt to identify a power authorizing the police action. Rather, it upheld the trial judge's quite general conclusion "that the police were acting in response to a real public safety concern and that their actions were justifiable and supported by the evidence" (para 61).

whether the intent of *Clayton* was to create an open-ended detention power, subsequent developments have held that it was.

### d) General Common Law Power to Detain

In *Mann*, the Court held that it was "not . . . appropriate for this Court to recognize a general power of detention for investigative purposes."[263] Eight years later in *Aucoin*, they said: "[t]he existence of a general common law power to detain where it is reasonably necessary in the totality of the circumstances was settled in *R. v. Clayton*."[264] The tendency of common law powers to expand readily is clearly demonstrated by this progression; there is, however, at least one hopeful sign in *Aucoin* which might help keep matters in check.

Aucoin was stopped because of an irregularity with a licence plate and then failed a roadside screening test. The officer decided to issue the accused a ticket and therefore asked the accused to sit in the back of the police vehicle. Because he was having the accused sit in the police vehicle, the officer searched the accused, claiming it to be for officer safety purposes. The officer felt something soft in the accused's pocket, asked what it was, and on receiving the reply that it was ecstasy, arrested the accused. On a further search the accused was found to be carrying cocaine and pills, and he was charged with possession for the purpose of trafficking. The central issue in the case was whether the officer had had the authority to place the accused in the back of the police vehicle in order to write him a ticket.

The officer had the power to detain the accused initially for the traffic violation; however, any justification for the search would have had to spring from the decision to have the accused sit in the police vehicle while the ticket was being written. The question was therefore whether the officer had that power to detain. The Court noted that the *Mann* power of investigative detention did not authorize the officer to do so, since the purpose of asking the accused to sit in the police vehicle was not to investigate his nexus to a recent or ongoing offence. It was in that context that they affirmed that *Clayton* had created a general power of detention for investigative purposes, and that was the power that was potentially relevant.

Having confirmed that the general power existed, however, the Court concluded that it did not authorize the particular detention. The general power only authorizes detentions that are "reasonably necessary in the totality of the circumstances," and this detention was not.

---

263 *Mann*, above note 182 at para 17.

264 *Aucoin*, above note 164 at para 36. Note that *Clayton* itself was only three years after the declaration in *Mann*.

Notably, the Nova Scotia Court of Appeal had upheld the trial judge's decision that the officer's actions were reasonable in the circumstances: the Supreme Court stressed that the issue is not whether it was reasonable, but whether it was reasonably *necessary*. In fact, they held, there were other reasonable means by which the officer could have addressed his concern that the accused might disappear into the crowd: for example, he could have waited one or two minutes for backup, which was close at hand, to arrive. Accordingly it was not reasonably necessary to detain the accused by placing him in the back of the vehicle and so that was an unlawful detention.

It is important to note that the ability from *Clayton* confirmed in *Aucoin* is not really a "power" at all, in the sense of an authority based on predetermined criteria such as the power to arrest, or for that matter, the *Mann* investigative detention power. Instead, it is simply a means of deciding, after the fact and on a case-by-case basis, whether to retroactively approve of the way the police behaved in a particular situation.[265]

However, the fact that the Court insisted on a detention being reasonably necessary, not merely reasonable, is an important feature with some potential to keep this much more expansive power in check.[266] In addition, another aspect of the reasoning in *Aucoin* is worth stressing.

In concluding that this detention was arbitrary, the Court observed that "in order to justify securing the appellant in the back seat — *knowing that this would also entail a pat-down search* — detaining the appellant in that manner had to be reasonably necessary."[267] That is, *Aucoin* makes clear that the *Charter* rights and liberty interests of the accused must be considered as part of the "totality of the circumstances."

---

265 Conceptually, one could see the broader *Clayton* power — simply "was it reasonably necessary" — as overtaking and replacing the *Mann* test, which requires other conditions to be met in addition to reasonable necessity. That is not how the cases are being applied in practice, however. Where an investigative detention is at issue, the *Mann* test continues to be applied, and *Clayton* tends to be applied when the circumstances are claimed to present an immediate threat to public safety.

266 See, for example, *R v Ali*, 2023 SKCA 127:

> [33] We accept, for the purposes of deciding Mr. Ali's appeal, that *R v Aucoin* stands for the proposition that if there were other less intrusive means for the police to continue with their investigation, other than asking Mr. Ali to leave his vehicle, that were reasonably available in the circumstances, then the police actions cannot be said to be reasonably necessary and a breach of s. 9 may have occurred.

See also *R v Fisher*, 2023 ONSC 6514.

267 *Aucoin*, above note 147 at para 39 [emphasis added].

The Court found, in effect, that the trial judge (who concluded there was no section 9 violation) reasoned backward. The proper approach was not to ask whether it was reasonable to search, given that the accused was to be put in the back seat: it was to ask whether it was reasonable to put the accused in the back seat, given that he would have to be searched. In other words, limits on the existence of the power must be read in specifically to respect *Charter* rights.

There is, it should be said, a different way of reading this passage. Recall that, as discussed in introducing powers of detention, the section 9 analysis has become a three-step approach: (1) Is the detention authorized by law? (2) Is the law non-arbitrary? (3) Is the manner in which the detention was carried out reasonable? As this particular power has developed, however, the distinction between those steps begins to break down.

The Court at one point in *Aucoin* described the "reasonably necessary" test as the means of satisfying step 1, that there *is* a power: "[t]he existence of a general common law power to detain where it is reasonably necessary in the totality of the circumstances was settled in *R. v. Clayton*."[268] However, it also posed the task in front of it as "considering whether its exercise was reasonably necessary in the circumstances of a particular case," which sounds much more like an analysis under step 3.[269]

That is, both the first and the third steps are determined by looking at whether the detention was reasonably necessary. This confounding of the first and third steps is quite understandable, in fact, given the nature of the general power to detain. The third step is meant to focus on the way in which the particular detention was carried out. But the general detention power, by saying that a police officer was authorized by law if the detention was reasonably necessary in the circumstances, makes the existence of the power dependent on the way in which the particular detention is carried out. The result is that it is often difficult to tell, in cases finding that there has been an arbitrary detention where

268 *Ibid* at para 36.

269 In *MacKenzie*, above note 198 at para 39 [emphasis added], the Court characterized *Aucoin* as being about the third step:

> [I]t is unnecessary to consider whether *the manner of* the appellant's detention was reasonably necessary in the circumstances. Unlike *R. v. Aucoin*, 2012 SCC 66, [2012] 3 S.C.R. 408, there is no suggestion here that the manner in which he was detained (being asked to sit by the side of the road while the sniff was conducted) was not reasonably necessary in the circumstances.

police have purported to rely on this power, exactly *why* their actions have failed the three step test.[270]

It is arguable that *Aucoin* tends to be factored into the impact on the accused's *Charter* rights at the third stage rather than the first stage, but much of the time it seems that the real answer is that courts are not turning their mind to that issue.[271] And ultimately, it might not be of great practical importance which approach is taken: if the detention is not reasonably necessary, then it violates section 9 in *some* way. This confusion does demonstrate, however, the conceptual difficulties that arise when police powers are left to be decided after the fact rather than determined in advance.

## 4) Postscript: Street Checks and Carding

The final topic to discuss is that of street checks, and the related issue of "carding." This is a useful topic to discuss at the end, because in addition to illustrating various aspects of the section 9 framework, it also points to ways in which police have begun to act in a way outside their powers, seemingly as a consequence of the existence of common law police powers. That is, although these practices have names and that makes it appear that they are police powers, they are not. Rather, the rise of street checks and carding over the past few decades is an unintended consequence of the failure to adhere strictly to the notion that police powers must be defined clearly and defined in advance. We will also see that, because the activities rest on very discretionary enforcement, there are clear indications of discriminatory enforcement against visible minorities: this makes the practices doubly problematic and could be seen as an instance of the manner of detention being unreasonable.

---

270 See, for example, *Barclay*, above note 248 at para 27, where the detention in question was not a brief one but should have been:

> The permitted duration of an investigative detention is determined by considering whether the interference with the suspect's liberty interest by his continuing detention was more intrusive than was reasonably necessary to perform the officer's duty, having particular regard to the seriousness of the risk to public or individual safety.

It would be possible to read that passage, and the decision generally, as saying that there is no power to detain for a long period of time. It would also be possible to read it as saying that there was a power of investigative detention, but that by detaining the accused for too long it was not carried out reasonably.

271 See, for example, *Adaikin v Calgary (Police Service)*, 2013 ABCA 333; *R v Azarnush*, 2016 ONCJ 355; *R v Baldwin*, 2016 ONCJ 589; or *R v Foster*, 2017 ONCJ 624. See also *Barclay*, above note 248.

Precisely because this topic does not concern defined powers, there is ambiguity over definitions, and no consistent usage.[272] "Street check" is a compendious term which captures a number of activities on the part of the police. At the most benign level, it can simply include police noting down observations they make about individuals they see on the street in order to retain that information in some kind of central database, without ever interacting with that individual. What most members of the public think of as a street check, however, is a subset of that, which police are more inclined to refer to as "carding": that is, stopping an individual on the street, without reasonable suspicion, in order to obtain information from that individual such as name and address, and sometimes then making a record of that information to be stored in a central database.[273] Exactly how intrusive the individual encounter might be varies: sometimes there might not be a request for identification, but sometimes the stop might involve a frisk search or request to look in a backpack. One could plausibly understand the term, especially from the perspective of the public, to include vehicle stops as well,[274] though those ought to be kept distinct: as discussed above, statutory and common law powers do exist allowing for vehicle stops, as long as they are conducted for particular purposes such as looking for impaired drivers or checking the mechanical fitness of a vehicle. The defining characteristic of a street check, however, is that it is conducted without such a specific goal, but rather for very general "intelligence gathering" purposes (though, it should be noted, there is good reason to doubt that they actually do gather useful information).[275] Still, the boundary is an amorphous one: if police approach a

---

272 See, for example, the discussion in The Honourable Michael H Tulloch, "Report of the Independent Street Checks Review" (11 December 2018), online (pdf): *Ontario Ministry of the Solicitor General* [Tulloch], www.mcscs.jus.gov.on.ca/sites/default/files/content/mcscs/docs/StreetChecks.pdf at 27; in Scot Wortley, "Halifax, Nova Scotia: Street Checks Report" (27 March 2019) [Wortley], online (pdf): *Human Rights Nova Scotia*, https://humanrights.novascotia.ca/sites/default/ files/editor-uploads/halifax_street_checks_report_march_2019_0.pdf at 7; or in Curt T Griffiths, Ruth Montgomery, & Joshua J Murphy, "City of Edmonton Street Checks Policy and Practice Review" (June 2018) [Griffiths et al], online (pdf): *Edmonton Police Commission* https://edmontonpolicecommission.com/wp-content/uploads/2019/02/EPS-Street-Check-Study-Final-REDACTED.pdf at 28.

273 See *Le*, above note 77 at para 10: "This common police practice of asking individuals who they are and demanding proof of their identities for no apparent reason has its own name. It is known as 'carding'."

274 Wortley, above note 272.

275 See Tulloch, above note 272, under the heading "Do Randoms Street Checks Actually Work?" at 96–105 or Wortley, above note 272, under the heading "*Garbage in, Garbage Out: The Quality of Street Checks*" at 85–89.

vehicle which is already parked, for example, and question all of the occupants, it seems that by anyone's definition that should be thought of as a street check.

By way of introduction, we can observe that two distinct problems arise with these activities. The first applies only to carding: it is unlawful, in the sense that no there is no lawful authority for it, and therefore it will virtually always violate section 9 of the *Charter* since it will fail to meet the "authorized by law" requirement. (It is quite likely that the practice would also violate section 8 by being an unreasonable search,[276] but it is easiest to see the issues by examining the detention necessary for the questioning to take place.) The second problem relates to the use of each of these activities. There is significant evidence that when police decide to do a stop, or even to do a less intrusive street check, they do so disproportionately in the case of visible minorities. This might well constitute racial profiling, but at a certain level it does not matter whether that is the case or not: the *impact* on the minority community is unfairly disproportionate no matter how it is classified, which would be a *Charter* violation.[277]

In recent years, these practices have come under increasing scrutiny and have been seen as more controversial. There have been calls for the practices to be banned or at a minimum regulated.[278] There is also evidence that police have felt institutional pressure to increase the number of street checks they perform in order to conform to some kind of informal quota or other internal pressures and, as a result, many of them are, even from the police perspective, of low value.[279] Street checks and carding seem to be of minimal value in preventing or investigating crime, and so even if they were not constitutionally problematic, there is little reason to defend them. We shall consider carding and broader street checks separately, to see the *Charter* problems with them.

As has been explained in this chapter, if a person is detained, then that detention will be arbitrary unless it is authorized by law. The only

---

276 Paul Socka, "Police Carding: Highly Unlikely to Satisfy *Charter* Standards for Consent Searches" (2018) 41 CR (7th) 76.

277 As noted in *Le*, above note 77 at para 81, "racial profiling looks inwards at what motivated the police interaction with a person," but even if that is not the *motive* behind disproportionate enforcement, the unjustified disproportion is a problem nonetheless.

278 See Tulloch, above note 272 at 96 or Wortley, above note 272 at 100.

279 See Tulloch, above note 272 at 96–105 or Wortley, above note 272 at 85–89. See also Griffiths et al, above note 272 at 208, noting that the Edmonton Police Services felt there had been a problem with quantity over quality in their street checks.

potential sources of authorization are statute, the common law, or consent. No statutory power authorizing street checks or carding exists. That is, no *Criminal Code* power authorizes them, and there do not appear to be any provincial statutes which create the authority for them either.

No common law power authorizes street checks. Indeed, in a sense the very point of a street check or carding is that it involves police doing what the common law has not authorized: if a roving random stop of a vehicle were involved, for example, or an investigative detention, then it would not be a street check/carding incident at all. Indeed, one could say not only that carding has not been authorized by the common law, but that it is exactly what the common law has *rejected*: the whole point of the powers discussed above is to say not only that, for example, police can detain if they have reasonable suspicion of a nexus between the individual and a recent or ongoing offence, but also to say that they *cannot* detain in the absence of meeting that standard. However, street checks and carding are consciously situations in which the criteria for none of the powers above are met, and so they are not authorized by common law.

That leaves only two possible arguments for the legality of carding. First, there would be no section 9 violation if the detention could be said to have been authorized by consent. Second, there would be no arbitrary detention if there were no detention at all: if the carding incident did not amount to a psychological detention.

It is not possible to assess either of these arguments on a categorical basis, since both rest on the circumstances of the individual encounter. However, both do raise quite similar issues. First, it seems safe to say that the very existence of outrage over carding, and the controversy of that practice particularly with regard to minority communities, suggests that a pretty significant number of people involved with them did not think they had any choice about the matter.[280] If that is so, then the argument that the person consented, and the argument that the person was not psychologically detained, both seem doomed to failure.

Based on arguments similar to this, and responding to concerns about street checks from the public, some provinces have acted to try to eliminate the problematic aspects. In Nova Scotia, an independent legal opinion obtained by the Human Rights Commission concluded

280 As the Court says in *Le*, above note 77 at para 109, "when individuals have repeated exposure to unwanted experiences from a more powerful source, they learn to simply acquiesce and try to get through the unwanted experience by getting it over with as quickly and peaceably as possible."

that street checks are illegal.[281] As a result, a Ministerial Directive there has ordered police not to conduct street checks or carding other than in circumstances where reasonable suspicion about involvement in criminal activity exists: that is to say, where lawful authority for the stop would exist.[282] In Ontario, originally a regulation was passed which was aimed at making individuals informed enough that the interaction would either be consensual or would not be a psychological detention.[283] However, in 2024 that regulation was replaced with a stricter one, aimed at limiting such interactions to those where an officer is "investigating an offence the officer reasonably suspects has been or will be committed."[284] In British Columbia, the Provincial Policing Standards require that "random or arbitrary police stops, which may or may not include a request for or the collection or recording of a person's identifying information, are not permitted, unless authorized by law or case law."[285]

The more important point to recognize is what has led to the concern about street checks which has led to them being banned in some provinces: discriminatory use of the technique. Although, as just discussed, carding would violate section 9 no matter to whom it was applied, in fact what has led to widespread concern about it is that it is disproportionately used in the case of visible minorities. This concern is especially acute when the individual is detained, as with carding, but is equally an objection to simple information-gathering in the broader sense of street checks. In the context of the section 9 framework it would be easy to see this as an illustration of the third step, on the basis that the manner of detention would be unreasonable if a power were used based on the race of the detainee. It is of course not perfectly straightforward to make that claim in this context, primarily because the practice could also be said to have already failed at either of the first two stages for exactly the same reason: there is no law purporting to create a power to detain on that

281 Former Chief Justice Michael MacDonald, "Independent Legal Opinion on Street Checks," October 15, 2019: https://cdn.halifax.ca/sites/default/files/documents/city-hall/boards-committees-commissions/191021bopc731.pdf.

282 *Minister's Directive – Street Checks Ban*, December 1, 2021: https://novascotia.ca/just/publications/docs/Minister-Directive-Street-Checks-Ban.pdf.

283 See the *Collection of Identifying Information in Certain Circumstances—Prohibition and Duties*, O Reg 58/16 [*CIICC*], issued under the *Police Services Act*, RSO 1990, c P.15.

284 *Collection of Identifying Information in Certain Circumstances — Prohibition and Duties*, O Reg 400/23 [*CIICC*], issued under the *Police Services Act*, RSO 1990, c P.15.

285 Provincial Policing Standards 6.2.1, issued under the *Police Act*, RSBC 1996, c 367, s 40.

basis, and if there were, that law would be unreasonable. However, it is probably best to think of it as a "manner of detention" issue, because that would have an impact on whether the violation could be saved by section 1: that is, an arbitrary law might be upheld (as in *Hufsky* or *Ladouceur*), but an arbitrary practice cannot be.[286]

There is significant reason to believe that these practices are differently employed. Tulloch points to various studies showing that visible minorities find themselves the subject of these practices at a rate far in excess of their percentage of the population in Ontario, ranging from around three times to seventeen times the rate one would expect based on their percentage of the population.[287] Griffiths found that in Edmonton, Indigenous peoples and visible minorities were stopped disproportionately.[288]

Disproportion compared to the general population, though, is not enough by itself to show conclusively that race is the sole, or a significant, explanation for that disproportion.[289] The Wortley Report is therefore of particular significance, as the most thorough statistical analysis of data dealing with this issue. That study looked at nearly 100,000 street checks over a twelve-year period, relying on the data gathered by the police themselves. The initial finding was that black people generally were six times more likely than white people to have been subject to a street check, black males were nine times more likely, and young black males were twenty times more likely to have been checked.[290] The study then looked for possible explanations of the data other than race, but found that no factors that could account for the difference.

For example, young people tend to be checked more frequently than older people, and the black population tended to be younger, but

---

286 The simple explanation for this is the requirement in s 1 that the violation must be "prescribed by law" before the rest of the s 1 test is completed. A law permitting an arbitrary detention (such as the driving stop in *Hufsky* based on no criteria) passes the "prescribed by law" portion of s 1, and then the importance of the goal to be achieved (highway safety) is balanced against the *Charter* violation (and in *Hufsky* meant the law was upheld). However, if there is an objectionable police *practice* in the use of a power, such as using a nominally "random" stop power for the purpose of racial profiling, that practice is not "prescribed by law." In that event the attempt to save the *Charter* violation under s 1 will fail at that stage and no further analysis needs to be done.

287 Tulloch, above note 272 at 43–44.

288 Griffiths et al, above note 272 at 88.

289 *Ibid* at 88, noted that it would require further data unavailable to that study to determine whether the cause of the disproportion was racial profiling.

290 Wortley, above note 272 at 115–16.

that did not account for the difference: young black males were more than four times as likely to be checked as young white males,[291] and in fact "Black people are grossly over-represented in street checks within each age category."[292]

The study also considered whether the overall figures could be skewed by the presence of a few individuals with either a significant criminal record (so that checks of those persons were quite possibly legitimate) or who simply happened to be checked frequently. However, comparing the rate at which black people without a criminal record were checked to white people without a record still showed a dramatic overrepresentation,[293] as did comparing black people who were checked only once to white people who were checked only once.[294] Similarly, there was the same kind of disproportion between black people checked multiple times and white people checked multiple times.

Wortley also considered the possibility that the issue was "place, not race":[295] that police tend to perform checks more frequently in areas with higher crime rates and minority populations are more likely to live in those areas.[296] If that were true then "1) White people residing in high-crime communities should be just as vulnerable to street checks as Black people within high crime communities; and 2) Black people residing in — or travelling through — low crime communities should be relatively immune from street checks."[297] In fact neither of those things turned out to be true on the data: black people were more likely than their white neighbours to be checked no matter what neighbourhood they lived in, and black people in predominantly white neighbourhoods experienced the greatest disproportion of all, at over thirteen times the rate one would expect.[298]

The Wortley Report is not alone in these types of findings. Expert reports in *Luamba*, for example, considering vehicle stops, found that "police are more likely to be influenced by racist stereotypes when they

---

291 *Ibid* at 115.

292 *Ibid* at 153.

293 *Ibid* at 133.

294 *Ibid* at 136.

295 *Ibid* at 142.

296 Griffiths et al, above note 272 at 15, also notes in the abstract the possibility that "stops are targeted at areas which have high concentrations of people from minority ethnic backgrounds," but does not conduct the same kind of analysis of the data as Wortley does.

297 Wortley, above note 272 at 142.

298 *Ibid* at 143.

act proactively"[299] (as in street checks) and that "the results are the same no matter where you look or how you look (police data, public surveys, citizen testimonials, type of intervention, etc.), whatever the period being studied: Black people are disproportionately targeted by law enforcement."[300]

The Supreme Court has defined "racial profiling" as including:

> Any action by a person in a situation of authority who applies a measure in a disproportionate way to certain segments of the population on the basis, in particular, of their racial, ethnic, national or religious background, whether actual or presumed.[301]

It seems impossible to interpret the figures from the Wortley Report in any other way than as matching that definition. Although they represent a rigorous analysis of figures from only one city, it is difficult to have high hopes that the *prima facie* disproportionate rates which have been reported in so many other locations somehow have a more innocent explanation.[302] It is also well-established that behaving in a way which would otherwise be lawful nonetheless becomes a *Charter* violation when the reason behind the behaviour is racial profiling.[303] Whether the practice involves the more intrusive stopping of individuals on the street or the less intrusive recording of information without direct interaction with the subject, then, it seems that both carding and street checks will violate the *Charter* on this basis as well. As the Court has said:

> The impact of the over-policing of racial minorities and the carding of individuals within those communities without any reasonable

---

299 *Luamba*, above note 208 at para 73.

300 *Luamba*, above note 208 at para 71.

301 *Le*, above note 67 at para 77, quoting *Quebec (Commission des droits de la personne et des droits de la jeunesse) v Bombardier Inc (Bombardier Aerospace Training Center)*, 2015 SCC 39 at para 33.

302 There is other evidence giving rise to concerns about racial profiling generally: see, for example, Ontario, Human Rights Commission, *A Collective Impact: Interim Report on the Inquiry into Racial Profiling and Racial Discrimination of Black Persons by the Toronto Police Service* (Ontario Human Rights Commission, Government of Ontario: November 2018), online: http://ohrc.on.ca/sites/default/ files/TPS%20Inquiry_Interim%20Report%20EN%20FINAL%20 DESIGNED%20 for%20remed_3_0.pdf#overlay-context=en/news_centre/ohrc-interim-reporttoronto-police-service-inquiry-shows-disturbing-results; or Yunliang Meng, "Profiling Minorities: Police Stop and Search Practices in Toronto Canada" (2017) 11:1 Human Geographies — Journal of Studies and Research in Human Geography at 5–23.

303 See, for example, *R v Storrey*, [1990] 1 SCR 241 at para 19 or *Le*, above note 77 at para 78.

> suspicion of criminal activity is more than an inconvenience. Carding takes a toll on a person's physical and mental health . . . Such a practice contributes to the continuing social exclusion of racial minorities, encourages a loss of trust in the fairness of our criminal justice system, and perpetuates criminalization.[304]

Some provinces have taken steps to eliminate carding and street checks, but there is good reason to argue that all jurisdictions in Canada should do so.

## D. THE ABILITY TO BREAK THE LAW: SECTION 25.1

A further set of provisions relating to police that needs to be examined is contained in sections 25.1 to 25.4 of the *Criminal Code*, which permit designated police officers to break the law. The sections are not explicitly phrased to create a power. Rather, they talk about such an officer being "justified" in doing particular things. That language is normally associated with defences, and the sections are found in the general part, under the heading "Protection of Persons Administering and Enforcing the Law." Nominally, all that these provisions do is protect particular officers from criminal liability in particular situations, and there are contexts in which that distinction matters.[305] Their genesis and the way they are structured, however, make them seem much more like a police power than a defence.

The provisions allow the federal or provincial minister responsible for police to designate certain officers. An officer so designated "is justified in committing an act or omission . . . that would otherwise constitute an offence,"[306] if two further conditions are met. The first condition

304 *Le*, above note 77 at para 95.

305 See, for example, *R v Roy and Biesinger*, 2017 ONSC 6020, where police officers had relied on s 25.1 in order to trespass and obtain information which was used in support of a warrant application. The trial judge seems to accept that the police's defence, which they only had because of s 25.1, did not mean that their behaviour in gathering the information had been lawful, and so the warrant application should have disclosed that illegality. The Court of Appeal agreed that the fact that the police had trespassed should have been disclosed, but the non-disclosure was not a serious omission, and the trespass authorized by s 25.1 was not an abuse of process: *R v Roy*, 2020 ONCA 18 [*Roy*].

306 Section 25.1(8).

is simply that the officer is investigating an offence or criminal activity.[307] The second condition is that the officer

> believes on reasonable grounds that the commission of the act or omission, as compared to the nature of the offence or criminal activity being investigated, is reasonable and proportional in the circumstances, having regard to such matters as the nature of the act or omission, the nature of the investigation and the reasonable availability of other means for carrying out the public officer's law enforcement duties.[308]

In other words, designated officers are permitted to break the law if, in their judgment, that is a reasonable choice.

Designations for this purpose are not made in relation to a particular investigation, but rather with regard to the particular officer.[309] The designation is to be made on the advice of a senior official, and there is provision for civilian oversight.[310] It is not explicitly stated in the section, but it is clear that this power is intended for officers performing undercover work.[311] It is also possible for other officers to be designated on an emergency basis by a senior official in exigent circumstances, but such a designation expires after a maximum of forty-eight hours.[312] Somewhat surprisingly, there is a statutory requirement to annually report the number of emergency designations made, but no similar obligation to report the number of "ordinary" designations.[313] There appears to be very little use of the particular powers for which there is a reporting requirement.[314]

There are some limits on the ability of designated officers to break the law. Section 25.1(11) states:

> a. Nothing in this section justifies
>    i. the intentional or criminally negligent causing of death or bodily harm to another person;

---

307 Section 25.1(8)(a).

308 Section 25.1(8)(c).

309 Section 25.1(4).

310 Sections 25.1(4), (3.1), and (3.2), respectively.

311 See, for example, *R v Nuttall*, 2018 BCCA 479 or *R v Baranec*, 2020 BCCA 156.

312 Section 25.1(6).

313 Section 25.3(a).

314 See, for example, *Annual Report on the Law Enforcement Justification Provisions* (Ontario: Ministry of the Solicitor General, 2018), online: www.mcscs.jus.gov.on.ca/english/Publications/PSAnnualReportLawEnforcementJustificationProvisions%E2 %80%932015.html; or *2017 Annual Report on the Law Enforcement Justification Provisions* (British Columbia: Ministry of Public Safety and Solicitor General, 2017), online: www2.gov.bc.ca/assets/gov/law-crime-and-justice/criminal-justice/police/publications/government/2017-law-enforcement-report.pdf.

ii. the wilful attempt in any manner to obstruct, pervert or defeat the course of justice; or
iii. conduct that would violate the sexual integrity of an individual.

There has been disagreement over whether the prohibition on causing "bodily harm" extends to psychological harm and, therefore, whether officers who make threats fall outside the ambit of the provisions.[315]

In addition, section 25.1(9) refers to actions "that would be likely to result in loss of or serious damage to property." Such actions are not forbidden, but alternative, additional conditions are attached to performing them. First, a designated officer can be authorized in writing by a senior official to commit the act. This senior official is to apply specified criteria in deciding — the section does not explicitly state "in advance" of the act, but that must be the intention.[316] That point is clear because the alternative, additional condition is that the officer believes on reasonable grounds that the grounds for obtaining written authorization exist, but the circumstances make it not feasible to obtain the authorization. The only specific circumstances that could justify an officer acting in this way are the need to

a. preserve the life or safety of any person,
b. prevent the compromise of the identity of a public officer acting in an undercover capacity, of a confidential informant or of a person acting covertly under the direction and control of a public officer, or
c. prevent the imminent loss or destruction of evidence of an indictable offence.[317]

There is again an annual reporting requirement as to how frequently these provisions are relied upon.[318]

This structure of designating officers, civilian oversight, emergency designations, authorizations in writing, and so on is far more consistent with a police power than a defence. It is also worth considering in this regard the way in which the provisions came about.

---

315 See *R v Lising*, 2007 BCSC 906 [*Lising*] at para 20, for the view that making threats is protected by the section, on the basis that what is meant is "bodily harm as specifically defined in s. 2 of the *Criminal Code*, as it has been interpreted in the cases." For the view that making threats is *not* protected, see *R v JJ*, 2010 ONSC 735 at para 336 [*JJ*], which points out that the definition of bodily harm in s 2 of the *Code* was interpreted by the Supreme Court of Canada in *R v McCraw*, [1991] 3 SCR 72, to include psychological harm.

316 Section 25.1(9)(a).

317 Section 25.1(b).

318 Section 25.3.

The provisions were a legislative response to a Supreme Court of Canada decision regarding police undercover work.[319] In a narcotics investigation, the police used what is referred to as a "reverse sting," which meant that they posed as the sellers of drugs rather than as buyers. The *Narcotic Control Act*,[320] the relevant statute at the time, did not specifically authorize the police to do this, and so they sought an opinion from the Department of Justice as to whether this technique would be legal. The real issue in the case was whether the accused were entitled to disclosure of that legal opinion. The argument of the accused, in seeking a stay of proceedings based on abuse of process, raised the issue of police good faith. In effect, it was agreed that if the police had acted in accordance with the legal advice that they had been given, then they had acted in good faith. The accused argued, though, that the police could not simply assert that they had followed the legal advice they were given. Rather, they had to either disclose that opinion or abandon their good faith claim. Disclosure, then, was really the central issue.

The Court concluded that the accused were entitled to disclosure of the opinion. In the course of reaching the decision, the Court did observe that "the conclusion that the RCMP acted in a manner facially prohibited by the Act is inescapable."[321] However, that was far from the central point of the analysis. The Court went on to observe that police illegality did not automatically lead to the conclusion that there had been an abuse of process, or to the conclusion that the accused were entitled to a remedy. The illegality in and of itself was a relatively small issue. To the extent that it was an issue at all, it was because of the question of whether the police had acted abusively in carrying out the investigation as they did, not whether the police were at risk of prosecution and therefore in need of a defence.

The provisions have been the subject of relatively little academic commentary, but that commentary has been critical. It has been firmly argued that the provisions are inconsistent with the rule of law and, therefore, threaten fundamental principles. It has also been argued that this cost has been paid for, effectively, no benefit, since the actual need for the police to break the law in the course of their investigations is small to non-existent.[322] There is little caselaw discussing the sections,

---

319 *R v Campbell*, [1999] 1 SCR 565 [*Campbell*].

320 RSC 1985, c N-1 [since repealed].

321 *Campbell*, above note 319 at para 25.

322 See Marc S Gorbet, "Bill C-24's Police Immunity Provisions: Parliament's Unnecessary Legislative Response to Police Illegality in Undercover Operations" (2004) 9 *Canadian Criminal Law Review* 35. Gorbet is a former RCMP

which is unsurprising. Prior to section 25.1 being introduced to the *Code*, the appropriate use of prosecutorial discretion meant that criminal charges were not laid against police for mere technical violations of the law in any event, and only in the event of egregious violations would they have been prosecuted. That fact alone makes section 25.1 largely redundant. More important, it also means that the circumstances in which the provisions might be pleaded and, therefore, discussed in court, rarely come to court. As a result, the chance for judicial scrutiny is greatly reduced.

In one case, the existence of the sections has, perhaps appropriately given their genesis, helped justify a stay of proceedings: that is, a stay was allowed, in part, because police allowed an agent to engage in illegal behaviour (as opposed to doing so themselves) without supervision, "thereby flouting all of the rules laid down in section 25.1 of the *Criminal Code*."[323] More frequently the argument for a stay fails.[324] One lower court judgment has broadly upheld the provisions, concluding that they do not violate section 7 of the *Charter*: they are not overbroad, not vague, and do not violate any other principles of fundamental justice.[325] Whether the provisions are unconstitutional does not seem to have reached any court of appeal.[326] However, a second judgment has interpreted the sections in a way that potentially narrows their scope in a way which would keep them better bounded. In *R v JJ* the trial judge engaged in an extensive discussion of the proper interpretation of section 25.1, including its legislative history, and concluded that it should not be treated as empowering the police, but rather should be strictly limited to the role of providing a justification if an officer were charged. In that case, the police were using a wiretap to investigate a murder. In an effort to stimulate discussion among the suspects, two undercover officers who purported to be associated with the murder victim approached one suspect, held him against a wall, and made death threats against those who had carried out the killing. The trial

---

undercover officer. See, as well, Grégoire Charles N Webber, "Legal Lawlessness and the Rule of Law: A Critique of Section 25.1 of the *Criminal Code*" (2005) 31 *Queen's Law Journal* 121.

323 *Brind'Amour v R*, 2014 QCCA 33 at para 75.

324 See *Roy*, above note 305; *Alkhalil c R*, 2020 QCCQ 4470; or *R v Nagtzaam and Brito*, 2023 ONSC 5832.

325 *Lising*, above note 315.

326 See *R v Khan*, 2024 ONCA 296, noting that in that case the accused had brought a challenge to the provisions at trial but had been denied standing on the basis that there was no illegal behaviour by the police in the course of their investigation (they had posted an ad offering the sale of sexual services, but it was not a genuine offer), and therefore s 25.1 was not engaged.

judge held that as section 25.1 was only a justification, it could not be said that the police had been empowered or authorized to make the threats. In that event, the accused was entitled to point to that behaviour as making the manner of executing the warrant unreasonable.[327] The Crown sought leave to appeal this ruling to the Supreme Court but was refused.[328]

## FURTHER READINGS

ALLMAN, ANTHONY. "Detention — What Does It Mean? A Comment on *R v Hawkins*" (1993) 18 *Criminal Reports* (4th) 17.

———. "Further Perspectives on Section 10(b) of the *Charter*: A Reply to Gold" (1994) 25 *Criminal Reports* (4th) 280.

BERGER, BENJAMIN L. "Race and Erasure in *R. v. Mann*" (2004) 21 *Criminal Reports* (6th) 58.

COUGHLAN, STEVE. "Search Based on Articulable Cause: Proceed with Caution or Full Stop?" (2002) 2 *Criminal Reports* (6th) 49.

———. "General Warrants at the Crossroads: Limit or Licence?" (2003) 10 *Criminal Reports* (6th) 269.

———. "Whither — or Wither — Section 9" (2008) 40 *Supreme Court Law Review* (2d) 147.

———. "Great Strides in Section 9 Jurisprudence" (2009) 66 *Criminal Reports* (6th) 75.

———. "*R. v. Ha*: Upholding General Warrants Without Asking the Right Questions" (2009) 65 *Criminal Reports* (6th) 41.

——— & ALEX GORLEWSKI. *The Anatomy of Criminal Procedure: A Visual Guide to the Law*, 2nd ed (Toronto: University of Toronto Press, 2026).

FISZAUF, ALEC. *The Law of Investigative Detention*, 2d ed (Markham: LexisNexis Canada, 2013).

GOLD, ALAN. "Perspectives on Section 10(b) — The Right to Counsel Under the *Charter*" (1993) 22 *Criminal Reports* (4th) 370.

GORBET, MARC S. "Bill C-24's Police Immunity Provisions: Parliament's Unnecessary Legislative Response to Police Illegality in Undercover Operations" (2004) 9 *Canadian Criminal Law Review* 35.

327 *JJ*, above note 315 at paras 303–8.
328 *R v JJ*, [2010] SCCA No 161.

GOTTARDI, ERIC V. "*R. v. Mann*: Regulating State Intrusions in the Context of Investigative Detentions" (2004) 21 *Criminal Reports* (6th) 27.

LAW REFORM COMMISSION OF CANADA. *Arrest* (Working Paper 41) (Ottawa: Law Reform Commission of Canada, 1985).

———. *Arrest* (Report 29) (Ottawa: Law Reform Commission of Canada, 1986).

MACKAY, A WAYNE. "Don't Mind Me, I'm from the R.C.M.P.: *R. v M.(M.R.)* — Another Brick in the Wall Between Students and Their Rights" (1997) 7 *Criminal Reports* (5th) 1.

MARIN, JOSEPH R. "*R. v. Mann*: Further Down the Slippery Slope" (2005) 42 *Alberta Law Review* 1123.

MCCOY, LESLEY A. "Liberty's Last Stand? Tracing the Limits of Investigative Detention" (2002) 46 *Criminal Law Quarterly* 319.

NICOL, JASON A. "'Stop in the Name of the Law': Investigative Detention" (2002) 7 *Canadian Criminal Law Review* 223.

PATEL, AMAN S. "Detention and Articulable Cause: Arbitrariness and Growing Judicial Deference to Police Judgment" (2002) 45 *Criminal Law Quarterly* 198.

QUIGLEY, TIM. "*Mann*, It's a Disappointing Decision" (2004) 21 *Criminal Reports* (6th) 41.

———. "Investigative Detention: Some Loose Ends Remain" (2009) 69 *Criminal Reports* (6th) 247.

———. "Was It Worth the Wait? The Supreme Court's New Approaches to Detention and Exclusion of Evidence" (2009) 66 *Criminal Reports* (6th) 88.

ROSE, DAVID. *Quigley's Criminal Procedure in Canada* (Toronto: Thomson Reuters, 2021) (loose-leaf) ch 6 and 8.

SANKOFF, PETER. "Articulable Cause Based Searches Incident to Detention — This *Cooke* May Spoil the Broth" (2002) 2 *Criminal Reports* (6th) 41.

SKIBINSKY, CHRISTINA. "Regulating *Mann* in Canada" (2006) 69 *Saskatchewan Law Review* 197.

STEWART, HAMISH. "The *Grant* Trilogy and the Right Against Self Incrimination" (2009) 66 *Criminal Reports* (6th) 97.

STRIBOPOULOS, JAMES. "A Failed Experiment? Investigative Detention: Ten Years Later" (2003) 41 *Alberta Law Review* 335.

———. "The Limits of Judicially Created Police Powers: Investigative Detention After *Mann*" (2007) 52 *Criminal Law Quarterly* 299.

———. "The Forgotten Right: Section 9 of the *Charter*, Its Purpose and Meaning" (2008) 40 *Supreme Court Law Review* (2d) 211.

STUART, DON. *Charter Justice in Canadian Criminal Law*, 7th ed (Toronto: Thomson Carswell, 2018) ch 4 & 5.

TANGUAY-RENAUD, FRANCOIS, "Doing Away with Racial Profiling in Policing without Doing Away with the Rule of Law" (2025) 62 *Osgoode Hall L.J.* 309.

TANOVICH, DAVID. "Operation Pipeline and Racial Profiling" (2002) 1 *Criminal Reports* (6th) 52.

TANOVICH, DAVID. "Using the *Charter* to Stop Racial Profiling: The Development of an Equality-Based Conception of Arbitrary Detention" (2002) 40 *Osgoode Hall Law Review* 145.

———. "*R. v. Griffiths*: Race and Arbitrary Detention" (2003) 11 *Criminal Reports* (6th) 149.

———. "The Colourless World of *Mann*" (2004) 21 *Criminal Reports* (6th) 47.

———. *The Colour of Justice* (Toronto: Irwin Law, 2006).

WEBBER, GRÉGOIRE CHARLES N. "Legal Lawlessness and the Rule of Law: A Critique of Section 25.1 of the *Criminal Code*" (2005) 31 *Queen's Law Journal* 121.

CHAPTER 6

# COMPELLING APPEARANCE AND JUDICIAL INTERIM RELEASE

## A. INTRODUCTION

Many aspects of criminal procedure are quite intricately linked. For example, the laying of an information in front of a justice serves several distinct functions. The laying commences the prosecution, and the information is the basis upon which either a preliminary inquiry will be based (if there is one) or a summary conviction trial will be held. It is also the foundation for a variety of methods to compel an accused to appear and answer to the charges laid out in the information. Yet, that initial appearance will not actually be for a trial on the charges, so the question arises as to what will happen to the accused in the interim. Thus, the *Criminal Code* provisions that set out the methods to make an accused first appear and those that deal with releasing or holding the accused pending trial form a whole, and both appear in Part XVI, "Compelling Appearance of Accused Before a Justice and Interim Release."

The issues related to the content of charges and the preferring of charges for trial will be discussed in Chapter 11. This chapter deals only with the procedure by which those charges are first laid. The charge is the focal point for various forms of compelling the appearance of the accused in court and determines issues of jurisdiction and many other features of pre-trial procedure.

Following the discussion of charges, we turn to the various mechanisms that may be used to compel the appearance of an accused person in court. The most obvious of those mechanisms is to arrest an accused, either with or without a warrant. Powers of arrest raise a host of issues of their own, particularly in light of section 10 of the *Charter*, which gives rights on arrest or detention. This chapter will not try to deal with all the issues surrounding powers of arrest — that will be the subject of Chapter 7. However, enough must be said here about arrest, with and without a warrant, to situate it in relation to the other methods of compelling appearance. As a result, there will be a certain amount of repetition between the two chapters, but not an excessive amount.

Finally, this chapter will turn to the topic of compelling an accused's appearance to answer to charges. In particular, the question of what to do with the person once they have appeared will be examined in a discussion of the principles governing judicial interim release.

## B. LAYING CHARGES

It is easy to see the laying of an information[1] as simply a technical requirement among so many other particular rules that must be followed in the course of criminal proceedings. In one sense that view is correct, but at the same time it is important to recognize the wider significance. The time when an information is laid before a justice marks a momentous occasion: it is the point at which some person passes from being a "suspect" to being an "accused." That transition has great consequences for the individual, for the individual's family, for the victim of the offence, for the criminal justice system, and for society as a whole. It means, for the most part, that the system has stopped trying to discover who committed an offence and will, from that point forward, be focused on proving the guilt of one particular person. Such a step should not be taken lightly.

The process of laying a charge consists of both a "ministerial" (administrative) and a judicial function. Under section 504 of the *Code*, the justice will perform the essentially bureaucratic and non-discretionary function of receiving the information. That step alone is of no consequence, however, unless the judge then takes discretionary and judicial action under section 507. It is worth looking at the two steps separately and in detail. (There is a parallel and functionally equivalent two-step process laid out in sections 505 and 508, which is used when an accused is given an appearance notice or released on an undertaking.

1 For an explanation of this issue in chart form, see Steve Coughlan & Alex Gorlewski, *The Anatomy of Criminal Procedure: A Visual Guide to the Law*, 2nd ed (Toronto: University of Toronto Press, 2026) [*Anatomy of Criminal Procedure*], Chart 1.3(b), "Compelling Appearance with Prior Judicial Scrutiny."

Differing in some practical details, it is discussed below in Section C(2), but the general principles behind it are the same as those set out here.)

With the exception of direct indictments, indictable offences are charged when an information is sworn, received, and approved by a judicial officer, in accordance with sections 504 and following of the *Code*.[2] This procedure applies equally to offences prosecuted by summary proceedings under Part XXVII.[3] When acting under section 504, the justice acts in a ministerial fashion and has no discretion over whether to receive the information.

An information may be sworn by any person who has reasonable grounds to believe that an offence has been committed. No person may be considered an accused person in the absence of a charge and, correspondingly, no court can have jurisdiction over the prosecution of an accused person in the absence of a charge.[4] In Canada, public prosecutions begin when an information is laid by a public officer. In some Canadian jurisdictions, charges are laid by peace officers, while in others they are laid by prosecutors after they have reviewed reports from the police or other authorities.[5] But, whether the informant is a peace officer, prosecutor, or private prosecutor, section 504 of the *Code* states some elementary requirements that must be met before a justice may receive and consider an information:

> 504. Any one who, on reasonable grounds, believes that a person has committed an indictable offence may lay an information in writing and under oath before a justice, and the justice shall receive the infor mation, where it is alleged
> (a) that the person has committed, anywhere, an indictable offence that may be tried in the province in which the justice resides, and that the person
> (i) is or is believed to be, or
> (ii) resides or is believed to reside, within the territorial jurisdiction of the justice;
> (b) that the person, wherever he may be, has committed an indictable offence within the territorial jurisdiction of the justice;

2 A direct indictment may be preferred at any time and may follow a charge that is first laid by way of an information.

3 See s 788ff.

4 See the definition of "accused" in s 493.

5 See the discussion of pre-charge screening in *R v Regan*, 2002 SCC 12, as well as Law Reform Commission of Canada, *Controlling Criminal Prosecutions: The Attorney General and the Crown Prosecutor* (Ottawa: Law Reform Commission of Canada, 1990).

(c) that the person has, anywhere, unlawfully received property that was unlawfully obtained within the territorial jurisdiction of the justice; or
(d) that the person has in his possession stolen property within the territorial jurisdiction of the justice.

Thus, an information must be in writing and under oath, and it must allege the commission of an offence by an identifiable person. It also must contain allegations that affirm the territorial jurisdiction of the justice before whom it is laid.[6]

Section 506 provides that the information may be laid in the manner set out in Form 2. Although this is phrased in a discretionary way, it is best for an information to be laid in this manner so that it complies with matters of form that are essential to jurisdiction, such as the date and place of the alleged offence, the date and place of the information, the identity of the informant, and the identity of the justice. On this topic, see also the discussion in Chapter 11, Section B, "The Charge Document," for analysis of the substantive rules governing the form of charges.

The informant must declare in the information that they have reasonable grounds to believe that an offence has been committed. Grounds for such a belief need not be based on the personal knowledge of the informant and may be based on reports that they have received: however, the person swearing the information must personally hold the necessary belief. It is not sufficient, for example, for a police officer to lay an information simply on the basis that they were instructed to do so by their superior: the officer must personally know enough to reasonably believe that the offence has been committed.[7]

Most prosecutions in Canada are public ones, which means that the informant is a peace officer or an agent of the attorney general, and the case is conducted by a Crown prosecutor (see, however, the discussion below of "private prosecutions"). Once the information has been received under section 504, the justice who received the information

---

6 "Territorial jurisdiction" is defined in s 2 of the *Code* as "any province, county, union of counties, township, city, town, parish or other judicial division or place to which the context applies." This quite open-ended definition creates the potential for ambiguity. In Ontario it has been determined that the "territorial jurisdiction" of a justice of the peace for purposes of this section is the entire province: *R v Ellis*, 2009 ONCA 483 [*Ellis*]. However, that decision is based, in part, on the legislation governing justices of the peace in that province, and so a different meaning might apply in other provinces. *Ellis* also observes that the fact that a justice has received an information in one place does not settle that any eventual trial will occur in that same location: see para 43.

7 *R v Pilcher* (1981), 58 CCC (2d) 435 (Man Prov Ct).

must consider the substance of the informant's allegations under section 507. In this judicial function, the justice exercises discretion as to whether it is appropriate to take any action or to require the accused person to answer the charges.[8]

This stage of the process is referred to as a "pre-enquete." It is performed *ex parte*, and so the justice will consider the allegations in the absence of the person or persons accused in the information. It also means that this hearing is generally not conducted in open court. Nevertheless, the justice must act judicially in the consideration of the information. They will examine the allegations of the informant and may ask questions of that person or any other witness where they consider such evidence necessary or desirable to ascertain the basis of the informant's belief that an offence was committed. Any evidence thus taken by the justice must be given under oath and recorded, but the justice is not obliged to observe the rules and principles governing the admissibility of evidence at a preliminary inquiry or trial.[9]

Upon considering the information, the justice must decide whether to endorse it. The *Code* does not state explicitly the standard that the justice must apply in this decision, but the justice must personally consider and agree that there are reasonable grounds to believe that an offence was committed by the person to be charged. The informant is not required to prove the allegations, however; nor is the justice required to make any judgment concerning the sufficiency of the case for prosecution. The justice must at least be satisfied that there are reasonable grounds, as disclosed in the information and any evidence adduced in support thereof, to believe that the offence was committed by the person named.[10] Some authority suggests that only when the information meets the higher standard of a *prima facie* case or something close to it should the justice be satisfied.[11] If the justice is satisfied, they will

---

8 *R v Allen* (1974), 20 CCC (2d) 447 (Ont CA) [*Allen*].

9 See, for example, *R v Edge*, 2004 ABPC 55 at para 63, relying on Tim Quigley, *Procedure in Canadian Criminal Law*, 2d ed (Toronto: Thomson Carswell, 2005) (loose-leaf).

10 *R v Mivasair*, 2025 ONCA 179 [*Mivasair*] at para 113:

> The standard to issue process is whether there is some evidence on each element of the offence: *McHale*, at paras. 5–11, 43–48, 64–71, and 74; *P.C.*, at paras. 27–30; *Criminal Code*, ss. 507 and 507.1. The standard for issuing process is also informed by the reasonable and probable grounds standard for a Justice of the Peace to receive an Information, set out in s. 504 of the *Criminal Code*.

11 See *R v Morton* (1993), 83 CCC (3d) 95 (Ont CA), aff'g (1992), 70 CCC (3d) 244 (Ont Ct Gen Div); *R v Fry* (1998), 38 RFL (4th) 328 (BCCA); or *S 507.1 Process Hearing — David-Kevin: Lindsay*, 2005 BCPC 176.

sign the information. This endorsement marks the moment at which a charge is formally laid and a prosecution begins. At this point, the person named in the information is an accused person before the court.

The judge must refuse to issue process if they are not satisfied that it establishes reasonable grounds to believe that an offence has been committed. However, a refusal to issue any process by one justice does not prevent the informant from seeking a summons or warrant from a different justice based on the information.[12]

Slightly different rules apply to the pre-enquete when an information is laid privately. These differences are meant to keep alive the option of private prosecutions while at the same time preventing their abuse. The hearing must be conducted by a judge or a specially designated justice, who is obliged to hear evidence, as opposed to merely having the discretion to do so.[13] The attorney general must be given a copy of the information, notice of the hearing, and an opportunity to attend and take part in it.[14] Further, if the justice does not issue a summons or warrant then (unlike a public prosecution), the private prosecutor is obliged to bring forward new evidence in order to have a new hearing.[15] Finally, the attorney general may intervene in any private prosecution, either to assume carriage of it, to stop it by means of a stay of proceedings, or to withdraw the charge.[16] The power to stay charges may be used any time after the information has been laid under section 504: in contrast, the power to withdraw charges may be exercised only after a pre-enquete has been held and cannot be used to

12 *Allen*, above note 8.

13 Section 507.1(3)(a).

14 Sections 507.1(3)(b)–(d).

15 Section 507.1(7).

16 The rules in this area are established somewhat oddly. Section 579 explicitly gives the provincial attorney general the authority to stay charges, without making any reference to whether the information was publicly or privately laid. Section 579.01 specifies that if the provincial attorney general intervenes in proceedings and does not stay them, they may call witnesses, examine and cross-examine, and so on. Those powers presuppose that the provincial attorney general can intervene in private prosecutions, but do not explicitly state that. Similarly, the attorney general has the ability to withdraw privately laid charges, but this power arises from the common law: *McHale v Ontario (Attorney General)*, 2010 ONCA 361 at para 53 [*McHale*]. On the other hand, s 579.1 explicitly states that the federal attorney general can intervene in private prosecutions of charges not laid under the *Code* (for example, drug prosecutions, which are prosecuted by federally appointed prosecutors). In addition it makes the ability to stay in s 579 available in such cases.

prevent a pre-enquete from taking place.[17] (See also the discussion of private prosecutions in Chapter 3, Section B(1)(b).)

# C. COMPELLING APPEARANCE

The compelling appearance and bail provisions in Part XVI of the *Code* operate by granting broad powers to police and judges to restrict the liberty of individuals but then attaching significant limitations on the use of those powers. The result is an attempt to satisfy the needs of the state to ensure that accused persons are present for their trials while, at the same time, using those powers with as much restraint as possible.[18] As the Court has said, "release — at the earliest opportunity and in the least onerous manner — is the default presumption in Canadian criminal law."[19] It is not clear that the system in fact works as intended as often as it should, but there is no doubt that using these powers with restraint is the *goal*.

That goal has always been implicit in the structure of the provisions: since 2019 it has become explicit. Section 493.1 of the *Code*, entitled "Principle of Restraint," directs that in all decisions under Part XVI, "a peace officer, justice or judge shall give primary consideration to the release of the accused at the earliest reasonable opportunity and on the least onerous conditions that are appropriate in the circumstances."[20] In making those decisions the actors are to give particular attention to the circumstances of Indigenous accused and accused who belong to a vulnerable population that is overrepresented in the criminal justice system and that is disadvantaged in obtaining release.[21]

---

17 *McHale*, *ibid*. The Court of Appeal noted that this result seems anomalous. They observe at para 90 that the common law rule around withdrawal of charges, infused by policy considerations, does not allow the attorney general to prevent a private prosecutor from at least having a pre-enquete before a judge or justice: the plain language of the statute, however, makes that possible in the case of a stay. Nonetheless, *McHale* was confirmed in *Mivasair*, above note 10 at para 116.

18 On this topic, see Steve Coughlan & Glen Luther, *Detention and Arrest*, 3d ed (Toronto: Irwin Law, 2024), in particular, the discussion in Chapter 4 under the heading "Restraint in Compelling Appearance."

19 *R v Myers*, 2019 SCC 18 [*Myers*] at para 1. See also *R v Zora*, 2020 SCC 14 [*Zora*] at para 26: "Restraint has a constitutional dimension, a legislative footing, and is not only recognized in case law, but was also recently expressly reinforced by the amendments that came into force on December 18, 2019."

20 This section was added by Bill C-75, *An Act to amend the Criminal Code, the Youth Criminal Justice Act and other Acts and to make consequential amendments to other Acts*, Royal Assent June 21, 2019.

21 Section 493.1(2).

As well as explicitly setting out the principle of restraint, Bill C-75 made adjustments to a number of provisions in ways that increased the likelihood of release of an arrested person.[22] In general, the kind of changes made were to give the discretion to release to any peace officer rather than to the officer in charge of a station, to expand the range of offences for which a person can be released, and so on. The most important thing to understand, of course, is what the law *now* states. Because so many of the changes have been accomplished through adjustments to the exact wording of particular provisions, however, it will not always be immediately apparent to a person who was already generally familiar with the rules to know exactly how they have changed. To an extent, therefore, the discussion below will not only describe what the law now is, but also how it has been changed. A particularly noteworthy change is the "judicial referral hearing," discussed below.

In general terms, the *Code* provides powers to police to require an accused to attend court through some type of written demand or by arresting the person, either with or without a warrant. The scheme "creates a ladder of increasingly coercive measures" to compel the appearance of an accused,[23] but preference is given to not detaining the person if possible. Peace officers are given the means to either not arrest, or if they have arrested, to release the person. If the person is not released they are taken to a justice, and the system is then designed to release the accused with as few restrictions as necessary. In short, the *Code* provides that, if possible, appearance should be sought without arrest or continued detention. Further, where Part XVI allows for an order for continued detention before trial, it also includes mechanisms for review of that detention. These issues will be discussed in Section D, below in this chapter.

A further demonstration of the restraint built in to Part XVI is seen in the fact that a police officer's decision that an accused should be made to attend court is usually not sufficient on its own: in most cases it is necessary for some judicial officer to confirm that decision. In some cases, the officer's initial interaction is with the individual accused of committing a crime. In that event, a justice must later review the

22 One set of changes, which does not specifically relate to the Compelling Appearance provisions but which nonetheless increases the likelihood of persons either not being arrested in the first place or being released afterward, relates to the classification of offences. In many instances discussed below, police officers will have increased discretion not to detain an accused if the offence is a hybrid one. Bill C-75 reclassified over 115 offences which formerly had been purely indictable ones to instead be hybrid, which means that discretion not to arrest or to release is now available for those offences as well.

23 *R v Penunsi*, 2019 SCC 39 at para 64, quoting *R v Nowazek*, 2018 YKCA 12.

officer's actions and (except in the instance of an arrest without a warrant) agree that charges should be laid. In other cases, the charges are laid in front of a justice first, and the police then seek out the individual. Although there are similarities between the two situations, it is convenient to consider them separately. Accordingly, we shall consider (1) the process for compelling an accused to appear when charges have not yet been laid and (2) the process that is used after charges have been laid. Before either of those, however, we shall look at the new option of a judicial referral hearing.

## 1) Judicial Referral Hearings

Judicial referral hearings, and the related concept of administration of justice offences, were the most innovative addition to the *Code*'s compelling appearance provisions in Bill C-75 and were intended as a response to a number of problems. The *Code* now contains a number of sections that piggyback on the various compelling appearance provisions: for example, section 145(3) makes it an offence for a person released on conditions to fail to comply with those conditions. While there is some argument that such behaviour can be seen as inherently wrongful enough to warrant being called a crime, one might equally argue that these offences are really just a method to see to it that the released person complies with the conditions.[24] In essence, these offences — which are identified in Bill C-75 as "administration of justice offences" — up the ante against the accused for any failure to comply.[25] Judicial referral hearings reflect a conclusion that those stakes can become too high, with detrimental effects for both accused and the criminal justice system as a whole, and therefore that another method should be used.

---

24 Parliament of Canada, *Legislative Summary of Bill C75: An Act to amend the Criminal Code, the Youth Criminal Justice Act and other Acts and to make consequential amendments to other Acts*, online: https://lop.parl.ca/sites/PublicWebsite/default/en_CA/ResearchPublications/LegislativeSummaries/421C75E#txt34 [C-75 Legislative Summary] notes that the purpose of these offences is "allowing accused persons to maintain their liberty, while ensuring that they keep the peace by abiding by certain conditions and appearing in court to respond to the charges against them."

25 See *Zora*, above note 19 at para 2:

> In many cases, an accused person faces criminal sanctions for conduct which, but for the stipulated bail condition, would be a lawful exercise of personal freedom. As the gravamen of the offence is a failure to comply with a court order, there is often no victim, no violence, or no direct harm to the public or property.

The impact on persons accused of these offences is to create a kind of "revolving door" of criminal liability. The initial charge against the accused might not have been especially serious, but if the accused fails to comply with conditions along the way or misses the court date, the accused will end up charged with two or three offences rather than just one. If the accused is found guilty, they will be convicted of several offences rather than just the one and sentenced accordingly: alternatively, the accused might even be found not guilty of the primary offence but still convicted of the administration of justice offences. In either case the accused ends up with a longer criminal record as a result, which has a long-term impact. This phenomenon can affect any accused, but has been noted as particularly having an impact on Indigenous accused.[26]

This also has an impact on the criminal justice system, simply because of the pure volume of such cases. Administration of justice offences make up something in the range of one quarter of the total caseload in criminal courts.[27] Of course if prosecution of those offences were truly effective then one might argue that the resources are well used, but the central purpose of prosecuting these offences is to deter non-compliance: the very fact that there are so many cases to prosecute suggests they are not having much effect. Given the pressures to make the court system more efficient,[28] removal of a significant number of cases from the system would be a further benefit.

In response, Bill C-75 introduced judicial referral hearings, which are a response to "the over-criminalization of bail breaches."[29] The

---

26 See, for example, Abby Deshman & Nicole Myers, *Set up to Fail: Bail and the Revolving Door of Pre-trial Detention* (Canadian Civil Liberties Association and Education Trust, July 2014): "The over-imposition of conditions of release and subsequent breaches are identified as major contributors to the over-arrest and incarceration of Aboriginal people." See also Sarah Runyon, "Correctional Afterthought: Offences Against the Administration of Justice and Canada's Persistent Savage Anxieties" (2020) 43 *Manitoba Law Journal* 5, 1–38.

27 C-75 Legislative Summary, above note 24:

> According to Statistics Canada, just over a million charges were completed in criminal provincial courts in 2015–2016, of which slightly more than 350,000 were for administration of justice offences — the largest number of these being failure to comply with an order (175,170). In 2014–2015, administration of justice offences represented 23% of cases completed in adult court.

See also *Zora*, above note 19 at para 60: "[I]n 2008/2009 it was estimated that one in five people in pre-trial detention were there because they failed to comply with conditions in a court order or probation order."

28 See the discussion of the right to a trial within a reasonable time, in Chapter 10, Section B(2)(c)(i).

29 *Zora*, above note 19 at para 27.

point of such a hearing is to allow the person's failure to comply to be considered by a judge or justice without necessarily resulting in a further criminal charge. Under this new approach, if a peace officer has reasonable grounds to believe that a person "has failed to comply with a summons, appearance notice, undertaking or release order or to attend court as required" but that the failure "did not cause a victim physical or emotional harm, property damage or economic loss," then rather than arrest the person for the offence the peace officer can issue an appearance notice requiring the person to appear at a judicial referral hearing.[30] At that hearing the judge or justice is, in effect, authorized to simply start over on the decision-making process about the accused's initial release. If the judge or justice is "satisfied" (which seems to suggest a balance of probabilities standard) that the accused failed to comply but did not thereby cause harm, then they can: cancel the previous document which imposed conditions on the accused and make a new release order; leave it in place; or order the accused detained in custody pending trial.[31] Importantly, though, if the judge chooses to do any of those things, no separate charge can be laid against the accused for the initial violation of conditions.[32] As a result, the accused's failure to comply with the earlier order might have consequences for the accused, but those consequences cannot include a longer criminal record.

A similar process already existed in the *Code* if, instead of issuing an appearance notice, a peace officer had in fact arrested an accused for contravening the conditions of their release or committing an offence while released.[33] Arrests for actual or imminent non-compliance can be made without a warrant, but a peace officer can also seek a warrant.[34] In that event, the accused will be ordered detained in custody unless they show cause why their detention is not justified, under the usual judicial interim release provisions.[35] These

30 Section 496.

31 Section 523.1. The judge or justice could also order the person remanded in custody for the purposes of the *Identification of Criminals Act*: s 523.1(c).

32 Sections 523.1(4) and (5), which respectively cancel any charge which had been laid and prevent any charge from being laid. Note as well that s 505, dealing with the timelines for laying charges after an appearance notice has been issued, does not refer to appearance notices issued under s 496, only those issued under s 497 (which are discussed below).

33 Section 524.

34 See ss 495.1 and 512.3, respectively.

35 Section 524(3) calls for the cancellation of the previous order, and s 524(4) imposes the burden on the accused to justify release in accordance with s 515(10).

procedures alone would have consequences for the accused which do not result in new charges being laid. However, unlike those governing judicial review hearings, there is no statutory bar to a new charge being laid in addition to this revocation of liberty. It might be that the general desire to increase efficiency by reducing the number of administration of justice offence charges laid will have an effect on practice in this area, but it now seems unlikely that that will be the case. If an officer had decided to arrest rather than use an appearance notice, the case is likely already regarded as more serious and so a new charge might be seen as appropriate. There is, however, a more fundamental problem.

Judicial referral hearings were designed not only to reflect the principle of restraint but also to address the problems of overcharging individual accused and overloading the justice system. They seemed to have the potential to be a valuable addition. Unfortunately, that potential has remained unrealized to date. Their use rests on referrals by Crown-side actors, and despite the support for such hearings from Parliament and the Supreme Court, in fact they have been very little used. Most Crown prosecution manuals contain no reference to them, and what little mention there is discourages rather than encourages their use.[36] In fact there has been very little use of judicial referral hearings to date, and there are no indications that that is likely to change.[37]

---

36 See Pascale Legault, "Bail and Indigenous Over-Representation in Canadian Detention Facilities: Do the 2019 Amendments to the *Criminal Code* Offer a Viable Solution?" (2025) 73 *CLQ* 84 [Legault], noting that only Alberta's manual makes reference to them and that:

> The inclusion of a section on judicial referral hearings in Alberta's *Crown Prosecutors' Manual* is less than a step in the right direction, though. Rather than encouraging the use of JRHs to curb Indigenous over-representation and lessen the impact of AOJOs on both the criminal justice system and on Indigenous offenders, the *Crown Prosecutors' Manual* provides a detailed protocol outlining all the ways in which s. 523.1 should be disregarded despite acknowledging the provision's purpose in reducing those identified issues.

37 Legault, above note 36:

> Five years after their introduction into the *Code*, there is limited evidence to show that judicial referral hearings are even being used, though Alberta's practice directives may make that unsurprising. Although articles and research continue to be published about the issue of Indigenous over-incarceration and the ongoing burden that AOJOs impose on the justice system, mentions of JRHs can only be found in footnotes as a passing consideration. The limited use of JRHs has also been remarked on by judges who express disappointment in the lack of JRH applications.

## 2) Compelling Appearance Pre-charge

If a peace officer decides that a person should be prosecuted, there are various ways to compel that person to attend court before an information is laid and the person is actually charged.[38] The most obvious is to make an arrest without a warrant, and powers of arrest are discussed at length in Chapter 7. A central point to note is that an arrest is not necessarily the only way, and is not the preferred way, to compel appearance, even if no charge has yet been laid. Other procedural mechanisms can be used, whether there has been an arrest without warrant or not. In effect, the *Code* provides that, pre-charge, a person may be required to attend court by means of an appearance notice or an undertaking.[39]

The principle of restraint, now explicit in section 493.1, has long been implicit in the structure of section 495, the primary provision dealing with warrantless arrest powers. A peace officer's power to arrest without warrant is created in section 495(1) and is quite broad. Section 495(2), however, goes on to suggest that in the case of less serious offences an officer should not use those arrest powers. "Less serious," in this context, is defined broadly to mean summary conviction offences, hybrid offences, or indictable offences listed in section 553 (those in the absolute jurisdiction of a provincial court judge).[40] In the case of those offences, the *Code* suggests that an officer should issue an appearance notice instead, unless there is a good reason to arrest.[41]

---

38 For an explanation of this issue in chart form, see *Anatomy of Criminal Procedure*, above note 1, Chart 1.3(d), "Arrest Without a Warrant" and Chart 1.3(f), "Release of Persons Arrested Without a Warrant."

39 Prior to Bill C-75, these *Code* provisions also allowed for release on a "promise to appear" or on a "recognizance." One of the goals of the Bill was to simplify the interim release procedures. Promises to appear no longer exist at all, and recognizances no longer appear in the interim release provisions (although they still exist in other contexts: see, for example, s 810). However, in large part that is a matter of terminology. A recognizance is a promise by a released person to pay a sum of money if they default on the terms of their release. The amended s 515(2)(b), dealing with bail conditions, now allows a justice to issue a "release order" which can include "the accused's promise to pay a specified amount if they fail to comply with a condition of the order."

40 Sections 495(2)(a), (b), and (c). Note that this exception has become larger, because one of the changes made to the *Code* by Bill C-75, above note 20, was to significantly increase the number of hybrid offences, by creating the option of using the summary conviction proceedings for many offences which had until then been purely indictable.

41 Section 497.

A "good reason to arrest" is limited to the possibilities that the person will not show up in court unless arrested or that there is a need to

- (i) establish the identity of the person,
- (ii) secure or preserve evidence of or relating to the offence, or
- (iii) prevent the continuation or repetition of the offence or the commission of another offence.[42]

Section 495(2)[43] is phrased in a confusing way, but the principle underlying it is that, for less serious offences, police officers should not arrest simply because they have the power to do so. The section had been understood not to *remove* the power to arrest, though, and so in practice it often occurs that the peace officer does make an arrest and then determines whether to release that individual or take him into custody.

If the officer decides, under section 495(2), not to arrest, section 497 authorizes the officer to issue an appearance notice. (As discussed above, an appearance notice can also be issued for the commission of some administration of justice offences, but in that case it will be issued under section 496.) An appearance notice names the accused, sets out the substance of the alleged offence, and directs the person to whom it is issued to appear in court at a specified time and place. It also indicates whether the accused is to appear at a judicial referral hearing, sets out the consequences of failing to appear either in court or at that hearing, and can require the person to appear for the purposes of the *Identification of Criminals Act*.[44] If the person does not appear for the purposes of the *Identification of Criminals Act*, a warrant for their arrest can be issued. However, consistent with the approach to judicial referral hearings, discussed above, that arrest warrant will simply relate to the offence for which the appearance notice was issued. Therefore, although there are consequences for an accused who does not comply with the demand, an additional criminal charge is not among those consequences.[45]

Even if a peace officer has arrested a person, that is not the end of the story. For some considerable period of time the *Code* contained relatively complex provisions allowing for the possible release of the arrested person, which varied according to the type of offence, by whether the power was given to the arresting officer at the scene or the officer in charge back at the station, and by the kinds of conditions which could

---

42 Sections 495(2)(d) and (e).

43 See Chapter 7 for further discussion on this section of the *Code*, and in particular the decision in *R v Carignan*, 2025 SCC 43, radically altering the approach to this section.

44 See s 500.

45 Section 512.2.

be imposed. Bill C-75 replaced all of this with provisions that push more strongly towards release. Section 498 simply provides that a peace officer (that is, it need not be anyone senior or in charge) can release a person arrested for anything but a section 469 offence (that is, the most serious ones), and shall do so as soon as practicable if the officer intends to seek a summons, issue an appearance notice, or have the person give an undertaking. The officer is not to do this if there are compelling reasons to keep the person in custody, which in this context amount to virtually the same reasons as in section 495(2), discussed above as affecting the decision whether to arrest or not. That is, the accused should not be released if their detention is necessary to determine their identity, secure or preserve evidence, prevent the continuation of that offence or another, or make sure the person will attend court. Section 498(1.1) adds only one additional consideration: the need to "ensure the safety and security of any victim of or witness to the offence."

Finally, section 503(2) grants a further release power to any peace officer, again applying to any offence not listed in section 469. This provision (sometimes referred to as "police bail")[46] is not entirely new, but is no longer as rigidly structured as it once was. The provision now simply indicates that the peace officer shall release the person if they are satisfied that the continued detention is no longer necessary, and shall issue an appearance notice (described above) or have the person give an undertaking (described in section 501). Both include setting out the name of the accused, the substance of the offence charged, and a condition that the accused attend court at a specified time and place. In addition, they can contain other conditions that are necessary to ensure the accused's attendance in court and to ensure the safety and security of any victim of or witness to the offence: these can include things like reporting at specified times, remaining within a territorial jurisdiction, depositing a passport, or promising to pay an amount of money for failure to comply with the undertaking.

If an accused was issued a section 497 appearance notice or has been released, an information is to be laid before a justice "as soon as practicable after the issuance or release, and in any event before the time stated" for appearing in court.[47] However, a failure to comply with that time limit is of very little consequence. If no charge is laid in time, an accused cannot be charged with failing to appear, because the failure to lay an information in the prescribed time meant that the particular process that was issued had no binding effect. However,

46 Both the accused and the Crown are entitled to apply to a justice to replace this undertaking: ss 503(2.2) and (2.3). See also *R v Oliveira*, 2009 ONCA 219.

47 Section 505.

nothing bars the police from simply laying a new information in order to have the person compelled to appear. The "as soon as practicable" requirement is meant to guarantee an opportunity for judicial intervention to cancel the process if it should not have been issued in the first place.[48] Therefore, failure to meet that requirement does not render the information null, cause the court to lose jurisdiction, or confer any free-standing right on the accused, even if the information has not been laid by the time the accused appears in court. To hold that a prosecution would be barred, it has been held, would amount to creating a time limit for the prosecution of an offence, which does not now exist in the case of indictable offences. The time requirements in the section "are steps in the process designed to bring an accused before the court on a timely basis and without the necessity of prior detention. They are not pre-conditions to the jurisdiction of the court to try the offence."[49] For the same reason, an irregularity at the ministerial stage, where the justice decides whether to confirm or cancel the process requiring the accused to appear, can result in a loss of jurisdiction over the person but not a loss of jurisdiction over the offence itself.[50] If the person *does* appear at the required time, the court recovers jurisdiction over the person, and since it always had jurisdiction over the offence the prosecution can proceed.

Once the information is laid it will be reviewed by a justice. This process is functionally equivalent to that outlined in Section B, above in this chapter, involving sections 504 and 507 of the *Code*, but is instead governed by sections 505 and 508. If the justice is not satisfied that there are reasonable grounds to believe that an offence has been committed, they will cancel any form or process that has been previously issued and will direct that notice be given to the person who had been issued such process. If the justice endorses the information, however, they can either confirm the form of process that has already been issued or can cancel it and issue a summons or warrant for arrest.[51]

One anomaly in these compelling appearance provisions should be noted. In the case of most methods by which a peace officer can start the process against an accused, the justice's reviewing role extends to assessing whether the person ought to be made to face charges at all. Surprisingly, the one circumstance in which this is not true is in the

---

48 *R v Gougeon* (1980), 55 CCC (2d) 218 (Ont CA). The caselaw around this issue was decided prior to Bill C-75, but nothing in the changes in that Bill should obviously have an impact on these results.

49 *R v Markovic* (2005), 200 CCC (3d) 449 (Ont CA).

50 *R v Ladouceur*, 2013 ONCA 328 at para 26 [*Ladouceur*].

51 Section 508.

case of an arrest without a warrant where the accused has not been released before being taken to the justice: that is, the most intrusive method of compelling appearance. Under either section 507 or 508, the justice has the ability to decide that charges should not be laid at all. However, section 507 does not apply "if an accused has already been arrested." In turn, section 508 only applies to an information laid under section 505, and section 505 only applies when a person is released rather than kept in custody. As a result, a person who is arrested and kept in custody will not see judicial scrutiny of their situation until a bail hearing, and that hearing will only look at terms of release, not at whether the charge should have been laid at all. An accused might pursue a tort claim for false imprisonment or claim a violation of the right to be free from arbitrary detention, but no direct judicial screening mechanism exists.[52]

## 3) Compelling Appearance Post-Charge

The foregoing discussion was concerned with the procedure where police interaction with the accused precedes the laying of charges (in essence, arrests without warrant and issuing appearance notices). One might conceptualize those situations as ones where the police have been present at the crime itself, such as a fight outside a bar, and have acted immediately to intervene and arrest or otherwise deal with those involved. In such a case, it is of necessity that a justice will review any charging decision after the fact. In other cases, the police (1) investigate a crime, (2) decide who they believe the guilty party is, and (3) lay a charge before a justice in order to compel that person to appear.[53] In such cases, the review by the justice will occur before the police interaction with the accused. In practice, the distinction is not so clear-cut — police might have interacted with someone and formed the grounds for a warrantless arrest but instead decide to first lay a charge and then seek a summons, for example — but that, at least,

52 See *R v Whitmore* (1989), 51 CCC (3d) 294 (Ont CA), or *Ladouceur*, above note 50 at para 26, as well as the discussion in James Stribopoulos, "Unchecked Power: The Constitutional Regulation of Arrest Reconsidered" (2003) 48 *McGill Law Journal* 225. Much of s 507 deals with the choice between a summons and a warrant: that might be why, in drafting, cases where the accused has already been arrested were excluded. If so, the drafting had the unintentional effect of removing judicial scrutiny from the decision to charge *at all* in the case of warrantless arrests.

53 For an explanation of this issue in chart form, see *Anatomy of Criminal Procedure*, above note 1, Chart 1.3(b), "Compelling Appearance with Prior Judicial Scrutiny" and Chart 1.3(e), "Release of Persons Arrested with a Warrant."

provides a rough guide to the reason that different sets of procedures are necessary.

In these latter cases, where interaction with the justice precedes interaction with the accused, the process of laying an information before a justice is followed (this is discussed in Section B, above in this chapter). The criteria in that regard are the same whether the police lay the charge before interacting with the accused or after. However, in these circumstances, the justice will issue process in the form of either a summons or a warrant for the arrest of the accused if the charge is endorsed.

A summons is a document issued by the court commanding the accused named therein to attend court at a specified time and place. It recites the offence or offences that the accused has been charged with, and it contains the same particulars as similar documents. In Form 6, it specifies the date to appear in court, a date to appear for purpose of the *Identification of Criminals Act*, and the consequences of non-appearance.[54] If the person does not appear as required for purposes of the *Identification of Criminals Act*, a justice can issue a warrant for the person's arrest. In line with the principle of restraint, however, and similar in philosophy to the approach behind judicial referral hearings, discussed above, this warrant will be for the original offence, not for a new offence of failing to appear.[55] That is, there is a consequence for non-appearance — a summons becomes an arrest warrant — but the consequence does not have the possibility of lengthening the person's criminal record. The summons is to be served in person or left with an adult at the person's last known address.[56]

An arrest warrant includes substantially the same details as a summons, but adds a command to peace officers within the local jurisdiction to arrest the person charged and to bring them to court. The warrant is addressed to all peace officers in the jurisdiction and remains in effect until it is executed.

The choice between a summons and an arrest warrant lies in the discretion of the justice. However, section 507(4) directs a justice to issue a summons unless there are reasonable grounds to believe that a warrant is necessary in the public interest. At a policy level, this is parallel to section 495(2), directing police officers to prefer the use of an appearance notice to an arrest for some offences. Nonetheless, it is a much more vague direction than that detailed provision and might

54 Sections 509(1), (4), and (5).

55 Sections 512.1, 512.2.

56 Section 509(2).

on that basis be subject to a *Charter* challenge.[57] However, given that it is now governed by the requirement in section 493.1 to "give primary consideration to the release of the accused at the earliest reasonable opportunity," it seems likely to be constitutional.

A justice will decide to issue a warrant in order to "compel the accused to attend before him or some other justice for the same territorial division."[58] This phrasing is not meant to permit a justice to say "when this person is arrested take them in front of no one but me." Rather, it simply intends that the person arrested is required to be brought before *some* justice.[59]

The *Code* allows the justice who issues an arrest warrant to endorse it for the specific purpose of authorizing the release of an arrested accused, pending their appearance in court.[60] Correspondingly, a peace officer is then authorized to release the accused.[61]

If a person is arrested and the police decide not to release under any of the various powers to do so outlined above, that person must be brought before a justice without unreasonable delay and, in any case, within twenty-four hours.[62] These deadlines are independent — the section does not give the police the right to automatically hold a person for twenty-four hours. Rather, the primary obligation is to take the person in front of a justice without unreasonable delay: twenty-four hours is set as the outer limit of what is reasonable.[63] Accordingly, a delay of twelve hours would be unreasonable if there was no good reason, on the facts of the particular case, not to have taken the accused in front of a justice in four hours. Indeed, reviewing courts have pointed to the need for police to anticipate that they will have to comply with this requirement and

57 See the discussion of this issue in Chapter 7.

58 Section 507(1)(b).

59 *R v Davidson* (2004), 26 CR (6th) 264 (Alta CA).

60 Section 507(6).

61 Section 499. Prior to Bill C-75, that release power more or less corresponded to that given to an officer in charge in the case of a warrantless arrest, which included attaching more restrictive conditions to the release. With Bill C-75 and its general move towards favouring release, if the warrant has been endorsed then any peace officer can release the accused by issuing an appearance notice or having the person give an undertaking.

62 Section 503. Note that this section specifically says that the obligation to take the accused in front of a justice arises if the accused has not already been released by the officer or officer in charge.

63 Judges have noted that police officers themselves often seem not to understand this point: see *R v MacDonald*, 2018 NSPC 25 at para 65 or *R v Raios*, 2018 ONSC 6867.

take steps in advance in order to be able to do so.[64] However, entering into how long a delay will be considered reasonable is a recognition that the police are entitled to interrogate and in other ways carry out some investigation during this arrest phase. In *R v Storrey*, for example, a lineup was arranged which involved witnesses who had to be brought in from outside the jurisdiction, and an eighteen-hour delay was reasonable.[65] That does not mean, however, that the police can always defer taking the accused in front of a justice because they are pursuing an investigation. A release within twenty-four hours might still have been unreasonably delayed.[66] Each case will depend upon its particular facts.

Setting a time limit for an arrested person to have the opportunity to be released by a justice is another reflection of the principle of restraint. As at other stages, though, that principle is not always implemented as it should be, and there are ongoing issues around compliance with the deadlines.[67]

The justice of the peace might decide, of course, that the accused should not be released. Similarly, the Crown (or the accused) could apply to the justice for an adjournment of the release hearing, during which time the accused will continue to be detained: this adjournment cannot be for more than three days without the consent of the accused.[68] Neither of these possibilities, however, relieves the police of their initial obligation to take the accused to a justice.[69] On the other

64 See, for example, *R v Mendez*, 2014 ONSC 498 [*Mendez*], or *R v Burgar*, 2013 BCPC 389 [*Burgar*].

65 [1990] 1 SCR 241.

66 See, for example, *R v Keats*, 2014 NSPC 108; *R v W(E)*, 2002 NFCA 49 [*W(E)*]; or *R v Koszulap* (1974), 27 CRNS 226 (Ont CA). Note, in particular, *Mendez*, above note 64, where police knew that justices of the peace would not be available after 2 p.m. but continued to question the accused, knowing the result would be that they could not comply with the twenty-four-hour deadline. At para 116 it was held: "It was not reasonable to choose to investigate at the expense of the rights of the accused to be brought before a court."

67 See *R v Reilly*, 2020 SCC 27, in which the Supreme Court upheld a stay of proceedings for an accused who had been held for more than twenty-four hours and where the case was "an instance of a systemic and ongoing problem that was not being satisfactorily addressed." See also *Reilly v Alberta*, 2024 ABCA 270, upholding the certification of a class for a class action lawsuit concerning non-compliance with s 503 of the *Code*. On the other hand in *Cirillo v Ontario*, 2021 ONCA 353, a similar class action suit was not allowed to proceed, but for reasons relating to the certification of a class rather than the non-existence of a problem.

68 Section 516.

69 See *W(E)*, above note 66; *R v Simpson* (1994), 29 CR (4th) 274 (Nfld CA), rev'd on other grounds [1995] 1 SCR 449 [*Simpson*]; *R v MacPherson* (1995), 100 CCC (3d) 216 (NBCA).

hand, the accused can waive the right to be taken in front of a justice within the time period.[70]

Courts were at one time divided on whether a failure to comply with the twenty-four-hour deadline resulted in an arbitrary detention, which would violate section 9 of the *Charter*.[71] However, the Supreme Court has since made clear that any unlawful detention is automatically an arbitrary detention.[72] It now seems to be uncontroversial and often conceded by the Crown that if an accused was detained beyond twenty-four hours there was a section 9 violation,[73] and the only issue concerns the appropriate remedy.[74]

Section 503 does provide for one situation in which the twenty-four hour outside limit does not apply: where no justice is available within that time, "the person shall be taken before a justice as soon as possible."[75] Lack of availability, however, cannot be argued on a simple administrative basis, such as that the courts do not sit on weekends.[76] The provision is intended to apply only in remote areas and similar situations.[77] Even in such cases, the provisions of sections 515(2.2) and (2.3) that allow an accused to appear in front of a justice by video or audioconference would need to be taken into account.

There is some ambiguity over the exact consequences of taking the accused in front of a justice. Some cases take the view that this step transfers the accused from the hands of the police and places them under the jurisdiction of the court and does so in order to protect the

---

70 *R v Montgomery*, 2016 BCCA 379 at para 217.

71 See, for example, *Simpson*, above note 69 at para 98 (Nfld CA); *W(E)*, above note 66; *R v Tam*; *R v Lai* (1995), 100 CCC (3d) 196 (BCCA); and *R v CK* (2005), 36 CR (6th) 153 (Ont Ct J).

72 *R v Grant*, 2009 SCC 32 at para 55.

73 See in particular *R v Salehi*, 2019 BCSC 197 [*Salehi*], rejecting the Crown's argument that it would be possible for an accused's detention in violation of s 503 to be unlawful but not arbitrary. See also *R v Frederickson*, 2013 BCSC 1992; *Burgar*, above note 64; *R v Kift*, 2014 ONCJ 454 [*Kift*]; *R v Brown*, 2014 BCSC 1872; or *Mendez*, above note 64.

74 See, for example, *R v Darling*, 2020 ONSC 6397; *R v Musara*, 2022 ONSC 3190; and *R v Noor*, 2022 ONCJ 140.

75 Section 503(1)(b).

76 See, for example, *Mendez*, above note 64, holding that where justices of the peace are not normally available after a certain hour, police must cease interrogating in order to take the accused before a justice while one is still available.

77 *Simpson*, above note 69 (Nfld CA).

accused's rights.[78] In practical terms this would mean that the police cannot take an accused before a justice and then take them back to the police station for further interrogation: rather, a bail order would have to be made and if the accused were still to be held in custody, it would be at some other facility.[79] Other courts reject that there is any such implication about the manner of detention.[80] In any case, the significance of this requirement is that the person is delivered from the custody of the police into the jurisdiction of the court to be dealt with according to law. At this point, therefore, it is necessary to turn to the final portion of this chapter, dealing with judicial interim release.

## D. JUDICIAL INTERIM RELEASE

The general philosophical approach to judicial interim release,[81] commonly referred to as "bail," has long incorporated a preference for interfering with liberty as little as necessary. This general principle is now stated explicitly in section 493.1 for all of Part XVI, but has also been made even more explicit in the bail provisions. The provisions are structured on the general assumption that an accused should be released pending trial and with as few restrictions as possible. Indeed, the *Code* creates what is usually referred to as a "ladder" approach to bail. In other words, an accused is presumed to be entitled to release without conditions and the Crown must justify each increasing step of intrusiveness. There are exceptions for section 469 and other offences, and they will be discussed below, but this is the general approach.

Bill C-75 made changes to the bail provisions, in part simply in terminology or to incorporate reference to other changes made by the Bill. However, the changes were in large part a reflection of comments made

---

78 See, for example, *R v Poirier*, 2016 ONCA 582:

> [58] Compliance with s. 503 is not simply a matter of form … If the police had complied with s. 503, the manner in which the appellant continued to be detained would have been subject to court supervision. The appellant's detention would have changed from being a detention pursuant to the execution of the general warrant to a court-monitored detention that ensured the ongoing protection of the appellant's *Charter* rights.

79 See *R v Precourt* (1976), 18 OR (2d) 714 (CA); *Kift*, above note 73; or *R v Ansari*, 2008 BCSC 1492.

80 See *R v Ashmore*, 2011 BCCA 18; *R v Chung*, 2011 BCCA 131; or *R v Bhandher*, 2012 BCCA 441.

81 For an explanation of this issue in chart form, see *Anatomy of Criminal Procedure*, above note 1, and the various charts in Part 2.1, Judicial Interim Release.

by the Supreme Court of Canada in *R v Antic*, a decision which criticized the way in which the bail provisions were being applied across the country, and the failure to adequately respect the way that the principle of restraint was already meant to be built in to them.[82] *Antic* was meant to send a message to bail courts to be more compliant with the *Code* scheme of using the least intrusive measure, to avoid cash bail, to view detention as a last resort, and so on,[83] And that has also been backed up by legislative change reinforcing what was already meant to be the proper approach. Nonetheless concerns have continued to exist.[84]

Further, at the time of this writing Bill C-14 has been introduced, which at a policy level seems to contain the message that bail should be granted *less* frequently.[85] For example, it proposes to add after the explicit statement of the principle of restraint that "For greater certainty, section 493.1 does not require the accused to be released."[86]

It is worth noting a rule that is slightly inconsistent with the policy of releasing an accused as readily as practicable. As noted above, an accused must be brought to a justice without unreasonable delay. This rule is meant to guarantee that person a speedy consideration of release; however, the justice that the accused is taken to can adjourn the bail hearing by up to three days without the consent of the accused.

---

82 *R v Antic*, 2017 SCC 27 [*Antic*].

83 See, for example, *R v Tunney*, 2018 ONSC 961 at para 57: "the *Antic* decision signals the need for a change in our bail culture. The message is clear. We need to do things differently." See also the discussion in Daniel Lerner, "*R. v. Antic* Did Change Something: Footnote 4 and the Role of Sureties" Ontario Bar Association, 20 November 2017. In addition, see Wayne K Gorman, "The Impact of the Supreme Court of Canada on the Law of Bail" (2017) 53:3 *Court Review* 92.

84 *Zora*, above note 19 at para 26:

> Many interveners drew attention to the widespread problems which continue to exist, even after this Court's decision in *Antic*, with the ongoing imposition of bail conditions which are unnecessary, unreasonable, unduly restrictive, too numerous, or which effectively set the accused up to fail. Any such practice offends the principle of restraint which has always been at the core of the law governing the setting of bail conditions.

See also Canadian Civil Liberties Association, *Still Failing: The Deepening Crisis of Bail and Pre-Trial Detention in Canada* (CCLA, 2024).

85 BILL C-14, "An Act to amend the *Criminal Code*, the *Youth Criminal Justice Act* and the *National Defence Act* (bail and sentencing)," First Reading, October 23, 2025 [Bill C-14].

86 Bill C-14, above note 85, art 14.

Longer delays are also possible, although in that case the consent of the accused would be required.[87]

At a bail hearing the onus will normally be on the Crown, though there are some exceptions that place the onus on the accused. In either case, the party with the onus is required to "show cause" for the result they are seeking, and so a bail hearing is often referred to as a "show cause hearing." The *Code* permits these hearings to be conducted by a "justice," which includes a justice of the peace, but quite commonly they are held in front of a provincial court judge.

In the ordinary case, where the onus is on the Crown to justify non-release, section 515(1) directs that the justice *shall* make a release order without conditions.[88] If the justice is persuaded not to do that, then section 515(2) of the *Code* sets out the conditions that could be attached to a release order. They are as follows:

(i) an indication that the release order does not include any financial obligations;
(ii) the accused's promise to pay a specified amount if they fail to comply with a condition of the order;[89]
(iii) the obligation to have one or more "sureties" — that is, a third party who promises to pay a specified sum if the accused does not appear as required — with or without the accused's promise to *pay* as well;[90]
(iv) the obligation to deposit money or other valuable security in a specified amount or value, with or without the accused's promise to pay a specified amount if they fail to comply with a condition of the order;[91] or

---

87 Section 516. See also *R v Zarinchang*, 2010 ONCA 286, in which institutional delays prevented an accused's bail hearing from being held until twenty-four days had passed. The Court of Appeal found that this violated the accused's right under s 9 of the *Charter* not to be arbitrarily detained and also his right under s 11(e) not to be denied reasonable bail without just cause. However, they overturned the remedy of a stay of proceedings which the trial judge had ordered and reduced the damage award to $3,600.

88 Bill C-75 has introduced the terminology of a "release order," though it does not reflect any substantive change and is merely the name for an order releasing the accused, either with or without conditions.

89 Such a promise to pay used to be referred to as a "recognizance," but Bill C-75 has adopted simpler language: see the discussion above in note 35.

90 See s 515.1 for the requirements around naming a person as a surety. In addition, see Part XXV, "Effect and Enforcement of Undertakings, Release Orders and Recognizances" for the rules governing the powers of sureties, their ability to have themselves removed, and so on.

91 Until Bill C-75, this option was only available with the consent of the prosecutor.

(v) if the accused is not ordinarily resident in the province in which they are in custody or does not ordinarily reside within 200 kilometres of the place in which they are in custody, the obligation to deposit money or other valuable security in a specified amount or value, with or without the accused's promise to pay a specified amount by the justice if they fail to comply with a condition of the order and with or without sureties.

The *Code* specifies that a justice cannot make an order under any of paragraphs (2)(b) to (e) unless the prosecutor "shows cause why an order containing the conditions referred to in the preceding paragraphs for any less onerous form of release would be inadequate."[92] That is what is meant by the "ladder approach": that the Crown must climb up to each increasing degree of intrusion on the accused's liberty. Bill C-75 added to that general approach two more specific requirements. Those are that a *promise* to pay should be preferred over an actual deposit of money,[93] and that a surety should only be required if the justice is satisfied that "this requirement is the least onerous form of release possible for the accused in the circumstances."[94] Both of these steps were responses to practice in bail courts, which were over-relying on cash bail and the use of sureties.

On the other hand, Bill C-75 also provided that a justice should consider two other relevant factors, which are more likely to militate towards greater restrictions on liberty: whether the offence related to the accused's intimate partner, and whether the accused has a criminal record.[95]

---

92 Section 515(2.01).

93 Section 515(2.02). The section requires that the accused "has reasonably recoverable assets" for this preference to apply. This particular provision is a reflection of *Antic*, above note 82, which held at para 49 that "Release with a pledge of money . . . has the same coercive power as release with a cash deposit."

94 Section 515(2.03). This provision is also a reflection of *Antic*, above note 82, which found an overreliance on the use of sureties and held at para 67 that "A recognizance with sureties is one of the most onerous forms of release. A surety should not be imposed unless all the less onerous forms of release have been considered and rejected as inappropriate."

95 Section 515(3). One of the other efforts in Bill C-75 was to take steps with regard to "intimate partner" offences, now defined in s 2 of the *Code*, which include changes at the bail and sentencing stages. Section 515(6)(b.1) also imposed a reverse onus in the case of a person who had previously been convicted of an intimate partner offences, and this provision was later broadened also to apply to persons who had received a discharge: *An Act to amend the Criminal Code and to make consequential amendments to another Act (interim release and domestic violence recognizance orders)*, SC 2024, c 22.

Sections 515(4) through 515(4.3) provide the various types of conditions that may, or must, be imposed when an order for release is made under section 515(2). All of these are, in principle, related to the objectives of ensuring the accused attends court, ensuring the safety of the community, or maintaining confidence in the administration of justice: that is, the grounds upon which an accused could potentially be detained under section 515(10).[96] They concern issues like reporting to a peace officer, remaining in a specified location, surrendering a passport, and so on. Conditions can also include not communicating with specified persons or staying away from particular locations, and the *Code* specifically directs the justice to consider whether those conditions are desirable in the case of certain offences.[97]

In crafting any individual release order, the Court has stressed that "[t]he setting of bail is an individualized process and there is no place for standard, routine, or boilerplate conditions."[98] They advised wariness about conditions that might be related to symptoms of mental illness or addiction since, for example, an abstinence condition that an accused cannot possibly abide by will not be reasonable.[99] Conditions intended to rehabilitate or help an accused person, such as "attend school," will not be appropriate unless necessary to address the risks posed by the accused.[100] They also advised caution around conditions such as to "keep the peace and be of good behaviour" or to obey the rules of a house and cautioned that some conditions such as not having a cell phone or staying away from certain areas can have perverse consequences.[101]

The ladder principle also applies in this context, and so no more conditions should be imposed than necessary.[102] The conditions imposed should be individualized to the particular accused, and "must be minimal, necessary, reasonable, the least onerous in the circumstances,

---

96 *Zora*, above note 19 at para 84:

> Only conditions which target those specific s. 515(10) risk(s) are necessary. If an accused is a flight risk, but poses no other risks, only those conditions that minimize their risk of absconding should be imposed. Similarly, if an accused poses a risk to public safety and protection, only the least onerous conditions to address that specific threat should be imposed.

97 The offences include things like terrorism offences or offences where violence was used or threatened: see ss 515(4.2)–(4.3).

98 *Zora*, above note 19 at para 100.

99 *Zora*, above note 19 at para 92.

100 *Zora*, above note 19 at para 93.

101 *Zora*, above note 19 at paras 94–97.

102 Zora, above note 19 at para 24.

and sufficiently connected to a risk listed in s. 515(10),"[103] though the Court has noted that this ambition is frequently not achieved in practice.[104] They have summarized the correct approach to be taken:

> In summary, to ensure the principles of restraint and review are firmly grounded in how people think about appropriate bail conditions, these questions may help structure the analysis:
>
> - If released without conditions, would the accused pose any specific statutory risks that justify imposing any bail conditions? If the accused is released without conditions, are they at risk of failing to attend their court date, harming public safety and protection, or reducing confidence in the administration of justice?
> - Is this condition necessary? If this condition was not imposed, would that create a risk of the accused absconding, harm to public protection and safety, or loss of confidence in the administration of justice which would prevent the court from releasing the accused on an undertaking without conditions?
> - Is this condition reasonable? Is the condition clear and proportional to the risk posed by the accused? Can the accused be expected to meet this condition safely and reasonably? Based on what is known of the accused, is it likely that their living situation, addiction, disability, or illness will make them unable to fulfill this condition?
> - Is this condition sufficiently linked to the grounds of detention under s. 515(10)(c)? Is it narrowly focussed on addressing that specific risk posed by the accused's release?
> - What is the cumulative effect of all the conditions? Taken together, are they the fewest and least onerous conditions required in the circumstances?[105]

These considerations apply even when there is a "consent" order to bail because the circumstances are such that an accused will have strong motivations to accept any form of release order rather than continue to be detained.[106]

---

103 *Zora*, above note 19 at para 24.

104 *Zora*, above note 19 at para 76:

> In practice, the number of unnecessary and unreasonable bail conditions, and the rising number of breach charges, undercut the claim that there is sufficient individualization of bail conditions.

105 *Zora*, above note 19 at para 89.

106 Zora, above note 19 at para 104:

> There are many compelling reasons a person in custody would "accept" suggested restrictions to secure release, even if such restrictions were overbroad. In addition to the universal human impulse towards freedom,

Well before *Zora* the governing principle was meant to be that release conditions should be realistic and workable for the accused, rather than "setting them up to fail."[107] *Zora* attempted to reinvigorate that principle, which was not represented in practice, but concerns over whether the proper approach is yet being taken remain.[108]

A particular issue is the imposition of cash bail, which the Court found to be too-frequently relied on by bail courts. A justice who orders cash bail must make inquiries into the means of the accused and cannot require a cash deposit so high that it amounts to a *de facto* detention order.[109] Further, there should be some type of causal relationship between the crime charged and the particular conditions imposed. However, this connection need not be so specific that, for example, a curfew cannot be imposed because the particular offence charge occurred during the day.[110]

The remaining possibility, beyond the various forms of release in section 515(2), is that the Crown might show cause as to why the accused should remain in custody until trial. Section 515(10) of the *Code* specifies that there are only three grounds on which continued detention of an accused may be ordered. The first two of these are relatively uncontroversial: (1) the detention is necessary to ensure the accused's attendance in court; or (2) the detention is necessary for the protection or safety of the public. In this context, "public" includes victims, witnesses, and any person under the age of eighteen, and the justice is directed to consider "all the circumstances, including any substantial likelihood that the accused will, if released from custody, commit a criminal offence or interfere with the administration of justice." These are sometimes referred to as the primary and secondary grounds for detention, though that terminology is a holdover from a

---

individuals are concerned with the effects continued detention would have on their families, their income, their employment, their ability to keep their home, and their ability to access medication and necessary services, as described above. When presented with a promise of release on what may appear to be "take it or leave it conditions" many accused simply acquiesce to avoid continued detention and/or a contested bail hearing.

107 *Zora*, above note 19 at para 87.

108 See Yule, C, & MacDiarmid, L (2024). 'It's a set up': Examining the Relationship Between Bail Conditions and the Revolving Door of Justice. *Current Issues in Criminal Justice*, 1–18. https://doi.org/10.1080/10345329.2024.2400825, arguing that despite some shifts, courts continue to assign conditions which accused have little realistic chance of complying with.

109 *Antic*, above note 82 at paras 56–59.

110 *R v Patko* (2005), 197 CCC (3d) 192 (BCCA).

previous version of the section and no order of priority is intended today.

The third possible ground for detention has been more controversial. An earlier version allowed for detention "in the public interest": it was struck down for violating the guarantee to reasonable bail found in section 11(e) of the *Charter* by being too vague and imprecise.[111] It was replaced by a section which allowed for detention "on any other just cause being shown" and in particular where it was necessary to maintain confidence in the administration of justice having regard to listed circumstances. This new section was also challenged and was upheld in part and struck down in part. The opening words of the section, "any other just cause" were struck out, on the ground of vagueness. The Court in *R v Hall* was divided over whether the same objection applied to the rest of the section, but, in a 5:4 split, upheld it.[112] The minority took the view that the enumerated considerations did not do enough to differentiate the new section from the old "public interest" criterion that had been found unacceptable. In contrast, the majority felt that the criteria delineated the risk-zone clearly enough that the vagueness claim was not made out. Following *Hall* Parliament amended the section to remove the portion that had been struck down, so it now says that detention can be ordered

> (*c*) if the detention is necessary to maintain confidence in the administration of justice, having regard to all the circumstances, including
> (i) the apparent strength of the prosecution's case,
> (ii) the gravity of the offence,
> (iii) the circumstances surrounding the commission of the offence, including whether a firearm was used, and
> (iv) the fact that the accused is liable, on conviction, for a potentially lengthy term of imprisonment or, in the case of an offence that involves, or whose subject-matter is, a firearm, a minimum punishment of imprisonment for a term of three years or more.[113]

Many courts were of the view that *Hall* had created a rule that this third ground should be used only in rare cases, though not all

111 *R v Morales*, [1992] 3 SCR 711 [*Morales*].
112 2002 SCC 64 [*Hall*].
113 Section 515(10)(c). In *R v St-Cloud*, 2015 SCC 27 at para 72 [*St-Cloud*], the Court noted that, given the French version of the statute, "confidence" should be read as "public confidence."

courts acted on this view.[114] However, in *St-Cloud* the Court indicated that there was no such rule: a consequence of applying the criteria in section 515(1)(c) might as a matter of fact be that detention on this ground occurred only rarely, but "only use it in rare cases" was not a precondition to its application or a criterion a court must consider.[115] Nor did the fact that *Hall* involved a horrific and inexplicable crime mean that the provision was confined to such cases: it applied to any type of crime, if the Crown proved that the detention of the accused was justified to maintain confidence in the administration of justice.[116] That decision included but was not limited to the circumstances explicitly listed in the section.[117]

Where the prosecutor justifies continued detention by showing cause, the justice must add a statement of the reasons for this decision to the warrant of committal.[118]

That is the general scheme for bail hearings, but, as noted above, there are some exceptions to this approach. The first one worth noting is created by section 515(6). That section lists a number of offences for which the onus is reversed.[119] That is, for the offences listed in that section, the justice is directed to order that the accused *shall* be detained unless the accused shows cause not to do so. These offences consist of: 1) a variety of criminal organization, terrorism, national security or weapons offences; 2) an intimate partner offence where the person has previously been convicted or discharged of an intimate partner offence; 3) an indictable offence committed by someone not ordinarily resident in Canada; 4) an offence related to failing to comply with some previous form of release order; and 5) an offence punishable by life imprisonment under sections 5 to 7 of the *Controlled Drugs and Substances Act*.[120] The last two reverse onuses on this list have been challenged under the *Charter* but were upheld.[121]

These provisions were changed slightly by Bill C-75. Previously, the *Code* specified that for some of these reverse onus situations, the accused

---

114 See Don Stuart & Joanna Harris, "Is the Public Confidence Ground to Deny Bail Used Sparingly?" (2004) 21 *Criminal Reports* (6th) 232.

115 *St-Cloud*, above note 113 at para 50.

116 *Ibid* at para 54.

117 *Ibid* at para 68.

118 Section 515(5).

119 Strictly, the list refers to offences falling into these categories that are not s 469 offences. That exception is made because a different reverse onus applies to s 469 offences: see the discussion immediately below.

120 SC 1996, c 19. Bill C-14, above note 85, proposes to add further offence to the list of those with a reverse onus around detention: see arts 23(8), (9), and (10).

121 See, respectively, *Morales*, above note 121, and *R v Pearson*, [1992] 3 SCR 665.

not only had to show cause that detention was not called for, but also had a reverse onus to "climb down" the ladder by showing that conditions should not be imposed. The *Code* now only says that the justice "shall make a release order under this section."[122] The natural reading of that, especially in light of the removal of a very clear reverse onus, is that if the accused rebuts the presumption of detention, then with regard to the release order the Crown is required to climb the ladder as subsection (2) requires. However, no court seems yet to have explicitly considered the issue, and Bill C-14 contains an amendment which will state that the Crown does not have to climb the ladder in reverse onus cases.[123]

The second exception to the general bail scheme applies to section 469 offences, the most common of which is murder. In this case, section 515(11) states that a justice has no authority to release the accused and must order them detained to be "dealt with according to law." That is not the end of the story, however. In this event, the accused will, in accordance with section 522, be taken before a judge of the superior court — no one else is authorized to release a person charged with a section 469 offence before trial. In this hearing, there is again a reverse onus, with the accused being required to justify release.[124] If the accused is ordered to be released, any of the ordinary conditions of release can be imposed.

A release order can be varied with the written consent of the accused, the prosecutor, and any surety.[125] A decision made by a justice concerning release or detention can be reviewed by a judge upon application of the accused or the prosecutor.[126] Applications of this kind are common, and there is no limitation on the number of such applications that can be made, except that following a review a further application cannot be brought for thirty days, unless the accused or the prosecutor has the leave of a judge. These reviews provide an opportunity to adjust or correct the order at the original bail hearing and also provide an opportunity to reconsider the appropriateness of the order if circumstances have changed. Where interim release has been denied for a non-section 469 offence, an accused person in custody is entitled to an automatic review if the trial has not commenced within ninety days.[127]

---

122 Section 515(7).

123 Bill C-14, above note 85 art 23(1).

124 Section 522(2).

125 Section 519.1

126 Sections 520–21.

127 Section 525(1): see ss 525(1)(a) and (b) for the precise point at which the clock starts ticking. Until Bill C-75 the deadline was only thirty days for summary conviction offences, but it is now ninety days for all non-section 469 offences.

There had been some suggestion that an accused was required to show some sort of unreasonable delay as a threshold to being permitted to bring a review application, but the Court has determined that that is not the case: the jailer (not the detainee) is obliged to bring an application immediately after the expiration of the ninety day time limit.[128] At such a review the judge can consider whether the prosecutor or the accused has been responsible for any delay and can give directions for expediting the proceedings, or can make a release order.[129] Somewhat surprisingly, no parallel provision *requiring* a review after a certain length of time exists for section 469 offences, though an accused is entitled to seek a review under section 680.

If not amended in some fashion, an order for judicial interim release lasts until the end of trial and, if an accused is found guilty of a non-section 469 offence, the term of the release will last until the time of sentencing. This remains the case even if, for some reason, a new information is laid in respect of an offence for which process has already been issued or a direct indictment is preferred.[130] However, a preliminary inquiry judge or trial judge can vacate any previous order (whether for detention or release) and substitute a different order where cause to do so is shown.[131]

The justice who conducts a bail hearing is not constrained by the rules and principles of admissibility that apply with respect to evidence at trial. Section 518, which sets out the principles of evidence at a bail hearing, concludes with a paragraph that allows the justice to "receive and base his decision on evidence considered credible or trustworthy by him in the circumstances of each case." This broad statement of admissibility is supplemented by more specific elements in section 518, such as the admissibility of wiretap evidence and evidence that relates both to the character and circumstances of the accused and the circumstances of the alleged offence. However, that section also specifies that a bail hearing may not be used to interrogate or examine the accused about the offence itself. Although the justice may conduct inquiries under oath of or about the accused, neither the justice nor the prosecutor may examine the accused about the circumstances of the alleged offence, unless the accused has elected to testify in the hearing at the invitation of their counsel or on their own decision. Of course, even at this stage an accused is entitled to protect themself against

128 *Myers*, above note 19. This requirement has now been made more explicit in s 525(1).

129 Sections 525(4) and (5).

130 Sections 523(1.1) and (1.2)

131 Section 523(2).

self-incrimination, and thus any questions put to the accused at the bail hearing should, in principle, be confined to matters that are relevant to a determination of the hearing. However, this can be a difficult issue to control at a bail hearing, especially as the prosecutor is specifically entitled to produce evidence of the alleged offence and the probability of conviction.

Finally, note that, where the Crown seeks to show cause for the accused to be detained pending trial, the accused is entitled to a mandatory publication ban on all evidence and representations made at the hearing.[132] Such a ban is justified under section 1 of the *Charter*, because it is a necessary measure to protect the accused's fair trial right given that at the bail hearing evidence that might be inadmissible at trial can be presented.[133]

## FURTHER READINGS

CANADIAN CIVIL LIBERTIES ASSOCIATION, *Still Failing: The Deepening Crisis of Bail and Pre-Trial Detention in Canada* (Toronto: CCLA, 2024)

COUGHLAN, STEVE, & GLEN LUTHER. *Detention and Arrest*, 2d ed (Toronto: Irwin Law, 2017).

COUGHLAN, STEVE, & ALEX GORLEWSKI. *The Anatomy of Criminal Procedure: A Visual Guide to the Law*, 2nd ed (Toronto: University of Toronto Press, 2026).

LAW REFORM COMMISSION OF CANADA. *Compelling Appearance, Interim Release and Pre-trial Detention* (Ottawa: Law Reform Commission of Canada, 1988).

———. *Controlling Criminal Prosecutions: The Attorney General and the Crown Prosecutor* (Ottawa: Law Reform Commission of Canada, 1990).

LEGAULT, PASCALE. "Bail and Indigenous Over-Representation in Canadian Detention Facilities: Do the 2019 Amendments to the Criminal Code Offer a Viable Solution?" (2025) 73 *CLQ* 84.

ROSE, DAVID. *Quigley's Criminal Procedure in Canada* (Toronto: Thomson Reuters, 2021) (loose-leaf) ch 5 and 9.

132 Section 517.

133 *Toronto Star Newspapers Ltd v Canada*, 2010 SCC 21

Runyon, Sarah. "Correctional Afterthought: Offences Against the Administration of Justice and Canada's Persistent Savage Anxieties" (2020) 43:5 *Manitoba Law Journal* 1–38.

Stribopoulos, James. "Unchecked Power: The Constitutional Regulation of Arrest Reconsidered" (2003) 48 *McGill Law Journal* 225.

Stuart, Don. *Charter Justice in Canadian Criminal Law*, 7th ed (Toronto: Thomson Carswell, 2018) ch 6.

——— & Joanna Harris. "Is the Public Confidence Ground to Deny Bail Used Sparingly?" (2004) 21 *Criminal Reports* (6th) 232.

Trotter, Gary. *The Law of Bail in Canada*, 3d ed (Scarborough: Carswell, 2010) (loose-leaf).

Yule, C., & MacDiarmid, L. (2024). 'It's a Set Up': Examining the Relationship Between Bail Conditions and the Revolving Door of Justice. *Current Issues in Criminal Justice*, 1–18 http://doi.org/10.1080/10345329.2024.2400825.

CHAPTER 7

# ARREST

This chapter deals with powers of arrest, which are mostly but not exclusively exercised by police. There is some overlap between this chapter and others. Obviously, arrest is one of the methods of compelling a person's appearance in court, and so the procedures here must be seen in light of the discussion in Chapter 6. In addition, the *Charter* guarantees particular rights on arrest *or* detention. Detention was discussed in Chapter 5, but section 10 issues were not discussed there at any length. Accordingly, the discussion of section 10 rights here is also relevant to that earlier chapter.

## A. INTRODUCTION

This section deals with powers of arrest, both those given to police officers and those available more broadly. Arrest powers are most important in the context of apprehending a person believed to have committed a crime, and so the major focus of this chapter will be the arrest powers found in Part XVI of the *Code*, "Compelling Appearance." However, other arrest powers for various purposes are also found in the *Code* and will be outlined briefly.

Arrest is only one of the methods that can compel the appearance of an accused before a court. Part XVI also contains provisions that allow an accused to be brought to court by two other methods: a summons or an appearance notice. Those techniques were discussed at greater length in Chapter 6, but it is useful to review them here.

Similar to powers of search and seizure, Part XVI of the *Code* is aimed at balancing legitimate state interests in prosecuting crime against individual freedom. On the one hand, it is sometimes necessary to require a person to answer to a criminal charge and therefore to appear in court to do so. On the other hand, our Western democratic principles hold that the state should not interfere with the liberty of individuals without good reason, and even then no more than is necessary. In large part, therefore, while Part XVI of the *Code* creates coercive powers given to the police, it endeavours to reflect the principle of restraint while doing so. This has long been the implicit governing principle, and since 2019 the Code has explicitly stated that in matters relating to arrest and bail "a peace officer, justice or judge shall give primary consideration to the release of the accused at the earliest reasonable opportunity and on the least onerous conditions that are appropriate in the circumstances."[1] This approach is an attempt to find the right balance between crime control and due process interests.[2]

Accordingly, in principle, a police officer should not be able to unilaterally compel the appearance of an accused in court. That decision should, at some stage, be confirmed by a judicial officer, typically a justice of the peace, and in all but one instance it is.[3] That confirmation can occur either before the officer deals directly with the accused person or afterward, but it will occur. Similarly, there are different levels of compulsion that can be directed towards the accused. The accused

1 Section 493.1, added by Bill C-75, *An Act to amend the Criminal Code, the Youth Criminal Justice Act and other Acts and to make consequential amendments to other Acts*, Royal Assent June 21, 2019 [Bill C-75]. See also *R v Zora*, 2020 SCC 14 at para 26:

> Restraint has a constitutional dimension, a legislative footing, and is not only recognized in case law, but was also recently expressly reinforced by the amendments that came into force on December 18, 2019.

On the other hand, at the time of this writing a Bill is before Parliament, primarily aimed at the bail provisions, which proposes to add to the Code the language "For greater certainty, section 493.1 does not require the accused to be released." See Bill C-14, "An Act to amend the *Criminal Code*, the *Youth Criminal Justice Act* and the *National Defence Act* (bail and sentencing)", First Reading October 23, 2025, art 14 [Bill C-14].

2 See Herbert L Packer, *The Limits of the Criminal Sanction* (Stanford: Stanford University Press, 1968) at 154–72 for a fuller discussion of these concepts.

3 The surprising exception is arrest without a warrant: see the discussion in Chapter 6, Section C(2).

may receive a request[4] in writing to appear in court on a particular day and be trusted to do so, or could, in contrast, physically be taken into control by the police officer and given no choice but compliance.

These two variables — judicial confirmation before or after, and a request in writing versus physical control — create four possibilities, which conform to the four methods of compelling an accused's appearance created by Part XVI.[5] At the least intrusive level, a police officer can show a justice that there are reasonable grounds to believe that a person has committed an offence and consequently obtain a summons requiring the accused to appear in court on a specified date.[6] Alternatively, the officer can first encounter a person on the street committing an offence and then require that person to appear in court by means of an appearance notice. This appearance notice must subsequently be confirmed by a justice.[7] These mechanisms were the subject of Chapter 6.

This chapter, however, deals with the more intrusive methods involved in taking physical control of the person, either after judicial authorization to do so has been issued or before (that is, arrest with or without a warrant). It is worth noting, however, that Part XVI has a number of rules aimed at having the state use the least intrusive, yet effective, means possible. Where a peace officer seeks judicial authorization first, for example, the justice is to issue a summons, unless it is shown to be necessary in the public interest to issue a warrant.[8] If a peace officer has arrested a person, with or without a warrant, various sections provide for that person's release at the earliest reasonable point.[9] These limitations reflect the principle of restraint in the use of police powers explicitly stated in the *Code*.[10] It will be seen that this principle is also reflected, in various ways, in the arrest powers themselves.

---

4 The word "request" is used here for the sake of contrast, but there are legal consequences for failing to appear or otherwise comply with an appearance notice, undertaking, or summons, which can include an arrest warrant being issued (s 512(2)) or being sent to a judicial referral hearing (ss 512.3 and 524). Judicial referral hearings were added to the *Code* in 2019 by Bill C-75, above note 1: see the discussion in Chapter 6, Section C(1).

5 For an explanation of these provisions in chart form, see Steve Coughlan and Alex Gorlewski, *The Anatomy of Criminal Procedure: A Visual Guide to the Law*, [*Anatomy of Criminal Procedure*], 2nd ed (Toronto: University of Toronto Press, 2026), Chart 1.3(a), "Compelling Appearance Matrix."

6 Section 507(1)(b). See s 509 for the contents of a summons.

7 Sections 497, 505, and 508(1)(b).

8 Section 507(4).

9 Sections 498, 499, and 503(1.1).

10 Section 493.1.

This section deals first with arrest with a warrant, arrest without a warrant, and the various supporting provisions affecting those powers. It then briefly considers the arrest powers outside of Part XVI. Finally, the constitutional and other rights that arise on arrest are outlined. These constitutional rights are also relevant to detentions.

As a final preliminary point, however, before looking at when the *power* to arrest exists, it should be made clear exactly what constitutes an arrest as a matter of fact. An arrest consists of either the actual seizure or touching of a person with a view to their detention, or words of arrest accompanied by the person submitting to the arrest.[11] The word "arrest" need not be used, provided the accused can be reasonably supposed to have understood that they were under arrest.[12] Although reducing arrest to touching the accused can make it seem like "a children's game" and could appear to make the arrest an instantaneous thing, arrest is a continuing act, starting with the moment of custody and extending until the person is either released from custody or brought before a justice and detained.[13] The primary significance of this conclusion is that the powers available to make an arrest originally, such as the use of force, continue to be available.

## B. ARREST WITH A WARRANT

As discussed in Chapter 6, a warrant[14] can be issued only after an information that sets out the reasonable grounds to believe that a person has committed an offence is laid before a justice. Section 504 creates this rule for indictable offences, and section 795 adopts the procedures of Part XVI for summary conviction offences. A personal appearance by the peace officer is not essential, and it is possible to lay an information electronically.[15] Where, having heard the allegations of the informant and the evidence under oath of any witnesses, a justice who is satisfied that a case for doing so is made out can issue either a summons or a

11 *R v Whitfield*, [1970] SCR 46.

12 *R v Latimer*, [1997] 1 SCR 217 [*Latimer*]. This rule is, in principle, reasonable, though its actual application in *Latimer* amounted to justifying a police action that was consciously intended not to be an arrest, as an arrest: see Stephen G Coughlan, "Developments in Criminal Procedure: The 1996–97 Term" (1998) 9 *Supreme Court Law Review* (2d) 273 at 290–93.

13 *R v Asante-Mensah*, 2003 SCC 38 at paras 33 and 43 [*Asante-Mensah*].

14 For an explanation of these provisions in chart form, see *Anatomy of Criminal Procedure*, above note 5, Chart 1.3(b), "Compelling Appearance with Prior Judicial Scrutiny."

15 Section 508.1.

warrant requiring the accused to attend before a justice to answer the charge. A summons, rather than a warrant, must be issued unless the evidence discloses reasonable grounds to believe that it is "necessary in the public interest" to issue a warrant.[16]

This "necessary in the public interest" criterion was also formerly used in section 515 of the *Code* in considering bail for an accused pending trial. In *R v Morales*, it was struck down as unconstitutionally vague and therefore a violation of section 11(e) of the *Charter*.[17] That subsection has since been replaced by a new provision that specifies criteria to be used in deciding whether an accused's detention is necessary to maintain confidence in the administration of justice. The new provision was upheld by the Court in a 5:4 decision that has attracted some criticism.[18] In the context of section 507(4), the public interest criterion has received relatively little attention but has been found to comply with the *Charter*.[19] It is now also, like everything in the Compelling Appearance Part, subject to the principle of restraint in section 493.1, requiring that primary consideration be given to the release of the accused at the earliest reasonable opportunity.

This relative lack of attention to the section may largely be due to the fact that, unlike a bail hearing, the application for an arrest warrant is made on an *ex parte* basis. The issue has occasionally arisen in complaints of a violation of the right to a trial within a reasonable time, and there is some lower court authority suggesting that if the police are going to claim that a warrant, rather than a summons, is necessary,

---

16 Section 507(4).

17 [1992] 3 SCR 711 [*Morales*].

18 *R v Hall*, 2002 SCC 64. See the discussion of the decision in Don Stuart, "*R v Hall*: Annotation" (2002) 4 *Criminal Reports* (6th) 201; and Tim Quigley, "*R v Hall*: Annotation" (2002) 4 *Criminal Reports* (6th) 202. The Court has since explained the workings of that section in more detail: *R v St-Cloud*, 2015 SCC 27.

19 In *R v Budreo* (1996), 104 CCC (3d) 245 (Ont Ct Gen Div), the trial judge found that the "public interest" criterion in s 507(4) differed from its unconstitutional use in s 515, and that it ought to be interpreted narrowly to mean only the two grounds for detention that had been upheld in *Morales*, above note 17: on that interpretation it was constitutional. The decision was affirmed on appeal (*R v Budreo* (2000), 142 CCC (3d) 225 (Ont CA)). In *R v Penunsi*, 2019 SCC 39 the Court did not explicitly comment on the constitutionality question: however they adopted from the Ontario Court of Appeal decision in *Budreo* the view that (in the context of arrest for a peace bond application), situations in which it will be "necessary in the public interest" to issue an arrest warrant will be limited to cases in which proceeding in this fashion is necessary to preserve the integrity of the [peace bond] proceeding. This will only be so when a case has been made out by the informant that the defendant will not otherwise attend court or that the defendant poses an imminent risk. (emphasis in *Penunsi*).

then they have an obligation to make reasonable efforts to effect the arrest.[20] Authorities conflict on whether issuing a warrant with respect to a person already in custody in order to preserve jurisdiction is in the public interest.[21] For the most part, however, little attention has been paid to the issue.

Warrants are directed only to peace officers, though that term has a relatively broad definition, including, of course, police officers, but also, in some cases, correctional officers, customs officers, fisheries officers, mayors, pilots in command of an aircraft, and others.[22] The peace officers to whom a warrant is directed must be within the territorial jurisdiction of the person who issues it[23] but in practical terms there are few real obstacles to the use of an arrest warrant anywhere in the country. A warrant issued by any court other than a justice or a provincial court judge can automatically be executed anywhere in Canada.[24] A warrant from a justice or provincial court judge can be executed anywhere in the province in which it is issued.[25] In the case of fresh pursuit, however, a warrant can be executed anywhere in Canada, and in any event, a peace officer to whom a warrant is directed can execute that warrant even when not in the territory for which that person is a peace officer.[26] Finally, a warrant issued in one jurisdiction can be endorsed by a justice of another jurisdiction and become executable there if the accused is believed to be in that other jurisdiction.[27]

A warrant must name or describe the accused, set out briefly the offence that the accused is charged with, and order that the accused be brought before a justice to be dealt with according to law. Arrest warrants do not expire, but simply remain in force until executed.[28] Section 29 of the *Code* requires an officer executing a warrant to have it where it is feasible to do so, and to provide it where requested. It also

---

20 *R v Yellowhorse* (1990), 111 AR 20 (Prov Ct); *R v Heidecker*, [1992] AJ No 91 (Prov Ct); *R v Kha*, 2016 ABPC 29.

21 Compare *R v Horton*, [2002] OJ No 1219 (SCJ), and *Re Inverarity and the Queen* (1984), 18 CCC (3d) 74 (Sask QB). In any case, it is more difficult under current *Code* provisions for a court to lose jurisdiction than it was in the past: see the discussion in Chapter 11.

22 Section 2. See *R. v. Chan*, 2025 MBCA 4, concluding that a provincially-appointed public health inspector was a "peace officer" for purpose of the *Criminal Code*.

23 Section 513. Territorial division includes a province, a county, a town, or any other judicial division appropriate to the context: s 2.

24 Section 703.

25 Section 703(2).

26 Section 514.

27 Section 528.

28 Section 511.

requires anyone who arrests, with or without a warrant, to give notice to the arrested person of "(a) the process or warrant under which he makes the arrest; or (b) the reason for the arrest."[29] One might naturally have read this section disjunctively, on the assumption that (a) applies to arrests with a warrant and (b) to arrests without a warrant. However, this was not the approach taken by the Court in *R v Gamracy*, a decision that removed much of the real force of the provision.[30] In that case, an officer made an arrest, but only told the accused that there was an outstanding warrant. The officer neither had the warrant nor knew what offence the warrant dealt with. The Court held that this was sufficient compliance with section 29. The arrest was not an arrest with a warrant, but a warrantless arrest under section 495(1)(c), to be discussed below. In that event, "there is a warrant" was held to be sufficient notice of the reason for the arrest.

*Gamracy* is a pre-*Charter* case, and section 10(a) of the *Charter* now creates the constitutional right to be informed promptly on arrest of the reasons for the arrest. That right requires that an accused be given sufficient information to decide whether to submit to the arrest and to make an informed choice about whether to exercise the right to counsel, and it seems unlikely that the amount of information provided by the officer in *Gamracy* would meet that standard. However, although there is a significant amount of caselaw around section 10(a) (discussed below in this chapter), this particular issue has not arisen, and so it is arguable that *Gamracy* still represents the state of the law.[31]

## C. ARREST WITHOUT A WARRANT

Warrantless arrests[32] are governed by sections 494 and 495 of the *Code*, which create a number of arrest powers available to three groups.

---

29 Section 29.

30 [1974] SCR 640 [*Gamracy*].

31 *Gamracy*, above note 30, has been followed post-*Charter* but has not been considered in connection with the s 10(a) issue: see, for example, *R v Kozoway* (1993), 142 AR 323 (QB), aff'd (1994), 157 AR 79 (CA). The early s 10(a) caselaw in particular tended to look at circumstances where the reason an accused was detained changed during the course of an investigation, possibly justifying a rewarning, rather than at the information given at the time of the arrest. See, for example, *R v Borden*, [1994] 3 SCR 145 [*Borden*]; *R v Smith*, [1991] 1 SCR 714 [*Smith* 1991]; *R v Evans*, [1991] 1 SCR 869 [*Evans*]; and *R v Black*, [1989] 2 SCR 138 [*Black*].

32 For an explanation of these provisions in chart form, see *Anatomy of Criminal Procedure*, above note 5, Chart 1.3(d), "Arrest Without a Warrant."

Section 494(1) creates arrest powers available to anyone, section 494(2) creates a special arrest power relating to property owners, and section 495(1) creates arrest powers available only to peace officers. Section 494 is sometimes spoken of as providing power for a "citizen's arrest," although it can in fact be used by anyone, peace officers included. Historically, it is section 494 that descends more directly from the common law powers of arrest, while section 495 creates additional powers for peace officers, an office which did not exist when powers of arrest first developed.[33]

The different powers of arrest are defined largely by two variables: arrests for indictable offences versus criminal (that is, any) offences, and "finds committing" powers versus "reasonable belief" powers. In each case, the former option is more limited than the latter.

Some arrest powers are limited to indictable offences (that is, ones that can be prosecuted by indictment, which in this context includes hybrid offences).[34] Other arrest powers apply to criminal offences in general and, therefore, include summary conviction offences as well. Indeed, many provinces have incorporated the *Criminal Code* arrest powers into their provincial offence acts, so as a practical matter some *Code* arrest powers apply to non-*Code* offences.[35]

---

33 See *R v Lerke* (1986), 49 CR (3d) 324 at 330 (Alta CA) [*Lerke*]: "The power exercised by a citizen who arrests another is in direct descent over nearly a thousand years of the powers and duties of citizens in the age of Henry II in relation to the 'King's Peace.'" See also *Asante-Mensah*, above note 13 at para 40: "The development of modern police forces brought about a transfer of law enforcement activities from private citizens to peace officers. But it is the peace officer's powers which are in a sense derivative from that of the citizen, not the other way around."

34 This rule is currently stated in the *Interpretation Act*, RSC 1985, c I-21, s 34(1)(a). Bill C-14, art 13 above note 1, proposes to add to the *Criminal Code* the following provision:

> 493.01 For greater certainty, a reference to an indictable offence includes an offence that may be punishable on summary conviction if it is also an offence that may be prosecuted by indictment, unless the prosecutor has elected to proceed by way of summary conviction.

35 In addition, other arrest powers exist in other statutes. See, for example, *Asante-Mensah*, above note 13, and its discussion of the arrest power given to private citizens (and, therefore, to private security firms) by Ontario's *Trespass to Property Act*, RSO 1990, c T.21, or the extensive review of federal non-*Criminal Code* and provincial arrest powers in Law Reform Commission of Canada, *Arrest* (Ottawa: Law Reform Commission of Canada, 1986) [Law Reform Commission].

The "finds committing" standard requires that the person arresting has witnessed the commission of the offence.[36] The requirement is read to mean "apparently" finds committing, in the sense that a subsequent acquittal of the accused on the charge for which they were arrested does not retroactively invalidate the arrest power. Thus, in *R v Biron*, for example, the accused was properly arrested for causing a disturbance since an officer witnessed the behaviour constituting the disturbance. The fact that Biron was eventually acquitted of that charge (because there was no proof at trial of the specific allegation of shouting) did not mean that he was illegally arrested, and so he was still guilty of resisting a peace officer in the execution of duty.[37] *Biron* is a pre-*Charter* case and so it may now be possible to argue that an arrest made when the accused is ultimately found not to have committed an offence violates the right, in section 9, to be free from arbitrary detention.

"Reasonable grounds to believe" that an accused has committed an offence requires that the person performing the arrest subjectively believes that the person has committed the offence and that the belief is objectively justifiable. In other words, a reasonable person standing in the shoes of the arresting officer would have also believed that grounds for arrest existed. The objective standard for a warrantless arrest, therefore, is the same as that required for obtaining an arrest warrant.[38] Whether the standard is met in an individual case is not always easy to determine and depends on the particular facts. More than mere suspicion is necessary, but the police are not required to have a *prima facie* case before arresting. Accordingly, although police cannot arrest simply in order to investigate and obtain reasonable grounds, the fact that an investigation continues after an arrest does not automatically mean that the arrest was not based on reasonable grounds.[39]

There is an aspect of the meaning of the "reasonable grounds to believe" standard which has developed oddly: exactly what level of

36 See *R v Abel*, 2008 BCCA 54 at para 52: "before invoking [the power to arrest on the basis of 'finds committing' in s 495(1)(b),] the arresting officer must have reasonable grounds to believe that the person to be arrested is apparently in the process of committing a crime in his or her presence."

37 [1976] 2 SCR 56 [*Biron*]. There is a further complicating factor in *Biron*: the officer who arrested the accused was not the officer who witnessed the apparent offence, but that does not affect the main point. *Biron* was distinguished in *R v Sharma*, [1993] 1 SCR 650, where the accused was found not to have been properly arrested when the offence for which he was arrested was found to be *ultra vires*. The Court held at para 32 that *Biron* "deals with apparent perpetration of an offence, not apparent offences."

38 *R v Storrey*, [1990] 1 SCR 241.

39 *Ibid*; *R v Duguay, Murphy and Sevigny*, [1989] 1 SCR 93.

probability it requires. Section 495 used to contain the phrase "reasonable and probable grounds," and despite the fact that the language was changed decades ago to simply say "reasonable grounds," caselaw very commonly still uses that term. The Court specifically considered whether the removal of the words "and probable" lowered the standard and concluded that it did not.[40] Nonetheless there was a view in some lower courts that the "reasonable grounds" standard could be met without reaching the level of "probability."

The Supreme Court did, at one point, very explicitly reject this interpretation. In *R v Loewen*, the Alberta Court of Appeal had held that the reasonable grounds standard for arrest had been satisfied without the accused's guilt being probable.[41] The Supreme Court upheld the result that the accused's arrest was lawful but specifically said that they did so *despite* the fact that the court below

> mistakenly held that the requirement of "reasonable grounds" in s. 495(1)(*a*) is different from the requirement of "reasonable and probable grounds."[42]

Despite this, some Court of Appeal decisions continued to state that the reasonable grounds standard did not require probability.[43] This was commonplace enough that the claim that reasonable grounds need not be more probable than not made its way into the kind of "boiler plate" instructions that are often repeated nearly verbatim from case to case. Eventually, in *R v Beaver* the Supreme Court quoted that instruction in such a boiler plate description of the law[44] and then two years later relied on that decision to conclude in *R v Campbell* that:

> The standard of reasonable and probable grounds requires the Crown to establish the reasonable probability of the claimed exigency, based on the experience and expertise of the police and the relevant facts before them; it does not require the Crown to establish the exigency

---

40 See *Baron v Canada*, [1993] 1 SCR 416 at para 55, talking about a parallel change to search warrant provisions and concluding that the earlier standard:

> required reasonable "and probable" grounds and simultaneously established that the two words import the same standard. "Reasonableness" comprehends a requirement of probability.

41 *R v Loewen*, 2010 ABCA 255.

42 *R v Loewen*, 2011 SCC 21 at para 5.

43 See, for example, *R v Ha*, 2018 ABCA 233; *R v Glendinning*, 2019 BCCA 365; *R v Omeasoo*, 2019 MBCA 43; *R v Chapman*, 2020 SKCA 11; or *R v Kinsella*, 2022 NLCA 40.

44 See *R v Beaver*, 2022 SCC 54 [*Beaver*] at para 72, where it described the principles set out as "settled."

on the balance of probabilities (see *R. v. Beaver*, 2022 SCC 54, at para. 72, discussing the standard of reasonable and probable grounds for a warrantless arrest).[45]

The result is that the reasonable grounds standard is now, apparently, something more than reasonable suspicion but something less than a belief on a balance of probabilities.

What is particularly remarkable about all of this is that, in *Beaver*, the Supreme Court cites as authority for that claim the Alberta Court of Appeal decision in *Loewen*: the decision where they had singled out this exact claim as the only error in the decision! At no point in either *Campbell* or *Beaver* does the Court acknowledge, or even seem to recognize, that they are overturning a point of law they had very deliberately decided earlier.

Because the belief need only be "reasonable," it is possible that an arresting officer might be mistaken about some aspect of the situation and yet still hold a reasonable belief: reasonableness does not demand perfection.[46] Indeed, an officer might be mistaken about the identity of the person being arrested, but if the belief was a reasonable one, the arrest will still be lawful.[47] However, only a mistake about the *facts* is permissible: a mistake about the law cannot be reasonable. In *R v Tim*, an officer arrested the accused for possession of a controlled substance when he found him in possession of a gabapentin pill. The officer was correct about the nature of the pill but incorrect that gabapentin was a controlled substance. Concluding that a lawful arrest cannot be based on a mistake of law, the Supreme Court held:

> The concept of "reasonable and probable grounds" for arrest relates to the facts, not the existence of an offence in law. A police officer makes a mistake of law when the officer knows the facts and erroneously

---

45 *R v Campbell*, 2024 SCC 42 at para 114.

46 See, for example, *R v Whitfield*, 2023 ONCA 479 [*Whitfield*] at para 21:

> The standard of "reasonable grounds" focuses on the officer's state of mind and the reasonableness of the officer's belief, rather than the actual state of affairs. Reasonable grounds can be "based on a reasonable belief that certain facts exist even if it turns out that the belief is mistaken": *R. v. St. Clair*, 2021 ONCA 895, 408 C.C.C. (3d) 117, at para. 26, leave to appeal to S.C.C. refused, 40270 (November 24, 2022); see also *R. v. Robinson*, 2016 ONCA 402, 336 C.C.C. (3d) 22, at para. 40.

47 See *R v Araya*, 2025 ABCA 61, where the police were planning to arrest a target individual. Araya had a similar physical description to the target, was in a vehicle with him, and fled at the same time. The officer who arrested Araya was found to have done so lawfully even though he thought Araya was the original target of the arrest. See also *Whitfield*, above note 46.

concludes that they amount to an offence, when, as a matter of law, they do not.[48]

Both the subjective and objective tests must be met. It is easy to see that an objectively unreasonable arrest should not be allowed simply because of the officer's personal belief. Equally, though, even if reasonable grounds for arrest exist on an objective basis, the arrest is improper if the officer does not have the necessary subjective belief. The issue is not simply whether grounds to arrest exist, but whether the officer *acts upon* such grounds.[49]

## 1) Section 494 Arrest Powers

The arrest powers in section 494(1) are given to anyone and are the most limited powers. Anyone may arrest a person whom they find committing an indictable offence. Alternatively, anyone may perform an arrest when they believe, on reasonable grounds, that some person has committed a criminal offence *and* is escaping and being freshly pursued by some other person with authority to arrest.

Section 494(2) creates a slightly broader arrest power for property owners and their designates. Anyone who owns or is in lawful possession of property can arrest not only for indictable offences, but also for any criminal offence they find being committed on or in relation to their property. "Property" is defined in section 2 of the *Code* to include real or personal property. This power was amended in 2013 to allow it to be exercised on something slightly broader than the "finds committing" standard which had previously applied. A property owner can arrest not only at the time of the offence but also within a reasonable time after the offence if it is not feasible for a peace officer to make the arrest.[50]

---

48 *R v Tim*, 2022 SCC 12 at para 36. See also *Kosoian v Société de transport de Montréal*, 2019 SCC 59 [*Kosoian*], which in the context of a civil action against the police noted at para 78 that "[t]he 'reasonable grounds' concept relates to the *facts*, not to the existence in *law* of the offence in question."

49 *R v Coles*, 2003 PESCAD 3. See also *S(VA) v Grace*, 2016 ABCA 45, where an arrest was found to be unlawful without even considering the objective grounds, on the basis that the arresting officer did not subjectively believe the arrestee had committed an offence. Similarly, see *R v Caslake*, [1998] 1 SCR 51, where the Court held that a search that would have been objectively justifiable as an incident to an arrest was unreasonable because that was not the officer's subjective purpose.

50 See the discussion in Steve Coughlan, "Citizen's Arrest, Property Owners, and Private Fiefdoms" (2014) 18 *Canadian Criminal Law Review* 1. See also *R v Wilson*, 2019 ABPC 176, where the accused was found not to fall within this power: although he made the arrest (if it was one) a reasonable time after the offence, he had not found the complainant committing it.

Anyone other than a peace officer who makes an arrest is required to deliver the arrested person to a peace officer "forthwith," that is, as soon as reasonably possible or practicable under all the circumstances.[51]

## 2) Section 495 Arrest Powers

Peace officers' arrest powers are much broader. Sections 495(1)(a) and (b) effectively allow a peace officer to arrest in any situation but two: (1) where the officer did not find the accused committing the offence, the offence is only a summary conviction one, and no arrest warrant has been issued, or (2) where the officer believes that a summary conviction offence is about to be committed.

Section 495(1)(a) permits a peace officer to arrest anyone who "has committed an indictable offence or who, on reasonable grounds, he believes has committed or is about to commit an indictable offence." Section 495(1)(b) permits a peace officer to arrest anyone they find committing a criminal offence. Finally, section 495(1)(c) permits a peace officer to arrest a person if they reasonably believe that a warrant exists for the person's arrest. Police have no power to arrest a person for investigative purposes: rather, "the s. 495 power to arrest is intimately related to bringing persons before justice to answer criminal charges."[52]

Read in one fashion, the first clause of section 495(1)(a) would make the second clause redundant. If a peace officer could arrest anyone who as a matter of fact has committed an indictable offence, it would be unnecessary also to have a power to make such an arrest on reasonable grounds. In practice, the section has not been interpreted in such a broad way. Section 495(1)(a) is taken to require that the officer has personally witnessed the offence, believes on reasonable grounds that the offence has been committed, or believes on reasonable grounds that the offence is about to be committed.[53]

Of those powers in section 495(1)(a) it is the "reasonable grounds" arrest that is by far the most common and the one about which there is the most caselaw. The Court has summarized the applicable principles.

The arresting officer must subjectively have reasonable grounds, and those grounds must be justifiable from an objective viewpoint. The

51 *R v Cunningham* (1979), 49 CCC (2d) 390 (Man Co Ct).

52 *R v Wilson*, 2025 SCC 32 at para 62.

53 *R v Klimchuk* (1991), 67 CCC (3d) 385 (BCCA). The court distinguishes witnessing the offence personally in s 495(1)(a) from the "finds committing" power in s 495(1)(b), on the basis that the former is restricted to situations where the officer witnessed the offence but could not prevent it before its completion, while "finds committing" requires that the arrested person still be in the process of committing the offence.

subjective grounds look at whether the arresting officer honestly believed that the suspect committed the offence, which is often established through the officer's testimony, and therefore involves a credibility assessment on the part of the trial judge. The objective assessment is based on the totality of the circumstances known to the officer at the time of the arrest and should be judged from the perspective of a reasonable person with comparable knowledge, training, and experience. Claims about training and experience should not be uncritically accepted nor approached with undue skepticism, and deference is not necessarily owed to an officer's view only because of their training or experience. It should also be taken into account that arrests often occur in rapidly changing circumstances and must be based on the available information, which might be less than complete. However, police cannot rely on evidence discovered after the arrest to justify either the subjective or objective grounds. Also, in some cases, the actual arrest is made by one officer at the direction of another. In such cases, it is the officer who directed the arrest who must have had reasonable grounds, and it does not matter whether the officer who carried out the arrest had such grounds.[54]

For many years it had been unclear whether the rule which applied to reasonable grounds in search warrant applications also applied to warrantless arrests: that unlawfully obtained evidence could not enter into those grounds. The Court ultimately concluded that the same rule does apply: "a principled approach to the *Charter* mandates that police cannot rely on unlawfully obtained evidence in order to conduct a warrantless arrest."[55] One effect of this is that it creates the potential for "consequential" *Charter* breaches where, for example, not allowing the results of an unlawful search to enter into the reasonable grounds for an arrest means that there will also be an unlawful detention.

The "finds committing" arrest power in section 495(1)(b) authorizes an arrest at any time where the officer witnesses the actual commission of a summary or indictable offence. Section 495(1)(c) adds the power to arrest without warrant on the basis that a warrant exists. The Law Reform Commission of Canada noted that this latter provision could seem contradictory but recommended its retention. They noted that, although an officer who encounters a suspect at a traffic check or while on routine patrol typically could not, as a practical matter, obtain a copy of the warrant, the existence of the warrant amounts to "judicially

54 *Beaver*, above note 44 at para 72. The Court also notes there that contemporaneous police notes are desirable but not mandatory.

55 *R v Zacharias*, 2023 SCC 30 at para 26.

certified" reasonable grounds.[56] Note that because section 495(1)(a) is limited to arrests for indictable offences, only sections 495(1)(b) and (c) can be used in the case of summary conviction offences.

The principle of restraint is further reflected in section 495(2) of the *Criminal Code*, attaching limits to the arrest powers in section 495(1). However, this point was not established until 2025, when the Supreme Court found in *R v Carignan* that the interpretation of that section which had prevailed for the previous half-century was incorrect.[57] The section had long been understood as providing guidelines to police about how to exercise their powers of arrest: *Carignan* concluded that its requirements were "binding and mandatory" and that failure to comply with them would mean that an arrest was unlawful.[58]

Section 495(2) is drafted in a very oblique fashion. It is structured as a triple, and sometimes a quadruple, negative. It applies only in the case of arrests for relatively less serious offences. That is, according to section 495(2)(a) through (c), it applies to indictable offences in the absolute jurisdiction of a provincial court judge, to hybrid offences, and to summary conviction offences. In those cases, section 495(2) directs peace officers not to arrest simply because an arrest power exists; rather, the section calls for some other factor to be present as well. The officer only has an arrest power in those cases if they believe on reasonable grounds that an arrest is the only way to do one of three things:

(i) establish the identity of the person,
(ii) secure or preserve evidence of or relating to the offence, or
(iii) prevent the continuation or repetition of the offence or the commission of another offence.[59]

Alternatively, the officer also has an arrest power if they reasonably believe that the person will not attend court unless arrested; that is,

56 Law Reform Commission, above note 35 at 23–24.

57 *R v Carignan*, 2025 SCC 43.

58 *Carignan*, above note 57 at para 3.

59 Section 495(2)(d). Strictly, the section includes only these factors among aspects of the public interest, and the criterion for not arresting is that the public interest can be satisfied without an arrest. In *Carignan* it was argued that this reference to the "public interest" would be unconstitutionally vague, as in *R v Morales*, [1992] 3 SCR 711. The Court rejected that argument on the basis that no constitutional challenge had been brought: see paras 80–81. Note that in *R v Fosseneuve* (1995), 43 CR (4th) 260 (Man QB), it was held that the section had to be read down to only the three criteria listed on the grounds that, otherwise, the "public interest" criterion permitted an arrest on unconstitutionally vague grounds.

under the circumstances it is evident to the officer that an appearance notice will not be sufficient.[60]

Until *Carignan* these requirements were understood essentially as advice to police officers, but no more than that. In *Carignan*, based on statutory interpretation, the Court concluded that the phrase "a peace officer *shall not* arrest a person without warrant" (emphasis added) at the start of section 495(2) did in fact impose a legal obligation:

> In short, the text of the provision suggests that, in practice, peace officers have an obligation, before making any arrest without warrant, to assess whether the public interest can be satisfied and the person's attendance in court ensured in some other way. This would therefore mean that peace officers should refrain from making such an arrest where they believe on reasonable grounds that these two conditions are met.[61]

The reason that section 495(2) was for so long understood only to be directory rather than mandatory was because of section 495(3), and the Court also considered — and corrected — the understanding of that provision. That section reads:

> (3) Notwithstanding subsection (2), a peace officer acting under subsection (1) is deemed to be acting lawfully and in the execution of his duty for the purposes of
> (a) any proceedings under this or any other Act of Parliament; and
> (b) any other proceedings, unless in any such proceedings it is alleged and established by the person making the allegation that the peace officer did not comply with the requirements of subsection (2).

Until *Carignan* the indication in that section that an officer was "deemed to be acting lawfully" was understood to mean that the arrest was still lawful despite non-compliance with subsection (2): i.e., that the subsection was not binding. *Carignan* concluded that the purpose of the section was much narrower. It was only meant to provide protection from liability for police officers who make otherwise lawful arrests that do not comply with subsection (2).[62] As the Court put it there, "[t]he lawfulness of the peace officer's *conduct* (in the context of a civil liability

60 Section 495(2)(e). Also note s 497, which authorizes the use of an appearance notice when an officer does not arrest by virtue of s 495(2).

61 *Carignan*, above note 57 at para 66. The Court also considered the legislative history of the provision to determine the intention of Parliament, as well as the context and purpose of the provision.

62 *Carignan*, above note 57 at para 89.

suit or criminal prosecution) would be a very different question than the lawfulness of the *arrest* under the *Criminal Code* and the *Charter*."[63] The arrest itself will be unlawful, and so as a result:

> Section 495(3) *Cr. C.* therefore does not apply in the criminal trial of the person arrested without warrant. Nor does it apply where a *Charter* motion is brought in the course of such a criminal trial. It follows that accused persons can assert in their own criminal trial that their arrest without warrant, which they believe to be contrary to s. 495(2) *Cr. C.*, constitutes an infringement of the *Charter*.[64]

## 3) Other *Criminal Code* Arrest Powers

The *Code* contains many other arrest powers, mostly with a warrant, though occasionally other warrantless ones as well. The majority are arrest powers intended to provide a measure of compulsion to the judicial process. For a very long time arrest powers were the method of dealing with an accused who did not appear for fingerprinting or who violated a condition of the undertaking by which they were released, though now the use of a judicial referral hearing would be the preferred method.[65] A person who has agreed to act as surety for an accused released pending trial can apply to be released from that obligation and is then empowered to arrest the accused.[66] An accused may fail to appear for trial, resulting in the issuance of a bench warrant.[67] Proceedings may also be adjourned, stayed, and so on and need to be recommenced later, with the result that the appearance of the accused must be compelled again, and an arrest warrant is typically an option at these stages as well.[68] Similarly, arrest warrants can sometimes be used to compel the appearance of witnesses.[69] Arrest warrants can also be used to help preserve the jurisdiction of the Court.[70]

Not all the other arrest powers simply support the court process, however. Section 199(2) of the *Code* creates a particular warrantless

63 *Carignan*, above note 57 at para 99.

64 *Carignan*, above note 57 at para 90.

65 See the discussion of judicial referral hearings in Chapter 6, Section C(1). As a matter of fact such hearings are rarely held: see Pascale Legault, "Bail and Indigenous Over-Representation in Canadian Detention Facilities: Do the 2019 Amendments to the *Criminal Code* Offer a Viable Solution?" (2025) 73 *CLQ* 84.

66 Section 766(2).

67 Section 597(1).

68 Section 578(1)(b).

69 Sections 698, 704, and 705.

70 Section 485(2).

arrest power for a peace officer who finds someone keeping a common gaming house or anyone found therein. In addition, section 31 allows a peace officer who witnesses a breach of the peace to arrest "any person whom he finds committing the breach of the peace or who, on reasonable grounds, he believes is about to join in or renew the breach of the peace." Note that a "breach of the peace" is not itself a criminal offence,[71] though, of course, much behaviour that would constitute a breach of the peace would equally meet the definition of some offence, such as causing a disturbance, rioting, or unlawful assembly.[72]

The power in section 31 is limited to breaches of the peace that have already occurred. There had been some authority suggesting that, at common law, police had a power to arrest to prevent an apprehended breach of the peace.[73] However, the Supreme Court of Canada rejected that suggestion.[74] The Court distinguished between arresting a person to prevent a breach of the peace by that person, and arresting a person because that person's actions might cause a breach of the peace by others. In the latter case, the creation of an arrest power could not get past the "reasonably necessary" stage of the ancillary powers doctrine.[75] In essence, there would be steps the police could initially take short of arresting the person which would prevent the breach of the peace, and so an arrest was not necessary. Alternatively, if the person interfered with the ability of the police to take those other steps then that would be an offence and a statutory arrest power would exist. In either event, though, no common law power was needed.[76] In the case of a power to arrest a person who personally was about to commit the breach of the peace, the Court did not decide that no such power existed (because the question did not arise on the facts) but Côté J did state that whether or not such a power had ever existed, "I seriously question whether a common law power of this nature would still be necessary in Canada today."[77] The core of their reasoning here was that so many statutory arrest powers exist to cover that situation that there was no legislative gap to be filled in by the common law.[78]

---

71 *Frey v Fedoruk*, [1950] SCR 517.

72 See Bruce P Archibald, "*Hayes v. Thompson and Bell*: Annotation" (1985) 44 *Criminal Reports* (3d) 316.

73 *Hayes v Thompson* (1985), 44 CR (3d) 316 (BCCA) [*Hayes*]; *Brown v Durham Regional Police Force* (1998), 21 CR (5th) 1 [*Brown*]; *Fleming v Ontario*, 2018 ONCA 160.

74 *Fleming v Ontario*, 2019 SCC 45 [*Fleming*].

75 See the discussion in Chapter 2, Section A(3)(b).

76 *Fleming*, above note 74 at para 99.

77 *Ibid* at para 60.

78 *Ibid* at para 61.

## D. SUPPORTING POWERS

A number of provisions in the *Code* provide additional power or protection to peace officers or others performing arrests. Anyone making a lawful arrest, for example, is justified in using as much force as necessary to do so, provided they act on reasonable grounds.[79] This power is set out in the *Code* for arrests under that Act, but the use of reasonable force is incidental to arrests in any case, such as those carried out under some provincial Act.[80] Latitude is permitted, since peace officers have a duty to act, sometimes in difficult and exigent circumstances.[81] Nonetheless, an officer is criminally responsible for using excessive force.[82] In addition, the use of excessive force can mean that an otherwise lawful arrest is an arbitrary detention and violates section 9 of the Charter.[83]

A special rule applies to the use of force likely to cause death or grievous bodily harm to effect an arrest. Such action is permitted only when, even if there is a warrant, a warrantless arrest would be allowable; the person has taken flight to avoid arrest; the person using the force believes on reasonable grounds it is necessary for the purpose of protecting the officer or some other person from imminent or future death or grievous bodily harm; and the flight of the person cannot be prevented in a less violent manner.[84]

Anyone arresting the wrong person under a warrant is not criminally responsible, provided they believed in good faith and on reasonable grounds that the correct person was being arrested. This same protection also applies to anyone called on to assist in the arrest.[85]

Police have the power to search a person who has been arrested (this issue is discussed in Chapter 4).

Special rules apply when the police enter a dwelling house to make an arrest because of the increased privacy interest in that situation. At common law, relatively little additional protection was provided to a

---

79 Section 25(1). Section 25 is phrased in the language of justification, meaning that, in principle, it creates a defence to a criminal charge rather than a power. Practically speaking, the distinction is of little importance.

80 *Asante-Mensah*, above note 13.

81 *Ibid*. See also *R v Nasogaluak*, 2010 SCC 6 at para 35.

82 Section 26.

83 *R v Squires*, 2016 NLCA 54. *Squires* concerns an investigative detention rather than an arrest, but the principle that the arrest or detention must have been carried out reasonably or there will be a s 9 violation is the same in either case. See *R v Le*, 2019 SCC 34.

84 Section 25(4).

85 Section 28.

suspect in this situation, but the Court held in *R v Feeney* that some of the common law rules did not pass *Charter* scrutiny.[86] Therefore, some of those common law rules have now been overridden by statute.[87] In essence, the judicial pre-authorization requirement that applied to entry to conduct a search now also applies to entry to effect an arrest.

Peace officers are now required to obtain specific authorization on an arrest warrant if they wish to enter a dwelling house in order to effect the arrest. The person issuing the warrant must be satisfied on reasonable grounds that the person to be arrested will be present in the dwelling house. In addition, the officer executing the warrant must have grounds to believe that the person to be arrested is present immediately before entering the dwelling house.[88] Similarly, a separate warrant that simply authorizes peace officers to enter a dwelling house can be issued if an arrest warrant already exists, or the person can be arrested without warrant.[89] In either case, the warrant can include any conditions the judge or justice feels are advisable to ensure that the entry is reasonable under the circumstances.[90]

A peace officer can enter without a warrant in exigent circumstances, which include situations where the officer has reasonable grounds to believe that the entry is necessary to prevent imminent harm or death to some person, or is necessary to prevent the imminent loss or destruction of evidence relating to an indictable offence. Even then, however, warrantless entry is allowed only where there are

---

86 [1997] 2 SCR 13 [*Feeney*]. In *Feeney*, the Court held that the common law requirements for entry into a dwelling house to effect an arrest were simply that the officer had reasonable grounds to believe that the person sought was within the premises; proper announcement was made; the officer believed reasonable grounds for the arrest existed; and reasonable grounds for the arrest did exist on an objective basis. These requirements amounted to little more than having grounds for arrest and reasonably believing the person was in the dwelling house, though the Court also suggested that, before forcing entry, police should have requested and been refused admission (paras 24 and 26). The Court held that privacy interests, of increasing importance with the introduction of the *Charter*, were not adequately respected by these rules.

87 See Renee M Pomerance, "Parliament's Response to *R v Feeney*: A New Regime for Entry and Arrest in Dwelling Houses" (1998) 13 *Criminal Reports* (5th) 84, and Robert W Fetterly & Daniel A MacRury, "Arrest of Persons in Dwelling-House (*Feeney* Warrants — The First Three Years)" (2001) 45 *Criminal Law Quarterly* 101 (Part I) and (2001) 45 *Criminal Law Quarterly* 360 (Part II), for discussion of these provisions. Even though they are now governed by a statutory scheme, the various entry warrants are often referred to as "*Feeney* warrants."

88 Section 529.

89 Section 529.1.

90 Section 529.2.

reasonable grounds to believe that the person is in the house and the conditions for obtaining a warrant exist but the exigent circumstances make it impracticable to obtain a warrant.[91] In assessing the practicability of obtaining a warrant, courts will need to have regard to section 529.5, which permits applications for entry warrants to be made by telephone or other means of telecommunications.

Normally, a peace officer entering a dwelling house to effect an arrest must first announce their presence. However, the *Code* does sometimes permit an officer who is lawfully entering, either with or without warrant, to omit the prior announcement.[92] The justice issuing the warrant must be satisfied on reasonable grounds that prior announcement would expose the peace officer or some other person to imminent bodily harm or death, or that prior announcement would lead to the imminent loss or destruction of evidence of an indictable offence. Even then, the peace officer executing the warrant (or entering in exigent circumstances without a warrant) must also have reasonable grounds to believe those same things immediately before entering without announcement.[93]

Although the *Code* explicitly permits warrantless entry only in exigent circumstances, there is also a common law exception in the case of hot pursuit. This exception was specifically held in *Feeney* to be justified despite the new rules required by the *Charter*. "Hot pursuit" refers to situations where there is "continuous pursuit conducted with reasonable diligence, so that pursuit and capture along with the commission of the offence may be considered as forming part of a single

---

91 Section 529.3. See Heather Pringle, "Kicking in the Castle Doors: The Evolution of Exigent Circumstances" (2000) 43 *Criminal Law Quarterly* 86 for criticism of this provision. She argues, at 108, that it creates a "dangerous extension of the exigent circumstances doctrine as it has been generally understood in Canada." In particular, she notes that s 529.3 reverses *Feeney*, above note 86, on the question of whether potential loss of evidence can constitute exigent circumstances. The Supreme Court has declined to hold that this definition of "exigent circumstances" should be adopted outside of s 529.3, specifically for the *Controlled Drugs and Substances Act*: *R v Paterson*, 2017 SCC 15.

92 See the discussion in *R v Brown*, 2024 ONCA 453, a case where the police obtained only an entry warrant but executed it on a no-knock basis, unaware of the difference between *Feeney* warrants and search warrants.

93 Section 529.4. Although the judge or justice issuing the warrant is required to have reasonable grounds to believe, in relation to either ground, the officer is only required to have reasonable grounds to *suspect* imminent bodily harm or death, though the standard of reasonable belief applies to the loss of evidence. Reasonable suspicion is a lower standard than reasonable belief, and of the different standards here reflect the greater consequences flowing from the risk of bodily harm than from the risk of lost evidence.

transaction."[94] There is no strict requirement that the officers personally witnessed the offence, although clearly the definition requires a connection approaching that. In such cases, entry without a warrant is justified on a number of grounds, including that the offender should not be rewarded for having fled or be encouraged to do so, that a person who is fleeing the police will not have their "domestic tranquility" interrupted by the entry, and that it might not be possible to identify the offender later if they are not arrested immediately. The hot pursuit exception is not limited to indictable offences but applies more broadly, including to provincial offences.[95] It remains unsettled as to whether there is a requirement of prior announcement when an officer in hot pursuit enters to arrest.

## E. RIGHTS ARISING ON ARREST

The word "rights" in this context is used broadly to include not only those rights guaranteed by the *Charter* on arrest, but also statutory provisions that apply once an arrest has occurred and that offer protection to an accused.

### 1) Statutory Protections

As noted above, the *Code* provisions that deal with compelling appearance try to balance state concerns with respect for the accused's liberty interest. The *Criminal Code* sets out several obligations on the part of police following an arrest. Generally speaking, these provisions reflect the principles of restraint and attempt to limit the use of coercive police powers to the extent possible. As discussed in Chapter 6, this principle is now not only implicit in the structure of the provisions, but explicit as section 493.1.

Several of these provisions mirror section 495(2), discussed above, and its approach of creating an arrest power while also providing guidelines around when not to use it. As discussed in Chapter 6, sections 498, 499, and 503(1.1) provide opportunities for a peace officer to revisit the decision to arrest and to release the accused on some other basis, such as an appearance notice or undertaking, instead. Where the officer does not do that, section 503(1) requires that the arrested person

94 *R v Macooh*, [1993] 2 SCR 802 at 817 [*Macooh*], quoting from Roger E Salhany, *Canadian Criminal Procedure*, 5th ed (Aurora, ON: Canada Law Book, 1989) at 44.

95 *Macooh*, above note 94.

be taken in front of a justice of the peace without unreasonable delay to consider the issue of release.[96]

Other specific rights arise with respect to young persons who are arrested. Section 25 of the *YCJA*[97] gives a young person the right to counsel on arrest, which, of course, is already guaranteed by section 10(b) of the *Charter* (see the discussion below). In addition, the *YCJA* requires that notice of the arrest be given to a parent of the young person. Further, specific statutory rules about interrogations of a young person after arrest provide that any statement is not admissible where the young person was not given the chance to contact counsel and a parent, or was not given the opportunity to have either or both present.[98]

## 2) *Charter* Rights Arising on Arrest

Section 10 of the *Charter* creates specific guarantees arising on arrest. Indeed, those rights arise on either arrest or detention, and so are relevant in that latter context as well. As a result, a person who is subject to an investigative detention is also entitled to the rights in section 10.[99]

Unlike section 8, which has had significant impact on the rules regarding searches and how they are to be conducted, the impact of section 10 has largely been to add additional requirements to the information to be given to an accused at the time of an arrest. There has also been an impact on the procedures followed afterward to facilitate actual contact by the accused with counsel. Most of this caselaw developed fairly early under the *Charter*, and section 10 now has a relatively settled jurisprudence.[100]

Section 10 contains three separate rights: the right to be informed of the reason for the arrest or detention in section 10(a), the right to counsel in section 10(b), and the right to *habeas corpus* in section 10(c).

---

96 See the more complete discussion of s 503 and of judicial interim release in Chapter 6.

97 *Youth Criminal Justice Act*, SC 2002, c 1.

98 *Ibid*, ss 146(2)(c) and (d).

99 *R v Suberu*, 2009 SCC 33. See the discussion in Chapter 5, Section C(1).

100 One particular issue that (surprisingly) remains unsettled is whether s 10 applies in the case of arrests not made by peace officers. In *Lerke*, above note 33, the Alberta Court of Appeal held that when one private citizen arrests another, *Charter* rights arise. Specifically, in that case, the right against unreasonable search and seizure was at issue. In contrast, in *R v J(AM)* (1999), 137 CCC (3d) 213, the British Columbia Court of Appeal decided that *Charter* rights did not arise on a citizen's arrest. In *Asante-Mensah*, above note 13, the Supreme Court of Canada noted the issue, but found that they were not required to address it: see para 77.

Only the first two are relevant in the context of arrests and so the discussion here will look at those sections. First, however, it is worth adding a brief note about the consequences of a breach.

As with the violation of any *Charter* right, there is the possibility of a remedy under section 24 of the *Charter*. Frequently the result of a section 10 violation will be that a statement is obtained from an accused person, and therefore the remedial issue is often whether that statement should be excluded. A threshold issue in that analysis is whether the statement was "obtained in a manner" that violated a *Charter* right: whether there is a temporal, contextual, or causal connection between the breach and the evidence.[101] Most of the time it will be obvious that if, for example, a detainee was not properly informed of their right to consult with counsel and then made a statement, then the threshold requirement is met.

On some occasions, however, the police will recognize that they have failed to comply with section 10 rights and will seek to repair that situation. Where there has been a failure to properly inform a person of their right to counsel or give them an opportunity to consult, for example, the police might make a "fresh start": that is, advise the detainee again of their rights, in an effort to sever any future statement from the prior violation. If they do make an adequate fresh start, then any future evidence will no longer have been obtained in a manner that violated the *Charter*, and no section 24 remedy will be available.

Whether a fresh start has been made in any given case is a factual determination, and it is not sufficient simply that the police advise the person properly of their rights at the later stage. The fundamental issue is whether any future statement or evidence can truly be seen to no longer have a connection to the prior breach or any evidence obtained because of it. Factors to consider in deciding whether there has been a fresh start or not include:

- whether the police informed the accused of the *Charter* breach and dispelled its effect with appropriate language;
- whether the police cautioned the accused after the *Charter* breach but before the impugned evidence was obtained, including telling the accused that they should not be influenced by anything they have already said to the police or the police have already said to them;
- whether the accused had the chance to consult counsel after the *Charter* breach but before the impugned evidence was obtained;

101 See, for example, *R v Mack*, 2014 SCC 58 at para 38.

- whether the accused gave informed consent to the taking of the impugned evidence after the Charter breach;
- whether and how different police officers interacted with the accused after the *Charter* breach but before the impugned evidence was obtained; and
- whether the accused was released from detention after the *Charter* breach but before the impugned evidence was obtained.[102]

### a) Section 10(a)

Section 10(a) provides that an accused is to be informed promptly of the reasons for the arrest or detention. The Court held in *R v Evans* that this right "is founded most fundamentally on the notion that one is not obliged to submit to an arrest if one does not know the reasons for it."[103] This section has provided less protection than it might, however. The test focuses on what the accused can be reasonably supposed to have understood, rather than on any precise words used.[104] In itself, that need not be objectionable, but it has been applied in a way with the potential to weaken the right. In *R v Latimer*, for example, the police decided not to arrest the accused and told him that he was being "detained for investigation" instead. That is, the police consciously purported to take the accused into custody on a basis not legally available (since no such power to detain for investigation existed) and offered that false explanation to the accused. The Court, nonetheless, relied on *Evans* to find that the accused knew he was in an extremely grave situation with regard to his daughter's death and, therefore, there was no section 10(a) violation.[105]

Similarly, in *R v Smith* (1991), the practical impact of section 10(a) was reduced. In that case, the accused was told that he was under arrest in connection with a shooting incident, but he was not told that the victim had died. The Crown conceded that section 10(a) had been violated, but relied on the accused's subsequent waiver of the right to counsel. The Court agreed, holding that, even if the accused was not

102 *Beaver*, above note 44 at para 103.

103 *Evans*, above note 31 at 886–87.

104 *Ibid* at 888. See, for example, *R v Mohamed*, 2014 SCC 63, aff'g 2013 ABCA 406, in which, during what began as a routine traffic stop, the officer told the accused that she smelled marijuana and asked him whether any was in the car: this was taken to be sufficient to convey that the officer was beginning a criminal investigation into an offence involving marijuana.

105 *Latimer*, above note 12 at para 31. Similarly see *R v Krieger*, 2015 BCCA 64 where the accused was arrested for importing narcotics into the country, but there was found to be sufficient compliance with s 10(a) when he was told he had been arrested for "smuggling." See also *R v Roberts*, 2018 ONCA 411.

aware of the specific charge, he had sufficient information to know the extent of his jeopardy, and therefore his waiver of counsel was valid despite the section 10(a) violation.[106]

Although allowing an accused to decide whether to submit to an arrest is described as the primary reason for section 10(a), from the start it has been acknowledged that a secondary reason is linked to the right to counsel in section 10(b): "[a]n individual can only exercise his section 10(b) right in a meaningful way if he knows the extent of his jeopardy."[107] This aspect of section 10(a) has received particular attention in cases where an accused is originally arrested for one reason, but the reason for their continued detention then changes. The Court has held that it can be necessary to re-advise the accused so that they can consider anew whether to seek legal advice.[108] See the discussion at the end of this chapter as to what type of change in circumstance is necessary to trigger section 10 a second time.

### b) Section 10(b)

Section 10(b) guarantees the right "to retain and instruct counsel without delay and to be informed of that right." The Court has noted that this protection is provided because the effective assistance of counsel is seen as crucial in our society, and, indeed, the right to it is a principle of fundamental justice.[109] The purpose of the right, the Court has said, is to provide an accused with an opportunity to be informed of their rights and obligations and to obtain advice on exercising those rights and fulfilling those obligations. In particular, upon arrest the accused has been deprived of liberty and may need legal assistance in regaining it. Equally, or even more important, the accused is at risk of self-incrimination and is in need of legal advice, particularly advice about the right to silence and how to exercise it.[110] For that reason the "without delay" requirement is usually treated quite seriously.[111] After

---

106 *Smith* 1991, above note 31.

107 *Black*, above note 31 at 152–53.

108 *Borden*, above note 31; *Smith* 1991, above note 31; *Evans*, above note 31; *Black*, above note 31.

109 See *Lavallee, Rackel & Heintz v Canada (Attorney General); White, Ottenheimer & Baker v Canada (Attorney General)*; *R v Fink*, [2002] 3 SCR 209; *R v GDB*, 2000 SCC 22.

110 *R v Bartle*, [1994] 3 SCR 173 at 191 [*Bartle*]; *R v Manninen*, [1987] 1 SCR 1233 at 1242–43 [*Manninen*]. See also *R v Grant*, 2009 SCC 32 at para 28.

111 See, for example, *R v Culotta*, 2018 ONCA 665, aff'd 2018 SCC 57 where the accused, following a boating accident, was arrested at 3:17 am, while she was in an ambulance receiving medical treatment. The officer followed the ambulance to the hospital and waited for a break in the medical treatment, at which point

the accused has been informed of the right to counsel, actual access to counsel can sometimes be delayed, but only as an exceptional step. There must be case-specific concerns for police safety, public safety, or the preservation of evidence in order to justify delay in providing access to counsel.[112] When there has been delay it is not always necessary to determine the exact point at which the right to counsel *should* have been offered: only that it was not offered soon enough.[113]

In practice, section 10(b) is effectively restricted to that purpose; that is, it was argued that a guaranteed right "to retain and instruct counsel" ought to include more than an initial consultation with counsel before being interrogated — it ought also to guarantee the assistance of counsel *during* the interrogation. The Court, however, concluded that this was not so. Rather, "an initial warning, coupled with a reasonable opportunity to consult counsel when the detainee invokes the right, satisfies s 10(*b*)."[114] In some circumstances, an accused might become entitled to a further opportunity to contact counsel mid-interrogation, but that is the extent of the right (see the discussion in Section E(2)(b), below in this chapter).

It is also worth observing that section 10(b) does *not* require the police to tell a detainee of their right to silence. Indeed, there is no absolute requirement that police inform every detainee of their right to silence. However, where a detainee is not told of that right there is a significant risk that any subsequent statement will be found not to be voluntary and to have been obtained in violation of the detainee's section 7 right against self-incrimination.[115] It is therefore common for police to advise a detainee of their right to silence, but the failure to do so is not a *Charter* violation.

---

he cautioned the accused. The Ontario Court of Appeal (upheld by the Supreme Court) concluded at para 35 that while the officer "may have had innocent — even benevolent — reasons for his delay, there can be no doubt that this suspension violated the appellant's rights to retain and instruct counsel 'without delay' (or 'immediately') upon detention."

112 *R v Griffith*, 2021 ONCA 302 at para 38. See also *R v Nguyen*, 2016 BCCA 32, or *R v Wu*, 2017 ONSC 1003, adopted in *R v Rover*, 2018 ONCA 745 at para 28, holding that delay is justified "where urgent and dangerous circumstances arise or where there are concerns for officer or public safety."

113 See *R v Thompson*, 2020 ONCA 264 at paras 67–71.

114 *R v Sinclair*, 2010 SCC 35, [2010] 2 SCR 310 at 311 [*Sinclair*].

115 *R v Tessier*, 2022 SCC 35 at para 79. The Court also holds at para 83 that if the person being questioned is a suspect — which is not the same as being a detainee (see the discussion of psychological detention in Chapter 5) — then "the absence of a police caution is not merely one factor among others to be considered. Rather, it is *prima facie* evidence of an unfair denial of the choice to speak to police."

Note that, like all *Charter* rights, the rights arising in section 10(b) are subject to the reasonable limits clause in section 1. In most cases, a failure to comply with one of the aspects of the right to counsel will not be saved under section 1, which makes *Charter* rights subject to "such reasonable limits *prescribed by law* as can be demonstrably justified in a free and democratic society."[116] The emphasized phrase requires that, if a *Charter* violation is to be saved, the police must have been given, either by statute or common law, the power to override the *Charter* right in question. Most commonly, if a police officer fails to give sufficient information to an accused about contacting counsel or some other aspect of section 10(b), that failure is not prescribed by law — it is simply an oversight. Therefore, section 1 analyses arise only infrequently with regard to the right to counsel, since they are typically settled at this relatively straightforward step, prior to getting into any difficult balancing of what sorts of limits are justifiable in a free and democratic society.

However, it is possible for a statute to prescribe a limit on section 10(b), like any other right, and in those cases the courts must consider whether the limit is justified. Accordingly, it was determined that statutory limits that prevent an accused from having access to counsel prior to blowing into a roadside screening device or performing roadside sobriety tests can be justified.[117]

In a typical case where section 10(b) rights have not been limited by section 1, however, various obligations have been imposed on the police at the time of the arrest or detention. The Court has divided these into "informational" and "implementational" obligations,[118] and it is convenient to discuss them under those headings.

### i) *Informational Duties*

Most obviously, section 10(b) specifically sets out the requirement that an accused must be informed of the right to retain and instruct counsel without delay. Police officers normally fulfill this duty by reading to the accused a "standard caution" which is distributed to them. This caution is intended to be as instructive and clear as possible, but in most cases, the police are not required to take any steps other than

---

116 *Charter*, s 1 [emphasis added].

117 *R v Thomsen*, [1988] 1 SCR 640; *R v Orbanski*; *R v Elias*, 2005 SCC 37. Note that in December 2018 all of the provisions concerning roadside screening and breathalysers that the previous caselaw had been based on were repealed and replaced with new provisions. It is not unlikely that many of these same right to counsel issues will therefore be relitigated around the new ss 320.27(1) and 320.27(2): see, for example, *R c Beaulieu*, 2019 QCCQ 3999.

118 *Bartle*, above note 110.

reading the caution to be sure that the accused has actually understood the right. Where special circumstances do exist, however, the police must take additional steps to be sure that the accused comprehends the right. Such special circumstances could include language difficulties, a known or obvious mental disability, or any genuine inability to comprehend the right on the part of the accused.[119] Conversely, exceptional circumstances can also justify delaying compliance with these informational duties.[120]

Other information must also be included in the standard caution. The police must give the accused information about access to counsel free-of-charge for persons who meet the financial criteria set by provincial legal aid plans. In addition, the accused should be given information about access to immediate temporary legal advice, irrespective of financial status.[121] In the latter case, the accused should also be told how to gain access to the service, for example, by telling the accused that they will be given the telephone number for duty counsel if they so wish.[122] However, police compliance with the duty to inform an arrested person of how to gain access is determined with regard to the circumstances of the case. In *Latimer*, for example, the Court held that there was no section 10(b) violation when the police did not give the accused the telephone numbers for either the duty counsel scheme in the province or the local legal aid office. They held that the former service was not available to the accused since it operated only outside normal business hours and that the telephone number for the latter service was easily available by looking in the phone book.[123] The Court did stress, though, that more might be required of the police in other cases.

Although the police must inform an accused of any existing duty counsel scheme in the province, the Court held in *R v Prosper* that section 10(b) does not impose an obligation on provinces to have such

---

119 *Evans*, above note 31; *Bartle*, above note 110. See, for example, *R v Polusmiak*, 2022 PECA 8, where the accused had obvious language difficulties and had to be shown rather than told how to comply with the ASD demand, which should have made clear to the officers that simply reading the accused her s 10 rights was insufficient.

120 *R v Mian*, 2014 SCC 54. In *Mian* the Court declined to decide whether protecting the integrity of a separate investigation would justify not immediately informing an accused of the reasons for arrest (thereby complying with s 10(a)) or allowing contact with counsel (thereby complying with s 10(b)). On the facts, it had not been shown that the separate investigation into drug trafficking that had occasioned the stop of the accused would have been jeopardized by giving him his s 10 rights.

121 *R v Brydges*, [1990] 1 SCR 190.

122 *Bartle*, above note 110 at 195. See also *R v Pozniak*, [1994] 3 SCR 310.

123 *Latimer*, above note 12.

a scheme.[124] Practically speaking, however, while formally refusing to create such a requirement, the Court left provinces with little realistic alternative. Relying on an implementational duty, discussed below, the Court held that, although there need not be a duty counsel scheme, police must nonetheless hold off from attempting to gain incriminatory evidence from an accused who expresses the wish to contact counsel until that person has had the opportunity to do so.[125] This holding would mean, for example, that police frequently could not administer breathalyzer tests unless a duty counsel system was in place. As a matter of fact, Nova Scotia, the province from which *Prosper* arose and which at the time lacked a duty counsel scheme, implemented one in the wake of that decision.

Further, if an accused who initially indicates a desire to speak to counsel later indicates they have changed their mind, an additional informational obligation is imposed on the police: they must rewarn that person of the right to a reasonable opportunity to consult with counsel, and more importantly must also inform the person of the obligation on the part of the police to hold off from eliciting evidence until that has occurred (see the discussion below of this obligation). Police are required to give this additional information (generally referred to as a "*Prosper* warning") so that an accused who nonetheless proceeds to speak with the police will understand what they are giving up.[126] The "change of mind" need only be apparent, in the sense that the issue is whether it appears to the officer that the accused has chosen not to speak to counsel, not whether the accused has in fact made that choice. Further, the accused need only be foregoing the right to an immediate consultation with counsel in order to be entitled to a *Prosper* warning, not waiving the chance to consult with counsel at any point.[127]

The police also must not act to undermine the right, by making disparaging comments about counsel's loyalty, commitment, availability, or the amount of legal fees, for example.[128] Similarly, offering a one-time-only plea bargain with a time limit that expires before an accused will be able to reach counsel is a section 10(b) violation. The Crown or police should offer any plea bargain to the accused's lawyer or to the accused with counsel present, unless there has been an express waiver

---

124 [1994] 3 SCR 236 [*Prosper*].

125 *Manninen*, above note 110.

126 *Prosper*, above note 124. This obligation was reaffirmed by the Court in *R v Willier*, 2010 SCC 37 [*Willier*].

127 See *R v Fountain*, 2017 ONCA 596 [*Fountain*] for both of these points.

128 *R v Burlingham*, [1995] 2 SCR 206 at 221 [*Burlingham*].

of counsel. This is a requirement in all cases, not simply in those where the offer has an expiration date.[129]

Finally, note that the informational aspects of the section 10(b) right arise in every arrest. All accused, whether they have expressed an interest in learning more about duty counsel or any other aspect of the right, are to be given all the information noted above.[130] This stands in contrast to the implementational requirements of section 10. Also, because the purpose of the right to counsel is to allow an accused to be protected against self-incrimination, section 10 rights are "triggered" again if there is a substantial change in the circumstances affecting the accused's degree of jeopardy. Failure to rewarn in such situations might violate section 10(a) and section 10(b).[131] Both of these issues are discussed in the next section.

*ii) Implementational Duties*

In addition to informing an accused of the right to counsel, two further correlative duties can arise on arrest. As is discussed further below, these duties only arise where an arrested person has in fact expressed a desire to contact counsel.

First, in such cases, the police must provide that person with a reasonable opportunity to speak with counsel. In *R v Manninen*, for example, the accused was arrested at a private business, and the Court found that there was no reason that the police could not have allowed him to use the telephone in that office, rather than wait until they returned to the police station. The accused was not required to ask to use the telephone; the obligation to facilitate contact with counsel meant that the police should have offered him its use. A police officer is not required to offer their own cell phone to an accused, but nonetheless has a duty to provide phone access as soon as practicable, in order to reduce the possibility of accidental self-incrimination.[132]

---

129 *Ibid* at 230. One might think of these aspects of the right to counsel as implementational rather than informational, but the Court speaks of them as the latter. Classifying them as informational does, in the Court's analysis, make them less easily subject to waiver: see Section E(2)(b), below in this chapter.

130 *Bartle*, above note 110. See the discussion of waiver of s 10(b) rights, below in this chapter.

131 *R v Paternak*, [1996] 3 SCR 607. The failure to rewarn would be a violation of the informational duties, but in addition, a violation of implementational duties would also arise, since the police would also have been obliged to facilitate the accused's renewed contact with counsel. See the discussion in Section E(2)(b), below in this chapter.

132 *R v Taylor*, 2014 SCC 50 at para 28. See also *R v Ector*, 2018 SKCA 46, holding that the duty to facilitate might require police to allow the accused to contact a third party in order to obtain the name of counsel.

The fact that a detainee has their own cell phone with them will be a relevant consideration, though it does not guarantee that the person should be permitted to use it immediately, for example from the side of the road.[133] The question will always be situation-dependent, and the onus will be on the Crown to show that a private phone conversation was not reasonably feasible in the circumstances.[134] In situations of urgency or other impracticality facilitating contact might temporarily be postponed, but otherwise the obligation should be complied with.[135] A reasonable opportunity to consult with counsel includes the right to do so in private, whether privacy is specifically requested or not.[136] Subject to the issue of reasonable diligence, discussed below, this right also includes the opportunity to contact the counsel of one's choice.[137] The reasonable opportunity might include internet access as a means of finding counsel.[138]

Second, when an arrested person has requested counsel, the police must hold off from questioning or otherwise seeking to elicit evidence from that person until they have had a reasonable opportunity to contact counsel. Thus, in *Manninen*, it was fairly clear that there was a section 10(b) violation when the police immediately questioned the accused and paid no attention to his expressed wish to speak to counsel. Equally, it meant there had been a violation in *R v Ross*, where the accused was required to participate in a lineup after having been unable to reach his counsel at 2 a.m. In that case, the Court held that it was unsurprising that counsel could not be reached at that hour, that there was no urgency or other compelling reason to conduct the lineup immediately, and, therefore, that the police were required to hold off.[139] As noted above, this duty to hold off also prevents the police from conducting breathalyzer tests without first giving the accused the reasonable opportunity to consult with counsel.[140] Indeed, the Court has found that a standard caution which concludes

133 *R v Tremblay*, 2021 QCCA 24.

134 *Ibid* at para 34.

135 *Manninen*, above note 110. See, for example, *R v Fan*, 2017 BCCA 99 where arrests were made at a remote location with no telephone or internet access, and the accused were not English speakers. The police provided the accused with written cards explaining their *Charter* rights, but no actual contact with counsel was facilitated until the accused were taken back to the station, where translators were available by telephone.

136 *R v Playford* (1987), 61 CR (3d) 101 (Ont CA).

137 *R v Ross*, [1989] 1 SCR 3 at 10–11 [*Ross*]; *Willier*, above note 126.

138 See, for example, *R v McKay*, 2014 ABQB 70; *R v Alaia*, 2017 ABPC 74; *R v Thompson*, 2014 ABPC 83; or *R v Bernesky*, 2014 ABPC 98.

139 *Ross*, above note 137.

140 *Prosper*, above note 124.

with the words "do you wish to say anything" violates the duty to hold off.[141] However, that the police cannot attempt to elicit evidence does not necessarily mean that they cannot ask *any* questions of the accused.[142]

These implementational duties differ in an important regard from the informational ones, in that they are not quite so firmly guaranteed. This is true in three separate but related ways: they do not arise for every accused, they can be waived, and they can be lost through a lack of reasonable diligence.

First, the implementational duties arise only when an accused has indicated a wish to speak to counsel. Unless there is evidence that suggests the accused did not understand the right to counsel, then the onus is on the accused to prove that they asked to speak to counsel but were denied the right, or that they were denied any opportunity even to ask to speak to counsel.[143] This qualification is distinct from the informational components of the right, all of which must be told to all accused whether they request information about, for example, legal aid or not.[144] This makes the analysis of whether, factually, the accused did or did not ask for counsel crucial, since it can settle whether there was a section 10 breach or not.[145]

Second, implementational duties and informational duties are treated differently when considering waiver. The latter virtually cannot be waived. A valid waiver requires that an accused have full knowledge of the right they are giving up. A person who has not yet received all the informational components of the right to counsel is therefore not in a position to waive the right.[146] Accordingly, even if an arrested person indicates that they do not want to hear the information in the standard caution, that will not normally be a valid waiver and the police have an obligation to inform them nonetheless. Before the police can choose to

141 *R v GTD*, 2018 SCC 7.

142 *R v Rowson*, 2015 ABCA 354, aff'd 2016 SCC 40 suggests at para 29 that, for example, police might need to ask a driver at the scene of an accident how much gas is in the tank of a vehicle or whether it contained dangerous goods before moving a damaged vehicle.

143 *R v Baig*, [1987] 2 SCR 537.

144 *Bartle*, above note 110.

145 In *R v Culotta*, 2018 ONCA 665, aff'd 2018 SCC 57, the accused was asked whether she wished to speak to a lawyer and replied "No, my parents should be here soon. We have a family lawyer." At both the Supreme Court of Canada and the Ontario Court of Appeal, the majorities took that statement to be declining counsel and therefore found no breach, while the dissents found it to be a request to speak to counsel — to a specific counsel — and therefore would have concluded there was a breach.

146 *Ibid* at 204.

forgo the obligation, it would not only be necessary for the person to have said that they understand the right to counsel, but there would also need to be reasonable grounds to believe that the claim was correct.[147]

In contrast, implementational duties can be waived. Most simply, an arrested person could explicitly decline to contact counsel after being given the opportunity to do so. Implicit waivers are also possible, though the standard is high and the waiver, though implicit, must be clear and unequivocal.[148] In particular, cooperating with the investigation by answering questions or participating in a lineup will not constitute a waiver.[149]

Finally, implementational duties can be lost. If an arrested person "is not being reasonably diligent in the exercise of his rights," then the correlative duties from *Manninen* are not a bar to the police continuing their investigation nonetheless.[150] This rule was laid down in *R v Tremblay*, a case where the trial judge found that the accused was actively obstructing the investigation, and the evidence suggested that he was using the right to counsel as a means of stalling a breathalyzer test. Even so, the Court found a section 10(b) violation in his case, though in *obiter* they created the "reasonable diligence" rule and did not exclude the breathalyzer evidence under section 24(2). Lack of reasonable diligence does not lead to a complete loss of section 10(b) rights. The arrested individual still has the right to speak to counsel. However, the police are no longer obliged to hold off their investigation until the arrested person has had a chance to do so. This is the case even if a person who has lost the right through lack of reasonable diligence subsequently reiterates the wish to speak to counsel.[151]

Because the accused is entitled to contact counsel of choice, the police must hold off from questioning until they have had a chance to do so. However, "reasonable diligence" is to be interpreted in context in such a case. That is, at this point the accused needs only preliminary advice, which raises simpler issues than choosing counsel for trial. Accordingly, at some point reasonable diligence will oblige the accused to speak to someone other than their counsel of choice,[152] but that does

147 *Ibid* at 206. The Court offers the example of a person who, after having already spoken to duty counsel, is rewarned of the right to counsel because of a change in circumstances during questioning. In such a case, it might not be necessary to tell the person once again of the existence of duty counsel.

148 *R v Clarkson*, [1986] 1 SCR 383 at 394–95 [*Clarkson*], quoting *Korponay v Attorney General of Canada*, [1982] 1 SCR 41.

149 *Manninen*, above note 110; *Ross*, above note 137.

150 *R v Tremblay*, [1987] 2 SCR 435 at para 9 [*Tremblay*].

151 *R v Smith*, [1989] 2 SCR 368 [*Smith* 1989].

152 *Ross*, above note 137: *Willier*, above note 126.

not happen automatically.[153] If an accused does agree to speak with some other lawyer (duty counsel, for example) and obtains advice, then the implementational duty has been complied with and the accused no longer has a right to wait to speak to counsel of choice.[154] However, this must be a genuine *choice* on the part of the accused: it is improper for the police to "steer" an accused towards duty counsel instead.[155]

Given the particular facts of *Tremblay* it is unfortunate that the Court chose to describe the accused's obstructionist behaviour as a lack of reasonable diligence. The real complaint in *Tremblay* seemed to be that the accused was asserting his *Charter* right not because he had any real interest in it, but as an improper means of avoiding responsibility. That objection is consistent with a purposive approach to the *Charter* and to the approach taken to other rights.[156] But phrasing the concern, in an understated way, as a lack of reasonable diligence has led to an expansion of the standard: a change to the detriment of all arrested persons. The result is to make the argument against the existence of the *Charter* rights plausible in a much wider range of cases.[157] In *Smith*, for example, the accused was arrested at 7 p.m. and, after several stops en route, he asked to call counsel at 9 p.m. upon arriving

---

153 See *Fountain*, above note 127, where after six and a half hours the accused was told that his lawyer would not be available until the next morning, and was asked whether he wanted to wait or to speak to a legal aid lawyer immediately. The Ontario Court of Appeal concluded at para 36 that "In this context, there was therefore nothing unreasonable in Mr. Fountain opting to wait until the next day" and therefore it could not be said he had either waived the right or failed to be reasonably diligent. In general, whether there was an obligation on the part of the police to wait for the accused's counsel of choice is a very fact-dependent question: see, for example, *R v Larson*, 2015 SKCA 143; *R v Rowson*, 2015 ABCA 354 or *R c Stevens*, 2016 QCCA 1707.

154 *Willier*, above note 126; *R v McCrimmon*, 2010 SCC 36 [*McCrimmon*].

155 See the discussion of this issue in *R v Jhite*, 2021 ONSC 3036 at pars 38ff.

156 In the context of disclosure, for example, the Court has required that an accused who is aware of undisclosed information must actively seek it out. An accused cannot choose to have their *Charter* right to disclosure violated so that they can then seek a remedy: see the discussion in Chapter 8. Similarly, in cases that deal with the right to a trial within a reasonable time, the Court's analysis has tried to prevent giving a remedy to an accused who does not genuinely want a prompt trial, but actually wants a *Charter* s 11(d) violation and a remedy therefore: see *R v Morin*, [1992] 1 SCR 771.

157 In *Prosper*, above note 124, it can hardly be surprising that the Court found the accused had been reasonably diligent when he made fifteen phone calls, all unsuccessful, to all twelve legal aid lawyers on the list given to him by the police. He was not also required "to call at random lawyers listed in the Yellow Pages late on a Saturday afternoon and plead for free or cut-rate legal advice": *Prosper* at para 56. In making this decision, however, the Court rejected the argument that had succeeded in the Court of Appeal.

at the police station. After being given a telephone book he decided not to call because only his lawyer's office number was listed, and he did not expect that his lawyer would be in the office at that time. The court split 4:3 as to whether the accused had complied with the reasonable diligence standard, with the majority finding that he had not. It is difficult not to think that a different decision would have been reached had the Court asked itself whether the accused was only pretending to assert his *Charter* rights as a way of obstructing the investigation.[158]

The rule that an implicit waiver of *Charter* rights must be clear and explicit is not, at a theoretical level, easily reconciled with the view that no implementational duties arise unless an accused requests counsel and that an accused must be reasonably diligent in exercising the right. All three are ways of deciding that the accused does not benefit from the implementational duties, but they set different standards for deciding the issue. The fact that silence would not be a clear and explicit waiver leads to the conclusion that the arrested person was entitled to the implementational duties. But silence would be a failure to request counsel, or a failure of reasonable diligence, which leads to the conclusion that the arrested person was not entitled to the implementational duties. Silence, or other ambiguous behaviour on the part of an accused, allows courts to apply either of the conflicting lines of authority, with conflicting results.[159] One might suggest that requiring police simply to ask the accused "Do you want to speak to a lawyer?" at the conclusion of a *Charter* warning would help resolve that ambiguity, but this suggestion has not been adopted.[160]

In conclusion, it is worth noting several things that are *not* part of the police's implementational duties. First, a person who has been arrested and has already spoken with counsel (or has waived the right)

---

158 *Smith* 1989, above note 151.

159 See, for example, *R v Hollis* (1992), 17 CR (4th) 211 (BCCA). This situation is particularly odd when one considers that a waiver must be considered in light of all the circumstances. To say "I know my rights" is not a valid waiver of the informational components. If an accused says, "I don't want a lawyer," that waiver cannot be taken at face value, and courts must decide whether the arrested person had a true understanding of the consequences: *Clarkson*, above note 148. The anomalous result is that there is greater protection under s 10(b) for an accused who expressly waives the right than for one who says nothing. See Stephen Coughlan, "When Silence Isn't Golden: Waiver and the Right to Counsel" (1990) 33 *Criminal Law Quarterly* 43. More recently see *R v Owens*, 2015 ONCA 652, concluding that the first question to be asked is whether the accused has requested counsel, and therefore that the question of waiver does not arise where the trial judge decides on the facts that there was no such clear request.

160 See *R v Knoblauch*, 2018 SKCA 15.

may then be questioned by the police. Even if the person later indicates that they do not wish to speak with the police, no duty is imposed on the police to stop their questioning. The person is not required to answer questions, but that does not mean the police are not entitled to ask them.[161]

Second, it was held in *R v Sinclair* that the fact a person being questioned wants to talk to counsel again does not, by itself, automatically trigger an obligation on the part of the police to allow such contact.[162] The "right to counsel trilogy" of cases[163] were quite restrictive in their approach to allowing a consultation with counsel a second time. Those cases found that it is only in certain changed circumstances that such an obligation will arise. Such changed circumstances include the use of new procedures involving the accused (for example, a lineup[164]); a change in the jeopardy facing the accused (for example, the death of an assault victim[165]); or, reason to believe that the accused might not have understood the right[166] (because, for example, the police have acted to undermine it[167]). Revealing evidence to the accused (real or false) is not sufficient, and the changed circumstances must be objectively observable in order to trigger additional implementational duties for the police.[168] The mere fact on its own that some questions might concern an offence other than the one for which the accused was arrested does not necessarily entitle the accused to be re-advised of their section 10 rights.[169] On the other hand, if the focus of the interrogation shifts to a new offence, particularly a more serious one, the accused must be advised again.[170] Courts tend to look to whether the suggested change was foreseeable or not at the time of the initial consultation with counsel as a significant factor in deciding whether a new consultation is required.[171]

---

161 *R v Singh*, 2007 SCC 48. The decision analyzes this question as an aspect of s 7 and the right to silence, but the analogy to s 10(b) is noted.

162 *Sinclair*, above note 114.

163 *Sinclair*, above note 114; *Willier*, above note 126; and *McCrimmon*, above note 154.

164 *Ross*, above note 137.

165 *Black*, above note 31.

166 *Sinclair*, above note 114 at para 52.

167 *Burlingham*, above note 128.

168 *Sinclair*, above note 114 at para 55.

169 *R v CJJ*, 2018 ABCA 7.

170 See, for example, *R v Heppner*, 2019 BCCA 108.

171 See, for example, *R v TGH*, 2014 ONCA 460, where the accused was confronted with a general warrant requiring him to submit to an unusual physical examination eleven months after his arrest: the *Sinclair* rule did not apply because

Further, the stated view of the Court has been that police are not expected to "look behind" the fact that an accused has had an opportunity to consult with counsel and try to assess the adequacy of that advice. If an accused person speaks with counsel (seemingly however briefly), then the police are entitled to assume that they have fulfilled their section 10(b) obligations. They have no obligation to ensure that the advice received was adequate, and unless the accused "diligently and reasonably" indicates that the advice was inadequate, the police are entitled to assume that they are satisfied with the exercised right to counsel and to commence their interrogation.[172] Indeed, it has been held that if the police have given the person an opportunity to contact counsel, they have no obligation to inquire whether the accused has actually done so.[173] This rule applies even if the charge is serious and the consultation with counsel has been only a matter of minutes.[174]

However, this attitude on the part of the Court might be changing. In *R v Lafrance*, the Court considered the last basis for allowing an additional consultation with counsel, that the accused might not have understood the right. They noted that two approaches to this question had been taken, one focusing solely on the fact of the earlier consultation but the other looking at the overall context to consider whether a detainee understood their right to silence and how to exercise it. In a 5:4 split the Court opted for the latter approach, one that in essence looks at whether the accused received a *benefit* from the consultation with counsel that occurred, rather than simply whether there was such

---

counsel could not have been expected to anticipate such an order and give the appropriate advice. On the other hand, in *United States of America v 'Isa*, 2014 ABCA 256, the accused was given the opportunity to consult with counsel when he was arrested by the RCMP but was not given a second opportunity when he was questioned by US authorities. This was found to be acceptable because the possibility of the second questioning was known to counsel during the first consultation.

Accused have had some success, at least at the trial level, in obtaining a second consultation with counsel when they had initially sought to speak to counsel of choice but had ended up speaking with duty counsel: see, for example, *R v Laverdiere*, 2014 ABQB 68; *R v Soomal*, 2014 ONCJ 220; or *R v WS*, 2014 ONSC 3144.

172 *Willier*, above note 126 at para 42.

173 See *R v Beauregard*, 2016 ABCA 37, relying on *Willier*, above note 126.

174 In *Willier*, above note 126, the accused was charged with murder and had two telephone conversations with duty counsel, one three minutes long and the other one minute. In *McCrimmon*, above note 1154, the accused was charged with a series of assaults and had a one-minute conversation with duty counsel. In *Sinclair*, above note 114, the accused was charged with murder and had two three-minute phone conversations with his lawyer.

a consultation.[175] The dissenters in *Lafrance* specifically objected that this was inconsistent with the approach of the right to counsel trilogy, which is perhaps the clearest demonstration that it is a loosening of the strictures of that approach.

## FURTHER READINGS


Burchill, John. "The Right to Counsel and the Right to Have Counsel Present" (2022) 45 *Manitoba Law Journal* 1.

Coughlan, Steve. "When Silence Isn't Golden: Waiver and the Right to Counsel" (1990) 33 *Criminal Law Quarterly* 43.

———. "Whither — or Wither — Section 9" (2008) 40 *Supreme Court Law Review* (2d) 147.

———. "Citizen's Arrest, Property Owners, and Private Fiefdoms" (2014) 18 *Canadian Criminal Law Review* 1.

———, "Is the Right to Counsel a Nuisance?" (2023) 27 *Canadian Competition law Review* 37.

———, & Glen Luther. *Detention and Arrest* 3d ed. (Toronto: Irwin Law, 2024).

——— & Alex Gorlewski. *The Anatomy of Criminal Procedure: A Visual Guide to the Law*, 2nd ed (Toronto: University of Toronto Press, 2026).

Fetterly, Robert W, & Daniel A MacRury. "Arrest of Persons in Dwelling-House (*Feeney* Warrants — The First Three Years) (Part I)" (2002) 45 *Criminal Law Quarterly* 101.

———. "Arrest of Persons in Dwelling-House (*Feeney* Warrants — The First Three Years) (Part II)" (2002) 45 *Criminal Law Quarterly* 360.

Friedland, Meryl, & Andrew Haag. "You Have the Right to Be Read Something That You Probably Won't Understand: Comprehensibility of the Right to Counsel" (2022) 70 *Criminal Law Quarterly* 485.

Gorlewski, Alex. "*R. v. Loewen* and Reasonable Grounds for Arrest: The Supreme Court's Overlooked Advice" (2012) 94 *Criminal Reports* (6th) 319.

Law Reform Commission of Canada. *Arrest* (Report 29) (Ottawa: Law Reform Commission of Canada, 1986).


175 *R v Lafrance*, 2022 SCC 32 at paras 74ff.

LEGAULT, PASCALE, "Bail and Indigenous Over-Representation in Canadian Detention Facilities: Do the 2019 Amendments to the Criminal Code Offer a Viable Solution?" (2025) 73 *Criminal Law Quarterly* 84.

PACKER, HERBERT L. *The Limits of the Criminal Sanction* (Stanford: Stanford University Press, 1968).

PENNEY, STEVEN. "State Action in Action: The Charter's Application in Criminal Investigations" (2023) 27 *Canadian Criminal Law Review* 61.

POMERANCE, RENEE M. "Parliament's Response to *R v Feeney*: A New Regime for Entry and Arrest in Dwelling Houses" (1998) 13 *Criminal Reports* (5th) 84.

PRINGLE, HEATHER. "Kicking In the Castle Doors: The Evolution of Exigent Circumstances" (2000) 43 *Criminal Law Quarterly* 86.

STRIBOPOULOS, JAMES. "Unchecked Power: The Constitutional Regulation of Arrest Reconsidered" (2003) 48 *McGill Law Journal* 225.

———. "The Forgotten Right: Section 9 of the *Charter*, Its Purpose and Meaning" (2008) 40 *Supreme Court Law Review* (2d) 211.

STUART, DON. "*R v Lafrance*: A 5-4 Majority Strengthens the s. 10(b) Right to Counsel" (2022) 81 *Criminal Reports* (7th) 293.

CHAPTER 8

# DISCLOSURE AND PRODUCTION

## A. INTRODUCTION

For many years, no effective right to disclosure of the Crown's case existed in Canada. Practice with regard to disclosure varied from court to court, and even from prosecutor to prosecutor. Despite calls for comprehensive disclosure schemes from the Law Reform Commission of Canada,[1] no statutory scheme was introduced. The problems that could arise from non-disclosure were made dramatically clear in the investigation of the wrongful conviction of Donald Marshall Jr, leading that Royal Commission to point to the need for consistent disclosure.[2] In general terms, that state of affairs changed in 1991 with the Supreme Court of Canada decision in *R v Stinchcombe*, which concluded that an accused person had a right, under section 7 of the *Canadian Charter of Rights and Freedoms*, to disclosure of the Crown's case.[3] The exact contours of this right have continued to be developed in subsequent caselaw, although *Stinchcombe* remains the leading case establishing

1 Law Reform Commission of Canada, *Discovery in Criminal Cases* (Ottawa: Law Reform Commission of Canada, 1974), and *Disclosure by the Prosecution* (Ottawa: Law Reform Commission of Canada, 1984).

2 Nova Scotia, Royal Commission on the Donald Marshall, Jr, Prosecution, *Commissioners' Report: Findings and Recommendations*, vol 1 (Halifax: Royal Commission on the Donald Marshall, Jr, Prosecution, 1989).

3 [1991] 3 SCR 326 [*Stinchcombe*].

the general principle. The Supreme Court has summarized the current state of affairs with regard to disclosure:

> The Crown must disclose all relevant information to the accused, whether inculpatory or exculpatory, subject to the exercise of the Crown's discretion to refuse to disclose information that is privileged or plainly irrelevant. Relevance must be assessed in relation both to the charge itself and to the reasonably possible defences. The relevant information must be disclosed whether or not the Crown intends to introduce it in evidence, before election or plea. Moreover, all statements obtained from persons who have provided relevant information to the authorities should be produced notwithstanding that they are not proposed as Crown witnesses. This Court has also defined the concept of "relevance" broadly . . . .[4]

As the law has subsequently developed, however, other schemes governing when the accused is entitled to have access to particular types of material have developed. *Stinchcombe* established a regime concerning "disclosure" that governs the Crown's first party obligation to give to the accused material in its possession. Subsequently, the Court was called upon to consider in what circumstances an accused ought to be entitled to material that is in the hands of third parties, rather than the Crown, which is referred to as "production." Production is governed by two regimes: the Court initially created rules around disclosure with its decision in *R v O'Connor*,[5] but in many circumstances, that scheme has been displaced by a statutory one. That statutory scheme is sometimes referred to as the "*Mills* Regime," after the case that found the provisions constitutional.[6] Finally, with its decision in *R v McNeil* the Court laid down rules that it characterized as a means of "bridging the gap between first party disclosure and third party production."[7]

Chronologically these various schemes each developed as a response to the state of the law at the time, addressing new issues as they arose. Looking at where the law has arrived, however, there are functionally two situations: first party disclosure of material that either is or should be in the hands of the Crown, and third party production of material in the hands of other parties (where special

---

4 *R v Taillefer; R v Duguay*, 2003 SCC 70 at para 59 [*Taillefer*] [page references omitted].

5 [1995] 4 SCR 411 [*O'Connor*].

6 *R v Mills*, [1999] 3 SCR 668 [*Mills*].

7 2009 SCC 3 [*McNeil*].

considerations apply to records in sexual offence prosecutions). As the Court has put it:

> to determine which regime is applicable, one should consider: (1) Is the information that is sought in the possession or control of the prosecuting Crown? and (2) Is the nature of the information sought such that the police or another Crown entity in possession or control of the information ought to have supplied it to the prosecuting Crown? This will be the case if the information can be qualified as being part of the fruits of the investigation or obviously relevant. An affirmative answer to either of these questions will call for the application of the first party disclosure regime. Otherwise, the third party disclosure regime applies.[8]

That amounts to saying that the first and last schemes created, the *Stinchcombe* and *McNeil* regimes, deal with disclosure, while the *O'Connor* and *Mills* regimes deal with production. This chapter will, however, discuss the development of each of the different schemes chronologically, because doing so makes clearer how each is a response to what had gone before.

# B. DISCLOSURE

## 1) Creation of the Right: *R v Stinchcombe*

In *Stinchcombe*, the Court found a duty on the part of the Crown to disclose its evidence to the accused. The Court rejected a number of arguments against disclosure.[9] It pointed out that the Crown's role is not to obtain a conviction but to lay all relevant evidence before the court. Any information in the hands of the Crown is therefore not a tool to convict the accused, but the property of the public to be used to ensure that justice is done. The Court also rejected the suggestion that Crown workloads would be increased by an obligation to disclose. It noted, as the Law Reform Commission studies found, that increased disclosure leads to an increase in cases settled, guilty pleas entered, and charges withdrawn, thereby decreasing Crown and court workloads. The Court acknowledged that some risk to informers may come from disclosure, but determined that this affects only the manner and timing of

---

8 *R v Gubbins*, 2018 SCC 44 at para 33 [*Gubbins*].

9 For an explanation of this issue in chart form, see Steve Coughlan and Alex Gorlewski, *The Anatomy of Criminal Procedure: A Visual Guide to the Law*, 2nd ed (Toronto: University of Toronto Press, 2026) [*Anatomy of Criminal Procedure*], Chart 2.3(a), "Disclosure."

disclosure, not the general principle. The Court also acknowledged that disclosure may allow an accused to tailor a defence to anticipate the prosecution's case, but held, nonetheless, that fairness to the accused requires that the accused see the evidence in advance.

This latter point is the most important in the Court's reasoning. Although policy arguments led them to conclude that routine disclosure is a desirable feature of the criminal justice system, it is the *Charter*, and in particular, the accused's right under section 7 to make full answer and defence, that is the mechanism by which that end is achieved. The Court concludes that "there is a general duty on the part of the Crown to disclose all material it proposes to use at trial and especially all evidence which may assist the accused even if the Crown does not propose to adduce it."[10]

The fact that this right is guaranteed by the *Charter* has been significant in much of the Court's later reasoning. For example, it means that the right potentially has application in any context where section 7 applies, not simply in domestic trials. In *Canada v Khadr* the Court found that the applicant (who was detained by the United States in Guantanamo Bay but had been interrogated there by Canadian officials) was entitled to disclosure of the material gathered by Canada. The more difficult issue was whether the *Charter* applied at all given the extraterritorial nature of the investigation. Once it was found that it did, however, section 7 imposed a disclosure obligation.[11]

## 2) Structure of the Right

First, the structure of the right as set out in *Stinchcombe* should be described. Whether evidence appears to be inculpatory or exculpatory is irrelevant to the obligation to disclose. The Crown is required to disclose on the request of the accused, made any time after a charge is laid. Disclosure ought to be made prior to election or plea, so that the accused can take the disclosed material into account in making a decision on those issues. The material to be disclosed includes all witness statements, whether the Crown intends to call the witness or not, and notes or "will say" statements where no actual statements exist. If there are no notes, the Crown should disclose the name, address, and

---

10 *Stinchcombe*, above note 3 at 338, quoting from *R v C(MH)* (1988), 46 CCC (3d) 142 (BCCA). See the discussion of *Canada (Justice) v Khadr*, 2008 SCC 28 [*Khadr*] in Chapter 3, Section B(2)(a).

11 *Khadr*, *ibid*. The Court also held at para 32 that the scope of that disclosure might differ from that in a domestic trial and would depend on the nature of Canadian authorities' involvement.

occupation of a witness and any information the prosecution possesses concerning the evidence that person might give. In later cases the duty to disclose has been described as "triggered whenever there is a reasonable possibility of the information being useful to the accused in making full answer and defence."[12]

The "first party" disclosure obligation includes both the Crown prosecutor and the police.[13] However, this is only true of the police to the extent that they are investigating the offence with which the accused is charged.[14] The obligation to disclose is a continuing one, and the Crown must disclose any additional information it receives. Equally, the defence has a continuing obligation to seek disclosure and is not entitled to assume that it has received all relevant information.[15] Where, following a review of disclosure by the trial judge, circumstances have changed, the appropriate approach for the Crown is to reapply to the trial judge concerning the issue, rather than to fail to disclose and argue the issue on appeal.[16]

The right to disclosure is very broad, but it is not absolute. First, the Crown "need not produce what is clearly irrelevant."[17] Second, it has the discretion to refuse to disclose information that is privileged.[18] Each of these should be discussed separately.

Evidence will be "relevant" in this context if it, for example, goes to meeting the case for the Crown, to advancing a defence, or to making

---

12 *R v Dixon*, [1998] 1 SCR 244 at para 21 [*Dixon*].

13 See *McNeil*, above note 7 at para 14: "the investigating police force, although distinct and independent from the Crown at law, is not a third party. Rather, it acts on the same first party footing as the Crown."

14 *R v Quesnelle*, 2014 SCC 46 at para 11 [*Quesnelle*]:

> For purposes of this "first party" disclosure, "the Crown" does not refer to all Crown entities, federal and provincial: "the Crown" is the prosecuting Crown. All other Crown entities, including police, are "third parties". With the exception of the police duty to supply the Crown with the fruits of the investigation, records in the hands of third parties, including other Crown entities, are generally not subject to the *Stinchcombe* disclosure rules.

See also *McNeil*, above note 7, and the discussion in Section D, below in this chapter.

15 *Dixon*, above note 12 at para 55. These two rules are to a certain extent contradictory and will, no doubt, give rise to disputes in practice: see the discussion of the need for due diligence by defence counsel in Section B(3)(b), below in this chapter.

16 *R v Khela*, [1995] 4 SCR 201 at para 10 [*Khela*].

17 *Stinchcombe*, above note 3 at 339.

18 The position is summed up in *R v Taillefer*, 2003 SCC 70 [*Taillefer*] at para 59: "The Crown must disclose all relevant information to the accused, whether inculpatory or exculpatory, subject to the exercise of the Crown's discretion to refuse to disclose information that is privileged or plainly irrelevant."

a decision about how to conduct the defence, such as whether to call evidence.[19] The Court said in *Stinchcombe* that "[i]nformation ought not to be withheld if there is a reasonable possibility that the withholding of information will impair the right of the accused to make full answer and defence."[20] In turn, full answer and defence will be impacted if "there is a reasonable possibility the non-disclosure affected the outcome at trial or the overall fairness of the trial process."[21] The outcome at trial will have been affected if "there is a reasonable possibility that, on its face, the undisclosed information affects the reliability of the conviction."[22] Looking at the overall fairness of the trial process requires "assessing, on the basis of a reasonable possibility, the lines of inquiry with witnesses or the opportunities to garner additional evidence that could have been available to the defence if the relevant information had been disclosed."[23]

Any privileged material need not be disclosed, and in practice informer privilege is the one which most frequently arises. The interaction between the disclosure rules and privilege is discussed at length below, in Section B(4).

Although disclosure is meant to be made before the accused is required to elect or plead, some other considerations might interact with that timing. The Crown might need to take steps to protect the identity of an informer for whom no claim of privilege could be made out, for example, which might give them some discretion over timing.[24] Further, the need to complete an investigation may justify the Crown in delaying some disclosure.[25] In many cases, of course, the Crown might be able to delay the laying of charges rather than delay the disclosure, particularly given the trial within a reasonable time ceilings which now exist.

The obligation to disclose evidence does not include a requirement that the Crown make its witnesses available for oral discovery.[26]

The Court has distinguished between evidence known to exist but which has not been disclosed, and evidence whose existence is in dispute. In the former case, the burden clearly rests with the

---

19 *R v Egger*, [1993] 2 SCR 451.

20 *Stinchcombe*, above note 3 at para 22.

21 *R v Dixon*, above note 12 at para 34 [*Dixon*].

22 *Dixon*, above note 12 at para 36.

23 *Dixon*, above note 12 at para 36.

24 Where the level of disclosure has already been reviewed by a court and an order made, however, the Crown no longer has discretion over the issue: see *Khela*, above note 16 at para 14, and the further discussion of this issue below.

25 *Stinchcombe*, above note 3 at 339.

26 *Khela*, above note 16 at para 18.

Crown to justify the non-disclosure of the evidence "by demonstrating either that the information sought is beyond its control, or that it is clearly irrelevant or privileged."[27] That is, where the documents are in the hands of the Crown, the onus is not on the accused to show that they are relevant in order to obtain disclosure, but on the Crown to show that they are clearly irrelevant if they wish to justify non-disclosure.[28] However, the Crown cannot be expected to justify the non-disclosure of evidence of which it is unaware or which it denies exists. In such circumstances, therefore, the defence is first required to show some basis that will allow the trial judge to conclude that potentially relevant further material exists.[29] The right to disclosure is not meant to allow fishing expeditions on the part of the defence, and so does not, for example, require the Crown to disclose whether the accused has been the subject of a wiretap unrelated to the charges laid.[30]

The rule of full disclosure, and its reliance on the accused's right to full answer and defence, has been applied in more specific contexts. In *R v Egger*,[31] for example, the Court was required to consider the former section 258(1)(d) of the *Criminal Code*, which allowed the Crown to rely on a certificate of a qualified technician as proof of the concentration of alcohol in the accused's blood, as determined from an analysis of a blood sample. That section required that the Crown have taken two samples of the accused's blood, one to be provided to the accused on request for analysis. However, the section did not explicitly require that the accused be given notice of the existence of the sample. The Court noted that "one measure of the relevance of information in the Crown's hands is its usefulness to the defence: if it is of some use, it is relevant and should be disclosed."[32] The various possible uses noted included "meeting the case for the Crown, advancing a defence or otherwise in making a decision which may affect the conduct of the defence such as, for example, whether to call evidence."[33] Accordingly, it concluded that the Crown was required to inform the accused of the existence of the sample, and to do so at a time when the accused can usefully act on the information.

---

27 *R v Chaplin*, [1995] 1 SCR 727 at para 25.
28 *R v Chu*, 2016 SKCA 156.
29 *Ibid* at para 30.
30 *Ibid*.
31 [1993] 2 SCR 451.
32 *Ibid* at para 20.
33 *Ibid*.

Similarly, in *R v Durette*[34] the Court held that the same principles apply in the context of wiretap applications:

> Apart from public interest concerns which may operate in a particular case, I see no reason why an accused should not be entitled to see exactly what the judge saw who relied on the affidavits to issue the authorization. Disclosure of the full affidavit should be the starting premise. Anything less potentially impairs an accused's ability to make full answer and defence and must be justified by the Crown in accordance with established principles. Editing of these affidavits is best viewed as a necessary evil.[35]

The existence of the right to disclosure has also affected the Court's analysis in other areas. In *R v Cook*,[36] for example, the Court concluded that the Crown had no obligation to call witnesses in order for all material facts to be brought forward. Given the accused's right to disclosure, the Crown's decision not to call a witness will not prejudice an accused. If the Crown decides not to call a witness whose testimony has changed from an earlier statement, for example, the accused will have received the earlier statement and will be entitled to the later one, due to the Crown's ongoing obligation to disclose.

Further, the Court has concluded that the Canadian Security Intelligence Service (CSIS) has, in the security certificate context, a duty to disclose similar to that in *Stinchcombe*. Although CSIS investigations are not criminal matters and do not lead to charges, seeking a security certificate with regard to a named person has serious implications for the liberty and security of the person concerned. These consequences include detention for an indefinite period or expulsion from the country. Accordingly, section 7 of the *Charter* is brought into play, and there is a duty to disclose. The exact nature of that disclosure obligation is not, however, identical to that in the criminal context. The Canadian Security Intelligence Service is required to retain all the information it uncovers and to disclose it to the ministers and the judge hearing the security certificate application. That judge is required to exclude any evidence that might pose a threat to national security and summarize the remaining evidence for the named person.[37]

---

34 [1994] 1 SCR 469 [*Durette*].

35 *Ibid* at 495, quoting Doherty JA in the court below.

36 [1998] 2 SCR 597.

37 *Charkaoui v Canada (Citizenship and Immigration)*, 2008 SCC 38. The Court also found that the CSIS policy of destroying their operational notes was invalid and that they had a duty to retain them when engaged in a targeted investigation.

## 3) Remedy for Breach of What Right: Disclosure or Full Answer and Defence?

The Court noted in *Stinchcombe* that the Crown's discretion with regard to disclosure can be reviewed by the trial judge if defence counsel disagrees with the way in which it has been exercised. In such a review, the onus would rest with the Crown to justify an exception to the rule of complete disclosure. Quite apart from issues of review by the trial judge, however, an issue which has frequently arisen is the effect of non-disclosure and the remedy that should flow from it. Most commonly, when non-disclosure arises during a trial, the remedy is simply an order for disclosure and possibly an adjournment. In *Stinchcombe*, where the trial was already over, the Court found that the accused might have conducted his defence differently by calling a particular witness, and that calling that witness could have affected the outcome of the trial. Accordingly, it ordered a new trial. Later cases have pursued the issue of remedy more fully, finding that, in some circumstances, a stay of proceedings is the appropriate remedy for non-disclosure. The most important cases since *Stinchcombe* to have discussed the issue of remedy are *R v Carosella*,[38] *R v La*,[39] *R v Dixon*,[40] and *R v Bjelland*.[41]

The Court has not been entirely consistent in its analysis of which *Charter* right is at issue when the Crown has failed to disclose relevant information. The earlier cases that considered this issue looked at whether disclosure was itself an independent *Charter* right or whether it was just an aspect of the right to full answer and defence. This seemed at first to matter on the assumption that one could proceed directly to the question of remedy once a breach of some *Charter* right had been found. As the Court's jurisprudence has developed, however, it has become apparent that, although disclosure is said to be a *Charter* right in its own right, no remedy will be given for that breach unless it also amounts to a breach of the right to full answer and defence.

### a) The Original Position: Remedy for Non-disclosure

*Carosella*[42] dealt with an accused charged with gross indecency. Before contacting the police, the complainant had visited a rape crisis centre and been interviewed by a social worker, who took notes of the conversation. The accused later applied for production of the records, but by

38 [1997] 1 SCR 80 [*Carosella*].
39 [1997] 2 SCR 680 [*La*].
40 Above note 12.
41 2009 SCC 38 [*Bjelland*].
42 Above note 38.

that time they had been destroyed (the centre had a policy of shredding files where there was police involvement before they were served with any application for production). The Court, therefore, had to determine whether the non-disclosure of the notes violated the accused's *Charter* rights and, if it did, whether a stay was the appropriate remedy.[43]

The first issue the Court needed to address, therefore, was exactly what *Charter* right was in play. The issue was whether disclosure is, in itself, a right implicit in section 7, or whether section 7 protects the accused's right to full answer and defence, one aspect of which is the need for disclosure. The Ontario Court of Appeal had held that disclosure was simply an aspect of the right to full answer and defence, a conclusion that L'Heureux-Dubé J, dissenting in the Supreme Court, agreed with. There was some justification for taking this view. In the earlier *R v O'Connor* decision, a majority had supported a portion of L'Heureux-Dubé J's judgment, in which she stated:

> the right of an accused to full disclosure by the Crown is an adjunct of the right to make full answer and defence. It is not itself a constitutionally protected right. What this means is that while the Crown has an obligation to disclose, and the accused has a right to all that which the Crown is obligated to disclose, a simple breach of the accused's right to such disclosure does not, in and of itself, constitute a violation of the *Charter* such as to entitle a remedy under s 24(1).[44]

The difference between the two possibilities is most important because of the effect it will have on the need for an accused to show prejudice arising from the non-disclosure. If the right in question is the right to full answer and defence, then non-disclosure might not harm the

---

43 *Carosella*, above note 38, ought strictly to be a production case rather than a disclosure one, and, indeed, L'Heureux-Dubé J argued in dissent that the rules around disclosure had nothing to do with the case since the files were never in the control of the Crown. The majority analyzed the issue primarily around the test for disclosure on the basis that "it is clear that the file would have been disclosed to the Crown. As material in the possession of the Crown, only the *Stinchcombe* standard would have applied" (para 41). On the issue of a remedy in such circumstances generally, see Paul Calarco, "What Happens When Evidence Has Not Been Recorded? Staying Charges to Ensure a Fair Trial" (2001) 44 *Criminal Law Quarterly* 514.

44 *O'Connor*, above note 5 at para 74, citing the British Columbia Court of Appeal decision (1994), 89 CCC (3d) 109 at 148–49. Until *Carosella*, above note 38, was handed down, there was no reason to think that the majority in *O'Connor*, who agreed with the portion of L'Heureux Dubé J's reasons in which this appeared, did not also ascribe to this particular passage. Courts of appeal had assumed it to be the majority position in the interim: see Graeme Mitchell, "R. v. *Carosella*: Difficult Cases Make Dangerous Law" (1997) 4 *Criminal Reports* (5th) 209.

accused in a particular case. For instance, the accused's ability to make full answer will not be affected by failure to disclose inculpatory information that does not form part of the Crown's case. However, if the accused has a *Charter* right to disclosure, then the non-disclosure of any information will automatically constitute a breach of that right. There will be no need to consider the actual effect of the non-disclosure on the accused. As L'Heureux-Dubé J had further noted in *O'Connor*:

> . . . the nondisclosure of information which ought to have been disclosed because it was relevant, in the sense there was a reasonable possibility it could assist the accused in making full answer and defence, will not amount to a violation of the accused's section 7 right not to be deprived of liberty except in accordance with the principles of fundamental justice unless the accused establishes that the non-disclosure has probably prejudiced or had an adverse effect on his or her ability to make full answer and defence.[45]

However, the majority in *Carosella* reached the opposite conclusion on both issues. They concluded that breach of the obligation to disclose "is a breach of the accused's constitutional rights without the requirement of an additional showing of prejudice . . . the breach of this principle of fundamental justice is in itself prejudicial."[46] In the particular circumstances in *Carosella*, it followed that "if the material which was destroyed meets the threshold test for disclosure or production, the appellant's *Charter* rights were breached without the requirement of showing additional prejudice."[47]

However, prejudice would remain relevant at the stage of determining remedy on this analysis. Remedies range, the Court notes, from adjournments to a stay of proceedings.[48] In *Carosella*, while reaffirming the principle that a stay should be granted only in the clearest of cases, the majority concluded that it was the appropriate remedy. In general, they held that stays can be justified on either of two bases: (1) where prejudice to the accused cannot be remedied, or (2) where there would be irreparable prejudice to the integrity of the justice system if the prosecution were continued.[49] The majority concluded that

45 *O'Connor*, above note 5.

46 *Carosella*, above note 38 at para 37.

47 *Ibid* at para 40.

48 *Ibid* at para 26. Other cases have found that costs can be an appropriate remedy: see, for example, *R v Lee*, [1996] OJ No 1276 (Gen Div); *R v SVL*, [1995] OJ No 2867 (Prov Div); and *R v Dix*, [1998] AJ No 419 (QB).

49 *Carosella*, above note 38 at para 51, quoting from *O'Connor*, above note 5. The test for a stay of proceedings has evolved since that time: see *R v Babos*, 2014 SCC 16.

both tests were met in this case. First, the Court noted the significance of the evidence destroyed, the trial judge's conclusion that it "would more than likely have assisted the accused in his defence,"[50] and the absence of any alternative remedy to cure this prejudice. Alternatively, the majority concluded, a stay could be justified because of the deliberate decision of an agency that receives government funds to destroy documents ("conduct designed to defeat the processes of the court").[51]

*Carosella* was a much discussed decision, and many people felt that the Court's obvious annoyance at the rape crisis centre's policy affected its reasoning too greatly.[52] It certainly is not clear that later decisions are easily reconciled with *Carosella*, but at the same time the Court has continued to frame the discussion in the terms set out there.

### b) The Current Position: Remedy for Failure of Full Answer and Defence

*La*,[53] decided only shortly after *Carosella*, reaffirms the principle that disclosure is an independent right guaranteed by section 7 of the *Charter*, not merely an aspect of the right to full answer and defence. However, in its actual result, it diminishes the significance of that principle.

In *La*, a police officer tape-recorded an interview with the complainant in a sexual assault case at a time prior to any charges being laid. The complainant was a thirteen-year-old runaway, and the interview was conducted in connection with a secure treatment application. By the time the accused came to trial, the police officer had lost the forty-five-minute tape, though he did testify that the complainant told a few lies on it. The trial judge held that the non-disclosure of the tape impaired the accused's ability to cross-examine the complainant and entered a stay of proceedings. On the face of it, the argument for a stay appears to be at least as strong as in *Carosella*. The accused did not receive disclosure, which alone was said to constitute a violation of section 7 without a showing of prejudice. The argument for prejudice is stronger here, in any case, since the evidence was a tape recording of the complainant herself, and it was known that she had lied in the interview. In *Carosella*, in contrast, the missing material was only another person's notes, and the complainant had consented to their production of the missing

---

50 *Carosella*, *ibid* at para 53, quoting the trial judge.

51 *Ibid* at para 56.

52 See Mitchell, above note 44; David Paciocco, "In Defence of *R. v. Carosella*: The Continuing Need for Prejudice" (1997) 4 *Criminal Reports* (5th) 199; Stephen G Coughlan, "Developments in Criminal Procedure: The 1996–97 Term" (1998) 9 *Supreme Court Law Review* (2d) 273.

53 Above note 39.

material and indeed was upset that they had been destroyed. There was less reason in *Carosella* to think that the missing material was of any use to the accused.

Nonetheless, what the majority found in *La* was that the accused's section 7 right was not violated at all. The Court found that, despite best efforts on the part of the police, evidence will sometimes be lost. Where the Crown can show that the reason the evidence was lost was not due to unacceptable negligence, the majority stated, the duty to disclose is not breached. It will still be possible for the accused's right to full answer and defence to be breached. However, this will be the case only if the accused can establish actual prejudice.[54] In this particular case, the majority held that the tape was relevant enough to meet the standard for disclosure in *Stinchcombe*, but fell short of establishing a serious impairment of the right to make full answer and defence.[55] (See the further discussion below of the rules arising from *La* for "lost evidence" cases.)

In practical terms, this decision removes much of the effect of the finding in *Carosella* that disclosure is a right in itself. The major significance of that finding was that it removed the need for the accused to show prejudice in order to show a *Charter* breach. But if there is no breach of that right where the Crown can satisfactorily explain the failure to disclose, then breach of the right to disclosure becomes less important. In many cases, given *La*, the accused will have to show a breach of the right to full answer and defence, and so will need to show some prejudice from the non-disclosure.[56]

This pulling away from the standard in *Carosella* can be seen clearly in *Dixon* and its companion cases.[57] Those cases arise from a set of complex facts, in which a number of accused were charged with assault in circumstances where there were many witnesses and many different accounts of what had occurred. None of the defence counsel had received copies of statements from four witnesses, although the pre-trial disclosure they had received included other information from which one could infer that these four people were potential witnesses.

54 *Ibid* at para 25.

55 *Ibid* at para 33.

56 See, for example, *R v Natsis*, 2018 ONCA 425, where an earlier draft of an expert report should have been retained and disclosed. Nonetheless, the Court of Appeal found no need for a remedy, because defence counsel had been able separately to establish everything that could have been established through the use of the draft.

57 *Dixon*, above note 12; *R v McQuaid*, [1998] 1 SCR 285; *R v Robart*, [1998] 1 SCR 279; *R v Smith*, [1998] 1 SCR 291 [*Smith*]; *R v Skinner*, [1998] 1 SCR 298 [*Skinner*].

During the trial several of the defence counsel became aware of the undisclosed statements, but decided, based on summaries, not to request copies of the statements themselves. Only after the trial was over did the defence counsel review the statements. Although two of the statements contained nothing relevant, the other two contained information that, while not of enormous significance, met the *Stinchcombe* threshold and should have been disclosed. The Court was therefore faced with a slightly new twist from that of *Carosella* or *La*. In those cases, it was known during the trial that there was undisclosed information. In *Dixon*, the failure to disclose did not become apparent until after the trial. This difference in timing is relevant both to whether there is a *Charter* breach and to the remedy to be granted. The case is therefore interesting both for how it shows the Court coping with the role of prejudice and for its approach to a remedy.

In *Carosella*, the Court had held that disclosure was an independent right guaranteed by section 7 and that prejudice was not relevant to whether that right had been breached — prejudice was relevant only at the remedy stage. Thus, in *Carosella*, the Court moved directly to determining a remedy after deciding the right to disclosure was breached. In *Dixon* the Court, in large measure, undid the main effects of having made disclosure an independent right. The Court held that "the right to disclosure is but one component of the right to make full answer and defence. Although the right to disclosure may be violated, the right to make full answer and defence may not be impaired as a result of that violation."[58]

Subsequently in *R v Taillefer; R v Duguay*, without adverting to the previous dispute over the issue, the Court held:

> Infringement of that right [disclosure] is not always an infringement of the right to make full answer and defence. There are situations in which the information not disclosed will meet the minimum test set out in *Stinchcombe* while having only marginal value to the issues at trial. To determine whether there is an infringement of the right to make full answer and defence, the accused will have to show that there was a reasonable possibility that the failure to disclose affected the outcome at trial or the overall fairness of the trial process.[59]

In each of these latter two cases, it was only after finding a breach of the right to full answer and defence that the Court considered remedy.

58 *Dixon*, above note 12 at para 31. On *Dixon*, generally, see Graeme G Mitchell, "*R. v. Dixon*: The Right to Crown Disclosure — A Roadmap for the Future" (1998) 13 *Criminal Reports* (5th) 260.

59 *Taillefer*, above note 4 at para 71 [references omitted].

Thus, the Court has changed the approach in *Carosella* to a three-part test: (1) Was the accused's right to disclosure breached? (2) If so, did that breach violate the accused's right to make full answer and defence? (3) If so, what remedy should be granted? Given this approach, it remains technically true, as stated in *Carosella*, that disclosure is an independent right and that it is not necessary to show prejudice to establish a breach of that right. However, as no consequences will attach to a breach of the right to disclosure alone, then in this context, the major consequences of those findings will have disappeared.

*Dixon* does not change the *Stinchcombe* standard for disclosure, and so the first question incorporates those rules. To decide whether the breach of disclosure affected full answer and defence, the Court set out a two-prong test. The accused must show a reasonable possibility that (1) the non-disclosure affected the outcome at trial or (2) it affected the overall fairness of the trial process.[60] The first prong of this test asks whether there is a reasonable possibility that the additional evidence could have created a reasonable doubt in the jury's mind.[61] The second prong considers whether the undisclosed evidence could have been used to impeach the credibility of a prosecution witness, or could have assisted the defence in its pre-trial investigations and preparations or in its tactical decisions at trial.[62]

With regard to both factors, the burden imposed on the accused is only that of showing a "reasonable possibility." That is, the question is not whether undisclosed evidence *would* have made a difference, only whether it *could* have.[63]

In assessing the first prong, whether undisclosed evidence could have affected the decision to convict, a court must look at the evidence as a whole and not at each undisclosed piece of information individually.[64] In *Dixon*, the Court decided that although the statements were relevant, they contained only relatively insignificant inconsistencies that could not affect the decision to convict. In *R v Smith*, in contrast, there was a reasonable possibility that one of the statements could have affected the outcome, since the witness said he did not see Smith hit anyone. The Court therefore ordered a new trial. Similarly, in *Taillefer* and *R v Illes* the defence could have used undisclosed evidence to challenge the credibility of important Crown witnesses, or to present an alternative theory about how the crime was committed.

60 *Dixon*, above note 12 at para 34. See also *Taillefer*, above note 4.
61 *Taillefer*, *ibid* at para 82; *R v Illes*, 2008 SCC 57 at para 25 [*Illes*].
62 *Illes*, *ibid* at para 27; *Dixon*, above note 12 at para 36.
63 *Illes*, above note 66 at para 25.
64 *Taillefer*, above note 4 at para 92ff.

The second prong of the *Dixon* test can overlap with the first prong. In *Illes*, for example, the same undisclosed evidence might have affected the jury's decision had it been used to cross-examine a Crown witness, but equally could be seen to have affected the fairness of the trial because the accused did not have the opportunity to conduct that cross-examination. The second prong, however, considers different issues. The failure to disclose evidence might, for example, affect a tactical decision such as whether to call evidence at trial — specifically the testimony of the witness whose evidence had not been disclosed.[65]

With regard to the fairness of the trial process, the Court stressed in *Taillefer* that the standard is only that of "reasonable possibility." In other words, a judge should not try to assess the evidence and decide whether it would have affected a jury's deliberations. It is sufficient that there be a reasonable possibility it would have done so for the fairness of the trial process to be affected.

The most significant factor relating to the "fairness of the trial" prong discussed in *Dixon* and its companion cases is due diligence on the part of defence counsel. In those cases, defence counsel knew or should have known, the Court said, of the possible undisclosed evidence. Upon becoming aware of the statements, the Court said, it is surprising that defence counsel did not request them. The Court concluded that "defence counsel is not entitled to assume at any point that all relevant information has been disclosed to the defence. Just as the Crown's disclosure obligations are ongoing, and persist throughout the trial process, so too does defence counsel's obligation to be duly diligent in pursuing disclosure."[66] More simply, at a certain point defence counsel was faced with a choice: "call for the statements or live without them."[67]

*Carosella* and later cases are not entirely consistent with one another, but a general consensus appears by confining *Carosella* to its own facts: *Dixon* sets out the general approach to disclosure, while *La* establishes the rules for the special case of "lost evidence."

As noted above, the loss of evidence which should have been disclosed will not always result in a finding that there was a *Charter* violation: "[t]he police cannot be expected to preserve everything that comes into their hands on the off-chance that it will be relevant in the

---

65 See, for example, *Illes*, above note 61, or *Skinner*, above note 57.

66 *Dixon*, above note 12 at para 55.

67 *Ibid*. In contrast, see *R v Pascal* (2020), 387 CCC (3d) 236 (Ont CA) at para 135 where the Ontario Court of Appeal found that it was "difficult to assign fault to defence counsel for a failure to request disclosure and information of which he was neither aware nor had any reason to suspect existed."

future."[68] The Crown does have an obligation to disclose all relevant information in its possession, which therefore gives rise to a duty to preserve relevant evidence. However, where there is no unacceptable negligence in the loss of the evidence, there is no breach of the right to disclosure. In deciding whether the Crown has satisfactorily explained the loss of the evidence, a Court should consider all the circumstances, including whether the evidence was perceived to be relevant at the time it was lost and whether the police acted reasonably in attempting to preserve it: the more relevant the evidence, the more care that should be taken to preserve it.[69] It has been noted that the preservation of evidence is especially important in the context of historical sexual assaults, where charges are sometimes only pursued decades later.[70] Even if there is a breach of the right to disclosure, of course, that does not settle the question of remedy: only in the clearest of cases is a stay the appropriate remedy.[71]

With regard to the issue of remedy, note that the complaint about non-disclosure in *Dixon* (as in other cases such as *Taillefer* or *Illes*) arose after the trial was completed. In such circumstances, the minimum remedy likely to be "appropriate and just" under section 24(1) of the *Charter* will be an order for a new trial. Where the non-disclosure is discovered before the trial is completed, the remedy is very likely only to be an order for disclosure accompanied by an adjournment.[72]

The Supreme Court has allowed for the possibility of something more than disclosure and an adjournment, but they have severely circumscribed that possibility. In *Bjelland* they acknowledged the availability of an order for exclusion of evidence under section 24(1) where non-disclosure is discovered mid-trial, but only in exceptional circumstances: (1) where the late disclosure renders the trial process unfair and the unfairness cannot be remedied by disclosure and an adjournment, or (2) where exclusion is necessary to maintain the integrity of

68 *La*, above note 39 at para 21.

69 See, for example, *R v Hersi*, 2019 ONCA 94 at para 32, where an undercover officer (UC) exchanged text messages with the accused but only saved some of them: "it is unacceptable that, almost thirty years after *Stinchcombe*, the UC could operate under the belief that he need save only relevant material that he viewed as significant." See also *R v Hillier* (2021), 71 CR (7th) 392 (Ont CA) or *R v KDS* (2021), 405 CCC (3d) 416 (Sask CA).

70 *R v Nygard*, 2025 MBPC 64. See also the review in that case of what has been found to be unacceptable negligence in other decisions.

71 See generally *R v FCB*, 2000 NSCA 35 at 547–48. See also *R v Bero* (2000), 151 CCC (3d) 545 (Ont CA).

72 *Ibid* at para 31.

the justice system.[73] The first circumstance might be met where the evidence is disclosed only after important and irrevocable decisions about how to conduct the defence have been made. The second might be met where an adjournment would significantly prolong the period of time an accused is held in custody pending the conclusion of the trial. In either instance, the Court placed the burden on the accused to show why exclusion was necessary and why disclosure and an adjournment would not be sufficient.[74]

## 4) Conflicting Protections: Disclosure and Privileged Information

The final point worth discussing in relation to disclosure is its interaction with the laws of privilege. Because the obligation to disclose is not absolute, "the Crown may justify non-disclosure in circumstances where 'the public interest in non-disclosure outweighs the accused's interest in disclosure.'"[75] Indeed, in *Stinchcombe* the Court stated that the right to disclosure was subject to the rules of privilege. In particular, noteworthy cases have considered informer privilege, solicitor–client privilege, and national security privilege.[76]

### a) Informer Privilege

Informer privilege is a long-standing common law rule, reiterated by the Court in *Bisaillon v Keable*[77] and other cases since. It arises when, in the course of an investigation, a peace officer guarantees protection and confidentiality to a prospective informer in exchange for useful information that would otherwise be difficult or impossible to obtain.[78] It is

---

73 *Bjelland*, above note 41 at para 24. Exclusion of evidence is normally considered under the *Charter*, s 24(2). The Court notes, however, that that subsection deals with excluding evidence that has been "obtained" by a *Charter* breach. Where the *Charter* breach is a s 7 violation due to failure to disclose, that subsection is not relevant and so the remedy must come (if at all) from s 24(1).

74 *Bjelland*, *ibid*, was a 4:3 decision of the Court with a vigorous dissent written by Fish J. The decision has been criticized as being too restrictive: see Paul Calarco, "*R. v. Bjelland*: No Effective Remedy for Crown Failure to Disclose" (2009) 67 *Criminal Reports* (6th) 219.

75 *Michaud v Quebec (Attorney General)*, [1996] 3 SCR 3 at para 47, quoting from *Durette*, above note 34.

76 For a discussion of other potential claims of privilege and their possible impact on an accused's right to disclosure, see Ian Carter, "Chipping Away at *Stinchcombe*: The Expanding Privilege Exception to Disclosure" (2002) 50 *Criminal Reports* (5th) 332.

77 [1983] 2 SCR 60 [*Bisaillon*].

78 *R v Basi*, 2009 SCC 52 at para 36 [*Basi*].

a near-absolute privilege and very broad in its scope because "[t]he tiniest and most seemingly innocuous of details could reveal the identity of an informer."[79] The identity of police informers is entitled to the highest level of protection not only to protect the individuals concerned, but also to preserve that investigative method. If those with confidential information about crimes were not confident that their identities would be protected, they would be far less likely to report that information to the police.

This type of privilege is unlike, for example, Crown privilege, in which the court can decide in the individual case whether it is more important to protect the privilege or the integrity of the trial. Rather, it is more absolute and so a successful claim of informer privilege gives a trial judge

> no power of weighing or evaluating various aspects of the public interest which are in conflict, since it has already resolved the conflict itself. It has decided once and for all, subject to the law being changed, that information regarding police informers' identity will be, because of its content, a class of information which it is in the public interest to keep secret, and that this interest will prevail over the need to ensure the highest possible standard of justice.[80]
>
> The privilege belongs to the informer and the Crown jointly — the Crown cannot disclose the informer's identity without her consent, but equally the informer herself cannot unilaterally waive the privilege.[81]

Informer privilege is more than just a rule of evidence and is not limited to the courtroom,[82] and courts should enforce the privilege where it is applicable whether it is claimed or not.[83] The privilege even applies to prevent a police officer who is charged with an offence from revealing the identity of an informer to their own counsel, barring a successful application to be permitted to do so (see the next paragraph).[84] It does not therefore follow, however, that an accused person is forbidden from making efforts outside the courtroom to determine who

79 *Canadian Broadcasting Corp v Named Person*, 2021 SCC 21 [*Canadian Broadcasting Corp*] at para 45.

80 *Bisaillon*, above note 77 at 98. This point has been continually emphasized by the Court: see, for example, *Named Person v Vancouver Sun*, 2007 SCC 43 at paras 19–23 [*Named Person*]; *Basi*, above note 78 at paras 22 and 37; and *R v Barros*, 2011 SCC 51 at para 30 [*Barros*].

81 *Named Person*, above note 80 at paras 23–25.

82 *Barros*, above note 80 at para 30.

83 *Bisaillon*, above note 77 at 84 and 88; *Basi*, above note 78 at para 38.

84 *R v Brassington*, 2018 SCC 37.

the informer is. Some such efforts might be improper if, for example, the purpose were to discover the identity of the informer in order to pressure the police into dropping charges: that could constitute the offence of obstruction of justice. However, discovering the identity of an informer can also play a legitimate role in making full answer and defence, since some informers might not be credible. Accordingly, there is no general prohibition on defence investigations into the identity of an informer.[85]

At common law, the only derogation from the rule of informer privilege is the "innocence at stake exception." Only if the evidence establishes a basis for this exception, such as that "the informer is a material witness to the crime, acted as an *agent provocateur*,"[86] or planted the material found under a search warrant,[87] will identifying information be revealed.[88]

In *R v Leipert*, the Court concluded that this "ancient and hallowed" common law rule was unchanged by the obligation of disclosure established in *Stinchcombe*.[89] *Stinchcombe* had held that disclosure was subject to privilege, and the Court found no inconsistency between that rule and the common law rule of informer privilege.[90]

Indeed, the Court reaffirmed the importance of the common law rule, stressing its particular application in the case of anonymous informers through programs such as Crime Stoppers. The privilege extends not only to the name of the informer, but to any information that may enable identification. However, it is "virtually impossible for the court to know what details may reveal the identity of an anonymous informer."[91] As a result, judges should not try to edit a tip sheet and order the edited tip sheet disclosed. Rather, a judge should simply uphold informer privilege and not require any information to be disclosed. Only if the accused can establish some basis to conclude that without the disclosure the accused's innocence is at stake, should the trial judge review the tip sheet and potentially order the disclosure of some portion of it. Even then, the Crown has the choice of staying the proceedings rather than making the disclosure.[92]

85 *Barros*, above note 80.
86 [1997] 1 SCR 281 at para 22 [*Leipert*].
87 *Ibid* at para 26.
88 See the further discussion of the innocence at stake exception in Section B(4)(b), below in this chapter.
89 *Leipert*, above note 75 at para 9.
90 *Ibid* at para 25.
91 *Ibid* at para 28. See, for example, *R v Hayes* (2020), 391 CCC (3d) 453 (Ont CA).
92 *Ibid* at para 33.

All of this applies, of course, on the assumption that a claim of informer privilege has been established. In many cases that claim depends on a guarantee of protection and confidentiality having been given. Since that guarantee might have been given only implicitly, it can be necessary for a judge to determine whether a claim of informer privilege ought to be granted. Whenever the issue of informer privilege arises (either by being claimed or by the judge raising the issue), the judge should settle the question with an *in camera* "first stage" hearing. Because of the importance of this type of privilege, the first stage hearing must be conducted on the assumption that the privilege does exist. At this stage even the existence of the claim cannot be publicly disclosed, and ordinarily only the putative informant and the Crown can appear. In certain circumstances (for example, where the interests of the informant and the Crown are aligned), it might be appropriate to appoint an *amicus curiae*.[93] The privilege must be established on a balance of probabilities.[94]

The accused and defence counsel are not entitled to be present at this first stage hearing. In particular, defence counsel cannot be present even if they undertake not to reveal any information to the client, and even if the client consents to that undertaking being made.[95] However, they should be excluded only to the extent necessary to protect the identity of the informant, and trial judges should adopt all reasonable measures to permit defence counsel to make meaningful submissions regarding what occurs in their absence. Reasonable measures might include inviting submissions on the scope of the privilege, allowing defence counsel to suggest questions to be put by the trial judge to any witness who will be called, or providing the defence with a redacted summary of the evidence taken in order to receive additional submissions on whether the privilege applies in the particular circumstances of the case.[96]

It is also possible to show that a claim of informer privilege is not established where it is shown that the interests it is meant to serve are

93 The Court developed these guidelines in a rather unusual factual situation in *Named Person*, above note 80, but has subsequently relied on them in *Basi*, above note 80. See also the more recent discussion in *Canadian Broadcasting Corp*, above note 79, though the issue there is focused on the interplay between such hearings and the open court principle. See also the discussion of publication bans in Chapter 11, Section F(2).

94 *Basi*, above note 80 at para 39.

95 *Ibid* at para 44. The Court held that defence counsel is outside the "circle of privilege" and therefore the privilege would be breached as soon as defence counsel knows, no matter what undertakings were given.

96 *Ibid*.

not in issue. Informer privilege is granted in order to assist in the investigation of crime and to further the interests of justice. Where a person has made an anonymous tip with the intention of furthering criminal activity or interfering with the administration of justice, for example by misleading the police, informer privilege does not arise. This will be so even if the person has been promised confidentiality.[97]

Where a claim of this sort is made, an *ex parte* hearing, similar to that described above, can be held to determine on a balance of probabilities whether the privilege exists, and the trial judge can review the tip itself. However, because of the moral and reasoning prejudice inherent in a suggestion that the accused made the tip with the intention of interfering with a police investigation, a judge can choose to require a preliminary *in camera* showing by the Crown that it is worth proceeding to such a hearing. This might include submissions by the Crown about the evidence it expects to adduce, which might lead the judge to decide no hearing is needed because the evidence is weak or speculative. Equally the preliminary hearing might require the Crown to demonstrate a realistic prospect that the probative value of the evidence will outweigh its prejudicial effect. However, there is no absolute requirement for such a hearing.[98]

#### b) Solicitor–Client Privilege

Solicitor–client privilege is also an ancient and hallowed doctrine that has existed at common law for hundreds of years.[99] Protecting as it does the ability of an accused person to gain legal advice in confidence, it has been recognized as occupying a unique position of fundamental importance. Indeed, it has been classified as a principle of fundamental justice.[100] However, an accused's right to full answer and defence, of which the right to disclosure is a part, is also a principle of fundamental justice. On occasion, it may be necessary for an accused to infringe another person's solicitor–client privilege in order to make full answer and defence. Neither principle will always prevail, and, therefore, in certain circumstances solicitor–client privilege will be required to give way.[101] Because of the importance of the privilege, though, that should occur only in limited, defined circumstances. The Court concluded in *R v McClure* that, just as with informer privilege, the obligation to

---

97 *R v Durham Regional Crime Stoppers Inc*, 2017 SCC 45.

98 *Ibid.*

99 See, for example, the discussion in *Descôteaux v Mierzwinski*, [1982] 1 SCR 860; *R v Solosky*, [1980] 1 SCR 821.

100 2001 SCC 14 at para 41 [*McClure*].

101 *Ibid* at para 38.

disclose[102] arises only when the accused's innocence is at stake. In a later decision they summarized the proper approach:

> The *McClure* test comprises a threshold question and a two stage innocence at stake test, which proceed as follows:
>
> - To satisfy the threshold test, the accused must establish that:
>   - the information he seeks from the solicitor–client communication is not available from any other source; and
>   - he is otherwise unable to raise a reasonable doubt.
> - If the threshold has been satisfied, the judge should proceed to the innocence at stake test, which has two stages.
>   - Stage #1: The accused seeking production of the solicitor–client communication has to demonstrate an evidentiary basis to conclude that a communication exists that could raise a reasonable doubt as to his guilt.
>   - Stage #2: If such an evidentiary basis exists, the trial judge should examine the communication to determine whether, in fact, it is likely to raise a reasonable doubt as to the guilt of the accused.[103]

In dealing with the threshold test, the Court has generally adopted a stringent position, as is consistent with protecting solicitor–client privilege as much as possible. The initial question asks whether the information is available *in an admissible form* from some other source. If it is not, the test could effectively never be met (if the accused did not know in some fashion that potentially useful evidence existed in a solicitor's file, no application would ever be made).[104] However, it must be clear that the other sources of information are not merely potentially inadmissible but genuinely unavailable. Thus, for example, if there is an issue as to whether other evidence might not be available because it is hearsay, a trial judge should first determine whether that evidence falls into any of the hearsay exceptions. The *McClure* application should be considered only after it has been decided that the other evidence is definitely unavailable.[105] If there is a possibility that the

---

102 Strictly, this will be a question of *production* of evidence from a third party, not *disclosure* of evidence in the hands of the Crown.

103 *R v Brown*, 2002 SCC 32 at para 4 [*Brown*].

104 Layton points out that, in most instances, the only people who are, in fact, likely to know of potentially exculpatory information protected by solicitor–client privilege are the other solicitor and client. See David Layton, "*R. v. Brown*: Protecting Legal-Professional Privilege" (2002) 50 *Criminal Reports* (5th) 37, for a discussion of voluntary release of privileged information by a lawyer.

105 *Brown*, above note 103 at paras 44–45.

third party has effectively waived solicitor–client privilege, then that too should be decided first.[106] A *McClure* application is intended to be a last resort.

The accused must also be unable to prove innocence in any other way. Once again, this means that all sources of evidence against the accused must be decided first. A case based entirely on circumstantial evidence is the least likely to succeed, and so infringement of solicitor–client privilege is less likely to be needed. But, if the Crown might strengthen its case by calling a jailhouse informant to report an alleged confession by the accused, the privileged information might be more needed, and so the Crown should make that decision before the *McClure* application.[107]

Whether the accused can prove innocence in any other way also affects the appropriate timing for a *McClure* application. Usually a trial judge should postpone the application at least until the Crown has closed its case. If the Crown has not proven its case beyond a reasonable doubt at that stage, the *McClure* application is unnecessary. Even then the trial judge may postpone the application further until the defence has presented its case, to see whether a reasonable doubt has arisen in some other way. Further, a *McClure* application can be renewed at a later stage of the trial if the defence feels it is then clearer that the accused has no other way to prove innocence.[108]

The first step in the innocence at stake test requires the accused to provide only an evidentiary basis that a communication exists that *could* raise a reasonable doubt. Mere speculation that such evidence may exist will not suffice, since the test is not meant to authorize fishing expeditions. However, the standard cannot be too high, since the accused is unlikely to have very precise information about the communication.[109] If the evidence suggested to exist merely challenges credibility or raises a collateral matter, it is unlikely to pass this part of the threshold test.

Where the first stage is passed, the trial judge should examine the record to determine whether there is useful evidence in it. At this stage,

---

106 *Ibid* at para 45.

107 *Ibid* at para 50.

108 *Ibid* at paras 52–54. There is some suggestion that a *McClure* application could also be brought to support an abuse of process claim rather than a claim of factual innocence. If that is so, the same principles would apply, but translated to the different context: broadly, the trial judge must be satisfied that there is no other way in which the abuse of process could be shown. See *R v Rutigliano*, 2015 ONCA 452.

109 *McClure*, above note 100 at para 52.

the higher standard, that the evidence *is likely to raise* a reasonable doubt about the accused's guilt, is applied:

> In most cases, this means that, unless the solicitor–client communication goes directly to one of the elements of the offence, it will not be sufficient to meet this requirement. Simply providing evidence that advances ancillary attacks on the Crown's case (e.g., by impugning the credibility of a Crown witness, or by providing evidence that suggests that some Crown evidence was obtained unconstitutionally) will very seldom be sufficient to meet this requirement.[110]

Nonetheless, the trial judge is not asking whether the evidence *will* raise a reasonable doubt, but merely whether it is likely to.[111]

In determining this question, the trial judge is not limited to the written materials in the file — the same principles govern solicitor–client communications whether they are oral or in writing. Accordingly, it is open to the trial judge to request that the solicitor providing the file also supply an affidavit stating that the file is a complete record or contains all other information necessary to complete the record.[112]

Evidence should not be disclosed from the file simply because it will strengthen the accused's case or it is more likely to be believed than other evidence. It cannot be released to corroborate other evidence the accused has led. The solicitor's file must be the *only way* for the accused to prove innocence.[113]

In deciding what information to disclose from the file, the trial judge should be similarly circumspect. The file should be edited to remove reference to any other offences or to other third parties, and only the information necessary to raise a reasonable doubt should be released.[114] Further, the information is to be released only to the accused, not to the Crown.[115] Finally, the person whose privilege is being infringed will enjoy use and derivative use immunity concerning the information released.[116]

---

110 *Ibid* at para 58. Layton is critical of this aspect of the Court's decision, arguing that, although described as the "innocence at stake" exception, the real issue is whether reasonable doubt is at stake. Therefore, information going to a witness's credibility, to admissibility of evidence, or to a stay application could be regarded as equally worthy of disclosure. See David Layton, "*R. v. McClure*: The Privilege on the Pea" (2001) 40 *Criminal Reports* (5th) 19.

111 *McClure*, above note 100 at 59.

112 *Brown*, above note 103 at para 65.

113 *Ibid* at para 72.

114 *Ibid* at para 77.

115 *Ibid* at para 84.

116 *Ibid* at para 99.

### c) National Security Privilege

National security privilege, unlike informer or solicitor–client privilege, is created by statute, specifically by the provisions of the *Canada Evidence Act* (*CEA*).[117] The *CEA* requires anyone who is required to disclose or expects to disclose "sensitive information" to give notice to the Attorney General of Canada of the possibility and the proceeding in which it might occur.[118] Pending action by the Attorney General the person giving notice cannot disclose the information, nor indeed the fact that notice has been given. However, the Attorney General can authorize the disclosure of any or all of the information. Alternatively, if the Attorney General does not wish to disclose the information, they can apply to the Federal Court for an order. The Federal Court judge can decide whether to hold a hearing and to whom notice of any such hearing should be given; the judge can also afford other people the right to make representations. If the judge is of the view that no injury to international relations, national defence, or national security would result, the judge can authorize disclosure. If such injury would result, the judge still can order disclosure, but only if the public interest in disclosure outweighs the public interest in non-disclosure. In such a case the disclosure can be subject to conditions and might take the form of the information itself, a summary of the information, or facts relating to the information. The judge may also order that notification of the decision be given to any person.

There is a limited right of appeal to the Federal Court of Appeal and beyond that to the Supreme Court of Canada.[119] More directly relevant, however, is a power given to the Attorney General of Canada when an order for disclosure has been made: despite that order, the Attorney General personally is, in those circumstances, entitled to issue a certificate prohibiting disclosure of the information.[120] In that event, notice of the certificate must be given to the judge presiding over the proceedings at which disclosure was proposed, every party to those proceedings, and others. The judge presiding at a criminal proceeding affected by such a certificate has the ability to make any order

117 RSC 1985, c C-5 (as amended) [*CEA*]. See, in particular, ss 38–38.16. A similar power exists in s 87 of the *Immigration and Refugee Protection Act*, SC 2001, c 27: see the discussion in *Canada (Attorney General) v Soltanizadeh*, 2019 FCA 202.

118 *Ibid*, s 38.01. "Sensitive information" is defined in s 38 as "information relating to international relations or national defence or national security that is in the possession of the Government of Canada, whether originating from inside or outside Canada, and is of a type that the Government of Canada is taking measures to safeguard."

119 *Ibid*, ss 38.09 and 38.1.

120 *Ibid*, s 38.13.

appropriate "to protect the right of the accused to a fair trial."[121] The *CEA* specifically contemplates that such orders might include dismissing specific counts, only allowing proceedings to continue on a lesser offence, or staying proceedings entirely.

This potential exception to disclosure is unusual in that the judge initially deciding whether material will or will not be disclosed to the accused is *not* the trial judge. The judge responsible for seeing to it that the accused's right to disclosure is respected has no direct control over the disclosure issue. Indeed, since the decision is made by a Federal Court judge, it will be made by a judge with no jurisdiction over criminal matters. Nonetheless, the Court held in *R v Ahmad* that, "properly interpreted,"[122] the scheme is constitutional, complying both with the division of powers in the *Constitution Act, 1867* as well as with the accused's right to disclosure under section 7 of the *Charter*.[123] It is the latter question that is relevant here.

A Federal Court judge has discretion under the *Canada Evidence Act* as to whether to give notice of the hearing to anyone. The Court concluded that the scheme had to be interpreted as requiring that, unless the Federal Court judge decides without a hearing that the information in question should be disclosed to the criminal court, there must be a hearing on the disclosure issues, and that notice of that hearing must be given to the criminal court. Similarly, absent compelling reasons to the contrary, the Federal Court judge should give notice of the proceedings to the accused as well.[124]

The scheme also authorizes disclosure to various parties on conditions. Given an accused's right to a fair trial and the trial judge's obligation to protect that right, the *CEA* scheme had to be interpreted as intending to make that possible. Accordingly, judges conducting a criminal trial had to be in a position to act judicially. This meant that a judge had to have enough information not only to see to it that an accused's right to a fair trial was not infringed, but also to see to it that prosecutions did not collapse unnecessarily. As such a trial judge ought to receive not only notice that a hearing about non-disclosure of sensitive information is occurring, but some basis for understanding what that information is and how it might have an impact on the

121 *Ibid*, s 38.14.

122 2011 SCC 6 at para 27 [*Ahmad*].

123 On these sections of the *CEA*, see, as well, *Canada (Attorney General) v Khawaja*, 2007 FCA 342.

124 The Court acknowledged that this did not immediately mesh well with the prohibition on giving notice of proceedings in s 38.02 but held that it was not necessary to pronounce in detail on that point in the case.

accused's trial. In some cases, a summary of the information might be sufficient while in other instances more extensive access will be required. In most cases, the Court held, disclosure of the information to the trial judge, on the condition that it not be revealed to the accused, will be the most appropriate option. The trial judge might also decide to hear submissions from Crown counsel or from a security-cleared special advocate on behalf of the accused in certain cases.

In the end, it will always remain up to the trial judge to decide whether an accused's right to disclosure has been adequately protected. If the trial judge concludes that it has not and that a stay of proceedings will therefore be necessary, the Crown should be notified. If further and better disclosure is not forthcoming, then a stay of proceedings will be the presumptively appropriate remedy.[125] A stay in such circumstances is contemplated by the statute and therefore need not meet the ordinary "clearest of cases" standard for a stay. It is this aspect of the statute, in effect, which allows the trial judge to protect the accused's right to disclosure even without the ability to govern disclosure:

> where the government is withholding information and the trial judge is unable to satisfy himself or herself that non-disclosure has not adversely affected trial fairness, and no lesser step or remedy can assure it, a stay of proceedings under s 38 must issue. Doubt, in this respect, should be resolved in favour of protecting the fair trial rights of the accused, including the right of full answer and defence.[126]

Thus, although trial judges are deprived of the ability to order disclosure, they do have the power to order a more drastic remedy.

# C. PRODUCTION

## 1) Introduction

As noted in the introduction to this chapter, in addition to the Court-created disclosure regimes dealing with material in the hands or reach of the Crown, there are also regimes governing an accused's right to access to material that is in the hands of third parties. The context that has driven the development of the law in this area is the issue of an accused's right to see psychiatric, medical, or other counselling

---

125 *Ahmad*, above note 122 at para 51.

126 *Ibid* at para 52.

records regarding a complainant, particularly complainants in a sexual assault trial.[127]

The reason special rules have been developed in this area is the presence of a competing concern to the accused's fair trial right, namely, the complainant's privacy and other rights. This situation is therefore similar to the interplay between disclosure and privilege. However, it is different because the type of privilege concerned is not a "class privilege," as informer privilege and solicitor–client privilege are. Although a complainant has a privacy interest in counselling records, those records are not automatically subject to the same kind of blanket protection. Rather, any claim of privilege was originally based on a case-by-case analysis according to the Wigmore test for privilege.[128] The right to disclosure automatically yields to a class privilege, but individual analysis and the weighing of interests are necessary when dealing with case-by-case privilege.

In addition, other factors distinguish production from disclosure, beyond the greater privacy interest in the material sought to be disclosed. Third parties, who are in control of the records, have no obligation to assist the defence. Further, the records are not part of the case the accused has to meet. All of these factors mean that the accused faces a higher burden than normal in obtaining access to this material, although not as high a burden as when a class privilege is in issue.

---

127 A great deal was written on the decisions handed down on this subject. See, for example, Jennifer Koshan, "Disclosure and Production in Sexual Violence Cases: Situating *Stinchcombe*" (2002) 40 *Alberta Law Review* 655; Lise Gotell, "The Ideal Victim, the Hysterical Complainant and the Disclosure of Confidential Records: A Case Study of the Implications of the *Charter* for Sexual Assault Law" (2002) 40 *Osgoode Hall Law Journal* 251 [Gotell]; Jamie Cameron, "Dialogue and Hierarchy in *Charter* Interpretation: A Comment on *R. v. Mills*" (2001) 38 *Alberta Law Review* 1051; Lise Gotell, "Colonization through Disclosure: Confidential Records, Sexual Assault Complainants and Canadian Law" (2001) 10 *Social and Legal Studies* 315; Karen Busby, "Third Party Records Cases since *R. v. O'Connor*" (2000) 27 *Manitoba Law Journal* 355; Peter Sankoff, "Crown Disclosure after *Mills*: Have the Rules Suddenly Changed?" (2000) 28 *Criminal Reports* (5th) 285; Don Stuart, "*Mills*: Dialogue with Parliament and Equality by Assertion at What Cost?" (2000) 28 *Criminal Reports* (5th) 275; Karen Busby, "Discriminatory Uses of Personal Records in Sexual Violence Cases" (1997) 9 *Canadian Journal of Women and the Law* 148; Heather Holmes, "An Analysis of Bill C-46, Production of Records in Sexual Offence Proceedings" (1997) 2 *Canadian Criminal Law Review* 71; Bruce Feldthusen, "Access to the Private Therapeutic Records of Sexual Assault Complainants" (1996) 75 *Canadian Bar Review* 537.

128 *McClure*, above note 100 at para 29.

As the law has developed, there are now two distinct sets of rules governing production. The first of these was created by the Court with its decision in *O'Connor*.[129] Subsequently a second regime was created when Parliament partly overrode the result in *O'Connor* with sections 278.1 to 278.9 of the *Criminal Code*, often called the *Mills* regime.[130] A proper understanding of the current state of the law, then, requires consideration of the Court's decision in *O'Connor*, the legislative response to that decision, and finally of *R v Mills*,[131] the Court's decision on a *Charter* challenge to the legislation.[132] The net effect of combining those two schemes, as we shall see, is that although applications under *O'Connor* initially could involve a difficult balancing of interests, most of the difficult cases have now been diverted to the *Mills* regime and *O'Connor* applications are less controversial than they originally were.

## 2) Production under *O'Connor*

In *O'Connor*,[133] the accused was charged with several counts of sexual assault. He obtained a pre-trial order for disclosure of the complainants' entire medical, counselling, and school records. When the accused was unsuccessful in obtaining all these records, the trial judge entered a stay of proceedings, eventually leading the Supreme Court to consider the question of the procedure to be applied when an accused seeks documents such as counselling records in the hands of a third party.

The Court created a two-stage process for deciding whether third-party records should be produced. At the first stage, the accused must persuade the judge to examine the records personally. At the second stage, having looked at the records, the judge is required to decide whether to release them or some portions of them to the accused. Most of the controversy has related to what factors should guide the decision at each stage.

---

129 *O'Connor*, above note 5.

130 As is discussed below, because of additions to the scheme, it now extends to s 278.97.

131 *Mills*, above note 6.

132 Layton observes that the number of standards applicable to third party production is "ever-growing": simple materiality in many cases; the *O'Connor* test where constitutionally protected privacy interests are at stake; ss 278.1–78.91 where those interests arise in the context of a sexual assault trial; and the "innocence at stake" standard of informer privilege and solicitor–client privilege. See Layton, above note 110.

133 For an explanation of this issue in chart form, see *Anatomy of Criminal Procedure*, above note 9, Chart 2.3(b)(i), "Production Orders Under *O'Connor*."

A majority of five judges held that at the first stage, it was necessary to consider not just the accused's right to make full answer and defence, but also to weigh the third party's privacy interests in the balance.[134] The accused must show that the records are likely relevant. On the one hand, "likely relevance" in this context was meant to set a higher standard than the standard for disclosure. On the other hand, likely relevance "is a lower threshold than 'true relevance', and has a 'wide and generous connotation' that 'includes information in respect of which there is a reasonable possibility that it may assist the accused in the exercise of the right to make full answer and defence'."[135] Rather, the accused must satisfy the trial judge "that there is a reasonable possibility that the information is logically probative to *an issue at trial or the competence of a witness to testify*."[136] The standard is not to be interpreted as onerous, since the accused will have to make submissions to the judge without knowing what is in the record.[137] It "is a first-step inquiry designed to prevent fishing expeditions, but nothing more."[138] Ultimately, asking the accused to show that a record is "likely relevant" demands more of the accused than the disclosure standard does, where the Crown would have to show the record was clearly *ir*relevant. However, it does not ask as much of the accused as the standard at the second stage of the test, where the judge who examines the records will order disclosed the parts that are truly relevant.

The Court's understanding of "likely relevance" has shifted over time. When the standard was first established in *O'Connor*, that was the only scheme governing production of third party records in any context, and so there was a need to have real protection for the greater privacy interests at stake. Since then the most controversial situations have been hived off to be dealt with under the statutory scheme, discussed below, and so *O'Connor* now deals with only relatively uncontroversial situations. In that evolved context, there is much less need for "likely relevance" to act as a significant filter.

In *O'Connor* itself, the majority suggested that evidence in counselling records might be relevant by containing information about the events underlying the charge, by revealing the use of a therapy

---

134 Provided the records were not already in the hands of the Crown. If that were the case, the majority held, the third party would no longer have a privacy interest.

135 *Gubbins*, above note 8 at para 27.

136 *O'Connor*, above note 5 at para 22 [emphasis in original].

137 *Ibid* at para 25.

138 *Gubbins*, above note 8 at para 28.

influencing the complainant's memory of the events, or by bearing on the complainant's credibility.

The majority specifically rejected the minority's suggestion that at the first stage, in addition to showing likely relevance, the accused should also have to satisfy the trial judge that the salutary effects of producing the documents outweigh the deleterious effects. That question, according to the majority, is confined to the second stage.[139]

At the second stage, where the trial judge decides whether to order any portion of the record produced, all the judges agreed that a number of factors were relevant to the decision:

> (1) the extent to which the record is necessary for the accused to make full answer and defence; (2) the probative value of the record in question; (3) the nature and extent of the reasonable expectation of privacy vested in that record; (4) whether production of the record would be premised upon any discriminatory belief or bias [and] (5) the potential prejudice to the complainant's dignity, privacy or security of the person that would be occasioned by production of the record in question.[140]

Four of the nine judges, however, unsuccessfully argued that two further factors should also be considered: "the extent to which production of records of this nature would frustrate society's interest in encouraging the reporting of sexual offences and the acquisition of treatment by victims" as well as "the effect on the integrity of the trial process of producing, or failing to produce, the record, having in mind the need to maintain consideration in the outcome."[141] A key point here is that the five factors all nine judges agreed on weigh the accused's interests against those of the particular complainant in the case: the majority wanted to limit the consideration to that. Taking into account things like the effect on reporting of sexual offences would be to weigh the immediate accused's interests against those of future, unrelated complainants. The majority said that the former consideration was a relevant but not paramount consideration,[142] and that the second consideration was relevant only in deciding admissibility of the evidence, not in deciding whether the material should be produced for the accused.

*O'Connor* created a scheme which was intended to engage in the potentially difficult balancing between an accused's fair trial interests and the privacy interests of others. As noted, the context for that decision

139 *O'Connor*, above note 5 at para 21.

140 *Ibid* at para 31.

141 *Ibid* at para 32.

142 *Ibid* at para 33.

pitted a strong third-party interest against that of the accused — the privacy interest of a sexual assault complainant with regard to therapeutic records. As we will see in the following section, that privacy interest and most similarly strong ones have since been "pulled" from the *O'Connor* regime by a statutory scheme. As a result, the cases left to be analyzed under *O'Connor* are only those where the competing interest is likely to be much less compelling than the accused's fair trial interest. Subsequent caselaw has recognized that point.

The Court has concluded, for example, that once "likely relevance" is made out in an application brought under *O'Connor* (rather than the *Mills* regime, to be discussed next), it is unlikely that a third-party privacy interest can defeat an application for production. It is possible that some redactions might be made or conditions imposed to ensure that there is no unnecessary invasion of privacy, but the production claim is likely to succeed. In effect, once an application has passed the likely relevance stage, the distinction between production and disclosure collapses:

> It may be useful to pose the question in this way: If the third party record in question had found its way into the Crown prosecutor's file, would there be any basis under the first party *Stinchcombe* disclosure regime for not disclosing it to the accused? If the answer to that question is no, there can be no principled reason to arrive at a different outcome on the third party production application.[143]

## 3) Production under the Statutory Scheme (the *Mills* Regime)

In response to the *O'Connor* decision, Parliament enacted sections 278.1ff of the *Criminal Code*. The exact details of that scheme will be detailed in a moment, but it is necessary first to provide an overview of how the two production regimes fit together. The *O'Connor* rules were developed in the context of counselling records, but they apply generally to all records in the hands of a third party. The statutory scheme applies only to *some* of the records in the hands of third parties and only for some offences — in essence, counselling and similar records for sexual assault complainants or witnesses. Accordingly, the *O'Connor* rules still govern production with regard to records not explicitly covered by the statutory scheme. Theoretically, the statutory scheme is

---

143 *McNeil*, above note 7 at para 42. See also the discussion in David Paciocco, "*Stinchcombe* on Steroids: The Surprising Legacy of *McNeil*" (2009) 62 *Criminal Reports* (6th) 26.

an exception to the "general" *O'Connor* regime: realistically, the exception applies far more often than the rule, since third party records, particularly counselling records,[144] have most often been sought in the context of sexual offence prosecutions. Further, because the *Mills* regime[145] encompasses records with a greater privacy, and in the context of more serious offences, the cases dealt with by it are more likely to be controversial.

Making the situation more complex is that the statutory scheme was itself subject to a *Charter* challenge in *Mills*.[146] Although the Court upheld the constitutionality of the statutory scheme, in the course of doing so they put a particular gloss upon the provisions which might make them more restricted than they at first glance seem to be. In addition, some adjustments were made to the provisions in 2015 with the *Victims Bill of Rights*, though these did not change the major thrust of the scheme.[147] Beyond that further changes were made in 2019 (see the discussion at the end of this section) though they simply added further provisions dealing with a related matter, rather than making any change to the third party record production scheme. In any event, it is necessary now to look in detail at the statutory scheme. In essence, those provisions enact the minority decision in *O'Connor*; that is, they follow the same general two-step approach adopted by the majority — indeed, by all judges — in that case, but require the trial judge also to take into account the factors the majority said should not be considered. On the face of it the provisions are broader than the majority decision in *O'Connor*, in the sense that they provide more protection to complainants' interests, in other ways as well.

---

144 Although a number of types of records are potentially subject to the statutory scheme, counselling records are consistently those sought most often: see Carly Jacuk and Hassan Rasmi Hassan, "Third Party Records: A Review of the Case Law from 2011–2017," Department of Justice, Victims of Crime Research Digest No 11 and Susan MacDonald, "Third Party Records: A Review of the Case Law from 2003–2010," Department of Justice, Victims of Crime Research Digest No 7.

145 For an explanation of this issue in chart form, see *Anatomy of Criminal Procedure*, above note 9, Chart 2.3(b)(ii), "Statutory Production Orders."

146 *Mills*, above note 6.

147 *Canadian Victims Bill of Rights*, SC 2015, c 13. For example, s 278.7(2) lists factors for a judge to take into account in deciding whether to order production to the accused: that list already included privacy and equality, but the *Victims Bill of Rights* added "personal security" there and in other sections. Similarly, the scheme already provided in s 278.4(2) that a complainant or witness was entitled to have counsel: s 278.4(2.1) added that the complainant or witness is to be informed of that right.

The majority in *O'Connor*, for example, was primarily concerned with "therapeutic records," which are "intensely private."[148] Even the minority only suggested that other documents, such as school records or private diaries, might also attract a reasonable expectation of privacy[149] and that this question "is inherently fact- and context-sensitive."[150] The statutory scheme, however, states that

> For the purposes of sections 278.2 to 278.92, *record* means any form of record that contains personal information for which there is a reasonable expectation of privacy and includes medical, psychiatric, therapeutic, counselling, education, employment, child welfare, adoption and social services records, personal journals and diaries, and records containing personal information the production or disclosure of which is protected by any other Act of Parliament or a provincial legislature.[151]

This definition could be read as taking a more categorical approach than the *O'Connor* rules did. That is, it could be read as saying that any third-party record of the listed type is one which attracts a reasonable expectation of privacy is covered by it. On that reading, all such records in the listed categories would be covered, not merely those found to attract a reasonable expectation of privacy after a fact- and case-sensitive analysis.[152] In addition, section 278.2 restricts the operation of this scheme to production in the context of prosecutions for various listed offences, all of which are sexual offences of one sort or another: in the case of any other offence, the *O'Connor* rules will still apply. As a practical matter, of course, it was primarily in the context of sexual offences that such applications have been made.

Further, the scheme in *O'Connor* was limited to records still in the hands of third parties. Those in the hands of the Crown no longer

148 *O'Connor*, above note 5 at para 7.

149 See the discussion of reasonable expectation of privacy in Chapter 4.

150 *O'Connor*, above note 5 at para 99.

151 Section 278.1. The list excludes "records made by persons responsible for the investigation or prosecution of the offence." In other words, documents prepared by the police in the investigation of the offence being prosecuted are not subject to the *Mills* regime; however, records prepared by police for other investigations are not excluded: *Quesnelle*, above note 14.

152 Note that until Bill C-51 was passed in 2018, the definition included the words "without limiting the generality of the foregoing": the removal of those words seems to limit the provisions only to the type of records explicitly listed, though that is of course quite a broad list. See *An Act to amend the Criminal Code and the Department of Justice Act and to make consequential amendments to another Act*, SC 2018, c 29, s 23 [Bill C-51].

attracted a reasonable expectation of privacy, the majority said, and therefore were subject to the ordinary *Stinchcombe* rules. The minority expressed no opinion on this issue.[153] Section 278.2(2), however, makes the statutory scheme applicable even to records already in the hands of the Crown, unless the complainant or witness has "expressly waived the application of those sections."

The accused's task at the first stage is to show that the record is "likely relevant," and section 278.3(4) lists some claims by the accused that would *not* be sufficient to meet this standard: for example that "the record relates to medical or psychiatric treatment, therapy or counselling that the complainant or witness has received or is receiving"[154] or that "the record may relate to the credibility of the complainant or witness."[155] In considering the first stage, section 278.5(2) of the *Code* requires the judge to balance the salutary and deleterious effects of producing the record for the judge's own inspection, as the minority in *O'Connor* wished. In particular, the accused is required not only to show that the record is likely relevant, but also that "the production of the record is necessary in the interests of justice."[156] Further, that section states that the trial judge "shall take . . . into account" the additional factors that the majority in *O'Connor* held should *not* be taken into account and states that the factors are to be applied at both the first stage (production to the judge personally) and the second (production to the accused), contrary to the approach taken in *O'Connor*. The intent, the Court has said, is to shift much of the balancing process from the second stage to the first.[157]

On the face of it, then, the statutory scheme departs from the *O'Connor* rules in a number of ways that were specifically considered and rejected by the majority of the Court. Given that the *O'Connor* rules were based on the accused's section 7 rights, it was therefore natural to wonder whether the statutory scheme violated the *Charter*.

In *Mills*,[158] the trial judge had found that the scheme violated an accused's section 7 and section 11(d) rights under the *Charter* and struck it down. When the issue reached the Supreme Court, the legislation was upheld. However, the Court explained its approach to the task by saying that "if legislation is amenable to two interpretations, a court should choose the interpretation that upholds the legislation

153 *O'Connor*, above note 5 at para 98.
154 Section 278.3(4)(b).
155 Section 278.3(4)(e).
156 Section 278.5(1)(c).
157 *McNeil*, above note 7 at para 32.
158 *Mills*, above note 6.

as constitutional"[159] and to a certain extent the decision could be seen as watering down what the legislation might have seemed to be saying to make the scheme depart less from the approach of the majority in *O'Connor*.[160] As time has passed, however, the scheme has not necessarily remained limited to that narrower initial reading.

In dealing with the statutory scheme's wider list of records covered by the scheme, the Court adopted the position of a lower court.[161] The list of records in section 278.1, they concluded, did not mean that *every* record of a type on that list was covered by the statutory scheme. Rather, only records of the type listed in which there was *also* a reasonable expectation of privacy would be governed by the scheme. In the immediate aftermath of *Mills*, some lower court judges ordered production on the basis that the statutory scheme was not applicable to the particular records in question.[162] Similarly in *Quesnelle*, more than a decade later, the Court held that the first question to be asked in deciding whether something is a "record" for purposes of the *Mills* regime was "does the document contain personal information for which there is a reasonable expectation of privacy?" and characterized the list in section 278.1 as "an illustrative list of some of the types of records that usually give rise to a reasonable expectation of privacy."[163]

On the other hand most recently the Court has described the *Mills* regime as applying to both enumerated and non-enumerated records, saying that the scheme applies to the records enumerated in section 278.1 "regardless of the specific content of the record."[164] They have also spent some time considering when records might be of a sort to which the *Mills* regime applies despite not being enumerated.[165] The approach to this particular aspect of the scheme has evolved.

---

159 *Mills*, above note6 at para 53

160 The Court speaks of itself in *Mills*, above note 6, as deferring to Parliament, but in its actual approach it is not genuinely deferential: see Steve Coughlan, "Complainants' Records after *Mills*: Same as It Ever Was" (2000) 33 *Criminal Reports* (5th) 300.

161 *R v Regan* (1998), 174 NSR (2d) 230 (SC).

162 Gotell, above note 127 at 283. See also *Quesnelle*, above note 14 at para 20, holding that the first question to be asked in deciding whether something is a "record" for purposes of the *Mills* regime is "does the document contain personal information for which there is a reasonable expectation of privacy?" and at para 22, describing the records mentioned as "an illustrative list of some of the types of records that usually give rise to a reasonable expectation of privacy."

163 *Quesnelle*, above note 14 at paras 20 and 22.

164 *R v JJ*, 2022 SCC 28 at para 39 [*JJ*].

165 *JJ*, above note 164 at para 42ff.

The statutory scheme is also broader than *O'Connor* because it applies to records already in the hands of the Crown. But this will not be the case where the complainant has expressly waived these protections, in other words, where a "fully informed complainant expressly waives the protection of the legislation, by declaration or *by voluntarily providing her records to the Crown*."[166] The Court interprets the legislative scheme as simply filling a void left by the *O'Connor* rules (how to deal with third-party records that come into the Crown's hands through a search warrant or similar means), but not as changing the *O'Connor* rules.[167] On the other hand, it is clear that the Crown might decide that records it has obtained to which the *Mills* regime applies should not be disclosed to the accused, in which case it will give notice to the accused.[168]

The statutory scheme requires the accused, at the first stage, to bring an application, and in that application to show that production is necessary in the interests of justice, a consideration motivated by the desire to give greater weight to a complainant's privacy interests.[169] The legislation lists claims that will not establish likely relevance, but in this context they consciously adopted what they thought of as the constitutional way of reading the provision. Section 278.3(4) does not *preclude* reliance on factors such as "the record may disclose a prior inconsistent statement of the complainant or witness":[170] it only requires that there be more than a bare assertion of the claim.[171] In *Mills*, the Court upheld this requirement by making it secondary to — and, indeed, in some ways converting it to — concern for the accused's right to make full answer and defence. A judge is required to protect that right of the accused. If it is necessary to examine the documents to see whether they should be produced to the accused, then production to the judge

---

166 *Mills*, above note 6 at para 106 [emphasis added].

167 *Ibid* at para 109.

168 Section 278.2(3). *Quesnelle*, above note 14, observes at para 16 that the Crown should in appropriate circumstances give an assessment of the likely relevance of such a record and, at a minimum, should advise if it intends to use any information contained in those records as part of its case.

169 Section 278.3. Initially s 278.3(5) required the accused to give fourteen days notice on the prosecutor, the record-keeper, and the complainant or witness: Bill C-51, above note 152, changed that to sixty days notice.

170 Section 278.3(4)(d).

171 *Mills*, above note 6 at para 118. See also *R v KC* (2021), 73 CR (7th) 240 (Ont CA), where the trial judge had erred by declining to look at the file even though the accused had presented case-specific information about some of the things in s 278.3(4), not simply attempted to rely on them in the abstract.

is necessary in the interests of justice.[172] The accused must have access to all documents that might be constitutionally required: "a production regime that denied this would not be production 'necessary in the interests of justice.'"[173] "Read correctly," this requirement is constitutional.[174]

Finally, the legislative scheme requires that the judge shall take into account at both stages the factors that *O'Connor* said were not to be considered at all, or were to be considered only at the second stage. The Court minimizes the practical effect of these changes by finding that the addition of these factors to the legislative scheme does not necessarily make any difference:

> s. 278.5(2) does not require that the judge engage in a conclusive and indepth evaluation of each of the factors. It rather requires the judge to "take them into account" — to the extent possible at this early stage of proceedings — in deciding whether to order a particular record produced to himself or herself for inspection. Section 278.5(2) serves as a check-list of the various factors that *may* come into play in making the decision regarding production to the judge.[175]

The Court makes clear that the accused's right to full answer and defence is not to be compromised by this change:

> Therefore, while the s. 278.5(2) factors are relevant, in the final analysis the judge is free to make whatever order is "necessary in the interests of justice" — a mandate that includes all of the applicable "principles of fundamental justice" at stake.[176]

In practical terms, following *Mills* the statutory scheme has resulted in some change, but not as much as it might. This is likely a reflection of the fact that, according to the Court, *Mills* did *not* intend to "shift the balance away from the *primary* emphasis on the rights of the accused."[177]

---

172 *Mills*, above note 6 at para 132.

173 *Ibid* at para 130. See Gotell, above note 127 at 286n: this aspect of the *Mills* reasoning has been frequently cited by lower courts as justification for production.

174 *Mills*, above note 6 at para 133.

175 *Ibid* at para 134 [emphasis added].

176 *Ibid*.

177 *R v Shearing*, 2002 SCC 58 [*Shearing*] at para 132 [emphasis in original]. See Heather Donkers, "An Analysis of Third Party Record Applications Under the *Mills* Scheme, 2012–2017: The Right to Full Answer and Defence versus Rights to Privacy and Equality" (2018) 41–4 *Manitoba Law Journal* 245, arguing that cases which order production are likely to follow the *Mills* gloss on the statutory scheme, while those not ordering production are more likely to follow the text of the provisions.

There are indications that because of the standard set in *Mills*, lower court judges decide less frequently that records meet the likely relevance standard, for example, and so do not examine the records personally.[178] This is as it should be, since — despite the fact that the same phrase is used in both tests — "likely relevance" is a higher standard under *Mills* than under *O'Connor*.[179] However, this does not necessarily mean that there is less production of records to the accused in the end: it might simply be that records that would not ultimately have been disclosed are filtered out at an earlier stage.[180] On the other hand, the *Mills* regime certainly does envisage that a trial judge might be persuaded to view the record but then decide not to produce it to the accused.[181]

Further, the type of analysis undertaken seems not to have changed dramatically. *Mills* itself asserts the relevance of the complainant's privacy *and* equality rights, and the legislative scheme includes factors intended to reflect broader societal interests.[182] Nonetheless, for a considerable period courts seemed reluctant to take into account any

178 Gotell, above note 127.

179 *McNeil*, above note 7 at para 30: "the common law likely relevance threshold in *O'Connor* differs significantly from the statutory likely relevance threshold set by Parliament for the production of records containing personal information in sexual assault proceedings under the *Mills* regime." See the elaboration at paras 31–32. In addition see *R v Batte* (2000), 34 CR (5th) 197 (Ont CA), holding at para 71 that "the mere fact that a complainant has spoken to a counsellor or doctor about the abuse or matters touching on the abuse does not make a record of those conversations likely relevant to a fact in issue or to a complainant's credibility," and at para 72 that such records "will pass the likely relevance threshold only if there is some basis for concluding that the statements have some potential to provide the accused with some added information not already available to the defence or have some potential impeachment value."

180 The Court noted in *McNeil*, above note 7 at para 32 that "while the *Mills* regime retains the two-stage framework set out in *O'Connor*, it differs significantly in that much of the balancing of the competing interests is effected at the first stage in determining whether production should be made to the court for inspection."

181 See, for example, *R v B(P)*, 2015 ONCA 738, where the trial judge was found to have erred in refusing to look at the counseling record: although the complainant testified that the account she gave to her psychologist and the one she gave in court were the same, it was her testimony itself which was being challenged, so that did not mean the records were not likely relevant. However, having examined the records themselves, the Ontario Court of Appeal agreed that the account in them was generalized and not inconsistent with the trial testimony, and therefore held they should not be produced.

182 See, for example, s 278.5(2) of the *Code*, including "society's interest in encouraging the reporting of sexual offences."

interest of a complainant other than privacy.[183] Once again, however, this might be an aspect of the approach which is changing. In *R v JJ*, in the course of upholding a small expansion to the scheme (see the discussion below) the Court stressed the dignity, equality and privacy interests of complainants in a number of places, for example by relying on the protection of those interests as showing that the legislation was not overbroad.[184]

Note as well that the statutory scheme has been held to apply even when third-party records are first sought as fresh evidence on appeal.[185] Further, the *Mills* regime applies only to *disclosure* of records: the Crown has a duty nonetheless to make reasonable inquiries and seek to *obtain* such potentially relevant material under *McNeil* (discussed in Section D, below in this chapter) which applies independently.[186]

One final issue should be mentioned in the context of the *Code's* statutory scheme for production of third party records. This last point relates to a significant change to the legislation made in 2018 by Bill C-51, though it is an evidentiary rather than a procedural issue.[187] As originally drafted, the statutory scheme only dealt with whether third party records should be *produced* first to the judge and then to the jury: it said nothing about whether such records would, if they ended up in the hands of the accused, be *admissible* at trial. That point was made by the Court in *R v Shearing*, where the accused was already in possession of a diary which had been written by the complainant and planned to use it to cross-examine her. The complainant argued that the diary should be returned to her and that the accused should then be required to bring an application under section 278.1ff for its production. The majority of the Court disagreed, holding that those provisions "address the *production* not the *use* or *admissibility* of personal information."[188]

However, in addition to the third party production regime, the *Code* has also contained for many years the "rape shield" provision in section 276 dealing with questioning a complainant about their sexual

183 Gotell, above note 127. In addition on the limited effectiveness of the provisions see also Lise Gotell, "When Privacy Is Not Enough: Sexual Assault Complainants, Sexual History Evidence and the Disclosure of Personal Records" (2006) 43:3 *Alberta Law Review* 743 and Lise Gotell, "Tracking Decisions on Access to Sexual Assault Complainants' Confidential Records: The Continued Permeability of Subsections 278.1–278.9 of the Criminal Code" (2008) 20:1 *Canadian Journal of Women and the Law* 111.

184 *JJ*, above note 164 at para 139.

185 *R v Rodgers* (2000), 144 CCC (3d) 568 (Ont CA).

186 *Quesnelle*, above note 14 at para 18.

187 Bill C-51, above note 152.

188 *Shearing*, above note 177 at para 94.

history, which does deal with admissibility. Such questions are either not permitted at all, or are only permitted following a successful application to lead such evidence.

Bill C-51, in essence, reversed the result in *Shearing* by creating rules about records already in the hands of the accused, and combining those with applications to lead evidence under the rape shield provisions. Section 278.92 of the *Code* now requires an accused who is already in possession of a record relating to a complainant (though not to a witness, which the third party production scheme includes) to bring an application if they wish to lead that record as evidence at a trial for a listed offence (again, a list of sexual offences). In part this also seems to have been a reaction to the high-profile acquittal in *R v Ghomeshi*, where the credibility of complainants was severely shaken when they were presented in cross-examination (to the apparent surprise of the Crown) with emails they had sent the accused. Section 278.93(4) requires that the application to use such evidence be brought at least seven days in advance, thereby eliminating the defence strategy of making use of such records by surprise.

The *Code* sets out the rules governing such applications and the criteria to be applied, and those rules are the same for applications under either section 276 or section 278.92. The criteria are not identical to those governing third party production applications, so *Shearing* has not literally been reversed, but many of the considerations are very similar between the two sets of provisions.[189] In addition, under the new regime complainants have been granted standing to make submissions and appear with respect to applications under sections 276 and 278.92 (a right they already had with respect to third party records applications under section 278.4).

These changes to the scheme were challenged on various bases, including that they impaired fair trial rights, were overbroad, infringed on the accused's right to silence, and improperly required defence disclosure, but the Court in *R v JJ* upheld the legislation.[190] They also spent some time explaining the process to be used for such applications, which govern applications both to lead sexual history evidence

---

189 See, for example, s 278.5(2)(d), asking "whether production of the record is based on a discriminatory belief or bias" and s 278.92(3)(e), speaking of "the need to remove from the fact-finding process any discriminatory belief or bias." Similarly, s 278.5(2)(f) asks a judge, in deciding on production, to consider "society's interest in encouraging the reporting of sexual offences," which is the same question asked in s 278.92(3)(b) in deciding admissibility of a record already in the hands of the accused.

190 *JJ*, above note 164.

and to use private records. The accused must prepare an application setting out detailed particulars of the evidence sought to be adduced, explaining the relevance of that evidence to an issue at trial. The judge will then determine, at stage one, whether that evidence is capable of being admissible based on the relevant threshold tests.[191] This stage one inquiry can proceed in writing, as an oral hearing, or both, as the judge decides. If the matter proceeds to a stage two hearing, the judge will then decide whether the evidence meets the test for admissibility, which in the case of private records applications is whether it "is relevant to an issue at trial and has significant probative value that is not substantially outweighed by the danger of prejudice to the proper administration of justice." This decision is governed by the factors listed in section 278.92(3) which, like those governing production under the *Mills* scheme, look both at the case at hand and the interests of future complainants.[192] Complainants have the right to appear and make submissions at the stage two hearing, with the assistance of counsel.[193]

## D. BRIDGING THE GAP (*R v MCNEIL*)

*McNeil* was a response to the fact that some documents, although not actually in the hands of the Crown and therefore not subject to *Stinchcombe* disclosure, ought clearly to be provided to the accused

---

191 Private record application are governed by ss 278.92(2)(a) and (b) while sexual history evidence is governed by ss 276(3) or 278.92(3).

192 The factors in s 278.92(3) are:

> (a) the interests of justice, including the right of the accused to make a full answer and defence;
> (b) society's interest in encouraging the reporting of sexual assault offences;
> (c) society's interest in encouraging the obtaining of treatment by complainants of sexual offences;
> (d) whether there is a reasonable prospect that the evidence will assist in arriving at a just determination in the case;
> (e) the need to remove from the fact-finding process any discriminatory belief or bias;
> (f) the risk that the evidence may unduly arouse sentiments of prejudice, sympathy or hostility in the jury;
> (g) the potential prejudice to the complainant's personal dignity and right of privacy;
> (h) the right of the complainant and of every individual to personal security and to the full protection and benefit of the law; and
> (i) any other factor that the judge, provincial court judge or justice considers relevant.

193 Section 278.94(2) and (3).

and certainly would be if an *O'Connor* application were brought: they are "obviously relevant." *McNeil* simplified the process for producing such records to the accused. In such cases (that is, where the Crown becomes aware of potentially relevant records in the hands of a third party), the Crown has a duty to inquire and obtain the evidence, rather than require the accused to pursue an *O'Connor* application.[194] This obligation has been evocatively referred to as the "duty to fetch."[195] As time has passed, it has simply come to be thought of as *part* of the Crown's disclosure obligation. It will be recalled that *Gubbins* said that the disclosure obligation applies when the information is in the hands of the Crown, or the nature of the information sought is such that the police or another Crown entity in possession or control of the information ought to have supplied it to the prosecuting Crown:[196] *McNeil* deals with the second of those situations.

The particular records in issue in *McNeil* were police disciplinary records and criminal investigation files relating to the main police witness. The Court rejected the suggestion that all state authorities, or even just the police and prosecutors, were indivisible for disclosure purposes. That assumption, it held, would require the Crown to make inquiries of every federal and provincial government department as well as every police force to see whether it might have relevant information. That does not mean, however, that the Crown can merely be passive. Rather, when aware of relevant information that it could obtain, the Crown has a duty to seek it out. This duty only applies, however, when the document is shown to exist. If the Crown does not concede the existence of the document in question, then the defence must establish a basis for the record's existence and relevance, or the Crown will have no duty under *McNeil*.[197]

In addition, the police have a corollary duty to disclose disciplinary records that could be relevant to the Crown, so that they can form part of the first-party disclosure package. The Court specifically listed five types of records that fell within this police duty:

a. Any conviction or finding of guilt under the *Canadian Criminal Code* or under the *Controlled Drugs and Substances Act* for which a pardon has not been granted;

---

194 *McNeil*, above note 7 at para 48ff.

195 David M Paciocco, "*Stinchcombe* on Steroids" (2009) 62 CR (6th) 26.

196 *Gubbins*, above note 8 at para 33. These two categories can also be thought of as "the fruits of the investigation" and material that is "obviously relevant to the accused's case": *Gubbins*, para 21.

197 *R v Awashish*, 2018 SCC 45.

b. Any outstanding charges under the *Canadian Criminal Code* or the *Controlled Drugs and Substances Act*;
c. Any conviction or finding of guilt under any other federal or provincial statute;
d. Any finding of guilt for misconduct after a hearing under the *Police Services Act* or its predecessor *Act*;
e. Any current charge of misconduct under the *Police Services Act* for which a Notice of Hearing has been issued.[198]

This list is usually referred to as the "Ferguson five." Records such as these ought to be provided by the Crown without prompting, although the officer concerned should be given notice of the intention to disclose and have the ability to make representations.

In the case of other types of records, the effect of the decision has in part been to create what amounts to a "*McNeil* hearing" to decide whether particular records should be treated in the same way. The issue is largely one of onus and the standard to be met. If the records in question are concluded to be first party records, they must be disclosed unless the Crown shows they are clearly irrelevant. But if they are found to be third party records, they will only be disclosed if the accused shows that they are likely relevant.[199] In practice, the latter standard is sometimes met on the basis that the records are obviously relevant, but even if that is not the case, an accused could show otherwise that they are likely relevant.[200]

It has been found, for example, that breathalyzer maintenance records do not meet the "obviously relevant" standard and neither do records relating to withdrawn disciplinary charges, but that the "rolling log" showing all evaluations conducted by a drug recognition expert and the testing and operating procedures for a speed measuring device do.[201]

Other cases have elaborated on further aspects of *McNeil*, such as that it cannot be used as a means of requiring the Crown to undertake an investigation on the accused's behalf;[202] that the Canadian Security Intelligence Service is not in the same category as police[203] but sheriffs

198 *McNeil*, above note 7 at para 57.
199 *R v Schirmer*, 2022 BCCA 214 at para 55 [*Schirmer*].
200 See, for example, *Schirmer*, above note 199.
201 See, respectively, *Gubbins*, above note 8; *Edmonton Police Association v Edmonton (City)*, 2017 ABCA 355; *R v Stipo*, 2019 ONCA 3; *York (Regional Municipality) v McGuigan*, 2018 ONCA 1062.
202 *R v Levin*, 2014 ABCA 142.
203 *R v Ahmad*, [2009] OJ No 6153.

are;[204] that disclosure can be postponed to avoid hampering an ongoing investigation;[205] and that an accused has no right to an adjournment to await the outcome of an investigation into an officer.[206]

A conclusion that the Crown has no duty to fetch under *McNeil* does not automatically lead to the conclusion that the accused is not entitled to the material: it only means that the accused must make an application for third party production, which might then succeed or fail.

Finally, note that the *McNeil* principles are not exhausted with trial, and that a *McNeil* application could be brought in the context of a fresh evidence application on appeal.[207]

## FURTHER READINGS

BUSBY, KAREN. "Discriminatory Uses of Personal Records in Sexual Violence Cases" (1997) 9 *Canadian Journal of Women and the Law* 148.

———. "Third Party Records Cases since *R. v. O'Connor*" (2000) 27 *Manitoba Law Journal* 355.

CALARCO, PAUL. "What Happens When Evidence Has Not Been Recorded? Staying Charges to Ensure a Fair Trial" (2001) 44 *Criminal Law Quarterly* 514.

———. "*R. v. Bjelland*: No Effective Remedy for Crown Failure to Disclose" (2009) 67 *Criminal Reports* (6th) 219.

CAMERON, JAMIE. "Dialogue and Hierarchy in *Charter* Interpretation: A Comment on *R. v. Mills*" (2001) 38 *Alberta Law Review* 1051.

CARTER, IAN. "Chipping Away at *Stinchcombe*: The Expanding Privilege Exception to Disclosure" (2002) 50 *Criminal Reports* (5th) 332.

COUGHLAN, STEPHEN G. "Developments in Criminal Procedure: The 1996–97 Term" (1998) 9 *Supreme Court Law Review* (2d) 273.

———. "Complainants' Records after *Mills*: Same as It Ever Was" (2000) 33 *Criminal Reports* (5th) 300.

---

204 *R v Collins*, 2010 ABPC 19.

205 *Duguay v R*, 2009 QCCA 1130.

206 *R v Huynh*, 2010 BCSC 1306.

207 See the overview of the process of a *McNeil* application, taking into account the appeal context, in *Schirmer*, above note 199 at para 54.

Alex Gorlewski. *The Anatomy of Criminal Procedure: A Visual Guide to the Law*, 2nd ed (Toronto: University of Toronto Press, 2026).

Donkers, Heather "An Analysis of Third Party Record Applications Under the *Mills* Scheme, 2012–2017: The Right to Full Answer and Defence versus Rights to Privacy and Equality" (2018) 41–4 *Manitoba Law Journal* 245.

Feldthusen, Bruce. "Access to the Private Therapeutic Records of Sexual Assault Complainants" (1996) 75 *Canadian Bar Review* 537.

Gotell, Lise. "Colonization through Disclosure: Confidential Records, Sexual Assault Complainants and Canadian Law" (2001) 10 *Social and Legal Studies* 315.

———. "The Ideal Victim, the Hysterical Complainant and the Disclosure of Confidential Records: A Case Study of the Implications of the *Charter* for Sexual Assault Law" (2002) 40 *Osgoode Hall Law Journal* 251.

Holmes, Heather. "An Analysis of Bill C-46, Production of Records in Sexual Offence Proceedings" (1997) 2 *Canadian Criminal Law Review* 71.

Hubbard, Robert W, Susan Magotiaux, & Suzanne M Duncan. *The Law of Privilege in Canada* (Aurora: Canada Law Book, 2006) (loose-leaf).

Law Reform Commission of Canada. *Disclosure by the Prosecution* (Ottawa: Law Reform Commission of Canada, 1984).

Layton, David. "*R. v. McClure*: The Privilege on the Pea" (2001) 40 *Criminal Reports* (5th) 19.

———. "*R. v. Brown*: Protecting Legal-Professional Privilege" (2002) 50 *Criminal Reports* (5th) 37.

Mitchell, Graeme G. "*R. v. Carosella*: Difficult Cases Make Dangerous Law" (1997) 4 *Criminal Reports* (5th) 209.

———. "*R. v. Dixon*: The Right to Crown Disclosure — A Roadmap for the Future" (1998) 13 *Criminal Reports* (5th) 260.

Paciocco, David. "In Defence of *R. v. Carosella*: The Continuing Need for Prejudice" (1997) 4 *Criminal Reports* (5th) 199.

———. "*Stinchcombe* on Steroids: The Surprising Legacy of *McNeil*" (2009) 62 *Criminal Reports* (6th) 26.

Rose, David. *Quigley's Criminal Procedure in Canada* (Toronto: Thomson Reuters, 2021) (loose-leaf) ch 12.

SANKOFF, PETER. "Crown Disclosure after *Mills*: Have the Rules Suddenly Changed?" (2000) 28 *Criminal Reports* (5th) 285.

STUART, DON. "*Mills*: Dialogue with Parliament and Equality by Assertion at What Cost?" (2000) 28 *Criminal Reports* (5th) 275.

———. *Charter Justice in Canadian Criminal Law*, 7th ed (Toronto: Thomson Carswell, 2018) ch 2.

CHAPTER 9

# PRELIMINARY INQUIRY

## A. INTRODUCTION

For many years, before an accused could be tried on any indictable offence in superior court, a preliminary inquiry was to be conducted, to see whether the accused should in fact be committed for trial. The assumption that there is such a two-stage structure is deeply embedded in the criminal justice system, affecting not only decisions about mode of trial or election and re-election,[1] but also the approach to determining whether a person's right to a trial within a reasonable time has been violated.[2]

However, the nature, scope, and purpose of the preliminary inquiry have been in flux for some time,[3] and they are becoming both less interesting and less important as a subject of discussion. Most notably, in 2019 they changed from a procedure available in the case of all indictable offences tried in superior court to one only available where the accused is charged with an offence punishable by imprisonment

1 See, for example, s 561, setting deadlines for re-election in relation to date of the preliminary inquiry. See also the discussion in Chapter 3, Section A(3).

2 See the discussion of this issue in Chapter 10, Section B(2)(c)(i).

3 See, for example, David Paciocco, "A Voyage of Discovery: Examining the Precarious Condition of the Preliminary Inquiry" (2003) 48 *Criminal Law Quarterly* 151.

of fourteen years or more.[4] Further, although in principle one of their central functions was to serve as a screening mechanism for unmeritorious prosecutions, as a matter of fact it is very uncommon for a preliminary inquiry to result in the accused not being ordered to stand trial.[5] Beyond that, even if the justice[6] does discharge the accused, the Crown has the ability to send the accused to trial despite a discharge, or without a preliminary inquiry having been held at all.[7] As a result, they do not genuinely serve as very much of a screening mechanism. Similarly, preliminary inquiries also long performed a type of disclosure function, but that need is now dealt with more directly by *Charter* decisions requiring the Crown to disclose all relevant evidence to the accused.[8] Some defence counsel see a benefit to being able to not only know the evidence that will come from a witness but to actually *test* that witness on the stand, but otherwise the discovery function is better satisfied in other ways. Further, as noted in Chapter 3, *Charter* remedies are not available at a preliminary inquiry. Finally, of course, the vast majority of criminal offences are tried in provincial court rather than superior court, and so the issue of a preliminary inquiry does not arise.[9]

---

4 This change was made in Bill C-75, *An Act to amend the Criminal Code, the Youth Criminal Justice Act and other Acts and to make consequential amendments to other Acts*, Royal Assent June 21, 2019.

5 See Department of Justice, "JustFacts: Preliminary Inquiries" June 2017, online: www.justice.gc.ca/eng/rp-pr/jr/jf-pf/2017/jun01.html:

> Research by Justice Canada found that holding a preliminary inquiry did not impact the likelihood of a trial taking place while Webster's research found some evidence to indicate that when a preliminary inquiry was held the likelihood of a trial taking place decreased.

6 A "justice" is defined in s 2 of the *Code* to mean either a justice of the peace or a judge of the provincial court. In virtually all jurisdictions of Canada, a preliminary inquiry is held by a provincial court judge.

7 Section 577.

8 See the decision of Côté and Rowe JJ in *R v Archambault*, 2024 SCC 35 [*Archambault*] at para 13:

> This constitutional right to the disclosure of all relevant information is distinct from the right to a preliminary inquiry, which is what led this Court to state in *S.J.L.*, at para. 23, that "the incidental function of the preliminary inquiry as a discovery mechanism has lost much of its relevance" since the enactment of the *Charter*.

9 See, for example, Canadian Centre for Justice Statistics, "Adult Criminal Court Processing Times, Canada, 2015/16," 13 February 2018. Based on the figures in Tables 1 and 3 in that report, there were 339,175 total cases (that is, one or more charges against the same accused) completed in provincial court in 2015/16, but only 3,099 cases in superior court: that is, roughly 99 percent of cases were in provincial court. Unfortunately, those figures are not reliable because they do not include superior court figures from five jurisdictions, including Ontario,

In short, over time legislative change has made preliminary inquiries less relevant. They were never available for matters to be tried in provincial court, which included not only summary conviction offences but indictable offences in the absolute jurisdiction of a magistrate.[10] For a long time they were frequently waived. Legislative change in 2004 made them available only on request, and only in relation to particular issues, which further marginalized the procedure. Legislative change in 2019 then changed the availability of preliminary inquiries so that they can only be held in the case of a relatively few most serious offences, those where the accused faces a penalty of fourteen years imprisonment or more. Availability is based on the situation of the *accused*, not the offence: that is, where a penalty has been increased to fourteen years since the time the offence was alleged to have occurred, meaning that the accused has a section 11(i) *Charter* right to the lower punishment, a preliminary inquiry will not be available.[11] Further, the preliminary inquiry justice has the ability to limit the issues which will be considered. Therefore, the discussion below should be seen in that light.

Until 2004 the preliminary inquiry was understood chiefly as a test of the sufficiency of the prosecution's case for trial. The central question was whether the prosecution could produce sufficient evidence on the whole of the case to warrant committal for trial.[12] Before facing trial in a superior court the accused was entitled, as of right, to a preliminary inquiry on the whole of the case and, in principle, the preliminary inquiry served important functions in screening out unsupportable charges and in providing the accused with a fuller understanding of the case to meet. Unless the accused waived the preliminary inquiry, the prosecution was required to produce sufficient evidence. A secondary

---

which has the most criminal cases. As a result, although a very strong tendency for cases to occur in provincial court can be pointed to, it is not possible to put a reliable percentage on it.

Note that it is possible for a case to be tried in provincial court after a preliminary inquiry, if the accused re-elects afterward, though in most cases this re-election would happen in order for the accused to plead guilty.

10 See the discussion in Chapter 3, Section A(3), "Mode of Trial."

11 *Archambault*, above note 8.

12 See, for example, *R v Hynes*, [2001] 3 SCR 623 [*Hynes*]. Evidence "on the whole of the case" means evidence on each element of an offence. It does not mean that the prosecution must tender all of the evidence that it can produce at trial: *R v Caccamo*, [1976] 1 SCR 786. Committal for trial can be ordered only if the evidence at the preliminary inquiry is sufficient in the sense that a jury, properly instructed, can find the accused guilty beyond reasonable doubt: *United States of America v Shephard*, [1977] 2 SCR 1067 [*Shephard*] (discussed in Section D, below in this chapter).

function of the inquiry was discovery: the inquiry afforded an opportunity to test the quality of evidence taken from witnesses under oath.[13] Among other advantages, this aspect of the inquiry allowed the parties, especially the defence, to have a record of sworn evidence that could later be used at trial to challenge the credibility of a witness.

As noted, since 2019 preliminary inquiries have been limited to a relatively small group of indictable offences. The major impetus behind this change was a concern about trial delay.[14] Since the 2016 decision in *R v Jordan*, ways of making the criminal justice system operate more efficiently have been on the minds of Parliament and the courts.[15] Precisely because of the doubts about the usefulness of preliminary inquiries mentioned above, and the extra time inherent in having one, their elimination has often been identified as a potential source of time-saving.[16] This would potentially speed up the system in two ways: by removing the need for the step of a preliminary inquiry in many cases, but also by reducing the workload of the provincial courts that would have conducted them. It was for that reason that Bill C-75 limited them. Indeed, the original version of the Bill would have limited them only to offences with a sentence of life imprisonment, but ultimately they were left available for those offences with fourteen years or more imprisonment as well. There seems likely to be no constitutional issue around this limitation, because there is no *Charter* right to a preliminary inquiry,[17] nor to cross-examine a particular witness at that preliminary inquiry.[18]

One issue arose because Bill C-75 contained no transitional provisions: were the changes relating to the availability of a preliminary inquiry retrospective or only prospective? In *Archambault* the two

---

13 *R v Skogman*, [1984] 2 SCR 93 at 105 [*Skogman*].

14 See *Archambault*, above note 8, where the Court noted at para 24 that:
the purpose of the legislative amendment is to reduce the number and length of preliminary inquiries in order to address the increase in court delays in criminal cases and alleviate the burden on witnesses and victims, who have to testify twice when such a procedure is used.

15 *R v Jordan*, 2016 SCR 27 [*Jordan*]. See generally the discussion in Chapter 10, Section B(2)(c)(i), "Trial Within a Reasonable Time."

16 See, for example, Senate, Standing Committee on Legal and Constitutional Affairs, *Delaying Justice Is Denying Justice: An Urgent Need to Address Lengthy Court Delays in Canada*, Final Report, June 2017, Priority recommendation 11, 8; and *ibid*, Recommendation 7, 48. See also *Jordan*, above note 15 at para 140: "Parliament may wish to consider the value of preliminary inquiries in light of expanded disclosure obligations."

17 *R v SJL*, 2009 SCC 14 [*SJL*]. The Court, in that case, noted that this rule was equally true for young persons charged with an offence.

18 *R v Bjelland*, 2009 SCC 38 at paras 34–37 [*Bjelland*].

accused had been charged with historical sexual offences: the charges were laid prior to the change coming into effect, but neither accused requested a preliminary inquiry until *after* the change was in effect. A majority of the Court concluded that the new rule did not apply to the two accused, but in a complex split that leaves the governing *rule* a bit ambiguous. All nine judges agreed that the rule was not simply a prospective one, and that an accused's right to a preliminary inquiry could have vested before the change came into effect. They disagreed over exactly when that time would be. The largest single cohort, of four judges, concluded that the right to a preliminary inquiry did not vest until an accused actually requested one: however, that was the dissenting judgment. The other five judges concluded that the right to a preliminary inquiry had vested either at the time of the alleged offence, at the time the charges were laid, or when the accused had reserved the right to elect mode of trial at a later date.[19] All of those dates preceded the coming into force of the changed provision, so the particular accused were not affected by the change. This leaves some lack of clarity, but fortunately that is a time-limited issue: six of the nine judges found that *some* sort of explicit step by the accused prior to the legislative change was necessary for the right to have vested, and the new provision came into force in September 2019.

In those cases where a preliminary inquiry is still available, the amendments to the *Code* that came into effect in 2004 altered its nature, and it can no longer be said that its primary function is to test the sufficiency of the prosecution case as a whole.[20] The central feature of those amendments was that a preliminary inquiry will be held only upon the request of a party. That party will almost always be the accused, but a request can be made by the prosecutor. In the absence of a request the accused will simply be committed to stand trial on a date fixed by the court.[21]

---

19 Justice Karakatsanis, writing for the dissent in *Archambault*, summed up the situation:

> [154] . . . My colleague Justice Martin concludes, like the Court of Appeal, that the new rule does not apply because it came into force after the time of the alleged offences. My colleagues Justices Côté and Rowe conclude that the new rule does not apply because it came into force after the respondents had been charged with those offences. Finally, my colleague Justice Kasirer concludes that the new rule does not apply because it came into force after the respondents reserved their right to elect their mode of trial at first appearance.

20 SC 2002, c 13.

21 Section 549.

Further, where a request is made, the inquiry will be conducted only with regard to issues and witnesses specified in advance.[22] It is contemplated that these points can and should be agreed upon between the parties, and the justice can order a hearing to encourage the parties to reach such agreement.[23] If there is an agreement of this nature, the *Code* provides that the justice can commit the accused without recording evidence on any other issues in the case.[24] Indeed, a change to the provisions in 2019 went further in limiting the inquiry: where the 2004 amendments gave the party requesting the preliminary inquiry the ability to request it only with regard to particular issues, the *Code* now provides that the justice personally has the ability to limit the scope of the preliminary inquiry to specific issues and limit the witnesses to be heard on these issues.[25]

The inquiry is thus no longer a test of the prosecution case as a whole because the sufficiency of the prosecution case is assumed, subject to any exception covered by a request. As now conceived, the preliminary inquiry is a limited examination of the sufficiency of the prosecution case with regard to specific issues and the evidence of specific witnesses.[26]

It is important to underscore the importance of the amendments that came into force in 2004. The changes were partly justified by extensive disclosure of the prosecution case to the accused before

---

22 Section 536.3. The New Brunswick Court of Appeal observed in *R v Gallant*, 2009 NBCA 84, that the French and English versions of s 536.3 are not parallel. The French version is unambiguous that an accused who requests a preliminary inquiry is to identify the issues upon which the *accused* wants to adduce testimony and a list of the witnesses the *accused* intends to call. The English version suggests that an accused requesting a preliminary inquiry is to point to the evidence they wish the *prosecutor* to adduce and the witnesses they want the *prosecutor* to call. The Court of Appeal found that it was unnecessary for them to decide the correct interpretation in that case.

23 Section 536.4. This is now commonly called a "focusing hearing."

24 Sections 536.4, 536.5, and 549.

25 Section 537(1.01).

26 In *Bjelland*, above note 18, the Court observed that:

> [24] The reforms effected by Parliament in 2002 — which made the preliminary inquiry optional, authorized agreements to limit the scope of the preliminary inquiry and authorized the holding of a prehearing conference, *inter alia* to promote a fair and expeditious inquiry — also tend to reduce the number of preliminary inquiries and their length (S.C. 2002, c. 13, particularly ss. 25 and 27, which came into force on June 1, 2004). These amendments show clearly that the trend is toward the adoption of mechanisms that are better adapted to the needs of the parties, not the imposition of more inflexible procedures.

plea.[27] Another justification was that, in practice, it has always been open to the defence to make admissions and to waive the right to a full preliminary inquiry in favour of a limited inquiry. A third justification was the growing length, in practice, of cross-examination. A fourth was that the right to a full preliminary inquiry was occasionally abused by counsel who, through lack of experience or judgment, could have waived the inquiry in whole or in part without prejudice to the accused. The 2004 amendments addressed those considerations.

Nevertheless, the reformulation of the preliminary inquiry as a limited examination of specific issues and witnesses significantly changed the nature of the order for committal. This limitation of the scope of inquiry effectively eliminated any test of the sufficiency of the prosecution case from the decision at the end of the inquiry. If the judge does not receive evidence on the case as a whole, it cannot sensibly be said that the decision to commit for trial is a decision based upon evidence that the whole of the case is sufficient. Where a limited inquiry is held on a specific issue, the decision to commit signifies only that the evidence presented on that issue meets the standard for committal. The plain design of the 2004 amendments allowing the parties to request that evidence only relate to particular issues, coupled with the 2019 amendments giving the justice the unilateral ability to make the same choice, shows that a limited inquiry is the norm. The only exception to this conclusion would be the rare case wherein a judge proceeds to conduct a preliminary inquiry on the whole of the case. It would be rare because the party that made such a request would seemingly have to assert that the case disclosed by the prosecution included no evidence on all essential elements of the offence charged. Because of this limited role which no longer matches the original justification for the procedure's existence, there is an argument that rather than simply limiting the availability of preliminary inquiries, Parliament should abolish them.[28]

Alternatively, one could argue that the function of the preliminary inquiry now is simply to afford the parties an opportunity upon request to test the evidence of specific witnesses on specific issues in preparation for trial. For all practical purposes the preliminary inquiry as it was known before 2004 has been reformed by Parliament as a limited and focused examination to obtain discovery of evidence under oath

---

27 This is the effect of jurisprudence after *R v Stinchcombe*, [1991] 3 SCR 326. The Court noted in *SJL*, above note 17 at para 23, that "the incidental function of the preliminary inquiry as a discovery mechanism has lost much of its relevance."

28 Parliament did consider this option even at the time it brought in the 2004 amendments: see the discussion in *R v PM*, 2007 QCCA 414 at para 72 [*PM*].

in the case of the most serious offences. It would therefore make sense for Parliament to undertake a more thorough reform of Part XVIII of the *Code* to redefine this procedure for what it now is. The purpose of such a reform would be to remove traces of the preliminary inquiry as a genuine test of the sufficiency of the prosecution case as a whole.

## B. JURISDICTION

The authority of a justice to conduct a preliminary inquiry is strictly statutory under Part XVIII of the *Code*.[29] In other words, there is no inherent jurisdiction, and the only powers that can be exercised by the judge are those that are explicitly granted in the *Code* or that are necessarily implicit in those provisions. The only additional authority they have to expand upon the express powers granted to them is found in section 537(1)(i). That section has provided for some time that the judge can conduct the hearing in any way that is consistent with the *Code*: Bill C-75 in 2019 amended that to add the ability to conduct it in a way "that appears to the justice to be desirable, including to promote a fair and expeditious inquiry." In particular, those amendments specify that in exercising that power the justice can limit the inquiry to specific issues and limit the witnesses to be heard.[30] It should be recalled that the changes in Bill C-75 were aimed at remedying delay in the system, and so judges are likely to focus particularly on the "expeditious" criterion.

The courts have said repeatedly that the preliminary inquiry justice has only the powers given by Parliament in Part XVIII of the *Code*. Thus, a judge who fails to comply with Part XVIII or who exceeds the authority given by the *Code* acts without jurisdiction and might be subject to review in the superior court.[31] This position was fuelled in some measure by the fact that preliminary inquiries were typically held, many years ago, before magistrates without formal legal training. It was also fuelled more generally by the idea that the provincial court is a statutory tribunal that has only those powers in criminal matters that are specifically accorded to it by Parliament. This approach to the jurisdiction of the provincial court is somewhat antiquated, in part, because preliminary inquiries are now routinely held before professional judges

29 *R v Doyle*, [1977] 1 SCR 597 [*Doyle*]; *R v Forsythe*, [1980] 2 SCR 268 [*Forsythe*].

30 Section 537(1.01).

31 *Skogman*, above note 13; *Forsythe*, above note 29. See *R v Deschamplain*, 2004 SCC 76 [*Deschamplain*], and *R v Sazant*, [2004] 3 SCR 635 [*Sazant*], for considerations of the scope of jurisdictional error at the preliminary inquiry.

in the provincial court and, in part, because those same judges are competent to exercise all functions for a proper trial. It is not surprising, therefore, that the powers of the justice at the preliminary inquiry have been expanded.

Nonetheless, a judge at a preliminary inquiry has no power to grant any remedy other than those contemplated by the *Code*.[32] The Supreme Court has specifically held that the judge cannot grant a remedy under the *Charter*, including remedies for delay, non-disclosure, or the production of evidence obtained in violation of a constitutional right.[33] A preliminary inquiry judge also does not have jurisdiction to make an order for production of third party records.[34]

## 1) Commencement

In some cases an accused has no election as to mode of trial for an indictable offence.[35] In the remaining cases, the *Code* now provides two separate forms of the election to be put to the accused: section 536(2) gives an accused charged with an indictable offence punishable by fourteen years or more imprisonment an election as to mode of trial and as to whether to request a preliminary inquiry if the trial will be in superior court, while section 536(2.1) simply gives an election as to mode of trial for the remaining indictable offences. Where it is available and requested, the justice has jurisdiction to proceed with a preliminary inquiry or to adjourn the preliminary inquiry to a later date. Almost invariably the matter is adjourned at the first appearance and, indeed, there can be frequent adjournments before the preliminary inquiry begins with the presentation of evidence.[36] The central point is that the possibility of having a preliminary inquiry in respect of an indictable offence will depend, first, on the classification of and available sentence for the offence and, second, on the election of the accused as to mode of trial.

There can be variations on the prototypical case in which an inquiry proceeds on a single count, in a single information, against a single accused. It is important to bear in mind that the jurisdiction of

32 *Hynes*, above note 12 at para 33. See also *R v Patterson*, [1970] SCR 409.

33 See the further discussion of this issue at Section B(5), below in this chapter.

34 *Ontario Provincial Police Commissioner v Mosher*, 2015 ONCA 722.

35 Specifically there is no such election for offences listed in s 553 which are in the absolute jurisdiction of the provincial court, and offences listed in s 469, which are in the exclusive jurisdiction of the superior court and will have a trial by judge and jury. See the discussion in Chapter 3, Section A, "Classification of Offences and Mode of Trial."

36 *Re R and Geszthelyi* (1977), 33 CCC (2d) 543 (BCCA).

the judge at the preliminary inquiry is to examine indictable offences charged by the prosecution or disclosed by the evidence (see the discussion of scope, below). Thus, even if the judge otherwise has jurisdiction over the offences, they cannot conduct a trial and a preliminary inquiry for the same accused simultaneously;[37] nor can they try one accused and at the same time conduct a preliminary inquiry in respect of a co-accused.[38] They can, however, conduct a preliminary inquiry in respect of charges in separate informations simultaneously.[39]

At the first appearance of the accused there is an arraignment, in the sense that the charge or charges will be read to the accused. An accused would not normally enter a plea at this stage, because nominally it is only after the justice has decided the accused should face trial that a plea is necessary. A formalistic reading of the *Code* suggests that the first appearance is the commencement of the preliminary inquiry.[40] In practice, it marks only a *pro forma* commencement of the inquiry at which the accused submits to the jurisdiction of the court, makes a provisional election as to mode of trial,[41] and sets a subsequent date for the actual commencement of the preliminary inquiry. For practical purposes, little turns on whether the preliminary inquiry formally commences at the first appearance or at a later date, such as the date on which the election is recorded. It is important, however, to note that on any account the judge presiding at the inquiry is seized of the matter as soon as evidence is adduced.[42] Until that time, the accused might appear before several justices or judges on various matters. Once evidence is adduced, though, the preliminary inquiry will normally continue to its conclusion before the same judge.[43]

## 2) Scope

The scope of the inquiry is defined by section 535 of the *Code*, which directs the justice or judge to inquire into the charge of any indictable offence and any other indictable offence in respect of the same transaction disclosed by the evidence taken in accordance with Part

---

37 *R v G(AM)* (2000), 142 CCC (3d) 29 (NSCA).

38 *R v Niedzwieki* (1980), 57 CCC (2d) 184 (BCSC).

39 *R v Rutherford*, [1968] 3 CCC 1 (BCSC).

40 *Doyle*, above note 29; compare *Re Danchella and the Queen* (1985), 19 CCC (3d) 490 (BCCA) [*Danchella*].

41 In some jurisdictions, there is not even a provisional recording of an election.

42 *Danchella*, above note 40.

43 Section 547.1 provides that when a justice is unable to continue to receive evidence, another justice may do so, if the record is otherwise complete and available, or may hear the case afresh.

XVIII. Until 1985, the jurisdiction to inquire was limited to the charge recited in the information or any included charge that might be disclosed by the evidence. Accordingly, the jeopardy of the accused in committal proceedings could be no greater than the charge or charges in the information. On a charge of second-degree murder, for example, the presiding judge had no jurisdiction to commit the accused for trial on a charge of first-degree murder.[44] The *Code* was amended in 1985 to allow the judge to commit the accused for trial on any indictable offence disclosed by the evidence at the preliminary inquiry.[45] This extension of jurisdiction implies that the presiding judge and the accused must, in principle, be alert throughout the preliminary inquiry to the possibility that offences other than those stated in the information might be disclosed by the evidence. At this point in time, however, this is one of the aspects of the preliminary inquiry provisions which is a relic of the past: it is based on the assumption that the justice will hear evidence on all elements of the offence, something that is no longer true.

Nonetheless, the scope of the preliminary inquiry is in principle not strictly limited to the offences as charged in the information. The inquiry can extend to any indictable offence disclosed by the evidence, provided that it arises from the same transaction. "Transaction" in this sense is not co-extensive with an offence. It refers to a narrative of conduct that might comprise several acts and might disclose several offences. If the information charges only one indictable offence, for example, but evidence of the transaction at the preliminary inquiry supports more, the judge can commit the accused to trial on all of them. The reference to the same transaction, however, is meant to limit the jeopardy of the accused at the inquiry to a narrative of conduct that is coherent in time or in some other manner.[46]

There is another sense in which the preliminary inquiry can extend beyond an examination of the sufficiency of the prosecution case on the charges in the information. The *Code* expressly allows the accused to call evidence, and this can include exculpatory evidence on a matter of defence.[47] For purposes of committal, however, this evidence will not be assessed by the presiding judge or weighed in favour of the accused, not least because the judge has no jurisdiction to examine the validity

44 *R v Chabot*, [1980] 2 SCR 985.

45 With regard to the scope of the inquiry, see Patrick Healy, "Chabotage: Expanding the Crown's Power to Prefer Additional Counts" (1984) 38 *Criminal Reports* (3d) 344.

46 See, for example, *R v Goldstein; R v Caicedo* (1988), 42 CCC (3d) 548 (Ont CA).

47 Section 541.

of defences.[48] The primary purpose of such defence evidence is to allow the accused the opportunity to test it and to record it in preparation for trial. Nothing in the amendments alters this.

The preliminary inquiry has also been used as an opportunity to lay an evidentiary foundation for an issue that can be decided only at trial. For example, although a justice has no power to order the production of third-party records at the preliminary inquiry, they can allow the accused to cross-examine the complainant on a range of facts that might later support an application at trial.[49] Similarly, although no remedy can be granted under the *Charter* at the preliminary inquiry, the judge can permit cross-examination of a prosecution witness to lay a basis for a motion under the *Charter* at trial: at least, that was clearly true until the 2004 amendments, though some courts have questioned whether the procedure is now more limited.[50] The judge also has discretion to allow the accused to call defence witnesses on trial matters.[51] All of this is consistent with the right of the accused to make full answer and defence, and with the discovery function of the preliminary inquiry, but it is also strictly beyond an inquiry into the sufficiency of the prosecution case for committal. There has been no serious challenge to the practice of allowing evidence on trial matters to be presented in examination or cross-examination.

The preliminary inquiry is rarely an occasion for formal challenges to the validity of charges in the information, and even then the only basis would be that the information fails to charge an indictable offence known to law.[52] The justice has no authority to question whether the information was properly sworn by inquiring into the grounds of belief asserted by the informant.[53] Further, the judge has no jurisdiction to inquire into any special plea based upon principles of double jeopardy.[54] Thus, the scope of inquiry is circumscribed by the content of the charges in the information and the evidence produced. This fact is only underscored by the application of section 601 to the preliminary inquiry. This provision, which is found among those relating to charges

---

48 *Hynes*, above note 12.

49 *R v B(E)* (2002), 162 CCC (3d) 451 (Ont CA) [*B(E)*].

50 See the varying opinions in *R v McGrath*, 2007 NSSC 255, aff'd on grounds of mootness 2008 NSCA 32 [*McGrath*]; *R v Tran*, 2008 ABPC 278 [*Tran*]; *R v Catellier*, 2016 MBQB 190 [*Catellier*]; or *Regina v Beers and Beers*, 2014 BCPC 45 [*Beers*].

51 *R v Dawson* (1998), 123 CCC (3d) 385 (Ont CA) [*Dawson*].

52 Section 546. See also *R v Gralewicz*, [1980] 2 SCR 493; *R v Bolduc* (1980), 20 CR (3d) 372 (Que CA), aff'd [1982] 1 SCR 573.

53 *Re Hislop and the Queen* (1983), 36 CR (3d) 29 (Ont CA).

54 *R v Prince*, [1986] 2 SCR 480.

at trial, allows for an application to be made to quash a count that fails to charge a known offence or that is otherwise defective on its face.[55]

Of greater importance, however, is that section 601 also gives the judge broad powers to amend the charges in the information at the preliminary inquiry. Thus, quite apart from the judge's jurisdiction to order committal on any indictable offence disclosed by the evidence at the preliminary inquiry, the judge can also amend the information to ensure that the charges conform with the evidence. Although the judge at the preliminary inquiry has no power to order the prosecution to furnish particulars in support of an information,[56] the power of amendment can compensate for this deficiency in all but the most egregious of cases. Challenges to quash the information at the preliminary inquiry will therefore succeed only in cases where there is a radical jurisdictional defect that lies beyond the power of amendment granted by section 601.[57]

## 3) Multiple Accused and Multiple Counts

In view of the limited statutory jurisdiction of judges at the preliminary inquiry, it seems clear that they have no power to order the severance of accused or counts.[58]

If multiple accused are charged in a single information, each is entitled to make a request for a preliminary inquiry (if it is available at all), as is the prosecution. If a request is made, the ensuing inquiry must be held in respect of all accused, and each of them will be entitled to participate.[59] In many instances, multiple accused will be concerned about the same issues, but there are also cases in which various accused persons wish to address different issues and hear evidence from different witnesses. In such cases, the preliminary inquiry will proceed on the issues and witnesses identified by the parties in the same manner as if there were only a single accused.[60] However, as the law favours prosecution of multiple accused together, the *Code* specifically empowers a judge not to record the election of an accused if it

55 *Dallas & Cassidy v the Queen* (1985), 21 CCC (3d) 100 (Ont HCJ); *R v Volpi* (1987), 34 CCC (3d) 1 (Ont CA).

56 *R v Chew*, [1968] 2 CCC 127 (Ont CA).

57 *R v Webster*, [1993] 1 SCR 3. The issue of sufficiency of an information is discussed at greater length in Chapter 11.

58 *Re R and Legg* (1993), 80 CCC (3d) 315 (NSSCTD); *Re Peters and the Queen* (1982), 2 CCC (3d) 278 (Sask QB); *R v Baksh*, 2014 ONCJ 591.

59 Section 536(4.2).

60 Of particular significance where there are multiple accused will be the cases in which one co-accused makes a request to hear the evidence of another.

would necessarily lead to severance of the accused.[61] As a result, even if only one accused elects a preliminary inquiry, that election will mean that an inquiry will occur for all.

Multiple counts can be joined in an information for purposes of a preliminary inquiry, provided that each of them could properly be the subject of a committal order, and a preliminary inquiry is available for each. When summary conviction or absolute jurisdiction offences have been combined in an information with an indictable offence, the result has hinged on the accused's election. That is, if the accused elected provincial court, the matters could be tried together (since that court would have jurisdiction over all of them), but if the accused elected superior court, the preliminary inquiry would proceed on the electable offences, and the others would have to be separately charged in another information.[62] Now that preliminary inquiries are less available, the situation is more complex. If an indictable offence carrying a penalty of fourteen years' imprisonment or more is combined in an information with an indictable offence carrying a lower penalty, the accused will have to be put to an election separately on each count: on the former to an election as to mode of trial and whether to have a preliminary inquiry (section 536(2)) and on the latter purely as to mode of trial (section 536(2.1)). However, in each case the accused would be able to elect superior court, either with or without a jury, as that mode of trial. The question therefore arises as to how to proceed when the accused elects superior court for both counts in the information and elects a preliminary inquiry for the count where that is available. One question is whether to sever the counts. On the one hand the superior court would have jurisdiction over both counts, so there is no obstacle there to an eventual joint trial, and the Crown must have felt that was the proper approach or they would not have put both counts in the same information. On the other hand, one count has an impediment to proceeding immediately to trial that the other does not, and so there might be a good argument that the trial which could proceed should proceed.

61 Section 567. Specifically, the judge can fail to record any election other than trial by judge with a jury, and so that will be the mode of trial for all the accused.

62 To be clear, the judge's power of committal is only as extensive as their power of inquiry, and thus there can be no order of committal on a summary-conviction offence. In Québec and Nunavut, the situation would appear to be slightly different because the judge with jurisdiction at the preliminary inquiry also has jurisdiction when the accused elects trial by judge alone. It would seem to follow that multiple counts could remain on the same information pending the outcome of the preliminary inquiry. In Québec, it has been decided that there is no objection in principle where the preliminary inquiry and the trial take place before the same judge of the Cour du Québec.

Considering the situation from the point of view of avoiding delay is not entirely helpful: holding a later joint trial will mean that the individual accused's trial on the counts without a preliminary inquiry will have been delayed unnecessarily, but holding separate trials will use more resources and contribute to overall delay. Separately, if there is no severance, it is reasonable to ask what the scope of the preliminary inquiry will be: is it strictly limited to the offence carrying the fourteen years imprisonment penalty or can it also concern the other offence? These matters have yet to be fully pursued by courts.[63]

## 4) Presence of the Accused

The accused is entitled to be present at the preliminary inquiry. For many years the courts took the view that the accused must be present.[64] Section 535 refers to an accused who is "before a justice," and this phrase was interpreted to mean that the justice's jurisdiction required the presence of the accused. This position has been changed by amendment of section 537(1)(j.1), which allows the judge a discretion to excuse the accused from all or part of the inquiry. If the judge does so the accused must be informed of the possibility that the evidence might nonetheless be used at trial.[65] Also, if certain conditions are met, the accused can appear by closed-circuit television or by videoconference at portions of an inquiry where the evidence of a witness is not being taken: this can always occur if the prosecutor and the accused agree, and the justice can require it in the case of an accused in prison.[66] Therefore, the accused has the right to attend the preliminary inquiry and will be required to attend unless excused by the justice. As a practical matter, this will follow either upon a request by the accused or the agreement of the parties.

If the accused absconds during the preliminary inquiry, section 544 provides that the accused is deemed to have waived the right to be present.[67] It also provides that the justice can continue the inquiry to

63 See *R v Craigg*, 2021 ONCJ 22, holding that legally the preliminary inquiry could only concern the charge eligible for one but that fairness might require allowing some questioning on other offences which were jointly charged if they were closely intertwined.

64 *Re McLachlan and the Queen* (1986), 24 CCC (3d) 255 (Ont CA).

65 Section 537(1.02).

66 See ss 537(1)(j) and 537(1)(k), respectively. In the latter case, an accused represented must be given the opportunity to consult privately with counsel.

67 In *Re Plummer and the Queen* (1983), 5 CCC (3d) 17 (BCCA), it was held that judicial acts undertaken after election by the accused as to mode of trial are acts "during the preliminary inquiry."

its conclusion or, if an arrest warrant has been issued, adjourn it. Even if it is adjourned, the justice can subsequently resume the inquiry. The accused cannot demand that the inquiry be reopened, although the justice is given discretion to make this order if exceptional circumstances justify it. Counsel for the accused is entitled to act for the absconding accused during the accused's absence if the inquiry is continued, and doing so includes calling witnesses. Most important, however, is that if the accused has absconded, the justice is entitled to draw an adverse inference.

## 5) Constitutional Issues

In *R v Mills*,[68] and again in *R v Hynes*,[69] the Supreme Court of Canada decided that a court conducting a preliminary inquiry is not a "court of competent jurisdiction" under the *Charter*. Thus, if the accused seeks to apply for a constitutional remedy under section 24 or 52, the only forum for such a motion is at trial. A preliminary inquiry judge might take *Charter* values such as freedom of religion into account in making decisions already within their power,[70] but cannot grant a *Charter* remedy.

One reason for reaching this decision was that the jurisdiction granted by the *Code* at the preliminary inquiry does not extend to constitutional issues. While this might be true, it raises the odd spectre that the allocation of jurisdiction under an ordinary statute can relieve the judge of the obligation to observe the supreme law of the country. The exclusion of *Charter* issues from the preliminary inquiry might be defensible as a matter of policy.[71] It is consistent with the idea that the function of the preliminary inquiry is modest: to ascertain whether the prosecution has enough evidence for the matter to be sent to trial. It is also consistent with some notion of economy and efficiency in criminal prosecutions because it would eliminate the time and effort necessary to resolve constitutional questions at a preliminary stage. Further, this position means that the judge at the preliminary inquiry cannot terminate a prosecution by granting a stay under the *Charter*. Particularly given the current limited scope of preliminary inquiries, there are arguments in favour of reserving decisions about *Charter* issues to the trial court.

---

68 [1986] 1 SCR 863 [*Mills*].

69 *Hynes*, above note 12.

70 *R v NS*, 2010 ONCA 670. The result in this case was affirmed, but this particular point was not in issue: 2012 SCC 72.

71 These arguments are rehearsed at some length by the majority in *Hynes*, above note 12.

Nonetheless, this position is anomalous in some regards. As is discussed below, a justice can exclude evidence from the preliminary inquiry on the basis that it does not comply with ordinary requirements for admissibility such as voluntariness. Why, then, should they be prevented from acting in the same way when the statement was obtained through a *Charter* violation? Further, the entitlement to seek a constitutional remedy at the preliminary inquiry would be consistent with a rich and robust concept of full answer and defence.[72] The rule prevents the accused from seeking an order for disclosure. It prevents any claim of unreasonable delay. In short, it deprives the accused of the opportunity to advance any constitutional claim that might have a material bearing on the outcome of the case. In some cases, efficiency might be better served by having such determinations made at as early a stage as possible.

## C. EVIDENCE

### 1) Admissibility

Evidence at the preliminary inquiry is taken under oath and recorded.[73] As at trial, prosecution witnesses are heard first and can be cross-examined by the accused or counsel. Subsections 540(2) and (3) refer to the taking of depositions before the presiding justice or judge, but this form of receiving evidence is almost never used. Depositions are statements made and sworn before the justice; they were commonly used long ago when court stenographers were few and there was no electronic means for recording the presentation of oral evidence. The modern practice is that evidence taken at the preliminary inquiry is recorded by a stenographer or by electronic means in the same manner as occurs at trial.

In general, evidence tendered at the preliminary inquiry must comply with principles and rules of admissibility that apply at trial (and indeed might later be admissible at trial because it was heard at the preliminary inquiry[74]). So, for example, any statement made by the accused to a person in authority must be proven to be voluntary beyond

---

72 *Ibid* at para 60ff, Major J, dissenting. See also *R v Howard*, 2009 PECA 27, holding that this rule also prevents a preliminary inquiry judge from granting costs as a *Charter* remedy.

73 Section 540. A court conducting a preliminary inquiry is a court of record.

74 See ss 715 and 715.1.

a reasonable doubt.[75] The proposition also means, more generally, that the procedure for receiving evidence at a *voir dire* applies at the preliminary inquiry. There are, however, important qualifications concerning the production and admissibility of evidence at the preliminary inquiry. One is that the presiding judge has no authority to call witnesses (other than on request of a party)[76] or to force the parties (notably the prosecution) to produce particular witnesses.[77] Also, as previously noted, the presiding justice or judge has no jurisdiction to hear matters relating to the *Charter*, and so has no jurisdiction to exclude evidence or to grant any other remedy under section 24.

There is, moreover, an important qualification on the application of the ordinary rules of admissibility, found in the power granted by section 540(7) of the *Code*: "A justice acting under this Part may receive as evidence any information that would not otherwise be admissible but that the justice considers credible or trustworthy in the circumstances of the case, including a statement that is made by a witness in writing or otherwise recorded."[78] This provision would potentially allow a party to tender "will-say" statements at the preliminary inquiry, or to introduce a videotaped version of a statement rather than calling a complainant to testify. This power to admit "credible or trustworthy" evidence, included as part of the 2004 amendments, was somewhat surprising, since the Supreme Court has said repeatedly that it is not part of the justice's function or jurisdiction to assess the credibility of evidence at a preliminary inquiry.[79]

This change was part of an effort to streamline pre-trial procedures.[80] The ability is very efficient for the prosecution, because when

---

75 *R v Pickett* (1975), 28 CCC (2d) 297 (Ont CA). See also s 545(1): "Nothing in this Act prevents a prosecutor giving in evidence at a preliminary inquiry any admission, confession or statement made at any time by the accused *that by law is admissible against him*" [emphasis added].

76 *Ibid*, ss 540(7) and 541(5).

77 *Re Phillips and the Queen* (1991), 66 CCC (3d) 140 (Ont Ct Gen Div); *Re R and Brass* (1981), 64 CCC (2d) 206 (Sask QB).

78 The section requires prior notice by a party of the intention to tender such evidence, although the judge is able to dispense with this requirement: s 540(8).

79 *R v Monteleone*, [1987] 2 SCR 154 [*Monteleone*]; *R v Yebes*, [1987] 2 SCR 168 [*Yebes*]; *R v Charemski*, [1998] 1 SCR 679 [*Charemski*]; *Hynes*, above note 12; *Sazant*, above note 31; *Deschamplain*, above note 31.

80 *Canadian Broadcasting Corp v Morrison*, 2017 MBCA 36 at para 85. See also *R v CMM*, 2017 MBCA 105 [*R v CMM*] at para 6: the intent "was to, without abolishing the preliminary inquiry altogether, streamline its use; reduce pre-trial delay; minimize inappropriate questioning of witnesses, particularly sexual assault complainants; and provide the Crown with 'an alternative method' of presenting its case than by the ordinary course of calling *viva voce* evidence."

it applies it eliminates the need to produce witnesses to give *viva voce* evidence. It carries a risk to the accused, however, since it is more difficult to challenge evidence that is presented only in that way. This concern about potential unfairness is offset to some extent by other provisions. First, the ability to introduce at a later trial evidence given at a preliminary inquiry does not apply to evidence admitted on this basis.[81] Second, the preliminary inquiry judge is entitled under section 540(9) to order the attendance for examination and cross-examination of any person who would otherwise not be required to appear because of section 540(7).

Although sections 540(7) and 540(9) have been in the *Code* since 2004, their exact interpretation has largely remained unsettled.[82]

The prevailing view is that, although it might be possible for the "sufficiency" aspect of a preliminary inquiry to be satisfied solely by filing documents, the amendments to the procedures were not meant to do away with the "discovery" function.[83] Therefore, in considering whether to allow a request by the accused under section 540(9) that a witness appear for examination, that discovery function should be taken

---

81 Sections 715(4) and 715.01(6). See the discussion below.

82 See, for example, *R v CMM*, above note 80 at para 7:

> The meaning of sections 540(7) and (9) has been the subject of much controversy in Manitoba. The parties cited numerous conflicting decisions of the Provincial Court, interpreting and applying sections 540(7) and (9), and also from the Court of Queen's Bench, deciding applications for *certiorari* relating to alleged errors committed in relation to these provisions. The decisions cited to us are disparate in approach and are irreconcilable.

Nonetheless that court decided at para 8 that, since it was dealing only with an appeal based on the jurisdiction to grant *certiorari* "it would not be appropriate to stray from the question of jurisdictional error and comment on the correctness of *any* of the previous interpretations of sections 540(7) and (9) that have been given by judges of the Provincial Court or Court of Queen's Bench."

83 More recently in *Archambault*, above note 8, Karakatsanis J noted at para 178:

> As this Court noted in *Hynes*, "[o]ver time, the preliminary inquiry has assumed an ancillary role as a discovery mechanism" (para. 31). Preliminary inquiries offer strategic benefits to the defence. They can be useful to test the evidence and gauge the strength of the Crown's case and to provide testimony on which to test credibility at trial (see, e.g., D. M. Paciocco, "A Voyage of Discovery: Examining the Precarious Condition of the Preliminary Inquiry" (2004), 48 *Crim. L.Q.* 151, at pp. 160-61; *R. v. N.S.*, 2012 SCC 72, [2012] 3 S.C.R. 726, at para. 40). The discovery function has, however, lost some of its significance given the Crown's constitutional disclosure obligations, following this Court's decision in *R. v. Stinchcombe*, [1991] 3 S.C.R. 326 (*R. v. S.J.L.*, 2009 SCC 14, [2009] 1 S.C.R. 426, at para. 23).

into account.[84] Exactly how to implement that principle has not been settled yet, however, and there is little caselaw beyond either the level of a preliminary inquiry judge or of a court hearing a *certiorari* application about such a decision. Courts have discussed and have often disagreed, for example, as to exactly how to determine whether evidence meets the "credible or trustworthy" standard,[85] whether a judge has the discretion to refuse to admit evidence even if it does meet that standard,[86]whether and on what standard to allow cross-examination,[87] the interplay between section 540(7) and 540(9) applications,[88] and so on.

In addition, since the section 540(7) provision creates an exception to the ordinary rules of admissibility, this raises the question of how far this exception extends.[89] For example, does it permit the justice to admit an involuntary statement by the accused to a person in authority if it is otherwise credible or trustworthy? Does it extend to any type of evidence that is specifically inadmissible by virtue of an exclusionary rule? Whatever its limits, this provision is unusual, especially in view of the reform in favour of a limited preliminary inquiry. It allows the

---

84 *R v Rao*, 2012 BCCA 275 [*Rao*] at para 95: "None of those authorities stand for the proposition that the discovery role has been extinguished or rendered obsolete." See also to the same effect *PM*, above note 28, or *R v Cowan*, 2015 BCSC 224. *Cowan* also holds however, that nothing in the amendments was meant to *expand* the discovery function of a preliminary inquiry.

85 Lower courts have attempted to articulate relevant factors: whether non-leading questions were used; whether the entire interview is to be introduced; whether the transcript is reliable; and, in the case of a child, the child's ability to understand the importance of telling the truth, for example. See *R v Vaughn*, 2009 BCPC 142 at para 15 [*Vaughn*], which contains a very thorough discussion of s 540(7). *Vaughn* has been relied on in that regard by subsequent cases: see, for example, *R v CAC*, 2011 BCPC 170; *Catellier*, above note 50; *R v Ryan No 2*, 2018 NLPC 1318 [*Ryan*]; or *R v SSS*, 2018 BCPC 366. Also on this standard, see *R v P (ML)*, [2008] BCJ No 1440 (Prov Ct); *R v Kirkpatrick*, 2011 ONCJ 112; *R v Piechotta*, 2016 BCPC 465; *R v Panfilova*, 2017 ONCJ 188; or *R v McKnight*, 2017 ABPC 250 [*McKnight*].

86 See *Catellier*, above note 50; *Ryan*, above note 85; *R v Martin*, 2017 MBQB 34; or *McKnight*, above note 85

87 See *R v Inglis* (2006), 208 CCC (3d) 85 (Ont Ct J). *PM*, above note 28; *CMM*, above note 80; or *R v Horswill*, 2015 BCPC 106. *CMM*, above note 80 at para 62 lists a number of considerations, including the suggestion that the governing question is whether "the proposed cross-examination has a realistic and reasonable chance of affecting the judge's determination as to whether there is some evidence upon which a reasonable jury or trier of fact properly instructed could convict." *McKnight*, above note 85, rejects that standard as too strict. See also *Rao*, above note 84, adopting a broader standard.

88 *Rao*, *ibid*; *R v Lavoie*, 2015 ABPC 30.

89 See *R v I(SP)* (2005), 27 CR (6th) 112 (Nun Ct J). See also *R v Canning*, 2005 ONCJ 144.

decision to commit at the preliminary inquiry to be based, at least in part, upon evidence that cannot be tendered at trial.

In large part no definitive answers have been given to these questions raised by the 2004 amendments. The 2019 amendments now significantly reduce the offences for which a preliminary inquiry will be available, limiting it to quite serious offences. On the one hand, this means that there will be fewer decisions about preliminary inquiries at all. On the other, it means that those decisions which are made will be in contexts where the stakes are higher and the need for fairness ought to take precedence over the push to efficiency. That might mean that the caselaw until this point will need to be revisited, but there is no sign of that having occurred.

## 2) Cross-Examination of Prosecution Witnesses

The accused is entitled to cross-examine prosecution witnesses called at the preliminary inquiry, either personally or through counsel.[90] This full right of cross-examination is constrained not only by a criterion of relevance to the scope of the inquiry as a whole, but also to the sufficiency of the prosecution evidence.[91] Thus, the accused is permitted to cross-examine a prosecution witness on any matter that could lead to the conclusion that the prosecution evidence is insufficient and is also permitted to cross-examine in a manner that might be useful in a subsequent trial. Until the 2004 amendments, it was clear that the accused could cross-examine a prosecution witness on a matter that might have central significance at the trial but that was wholly outside the scope of the preliminary inquiry.[92] This occurred most frequently when an accused cross-examined for the purpose of a subsequent challenge at trial to the credibility of a witness, or for the purpose of laying the factual foundation for an issue under the *Charter* to be raised at trial. However, whether this statement remains true after the 2004 amendments has been a matter of some disagreement in lower courts. Some courts have concluded that the rule remains unchanged, while others have concluded that the streamlining of the preliminary inquiry now means that such matters must be left for trial.[93] Courts have also

---

90 *Re Zaor and the Queen* (1984), 12 CCC (3d) 265 (Que CA).

91 *R v Bayne* (1970), 14 CRNS 130 (Alta SCAD).

92 *B(E)*, above note 49; *Dawson*, above note 51. See also *Re Ward and the Queen* (1976), 31 CCC (2d) 466 (Ont CA); *R v George* (1991), 69 CCC (3d) 148 (Ont CA).

93 See, for example, *McGrath*, above note 50; *Tran*, above note 50; *Catellier*, above note 50; or *Beers*, above note 50. It has been argued that any efficiencies gained

commented on cross-examination of a complainant about sexual history at a preliminary inquiry, concluding that it is either not permitted at all or that it might occur rarely if at all.[94,95]

With respect to examination and cross-examination, but especially the latter, the justice has the express power to immediately stop any part of it that is, "in the opinion of the justice, abusive, too repetitive or otherwise inappropriate."[96] This power is broad. While protection against abuse or undue repetition is necessary, it is not clear what is intended by the sweeping phrase "otherwise inappropriate." Given that the *Code* encourages limitations on the scope of preliminary inquiries, this phrase should not be interpreted to restrict the ability of the parties to discover the nature and quality of the opponent's evidence.

In the amendments that came into force in 2004, there was a conspicuous gap that Parliament should have filled regarding the right of cross-examination. If the defence makes a request to hear a prosecution witness on a specific issue, it presumably wishes to cross-examine that witness, but nothing in the *Code* makes it clear that such a witness is a prosecution witness for the purposes of cross-examination at the preliminary inquiry. A judge cannot call a witness and has no jurisdiction at the preliminary inquiry to order the prosecution to call a witness, and so, seemingly all that the judge can do is ask the prosecutor to consent to call a witness for the purpose of cross-examination by the accused. It is also arguable that a request from the defence can be considered to have the effect of challenging the prosecution case with regard to a specific witness and specific issue and this, in turn, can be taken to require the prosecution to call its witness on that specific issue.

---

at the preliminary inquiry stage by refusing to permit evidence to be called on matters not going strictly to whether the accused should be committed for trial would result in greater inefficiencies from unnecessary applications at trial: Tim Quigley, "*R. v. Tran*: Annotation" (2008) 63 *Criminal Reports* (6th) 345.

94 The British Columbia Court of Appeal has concluded that questions can only be asked about sexual history after a successful application to be permitted to do so, and that those statutory provisions limit applications to the time of trial: *R v MPS*, 2014 BCCA 338. The Ontario Court of Appeal has held that as a matter of law an application could be made at a preliminary inquiry but that "[i]t is likely that tactical considerations dissuade counsel from bringing s. 276 applications at preliminary inquiries or during bail proceedings. Even if successful, evidence of the complainant's prior sexual history will be of no value at a preliminary inquiry in terms of committal; nor will it have much, if any, impact on the apparent strength of the Crown's case in the context of bail proceedings": *R v Kuzmich*, 2020 ONCA 359 at para 35.

95 *R v MPS*, 2014 BCCA 338.

96 Section 537(1.1).

## 3) Address to Accused

At the close of the prosecution evidence the *Code* requires the justice to address an accused who is not represented by counsel as follows, or in like terms:

> Do you wish to say anything in answer to these charges or to any other charges which might have arisen from the evidence led by the prosecution? You are not obliged to say anything but whatever you do say may be given in evidence against you at your trial. You should not make any confession or admission of guilt because of any promise or threat made to you but if you do make any statement it may be given in evidence against you at your trial in spite of the promise or threat.[97]

This caution is a vestige of ancient law in which magistrates were required to conduct investigations of alleged criminal activity, typically after arrest and before considering bail. As the preliminary inquiry later became a judicial examination of the sufficiency of the prosecution case, the investigative role of the magistrate disappeared. The caution is also a vestige of an era in which an accused person was not competent to testify. For both of these reasons the caution is largely an anachronism.

Section 541(2) requires this caution to be given only to an unrepresented accused, presumably on the assumption that an accused with representation will be competently advised of their position, thus dispensing with the need for the address. Nonetheless, there seems to be no harm in the judge reciting the required address in all cases, unless the defence makes clear that the accused has been apprised of the content of the address. In any case, as a practical matter it is rare for the accused to make a statement after caution, not least because anything they might say by way of defence will not be considered in the decision to commit for trial or discharge.[98] Since the 2019 amendments limiting preliminary inquiries to a small set of serious offences, it is also much less likely that an accused will be unrepresented.

## 4) Defence Evidence

The defence is also entitled to adduce evidence on behalf of the accused, including testimony by the accused, but it is not obliged to

97 Section 541(2).

98 Moreover, the accused who makes a statement after caution cannot be cross-examined, unlike the accused who testifies.

call witnesses.[99] As the preliminary inquiry is not a trial and cannot lead to a judgment of acquittal, it is comparatively rare that the accused is discharged at the preliminary inquiry solely on the basis of evidence called by the defence. Indeed, the tactical position of the defence at the preliminary inquiry can be delicate. There is no obligation on the accused to make disclosure of its case, and the production of witnesses for the defence can have not only the effect of making disclosure but also of exposing the accused at trial to any weaknesses that might emerge in the evidence of such witnesses.

There is, however, often some advantage in the preparation of the defence case if the accused calls evidence of potential prosecution witnesses. Such witnesses might not be essential for the prosecution to succeed at the preliminary inquiry, but they might still be useful for the defence. The advantage lies in hearing and seeing those witnesses, and thus assessing what they can give in evidence and the credibility with which they give it. Even if the effect of calling such evidence is, in some cases, to disclose the strategy of the defence, there might be no disadvantage in doing so if the net effect is to gain a stronger basis for preparing a defence at trial. Once again, these considerations illustrate that the preliminary inquiry provides an opportunity for the defence to acquire further discovery of the case as a whole.

This opportunity can be especially important where there is a real risk that the evidence in issue might not be, for any reason, available at trial, and the accused wishes to preserve it. On the other hand, in some cases an accused might be quite content that certain evidence will not be available later. In either event, it is important to take note of the fact that evidence led at the preliminary inquiry (whether by the defence or the Crown) may be admitted at trial.

## 5) Preliminary Inquiry Evidence at Trial

Section 715(1) of the *Code* provides that if evidence was taken at the preliminary inquiry in the presence of the accused, and the witness either refuses to testify or is dead, insane, too ill to travel, or absent from Canada, then that evidence can be introduced at trial. This statutory rule does not apply to normally-inadmissible evidence which was admitted on the basis that it was credible or trustworthy (under section 540(7)), and requires that the accused had a full opportunity to cross-examine the witness. Generally such an opportunity will only fail to have been provided where, physically, no such complete

99 Section 541.

cross-examination takes place: where the witness refuses to answer, disappears, or the trial judge wrongly limits cross-examination, for example.[100] Where the failure to cross-examine only stems from the accused's ignorance of potentially useful information, even through lack of disclosure, or from the failure to appreciate the significance of particular evidence at the time, a full opportunity will generally be found to have been provided.[101] Note also that the accused's excused absence does not prevent the use of this section, and the justice is required to inform the accused of that point.[102] Even if all the statutory criteria for admission are met, however, the decision is still a discretionary one on the part of the judge, who must decide whether admitting the evidence would cause unfairness to the accused.[103]

Section 715, however, does not set out a "comprehensive code" on when preliminary inquiry testimony is admissible. As a result, in some cases, it is also possible to admit preliminary inquiry testimony through the principled exception to the hearsay rule. In *R v Hawkins*, for example, a witness testified at the preliminary inquiry, but then married the accused and so was incompetent to testify at trial. The Court held that this did not mean she was "refusing" to testify, and so section 715 did not apply to allow her evidence to be led at trial. Nonetheless, her preliminary inquiry testimony was admissible because it met the criteria of necessity and reliability that make up the principled exception.[104]

Bill C-75 has — again, seemingly as a trial efficiency measure — slightly expanded the evidence from a preliminary which can be used

---

100 *R v Lewis (KT)*, 2009 ONCA 874 [*Lewis*].

101 *Lewis, ibid*; *R v Roulette*, 2015 MBCA 9; *R v Jones-Solomon*, 2015 ONCA 654. In contrast, see *R v Assoun*, 2006 NSCA 47, in which the accused was unaware at the time of the preliminary inquiry that a witness claimed to have obtained some of her information through "psychic visions." In *Assoun* it was found that cross-examination on that point would not likely have changed the evidence of the witness, and so it was found not to have been wrongly admitted at trial, and the accused's conviction for murder was upheld. Many years later he was granted a re-trial and in 2019 the Crown discontinued proceedings against him: Innocence Canada, "Glen Assoun Acquitted of 20-Year-Old Murder Conviction" (27 February 2019), online: www.innocencecanada.com/the-latest/newspress/20-year-old-conviction-quashed-for-glen-assoun/.

102 Section 537(1.02).

103 *R v El Hajj Ahmad*, 2024 ONSC 5795 [*El Hajj Ahmad*].

104 [1996] 3 SCR 1043. This precise result might now be questionable, given the Court's subsequent ruling on spousal incompetency and the principled exception in *R v Couture*, 2007 SCC 28 [*Couture*]. However, nothing in *Couture* casts doubt on the general approach that s 715 is not a complete code and that preliminary inquiry evidence is potentially admissible under the principled exception.

directly at trial. Under section 715.01, a transcript of the testimony of the evidence of a police officer (as defined in section 183) can be used as evidence at trial without meeting all the requirements of section 715(1). The only conditions for the use of that evidence are that the testimony was given in the presence of the accused during a *voir dire* or preliminary inquiry and that notice is given. This section is also slightly broader than section 715(1) in another way: it permits the prior evidence to be used "in relation to the accused's trial," where section 715(1) only allowed the evidence to be used if it came from "the preliminary inquiry into the *charge*." Therefore, even if there were no preliminary inquiry into the particular charge (because, for example, a preliminary inquiry was not available for that offence) evidence coming from a preliminary inquiry into a jointly-laid charge might still be admitted under this section.[105] Once again, the decision is a discretionary one and should not work unfairness. One method of addressing that concern is in section 715.01(3), that the judge can require that the officer be made available for cross-examination. Although the section says the evidence must have been given in the presence of the accused, if the accused had been permitted to be absent from the preliminary inquiry during that officer's testimony, it can still be used. Further, if the testimony was taken while the accused had absconded, they are deemed to have been present.[106]

## 6) Publication Bans

As in all other aspects of criminal procedure, proceedings are open unless there is some specific basis for an exception. Thus, the presentation of evidence is conducted in open court and might be the subject of public comment, unless the judge orders otherwise. The *Code* gives the judge discretion to exclude the public from court.[107] This power is occasionally used, but it is comparatively rare at preliminary inquiries.

---

105 See, for example, *El Hajj Ahmad*, above note 103, where the accused was charged with both drug and firearm offences. He was only eligible for a preliminary inquiry on the drug charges, but evidence from that could, in principle, be led at trial in relation to the drug charges. In fact the trial judge declined to allow the evidence to be used, on the basis that the accused had not been able to cross-examine the police officer on the firearm charge at the preliminary inquiry, and so admitting it would be unfair.

106 Sections 715.01(4) and (5). Note that s 537(1.02) requires that if a justice permits an accused to be absent (under s 537(1)(j.1)) they must inform the accused of this possibility.

107 Sections 537(1)(h) and 486.

As distinct from the general public, witnesses are routinely excluded, at least until they have given their evidence.[108]

Typically, the presentation of evidence at the preliminary inquiry is the subject of a ban on publication. The legislative rationale for these orders is that the accused, who is presumed innocent and is not in jeopardy of conviction at the preliminary inquiry, should be shielded from adverse publicity before trial. The same might be said of other witnesses, especially the complainant. Indeed, there is a general argument that the fairness of any subsequent trial can be ensured only if there is a publication ban at the preliminary inquiry.

A publication ban is imposed by order of the justice before any evidence is taken — it is discretionary, if sought by the prosecution, and mandatory, if sought by the accused.[109] It has been held that if the order is sought after the presentation of evidence has begun, the presiding judge has discretion in the matter, but there is little apparent justification for this position.[110] If the rationale for allowing any publication ban has force in the first place, there is no reason why that rationale should not be given effect after the presentation of evidence has begun.

If an accused is not represented by counsel, the *Code* obliges the judge to inform the accused of the right to seek a publication ban.[111] When ordered, the ban remains in effect until the accused is discharged or, if the accused is committed for trial, the trial is ended. Although such bans infringe the freedom of expression and the right to know what transpires in the public proceedings of courts, the courts have ruled that they are reasonable limitations upon those rights.[112]

## D. COMMITTAL

Section 548 of the *Code* directs the justice or judge at the preliminary inquiry to commit the accused for trial on any indictable offence if the evidence in support of that charge is sufficient. It also requires that the accused be discharged in respect of any charge on which the

108 *Re Collette and the Queen; Re Richard and the Queen* (1983), 6 CCC (3d) 300 (Ont HCJ); *R c M(AG)* (1993), 26 CR (4th) 379 (Que CA); compare *Re Armstrong and State of Wisconsin* (1972), 7 CCC (2d) 331 (Ont HCJ).

109 Section 539.

110 *R v Harrison* (1984), 14 CCC (3d) 549 (Que SP).

111 Section 539(2).

112 See, for example, *Dagenais v Canadian Broadcasting Corp*, [1994] 3 SCR 835; *Canadian Broadcasting Corporation v New Brunswick (Attorney General)*, [1996] 3 SCR 480; and *R v Mentuck*, [2001] 3 SCR 442.

evidence is not sufficient. Everything turns, therefore, on what is meant by "sufficient" evidence. The courts have provided a test that has been consistently applied for many years, though there is some basis to challenge whether it is the correct test. (Note, of course, that this test is based on the no-longer-correct assumption that the judge is assessing the entire case against the accused.)

In *R v Shephard*, the Supreme Court stated that the test of sufficiency at the preliminary inquiry, as for a directed verdict and for committal in extradition matters, was whether a reasonable jury, properly instructed, could find the charge proved beyond reasonable doubt.[113] Where the Crown has adduced direct evidence on all the elements of the offence, the accused must be committed for trial. Where the evidence includes circumstantial evidence, the judge is to engage in a limited weighing of the whole of the evidence to determine whether a reasonable jury properly instructed could return a verdict of guilty. However, that limited weighing does not include drawing inferences from the facts or assessing credibility. Rather, the judge is to decide whether, if the Crown's evidence is believed, it would be reasonable for a properly instructed jury to infer guilt. As the Court has noted, "this task of 'limited weighing' never requires consideration of the inherent reliability of the evidence itself. It should be regarded, instead, as an assessment of the reasonableness of the inferences to be drawn from the circumstantial evidence."[114] One could easily question whether denying the preliminary inquiry justice any ability to consider the probative force of the evidence is the right decision. It is arguable that the presiding judge should assess the force of the evidence.

A convenient fashion in which to examine the test of sufficiency is to look at the criteria of completeness and weight. The first of these means only that the prosecution leads evidence corresponding to each of the elements of the offence as defined in the substantive criminal law, including identification.[115] In a case of assault, for example, this would mean that there was evidence led that the accused intentionally applied force to another person without that person's consent. In the general run of cases, the criterion of completeness poses few difficulties.

It is the criterion of weight that is problematic. The Supreme Court and other courts have said repeatedly that the judge is not to assess the weight of evidence at the preliminary inquiry.[116] Accordingly, a judge

---

113 *Shephard*, above note 12.

114 *R v Arcuri*, [2001] 2 SCR 828 [*Arcuri*] at para 30. See also the discussion in *R v Jackson*, 2016 ONCA 736.

115 *Skogman*, above note 13; *Deschamplain*, above note 31 at para 23.

116 *Monteleone*, above note 79; *Yebes*, above note 79.

must not assess the credibility of witnesses who testify.[117] In response, some courts have asserted that if there is any evidence on all essential elements in the charge, there should be an order of committal.[118] The reason most commonly invoked for this assertion is that the justice or judge at the preliminary inquiry must not usurp the functions of the jury or judge at trial in determining the strength of the case.[119]

On the other hand, if the prosecution evidence is such that no reasonable jury, properly instructed, could find the charge to be proven beyond a reasonable doubt, that seems like it should be a relevant consideration. Even given that a judge is not entitled to assess the credibility of a witness, one might argue that they should discharge the accused if no reasonable trier of fact could find the accused guilty on the evidence adduced by the prosecution. To reach such a conclusion would not be to usurp the role of the ultimate trier of fact.

The resolution of this problem depends upon the perceived purpose of having preliminary inquiries. If the test of sufficiency is restricted to the criterion of completeness, as discussed above, the justice should not weigh the evidence adduced at the preliminary inquiry. It would also follow from this that the test of sufficiency stated in *Shephard* should be reformulated to require that the prosecution evidence need only support an air of reality as regards each of the elements of the charge. But if the primary purpose of the preliminary inquiry is to test the sufficiency of the prosecution case, and thus to protect the accused from being placed on trial pointlessly, then the judge must be able to discharge the accused in a case where no reasonable trier of fact could find the prosecution case proved beyond reasonable doubt.

Further, and once again in the context of an extradition case, the Court has commented in *United States of America v Ferras*:

> [40] . . . I take as axiomatic that a person could not be committed for trial for an offence in Canada if the evidence is so manifestly unreliable that it would be unsafe to rest a verdict upon it. It follows that if a judge on an extradition hearing concludes that the evidence is manifestly unreliable, the judge should not order extradition under s 29(1). Yet, under the current state of the law in *Shephard*, it appears that the judge is denied this possibility.[120]

---

117 See, for example, *Arcuri*, above note 114; see also, *Deschamplain*, above note 31; and *Sazant*, above note 31.

118 An extreme illustration is *Charemski*, above note 79.

119 *Monteleone*, above note 79.

120 2006 SCC 33 [*Ferras*].

In *Ferras* the Court went on to modify the *Shephard* test in the extradition context, but in doing so it indicated that there was no longer symmetry between the extradition and preliminary inquiry tests.

There would be value in the standard of sufficiency being further reviewed by the Supreme Court, specifically in the context of preliminary inquiries. A purposive interpretation of this test would be that a justice should discharge the accused if no reasonable trier of fact could find the essential elements of the offence proven beyond a reasonable doubt. Given the more limited role that has been provided for preliminary inquiries, first by limiting the issues that can be considered and second by limiting their availability, however, it is unlikely that major change of this sort is forthcoming.

Assuming that the prosecution case at the preliminary inquiry meets the test of sufficiency, the judge will order committal on any indictable offence charged or supported by the evidence. Ordering committal is done by endorsing the information in a manner that identifies the appropriate offences.[121] It will be recalled that the judge is not limited to committal on the offences charged in the information or to lesser or included charges, but is limited to committal upon charges in respect of the same transaction.[122] In general, this limitation means that the committal order must refer to offences that are related to the event or sequence of events that form the factual basis of the charges in the information at the preliminary inquiry. There is some margin in this for flexibility, and thus it has been held that if the evidence identifies another victim than that identified in the original charge, there might be an order of committal for an offence in relation to that victim, provided, of course, that the offence occurred in respect of the same events.[123]

If the accused is discharged at the preliminary inquiry, there is no acquittal and thus they cannot claim protection against double jeopardy if the prosecution should subsequently proceed against them on the same charge or a related charge, either by means of a fresh information or a direct indictment. As the accused was never in jeopardy of

---

121 It is not adequate for the judge simply to say that the accused is committed for trial. Specific offences must be enumerated in the endorsement.

122 The judge has no jurisdiction to commit the accused for trial on any summary conviction offence that is disclosed by the evidence, but he can commit for any indictable offence, including one that lies within the absolute jurisdiction of the provincial court.

123 *R v Stewart* (1988), 44 CCC (3d) 109 (Ont CA).

conviction at the preliminary inquiry, the discharge cannot constitute a final judgment.[124]

If the accused is committed for trial, the justice who presided at the preliminary inquiry is required to immediately transmit the record of the inquiry to the court of trial.[125] The record comprises the information as endorsed, the evidence (including exhibits), any statement made by the accused after the justice's address, and any paper process relating to compelling the appearance of the accused.

## E. REVIEW OF PRELIMINARY INQUIRY DECISIONS

The *Code* sets out no procedure for appealing the decision to commit or discharge at a preliminary inquiry, and so no appeal is possible. As a result, review of such a decision can be made only on the basis of an action for *certiorari*. Part XXVI of the *Code* regulates the use of extraordinary remedies in the criminal justice system and attaches some limits on the occasions when *certiorari* is available,[126] but it does remain available in the case of decisions at a preliminary inquiry. In principle, it is open to the Crown to seek *certiorari* in the case of a discharge, and this does sometimes occur.[127] As a practical matter, the Crown also has the usually simpler option, under section 577, of preferring a direct indictment despite the discharge, so more frequently *certiorari* applications involve an accused seeking review of a decision to commit.

Because the preliminary inquiry decision is reviewed by way of *certiorari* rather than appeal, it is not sufficient to show an error of law on the part of the preliminary inquiry judge. Rather, *certiorari* will be granted only if the judge has fallen into jurisdictional error: that is, "where the presiding judge fails to observe a mandatory provision of the *Criminal Code* or denies a party natural justice."[128] Many errors of law will simply be errors within a judge's jurisdiction. Erroneously excluding evidence at the preliminary hearing is unlikely to be a jurisdictional error (for example, an error with respect to the application of

---

124 *R v Ewanchuk* (1974), 16 CCC (2d) 517 (Alta SCAD); *R v Fields* (1979), 12 CR (3d) 273 (BCCA).

125 Section 551.

126 See s 776.

127 See, for example, *R v Dubois*, [1986] 1 SCR 366 [*Dubois*]; *Sazant*, above note 31; *PM*, above note 28.

128 *CMM*, above note 80 at para 10.

the rules of evidence will not be a jurisdictional error unless it rises to the level of a denial of natural justice).[129]

Apart from denying natural justice, it is also a jurisdictional error if a trial judge fails to comply with a mandatory provision of the *Code*. In particular, section 548 of the *Code* requires a judge to commit the accused for trial if "there is sufficient evidence." Cases have held that this means there must be at least some basis in the evidence at the preliminary inquiry that supports the decision to commit.[130] It has also been taken to mean, since a preliminary inquiry judge does not weigh evidence, that where the Crown has adduced direct evidence on all the elements of the offence, the preliminary inquiry judge must commit the accused even if the defence has offered exculpatory evidence.[131] If there is no evidence on some essential element of the charge, however, it will be a jurisdictional error for the preliminary inquiry judge to commit the accused to trial.[132] Once again, however, this older caselaw is of limited relevance when related to a preliminary inquiry which is now usually limited only to particular issues, not sufficiency of the case as a whole.

The existence of evidence at the preliminary inquiry must be understood broadly. Even if the Crown has indicated that evidence led through a preliminary inquiry witness will not be led at trial, that evidence must nonetheless be considered in the decision to commit, and it would be a jurisdictional error to fail to consider it.[133]

Section 548 also requires a preliminary inquiry judge to discharge the accused if "on the whole of the evidence no sufficient case is made out." In other words, if a preliminary inquiry judge grants a discharge without considering "the whole of the evidence," that will also be a jurisdictional error.[134] The action would constitute a failure to comply with a mandatory statutory provision and would therefore allow a reviewing court to intervene.

Some guidance on the type of mistakes that can lead to jurisdictional errors was provided by the Court with its decision in

---

129 *Dubois*, above note 127 at 377; *Forsythe*, above note 29 at 272; *Attorney General (Quebec) v Cohen*, [1979] 2 SCR 305.

130 *Dubois*, above note 127 at 377.

131 *Arcuri*, above note 114 at para 29.

132 *Skogman*, above note 13 at 104. For discussion of jurisdictional error generally, see William Poulos, "The Preliminary Inquiry: Staying Within the Zone of Protection" (2015) 62 *Criminal Law Quarterly* 365.

133 *R v Papadopoulos* (2005), 201 CCC (3d) 363 (Ont CA), leave to appeal to SCC refused [2005] SCCA No 314.

134 *Deschamplain*, above note 31 at para 18.

*R v Sazant*.[135] The accused had been discharged at the preliminary inquiry on a charge of sexual assault. The preliminary inquiry judge had said there was "absolutely no evidence of non-consent." In fact, the complainant had testified that he did not want to take part in the sexual activity, and so there was no dispute that the preliminary inquiry judge had made an error. The issue was whether the error was jurisdictional.

The Court held that there were three possible explanations for the preliminary inquiry judge's mistake. He might have misunderstood the elements of the offence and given effect to a non-existent defence. In that event, he would not have tested the Crown's evidence against the actual elements of the offence charged, which would be a jurisdictional error. Second, the preliminary inquiry judge might have found the complainant's statement to be ambiguous, capable of interpretation either as an expression of "after-the-fact" regret, or as a statement of "during-the-fact" non-consent. If that were the case, though, it was not open to the preliminary inquiry judge to decide which interpretation he preferred — that would be an issue for the trial judge. In that event, the preliminary inquiry judge would again have fallen into jurisdictional error by deciding an issue reserved for another forum.[136] Finally, the preliminary inquiry judge might have simply overlooked the evidence of non-consent in the complainant's testimony. In that event he would have failed to consider "the whole of the evidence" as required by section 548, and so again would have committed a jurisdictional error.

An accused who wants to bring a *certiorari* application must do so before entering a plea to the charge upon which they were committed to trial. Once the plea is entered, jurisdiction is transferred to the superior court for trial, and the issue becomes whether the Crown can prove its case, not how the accused came to be there.[137]

## FURTHER READINGS

HEALY, PATRICK. "Chabotage: Expanding the Crown's Power to Prefer Additional Counts" (1984) 38 *Criminal Reports* (3d) 344.

---

135 *Sazant*, above note 31.

136 This had also been the rationale in *Dubois*, above note 127, where the preliminary inquiry judge was taken to have decided whether the evidence was capable of proving the Crown's case beyond a reasonable doubt, a decision reserved for the trial judge.

137 *R v Tippett*, 2010 NLCA 49

PACIOCCO, DAVID. "A Voyage of Discovery: Examining the Precarious Condition of the Preliminary Inquiry" (2003) 48 *Criminal Law Quarterly* 151.

POULOS, WILLIAM. "The Preliminary Inquiry: Staying Within the Zone of Protection" (2015) 62 *Criminal Law Quarterly* 365.

QUIGLEY, TIM. "*R. v. Tran*: Annotation" (2008) 63 *Criminal Reports* (6th) 345.

ROSE, DAVID. *Quigley's Criminal Procedure in Canada* (Toronto: Thomson Reuters, 2021) (loose-leaf), ch 14–15.

CHAPTER 10

# PRELIMINARY MATTERS AND REMEDIES

A number of matters can or must be dealt with prior to the start of prosecution. First, in some cases, an offence is not dealt with by way of prosecution at all, but rather through some alternative. Next, assuming that a prosecution is to occur, some administrative and other matters can be dealt with before the trial begins, either through a pre-trial motion or a pre-trial conference. Finally, in a case that will be tried by a jury, that jury must be selected. These issues will be dealt with in this chapter.

## A. ALTERNATIVES TO PROSECUTION

In an informal sense, an alternative to prosecution has long existed through the exercise of discretion by police to not lay charges in the first place, or by Crown prosecutors to not continue them.[1] Only relatively recently has that discretion been more formalized in a system of alternative measures authorized by statute.

1 The general view of the legitimacy of exercising that discretion has varied over time: see the discussion in Bruce Archibald, "Prosecutors, Democracy and the Public Interest: Prosecutorial Discretion and Its Limits in Canada" (Paper delivered at the XVIth Congress of the International Academy of Comparative Law, Brisbane, Australia, 14–22 July 2002) at 17–22.

Statutory alternative measures to prosecution began in 1985 with the *Young Offenders Act*,[2] though under that Act they were available only to young persons. Subsequently in 1995, the provisions of section 4 of the *YOA* were adopted into the *Criminal Code*, thereby creating the potential use of alternative measures for adults as well. The essential theory behind these schemes is that, in certain cases, the interests of society might be adequately protected through measures that are less intrusive to the person alleged to have committed an offence than prosecution. If the person fails to comply with the requirements of the alternative measures program, however, criminal charges can still be laid.

Section 717 of the *Code* does not require that an alternative measures program exist, but it authorizes the attorney general of a province to create such a program, and most provinces have done so.[3] The use of these measures is subject to various conditions, in particular, the general directive that the use of such measures cannot be inconsistent with the protection of society, and that the person considering their use is satisfied that they are appropriate given "the interests of society and of the victim."[4] Other provisions are aimed at protecting the interests of the person who would otherwise be the "accused." In large part, these provisions are aimed at ensuring that alternative measures are used only in cases that would otherwise have proceeded to prosecution, rather than being used in cases that simply would not have occupied the justice system at all. That is, alternative measures are intended to be a way of diverting some cases out of the criminal justice system, not a way of expanding its scope.

Consistent with this approach, alternative measures cannot be used unless the prosecutor believes that there would be sufficient evidence to proceed with a prosecution and that the prosecution is not barred at law in any way.[5] The person involved must have been advised of the right to counsel, must accept responsibility for the act or omission

2 RSC 1985, c Y-1, enacted as SC 1980–81–82–83, c 110 [*YOA*].

3 See, for example, the programs in Saskatchewan (https://publications.saskatchewan.ca/api/v1/products/73150/formats/81682/download), Quebec (https://equijustice.ca/en/restorative-justice-services/general-alternative-measures-program), or Newfoundland and Labrador (https://www.gov.nl.ca/releases/2019/jps/0311n06/). See also the discussion in Canadian Resource Centre for Victims of Crime, *Restorative Justice in Canada: What Victims Should Know* (https://crcvc.ca/wp-content/uploads/2021/09/Restorative-Justice_DISCLAIMER_Revised-July-2022_FINAL.pdf). At the time of this writing, Bill C-16, *An Act to amend certain Acts in relation to criminal and correctional matters (child protection, gender-based violence, delays and other measures)*, first reading December 9 2025 [Bill C-16] has been introduced. If passed in its current form, it will introduce into the *Code* Part XXII.2, "Alternative Measures and Restorative Justice Processes."

4 Section 717(1)(b).

5 Sections 717(1)(f) and (g).

constituting the offence, and must fully and freely consent to participate.[6] Alternative measures cannot be used where the person denies involvement in the offence or wants a charge dealt with in court.[7] Further protection for the individual is provided by the rule that no admission, confession, or statement made by a person as a condition of being dealt with by alternative measures is admissible against that person in any later proceedings.[8]

If a person completes the alternative measures, the court must dismiss any charges laid against that person later in respect of the offence. If charges are later laid against a person who has only partly completed the alternative measures, a court can still stay the charges if it is of the view that "the prosecution of the charge would be unfair, having regard to the circumstances and that person's performance with respect to the alternative measures."[9]

In practice, provinces have tended to consider the use of alternative measures according to various categories of offences. Typically, alternative measures simply will not be used for serious violent offences, serious sexual offences, spousal violence, drug trafficking, organized crime, and so on. Many minor offences presumptively will automatically be referred to alternative measures, while a group of offences in the middle continue to depend on prosecutorial discretion. Normally, this discretion is to be exercised in accordance with criteria established within the province's prosecution service.[10]

Alternative measures programs usually ask the person to undertake community service, personal service for the victim, specialized education programs, counselling, or to write a letter of apology.[11] More ambitious alternatives are also available. In Nova Scotia, for example, relying on the authority of section 717 of the *Code* and section 4 of the *YOA*, the province created a restorative justice program. This program creates the possibility for conferences between the offender, the victim, supporters of each of those people, and, potentially, other members of the community or police officers. Supporters of restorative justice argue that the outcomes of such conferences can ultimately be far more beneficial to the offender, the victim, and society as a whole.[12]

---

6 Sections 717(1)(c), (d), and (e).
7 Section 717(2).
8 Section 717(1)(3).
9 Section 717(4)(b).
10 See the discussion in Archibald, above note 1 at 29–30.
11 *Ibid* at 29.
12 *Ibid* at 34.

Subsequently, the *YOA* was replaced by the *Youth Criminal Justice Act*.[13] That Act now refers not to "alternative measures" but to "extrajudicial measures." For the most part, the features noted above are unchanged,[14] though they are now classed as "extrajudicial sanctions." However, various additional features, other than sanctions, have been added to the scheme. Most notable is the declaration of principles, in addition to those governing the *YCJA* generally, and specific to extrajudicial measures and clearly aimed at encouraging greater use of the measures. They affirm that extrajudicial measures are often the most appropriate and effective way to address youth crime, and that they allow for effective and timely intervention. In particular, they affirm that extrajudicial measures are presumed to be adequate for non-violent offences where the young person has not previously been found guilty of an offence, and that they can be used even if the young person has previously been dealt with by extrajudicial measures or has been found guilty of an offence.[15]

Consistent with a restorative approach, the *YCJA* also encourages the use of extrajudicial measures that aim to involve the families of the young person, the victim, and the community in their design and implementation.[16]

The *YCJA* also creates a system of what might be termed "pre-alternative measures," by allowing the attorney general of a province to create a system whereby police or prosecutors can administer a caution to a young person rather than commencing judicial proceedings. Under the *YCJA*, before starting judicial proceedings or taking any other measures, police are to consider the principles set out above and decide whether it would be sufficient to issue a caution. Police can also, with consent, refer a young person to a community agency "that may assist the young person not to commit offences."[17] Provincial programs authorizing Crown prosecutors to administer cautions rather than con-

---

13 SC 2002, c 1 [*YCJA*].

14 Two differences should be noted. Section 10(2)(d) of the *YCJA*, *ibid*, requires not only that the young person be informed of the right to consult with counsel, but also that there be a reasonable opportunity to do so. Further, in s 10(2)(b), although the person considering whether to refer must still consider the interests of society, any explicit reference to the interest of the victim has been removed.

15 *Ibid*, s 4. In 2019 s 4.1 was added, stating that the presumption does not apply in the context of "failure to comply" charges where "(a) the young person has a history of repetitive failures or refusals; or (b) the young person's failure or refusal caused harm, or a risk of harm, to the safety of the public."

16 *Ibid*, s 5.

17 *Ibid*, s 6(1).

tinue proceedings are also envisioned.[18] The relatively informal, low seriousness of this response to a young person's actions is stressed by the requirement that evidence of a caution or referral given to a young person is not admissible to prove prior offending behaviour in any later proceedings.[19]

It has been argued that these measures around restraint in the youth justice have been very successful, and that there are lessons which could be adopted to the adult criminal justice system.[20]

In addition to these programs, many provinces or cities have developed drug treatment or mental health courts.[21] The exact criteria differ from location to location, but they all share the underlying goal of dealing with offenders whose criminal behaviour is associated with either addiction or mental health issues by confronting those underlying issues directly, rather than simply prosecuting the accused for the behaviour. Typically, the Crown must be able to show that it would be possible to obtain a conviction, or the accused must be willing to plead, or actually plead, guilty to the offence. The offender is then referred to the appropriate court and becomes subject to a close monitoring scheme, often by means of bail conditions. Such courts are not located in every province but are becoming increasingly common.

Finally, the *Code* has since 2018 provided for "remediation agreements," which are specifically designed for organizations which have committed an offence on a list of economic crimes. Before negotiating a remediation agreement with an organization the prosecutor must believe certain conditions are met, including that there is a reasonable prospect of conviction, that the offence did not cause bodily harm, death, a threat to national security or involve a criminal organization or terrorist group, and that an agreement is in the public interest. If an agreement is negotiated, it must include a number of things, including a statement of facts about the offence, the organization's admission of

---

18 *Ibid*, s 8.

19 *Ibid*, s 9.

20 See Richard Barnhorst, "Achieving Restraint in the Use of the Criminal Justice System: Canada's Youth Criminal Justice Act" (2024) 72 *CLQ* 5.

21 According to Department of Justice Canada, *Legal Aid in Canada 2022-23* (https://www.justice.gc.ca/eng/rp-pr/jr/aid-aide/2023/docs/2024-legal-aid-in-canada-2022-23-eng.pdf), eleven jurisdictions have mental health courts (all but PEI and Nunavut), eleven have drug treatment courts (all but New Brunswick and PEI), eight have Indigenous Peoples courts/Gladue Courts (there are none in PEI, Newfoundland, or in the territories), and eleven have domestic violence courts (all but PEI and Nunavut). See also Richard D Schneider, Hy Bloom, & Mark Heerema, *Mental Health Courts: Decriminalizing the Mentally Ill* (Toronto: Irwin Law, 2007).

responsibility, terms about forfeiture, restitution, payment of penalties, an obligation to cooperate in investigating and prosecuting wrongdoing associated with the offence, and a deadline for completion. A remediation agreement must then be approved by a court. Criminal proceedings can be recommenced if the organization breaches the agreement, but if it is successfully completed, then the charges are deemed never to have been commenced and further proceedings are barred.[22]

## B. PRE-TRIAL MOTIONS AND CONFERENCES

### 1) Timing and Means

Authority over pre-trial motions and conferences is not set out as clearly in Canadian law as one might wish. Potential ambiguity arises even with the concept of what counts as "pre-trial." The Supreme Court has held on a number of occasions that the phrases "charged with an offence" and "commencement of trial" do not have fixed meanings and will be adjusted to suit particular contexts.

In *R v Chabot*, for example, the Court found the key transition point to be when an indictment was "lodged with the trial court at the opening of the accused's trial, with a court ready to proceed with the trial."[23] In *R v Kalanj*, in contrast, the Court notes that the word "charged" has no precise meaning in law and could reasonably range from being told that one will be charged with an offence to being called upon to plead in court.[24] In the context of the *Charter* section 11(b) right to trial within a reasonable time, the Court rejected the *Chabot* position, holding instead that a person is "charged" for section 11 purposes when an information is sworn or a direct indictment is laid.[25] Similarly, in *Spek v the Queen* the Court noted that the time of commencement of a jury trial will vary depending on which *Code* section is being considered and

---

22 See generally Part XXII.1 of the *Code*, ss 715.3–715.43, as well as *SNC-Lavalin Group Inc v Canada (Public Prosecution Service)*, 2019 FC 282, discussing the provisions.

23 [1980] 2 SCR 985 at 999 [*Chabot*].

24 [1989] 1 SCR 1594 at para 11 [*Kalanj*].

25 The Court rejected the argument that the time should run from the accused's arrest, eight months prior to the laying of charges. Compare *R v Connors* (1998), 14 CR (5th) 200 (BCCA), which held that for purposes of the *Identification of Criminals Act*, RSC 1985, c I-1, an accused had been charged with an offence when he had failed a breathalyzer test and was asked to give fingerprints at the time or return later to do so.

what interests are at stake.[26] For example, in dealing with an accused's right to be present for trial, the Court has considered jury selection to be part of the trial,[27] but in dealing with the power to replace a juror, the Court has held that the trial does not commence until the accused is placed in the charge of the jury.[28]

In the context of pre-trial motions, the Court had held that only the trial judge should hear applications to sever counts. In reference to the *Chabot* case in *R v Litchfield*,[29] the Court held that only the trial judge has jurisdiction to issue severance orders. However, the Court noted that as long as a trial judge had been assigned, there was no need to wait until the actual trial date to bring the application. Section 645(5) of the *Code* specifically authorized a trial judge in a jury trial, before the jury has been selected, to deal with any matter that would be dealt with in the absence of the jury. The Court noted that a similar power "was always open to a trial judge in a case of trial by judge alone to hear pre-trial motions before preparing to hear evidence."[30]

As a matter of common law, it is very likely that the *Litchfield* ruling would have applied to pre-trial motions generally, preventing most such applications from being brought other than to the trial judge. However, concerns about making the system operate more efficiently in an effort to avoid delay have led to a change in the law. The Supreme Court has suggested that trial courts should review their case management regimes to ensure that they provide the tools for parties to collaborate and conduct cases efficiently.[31] More importantly, in response to that same concern, Parliament has amended the provisions in the *Criminal Code* dealing with case management to make it possible for most issues to be dealt with at an earlier stage. Section 551.1 of the *Code* permits the appointment of a case management judge where "it is necessary for the proper administration of justice."[32] This measure was introduced in response to the difficulties and delays that arise with regard to so-called "mega trials" and was at first not routinely taken. However, because of increased concerns about trial delay (see the discussion below in Section B(2)(c)(i), "Trial Within a Reasonable Time"), the appointment of case management judges is now looked

26 [1982] 2 SCR 730 [*Basarabas*].
27 *R v Barrow*, [1987] 2 SCR 694 [*Barrow*].
28 *Basarabas*, above note 26.
29 [1993] 4 SCR 333 [*Litchfield*].
30 *Ibid* at para 27.
31 *R v Jordan*, 2016 SCC 27 at para 139 [*Jordan*]. See also *R v Haevischer*, 2023 SCC 11 [*Haevischer*], discussing the standard for summary dismissal of applications.
32 See also the discussion of case management judges in Chapter 2, Section B(4).

to as a method of making the system operate more efficiently. Until 2019, for example, a case management judge could not be appointed until after an indictment had been preferred, but that limitation has now been removed, with the expectation that they will be appointed at an early point in the process.[33] Where a case management judge is appointed, that judge can take steps to make the process more efficient, for example by encouraging the parties to make admissions and reach agreements, or establishing schedules and imposing deadlines. In addition, the case management judge can adjudicate issues such as severance of counts or accused, disclosure, admissibility of evidence, or change of venue.[34] Any such decision is binding on the parties and the trial judge, barring circumstances such as fresh evidence arising.[35] Indeed, it is open to a trial judge, during the trial, to refer such questions to the case management judge for decision.[36]

A further forum in which matters can be discussed pre-trial is through a pre-hearing conference. Section 625.1 of the *Code* permits such hearings "to consider matters that to promote a fair and expeditious hearing, would be better decided before the start of the proceedings, and other similar matters, and to make arrangements for decisions on those matters."[37] Such conferences are mandatory in the case of jury trials[38] and generally have been described as "an invaluable ally in the struggle to promote a fair and efficient criminal trial process."[39]

Pre-hearing conferences provide an opportunity for the parties and the court to see whether an agreement can be reached on issues that will expedite the trial. The conference gives the judge a chance to determine, for example, whether the voluntariness of statements will be admitted, whether identity will be an issue, or whether continuity of exhibits will be challenged.[40]

---

33 Bill C-75, *An Act to amend the Criminal Code, the Youth Criminal Justice Act and other Acts and to make consequential amendments to other Acts*, [Bill C-75], Royal Assent June 21, 2019, repealed what had been s 55.1(3), imposing that temporal limit.

34 Section 551.3(1).

35 Section 551.3(4).

36 Section 551.6.

37 Section 482(1) of the *Code* creates the authority for superior courts of criminal jurisdiction to create rules of court, and s 482(2) permits courts of criminal jurisdiction to do so. Section 482(3)(c) specifically authorizes rules concerning pre-hearing conferences. Superior courts in every province have, in fact, made such rules.

38 Section 625.1(2).

39 *R v Nguyen*, 2013 ONCA 169 at para 54.

40 *R v Christensen* (1995), 100 Man R (2d) 25 (CA) [*Christensen*].

However, in contrast to pre-trial motions, pre-hearing conferences are not intended to determine matters: "s. 625.1 does not bind either the Crown or defence to a particular position."[41] Thus, for example, a Crown prosecutor might indicate at a pre-hearing conference a lack of intention to use a statement given by the accused, but then at trial seek to introduce the statement. Provided that on the particular facts there is no threat to the accused's fair trial right (for example, that the accused has not chosen a jury trial relying on the fact that the statement would not be tendered), the prosecutor is entitled to change strategy despite representations made at the pre-hearing conference.[42] Similarly, a Crown prosecutor can decide after a pre-hearing conference on a joint indictment to file separate indictments against each accused.[43]

The defence is also not bound by representations made at a pre-hearing conference and can, for example, indicate at a conference that the issue in a sexual assault trial will be consent, but then argue at trial that no sexual relations occurred.[44] Similarly, because the pre-hearing conference is held on a without prejudice basis, indicating an intent to request a transfer hearing to youth court during the conference does not constitute an application.[45]

## 2) Particular Pre-trial Motions

Pre-trial motions can cover a wide variety of topics, and so the details of each will not be dealt with here. The substantive issues relevant to an application challenging the form of an indictment, or seeking a publication ban, can be found in Chapter 11. Similarly, pre-trial applications dealing with *Charter* issues, such as search and seizure issues or motions regarding disclosure, are dealt with in the chapters that correspond to those topics. However, some pre-trial motions will be discussed at greater length here, in particular, applications for change of venue, applications regarding fitness to stand trial, and *Charter* applications regarding the right to a trial within a reasonable time.

---

41 *R v Begrand-Fast* (1999), 180 Sask R 271 (CA), leave to appeal to SCC refused [1999] SCCA No 583 [*Begrand-Fast*].

42 *R v K(MA)* (2002), 166 Man R (2d) 205 (CA).

43 *Begrand-Fast*, above note 41.

44 *Christensen*, above note 40. The Court questions the wisdom of such a strategy, at least without giving prior notice to the court and the Crown of the changed approach.

45 *R v AWD* (1999), 126 OAC 334 (CA).

### a) Change of Venue

At common law, trials are to be held in the area in which the offence occurred. Trial judges typically have jurisdiction throughout the province in which they are appointed, and the only real territorial limitation is that courts should not hear trials of offences committed entirely in another province.[46] Nonetheless, the practice continues to be that trials are normally held in the area where the offences occurred, on the basis that this approach serves the interests of both the accused and the community.[47]

In some circumstances, however, it is possible to apply to change the venue in which the trial will be held,[48] in accordance with section 599 of the *Code*. That section allows either the defence or the Crown to apply for a change of venue on the grounds that

> (a) it appears expedient to the ends of justice, including
>    (i) to promote a fair and efficient trial, and
>    (ii) to ensure the safety and security of a victim or witness or to protect their interests and those of society; or
>
> (b) a competent authority has directed that a jury is not to be summoned at the time appointed in a territorial division where the trial would otherwise by law be held.[49]

As a practical matter, change of venue applications have most often turned on whether there was pre-trial publicity of a type that made it too difficult for an accused to obtain a fair trial without one.[50] The

---

46 Section 478(1), but see the various special jurisdiction rules in ss 7, 476, 477.1, and 478(2) and (3).

47 *R v Suzack* (2000), 30 CR (5th) 346 at para 30 (Ont CA) [*Suzack*].

48 For an explanation of this issue in chart form, see Steve Coughlan & Alex Gorlewski, *The Anatomy of Criminal Procedure: A Visual Guide to the Law*, 2nd ed (Toronto: University of Toronto Press, 2026) [*Anatomy of Criminal Procedure*], Chart 2.5(b), "Change of Venue."

49 Note that s 2 of the *Code* defines "territorial division" as "any province, county, union of counties, township, city, town, parish or other judicial division or place to which the context applies." Note, as well, that s 599 is incorporated by reference to apply to summary conviction offences: s 795.

50 *R v Nassr*, 2025 ONSC 934, notes that:

> [26] Prior cases where change of venue applications have been successful provide helpful examples of the types of prejudicial circumstances that can warrant such an order. They typically include some combination of extensive media coverage both leading up to and shortly before the trial; the publication or broadcast of highly prejudicial inadmissible information; a victim who is a beloved or prominent member of the community; inflammatory comments made by elected officials or other public figures; law reform efforts inspired by the crime; fundraising for the victim's family or to

essential issue is whether there is strong evidence of a general prejudicial attitude in the community as a whole.[51] In addition, that prejudice must not be capable of being cured by safeguards in jury selection, by instructions from the trial judge to the jury panel, or by the rules of evidence.[52] Because the remedy is discretionary, the judge hearing the application must consider all relevant factors.

The difficulty in obtaining jurors in a venue can justify a change.[53] However, the existence of the challenge for cause process, for example, and the ability in some circumstances to question jurors to determine whether pre-trial publicity has affected their ability to be impartial, has been relied on to dismiss change of venue applications.[54] Indeed, in cases where pre-trial publicity has been province-wide, it has been held that leaving the trial in a larger centre and using the challenge for cause process is more likely to protect the accused's rights than changing the venue to a smaller centre.[55] The date of the media coverage will also be relevant: prejudicial publicity from a year prior might not justify a change in venue.[56] In *R v Eng* the British Columbia Court of Appeal upheld a decision not to change venues on a retrial, even though a change of venue had been allowed on the original trial, on the basis that the passage of time had mended any prejudice caused by the media coverage.[57] Further, a change of venue will not be granted if the source of prejudice is the information to come out at trial, rather than the fact of pre-trial publicity "where the real potential for prejudice lies in the evidence which the jury eventually selected to try the case will hear, a change of venue does not assist in protecting an accused's right to a fair trial."[58]

---

memorialize the victim in some way; and, quite often, comparatively smaller communities.

One distinct circumstance worth noting is when a change of venue is sought under s 531 of the *Code* to allow a trial to take place more easily in the official language of Canada that is the language of the accused.

51 *R v Munson*, 2003 SKCA 28 [*Munson*]; *R v English* (1993), 84 CCC (3d) 511 (Nfld CA) [*English*]; *R v Alward and Mooney* (1976), 39 CRNS 281 (NBSCAD).

52 *Suzack*, above note 47 at para 35.

53 See, for example, *R v Anugaa*, 2018 NUCJ 2, where jurors had already been summoned four times and two trials had started, in a community of fewer than 900 people: the trial judge ordered a change of venue for the third trial.

54 See, for example, *ibid* and *Munson*, above note 51. For further discussion of pretrial publicity and challenges for cause, see Section C(3)(c), below in this chapter.

55 *Munson*, above note 51.

56 *Suzack*, above note 47.

57 (1999), 138 CCC (3d) 188 at para 6 (BCCA).

58 *Suzack*, above note 47 at para 38.

Although pre-trial publicity is the most common reason for a change in venue application, the criterion is whether the change is "expedient to the interests of justice," which can include other matters.[59]

Where an accused applies for the change in venue,[60] the accused must show that the change is needed. Although this might be considered to place an onus on the accused, the provision has been held not to violate the *Charter*.[61]

### b) Fitness to Stand Trial

Another motion potentially made on a pre-trial basis concerns the fitness of the accused to stand trial.[62] This issue looks at whether the accused suffers from a mental disorder, and so it is related to the ultimate issue of whether an accused will be found not criminally responsible under section 16 of the *Code*. However, it is a distinct question, because a not criminally responsible defence inquires into the accused's mental state at the time of the offence, while fitness is strictly focussed on the time of trial.[63] The fitness to stand trial provisions are found in Part XX.1 of the *Code*. The majority of that part sets out the procedures to deal with accused who have been found not criminally responsible based on a state of mind at the time of the offence, while the fitness provisions focus on the accused's mental state at the time of trial and whether it is fair to proceed.[64]

Everyone is presumed to be fit to stand trial.[65] The definition of "unfit to stand trial" in section 2 of the *Code* requires first that the accused suffers from a mental disorder (the same requirement as in section 16 for an accused to be not criminally responsible). The second requirement is

---

59 See, for example, *R v Graham*, 2024 ONSC 6462, where a five-week murder trial for an in-custody accused was to be held on Manitoulin Island, which would necessitate five hours of travel each day during the worst part of winter. The Crown and the defence both agreed the venue should be changed, though they disagreed as to where. Similarly see *R v McIntyre*, 2024 BCSC 774, where the venue was changed so that an accused in ill health would not have to spend eight weeks detained in a cell at an RCMP detachment rather than a remand centre.

60 This is the typical case, though it is open on the terms of s 599 for the Crown to apply: see *R v Ponton* (1899), 2 CCC 417 (Ont HCJ).

61 *Suzack*, above note 47 at para 43.

62 For an explanation of this issue in chart form, see *Anatomy of Criminal Procedure*, above note 48, Chart 2.5(c), "Fitness to Stand Trial."

63 *R v Bharwani*, 2023 ONCA 203, aff'd in the result in *R v Bharwani*, 2025 SCC 26 [*Bharwani*].

64 Section 141 of the *YCJA*, above note 13, incorporates Part XX.1 of the *Criminal Code* except where those provisions conflict with rules in the former Act.

65 Section 672.22.

that the accused is unable on that account to conduct a defence at any stage of the proceedings before a verdict is rendered or to instruct counsel to do so, and, in particular, unable on account of mental disorder to

(a) understand the nature or object of the proceedings
(b) understand the possible consequences of the proceedings, or
(c) communicate with counsel.

More simply, the section asks: (1) Does the accused have a mental disorder and, (2) if so, does that mental disorder render the accused unable to conduct a defence or to instruct counsel to do so?[66] This provision is a codification of common law rules concerning fitness.[67]

For several decades the leading authority on fitness to stand trial was the Ontario Court of Appeal decision in *Taylor*.[68] It set a consciously low standard: or put another way, it is relatively difficult to establish that the accused is *not* fit to stand trial. This is because a finding of unfitness can result in profound limitations on an accused's liberty, since an unfit accused will be placed under the jurisdiction of a Review Board until they are either found fit to stand trial or permanently unfit to stand trial.[69] A theme which has regularly, but unsuccessfully, arisen is that an accused should have to meet a higher "analytical capacity" test. However, the test set in *Taylor* only required that the accused have the "limited cognitive capacity to understand the process and to communicate with counsel . . . provided the accused possesses this limited capacity, it is not a prerequisite that he or she be capable of exercising analytical reasoning in making a choice to accept the advice of counsel or in coming to a decision that best serves her interests."[70] This test had traditionally been referred to as the "limited cognitive capacity" test, though in substantially agreeing with *Taylor* the Supreme Court suggested that to avoid confusion caused by vague expressions, it should simply be termed the "fitness to stand trial" test.[71]

---

66 *Bharwani*, above note 63 at para 50.

67 *R v Taylor* (1992), 11 OR (3d) 323 (CA) [*Taylor*]; *R v Brigham* (1992), 18 CR (4th) 309 (Que CA). The words "in particular" indicate that other circumstances could also be relevant: *Bharwani*, above note 63.

68 *Taylor*, above note 67.

69 *Bharwani*, above note 63 at para 73.

70 *R v Whittle*, [1994] 2 SCR 914 at para 33 [*Whittle*], describing *Taylor*, above note 67 as setting out the correct test for fitness. *Taylor* has been interpreted as requiring only that the accused be able to communicate the facts relating to the offence to counsel: see, for example, *R v Jobb*, 2008 SKCA 156. More commonly the test is taken to be whether the accused is able to participate meaningfully in the trial: see *R v Morrissey*, 2007 ONCA 770 interpreting *Taylor* and the discussion of the competing lines of authority in *R v Daley*, 2019 NBCA 89.

71 *Bharwani*, above note 63 at para 50.

It is the second part of the test, whether the accused is able to "conduct a defence," that is central to the fitness to stand trial test. A "defence" consists of various key decisions, such as how to plead or elect, whether to testify, whether to retain counsel, and other decisions encompassed within the right to full answer and defence. It includes at least: 1) the right to challenge the Crown's case; 2) the right to advance a defence; and 3) the right to address the trier of fact.[72] The ability to conduct that defence requires a reality-based understanding of the nature or object and possible consequences of the proceedings, the capacity to make decisions, and the capacity to intelligibly communicate with the court and counsel.[73] In particular, "[t]he accused is not required to make decisions in their best interests, but cannot be overwhelmed by delusions, hallucinations, or other symptoms of their mental disorder when making and communicating these decisions."[74]

The Court, having jurisdiction over the accused, can order a fitness hearing on its own motion, or on application by the prosecutor or the accused. A party arguing that the accused is unfit has the burden of proof, on a balance of probabilities.[75] The fitness hearing itself is a two-stage process. First, the judge must consider whether there are reasonable grounds to decide whether the accused is unfit to stand trial. If this threshold is met, then the actual question of fitness is decided.[76] A court can order an assessment to help determine whether an accused is fit to stand trial.[77] This assessment can be ordered on the court's

---

72 *Bharwani*, above note 63 at para 63.

73 *Bharwani*, above note 63 at para 70.

74 *Bharwani*, above note 63 at para 77. The Court added:

> [81] This level of capacity falls short of requiring effective or wise decisions. That an accused may make objectively poor decisions in the conduct of their defence is irrelevant to the issue of their fitness to stand trial. The fact that an accused is "unable" to mount a defence due to being legally untrained, unsophisticated, or driven by motivations unrelated to the truth-seeking function of the trial (such as vengeance, religious devotion, or obstruction) plays no role in the inquiry.

75 Sections 672.22 and 672.23(2).

76 *R v Lovie* (1995), 24 OR (3d) 836 (CA); *R v Bain* (1994), 130 NSR (2d) 332 (CA). See the useful review of caselaw in *R v Chemama*, 2024 QCCA 405 [*Chemama*] where, in a jury trial, the trial judge was found to have properly decided there were no reasonable grounds for a fitness assessment, rather than to have wrongly usurped the jury's role in deciding the assessment showed the accused to be fit.

77 Section 672.11(a). It can be an error for a judge, even in the absence of a request from counsel, to fail to do so where the circumstances make it apparent an assessment should be done: see *R v Walker*, 2019 ONCA 765.

own motion or on application by the prosecutor or the accused. Where the prosecutor applies for an assessment order in a summary conviction case, the court cannot grant the application unless the prosecutor shows reasonable grounds to believe that the accused is unfit or the accused raises the issue.[78]

In non-jury trials or at a preliminary inquiry the judge determines whether the accused is fit.[79] In jury cases where the accused has already been given in charge to the jury, the jury decides fitness.[80] In jury cases where the accused has not been given in charge to the jury, a jury must be sworn to decide the fitness issue, though with consent of the accused that jury can also hear the trial, if one occurs.[81]

Fitness applications need not be made pre-trial and can be brought any time prior to verdict, but there are some restrictions on timing. If the offence in question is a hybrid one, the judge must postpone the fitness hearing until after the Crown has elected whether to proceed summarily or by indictment.[82] If the application is brought during a preliminary inquiry, the judge can postpone the application until the time the accused is called upon to answer the charge.[83] Similarly, if the application is brought at trial, the judge has discretion to postpone the application until the opening of the accused's case.[84] The rationale for these delays is found in section 672.3, which notes that, if the accused is discharged at the preliminary inquiry or acquitted at the close of the Crown's case, the fitness issue will not be tried at all. Consistent with this approach is the obligation on the judge, in exercising the section 672.25(2)(b) discretion, to consider first whether the Crown can prove that the accused committed the act alleged in the indictment. If there is dispute over this question the judge

> may proceed with the trial proper and postpone the fitness inquiry, or he or she may require the Crown to demonstrate at the outset of the fitness hearing that it is in a position to establish that the accused committed the act or acts alleged in the indictment. In either case, a finding that an accused is not fit to stand trial should not be made in the absence of any basis to put that accused on trial.[85]

---

78 Section 672.12(2).
79 Section 672.27.
80 Section 672.26(b).
81 Section 672.26(a).
82 Section 672.25(1).
83 Section 672.25(2)(a).
84 Section 672.25(2)(b).
85 *Taylor*, above note 67.

In addition, the fitness question "must be assessed holistically, recognizing that an accused's mental state may fluctuate."[86] That is, a transient mental state or a momentary delusion that prevents an accused from making reality-based decisions might not render the accused unfit, if the trial judge and others can help the accused get back on track by the time important decisions are to be made.

If the accused is found unfit, however, that bars proceeding with any other aspects of the matter, not merely the trial proper. The section talks about an accused being unfit "at any stage of the proceedings," and therefore no bail hearing or preliminary inquiry could be conducted for an unfit accused, and sentencing could not occur if a fit accused had become unfit after trial.[87]

If the accused is unrepresented, counsel shall be appointed.[88] If the accused is found fit to stand trial, matters continue as if no application had ever been made.[89] If the accused is found unfit, however, then a disposition hearing concerning the accused must be held. This hearing is conducted in accordance with essentially the same rules as disposition hearings for an accused found not criminally responsible, under section 16, at the conclusion of trial. The accused cannot be discharged absolutely, but can be confined in a hospital or discharged subject to conditions.[90] Treatment other than electroconvulsive therapy can be ordered for up to sixty days, provided there is specific evidence from a medical practitioner that the treatment will help make the accused fit for trial.[91] The consent of the accused is not required, but a treatment order is subject to the consent of the hospital where the treatment will take place: this includes consent not only to the treatment itself but to other conditions in the order, such as the commencement date.[92]

Whether an accused is fit to stand trial is a time-dependent issue. An accused might seem unfit at a certain point but that concern could disappear.[93] Alternatively, an accused could be found fit to stand trial

86 *Bharwani*, above note 63 at para 78.

87 *R c RL*, 2017 QCCA 933.

88 Section 672.24.

89 Section 672.28.

90 Section 672.54.

91 Sections 672.58 and 672.61.

92 Section 672.62 requires the consent of the facility. In *R v Conception*, 2014 SCC 60, the Court concluded that this gives the facility the ability to refuse consent to an order for treatment to begin "forthwith."

93 See, for example, *Chemama*, above note 76, where the trial judge raised the issue of fitness before there was a suspension of the trial but was found properly not to have returned to it when the trial resumed.

but for there to be a change in circumstances leading to a later application concerning the same issue.[94] If an accused is found unfit to stand trial, there must be regular reviews in which the Crown must show that it could still prove its case against the accused if called upon to do so. These reviews must occur at least every two years, or earlier if the accused shows reason to doubt that the Crown is still able to prove its case.[95] Evidence at these hearings can be by way of affidavits or transcripts, and the exact procedure is not specified in the *Code*. If, at any review, a *prima facie* case against the accused cannot be made out, the accused is entitled to an acquittal.

The defence and the Crown are each entitled to appeal the decision of a fitness hearing.[96]

### c) *Charter* Motions

Many different *Charter* motions can be brought, not necessarily on a pre-trial basis. Applications dealing with a violation of an accused's right to be free from unreasonable search and seizure, for example, might well occur either at the start of a trial or during its course. This chapter will not attempt to deal with all the various substantive issues that could arise on *Charter* motions. Only two motions will be considered here: (1) applications concerning the right to a trial within a reasonable time and (2) applications dealing with abuse of process.

#### i) *Trial Within a Reasonable Time*

Section 11(b) of the *Charter* guarantees any person charged with an offence the right "to be tried within a reasonable time." As a general rule this is an application which should be brought before trial, though that is not an absolute requirement.[97] For decades this right had — except for a very short period — minimal impact on the system, because of the way in which it had been interpreted. With the 2016 Supreme Court of

94 See, for example, *R v LSC*, 2003 ABCA 105.

95 Section 672.33. This is one of the few places in which the rules for young persons are different. Section 141(10) of the *YCJA*, above note 13, requires that such reviews happen at least every year.

96 Sections 675(3) and 676(3).

97 *R v JF*, 2022 SCC 17 at para 36 [*JF*]. Under the current approach it is expected that by the time trial dates are set the parties will be able to predict whether there will be a s 11(b) violation. Exceptionally an application can be brought later. Previously the view was that the motion could be brought at any time the delay had become unreasonable, including after the close of the Crown's case: *R v Rahey*, [1987] 1 SCR 588 [*Rahey*].

Canada decision in *R v Jordan*[98] that situation changed, and the right to a trial within a reasonable time is having significant impacts at every stage of the criminal justice system, across the country. Although the approach to section 11(b) from *Jordan* can be described and understood in its own right, some background is helpful to understand exactly *why* the Court adopted the approach it did, and therefore the spirit which is to be brought to bear in using that approach.

Although the section is not drafted in a way to require this reading, it is useful to distinguish between exceptional delay and institutional delay. "Exceptional delay" refers to delay that is out of the ordinary. For example, in *R v Rahey*,[99] a decision that normally would have been made in a few days was adjourned nineteen times and took eleven months. In *R v Godin*, a "straightforward" case that "needed only modest amounts of court time" was not even scheduled to begin until two and half years after charges were laid.[100] In both *R v Stensrud*[101] and *R v Smith*,[102] delays relating to preliminary inquiries (the preparation of a transcript and the actual scheduling of the inquiry, respectively) were unusual compared to the norm in those jurisdictions. In all those cases, it was not difficult for a court to conclude that the particular delay was unreasonable, because there was an obvious external measure against which to judge. "Institutional delay," on the other hand, refers to delay that is inherent to the system itself. That is, in institutional delay cases the problem is not that a particular case took too long compared to the norm, but that the norm itself is too long. This is inherently a more difficult claim to assess, because there is no external standard that unambiguously determines how long is too long.

As section 11(b) has developed, institutional delay cases have become the dominant issue. Broadly, at a relatively early stage the Court adopted an approach under section 11(b) to institutional delay that made it very difficult for any such claim to succeed. The unintended consequence of that was that the primary impetus to prevent delay in the system was removed, and as a result the system became slower and slower: ironically, the right to a trial within a reasonable time caused trials to be slower. After more than two decades of this, because of the crisis that trial delay had become, in 2016 the Court threw out the old approach and adopted a radically new one with its decision in *Jordan*. While many details of that new approach still need to be

---

98 *Jordan*, above note 31.
99 *Rahey*, above note 97.
100 2009 SCC 26 at para 16 [*Godin*].
101 *R v Stensrud*, [1989] 2 SCR 1115.
102 *R v Smith*, [1989] 2 SCR 1120 [*Smith*].

worked out,[103] it is clear that the primary effect has been to energize all actors in the system to try to eliminate delay. A little bit needs to be said about pre-*Jordan* caselaw, though it is no longer necessary to understand that set of rules in any detail. *R v Askov* was the first occasion on which the Supreme Court dealt with institutional delay.[104] In that case the Court suggested that, as a guideline, a case should take no more than six to eight months from committal to trial (that is, at the superior court level). The Court had previously determined that the minimum remedy for a violation of section 11(d) is a stay of proceedings: it is not possible to find that a reasonable time in which to have a trial has already passed but to put the accused on trial nonetheless.[105] The immediate result was that charges against Askov were stayed.

However, the case had a much broader impact: based on the guideline, in a period of less than a year, 47,000 charges did not go to trial in Ontario alone. The majority of these charges were minor ones and were withdrawn by Crown prosecutors rather than stayed by judges in accordance with the *Askov* guidelines. Nonetheless, the situation was perceived very negatively by the public, and the Court appeared to feel some pressure over this result.[106] Eighteen months later, in the next case to deal with institutional delay, *R v Morin*, they adopted a stricter test than had previously existed. That test gave judges a great deal of discretion to allocate individual portions of the time taken in various ways that did not count towards finding a violation, such as to actions of the defence, to the inherent time requirements of the case, or to the limits on institutional resources, and then to decide whether there was a violation or not.[107] On the face of it, the steps in the test were not greatly changed from *Askov*. Indeed, *Morin* also proposed a guideline:

103 See *R v King*, 2018 NLCA 66 [*King*] at para 33, listing twenty-eight questions arising from *Jordan*.

104 [1990] 2 SCR 1199 [*Askov*].

105 That is the simplest way to understand the conclusion, but not the only one. Six judges in *Rahey*, above note 97, reached the conclusion that a stay is the minimum remedy for a breach of s 11(b), but for three different sets of reasons. Four of them suggest that a s 11(b) violation removes the jurisdiction of a court to put the accused on trial. Bill C-16, above note 3, if passed in its current form will add s 492.22 saying that a finding of unreasonable delay will not lead to a loss of jurisdiction. This is presumably intended to make available remedies other than a stay.

106 See Peter McCormick, *Canada's Courts* (Toronto: James Lorimer and Company, 1994) at 184: "So great was the outcry that Mr. Justice Cory took the unusual step of using the occasion of a speech in England the following summer to respond to some of the complaints"

107 [1992] 1 SCR 771 [*Morin*]. Other than in one particular circumstance, which becomes less relevant as time passes, it is no longer important to know the structure of the *Morin* test. However, the Court there held at para 26 that:

eight to ten months at the provincial court level. What made *Morin* "stricter" was more a reflection of the attitude toward delay reflected in the case. First, as though to signal the unimportance of the eight to ten-month guideline, the Court found no section 11(b) violation despite the fourteen months actually taken in the case. Second, the Court adopted a very different attitude towards the issue of "prejudice to the accused."

Three separate types of prejudice have been identified as relevant in section 11(b) cases, reflecting different interests: prejudice to security of the person due to the stress and cloud of suspicion accompanying a criminal charge; prejudice to the liberty interest because of pre-trial custody or bail conditions; and prejudice to the right to make full answer and defence because of possible lost evidence and so on.[108] An early view of Lamer J (as he was at the time) was that prejudice to the security interest was the only relevant form of prejudice. In his view, the existence of section 11(b) was an acknowledgement that being charged with an offence carried harms which the right to a trial within a reasonable time was meant to minimize.[109] The other forms of prejudice were relevant to other rights, such as section 7, but evidence of them should not even be allowed in section 11(b) cases. His logic was that if evidence of those sorts of prejudice was allowed to make some cases seem stronger, then cases without that sort of evidence would seem weaker, but that that could not be the case: security interest prejudice *by itself* was sufficient. Therefore, to allow evidence of those other sorts of prejudice risked undermining the purpose of the right.

The majority of the Court, however, did not share that fear, and allowed all three forms of prejudice to be considered relevant.

---

> While the Court has at times indicated otherwise, it is now accepted that the factors to be considered in analyzing how long is too long may be listed as follows:
>
> 1. the length of the delay;
> 2. waiver of time periods;
> 3. the reasons for the delay, including
>    (a) inherent time requirements of the case,
>    (b) actions of the accused,
>    (c) actions of the Crown,
>    (d) limits on institutional resources, and
>    (e) other reasons for delay; and
> 4. prejudice to the accused.

108 *Godin*, above note 100 at para 30.

109 See *Rahey*, above note 97 at para 36:

> prejudice is part of the rationale for the right and is assured by the very presence of s. 11 (*b*) in the *Charter*. Consequently, there exists an irrebuttable presumption that, as of the moment of the charge, the accused suffers a prejudice the guarantee is aimed at limiting, and that the prejudice increases over time.

The *Morin* decision showed Lamer J's fear to be justified: the majority dismissed her claim in large part based on the absence of any prejudice: that is why it did not matter that the time taken for her case was well outside the guideline. What they really *meant*, however, was that she had not led evidence of prejudice to her fair trial or liberty interests: they did not consider prejudice to her security interest.[110] That established a pattern for the cases subsequent to *Morin*, where for practical purposes an accused who could not show some infringement of their liberty or fair trial interests would almost certainly fail in a section 11(b) claim: security interest prejudice alone was not enough.

The effect of that approach was to downplay any importance of timeliness in a trial: restrictive bail conditions or the loss of evidence might be a concern, but delay in and of itself was not. That alone helped undermine the section 11(b) right, but *Morin* also implemented a more subtle attitudinal change regarding prejudice. Specifically, the Court adopted the viewpoint that accused persons did not actually *want* a trial within a reasonable time: instead "[h]is interest lies in having the right infringed by the prosecution so that he can escape a trial on the merits."[111] They classified those who would not want a timely trial as "the majority group" for whom "the delay benefited rather than prejudiced the accused."[112]

The attitude underlying these comments goes well beyond saying that prejudice to an accused's security interest is not sufficient: it is saying that security prejudice is not prejudice *at all*, but a benefit to the accused. Because of that, section 11(b) claims became functionally limited to cases of individual, as opposed to institutional, delay, and the system no longer had any incentive to deal with institutional delay. Because *most* accused were presumed not to be worried about delay, the interests protected by section 11(b) could be satisfied by finding the few individuals who complained and moving them to the front of the queue, while letting the rest of the system chug along as slowly as it liked.

*Morin* created a test which gave judges a great deal of discretion to attribute portions of delay to neutral factors which did not count in favour of a section 11(b) claim. It also said to adopt an attitude of skepticism towards an accused who claimed to be worried about a section 11(b) violation. Effectively, courts were invited to *explain*

---

110 As Lamer J pointed out in dissent, the Crown "has not even attempted to show that her security interests have not been affected": *Morin*, above note 107 at para 95.

111 *Ibid* at para 57, in part quoting a paper written by Doherty J.

112 *Ibid* at para 59.

*away* and justify the amount of time cases had taken, rather than to speed them up. It could hardly be surprising that after more than two decades of operating under that approach, it became true that "a culture of complacency towards delay has emerged in the criminal justice system."[113]

The *Jordan* approach addressed head-on the implicit features of the *Morin* approach that led to that situation. Specifically, it created a test which removed a great deal of the discretion judges had, imposed "presumptive ceilings" which are to be more strictly adhered to than the "guidelines" in *Askov* and *Morin*, and removed any explicit consideration of prejudice, so that the purported absence of prejudice can no longer lead to the failure of a section 11(b) claim. Put another way, the *Morin* approach was intended to reduce the number of successful section 11(b) claims by making the test difficult to satisfy: the *Jordan* approach is intended to reduce the number of successful section 11(b) claims by making the system faster. As the Court has later put it, "[t]he new framework marks a shift away from a retrospective approach and adopts a prospective standpoint that allows the various participants to know the bounds of reasonableness from the outset of the proceedings."[114] As a result, the parties are motivated to move proceedings along so that no violation takes place, rather than argue after the fact whether there was one.

It is worth noting before going further that *Jordan* was intended to revitalize section 11(b), but it does not govern the full scope of the right to a trial within a reasonable time. The right protects a person "charged with an offence" and therefore applies from the time a charged is laid until the completion of sentencing.[115] The specific framework established in *Jordan*, however, does not cover *all* of that period: it governs the period from the laying of charges to the end of trial, which in this context is the end of the presentation of evidence and argument.[116] The effect of that is that although the time taken by the judge's deliberation and by sentencing are also protected by section 11(b), they are not part of the *Jordan* framework. We will therefore first discuss *Jordan*, which has attracted the great majority of the caselaw, and then look at deliberation time and sentencing. Note as well that during an appeal the appellant is not "a person charged with an offence" and so section 11(b) has no application: however, if a new

---

113 *Jordan*, above note 31 at para 40.

114 *JF*, above note 97 at para 31.

115 *JF*, above note 97 at para 23.

116 *R v KGK*, 2020 SCC 7.

trial is ordered the *Jordan* framework applies once again.[117] This issue will also be discussed below.

The *Jordan* approach sets a presumptive ceiling of eighteen months for cases tried in provincial court and thirty months for cases tried in superior court. The first step is to calculate the total time from the laying of the charge to the anticipated end of trial. From that deductions will be made for any defence delay: "defence delay" consists of periods of delay either waived by the defence or caused solely by the conduct of the defence. If that net time is above the ceiling, then the delay is presumed to be unreasonable and there will be a section 11(b) violation, unless the Crown can rebut that presumption by showing "exceptional circumstances." Exceptional circumstances fall into two categories: first, they include circumstances that "lie *outside the Crown's control* in the sense that (1) they are reasonably unforeseen *or* reasonably unavoidable, *and* (2) Crown counsel cannot reasonably remedy the delays emanating from those circumstances once they arise."[118] Second, exceptional circumstances included "particularly complex cases." In the case of the first type of exceptional circumstance, the delay caused by the unforeseeable event will be deducted from the total, which might result in the total delay now being below the ceiling. In a particularly complex case, the judge has the ability to decide in a more discretionary way that this simply was not a case which could reasonably have been completed within the ceiling.

That is the essence of the scheme, and we shall pursue each of those steps individually in a moment, but a few other things are worth noting. The first is the way in which the absence of taking prejudice into account manifests itself. That is — unlike with the *Morin* approach — it is not possible for a court to decide that a case took longer than the ceiling but there was no section 11(b) violation because there was no prejudice. Rather, the ceilings are themselves a reflection of the prejudice to the accused's interest from the delay itself.[119] Therefore (unless it is a particularly complex case), if time for defence delay and

---

117 *JF*, above note 97.

118 *Ibid* at para 69 [emphasis added].

119 *Ibid* at para 54:

> Third, although prejudice will no longer play an explicit role in the s. 11(*b*) analysis, it informs the setting of the presumptive ceiling. Once the ceiling is breached, we presume that accused persons will have suffered prejudice to their *Charter*-protected liberty, security of the person, and fair trial interests. As this Court wrote in *Morin*, "prejudice to the accused can be inferred from prolonged delay" (p. 801; see also *Godin*, at para. 37). This is not, we stress, a rebuttable presumption: once the ceiling is breached, an absence of actual prejudice cannot convert an unreasonable delay into a reasonable one.

unforeseeable circumstances has been deducted but the total time is still over the ceiling, then that is the end of the analysis — the accused's right was violated.[120]

Second, although a violation is presumed once the time exceeds the ceiling and can only be rebutted as explained above, that is not to say that a violation could not have occurred below the ceiling. As the Court noted, those ceilings are not set to indicate how long a case should take, but the point at which it has clearly taken too long.[121] Even below the ceiling it is open to an accused to show that there has been a violation of their section 11(b) right: this is so whether the case was resolved in a period of time below the ceiling, or whether the time counts as below the ceiling once deductions for defence delay and exceptional circumstances have been made. We shall explore this issue below as well.

Finally, having in mind the unfortunate consequences of the guideline in *Askov*, and in order to prevent the same sort of thing from occurring again, the Court created a "transitional exception." The essence of this exception was to recognize that the new *Jordan* regime had to be eased into the system in order to give participants a chance to amend their practices and attitudes, but that in the short term remedies should not be granted because the criminal justice system did not comply with rules which had not been formulated at the time. The point, essentially, is that if the parties — primarily the courts and the Crown — had been reasonably relying on the previous state of the law and complied with it, then no section 11(b) remedy should be given.[122] In practical terms, this has meant that if the case entirely or largely took place while *Morin* was the governing law, then it should still be governed by *Morin*. On

---

120 *R v Long*, 2023 ONCA 679 observed that "the *Jordan* ceiling is a hard one" and therefore that "18 months and 1 day would exceed the presumptive ceiling" (paras 51 and 52). On the facts they found the delay to be shorter than that, however.

121 *Ibid* at para 56 says of the ceiling:

> It is not an aspirational target. Rather, it is the point at which delay becomes presumptively unreasonable. The public should expect that most cases can and should be resolved before reaching the ceiling.

122 *Ibid* at para 96: "This transitional exceptional circumstance will apply when the Crown satisfies the court that the time the case has taken is justified based on the parties' reasonable reliance on the law as it previously existed." This does not mean, of course, that no transitional cases could succeed in a s 11(b) claim. In *R v Thanabalasingham*, 2020 SCC 18, for example, most of the proceedings took place before *Jordan*, but even on the *Morin* approach the delay — which included the accused spending nearly five years in custody awaiting trial — was unreasonable.

the other hand, if the parties had had enough time that they *should* have adapted, the transitional exception does not apply.[123]

Each of the individual factors making up the *Jordan* regime should now be considered. Even though the test is nearly a decade old at the time of writing, some of the rules are still being fine-tuned, and some issues have yet to be settled.

The first thing to note is the length of the ceilings: eighteen and thirty months, depending on whether the trial is to take place at the inferior or superior court level. Although *Jordan* does not state the rationale explicitly, it is apparent that the different deadlines apply based on the existence of a two-stage process, separated by the preliminary inquiry, when a matter is to be tried in superior court: that was the reason that the guideline in *Askov* governed the period running from "committal" to trial. As straightforward as that distinction seems, it does create some scope for ambiguity. For example, there might not in fact be a preliminary inquiry in many cases, either because the accused waives that right or because the Crown proceeds by way of direct indictment: to date, the view is that the longer ceiling would apply to a trial in superior court nonetheless.[124] Similarly, it has been held that if an accused re-elects from superior court to inferior court close to the date the preliminary inquiry was to be held, the longer deadline still applies.[125]

Further, it is arguable that this issue should be revisited because of changes to the *Criminal Code* made by Bill C-75.[126] That Bill dramatically reduced the number of cases where an accused is entitled to request a preliminary inquiry at all, which is aimed at making the

123 See *R v Hanan*, 2023 SCC 12 [*Hanan*], where charges were laid about seven months before *Jordan* was decided but where the parties initially scheduled the trial with the *Jordan* ceilings in mind. An adjournment before trial pushed the dates back well past the ceiling, and the Court found that the trial judge had erred in finding the transitional exception to apply:

> [7] . . . The delay beyond the ceiling was due not to a lack of time for the system to ameliorate ingrained institutional delays, but to the Crown's refusal to agree to a trial by judge alone, despite being warned of the possible consequences of delay, and despite *Jordan* having been decided almost two and a half years earlier. Were it not for the Crown's decision, the trial would have occurred within the ceiling.

124 See *R v Schenkels*, 2017 MBCA 62 [*Schenkels*] and the discussion at paras 43–50. See also *R v Bulhosen*, 2019 ONCA 600 and *R v Perdomo*, 2020 ABCA 404, in both of which the Crown used a direct indictment, thus avoiding the "first stage" but nonetheless the thirty month ceiling was found to be applicable.

125 *DMS v R*, 2016 NBCA 71 [*DMS*].

126 Bill C-75, above note 33. Various provisions came into force either on Royal Assent, or thirty, sixty, or 180 days later: see ss 405–7.

criminal justice system more able to comply with the *Jordan* ceilings.[127] To some extent that is just intended as a general efficiency matter: if provincial courts have fewer preliminary inquiries to conduct, they have more time and resources to devote to other cases. However, it has an uncertain impact on the thirty-month ceiling for superior court cases. That ceiling was based on the expectation that a preliminary inquiry was routinely available to all cases tried in superior court: if that expectation is removed, most of the rationale for the higher ceiling also disappears. Nonetheless, there seems to be no move to reconsider the ceilings on this basis, and such an argument is unlikely to succeed.

Another question arises because the length of the ceilings is partly justified by "baking in" consideration of prejudice. One argument which was made was that there should be shorter ceilings for cases involving young persons, on the basis that there should be less tolerance for prejudice to that group.[128] However, the Court concluded in *R v KJM* that, although special considerations arise for young persons, those considerations could be accommodated under the ordinary framework. Specifically this could be done by looking at the rules for cases which in fact took less time than the ceiling. As will be discussed below, a violation can still be found in those cases where the defence took meaningful steps to expedite the proceedings and the case took markedly longer than it reasonably should have. In that context, "the enhanced need for timeliness in youth matters is simply one 'case-specific factor' to consider when determining whether a case took (or is expected to take) markedly longer than it reasonably should have."[129] For similar reasons about the acceptable level of prejudice, it has been argued that the ceilings should be lower for provincial offences such as speeding,[130] but given the result in *KJM* it seems unlikely that that approach will be adopted.

---

127 Bill C-75 as passed by the House called for preliminary inquiries to be limited to offences with a potential penalty of life imprisonment, which would be very few. Following proposed amendments from the Senate the Bill was passed in a form that also allowed preliminaries for any offence with a penalty of fourteen years' imprisonment or more, which made them still available for a further eighty-six offences.

128 In *R v JM*, 2017 ONCJ 4, Paciocco J (as he then was) suggested that in youth matters the ceiling should be either twelve or fifteen months, but he did not decide the point. In *R v KJM*, 2018 ABCA 278 the dissenting judge held that a fifteen-month ceiling should apply in youth cases, but the majority (for two different sets of reasons) did not agree.

129 *R v KJM*, 2019 SCC 55 at para 74.

130 *York (Regional Municipality) v Tomovski*, 2017 ONCJ 785.

The ceiling governs the period from the laying of charges to the end of trial. For purposes of the *Jordan* ceiling, the end of trial is the end of the presentation of evidence and argument.[131] Although on the face of it "from the start to the finish" seems like a simple concept, there is some ambiguity.

The notion that the right to a trial within a reasonable time does not include pre-charge delay has been adopted from the very earliest cases,[132] and *Jordan* simply continues that approach, so that the clock starts ticking when the charge is laid, as opposed to some other date such as the date the accused was arrested. Some lower courts had pushed back against that approach both pre- and post-*Jordan*[133] but without success.[134] However, there is still the difficulty that sometimes more than one charge could be laid, at different times, and subsequent charges might either replace, amend, or be added in addition to the original charge. One view is that the clock runs separately on each charge,[135] but another is that the Crown cannot unilaterally reset the clock by amending or substituting a new information.[136] In the particular context of a charge being withdrawn and a later charge then being laid, the prevailing view is that the relevant period is only when there are active charges outstanding: unless, that is, the withdrawal and re-laying seems to be an attempt to avoid the impact of the ceilings.[137]

---

131 *R v KGK*, above note 116. This does not mean that the s. 11(b) right only applies until the end of the presentation of evidence and argument. See the discussion of deliberation and sentencing delay, below.

132 *Kalanj*, above note 22 at para 11. In *Kalanj* the accused was arrested and fingerprinted, but no charges were laid for eight months, and the Court held that that delay should not be calculated into the s 11(b) equation. In *R v L(WK)*, [1991] 1 SCR 1091, the Court rejected an application based on pre-charge delay and an alleged violation of s 7 in terms that suggest such motions, while not absolutely barred, are unlikely to succeed and would require something more than just delay.

133 See, for example, *R v Egorov*, [2005] OJ No 6171 (Ct J); *R v Nash*, 2014 ONSC 6025; or *R v Swaminathan*, 2015 ONCJ 394, suggesting that the clock should start when an accused becomes subject to conditions in a recognizance or similar document, even if the formal charge is not laid until later. See also *R v Gleiser*, 2017 ONSC 2858; *R v Bolé*, 2019 ONCJ 141; or *R v Elakrat*, 2020 ONCJ 343.

134 See *R v Boima*, 2018 BCCA 297; *R v Allison*, 2022 ONCA 329; and *R v Doak*, 2022 NBCA 48.

135 *R v Kaulback*, 2018 NLCA 8 [*Kaulback*].

136 *R v TML*, 2019 ABCA 176. See also *Guimont c R*, 2017 QCCA 1754 [*Guimont*].

137 See *R v Kanda*, 2021 BCCA 267 at para 115. See also paras 105–06: "where the charge is stayed or withdrawn, one must look at the reason for doing so, and the surrounding circumstances . . . In *Curry* and *Scott*, the courts considered

On the same logic, the clock keeps running when a mistrial is declared, because in that case the accused *is* still facing charges.[138]

Second, there is some caselaw suggesting that periods of time occurring in between the start and the finish might simply not be counted, on bases not mentioned in *Jordan*. Pre-*Jordan*, it had been held in lower courts that in unusual circumstances, even some portion of the delay after charges are laid might not be taken into account in a way completely separate from the section 11(b) analysis,[139] though now it seems likely that those cases would be subsumed into the exceptional circumstances analysis. However, there is dispute over how to proceed when a judge is called upon to make interlocutory decisions. Pre-*Jordan*, that time counted towards a section 11(b) claim,[140] and there seems no reason that should not continue to be the case. However, it has been argued that interlocutory decision-making time should simply not be counted in the first place.[141] The better view, however, is that the time should count, but that in appropriate cases (where there are a great many decisions to be made, or they are complex) such decision-making time might be an exceptional circumstance.[142] The important difference between those approaches is that the latter makes it more likely that the onus will remain on the Crown to justify the length of time taken in a case. A consistent approach to this issue needs to be adopted.[143]

---

that the section 11(b)-protected interests were engaged because, as I read the judgments, the stay was, in essence, an end run around *Jordan*."

138 *R v Way*, 2022 ABCA 1. The mistrial might be an exceptional event and affect the ceiling in that way, but it does not reset the clock to zero.

139 In *R v Cisar*, 2014 ONCA 151, charges were laid against an accused while he was out of the country. He was unaware even of the existence of those charges until eight years later, when he was back in Canada. The Ontario Court of Appeal held that there was no s 11(b) violation during that eight-year period, because the interests s 11(b) was meant to protect were not affected on the facts. His security of the person and liberty interests could not have been affected since he had not been arrested or even made aware of the charges, and his fair trial interests were not on the facts affected, since he was in no worse a position to mount a defence.

140 In *Rahey*, above note 97, the *only* time complained of related to an interlocutory decision.

141 See the view of Slatter J in *R v Mamouni*, 2017 ABCA 347 [*Mamouni*].

142 See, for example, *R v Corner*, 2023 ONCA 509, where an interlocutory decision was appealed to the Supreme Court of Canada, occasioning a five-month delay which was subtracted as an exceptional circumstance. See also the view of Watson J in *Mamouni*, ibid, and of Hamilton J in *R v KGK*, 2019 MBCA 9 [*KGK*].

143 See also *R v Manasseri*, 2016 ONCA 703, where the accused was discharged at the preliminary inquiry but that decision was eventually overturned on a *certiorari* application. Based on the agreement of the parties, the time between

Once the total delay is calculated, the first task is to deduct defence delay. This is the most sensitive part of the new test, in the sense that it carries the greatest danger of *not* reversing the culture of complacency. That is, the more that the time taken is attributed to the defence, the more that courts are simply allowing cases to proceed slowly rather than requiring the system to become faster. It is important, therefore, that matters not too readily be declared defence delay.

The first category of defence delay is delay which has been waived. In this context, as with most *Charter* rights, the waiver can be either explicit or implicit, but must be "clear and unequivocal" and the accused must have full knowledge of their rights and the effect of the waiver.[144] Pre-*Jordan* caselaw held that consent to a trial date might but does not necessarily constitute a waiver,[145] and that an accused was not required to make an entirely *pro forma* objection if there is no reason to think that an earlier trial date would be available.[146] The Court has, post-*Jordan*, relied on many previous observations about what does not constitute waiver: in particular silence or inaction do not by themselves constitute waiver, though lateness in bringing a section 11(b) application can be relevant.[147]

In the early post-*Jordan* period some Crowns adopted the approach of asking accuseds for explicit waivers, on the record, whenever they asked for an adjournment to review disclosure or make similar applications. It remains the case that explicit waivers are sometimes put on the record, but a practice of pushing the defence to routinely waive *all* delays does not seem to have developed. This is fortunate, since it would have run completely contrary to the spirit of *Jordan*. The point of *Jordan* was to speed up the system rather than continuing the culture of complacency: routinely requiring waiver of the right would have been to adopt complacency as the dominant approach.

The second category of defence delay is that caused by the defence, and this is the area where courts must take most care to apply *Jordan* in a way that reduces delay rather than justifies and excuses it. The message

---

discharge and the accused being ordered to stand trial after all was not counted in that case, but the Ontario Court of Appeal noted that the question should be considered an open one. See the discussion at paras 335–41. On the same point see *R v Brezden and Mulligan*, 2017 ONSC 6376 and *R v Kozma*, 2017 ABQB 723.

144 See generally the discussion of caselaw concerning waiver under *Jordan* in *R v Herman*, 2023 ABCA 52.

145 *Smith*, above note 102.

146 See, for example, *R v Mills*, [1986] 1 SCR 863; *Rahey*, above note 97; or *Askov*, above note 104.

147 *JF*, above note 97 at paras 43–52

coming from *Jordan* was that "defence applications and requests that are not frivolous will also generally not count against the defence."[148]

As the Court stressed in *Cody*, its follow-up decision reaffirming the *Jordan* approach one year later:

> [29] not all delay caused by defence conduct should be deducted under this component. In setting the presumptive ceilings, this Court recognized that an accused person's right to make full answer and defence requires that the defence be permitted time to prepare and present its case.

That is, the mere fact that an accused has made an interlocutory motion or taken time in some other way should not, by itself, be counted as defence delay: the purpose of the high ceilings was to allow for just such actions.[149] Rather, the concern is more with "[d]eliberate and calculated defence tactics aimed at causing delay, which include frivolous applications and requests."[150] In *Cody* an application based on alleged bias on the part of the trial judge was found to be frivolous and was defence delay, and there are other clear-cut cases.[151] Delay caused by an application might also be characterized as caused by the defence even if the application is legitimate, depending on the manner in which it is brought.[152] Against that, many cases do not count delay against

---

148 *Jordan*, above note 31 at para 65.

149 See, for example, *Regan*, 2002 SCC 12 [*Regan*]:

> [62] The *Jordan* framework recognizes that defence lawyers need time to review disclosure. Just as the Crown cannot be expected to provide full disclosure the same day the accused sends in his disclosure request, defence counsel cannot be expected to drop everything and pour [sic] over the witness interviews and police reports the moment they arrive. Lawyers require a reasonable amount of time to prepare, and this preparation time does not count as defence delay.

150 *Jordan*, above note 31 at para 63.

151 See, for example, *R v Burke*, 2018 ONCA 594 where the accused fled after charges were laid, or *R v Faulkner*, 2018 ONCA 174, where a third-party records application was found to have been undertaken for the purpose of stalling proceedings.

152 See, for example, *R v Boulanger*, 2022 SCC 2 [*Boulanger*], where the accused did not bring a motion relating to redactions in a document until fifteen months after receiving it, even though redactions in other documents were already a subject of discussion. Similarly in *R v Lai*, 2021 SCC 52, the accused re-elected at a late date and lost trial dates, well after being advised that he could keep those trial dates by re-electing earlier. See also *R v Kirby*, 2024 NBCA 32. Bill C-16, above note 3, if passed in its current form will require that the time taken for applications under various applications relating to records in sexual offence cases not be counted if notice of the application is not given in accordance with the "60 days in advance" requirement.

the defence if it does not seem like a tactic to slow things down.[153] *Cody* stresses that the only delay to be attributed to the defence is "that which: (1) is solely or directly caused by the accused person; and (2) flows from defence action that is *illegitimate* insomuch as it is not taken to respond to the charges,"[154] but also notes that determining whether action is illegitimate is not an exact science. They hold:

> [32] Defence conduct encompasses both substance and procedure the decision to take a step, *as well as the manner in which it is conducted*, may attract scrutiny. To determine whether defence action is legitimately taken to respond to the charges, the circumstances surrounding the action or conduct may therefore be considered. The overall number, strength, importance, proximity to the *Jordan* ceilings, compliance with any notice or filing requirements and timeliness of defence applications may be relevant considerations. Irrespective of its merit, a defence action may be deemed not legitimate in the context of a s. 11(*b*) application if it is designed to delay or if it exhibits marked inefficiency or marked indifference toward delay.

One particular issue arises when defence counsel declines a particular offered date. *Jordan* said that when the Crown and the court are ready to proceed but the defence is not, that is defence delay:[155] some early cases took that to mean that if the defence refused a particular date, they were responsible for all of the delay until the matter was actually scheduled.[156] However, the Supreme Court rejected that "bright line rule," concluding instead that "[a]ll relevant circumstances should be considered to determine how delay should be apportioned among the participants."[157] In *Boulanger*, for example, defence counsel was unavailable for a four-month period when new dates were being scheduled, but that there would be a need for additional time had been brought to the judge's attention months before that time. Other relevant circumstances included the prosecution's changes in strategy,

153 See, for example, *Regan*, above note 149, where the unusual length of time taken to obtain instructions could not be attributed to the defence where the accused was in prison on other side of country. Similarly, in *DMS*, above note 125, going through the legal aid application process to obtain representation took time, but this was not defence delay. See also *Javanmardi c R*, 2019 QCCA 576, where a defence challenge to admissibility of some evidence was found not to be defence delay.

154 *R v Cody*, 2017 SCC 31 at para 30 [*Cody*] [emphasis added].

155 *Jordan*, above note 31 at para 64 and *Cody*, above note 154 at para 30.

156 See, for example, *Dupuis c R*, 2016 QCCA 1930 or *Schenkels*, above note 124.

157 *Hanan*, above note 123 at para 9, citing *R v Boulanger*, above note 152.

institutional delay, and the court's lack of initiative, and so only half of the four-month delay was attributed to the defence.[158]

Within that issue of scheduling, a particular issue which has not yet been settled by the Court relates to cases where there are several co-accused.[159] *Cody* describes defence delay as that "solely" caused by the accused, and the general view is that if a matter is delayed because of one co-accused, that should not be attributed to other co-accused.[160] However, there can be circumstances in which delay caused by one co-accused will be attributed to all, if for example it appears that the other co-accused were happy to have the benefit of the delay, or that the co-accused were conducting their defence jointly.[161] In general, though,the section 11(b) claim of each co-accused must be assessed separately, which could sometimes mean that the trials of co-accused need to be severed in order not to violate the section 11(b) rights of some. Alternatively, in some cases the joining of a number of co-accused in the same trial, if justified, could mean that the case qualifies as a "particularly complex" one and that there is no section 11(b) violation for that reason.[162] This is not necessarily the case, however.[163]

If, after the deduction of any defence delay, the case is still over the ceiling, the onus is on the Crown to show that there is not a section 11(b) violation by showing exceptional circumstances. The first

158 Note that even pre-*Jordan* it had been held that defence counsel is not required "to hold themselves in a state of perpetual availability": *Godin*, above note 100 at para 23.

159 *R v Yusuf*, 2021 SCC 2 [*Yusuf*] at para 4: "we have chosen to leave for another day . . . whether and in what circumstances multiple accused should be treated communally as opposed to individually when assessing defence delay under s. 11(*b*) . . ."

160 *R v Gopie*, 2017 ONCA 728 [*Gopie*]. See also *R v Gatt*, 2017 ONSC 3563 [*Gatt*] or *R v Beaulieu*, 2017 ONSC 6543.

161 See, for example, *R v Albinowski*, 2018 ONCA 1084 [*Albinowski*] or *R v Brissett*, 2019 ONCA 11.

162 *Gatt*, above note 160. See also the discussion of this issue in *R v Tran*, 2023 ONCA 532. Another challenge relating to scheduling concerns the availability of Crown counsel. Particularly in larger cases, Crown prosecution services understandably prefer to have the same prosecutor or prosecutors take charge of the file from start to finish. Sometimes, however, the simplest way to avoid a s 11(b) violation is to schedule a matter for an earlier date than the assigned prosecutor is available, with the expectation that a different member of the prosecution service will take care of it. Delay in such a case would obviously not be caused by the defence, but there might sometimes be an argument that it goes to particular complexity.

163 *R v Roberts*, 2020 BCCA 307 at para 96:

> While it is no doubt true that cases involving more than one accused will often require additional time, the possibility that such time may be required was taken into account by the Supreme Court of Canada in setting the presumptive ceilings. That the Supreme Court expects trials in most multiple-accused cases to be completed within the presumptive ceilings is evinced by *Jordan* itself.

category of exceptional circumstances are unforeseeable discrete events, which might cause the deduction of particular periods of time. Recall that *Jordan* set two requirements for such discrete events: they must be reasonably unforeseen or reasonably unavoidable, *and* the delays emanating from them cannot reasonably be remedied by the Crown.[164] It is important to bear in mind that both criteria must be met. In *Cody*, for example, the accused's defence counsel was appointed to the bench, and all agreed that that was both unforeseeable and that the delay caused by it was as short as it could reasonably be. However, there was also a delay caused by the discovery of an error in the agreed statement of facts. Such an error could qualify as reasonably unforeseeable, since the standard is not perfection.[165] However, it took seven and a half months to resolve the issue when it could have been resolved in as little as a day, and so it did not justify the deduction of the time actually taken.

Many cases have considered whether particular discrete events qualify as exceptional circumstances. In *Coulter*, for example, the Crown prosecutor was in a car accident the morning the trial was to proceed and the matter was adjourned to the first available date: the period of delay caused by that adjournment was deducted.[166] Few cases are as straightforward as that,[167] and so courts have also had to determine whether things like a mistrial,[168] a co-accused becoming a Crown witness,[169] or an overcrowded docket due to a shortage of judges[170]

---

164 *Jordan*, above note 31 at para 69.

165 *Cody*, above note 154 at para 58. See also *R v Coates*, 2023 ONCA 856 at para 46: "The Crown does not have to show that the steps it took were successful, only that it reasonably attempted to avoid the delay."

166 *R v Coulter*, 2016 ONCA 704. See also *DMS*, above note 125 and *Gopie*, above note 160, where the illness of the accused and of a witness, respectively, were exceptional circumstances.

167 Though some are: in *Mamouni*, above note 141, trial dates were lost due to the Calgary flood of 2013.

168 *Mallozzi*, 2017 ONCA 644: two mistrials were unanticipated events.

169 *R v Gordon*, 2017 ONCA 436: the delay caused when a co-accused changed their plea and cooperated with police, leading to a new trial for the remaining accused, was an exceptional circumstance.

170 *R v Brown*, 2018 NSCA 62: the absence of one judge from a jurisdiction because they had been seconded to a different jurisdiction because of illness was *not* a discrete exceptional event. The Nova Scotia Court of Appeal held:

> [70] . . . while it was not within the power of the trial judge, the Crown, or the defence to mitigate a situation that needed the provision of additional judicial resources, it was a problem that the justice system had a responsibility to address. That is one of the directives to come out of *Jordan* and *Cody*. It is not only justice participants who have to respond to a new delay-sensitive regime, the justice system itself has to change. If docket problems arise

constitute discrete exceptional events.[171] A relatively common issue is the failure to appear of a Crown witness, and courts have tried to create guidelines around that problem.[172]

The second type of exceptional circumstance is the particularly complex case. It differs from the discrete event category in the way in which it is taken into account: rather than calling for the deduction of some particular period of time, in a particularly complex case the judge has discretion to decide that the case could not reasonably have been completed within the ceiling. This category again would have the potential to undermine the spirit of *Jordan* if judges too readily resorted to it, but the Court has tried to make clear that it is a very limited exception. The case must be not merely complex but "particularly" complex, and *Jordan* noted that the typical murder trial would not qualify.[173] The exception only applies to a case that, because of the nature of the evidence or the nature of the issues, will "require an inordinate amount of trial or preparation time,"[174] and further applies "only where the case *as a whole* is particularly complex."[175] In *Cody*, for example, there was voluminous disclosure, but the rest of the case was not out of the ordinary, and so it did not qualify as a particularly complex case. Courts have found cases to meet the particularly complex criterion most often when there is a combination of features such as multiple accused and many witnesses, voluminous disclosure, a large number of pre-trial applications, or parallel proceedings which affect scheduling.[176]

In the long term, if a case took longer than the ceiling and the Crown could not satisfy its onus based on one or the other exceptional circumstance, then the section 11(b) application will be successful and a stay of proceedings will be ordered. In the shorter term, the Crown might also satisfy its onus based on the transitional exception: "that the time the case has taken is justified based on the parties' reasonable reliance on the law as it previously existed."[177] The central point is that

---

because judicial resources have been stretched too thinly then additional judges need to be brought in to alleviate the problem.

171 See the discussion in *Doudou-Traoré c R*, 2018 QCCA 2020 at para 58 of situations considered by various courts to be a discrete exceptional circumstance. In that case itself the need to obtain expert reports was not a discrete unanticipated event.

172 See, for example, *R v Mavros*, 2020 ABCA 436, or *R v MS*, 2023 MBCA 90.

173 *Jordan*, above note 31 at para 78.

174 *Ibid* at para 77.

175 *Cody*, above note 154 at para 64 [emphasis added].

176 See, for example, *Gopie*, above note 160; *R v Baron*, 2017 ONCA 772; *Agostini c R*, 2018 QCCA 373; *King*, above note 103; or *R v Chan*, 2019 ABCA 82.

177 *Jordan*, above note 31 at para 96.

the more of a particular case that took place while the *Morin* framework governed, the more the delay should be judged against that *Morin* framework. For a decision made a month after *Jordan*, for example, the parties would have been expecting *Morin* to govern the application, and so the presumptive ceiling would be largely irrelevant. This transitional exception proved very effective as a mechanism to prevent chaos in the change from one system to another: for at least the first six months after *Jordan*, there was not a single case of a successful section 11(b) application under *Jordan* where the trial judge did not also find that a stay would have been ordered under *Morin* as well.[178] As we get further from the time *Jordan* was decided, the less important that transitional exception becomes, since as a practical matter cases where any portion of the proceedings pre-date *Jordan* are diminishingly few.

The only remaining issue to discuss is an application by an accused claiming a violation of the right to a trial within a reasonable time even though the time taken falls below the presumptive ceiling. It is important that such a possibility exist, because the presumptive ceilings were set to be quite high. In provincial court the ceiling is eighteen months, or about 550 days: the *median* time that such cases took at the time, however, was only 112 days,[179] which means that the ceiling only became relevant when a case had taken about *five times* the median.

In part the presumptive ceiling is about onus: if the ceiling is exceeded the onus is on the Crown to show there was no violation, and that can only be done as shown above. Below the ceiling, the onus is on the accused to prove the violation. Specifically, the defence must show that "(1) it took meaningful steps that demonstrate a sustained effort to expedite the proceedings, *and* (2) the case took markedly longer than it reasonably should have."[180] Note that how long the case "should have" taken is not a reference to the presumptive ceiling, but to a more abstract notion of a reasonable time.[181] Although this analysis does not explicitly take prejudice into account, implicitly the notion is that only an accused who objects to the pace at which matters are proceeding can make an application under the ceiling. Cases do tend

178 See Jessica Patrick, "Six Months of *Jordan*: A Statistical Overview" (2017) 35 CR (7th) 348.

179 Ashley Maxwell, "Adult Criminal Court Processing Times, Canada, 2015/2016," Juristat, Vol 38, No 1.

180 *Jordan*, above note 31 at para 82 [emphasis in original]. Note that the relevant length of time here is the net delay *after* any periods have been deducted, not the total time: *R v Musclow*, 2024 ONCA 565.

181 Because of this, the date a case is first scheduled for is not necessarily an indication of how long it "should" take: *R v Campbell*, 2022 ONCA 223 at paras 25–28 [*Campbell*].

to deny a remedy under this branch to an accused if there was no clear sign that they were not themselves content with the pace at which things were proceeding.[182] On the other hand, defence counsel is not required to take every possible step to expedite matters.[183]

The *Jordan* framework is structured around various factors, but it seems fair to say that in its design, and in the way it is being applied, it is much more about changing *attitudes*. This was explicit in *Jordan* itself, of course, which spoke about changing the culture of complacency about delay and imposed obligations on all parties.[184] It can also have an impact on how the various stages of the test are applied. An application by the defence which is reasonable in itself might nonetheless be counted as defence delay depending on when it was brought.[185] Indeed, an application by the defence which will cause delay can be refused on that basis, even if the defence were willing to concede that the delay caused should be deducted from the total time.[186] Exercises of prosecutorial discretion which are not improper in the abstract might nonetheless mean that delay has become unreasonable.[187] This also affects when an application for a section 11(b) remedy itself should be brought: in a timely manner, which as a general rule will mean before

---

182 See, for example, *R v Stephan*, 2017 ABCA 380; *Albinowski*, above note 161; or *Kaulback*, above note 135.

183 See *Campbell*, above note 181 at para 23: "requiring an accused person to demonstrate that they have taken sustained, meaningful steps to expedite proceedings does not include requiring them to bring motions that are doomed to fail."

184 *Jordan*, above note 31 at para 137: "[r]eal change will require the efforts and coordination of all participants in the criminal justice system." See also *JF*, above note 97 at para 30: "everyone must take proactive measures to remedy any delay and to ensure that the accused is tried in a timely manner."

185 See *Boulanger*, above note 152, where the defence brought an application relating to redactions in a document but not until fifteen months after receiving the document.

186 *Thanabalasingham*, above note 122 at para 9:

> where the defence seeks an adjournment, a court may deny it "on the basis that it would result in unacceptably long delay, even where it would be deductible as defence delay" (*Cody*, at para. 37).

187 See, for example, *Hanan*, above note 123, where the trial could have been completed within the ceiling despite an exceptional circumstance if the Crown had agreed to proceed by way of judge alone. In contrast, see *R v JS*, 2024 ONCA 794 where a judge's unavailability for a three-month period extended the time the trial took. However, in attempting to complete the trial earlier Crown counsel had cancelled a vacation day, offered to reschedule other matters, and was willing to call the complainant earlier than planned despite the possibility that the complainant would therefore have to testify twice. Her non-complacent attitude was central to the court of appeal finding that the exceptional circumstance had been adequately dealt with.

the trial begins.[188] Only exceptionally could a section 11(b) application be brought on appeal.[189]

As noted earlier, the *Jordan* ceilings cover the period from the laying of the charge to the completion of evidence and argument. However, that is not the sole impact of section 11(b): the time a judge takes to decide a case can also affect that right. *Jordan* was aimed at addressing the culture of complacency in the criminal justice system, but the Court has held that there was no evidence that judicial decision-making time contributed to that culture, and so this aspect of the section 11(b) right is not governed by the *Jordan* framework. They also noted that including decision-making time in the ceiling would have the paradoxical result that the more complex the trial, the longer it would take, with the result that the judge would have less time to deliberate than in simpler cases.[190]

Accordingly there is a separate test governing delay in deliberation time. Trial judges are in the best position to assess how much time is needed in the circumstances of the case and to balance the need for timeliness and trial fairness with practical considerations. Further, in the trial context time can be "the enemy of trial fairness"[191] because of the risk of losing evidence, but once the record is set the necessary time for the judge to assess the evidence, research points of law, and write reasons works to ensure fairness. Therefore the test in this context is whether the deliberation time took markedly longer than it reasonably should have in all of the circumstances.[192] There is a presumption that the verdict did not take longer than necessary, and the burden is on the accused to rebut that presumption.[193] This is a "high bar" because judges benefit from the presumption of integrity and because the result of finding a violation will be a stay of proceedings, which should occur only in the clearest of cases.[194] Factors to be taken into account in deciding the issue included the length of time taken by deliberation, how close the case was to the *Jordan* ceiling prior to that point, the complexity of the case, and, potentially, deliberation time typically taken in similar cases.[195]

---

188 *JF*, above note 97 at para 36.

189 *JF*, above note 97 at para 42.

190 *KGK*, above note 142. In addition the Court observed that it would be inappropriate to include decision-making time in the ceiling since the Crown would have no way of estimating what it might be, nor any way to justify a delay.

191 *KGK*, above note 142 at para 60.

192 *KGK*, above note 142 at para 54.

193 *KGK*, above note 142 at para 56.

194 *KGK*, above note 142 at para 65.

195 *KGK*, above note 142 at paras 67–73.

Section 11(b) also applies during the sentencing period, though again it is not covered by the *Jordan* ceiling.[196] To date the Supreme Court has not established a test for how the right to a trial within a reasonable time applies in the sentencing context.[197] The Supreme Court in *KGK* had consciously declined to set a particular time period as a ceiling for deliberation, and many of their rationales for not doing so — the presumption of judicial integrity, individual judges' workloads, varying institutional resources — would apply equally to sentencing. Some provincial Courts of Appeal have addressed post-conviction delay, with varying results. The Ontario Court of Appeal has set a presumptive ceiling of five months between the date of conviction and the date of sentencing.[198] The Quebec Court of Appeal, however, rejected that approach, preferring the more flexible question of asking whether the proceedings were "unduly prolonged."[199] British Columbia has found that the *Morin* framework should be used.[200]

As noted earlier, the remedy for a breach of the right to a trial within a reasonable time is a stay of proceedings and has been since the earliest cases.[201] That rule clearly applies when the trial itself is not completed within a reasonable time, and *KGK* applied the same rule to decision-making delay.[202] However, the Court left open the question of whether a remedy other than a stay could be appropriate for a breach of section 11(b) in the sentencing context.[203] Some lower courts have held that other remedies are available in this situation.[204] The Supreme Court has given leave to a case which might cause them to decide on both the section 11(b) test for post-conviction appeals and the appropriate remedy.[205]

Also worth noting on the issue of remedies is the possibility of granting a remedy other than a stay in order to *avoid* a violation of section

196 *JF*, above note 97 at para 27, notes that *Jordan* was explicit about s 11(b) applying to sentencing, but neither case sets out any specific rules.

197 In *R v Yusuf*, above note 159, the Court consciously declined to consider whether a s 11(b) claim could be brought post-conviction. On this issue, see Derek Spencer, "Extending *Jordan* to Consider Verdict and Sentencing Delays" (2019) 50 CR (7th) 30.

198 *R v Charley*, 2019 ONCA 726.

199 See *Deblois c R*, 2021 QCCA 1093 at para 134, relying on *Demers c R*, 2018 QCCA 617. See also *Lévesque Paquette c R*, 2023 QCCA 1047.

200 *R v SCW*, 2018 BCCA 346.

201 See the discussion above at fn 107. Bill C-16, above note 3, if passed in its current form will contain provisions in a new s 492.31 structuring when a stay of proceedings can be ordered as a remedy.

202 See *KGK*, above note 142 at para 65.

203 *Yusuf*, above note 159 at para 4.

204 See, for example, *R v Hartling*, 2020 ONCA 243 and *R v RB-C*, 2024 ONCA 930 [*RB-C*] in both of which the remedy was a sentence reduction.

205 The Court granted leave in *RB-C*, above note 204 on May 15, 2025.

11(b), an option which is in keeping with *Jordan*'s spirit of encouraging the system to move more efficiently. In *Varennes*, a murder trial scheduled during the height of the COVID-19 pandemic and before a vaccine had been developed, the accused sought to have a judge alone trial, but the Crown did not consent. The trial judge, citing the potential risks and delays in trying to hold a jury trial in the circumstances, ordered a judge-alone trial nonetheless, and the Court upheld that decision. The trial judge had jurisdiction to make that order as a section 24(1) remedy, to avoid a probable future violation of section 11(b) and the need to order a stay if that occurred.[206]

Section 11(b) does not apply to appeals because the person is not at that time a "person charged with an offence."[207] If a new trial is ordered, then the clock is reset to zero, and any delay from the first trial can no longer be considered.[208] The same ceilings apply to the retrial, but in deciding that point the Court reiterated that the ceilings are *ceilings* and that most trials should occur more quickly. It is possible to find that there was a section 11(b) violation even under the ceiling, and that is a particularly relevant issue for retrials. Special care should be taken to prioritize retrials, especially as they can be expected to take less time than the original trial. Further, even though delay from the first trial cannot be taken into account in the calculations, the amount of prior delay can form part of the context affecting how much retrial delay is reasonable.[209]

To conclude this discussion, it is worth recalling that although *Jordan* created a test that is more easily met by an accused, the goal of the decision was not to have more successful section 11(b) applications: it was to speed up the system so that there would be fewer violations of the right in the first place. In that regard, the real goal of the decision was to displace the culture of complacency about delay. One of the primary advantages of the presumptive ceilings over the previous much more discretionary approach is that the parties can see the problem coming under *Jordan*, whereas under *Morin* it was just a matter of arguing after the fact whether there had been a violation, at a point when it was too late to do anything to prevent it. Now, if for some reason a matter has to be adjourned, or there have been a number of delays along the way, the Crown and the courts especially can more readily see when there will presumptively be a section 11(b) violation, and can take steps to prevent that. In the past, if a matter had to be adjourned, it would normally have just been scheduled

---

206 *R v Varennes*, 2025 SCC 22.
207 *JF*, above note 97.
208 *JF*, above note 97.
209 *JF*, above note 97.

for whatever the next available date happened to be. Now, if that date would be too far in the future, special arrangements will be made to find something earlier.[210] Similarly, courts are beginning to take other measures, such as limiting unduly long cross-examination, deciding or dismissing motions early,[211] and otherwise taking more active control of proceedings in order not to allow matters to lengthen unnecessarily.[212] In addition, Parliament has taken action in response to the *Jordan* decision. Bill C-75 made a number of changes to the criminal justice system which were designed to have an impact on its general efficiency. That Bill dramatically limited how often preliminary inquiries would be available, though as noted above that is a measure which is largely at odds with the rationale for the higher ceiling in superior court. In addition, Bill C-75 expanded judges' case management powers,[213] allows some "routine" police evidence to be presented in writing rather than through oral testimony,[214] and allows for remote rather than in-person appearances in some circumstances,[215] among other things. In addition, that Bill created "administration of justice offences" as a means of dealing with failures to appear for court or comply with other conditions.[216]

Despite these measures and the greater effort not to be complacent about delay, however, there are countervailing issues. In fact the option to divert administration of justice offences has not been taken up. Further, some areas of the law, especially related to sexual offences and sexual history evidence, have become complex and have added to the burden on courts.[217] Whether for those reasons or others, it is not apparent that there has been much success in actually speeding the system up. In 2015–2016, just prior to *Jordan*, for cases that required more than seven days the median length of trial was 160 days. In 2019–2020 that median had risen to 177 days. The median rose even further to 232 days by 2022–2023, but of course by then the confounding factor of the COVID-19 pandemic was having a significant effect.[218]

---

210 See, for example, *R v MacIsaac*, 2018 ONCA 560.

211 See the discussion of *Haevischer*, above note 31, in Chapter 11, Section F(1).

212 See, for example, *R v Brissard*, 2017 ONCA 891; *R v Podolski*, 2018 BCCA 96; *R v Vorobiov*, 2018 ONCA 448; or *R v Breton*, 2018 ONCA 753.

213 Bill C-75, above note 33, clauses 252, 253, and 269.

214 *Ibid*, clauses 278 and 294.

215 *Ibid*, clauses 1(2), 190, 218, 227(2), 293, and 295.

216 *Ibid*, clauses 214 and 236.

217 *R v Kinamore*, 2025 SCC 19 at para 1. Bill C-16, above note 3, if passed in its current form will will make special rules concerning delay and applications specific to sexual offences.

218 See the discussion in Ben Hoskins, "Remedying Delay Without a Stay: Revisiting the Remedy for Section 11(b) *Charter* Violations" (2025) 28 *Canadian Criminal Law Review* 213.

Nonetheless, it is difficult to say with any certainty whether *Jordan* has had the "bottom line" effect that was looked for.

#### ii) *Abuse of Process and Fair Trial Rights*

Although the doctrine was in doubt in Canada for many years, the Supreme Court has unequivocally concluded that

> there is a residual discretion in a trial court judge to stay proceedings where compelling an accused to stand trial would violate those fundamental principles of justice which underlie the community's sense of fair play and decency and to prevent the abuse of a court's process through oppressive or vexatious proceedings.[219]

Motions for a stay based on abuse of process need not be brought on a pre-trial basis and, indeed, most typically would not be (many claims, such as entrapment, will depend on the evidence that emerges at trial).[220] However, they are potentially available at a pre-trial stage because the issue in deciding whether to grant a stay for abuse of process is not whether the prosecution can prove its case, but whether the case is "tainted to such a degree that to allow it to proceed would tarnish the integrity of the court."[221] Thus, for example, it is possible to obtain a stay even at the stage of an extradition hearing to face charges in another country.[222]

Two separate issues arise here: (1) whether there was an abuse of process, and (2) if there was, whether a stay is the appropriate remedy. For a very long time the caselaw tended to treat these as a single question and to assume that if there was an abuse of process then the result had to be a stay of proceedings. As a result, to a certain extent the reluctance to use the extreme remedy of a stay of proceedings held back the development of the abuse of process doctrine itself. As we will see below, however, the Court has now separated the two questions more clearly, quite specifically allowing for the possibility of an abuse of process with a remedy other than a stay.[223] It is therefore appropriate to discuss those two issues independently.

---

219 *R v Jewitt*, [1985] 2 SCR 128 at 135 [*Jewitt*].

220 Indeed, the Court held in *R v Mack*, [1988] 2 SCR 903 [*Mack*], that an abuse of process claim could not be considered until after the judge had decided whether the Crown had proven the accused guilty beyond a reasonable doubt.

221 *R v Conway*, [1989] 1 SCR 1657 at 1667.

222 *United States of America v Cobb*, [2001] 1 SCR 587 [*Cobb*].

223 See generally the discussion in Steve Coughlan, "Threading Together Abuse of Process and Exclusion of Evidence: How It Became Possible to Rebuke Mr. Big" (2015) 71 SCLR 415.

### a. Abuse of Process

Abuse of process has had something of a laboured history in Canadian law. It seemed for many years that, as a common law doctrine, it did not exist in Canada.[224] It was later affirmed first, that such a common law power did exist,[225] and then later, that the common law power to stay for abuse of process and the ability of a court to grant the *Charter* remedy of a stay of proceedings were largely co-extensive.[226] As initially developed, the test had two branches with slightly different tests, a main category which was forward-looking and a "residual" category which was backward-looking.[227] Eventually, however, the residual category was given somewhat more credence, and the same test was made to apply to both categories.[228]

The two categories of abuse of process are as follows:

> (1) where state conduct compromises the fairness of an accused's trial (the "main" category); and (2) where state conduct creates no threat to trial fairness but risks undermining the integrity of the judicial process (the "residual" category).[229]

The first category is forward-looking in the sense that it asks whether there is any ongoing unfairness to the accused.[230] It is the main category because typically the questions of whether there was an abuse and whether there should be a stay were treated as essentially the same question, and the view of the Court was that "the mere fact that the state has treated an individual shabbily in the past is not enough to warrant a stay of proceedings."[231]

One particular area in which the first category of abuse of process trial fairness has been pursued is when the Crown repudiates a plea agreement.[232] A bare allegation that there has been an abuse of process is not sufficient to cause a court to inquire into the exercise of

---

224 See, for example, *R v Rourke* (1977), [1978] 1 SCR 1021.

225 *Jewitt*, above note 219.

226 *R v O'Connor*, [1995] 4 SCR 411 [*O'Connor*]. The Court held at para 70:

> the only instances in which there may be a need to maintain any type of distinction between the two regimes will be those instances in which the *Charter*, for some reason, does not apply yet where the circumstances nevertheless point to an abuse of the court's process.

227 See, for example, *O'Connor*, *ibid*, or *Canada (Minister of Citizenship and Immigration) v Tobiass*, [1997] 3 SCR 391 at para 91 [*Tobiass*].

228 *R v Babos*, 2014 SCC 16 [*Babos*].

229 *Ibid* at para 31.

230 *Ibid* at para 34.

231 *Tobiass*, above note 227 at para 91.

232 *R v Nixon*, 2011 SCC 34.

prosecutorial discretion: there is a threshold burden on the accused to satisfy the court that there is a serious issue to look into. The allegation that the Crown was pursuing charges against one accused but not against another, for example, would not be sufficient. Where the Crown repudiates a plea agreement, however, that threshold burden is met because such action on the part of the Crown is rare and exceptional. Although the ultimate burden to show an abuse of process rests with the accused, where the Crown has resiled from a plea agreement, there is an evidentiary burden on them to explain why they have failed to honour the bargain, and failure to meet it can weigh heavily in the decision.[233]

A pre-trial motion seeking a stay has sometimes been sought on the basis that it will be impossible to empanel an impartial jury, most probably due to pre-trial publicity, though not necessarily only on those grounds.[234] The Court has not completely precluded such a motion, although they did hold that such an application brought before jury selection had begun was premature:

> It is only at the stage when the jury is to be selected that it will be possible to determine whether the respondent can be tried by an impartial jury In an extreme case (and the present certainly qualifies), such publicity should lead to challenge for cause at trial, but I am far from thinking that it must necessarily be assumed that a person subjected to such publicity will necessarily be biased.[235]

On this issue, see the further discussion in Section C(3)(c), below in this chapter, of challenge for cause in the jury selection process.

In dealing with the second category, undermining the integrity of the judicial process, the question is "whether the state has engaged in conduct that is offensive to societal notions of fair play and decency and whether proceeding with a trial in the face of that conduct would be harmful to the integrity of the justice system."[236] Although this category looks to past misconduct, it is still intended to have a prospective aspect to it: a court should ask whether proceeding in light of the impugned conduct would do *further* harm to the integrity of the justice system.[237]

In *R v Jewitt* the issue was whether the accused had been entrapped, and the Court has subsequently elaborated on entrapment as one of the

233 *Ibid* at paras 62–63.
234 See *English*, above note 51; *R v Vermette*, [1988] 1 SCR 985 [*Vermette*].
235 *Vermette*, *ibid* at 992–93.
236 *Babos*, above note 228 at para 35.
237 *Ibid* at para 38.

circumstances that might lead to a stay of proceedings based on abuse of process.[238] The list of potential abuses is open-ended, and accused have made applications based on conflict of interest for the accused's lawyers,[239] pre-charge collaboration between police and Crown prosecutors that was alleged to have led to a loss of objectivity on the part of the Crown,[240] reliance by police on advice as to whether their investigation would be illegal,[241] threats of sexual violence for contesting extradition,[242] and non-disclosure of evidence.[243] One area of particular interest relates to mistreatment of arrested persons by police which, on the face of it, seems like shabby past treatment and therefore not something falling within the doctrine. However, many lower courts tended to grant stays to accused who were subject to violence or other mistreatment, even while recognizing that this was difficult to reconcile with the rules the Court had laid down.[244] Eventually the Supreme Court, while not changing the law in this area, acknowledged that trial judges could properly conclude that past abuse of this sort was serious enough that public confidence in the administration of justice could be undermined by the mere act of carrying forward in light of it.[245]

This greater acknowledgement of the significance of past misbehaviour perhaps prompted the Court in *R v Hart* to suggest that the abuse of process doctrine should be "reinvigorated" in the context of Mr. Big undercover operations.[246] A Mr. Big operation targets an accused by trying to lure them into joining a fictitious criminal organization. The prospect of significant reward is held out, and often there are implicit threats about disloyalty; ultimately, the accused is presented with the need to confess previous involvement in whatever crime the police were investigating to "Mr. Big," the putative head of the organization, in order to be accepted: that confession is then used as evidence.[247] The

238 *Mack*, above note 220; *R v Barnes*, [1991] 1 SCR 449.

239 *R v Neil*, 2002 SCC 70.

240 *R v Regan*, above note 127. The majority held that any alleged misbehaviour on the part of the Crown had no ongoing effect (para 104), but the dissent argued that the existence of the proceedings *at all* was the ongoing effect (para 219).

241 *R v Campbell*, [1999] 1 SCR 565.

242 *Cobb*, above note 222.

243 *O'Connor*, above note 226, although the *O'Connor* analysis deals with the issue as implicating the accused's s 7 rights.

244 See the discussion in *R v Walcott* (2008), 57 CR (6th) 223 (Ont SCJ), and in Tim Quigley, "Stays of Proceedings Due to Police Misconduct" (2011) 79 *Criminal Reports* (6th) 124.

245 *R v Bellusci*, 2012 SCC 44.

246 2014 SCC 52 at para 114 [*Hart*].

247 Among the many Mr. Big cases, see *Hart*, *ibid*; *R v Mack*, 2014 SCC 58; *R v Grandinetti*, 2005 SCC 5; or *R v Mentuck*, [2001] 3 SCR 442.

Court observed that the abuse of process doctrine had never succeeded as an objection to Mr. Big cases, but that courts should be more open to the possibility. They observed that the technique could become abusive when the use of inducements or threats becomes coercive, or when the technique preys on vulnerabilities such as mental health problems, substance addictions, or youthfulness.[248] This appears not to have had a significant impact to date on the results in Mr. Big cases.[249] However, some stays have been issued in the case of abusive investigations which were similar to, but not precisely, Mr. Big operations.[250]

In most cases, claims based on the residual category are not ultimately successful because the issues of whether there was an abuse and whether there should be a stay have been closely linked. This has limited the doctrine because a stay of proceedings can be granted only in the "clearest of cases."[251] So, when should a stay be granted?

b. *Stay of Proceedings*

The same test is used no matter which category of abuse is alleged:

> (1) There must be prejudice to the accused's right to a fair trial or the integrity of the justice system that "will be manifested, perpetuated or aggravated through the conduct of the trial, or by its outcome" . . .;
> (2) There must be no alternative remedy capable of redressing the prejudice; and
> (3) Where there is still uncertainty over whether a stay is warranted after steps (1) and (2), the court is required to balance the interests in favour of granting a stay, such as denouncing misconduct and preserving the integrity of the justice system, against "the interest that society has in having a final decision on the merits."[252]

---

248 *Hart*, above note 246 at paras 115–18.

249 Courts of Appeal have declined, post-*Hart*, to issue stays based on Mr. Big operations in *R v Johnston*, 2016 BCCA 3; *R v Randle*, 2016 BCCA 125; *R v Magoon*, 2016 ABCA 412; *R v Kelly*, 2017 ONCA 621; and *R v Pearson*, 2024 ABCA 245. A retrial was ordered in *R v Jeanvenne*, 2016 ONCA 106, though primarily for other reasons.

250 See *R v Derbyshire*, 2016 NSCA 67 and *R v Nuttall*, 2018 BCCA 479. The Court did anticipate this possibility in footnote 5 to *Hart*, above note 246: "Time will tell whether, in a future case, the principles that underlie this rule warrant extending its application to another context." See also *R v Amin*, 2024 ONCA 237 which ordered a new trial in a Mr Big case, but not because of Mr Big issues.

251 *Jewitt*, above note 219 at 137.

252 *Babos*, above note 228 at para 32.

The first step in this test amounts to asking whether there was an abuse of process based on either the main or the residual category. If there is, and since a stay is limited to the clearest of cases, the question becomes whether any other remedy is sufficient. Because abuse of process and the section 7 right to a fair trial are closely aligned, most cases of abuse of process mean that, without a remedy, the trial would not be fair: however, in most of those situations some other remedy, such as an order for further disclosure and an adjournment, or in more extreme cases an order for a new trial, perhaps with the exclusion of particular evidence, is an adequate solution. Therefore, a stay is not the most likely remedy for the main category. It is more likely to be a remedy for the residual category.

In the residual category, however, the focus of the remedy is not to provide redress to the accused for the wrong, but to consider whether an alternative remedy short of a stay of proceedings will adequately dissociate the justice system from the impugned state conduct going forward.[253] In those circumstances, a remedy aimed at restoring the reputation of the justice system might take the form of a judicial rebuke of the state behaviour or some type of external inquiry into the misbehaviour, and if that were an adequate remedy then no stay would be ordered.[254] On the one hand that could be seen as disadvantageous for the accused, since they receive no personal benefit from the remedy given. On the other hand, this approach has expanded the potential *standing* of accused persons to apply for a remedy. Because the harm being remedied is the harm to the integrity of the justice system, an accused might be able to seek the remedy even if their own *Charter* rights were not infringed. All that is necessary is that the proceedings against the accused have been "tainted" by the abusive state conduct in question.[255]

If there is any doubt about granting a stay after these two steps, then the third step requires balancing the interest of society in a final decision on the merits against the accused's interests. In *R v Babos* a

253 *Ibid* at para 39.

254 See, for example, *R v Gowdy*, 2016 ONCA 989, where police publicly released private medical information about the accused, but it was found that a remedy short of a stay would be sufficient to demonstrate that the justice system disapproved of and disassociated itself from the wrongful conduct.

255 *R v Brunelle*, 2024 SCC 3 at para 55. In *Brunelle*, over 250 police officers had carried out arrests and searches of thirty-one individuals as part of a single operation. The operation as a whole was marked by many s 8 and s 10 violations. The point of the ruling was that an individual accused had standing to apply for a stay based on the residual ground whether their own ss 8 or 10 rights were violated or not.

Crown prosecutor had made threats to lay more charges in order to apply pressure to the accused. The Court said that behaviour was reprehensible and should not be repeated by any Crown, but did not issue a stay. Instead, they concluded that even though no alternative remedy was available, a stay of proceedings was not warranted when balanced against society's interest in a trial on the twenty-two charges related to firearms, illegal drugs, and organized crime.[256]

# C. JURY SELECTION

## 1) Introduction

The *Criminal Code* provides for several methods of trial, in particular, trial by provincial court judge, trial by superior court judge alone, and trial by superior court judge with a jury (see the discussion in Chapter 3, Section A). Section 471 of the *Code* provides that every indictable offence shall be tried by a judge and jury "except where otherwise expressly provided by law." As a matter of fact, various *Code* sections readily provide otherwise for every offence except those listed in section 469, and provide that even those offences might not have a jury trial if the Crown consents.[257] The net effect is that a few offences, such as murder and treason, are normally required to be tried by jury, while a few indictable offences, such as theft not exceeding $5,000, cannot have a jury. For all other indictable offences, an accused can choose between any of the three modes of trial.[258]

---

256 See Tim Quigley, "*Babos*: Balancing Test Unnecessarily Restricts Residual Category for Stay as Abuse of Process" (2014) 8 *Criminal Reports* (7th) 55, and HA Kaiser, "*Babos*: Further Narrowing Access to Stay of Proceedings Where the Integrity of the Judicial Process Is Implicated" (2014) 8 *Criminal Reports* (7th) 59, both criticizing the approach in *Babos*. On this third step, see also *R v Haevischer*, 2014 BCSC 2172 where, among other things, the accused were subjected to "serious, prolonged and systemic" (para 145) mistreatment while being kept in solitary confinement for a long period of time, but this was outweighed by society's interest, since the accused were guilty of six execution-style killings. The trial judge there had summarily dismissed the application, but the Supreme Court found it to have been an error not to have conducted a full hearing of the application: *Haevischer*, *ibid*.

257 See the discussion in Chapter 3, Section A(3), "Mode of Trial."

258 Note, as well, that s 11(f) of the *Charter* guarantees an accused the right to "the benefit of trial by jury" for any offence with a punishment of five years' imprisonment or more. In *R v Turpin*, [1989] 1 SCR 1296, the Court held that although an accused could waive that right, waiver of the right to trial by jury did not amount to a right to trial by non-jury. Accordingly, the *Code* provisions

There are three stages to the jury selection process: assembling the jury roll, which is as far as possible a list of all eligible jury members in the region; from the jury roll selecting a jury panel (or array[259]), which is the pool from which a trial jury is selected; and from the jury panel selecting the trial jury (sometimes called the "petit jury") for a particular criminal trial.[260] Those stages are governed by a mixture of federal and provincial legislation. Section 92(14) of the *Constitution Act, 1867*[261] gives each province jurisdiction over the administration of justice in the province. In each province and territory, a jury act sets out the rules by which the jury roll is to be assembled and the jury array is to be summoned to the courtroom. These rules include such matters as qualifications and disqualifications for being a juror, sources from which the jury roll is assembled, and compensation for jurors. Once the prospective jurors are in the courtroom in a criminal matter, the provisions of the *Code* then govern the selection of the jury for the particular trial. These *Code* rules deal with challenges for cause, excusing jurors, and other matters.[262] Jury selection is an area where there has been significant relatively recent statutory change and arguably a change in underlying attitudes. The statutory changes came with Bill C-75 in 2019, when substantial alterations were made to the portions of jury selection governed by the *Criminal Code*.[263] These changes were prompted by a controversial acquittal in a second degree murder case, where the victim was an Indigenous person and the accused was

---

preventing an accused from electing trial by judge alone in a murder case did not violate s 11(f).

259 The *Code* uses both the terms "array" and "panel" to refer to this group: see, for example, s 629, which speaks about challenging a jury panel, but appears under the heading "Challenging the Array."

260 *R v Kokopenace*, 2015 SCC 28 at para 8 [*Kokopenace*].

261 (UK), 30 & 31 Vict, c 3.

262 In *Barrow*, above note 27, the Court notes that the provinces have jurisdiction over the "administrative" aspects of jury selection, specifically the authority to assemble the array. See, for example, *R v Montague*, 2010 ONCA 141, where the accused objected that some potential jurors had been excused in his absence. The Court of Appeal rejected the appeal on the basis that the potential jurors had been excused on administrative grounds under the relevant provincial legislation, not by means of the power to excuse jurors in s 632 of the *Code*. Accordingly, it had been done as part of assembling the jury panel in the first place, not excusing someone from the jury panel, and so the accused had no right to be present.

The precise constitutional dividing line between federal and provincial jurisdiction is not entirely clear: see David Pomerant, *Multiculturalism, Representation and the Jury Selection Process in Canadian Criminal Cases* (Ottawa: Department of Justice Canada, Research and Statistics Directorate, 1994).

263 Bill C-75, above note 33.

a white person: although the jury panel had included Indigenous persons, the jury actually selected consisted only of white people.[264] In response, and as will be discussed below, virtually all of the rules of jury selection which affected how the jury is chosen from the jury panel were changed. More subtly, the approach of courts to implementing those rules had long rested on the strong belief that the vast majority of potential jurors are able to and will act impartially, no matter whom the accused. More recent caselaw applying the new jury selection procedures has fallen away from that assumption, though it has not disappeared entirely. This is reflected most obviously in the Court's more recent commentary on challenge for cause but has impacts at other stages as well. As a result, and as will be discussed at various points below, there is room for some level of uncertainty around whether the established approaches will continue unchanged.

## 2) Provincial Legislation Jury Selection Procedures — Creating the Jury Array

Each province has jurisdiction over the administration of justice in the province, and section 626 of the *Code* specifies that jurors must be qualified in accordance with the laws of the province.[265] That section also states that, notwithstanding any law of a province, no person can be disqualified from jury service based on sex. To comply with constitutional requirements, the jury roll must be assembled by a process that provides

---

264 On 9 February 2018, Gerald Stanley was found not guilty by a jury of the second-degree murder of Colten Boushie. The deceased was in a vehicle on the accused's land at the time and was killed by a gunshot from a gun the accused was holding. As the trial was by jury there are no reasons for the acquittal, but the arguments between the Crown and the defence focused on whether the fatal shot had been fired intentionally or by accident.

265 The Court describes this provision in *R v Sherratt*, [1991] 1 SCR 509 [*Sherratt*], as avoiding jurisdictional conflict, but it could equally be seen as contributing to the ambiguity of the situation. It is true that the provision leaves no doubt as to which statutes govern the out-of-court portion of jury selection. However, the existence of s 626 creates doubt as to *why* the provincial jury acts govern the situation. If the provinces have jurisdiction to create those statutes by virtue of s 92(14) of the *Constitution Act, 1867*, above note 261, then s 626 is unnecessary: its existence could imply that the *Code* is the ultimate foundation of authority for the rules in the provincial jury acts. In this regard, the situation could be similar to the definition of "Attorney General" in s 2 of the *Code*, which in *Canada (Attorney General) v Canadian National Transportation Ltd*, [1983] 2 SCR 206, was held to be the provincial attorney general, not because the province had original jurisdiction over prosecutions, but because valid federal legislation designated the provincial attorney general. See generally, Pomerant, above note 262, for more on this issue.

a fair opportunity for a broad cross-section of society to participate.[266] This goal is manifested in different ways within various statutes. In Nova Scotia, for example, the legislation explicitly states that the list should be drawn from a "data base that to the extent possible shall include the entire population."[267] Prince Edward Island, on the other hand, specifies that the *Health Services Payment Act*[268] list should be used.[269] Manitoba directs the sheriff to use "appropriate lists."[270] Other provinces do not specify what source is to be used in assembling the array.

The goal of assembling this list is representativeness, but that concept has a particular meaning in the context of jury selection: or at least, it is clear that it used to have a particular meaning, but this is one of those areas where it is possible that underlying attitudes are shifting. The Supreme Court of Canada considered this stage of the process in *R v Kokopenace*, concluding that representativeness did *not* mean that the jury roll had to be proportionally representative of the province's or region's population nor that the ultimate jury selected needed to include members of any particular group.[271] Rather than having substantive content, representativeness was found to focus on the *process* used to assemble the list. The Court held:

> To determine if the state has met its representative obligation, the question is whether the state provided a fair opportunity for a broad cross-section of society to participate in the jury process. A fair opportunity will have been provided when the state makes reasonable efforts to: (1) compile the jury roll using random selection from lists that draw from a broad cross-section of society, and (2) deliver jury notices to those who have been randomly selected. In other words, it is the act of casting a wide net that ensures representativeness. Representativeness is not about targeting particular groups for inclusion on the jury roll.[272]

---

266 *Kokopenace*, above note 260 at para 2. The *Charter* rights implicated are s 11(d) (the right to a fair trial by an impartial tribunal) and s 11(f) (the right to a trial by jury for offences punishable by imprisonment of five years or more).

267 *Juries Act*, SNS 1998, c 16, s 7(1).

268 RSPEI 1988, c H-2.

269 *Jury Act*, RSPEI 1988, c J-5.1, s 8(1).

270 *Jury Act*, CCSM c J30, s 6(1). The Regulations to that Act define "appropriate lists" as "a) the list maintained by the Minister of Health and Seniors Care of residents registered with the Minister of Health and Seniors Care under *The Health Services Insurance Act*; and (b) the list of persons who are qualified as electors in the Francophone School Division under section 21.37 of *The Public Schools Act*."

271 *Kokopenace*, above note 260 at para 59.

272 *Ibid* at para 61.

If these criteria are met, *Kokopenace* held, then representativeness is satisfied "provided that the state has not deliberately excluded members of a particular group."[273]

On the legal standard for assembling the jury array *Kokopenace* remains the law. It does illustrate, however, how underlying attitudes might be changing. The approach in *Kokopenace* — that all that mattered was random selection from a random cross-section — rested on assumptions about impartiality. That case noted that "[o]ur criminal justice system has a strong presumption of juror impartiality"[274] and that "there is no empirical data to support the proposition that jurors of the same race as the accused are necessary to evaluate the evidence in a fair and impartial manner."[275] This presumption that anyone can fairly act as a juror for anyone leads to the conclusion that randomness and no *deliberate* exclusion is all that is required for fairness. It is that underlying attitude that seems to be shifting.

This will be discussed in more depth below, particularly when considering challenge for cause but is observable even in later comments about *Kokopenace*. *R v Chouhan* is a decision with five judgments among the nine judges and complicated divisions, but several judges there speak in a way that challenges the assumption *Kokopenace* is built on. Justice Martin, for example, described *Kokopenace* as setting a constitutional *minimum* but argued that "that case did not address whether Parliament could implement further measures for assuring representativeness and impartiality, including measures to deliberately *include* underrepresented groups."[276] Similarly Côté J argued that "[w]hile I accept that *Kokopenace* set the constitutional minimum required for representativeness, it did not exhaustively define representativeness."[277] Separate from the issue of assembling the initial list is the task of making exclusions from that list. There is a reasonable degree of uniformity across the country concerning which people are qualified for jury service. Normally, a juror is required to be of the age of majority in the province, a resident of that province, and a Canadian citizen.[278] Disqualifications frequently appear to be based on two general justifications: (1) that the potential juror would face a conflict in serving on

273 *Kokopenace*, above note 260 at para 40.
274 *Kokopenace*, above note 260 at para 53.
275 *Kokopenace*, above note 260 at para 52.
276 *R v Chouhan*, [2021] 2 SCR 136 [*Chouhan*] at para 115. Justice Martin was concurring in the result for three judges.
277 *Chouhan*, above note 276 at para 273. Justice Côté was dissenting in the result.
278 Note, though, that Manitoba, for example, has repealed the citizenship requirement: *Charter Compliance Statute Amendment Act*, RSM 1987 Supp, c 4, s 14.

a jury, or (2) that what the juror does in everyday life is more important than, or for some other reason justifies a general exemption from, serving on a jury. For example, people involved in law enforcement are typically disqualified from jury service, though the exact list of which personnel do and do not qualify varies from province to province. Similarly, judges and lawyers are routinely excluded from juries, as sometimes are articled clerks or those who are attending or have attended law school. Disqualifications based on some types of criminal record are also routine though again, with variation between provinces.[279] On a different note, jury acts regularly disqualify the Governor General, the Lieutenant Governor, members of Parliament, members of the provincial government, senators, and so on. In some provinces, doctors, veterinarians, or other health professionals are also disqualified. In addition, most jurisdictions provide scope for an individual assessment of whether it will create a hardship for a particular person to serve on a jury, allow for exemptions based on reasons of religion or conscience, and exclude those with a physical or mental disability that would prevent the person from fulfilling the role of a juror.

## 3) *Criminal Code* Jury Selection Procedures — Choosing the Jury from the Jury Array

### a) Mechanics of Selecting Jurors

Once the jury array has been assembled in court, the *Criminal Code* provisions govern the remaining selection procedures.[280] It is possible for either the accused or the prosecutor to challenge the array, but doing so can be based only on "partiality, fraud or willful misconduct on the part of the sheriff or other officer by whom the panel was returned."[281]

279 For example, s 3(p) of the *Jury Act*, RSBC 1996, c 242 disqualifies anyone "convicted of an offence under the *Criminal Code*, the *Cannabis Act* (Canada) or the *Controlled Drugs and Substances Act* (Canada) unless a pardon was granted or issued," while s 4(e) of the *Juries Act*, SNS 1998, c 16 disqualifies "a person who has been convicted of a criminal offence for which the person was sentenced to a term of imprisonment of two years or more."

There is an interplay here with s 638(1)(c) of the *Criminal Code*, which creates a challenge for cause on the basis that "a juror has been convicted of an offence for which they were sentenced to a term of imprisonment of two years or more and for which no pardon or record suspension is in effect." It has been found that there is no constitutional impediment to provinces creating a stricter disqualification than that found in the *Code*: *R v Hoffman*, 2019 ONSC 2355, aff'd without reasons 2021 ONCA 781.

280 For an explanation of this issue in chart form, see *Anatomy of Criminal Procedure*, above note 48, Chart 3.2(a), "Jury Selection."

281 Section 629.

The same notion of representativeness that governed creating the jury roll — that is, that it does not include targeting particular groups — also governs at this stage. As a result, efforts either to increase *or* decrease the number of members of a particular group on the array will create grounds for a successful challenge.[282]

If the array has been accepted, then the selection procedure itself begins: potential jurors are chosen randomly from those present in accordance with the procedures set out in section 631 of the *Code*.[283] This procedure continues until, after the methods of excluding jurors (discussed at Section C(3)(b), below in this chapter) have been considered, enough jurors have been selected. Some protection for the privacy of jurors is found in the expectation that those called will be identified only by number, not name, for selection purposes.[284] Indeed, the judge can, if satisfied that it is necessary for the proper administration of justice, order a publication ban on the identity, or otherwise limit the use of information that would reveal the identity, of a juror. This provision was added to protect jurors from the risk of intimidation.[285]

---

282 See, for example, *R v Butler* (1984), 3 CR (4th) 174 (BCCA) [*Butler*], where the sheriff deliberately excluded Indigenous people from the array, or *R v Born With a Tooth* (1993), 22 CR (4th) 232 (Alta QB) [*Born With a Tooth*], where the sheriff took steps to guarantee that they were included: both resulted in successful challenges.

283 Section 631 provides that juror's names are to be written on card, put in a box, and "thoroughly shaken together." However, in 2022 s 631.1 was added to the Code allowing "electronic or other automated means" to be used, as long as the selection is still random. Section 631 also sets out quite precise guidelines concerning how many names are to be randomly drawn at a time, the order in which potential jurors are to be sworn, and so on. However, s 643(3) provides that failure to comply with s 631, 635 (order of challenges), or 641 (calling jurors who have been stood by) does not affect the validity of the proceedings. In essence, this saving provision is meant to protect only against harmless errors: not if the error has deprived the accused of a statutory right or deprives an accused of the right to a trial by a jury lawfully constituted: *R v Rowbotham* (1988), 63 CR (3d) 113 (Ont CA).

284 Section 631(3) provides that the clerk of the court will draw a card and call only the number, although s 631(3.1) permits a judge to order that the name and number be called where that is necessary for the proper administration of justice.

285 Section 631(6). See, for example, *R v Jacobson* (2004), 196 CCC (3d) 79 (Ont SC), where the circumstances led the judge to order a ban on identifying information: two accused were on trial for a home invasion and murder which had been carried out by more than two people, and a witness had been shot to prevent him from testifying. Less dramatic circumstances can also lead to a publication ban. See, for example, *R v Shaw*, 2024 ONCA 119, where a jury secrecy issue arose because a juror had visited the scene of the murder on his bike and posted pictures to social media: a ban on the juror's identity was imposed.

When there is a challenge for cause, there is a need for someone to decide that challenge. This is an area where the law was significantly changed by Bill C-75, and the new rule is easily stated: the judge decides.[286] Prior to that, the challenge was decided by two lay people: typically the two previously-sworn jurors (which was referred to as the "rotating triers" approach) but as of 2008 it also had become possible for two unsworn jurors to be sworn in to decide all the challenges (the "static triers" approach). There was a long-running disagreement among trial courts as to whether, given the wording of the *Code* and the inherent powers of a trial court, both sworn and unsworn jurors could be excluded, whether that could be done under both methods or only on the static triers approach, who could initiate such a procedure, and what the standard was.[287] The purpose of the exclusion was to prevent potential jurors from becoming "contaminated" by hearing other challenges for cause and the issues that arise. Under the changed legislation that issue has been anticipated, and the trial judge has the ability, on the application of the accused or prosecutor or on the judge's own motion, to order the exclusion of all jurors, sworn and unsworn, if the judge "is of the opinion that the order is necessary to preserve the impartiality of the jurors."[288] The Supreme Court has suggested that trial judges should as a rule exclude prospective jurors, but for a different reason: "[j]urors would be understandably reluctant to acknowledge a bias or prejudice publicly, and therefore, the risk of empanelling a biased juror increases where exclusion orders are not made."[289]

If the entire jury array is run through without a sufficient number of jurors having been selected, section 644 of the *Code* allows the judge to order the sheriff to summon "without delay" other jurors to the courtroom. As a practical matter, the sheriff will simply go to the street and require passersby to attend for potential jury selection or go to a location where they expect to find sufficient numbers of people. This provision allows for persons to be summoned "whether qualified jurors or not," and the sheriff cannot be delegated the authority to engage in pre-screening.[290] Because of the goal of randomness in selection

286 Section 640. This change was challenged as violating the *Charter* but was upheld in *R v Chouhan*, 2020 ONCA 40. That issue was not argued when *Chouhan* was appealed to the Supreme Court.

287 This was eventually settled by the Supreme Court of Canada in *R v Esseghaier*, 2021 SCC 9, but the conclusion they reached — that there was a common law discretion to exclude prospective jurors when using rotating triers — is at this stage only of historical interest.

288 Section 640(2).

289 *Chouhan*, above note 276 at para 67.

290 *R v Mid valley Tractor Sales Ltd* (1995), 101 CCC (3d) 253 (NBCA).

the sheriff has very little discretion about whom to summon, though they do have a limited discretion not to summon people who cannot attend jury selection due to some immediate conflict such as a medical appointment.[291] These jurors are known as "talesmen," and once in court are selected from in the same manner as the original array.

A jury normally has twelve members; however, various provisions in the *Code* allow that number to go as high as fourteen (indeed, arguably sixteen) and as low as ten, depending upon the particular stage.[292] This flexibility is a response to practical challenges posed to juries in big cases. Some trials can last many months or even years, and jurors can die or fall ill. Further, in some cases, they might seek to be discharged due to personal hardship or other reason, or, alternatively, dissension can arise among jury members and the trial judge might conclude that it lies at the feet of one juror. It is possible, in such instances, for a trial judge to discharge a juror during the trial "by reason of illness or other reasonable cause."[293] Anticipating the possibility of the attrition of jurors in some trials, therefore, a judge can direct that one or two "additional" jurors be selected at the start.[294] As a result, it is possible for as many as fourteen jurors to be sworn in at the start of trial and to listen to all the evidence. However, once the evidence is complete and the jury is to begin deliberating, that number must be reduced to twelve: if there are more than that number, the trial judge randomly selects names from all the jurors sworn in and discharges them until only twelve remain, and those twelve deliberate.[295] The point of choosing randomly at that stage is so that, during the trial itself, no juror

---

291 *R v Blackduck*, 2014 NWTSC 48.

292 For an explanation of this issue in chart form, see *Anatomy of Criminal Procedure*, above note 48, Chart 3.2(c), "Number of Members of a Jury."

293 Section 644(1). This power should not be exercised lightly. The Supreme Court noted in *R v Pan; R v Sawyer*, 2001 SCC 42 at para 97, that s 644 only permits jurors to be discharged in the course of the trial where a serious issue arises as to their fitness as a juror. It is not designed to encourage jurors to bring trivial complaints about their fellow jurors to the attention of the trial judge in the course of the trial, nor does it contemplate the discharge of jurors over minor concerns.

In *R v Kum*, 2015 ONCA 36 (in which a majority of jury members wrote to the judge with concerns about two other members), the Ontario Court of Appeal suggested that because of concerns about jury secrecy, a trial judge is best advised to initially approach such situations by recharging all the jurors about their duty and responsibilities. It is open to a judge to conduct an inquiry with one or more jurors, but that is not usually the best starting point.

294 Section 631(2.2).

295 Section 652.1(2).

should think of themselves as the "spare" who might not need to take part in deliberations.

There is another potential issue leading to attrition among jury members, which is the possibility of a long gap between the commencement of the trial, when jurors are selected,[296] and the commencement of calling evidence. Particularly given the number of *Charter* applications that are brought in criminal trials and that must be heard in the absence of the jury, it is possible that a jury will be selected but then directed to withdraw for some significant period of time before the trial begins in earnest. Once again this is a situation which can result in changing circumstances, with the result that some jurors who were selected might no longer be available when evidence is called.

The *Code* contains several responses to this problem. First, the *Code* permits the selection of one or two "alternate" jurors.[297] The role of alternate jurors differs from that of additional jurors: they are chosen at the time of jury selection but are not sworn in. Rather, they return at the commencement of evidence, at which point it is determined whether they are needed. If they are needed to complete a full jury (whether that is twelve, thirteen, or fourteen members), then they are sworn in, but if they are not needed at that stage, then they are excused.[298] Alternatively, even if no alternate jurors were selected, as long as no evidence has been heard, it is open to a trial judge to reopen the jury selection process and choose a replacement juror either by selecting a juror from some other jury array that happens to be available or by using the procedure for selecting talesmen.[299] Finally, there is no absolute requirement that a verdict be rendered by a jury of twelve. Rather, unless the judge orders otherwise, the jury remains properly

---

296 The Court has noted that the "commencement of trial" is not a single fixed point and will vary depending on the *Code* section and interests in question. The accused's right to be present for the entire trial, for example, should be construed to allow the accused to be present for the selection of the jury. In the context of replacing jurors, though, the Court has designated the commencement of trial as the point at which evidence is first heard. See *Basarabas*, above note 26.

297 Section 631(2.1).

298 Section 642.1. If the full numbers of both alternate and additional jurors are employed, then up until the time the jury begins to hear evidence, there could be sixteen people who might eventually be part of the twelve who decide the case.

299 See s 644(1.1). In *R v Paterson* (2001), 41 CR (5th) 278 (BCCA), the trial occurred before s 644(1.1) had been placed in the *Code*, though, in fact, the trial judge did select a replacement juror from a different jury array. The British Columbia Court of Appeal held that s 644(1.1) merely codified what had already been the law.

constituted and can render a verdict provided the number of jurors is not reduced below ten.[300] Indeed, should the number fall below ten, the trial can continue on a judge alone basis if the parties agree.[301]

There are now only two mechanisms by which a member of the jury array might be excluded from the jury: exemptions and challenges for cause, each of which are discussed below. Until Bill C-75 there was a third method, called a peremptory challenge, which allowed each of the Crown and the defence to unilaterally exclude a certain limited number of jurors without being required to offer an explanation. Those challenges are also discussed below, though the important point to come out of that discussion relates more to the reasons the Supreme Court found there to be no *Charter* violation with their abolition. The *Code* does not specify an order in which the steps take place, but in the past applications for an exemption were decided first so that the parties would not be required to use up their peremptory challenges on jurors who might not have served in any case.[302] That particular rationale no longer exists, but there seems no reason that the current order should be changed.

### b) Exemptions

Section 632 of the *Code* allows a trial judge to excuse jurors[303] based on any of three grounds: personal interest in the matter to be tried; relationship with the judge, prosecutor, accused, counsel for the accused, or a prospective witness; and personal hardship or other reasonable cause. Typically, this procedure is carried out before the names of individual jurors are called, by the judge asking whether any jurors wish to be excused. Although this task is in a sense administrative, it is a part of the trial, and the accused is entitled to be present for it.[304]

Strictly the first two grounds upon which jurors can be excused relate to potential partiality, which, in general, must be dealt with by way of the challenge for cause procedures in the *Code*. However, these grounds are limited to such "obvious situations of non-indifference" that the consent of counsel to the exclusion of the juror can be presumed.[305] In any event, it was found to be acceptable for the judge to

300 Section 611(2).

301 Section 644(3). This provision was added by Bill C-75, above note 33: until this change there would have been a mistrial if the number of jurors fell below ten.

302 *R v Douglas* (2002), 12 CR (6th) 374 (Ont CA) [*Douglas*].

303 Throughout this section, references to a "juror" should be understood where appropriate to mean a "prospective juror": that is, a person on the array whose name is called out for possible selection to a jury.

304 *Barrow*, above note 27. See also *R v Kakegamic*, 2010 ONCA 903.

305 *Sherratt*, above note 265 at 534.

decide these putative applications at a time when "cause-based" challenges had to be decided by other triers of the challenge: now that such challenges will be decided by the judge, this situation is less anomalous.[306] In any circumstance other than these obvious ones, the challenge for cause procedures must be used. In addition, nothing prevents a party from challenging for cause a juror whose request to be excused was not granted by the trial judge.[307]

The trial judge has a further related power under section 633 of the *Code*. Rather than excusing the juror completely, the trial judge can have a juror "stand by."[308] In that event, jury selection continues with the remaining members of the array. In essence, when a juror has asked to be excused, a judge has three choices: where there is a good case for being excused, say yes; where there is not a good case for being excused, say no; or, where there is some case but not clearly a good enough one, put the juror to the end to give them a chance to avoid jury duty without actually being excused. Jurors that are required to stand by are only re-called for possible selection if the array is exhausted without a complete jury. In that event, those jurors are re-called in the order in which they were first called, at which point the judge will decide whether to grant the exemption, and if the judge does not, then the juror will be subject to the normal challenge process.

The section states that it can be used only when a juror is individually called under section 631, rather than in the global manner used for excusing jurors. However, in *R v Krugel* the Ontario Court of Appeal found that an accused had suffered no prejudice when a trial judge departed from that approach,[309] and in *R v Douglas* it appeared to approve the practice of a trial judge who, with no objection from counsel, adopted the administrative convenience of informally standing aside, as a group, all jurors who indicated that they would seek an exemption if they were asked.[310]

---

306 See, for example, *R v Riley*, 2017 ONCA 650, which considered the extent to which a judge could "vet" potential jurors given the interplay between the power to excuse (given to the judge) and the power to decide challenges for cause (at the time given to triers).

307 *Ibid*.

308 At one point the *Code* gave the Crown the power to stand by jurors in a similar fashion, though this was found to violate the *Charter* in *R v Bain*, [1992] 1 SCR 91 [*Bain* SCC]. This process was frequently referred to as causing jurors to "stand aside," and presumably because of this former power, the "stand aside" terminology is often used interchangeably with "stand by" when speaking of the power in s 633: see, for example, *R v Matthew Raymond (Ruling #4)*, 2019 NBQB 203.

309 *R v Krugel* (2000), 31 CR (5th) 314 (Ont CA) at para 36 [*Krugel*].

310 *Douglas*, above note 302.

As originally drafted, the exemption section was limited to having jurors stand by based on personal hardship or other reasonable cause, which is the third of the three grounds upon which jurors can be excused under section 632. On that version of the section, the Ontario Court of Appeal had held that "other reasonable cause" could include potential partiality on the part of the juror.[311] The point to note is that any given "stand by" was to be based on something about the individual juror in question. However, Bill C-75 amended the section to also allow a judge to have a juror stand by for the reason of "maintaining public confidence in the administration of justice." It must be said that this is a confusing provision and difficult to reconcile with other jury selection mechanisms. First, it is surprising that a provision which focuses on public confidence is mixed in with grounds which have otherwise rested on a feature of an individual juror. However, that is not the most difficult part to understand. As noted above, the genesis of this change was a trial in which an all-white jury tried a white accused charged with killing an Indigenous man. The natural inference, therefore, is that that was the "problem" this change was meant to solve. Indeed, in introducing Bill C-75 the Minister of Justice explicitly said that this particular change was meant to "strengthen the power of judges to stand aside some jurors in order to make room for a more diverse jury."[312] If so, that would suggest that judges should use this ability for things like influencing the racial makeup of a jury: for example, if as yet no visible minority jurors have been randomly selected from the jury array, the judge could stand by all the white jurors whose names are called until a visible minority juror's name is called.

The immediate difficulty is that if that were the approach meant to be adopted, it would rest on an understanding of "representativeness" which is not only different from that which has been adopted until now, but is in fact the very understanding which has been *rejected*. The Court has noted that "[c]ourts have consistently rejected the idea that an accused is entitled to a particular number of individuals of his or her race on either the jury roll or petit jury"[313] and that "representativeness is not about targeting particular groups for inclusion on the jury roll."[314] An accused cannot insist that the jury or jury array contain members of the accused's race.[315]

311 *Krugel*, above note 309.

312 *Chouhan*, above note 276 at para 108.

313 *Kokopenace*, above note 260 at para 39.

314 *Ibid* at para 61.

315 *R v Kent, Sinclair and Gode* (1986), 27 CCC (3d) 405 (Man CA).

The view until now has been that representativeness is to be equated with randomness, and therefore that it is the latter that is to be protected.

Nonetheless, in the view of some members of the Supreme Court, this change to the stand-by power *did* signal a fundamental change in approach. In *Chouhan*, Martin J argued that "I would caution against placing undue weight on the principle of random selection."[316] Holding that "public confidence" should be measured by looking at the reasonable observer, she maintained that "[t]he reasonable observer would be aware that the amendments in Bill C-75 respond to long-standing concerns about inadequate Indigenous representation on juries and the resulting impacts on public confidence."[317] Similarly Abella J argued that "[t]he legislative intent behind the new stand-aside power was to empower trial judges to ensure impartiality and 'to make room for a more diverse jury'" and that "[i]t is based on an understanding of representativeness which looks to the actual composition of the jury, as opposed to the randomness of the selection process."[318]

The majority in *Chouhan*, however, rejected this view:

> [W]e respectfully reject our colleague Abella J.'s suggestion that trial judges use the stand-aside power to "actively promote jury diversity" and to approximate "Canada's kaleidoscope of human diversity" (para. 164). Parliament did *not* write into law that the stand-aside power is to be used to bolster jury diversity as our colleague has conceived of it, but, again, for "maintaining public confidence in the administration of justice". As a matter of law, we cannot accept that public confidence in the administration of justice depends on achieving a jury that approximates the diversity of Canadian society.[319]

---

316 *Chouhan*, above note 276 at para 113. Justices Karakatsanis and Kasirer concurred in her judgment.

317 *Chouhan*, above note 276 at para 116.

318 *Chouhan*, above note 276 at para 162.

319 *Chouhan*, above note 276 at para 74. There is some scope to argue whether Moldaver and Brown JJ were in fact writing for the majority here. Chief Justice Wagner also signed on to their reasons, and although Côté J dissented in the case, she specifically agreed with this aspect of the majority reasoning. Justice Rowe concurred with the majority on the issue in the case, that the abolition of peremptory challenges was constitutional. It is *arguable* that these comments on the stand-aside power were *obiter* and that Rowe J's concurrence therefore does not apply to them. However, the Ontario Court of Appeal has rejected that argument, holding that this portion of *Chouhan* is binding majority opinion, not *obiter*, and that the stand-aside power cannot be used to create "representativeness": see *R v Azzi*, 2022 ONCA 366. See also *R v SJL*, 2024 NBCA 76, adopting *Azzi* on this point.

Given that the majority in the Supreme Court has rejected the purpose the Minister of Justice said the change intended,[320] that does leave the question of what the "public confidence" stand-aside power is in fact to be used for. The majority in *Chouhan* said that this will need to be worked out on a case-by-case basis, offering only the example of excluding a juror where there are still doubts about their partiality despite them having survived a challenge for cause. However, that potential use of the stand-aside power already existed without the addition of the "public confidence" ground.[321] It is also a situation much less likely to arise since Bill C-75, since one of the other changes made by it was to have challenges for cause decided by the trial judge, not by someone else: it is difficult to see how the trial judge could simultaneously find the juror impartial but also have them stand aside because of doubts about whether they were impartial.[322] Beyond that, the majority suggest only that public confidence will not easily be lost and that it would require something egregious,[323] so perhaps the real lesson of *Chouhan* for the stand-aside power is that the addition of the "public confidence" ground will have little practical impact.

A final point around this additional ground is the question of who invokes it. Although the section is not explicit on this point, until now it has focused on hardship, and so implicitly the request would have come from the juror personally. A concern over "maintaining public confidence," however, seems likely to be raised by one of the parties or by the judge personally. Nothing in the language of the section would prevent that.

---

320 *Chouhan*, about note 276 at para 81:

> This, in turn, calls into question the statement of the then-Minister of Justice that the amended stand-aside power would enable judges to "make room for a more diverse jury."

321 *Krugel*, above note 309.

322 See, however, the procedure adopted in *R v RO*, 2021 ONSC 6331 [*RO*] at para 3:

> 11. The stand aside power may be used to address potential bias or other grounds of partiality. Once a juror is found to be acceptable after the challenge for cause, I will turn to counsel to ask if there are any submissions. If counsel do not wish to make submissions, the prospective juror shall be sworn as a juror. If counsel wish to make submissions pursuant to s. 633 of the *Criminal Code*, I will invite the prospective juror to leave the courtroom and then invite the parties to make submissions or propose defined questions, where appropriate. There must be some objective rationale for standing the juror aside. If the prospective juror is stood aside, reasons will be given. The prospective juror will then be invited back into the courtroom and may be asked further questions. They will either be directed to stand aside or be sworn as a juror to try the case.

323 *Chouhan*, above note 276 at para 72–73.

### c) Anti-bias Instructions and the Abolition of Peremptory Challenges

Section 634 of the *Criminal Code* (repealed by Bill C-75 in 2019) created "peremptory challenges," which allowed the accused or the Crown to dismiss a potential juror without explanation. Each party was allocated a certain number of such challenges, depending on the seriousness of the offence: in the case of first-degree murder, for example, an accused would have twenty peremptory challenges, and any co-accused would also have that same number. The Crown had the same number of peremptory challenges as all the accused combined. In serious cases — and jury trials are most likely in serious cases — there could therefore be a very large number of peremptory challenges.

There was no real debate that the accused's use of peremptory challenges was unconstrained. Blackstone offered two rationales for their existence, which were frequently cited:

> 1. As every one must be sensible what sudden impressions and unaccountable prejudices we are apt to conceive upon the bare looks and gestures of another, and how necessary it is that a prisoner (when put to defend his life), should have a good opinion of his jury, the want of which might totally disconcert him, the law wills not that he should be tried by any one man against whom he has conceived a prejudice, even without being able to assign a reason for such his dislike. 2. Because, upon challenges for cause shown, if the reasons assigned prove insufficient to set aside the juror, perhaps the bare questioning his indifference may sometimes provoke a resentment, to prevent all ill consequences from which the prisoner is still at liberty, if he pleases, peremptorily to set him aside.[324]

It was less clear whether the Crown was equally unconstrained in its use of peremptory challenges, though this point was never fully settled. There was some caselaw considering actions by the Crown to "construct" a jury with a particular make up, though the Supreme Court never authoritatively grappled with this issue.[325]

---

324 See *R v Cloutier*, [1990] 1 SCR 158 at 720.

325 In *R v Pizzacalla* (1991), 7 CR (4th) 294 (Ont CA) the Ontario Court of Appeal ordered a retrial in a case where the Crown used a discretionary power to produce an all-female jury in a sexual assault case: the Supreme Court in *Bain*, above note 308, seems to endorse the view that this action by the Crown had been improper. On the other hand in *R v Biddle*, [1995] 1 SCR 761, another case in which the Crown had created an all-female jury for a sexual assault case, the majority declined to comment on the issue, while Gonthier and McLachlin JJ took opposing views on whether the action was acceptable.

In any event, that debate demonstrates the potential issue with peremptory challenges, which was that they were at odds with the notion of "representativeness through randomness." They were quite consciously *not* random and had the potential to have a significant impact on the make-up of the jury. Random selection will mean, for example, that there will be fewer members of a minority community in the jury array. A party wishing to exclude all members of that group from a jury might have had enough peremptory challenges to exclude all of them. Indeed, the abolition of peremptory challenges was sparked by the Gerald Stanley trial, a white accused charged with the murder of an Indigenous man, where exactly this was perceived to have happened. It was reported that Stanley's defence counsel used peremptory challenges when potential jurors who appeared to be Indigenous were called: whether that is the case or not, certainly no Indigenous people ended up on the jury.[326]

The abolition of peremptory challenges was challenged as violating sections 11(d) (right to an independent and impartial jury) and section 11(f) (right to trial by jury) in *Chouhan*, but the Supreme Court found no violations and upheld the abolition.[327] What is arguably most interesting about that decision is not the final result but the additional guidance that the Supreme Court gave about jury selection generally. Some aspects relating to challenge for cause will be discussed under the next heading, but a major point raised by the Court was to encourage the use of "anti-bias instructions."

Perhaps the major argument in favour of peremptory challenges was that, despite the risks of excluding visible minorities from a jury, they were also a tool available *to* visible minority accused seeking to avoid

326 Given the demographics of the community where the trial occurred and estimates of the number of Indigenous people on the jury panel, it has been estimated that the probability of an all-white jury occurring randomly in a case like this would be one in 133. See Christian A Miller, "Peremptory Challenges During Jury Selection as Institutional Racism: An Investigation Within the Context of the Gerald Stanley Trial (*R v Stanley*, 2018 SKQB)" (2019) 67 *Criminal Law Quarterly* 215. The *Stanley* case is not the only instance of such behaviour being suggested: see, for example, *R v Cornell*, 2017 YKCA 12, where defence counsel suggested that the Crown was using peremptory challenges to prevent any Indigenous people from appearing on the jury. In *Cornell* there was found to be no evidence that the Crown had in fact behaved in that way. See also *R v Gayle* (2001), 154 CCC (3d) 221 (Ont CA) [*Gayle*].

327 *Chouhan*, above note 276.

jurors who might have conscious or unconscious biases.[328] The majority in *Chouhan*, in finding that there was no violation of the accused's right to an impartial jury, therefore spent some time considering other aspects of the jury selection process aimed at impartiality. One of these, and one which has potential for a significant impact, was the expanded use of anti-bias instructions.

*Chouhan* noted that trials do not take place in a social vacuum, and that many biases are unconscious. To help ensure impartiality, therefore, two types of anti-bias instructions were proposed: general instructions on biases and stereotypes and instructions on specific biases and stereotypes that arise on the facts of the case.[329]

General anti-bias instructions should be given before the presentation of evidence or at any other appropriate time, including before jury selection to the entire panel:

> We suggest that trial judges begin by pointing out that as members of society, each juror brings a variety of beliefs, assumptions, and perceptions to the court room. These assumptions will often be based on characteristics such as gender, race, ethnicity, sexual orientation, or employment status. Trial judges ought to highlight that jurors may be aware of some of their biases while being unaware of others.[330]

Trial courts have begun acting on this advice, and general anti-bias instructions are becoming a feature of jury trials.[331]

Instructions on specific biases and stereotypes are meant to be tailored to the individual trial and the issues which might plausibly arise. They could relate to myths and stereotypes about sexual assault or to views on Indigenous women who perform sex work,[332] to bias

---

328 See the dissenting reasons of Côté J in *Chouhan*:

> [227] There is a sad irony to this case. Parliament eliminated peremptory challenges because it saw them as an arbitrary tool used to perpetuate systemic racism and discriminate against jurors who are racialized or other marginalized persons. The reality is, however, that peremptory challenges are far from arbitrary. More particularly, for accused persons who are racialized or otherwise marginalized, they are a lifeline to combat unconscious biases and discrimination.

329 *Chouhan*, above note 276 at para 52.

330 *Chouhan*, above note 276 at para 53.

331 See, for example, the instructions set out in *R v Bhogal*, 2021 ONSC 4925 [*Bhogal*] by Pomerance J, as she then was, and adopted in *R v Martin*, 2021 ONSC 5333 [*Martin*]. See also *R v RO*, 2021 ONSC 6331 [*RO*], setting out general instructions to be given before jury selection, and then further anti-bias instructions to be given to the jury once selected.

332 *Chouhan*, above note 276 at para 57, pointing to *R v Barton*, 2019 SCC 33.

against men of East Indian heritage, the stereotype that men of colour are more prone to violence than white men or that persons who consume drugs are likely to commit violent crimes,[333] or "conscious and unconscious negative feelings or assumptions about gender, race, ethnicity, religion, sexual orientation, age or employment status."[334] The specific anti-bias instructions to be given will depend on the individual trial: "[i]nformed by recent case law and a modern understanding of impartiality, trial judges may therefore draw on their own professional experiences and good sense in deciding whether anti-bias instructions are required, and the submissions of counsel will be helpful in identifying appropriate cases for such instructions."[335]

### d) Challenges for Cause

Section 638 of the *Code* sets out the grounds upon which a juror can be challenged for cause.[336] Both the Crown and the accused are entitled to an unlimited number of challenges for cause, but the grounds upon which those challenges can be made are exhaustively defined in subsections (a) through (f) of section 638(1). Some of the grounds are simply factual questions, such as that the juror's name does not appear on the panel, the juror is not a Canadian citizen, or the juror has been convicted of an offence for which they were sentenced to a term of imprisonment of two years or more and for which no pardon or record suspension is in effect.[337] A juror can also be challenged on the basis

---

333 *Bhogal*, above note 331.

334 *RO*, above note 331 at para 26. To similar effect see *R c Boudreau-Chartrand*, 2023 QCCS 3820.

335 *Chouhan*, above note 276 at para 50. See, for example, *RO*, above note 331, where it was agreed only general anti-bias instructions were required. See also *R v Necan*, 2024 ONCA 751, where the failure to refer to the accused's Indigenous status was found not to be an error, in part because the trial pre-dated *Chouhan*, but also because the accused's Indigeneity was not seen to be a significant enough factor in the trial. The accused had not requested a challenge for cause procedure on that basis, for example.

336 For an explanation of this issue in chart form, see *Anatomy of Criminal Procedure*, above note 48, Chart 3.2(b), "Challenge for Cause."

337 This particular limitation was changed from one year's imprisonment to two with Bill C-75, above note 33. This change was motivated by several concerns, one of which was that the lower penalty excluded potential jurors with relatively minor criminal offences, which tended to adversely affect the number of potential Indigenous jurors. In addition, another provision of Bill C-75 raised the default penalty for summary conviction offences from six months to two years less a day: increasing the "disqualification level" for jurors to two years meant that conviction for a summary conviction offence would continue to not be a disqualification. Bill C-75 also changed the language of s 638(1)(d) to "is not a Canadian citizen" from "is an alien."

either of physical incapacity to perform the duties of a juror, or of an inability to speak the language in which the trial will occur.[338] The only ground that has attracted real controversy is section 638(1)(b), a challenge on the basis that the juror "is not impartial." Until June of 2019 this requirement was phrased in the *Code* as an objection that the juror "is not indifferent between the Queen and the accused." The change in wording is not meant to create any change in meaning: "not indifferent" had been defined in the caselaw to mean "not impartial," or prejudiced.[339] However, it is necessary to know of the change in terminology because the existing caselaw generally speaks in terms of whether the juror was indifferent.

The attitude of the criminal justice system to challenge for cause is arguably in a state of fluctuation at present. The Supreme Court of Canada had for a very long time consciously set a limited role for this ground.The Court had observed that there are two approaches to deciding whether a juror is not impartial:

> The first approach is that prevailing in the United States. On this approach, every jury panel is suspect. Every candidate for jury duty may be challenged and questioned as to preconceptions and prejudices on any sort of trial. . . . Canada has taken a different approach. In this country, candidates for jury duty are presumed to be indifferent or impartial. Before the Crown can challenge and question them, they must raise concerns which displace that presumption.[340]

In other words, challenge for cause is automatic in the United States, and there is a right from the start to question each potential juror to see whether that person is appropriate. Effectively the opposite was true in Canada, where it is presumed that any person can be an impartial juror for any other person. As a result, counsel will not be allowed to ask any questions regarding a challenge for cause

---

338 This requirement is generally (though not uniformly) a provincial criterion for inclusion on a jury array initially, as one might expect. The particular motivation for s 638(1)(f) is s 530 of the *Code*, under which a trial can be directed to be in the official language of the accused. That provision is designed for situations where an accused speaks an official language of Canada that is not necessarily the language used daily in the courts of that province and therefore the trial might not ordinarily be in the accused's language. Section 638(1)(f) guarantees that when a trial is ordered to be in one of Canada's official languages, all the jurors will speak that official language. It has been proclaimed only in Manitoba, New Brunswick, the Northwest Territories, Ontario, and the Yukon Territory.

339 *R v Hubbert*, [1977] 2 SCR 267, aff'g [1975] OJ No 2595 (CA) [*Hubbert*].

340 *R v Williams*, [1998] 1 SCR 1128 at paras 12–13 [*Williams*].

without first satisfying the judge that there was some reason to doubt the juror's impartiality.

In practical terms, for a very long time the only basis upon which questions towards a challenge for cause were allowed was where there had been extensive and discreditable pre-trial publicity. For some decades now it has also been permissible to ask questions of potential jurors where there is a possibility of prejudice against an accused based on their race. Until recently it would have been correct to say that any other types of challenges were unlikely to be allowed because of the very strong presumption of juror impartiality. However, the Supreme Court's 2021 decision in *Chouhan* seems to signal a conscious departure, at least to some extent, from that strong presumption, and so it appears that questions aimed at a challenge based on partiality are available more broadly. The contours of this shift are still being worked out. It is easiest to explain this by looking at how challenges for cause have evolved over time.

The Court has suggested that there are four relevant types of potential juror prejudice.[341] Interest prejudice arises when the juror has a direct interest in the trial, that is, where "the juror is the uncle of the accused, or the wife of a witness," for example.[342] Excluding a juror for this type of prejudice is not controversial, and, as noted above in Section C(3)(b), a trial judge can simply ask about any such relationships and excuse jurors before jury selection commences in such instances with the presumed consent of counsel.[343] Potentially more controversial are the other types: (1) specific prejudice, which consists of attitudes or beliefs about the particular case, gained through media coverage or some other source, that might prevent the juror from being impartial; (2) generic prejudice, consisting of stereotypical attitudes about the accused, victims, witnesses, or the nature of the crime; and (3) conformity prejudice, when a juror might feel influenced by strong community feelings about an expected outcome.[344] It is in those contexts that the presumption of impartiality has its most notable impact.

Challenge for cause is not intended to be a means for counsel to find out what type of person the juror is.[345] Although the Court had

---

341 *Williams*, *ibid* at para 10, relying on Neil Vidmar, "Pretrial Prejudice in Canada: A Comparative Perspective on the Criminal Jury" (1996) 79 *Judicature* 249.

342 *Sherratt*, above note 265 at 534, quoting from the Ontario Court of Appeal level decision in *Hubbert*, above note 339.

343 See s 632 of the *Code* and *Sherratt*, above note 265; *Barrow*, above note 27.

344 *Williams*, above note 340 at para 10.

345 *Hubbert*, above note 339.

resisted saying that challenge for cause is limited to extreme cases,[346] the presumption of impartiality means that counsel is not permitted to *routinely* challenge jurors. Rather, a two-step process is involved. First, counsel must satisfy the trial judge that the challenge for cause should be permitted: counsel must tell the trial judge the basis for the challenge.[347] If the trial judge is not satisfied that counsel has provided sufficient reason to doubt the juror's impartiality, the challenge will not occur. This would be true whether counsel wishes to challenge an individual juror or the jury array as a whole. At this stage of the process, the test is whether there is a realistic possibility for partiality.[348] Demonstrating a realistic potential for partiality (when dealing with a challenge to all members of the array) involves two components: showing "(1) that a widespread bias exists in the community; and (2) that some jurors may be incapable of setting aside this bias, despite trial safeguards, to render an impartial decision."[349] These two components are referred to as the "attitudinal" and "behavioural" components of partiality. The second stage is the challenge itself, where counsel is permitted to ask questions of the jurors to determine whether the juror will in fact be able to act impartially. Even at this stage, counsel will not have an unrestrained right to question jurors (in some cases, only one or two predetermined questions will be allowed).[350]

Because counsel must state the basis for challenging the juror beforehand but will likely know little about the individual juror, there have been practical obstacles preventing challenges for cause from even occurring, let alone succeeding (see, however, the discussion of jury-vetting, below). Therefore, cases have most commonly concerned challenges that are relevant to the array as a whole, rather than having particular regard to some individual juror.[351] For example, in *R v Hubbert* the accused wanted

346 *Sherratt*, above note 265.

347 *Hubbert*, above note 339 at para 35 (CA): "The *Code* does not require that a challenge, oral or written, be particularized . . .. But counsel must have a reason, even a generalized one."

348 *Williams*, above note 340 at para 32.

349 *R v Find*, [2001] 1 SCR 863 at para 32 [*Find*].

350 See, for example, *Hubbert*, above note 339, or the jury selection in the initial trial in *Williams*, above note 340. At the Supreme Court in *Williams*, the Court spoke about "confin[ing] the challenge to two questions, subject to a few tightly controlled subsidiary questions" as "a practice to be emulated" (para 55). See also the discussion of this approach in *Gayle*, above note 326.

351 Because of the rise of social media, it is ceasing to be true that counsel have little ability to find out information about individual jurors. This makes it more plausible that challenges based on factors unique to a particular juror will occur, and it is possible that this will come to have an impact on the caselaw or the justice system generally. See, for example, *R v Way*, 2019 ABQB 271,

to question every juror to determine whether that juror would be prejudiced by learning that the accused had been detained in a mental health institution. Pre-trial publicity has also been a basis upon which counsel have sought to ask questions with a view to making challenges. *R v Sherratt*, for example, concerned a murder that was particularly notorious in the community, and the accused sought, unsuccessfully, to question jurors to determine whether the pre-trial publicity would prevent them from being impartial. The Court refused to allow the challenge in that case, holding that there was a distinction between mere publication of the facts of a case, on the one hand, and misrepresentation of evidence by the media, wide publicization of discreditable facts from an accused's past, or speculation about the accused's guilt or innocence, on the other hand.[352] It is fair to say that, at least until recently, counsel generally have had difficulty persuading judges that it is reasonable to question every member of a jury array with regard to possible prejudice.[353] Precisely because the Canadian approach presumes the impartiality of every juror, showing a realistic potential of partiality is difficult.

The Court did, however, create one exception to this generalization, dealing with situations where partiality might arise due to attitudes about the race of the accused. In *R v Williams*, the accused was Aboriginal and his counsel wanted to challenge jurors for cause based on racial attitudes. The accused did not offer evidence that the particular people on the jury array had racist attitudes. Rather, he led evidence showing that there was widespread bias against Aboriginal peoples in the community. The trial judge accepted that evidence, but held that evidence of general bias in the community did not establish a realistic potential of partiality on the part of jurors at trial, in part, because jurors could be expected to set aside their biases. The British Columbia Court of Appeal upheld the decision on the basis that general bias was not the equivalent of a racist attitude of particular concern to a criminal trial.

---

challenging a practice of the jury list only being available as of the morning of trial. Counsel successfully applied for a change in practice to make the list available five days in advance, specifically in order to allow an opportunity to investigate the social media accounts of prospective jurors.

352 For other cases dealing with pre-trial publicity as a ground for challenge, see *R v Merz* (1999), 140 CCC (3d) 259 (Ont CA); *Gayle*, above note 326; *R v Proulx* (1992), 76 CCC (3d) 316 (Que CA); and *R v Keegstra* (1991), 3 CR (4th) 153 (Alta CA).

353 See V Gordon Rose & James RP Ogloff, "Challenge for Cause in Canadian Criminal Jury Trials: Legal and Psychological Perspectives" (2002) 46 *Criminal Law Quarterly* 210, for an overview of types of evidence that have, and have not, been successful in permitting counsel to challenge for cause, as well as a discussion of the potential role of psychologists in such challenges.

The Supreme Court of Canada overturned this result for a number of reasons. It held that the lower courts had set too high a standard for showing a realistic possibility of prejudice in these circumstances. Looking for attitudes particularly relevant to the justice system was an unrealistic test, it held, as was the expectation that juror attitudes would be "cleansed" by instructions about how they should discharge their duties. Racist attitudes, the Court pointed out, are insidious and sometimes unconsciously held — a juror might not be *able* to set them aside, even when trying to do so. Further, the potential effect of the attitude is unpredictable and, therefore, hard to guard against:

> It may incline a juror to believe that the accused is likely to have committed the crime alleged. It may incline a juror to reject or put less weight on the evidence of the accused, or it may, in a general way, predispose the juror to the Crown, perceived as representative of the "white" majority against the minority-member accused, inclining the juror, for example, to resolve doubts about aspects of the Crown's case more readily.[354]

Essentially, with *Williams* the Court signalled that trial judges should be more open to being persuaded that there is a realistic potential for partiality (that is, that the first phase of the challenge for cause process is fulfilled) when the challenge is based on possible attitudes about race.[355] Indeed, the Court went so far as to note that widespread racial prejudice, as a characteristic of a community, could be the subject of judicial notice. Once widespread prejudice has been proved in one case, judges in later cases can take judicial notice of it or indeed simply find that widespread prejudice in a particular community is proven by events of indisputable accuracy, without any need for an accused to provide evidence.[356] Lower courts carried this finding to its logical conclusion, in a way likely to be approved by the Supreme Court, should the issue even reach there. For example, in *R v Parks* the Ontario Court of Appeal had reached a conclusion similar to that in *Williams*, though that case dealt with a black person accused in the city of Toronto.[357] In

354 *Williams*, above note 340 at para 11.

355 On *Williams*, *ibid*, generally, see David M Tanovich, "The Future of Challenge for Cause in the Wake of *Williams*" (1998) 15 *Criminal Reports* (5th) 250, and Stephen G Coughlan, "Developments in Criminal Procedure: The 1997–98 Term" (1999) 10 *Supreme Court Law Review* 273.

356 *Williams*, above note 340 at para 54.

357 (1993), 24 CR (4th) 81 (Ont CA) [*Parks*]. The Supreme Court refused leave to appeal in *Parks*, but subsequently relied heavily on its reasoning in deciding *Williams*, above note 340. The Court was also able to note in *Williams* that post-*Parks* experience in Ontario had shown no significant delay in jury selection

*R v Wilson*, that court subsequently decided that challenges for cause based on the realistic potential for racist attitudes should be allowed to any black person accused in Ontario, not merely Toronto, without further empirical evidence of racism.[358] Later in *R v Koh*, that court expanded the finding to allow challenge for cause by any accused belonging to *any* visible minority. Its intention was not to do away with the need for a finding of a realistic potential for prejudice, but "to find that in the light of the numerous trial and appellate decisions in this jurisdiction concerning various categories of visible minorities, this test has been met wherever the accused is a member of a visible racial minority."[359]

The Supreme Court did not, with *Williams*, intend to make challenge for cause more easily available outside the context of racial prejudice, however. This position was clear from the post-*Williams* decision in *R v Find*.[360] In that case the accused wished to be allowed to question jurors in order to decide whether to challenge them for cause, on the basis that the case concerned sexual assaults against children. The accused argued that there was a realistic potential that some jurors would be unable to act impartially because of the nature of the charges. In *Williams*, the Court described racial prejudice as "generic prejudice," which, in turn, it described as "stereotypical attitudes about the defendant, victims, witnesses or the nature of the crime itself."[361] Therefore, *Find* was an attempt to apply the approach in *Williams* to a relatively similar situation (another type of generic prejudice).

The Court rejected the appeal. The accused had argued that there was a realistic potential for partiality on a number of grounds: the widespread incidence of sexual abuse, which meant that previous victims or those close to them were likely to be on the panel; the politicized and gender-based nature of views about sexual assault; myths and stereotypes about sexual assault; the emotional nature of sexual assault trials; the history of challenge for cause in Ontario, which showed that when challenge for cause on this basis was allowed, roughly one third of jurors challenged were disqualified; and social science evidence suggesting widespread bias. Nonetheless, the Court

procedures despite the relaxing of the first stage in this context. Given that the efficiency of the system and the spectre of "US style" challenges for cause are a regular concern of the Court, it appears possible that leave to appeal might have been refused in *Parks* precisely to discover what the practical impact of the change would be.

358 (1996), 47 CR (4th) 61 (Ont CA).

359 (1998), 21 CR (5th) 188 at para 31 (Ont CA).

360 *Find*, above note 349.

361 *Williams*, above note 340 at para 10.

was not persuaded on any of these grounds to permit the questioning towards challenge for cause to occur. It found that the evidence presented did not show a realistic possibility of prejudice and held as well that such a possibility could not be the subject of judicial notice. Further, they concluded that, unlike racial prejudice, any prejudice of this sort could be cured by judicial direction to jurors or other trial safeguards. Although the decision acknowledged the possibility of better evidence being presented in some future case, the case clearly indicated that outside the context of potential racial prejudice against the accused, challenge for cause was intended to be no more freely available than it was pre-*Williams*.[362]

Further, in *R v Spence*,[363] another post-*Williams* case, the Court refused to allow a *Parks*-like question which was based on the theory that witnesses might fail to be impartial because they would feel a race-based sympathy for a victim rather than a race-based antipathy to the accused, as in *Williams* and *Parks*. The accused in *Spence* was black and the victim of the robbery was East Indian. The trial judge allowed the accused to challenge potential jurors on the issue of possible bias against him because of his race, but he was not allowed to ask whether jurors would be affected by the fact that he was accused of robbing an East Indian victim. The accused argued that potential East Indian jurors might feel a natural sympathy for the victim, and that asking this question was simply a natural progression of the *Williams/Parks* approach.

The Court held that the trial judge had acted correctly in refusing to allow the question. It held that the previous cases had dealt only with the issue of potential prejudice *against* a member of a visible minority and that none of the social science evidence presented in those cases established any kind of bias *in favour of* members of a particular group. The Court also held that no evidence establishing such a "natural sympathy" had been presented, and that it was not a matter of which a court could take judicial notice. Accordingly, they rejected the accused's argument.[364] In doing so they reasserted the long-standing

---

362 Further on this issue, see Steve Coughlan, "*R v Find*: Preserving the Presumption of Innocence" (2001) 42 *Criminal Reports* (5th) 31, and Michael Plaxton, "The Biased Juror and Appellate Review: A Reply to Professor Coughlan" (2001) 44 *Criminal Reports* (5th) 294.

363 [2005] 3 SCR 458 [*Spence*].

364 It is worth noting the implication of this conclusion on the Stanley trial, above note 326, and therefore the way in which it might have contributed to the changes to the jury system made in Bill C-75. It was noted above that defence counsel was said to have used peremptory challenges to exclude potential jurors who appeared to be Indigenous. One impact of the decision in *Spence* is that,

view that challenge for cause is far from automatic, and that jurors are presumed to be impartial:

> Our criminal law is premised on the ability of 12 jurors to do their job with "indifference" as between the Crown and the accused. We do not start with the idea that it is up to the potential juror to demonstrate his or her impartiality. Our procedures in this respect differ from the American approach. In this country, people called for jury duty benefit from a presumption that they will do their duty without bias or partiality.[365]

It was in this context that the decision in *Chouhan* came along, but it seems implicitly to back away from this strong presumption. The actual issue in *Chouhan* was whether the abolition of peremptory challenges violated sections 11(d) (right to an independent and impartial jury) and section 11(f) (right to trial by jury) of the *Charter*: the majority of the Court concluded that it did not. However, reaching that conclusion required the court to consider *other* aspects of jury selection which protected those rights, including challenge for cause. In addition, there were five separate judgments, with the result that on some aspects of the decision there is no clear majority.[366] However, all five judgments make some observations which go to the underlying attitude that judges should adopt, and even the most modest of those suggests a departure from the status quo.

The majority judgment on the ultimate issue is that of Moldaver and Brown JJ. In general, that judgment departs least from the settled orthodoxy, in the sense that most of the other judgments call for greater departures from the current approach. But even Moldaver and Brown JJ speak about challenge for cause as though it should be more freely available than previous caselaw has suggested. Rather than insisting on social science evidence or a particular type of prejudice or even requiring that the standard for judicial notice be met, they say:

> While widespread bias cannot be presumed in all cases, the parties do not face an onerous burden for raising a challenge for cause. The accused person or the Crown must merely demonstrate a reasonable possibility that bias or prejudicial attitudes exist in the community, with respect to relevant characteristics of the accused or victim,

---

had defence counsel thought that some jurors would have a race-based sympathy for the victim, challenge for cause would not have been available, and so the use of peremptory challenges would have been the only available option.

365 *Spence*, above note 363 at para 21.

366 See the discussion in Steve Coughlan, "*R v Chouhan*: Signs of Seismic Shift in Jury Selection" (2021) 72 *Criminal Reports* (7th) 125.

> and could taint the impartiality of the jurors. In most cases, expert evidence will not be necessary: challenges for cause must be available wherever the experience of the trial judge, in consultation with counsel, dictates that, in the case before them, a realistic potential for partiality arises.[367]

*Chouhan* also speaks about challenge for cause being available on bases other than those which have been generally accepted to date: they say that it might be based on "characteristics of the accused, complainant or victim, such as race, addiction, religion, occupation, sexual orientation or gender expression."[368]

Trial courts have begun to take this broader approach to allowing questions to be asked on a challenge for cause on bases that likely would not have been permitted in the past. Beyond general questions about pre-trial publicity or race, questions have been allowed going to whether jurors have beliefs about men of colour charged with crimes against white women, about drug users, or about people who either engage in sex work or pay for sex.[369] An issue which remains the subject of some debate in lower courts is whether the new direction given by *Chouhan* overrides that in *Find*: that is, whether it is now possible to have challenge for cause questions based on the nature of the offence.[370]

Separate from the issue of when challenge for cause is to be allowed at all is the issue of the procedure to be used.

When challenge for cause is allowed, the process to be followed is primarily set out in the *Code*. The *Code* provides that the challenge itself is decided by the trial judge,[371] and in *Chouhan* the Court suggested that it would be appropriate for the trial judge, "as an impartial person adjudicating impartiality," to be the person who poses the questions to the jurors.[372] For the first juror, the accused decides whether to challenge for cause before the Crown, and from that point on they alternate who goes first.[373]

---

367 *Chouhan*, above note 276 at para 62.

368 *Chouhan*, above note 276 at para 64.

369 See *Bhogal*, above note 331, and *Martin*, above note 331.

370 See *Bhogal*, above note 331; *Martin*, above note 331; *R v Coban*, 2021 BCSC 2154; and *R c Boudreau-Chartrand*, 2023 QCCS 3820.

371 This is a new innovation with Bill C-75, above note 33: see the discussion above under Section C(3)(a), "Mechanics of Selecting Jurors."

372 *Chouhan*, above note 276 at para 67. Trial courts have not all seen this as mandatory: see *Martin*, above note 331.

373 When there is more than one accused, the accused alternate with the Crown as a group, though each accused is separately entitled to challenge: s 635(2). The accused are required to decide whether to challenge in the order that their names appear on the indictment, unless they agree on a different order. Although this requirement might place the first accused at a tactical

The judge has discretion to permit submissions by counsel following the questioning.[374]

It will generally be an error that leads to a new trial if the *Code* provisions for challenge for cause are not followed. In *Barrow*, for example, the trial judge permitted jurors to request exemption on the basis that they would be unable to decide impartially, not simply on obvious grounds such as relation to the accused, but based on pre-trial publicity. These exemption requests took place without the accused and were held to usurp a portion of the challenge for cause process.[375] Similarly, in *R v Guérin* the trial judge largely took over the roles of questioning jurors and deciding their impartiality.[376] In each case a new trial was ordered.

One last issue that arises in the context of challenges should be discussed: the amount of information that the parties have about the potential jurors. Typically parties have been unlikely to know much about the members of the jury panel. This situation — or more accurately efforts by the Crown to avoid it — has led to litigation.

This issue first reached the Supreme Court in *R v Latimer*,[377] where the RCMP, having prepared a questionnaire in cooperation with the Crown prosecutor, administered it to thirty prospective jurors. The questionnaire asked the views of the prospective jurors on a number of issues, including religion, abortion, and euthanasia. The Crown did not disclose the questionnaire or the direct contact with jurors to the defence or the trial judge. In very brief reasons, the Court described this as a "flagrant abuse of process and interference with the administration of justice," which warranted a new trial.[378] The issue, it held, was not whether the RCMP's behaviour influenced the jury's deliberations, but that it violated the principle that justice must not only be done, but be seen to be done.

---

disadvantage compared to fellow accused, it does not violate the *Charter*: *Suzack*, above note 47.

374 *Hubbert*, above note 339; *R v Moore-McFarlane* (2001), 47 CR (5th) 203 (Ont CA). These decisions were based on the old system where the triers of the challenge were other jurors, but there is no obvious reason submissions should not be available when the judge decides.

375 *Barrow*, above note 27.

376 (1984), 13 CCC (3d) 231 (Que CA). Since Bill C-75 that would of course be the correct procedure, but it was not at the time.

377 [1997] 1 SCR 217 [*Latimer*].

378 *Ibid* at para 43. Interestingly this seems to be the only instance of the Court finding an abuse of process and ordering a new trial as opposed to ordering a stay of proceedings prior to the decision in *Babos*, above note 228, finding that the two were not intrinsically linked. However, that point is not relevant to the jury screening issue.

Perhaps surprisingly, given the strong language of the Court in *Latimer*, similar issues continued to arise. In some cases, despite a Practice Memorandum directing them not to do so, Crown prosecutors asked police officers for information concerning prospective jurors and then acted on it. The practice led to an investigation by Ontario's Information and Privacy Commissioner,[379] and eventually to a trilogy of cases at the Supreme Court: *R v Yumnu*,[380] *R v Emms*,[381] and *R v Davey*.[382] The result of those decisions is what has generally been regarded as a relaxation of the strong position taken in *Latimer* against "jury-vetting."

The Court concluded that, since having a criminal record is a basis for exclusion from a jury and self-reporting is not necessarily successful as a screening method, it is acceptable for the Crown to ask police to do a criminal record check on prospective jurors. That was the primary thing that police had been asked to do in the trilogy, and it was a "far cry from the conduct at issue in *Latimer*."[383] The police cannot be *asked* to do more than that, but if they discover other relevant information in the course of a criminal record check, they can give this information to the Crown. The Court noted in *Yumnu* that such information might be relevant not only to whether to peremptorily challenge (a point that is no longer relevant), but also to whether to ask the judge to remove the juror as obviously partial or to make a challenge for cause.[384] Indeed, the Court noted that the information might be relevant for the Crown to ask the judge to have the juror stand aside, a justification which is now more relevant given the added "maintaining public confidence" ground in section 633.

If the Crown does receive any such information from the police, it is required to give that to the defence, in accordance with its ordinary disclosure obligations. However, independent of asking the police to check official records, Crown prosecutors are also entitled to ask police officers, as part of the "prosecution team," for their general impressions of potential jurors, and there is nothing wrong with using this collective experience and judgment in exercising discretionary decisions. These sorts of general impressions or public knowledge need not be

---

379 Information and Privacy Commissioner, *Excessive Background Checks Conducted on Prospective Jurors: A Special Investigation Report* (Toronto: Information and Privacy Commissioner of Ontario, 2009).

380 2012 SCC 73 [*Yumnu*].

381 2012 SCC 74 [*Emms*].

382 2012 SCC 75 [*Davey*].

383 *Emms*, above note 381 at para 49.

384 *Yumnu*, above note 380 at para 54.

disclosed to the defence, since they are not linked to the prosecution's role as an agent of the state.[385]

Despite this further guidance from the Supreme Court, improper investigations into potential jurors by the police have not ceased entirely.[386]

## FURTHER READINGS

Archibald, Bruce. "Prosecutors, Democracy and the Public Interest: Prosecutorial Discretion and Its Limits in Canada" (Paper delivered at the XVIth Congress of the International Academy of Comparative Law, Brisbane, Australia, 14–20 July 2002).

Baar, Carl. "Criminal Court Delay and the *Charter*: The Use and Misuse of Social Facts in Judicial Policy Making" (1993) 72 *Canadian Bar Review* 305.

Barnhorst, Richard. "Achieving Restraint in the Use of the Criminal Justice System: Canada's Youth Criminal Justice Act" 2024 72 *Criminal Law Quarterly* 5.

Cournoyer, Guy. "Case Management Powers: From Felderhof to Jordan" in Benjamin L Berger, Emma Cunliffe, & James Stribopoulos, *To Ensure that Justice is Done: Essays in Memory of Marc Rosenberg* (Toronto: Thompson Reuters, 2017).

Coughlan, Steve. "*R. v. Find*: Preserving the Presumption of Innocence" (2001) 42 *Criminal Reports* (5th) 31.

———. "Making Trial Within a Reasonable Time a Right Once More" (2017) 81 *Supreme Court Law Review* 213.

———. "Patterns in the *Jordan* Case Law One Year After *Cody*" (2018) 42 *Criminal Reports* (7th) 342.

———. "Threading Together Abuse of Process and Exclusion of Evidence: How it Became Possible to Rebuke Mr. Big" (2015) 71 *Supreme Court Law Review* 415.

---

385 *Davey*, above note 382 at paras 38–46.

386 See *R v Oland*, 2018 NBQB 258, where a police officer who was assisting the Crown conducted improper investigations on both potential and sworn jurors. Upon discovering the action Crown counsel disclosed it to the defence, who successfully applied for a mistrial. By consent the trial was begun again on a judge-alone basis.

———. "*R v Chouhan*: Signs of Seismic Shift in Jury Selection" (2021) 72 *Criminal Reports* (7th) 125.

——— & Alex Gorlewski. *The Anatomy of Criminal Procedure: A Visual Guide to the Law*, 2nd ed (Toronto: University of Toronto Press, 2026).

Kaiser, HA. "*Babos*: Further Narrowing Access to Stay of Proceedings Where the Integrity of the Judicial Process Is Implicated" (2014) 8 *Criminal Reports* (7th) 59.

Law Reform Commission of Canada. *Trial Within a Reasonable Time: A Working Paper* (Ottawa: Canada Communication Group, 1994).

Miller, Christian A. "Peremptory Challenges During Jury Selection as Institutional Racism: An Investigation Within the Context of the Gerald Stanley Trial (*R v Stanley*, 2018 SKQB)" (2019) 67 *Criminal Law Quarterly* 215.

Patrick, Jessica. "Six Months of *Jordan*: A Statistical Overview" (2017) 35 *Criminal Reports* (7th) 348.

Plaxton, Michael. "The Biased Juror and Appellate Review: A Reply to Professor Coughlan" (2001) 44 *Criminal Reports* (5th) 294.

Pomerant, David. *Multiculturalism, Representation and the Jury Selection Process in Canadian Criminal Cases* (Ottawa: Department of Justice Canada, Research and Statistics Directorate, 1994).

Quigley, Tim. "Have We Seen the End of Improper Jury Vetting?" (2013) 98 *Criminal Reports* (6th) 109.

———. "*Babos*: Balancing Test Unnecessarily Restricts Residual Category for Stay as Abuse of Process" (2014) 8 *Criminal Reports* (7th) 55.

Rose, David. *Quigley's Criminal Procedure in Canada* (Toronto: Thomson Reuters, 2021) (loose-leaf), ch 16, 19, & 20.

Rose, V Gordon, & James RP Ogloff. "Challenge for Cause in Canadian Criminal Jury Trials: Legal and Psychological Perspectives" (2002) 45 *Criminal Law Quarterly* 210.

Ruby, Clayton. "Trial Within a Reasonable Time Under Section 11(b): The Ontario Court of Appeal Disconnects from the Supreme Court" (2013) 2 *Criminal Reports* (7th) 91.

Schneider, Richard D, Hy Bloom, & Mark Heerema. *Mental Health Courts: Decriminalizing the Mentally Ill* (Toronto: Irwin Law, 2007).

SPENCER, DEREK. "Extending *Jordan* to Consider Verdict and Sentencing Delays" (2019) 50 *Criminal Reports* (7th) 30.

STUART, DON. *Charter Justice in Canadian Criminal Law*, 7th ed (Toronto: Thomson Carswell, 2018) ch 2 and 6.

TANOVICH, DAVID M. "The Future of Challenge for Cause in the Wake of *Williams*" (1998) 15 *Criminal Reports* (5th) 250.

VIDMAR, NEIL. "Pretrial Prejudice in Canada: A Comparative Perspective on the Criminal Jury" (1996) 79 *Judicature* 249.

WILSON, BERTHA. "Will Women Judges Really Make a Difference?" (1990) 28 *Osgoode Hall Law Journal* 507. http://doi.org/10.60082/2817-5069.1764.

CHAPTER 11

# THE TRIAL PROCESS

## A. INTRODUCTION

This chapter focuses on the actual process of a trial. That discussion must begin at the pre-trial stage, with reference to the charging documents that bring a person to court and set out the case to be met at trial. From there we move to a discussion of the pleas an accused can enter, and the various stages of a trial, including opening statements, examination of witnesses, closing arguments, and charging of the jury. We will then consider the rules surrounding jury deliberations and finally conclude with a discussion of the various powers a judge can exercise during the trial.

## B. THE CHARGE DOCUMENT

### 1) Informations, Indictments, and Direct Indictments

When a person is put on trial for an offence, there must be some particular document specifying the charge against that person. Initially, charges are laid by means of an information,[1] which was discussed in Chapter 6. When an accused is tried by a provincial court judge, that information is the relevant trial document, whereas when the accused

1 *Criminal Code*, ss 504 and 505.

is tried in a superior court, a different document — an indictment — is prepared.[2] Conceptually, the transition from provincial court to superior court is by means of a preliminary inquiry in the provincial court, following which the accused would (or on rare occasions would not) proceed to trial in the superior court: see Chapter 9, Preliminary Inquiry. The *Code* provisions have therefore been structured around the assumption that the indictment is prepared following the preliminary inquiry, that a preliminary inquiry is routinely held, and that that preliminary inquiry considers the sufficiency of the entire case against the accused and decides whether the accused should stand trial or not.

For that reason the *Code* provides, for example, that the indictment can include not only the charge on which the person was ordered to stand trial, but also any charge founded on the facts disclosed at the preliminary inquiry.[3] That rule — that an indictment can be preferred on a charge where the facts making it out are disclosed at the preliminary inquiry — does not allow a prosecutor to prefer an indictment on the very charge for which the accused is discharged. Rather, that power is intended to allow the preferment of charges for other offences that are disclosed at the preliminary inquiry.[4] Nonetheless, the Crown *can* lay an indictment concerning the offence for which an accused has been discharged: section 577 of the *Criminal Code*, discussed below, permits exactly that, although it requires the personal consent in writing of the attorney general or deputy attorney general.[5]

In fact, however, the assumption that a preliminary inquiry is a relatively wide-ranging inquiry into all the facts related to the case has not been accurate for some time. Amendments to the *Code* in 2004 meant that preliminary inquiries were limited to the specific issues about which the parties (most likely the accused) requested evidence be led. Amendments in 2019 gave the judge the ability to unilaterally limit the inquiry to particular issues.[6] Both of those rules limit the likely applicability of a rule permitting an indictment based on the facts

---

2 Section 566(1). Note that the power in s 577 to proceed by direct indictment means that there could be occasions when an indictment is the first charge document prepared.

3 Section 574.

4 *R v Tapaquon*, [1993] 4 SCR 535.

5 See the discussion in Chapter 3, Section B(1)(a) concerning consent of the attorney general.

6 See s 537(1.01), added by Bill C-75, *An Act to amend the Criminal Code, the Youth Criminal Justice Act and other Acts and to make consequential amendments to other Acts*, Royal Assent June 21, 2019. That Bill also limited preliminary inquiries to offences punishable by fourteen years imprisonment or more, which means that they will be much less common to begin with.

disclosed, because not very many "extraneous" facts are likely to be disclosed.

Further, the primary rule around indictments in section 574(1) talks about what the prosecutor can do in relation to the charges and evidence at the preliminary inquiry, which reflects an assumption that there normally will *be* such a proceeding. That assumption too is no longer correct. The amendments in 2004 made preliminary inquiries only available on request (typically of the accused). The amendments in 2019 limited preliminary inquiries to offences punishable by fourteen years or more imprisonment, which is a small subset of all indictable offences. Accordingly there is a need for a separate power to prefer indictments, which is found in section 574(1.1): when no preliminary inquiry was requested or was available, the prosecutor can prefer an indictment in respect of a charge set out in an information or informations.

In a sense, given the current limited availability of preliminary inquiries, this power in section 574(1.1) to prefer an indictment without a preliminary inquiry should be regarded as the norm. At one point, however, to do so was seen as a discretionary and unusual step, provided for in section 577. That prosecutorial power continues to play a relevant role, because it allows the Crown in some circumstances to override the accused's choice or the preliminary inquiry justice's decision.

Section 577 allows for "direct indictments," which is a special power that in effect overrides procedures that the accused would otherwise be entitled to benefit from, That is, it permits the prosecutor to prefer an indictment if the preliminary inquiry has been commenced but not concluded,[7] or even if the accused was discharged following the preliminary inquiry. This power also applies where a committal for trial has been quashed,[8] or where a trial judge has specifically declined to order an accused to stand trial on a charge not laid but disclosed in the evidence at the preliminary inquiry.[9] The section also says that the power can be used "even if the accused has not been given the opportunity to request a preliminary inquiry," but that language pre-dates the 2019 amendments which removed the right to request a preliminary inquiry from the accused for the great majority of offences: the interplay between that old wording and the new rule might need to be

---

7 Courts had already held that the power was available in this situation, but the *Code* has since been amended to explicitly state it. See *R v Stewart (No 2)* (1977), 35 CCC (2d) 281 (Ont CA).

8 *R v Charlie* (1998), 126 CCC (3d) 513 (BCCA).

9 *R v McKibbon*, [1984] 1 SCR 131.

sorted out. This is particularly so because, since a direct indictment normally overrides what would otherwise be the accused's entitlements, it can only be preferred with the personal consent in writing of the attorney general or deputy attorney general.[10] Where the reason the accused could not request a preliminary inquiry was that it is not available statutorily, the accused was deprived of nothing and there is no reason such special protection is required.

The attorney general's power to authorize a direct indictment cannot be reviewed by a court.[11] It does not violate the *Charter*, provided that the accused receives full disclosure and nothing else in the circumstances makes the action an abuse of process.[12] Indeed, the power is seen as having potentially beneficial effects, such as protecting an accused's right to a trial within a reasonable time, protecting the physical or psychological health of witnesses, preserving Crown evidence, avoiding multiple proceedings when there are co-accused, and so on.[13]

Once it is preferred, the indictment provides a fresh starting point upon which the future proceedings are based, and an accused is no longer entitled to look behind it, for example, to attempt to quash by *certiorari* the committal for trial. The indictment is preferred and then acts as a type of barrier, once it is lodged with the trial court at the start of the accused's trial, in front of a court ready to proceed.[14]

Whether the trial proceeds by information or indictment, the document is the starting point for the trial and sets out the case the accused has to meet. The rules set out in Parts XVI and XX of the *Code* that

---

10 Section 577(b) also permits direct indictments in private prosecutions where a judge of the court permits the direct indictment to be preferred.

11 *R v Balderstone* (1983), 8 CCC (3d) 532 (Man CA), leave to appeal to SCC refused [1983] 2 SCR v; *R v Stolar* (1983), 32 CR (3d) 342 (Man CA), leave to appeal to SCC refused [1983] 1 SCR xiv [*Stolar*].

12 *R v Ertel* (1987), 58 CR (3d) 252 (Ont CA), leave to appeal to SCC refused (1987), 61 CR (3d) xxix; *R v Arviv* (1985), 45 CR (3d) 354 (Ont CA), leave to appeal to SCC refused [1985] 1 SCR v; *Stolar*, above note 11.

13 *R v SJL*, 2009 SCC 14 [*SJL*]. The Court refers at para 38 to ten reasons often cited in support of direct indictments, acknowledging that some are vaguely worded and that not all will be relevant in a given case. The Court also concludes in *SJL* that direct indictments are available in the case of young persons in the relatively few cases where they can be prosecuted by way of indictment.

14 *R v Chabot*, [1980] 2 SCR 985. See also *R v Regan*, 2002 SCC 12, where a 5:4 majority of the Court were of the view that the direct indictment in that case acted to "cleanse" any concerns about loss of objectivity at an earlier stage. Since the attorney general personally needed to consent, it was reasonable to conclude that a fresh, careful, and objective review of the case must have taken place.

govern compelling appearance and jury trials also apply to summary conviction offences by virtue of section 795, with only minor variations, so the requirements for an information and an indictment can be discussed together. The Supreme Court has stressed the importance of this document, holding that "it is fundamental to a fair trial that an accused know the charge or charges he or she must meet."[15] As we will see in subsection B(5) below, though, the general tenor of the caselaw has been to considerably downplay the significance of the technical requirements for these documents or any failures to comply with those requirements.

## 2) Joinder and Severance of Counts

Although many rules surrounding indictments were originally developed to a great extent at common law, they are now primarily set out in the *Code*. There are many rules in the *Code* and there has been a good deal of litigation over these issues, but a good general guideline is that relatively few firm limitations are imposed on the structure of indictments. An indictment (Form 4 from the *Code*) can contain any number of "counts."[16] Each count is to cover a single transaction, though this rule is specifically said to apply "in general."[17] The concept of a "single transaction" has so far been given a broad interpretation, but there are questions as to whether that is the proper approach.[18] Further, although for many years a trial could not concern more than one indictment, the Court has relaxed that requirement. It is now possible to hold a trial on one or more indictments simultaneously,[19] provided that the accused consents, or the trial judge feels that it is in the

15 *R v GR*, [2005] 2 SCR 371 at para 2.

16 "Count" is defined in s 2 of the *Code* as a "charge in an information or indictment."

17 Section 581(1).

18 See the discussion of *R v Lilly*, [1983] 1 SCR 794 [*Lilly*] at Section B(5)(c), below in this chapter, in which twenty-one separate withdrawals from a trust account were the foundation for a single count of fraud and, in general, the discussion of division of counts. See also *R v MRH*, 2019 SCC 46 [*MRH*], where the Court held:

the Crown practice of drafting a single count of an indictment to capture multiple distinct incidents creates the risk that the accused may be convicted without the jurors' unanimous agreement on any one underlying incident. We leave for another day whether the law supports such a practice.

19 For an explanation of this issue in chart form, see Steve Coughlan and Alex Gorlewski, *The Anatomy of Criminal Procedure: A Visual Guide to the Law* (Toronto: Irwin Law, 2019) [*Anatomy of Criminal Procedure*], Chart 3.1(d), "Joinder and Severance of Counts."

interests of justice and the charges could have been jointly charged in a single indictment.[20] This latter requirement imposes few restrictions.[21] Section 589 prevents any charge from being joined with murder, though even this rule is subject to exceptions if the other offence arises out of the same transaction or the accused consents to the joinder.[22] Summary conviction and indictable offences can be tried together, provided the accused consents and the accused's election and the other procedures make it possible to do so.[23] Provincial offences and summary conviction offences can also be joined in a single trial, since the same court has jurisdiction to try each separately.[24] Otherwise, the limits on joinder of counts are case by case, according to the criteria in section 591(3) of the *Code*. That provision allows a judge to order an indictment to be severed in order to send some counts or some co-accused to a separate trial.

A preliminary inquiry judge does not have jurisdiction to sever.[25] Until recently the rule was that severance decisions had to be made by the trial judge, though changes to the *Code* in 2019 make it possible for a case management judge to deal with this issue.[26] The judge's decision is subject to review on appeal, but it is not to be interfered with unless the judge has acted unjudicially or the ruling resulted in an injustice.[27] The former question looks at the circumstances at the time the ruling was made, while the latter takes into account as well the unfolding of the trial and of the verdicts.[28] Normally, an application to sever is made

---

20 *R v Clunas*, [1992] 1 SCR 595 [*Clunas*].

21 See, for example, s 574 or s 789(1)(b) of the *Code*.

22 See the thorough discussion of this section in *R v Riley* (2008), 229 CCC (3d) 266 (Ont SCJ). See also s 473(1.1), which permits an offence in s 469, which otherwise must be tried by a judge and jury, to be joined with any other offence and tried without a jury, provided the Crown and accused both consent. See also *R v Manasseri*, 2016 ONCA 703 [*Manasseri*], finding the "same transaction" rule to be satisfied when two accused separately assaulted the victim, but the assaults were only a few minutes apart, were in the same general location, and were causally connected.

23 *Clunas*, above note 20. Effectively, this requires the trial to be in a provincial court, since that is the only option properly available to the accused for a summary conviction offence.

24 *R v Sciascia*, 2017 SCC 57.

25 *R v Hynes*, [2001] 3 SCR 623 [*Hynes*].

26 Section 551.1. See the discussion of this issue in Chapter 10, Section B(1).

27 *R v Litchfield*, [1993] 4 SCR 333 [*Litchfield*]. See also *R v Cumor*, 2019 ONCA 747 at para 56: "A trial judge's severance ruling is entitled to deference and will only be interfered with on appeal if the judge acted unreasonably or if the ruling resulted in an injustice."

28 *R v Last*, 2009 SCC 45 at para 15 [*Last*].

on a pre-trial basis because the decision will dictate the course of the trial.[29] However, section 591(4) permits the order to be made before or during the trial, with the jury being discharged with regard to any counts or accused that are severed during trial.

The *Code* gives little in the way of guidance regarding the criteria for severance decisions, stating only that the court can do so where "the interests of justice so require."[30] The Supreme Court has developed considerations to take into account when deciding whether to sever counts. These include

> the general prejudice to the accused; the legal and factual nexus between the counts; the complexity of the evidence; whether the accused intends to testify on one count but not another; the possibility of inconsistent verdicts; the desire to avoid a multiplicity of proceedings; the use of similar fact evidence at trial; the length of the trial having regard to the evidence to be called; the potential prejudice to the accused with respect to the right to be tried within a reasonable time; and the existence of antagonistic defences as between coaccused persons.[31]

Because society has an interest in avoiding a multiplicity of proceedings, the onus is on the accused, on a balance of probabilities, to show that separate trials should be held.[32] The obvious risk in holding a joint trial is that evidence admissible on only one count will affect the decision on another count. A trial judge can give a limiting instruction about the appropriate use of evidence to the jury, but if that was seen as always being a sufficient safeguard, then prejudice would essentially cease to be a relevant factor in the analysis.[33] Further, trial judges must take great care in distinguishing the two issues of severability and similar fact evidence, particularly as the onus is on the accused for the first, but on the Crown for the second.[34]

Where an application to sever is made later in the trial, it ought to be based on some prejudice that was not apparent at the start.[35] For example, an accused could decide at the close of the Crown's case that the Crown's witnesses were not credible on some counts. The accused might therefore feel that it was not necessary to take the stand with

---

29 *Litchfield*, above note 27.

30 Section 591(3).

31 *Last*, above note 28 at para 18.

32 *R v Cross* (1996), 112 CCC (3d) 410 (Que CA) [*Cross*].

33 *Last*, above note 28 at para 16.

34 *R v Arp*, [1998] 3 SCR 339.

35 *R v DAC* (1996), 72 BCAC 227 (CA), aff'd [1997] 1 SCR 8 [*DAC*].

regard to those counts, but that it was necessary to testify with regard to other counts. In such circumstances, the accused's fair trial right and right to silence might be brought into conflict if the counts were not severed. At such a late stage, however, the burden on the accused is very heavy and an assertion that the accused wished to testify on some counts but not on others would not be sufficient. The accused would be required to outline the basic nature of the proposed defence to justify severance and the consequent retrial on the severed charges.[36]

## 3) Joinder and Severance of Accused

Similar considerations arise in deciding whether to sever multiple accused from the same indictment and hold separate trials, though there are additional issues.[37] Even more strongly in these circumstances, the practical goal of avoiding multiple proceedings favours not holding separate trials over the same facts unless it is necessary. The general rule is that accused who are alleged to have committed a crime together should be tried together.[38] This principle is adhered to quite firmly. When co-accused blame one another, they might be able to cross-examine one another in ways not available to the Crown, for example, with regard to propensity or similar issues.[39] This could result in the fair trial right of one accused conflicting with the pre-trial right to silence of a co-accused, if one accused wants to point to the failure of the other to cooperate with the police. Even then, the Court has held that the solution in such situations is not to sever the trials, but to balance the competing rights of the two accused along with the interest of the state in a joint trial. The Court has held that in such circumstances of a "cut-throat defence," the policy reasons favouring a joint trial apply with equal or greater force than normally.[40]

Nonetheless, there are exceptions to the joint trial rule. First, a young person and an adult cannot be tried together.[41] More generally, a trial judge has discretion to sever the trials of co-accused in accordance

---

36 See *DAC*, *ibid*, and *Cross*, above note 32.

37 For an explanation of this issue in chart form, see *Anatomy of Criminal Procedure*, above note 19, Chart 3.1(c), "Joinder and Severance of Accused."

38 *R v Chow*, 2005 SCC 24. See also *R v Torbiak and Gillis* (1978), 40 CCC (2d) 193 (Ont CA) [*Torbiak*]; *R v Miller and Cockriel* (1975), 33 CRNS 129 (BCCA), aff'd on other issues (1976), 70 DLR (3d) 324 (SCC); *R v Agawa and Mallett* (1975), 31 CRNS 293 (Ont CA) [*Agawa*].

39 *R v Kendall* (1987), 57 CR (3d) 249 (Ont CA).

40 *R v Crawford; R v Creighton*, [1995] 1 SCR 858 [*Crawford*]. See, for example, *R v Brincheski*, 2016 MBCA 73 or *R v Zvolensky*, 2017 ONCA 273.

41 *SJL*, above note 13.

with section 591(3) where it is required in the interests of justice. In deciding the issue, courts should consider not only whether the co-accused will have antagonistic defences, but also other issues, such as the possibility of inconsistent verdicts from separate trials (which militates against severance), whether evidence admissible against one accused is inadmissible against another,[42] as well as the cost of multiple trials to the participants and the criminal justice system and impairment of the truthseeking function of the trial.[43]

The fact that one of the accused would be a compellable witness for the other accused in a separate trial but not in a joint trial is relevant, but not determinative. In *R v Agawa and Mallett*, for example, the Ontario Court of Appeal upheld the trial judge's decision not to grant separate trials in such circumstances because there was not sufficient evidence that the co-accused would have given evidence useful to the applicant even if he were made compellable.[44] The question is whether the co-accused's evidence could reasonably affect the verdict by creating a reasonable doubt.[45] As with many issues, cases have divided on the proper way to proceed. Some decisions have held that counsel's assertion that a co-accused has made out-of-court statements that would be helpful must be taken at face value and justify severance. Others have held that granting severance simply on the allegation that one co-accused might give evidence in defence of the other is to reverse the presumption in favour of joint trials. Some authority suggests that if an accused shows that a co-accused's evidence is likely to raise a reasonable doubt, there is no longer any discretion not to grant the severance application. Much will depend on the facts of the individual case.[46]

The fact that some evidence will be admissible against one accused but not others is also relevant, but again it is not sufficient to require severance. Where several accused have all made statements, for example, the content of each statement might become admissible for its truth against the accused making it, but not against each of the co-accused. Particularly in jury trials, the trial judge then has the "added and heavy

42 *DAC*, above note 35; *Cross*, above note 32.

43 *R v Baranec*, 2020 BCCA 156 at para 210 [*Baranec*].

44 *Agawa*, above note 38.

45 *Torbiak*, above note 38. In that case, the trial judge did not apply this test and refused to sever because the co-accused's testimony would only be corroborative. The Court of Appeal found this to be an error but declined to grant the appeal nonetheless, on the basis that the error did not amount to a miscarriage of justice.

46 See generally *R v Boulet* (1987), 40 CCC (3d) 38 (Que CA), leave to appeal to SCC refused [1989] 1 SCR vi; *R v Szczerba* (2002), 314 AR 114 (QB); and the cases discussed in those cases.

burden of complete and proper instruction to the jury on the precise limits of the evidence admissible against each of the accused, and hence the limited use to which these statements can be put."[47] The Court has suggested that in conspiracy trials where the evidence is much stronger against one accused, and particularly where a damaging statement will be admissible against one but not the other, the safer course is to order separate trials.[48] But that does not mean separate trials are always required, and a judge could correctly conclude that any prejudice can be sufficiently guarded against through clear instructions as to the use they can and cannot make of evidence.[49] There is a strong presumption that jurors are capable of understanding and following such instructions.[50]An additional consideration in the decision whether to sever accused is the right to a trial within a reasonable time. In *R v Jordan*, the Supreme Court adopted an approach to that right which imposed presumptive ceilings on the length of time a trial could take before there would be a section 11(b) violation.[51] That analysis takes into account whether delay has been "caused solely by the conduct of the defence," which will decrease the likelihood that that accused will be found to have had their right violated.[52] When there are co-accused, however, and one of them has requested an adjournment or otherwise created delay, that delay will not be seen as having been caused by the other co-accused. In that event the ceiling for conducting a trial with regard to those other accused might be exceeded if the trial remains a joint one, which creates pressure in some cases to sever the accused.[53] However, in such situations there still might not be a section 11(b) violation if exceptional circumstances are established. It has been held that in this context to show exceptional circumstances:

> the Crown must establish that: (1) the joint trial is being undertaken in the interests of justice; (2) the delay has arisen because of the joint

47 *R v McFall*, [1980] 1 SCR 321 at 338. The quote is from Estey J, who dissented in the result because the majority held that any errors were harmless ones covered by the curative provisions in the *Code*.

48 *R v Guimond*, [1979] 1 SCR 960.

49 See, for example, *R v Boima*, 2018 BCCA 297.

50 *Baranec*, above note 43 at para 214.

51 *R v Jordan*, 2016 SCC 27.

52 *Ibid* at para 63.

53 See, for example, *Manasseri*, above note 22, holding at para 373 that "A joint trial is not some magic wand the Crown can wave to make a co-accused's s. 11(b) rights disappear." However, see also *R v Singh*, 2016 BCCA 427 81: "Severance is not a panacea when delay issues arise in a multi-party indictment." In addition see *R v Gopie*, 2017 ONCA 728, *R v Jurkus*, 2018 ONCA 489, or *R v Brissett*, 2019 ONCA 11.

> trial; (3) the delay is unforeseen or reasonably unavoidable; and (4) the Crown could not reasonably have ameliorated that delay.[54]

When co-accused are tried together, the order in which their names appear on the indictment settles the order in which they will be called upon to do many things at trial, such as exercise challenges, question witnesses, decide whether to call a defence, and make closing addresses. The Crown has discretion over what order to choose for the indictment and in doing so can make tactical decisions that it is not called upon to explain, short of an abuse of process.[55]

## 4) Content of Charges

Any given count, whether it is in a multi-count information or dealt with individually, "shall contain in substance a statement that the accused or defendant committed an indictable offence therein specified."[56] Section 581 continues by setting out some rules for that statement, which can be "in popular language without technical averments," in the words of the *Code* provision, or in words that give the accused notice of the offence that they are charged with.[57] Whatever is done, however, the key rule from section 581(3) is that

> a count shall contain sufficient detail of the circumstances of the alleged offence to give to the accused reasonable information with respect to the act or omission to be proved against him and to identify the transaction referred to but otherwise the absence or insufficiency of details does not vitiate the count.

The *Code* then offers further detail to help determine whether this standard is met. The count can refer to the particular section under which the accused is charged, as a way of helping to give sufficient

---

54 *R v Tran*, 2023 ONCA 532 at para 40. In that case there had been delays caused by two of Tran's co-accused, with the result that the trial did not complete until nine days after the presumptive ceiling. The Ontario Court of Appeal held at para 43 that "it would have been thoroughly unreasonable to expect the Crown to abandon a joint trial format that was undertaken in the interests of justice to avoid a nine-day delay." However, they acknowledged that other circumstances, such as those in *Manasseri*, above note 22, could mean that the Crown was required to abandon a joint trial plan.

55 *R v Sandham* (2009), 248 CCC (3d) 392 (Ont SCJ).

56 Section 581(1).

57 For an explanation of this issue in chart form, see *Anatomy of Criminal Procedure*, above note 19, Chart 3.1(a), "Contents of Charges: Duplicity" and Chart 3.1(b), "Contents of Charges: Insufficiency."

notice.[58] Further, the *Code* specifies that the absence of details does not automatically render a count insufficient and lists particular omissions that are not fatal, such as that "it does not name the person injured or intended or attempted to be injured," "it does not specify the means by which the alleged offence was committed," or "it does not name or describe with precision any person, place or thing."[59] The issue of sufficiency of counts is discussed in greater detail at Section B(5)(b), the section immediately below in this chapter, and the rules here are closely connected to those issues.

The Court has noted that there are two interrelated rules dealing with indictments: section 581(3), dealing with insufficient detail, and the "surplusage rule," dealing with additional unnecessary detail.[60] The general rule is that the purpose of each count in an indictment is to put the accused on notice of the case to be met: the goal is to avoid the excessive technicalities of old rules while seeing to it that the accused understands the real nature of the allegation. Accordingly, a count must have sufficient detail, and an accused is normally entitled to expect that the Crown will be required to prove all the details of any allegation made. However, it is open to a court to find that a detail actually provided in a count is "surplusage," and therefore that some fact need not be proven despite being alleged. It is not always clear in practice whether a detail is mere surplusage.

For example, in *R v Saunders* the Crown charged a number of accused with conspiracy to import heroin. The charge would have been perfectly acceptable had it not specified which narcotic was to be imported. However, having specified heroin, the Crown was obliged to prove that the conspiracy related to that narcotic in particular.[61] Similarly, in *R v NC*[62] the accused was charged with trafficking in cocaine, though the evidence at trial showed that the substance she had claimed to be cocaine was actually a mixture of baby powder and aspirin. This would have been an offence nonetheless, since the *Narcotic Control Act* provision also made it an offence to traffic in any substance held out to be a narcotic.[63] However, the Québec Court of Appeal held that, having

58 Section 581(5).

59 Section 583. The *Code* also creates special rules for some particular situations, such as that no one can be convicted of high treason (rather than treason) or first-degree murder (rather than second-degree murder) without having been specifically charged with that offence: s 582. See also the special rules in ss 581(4), 584, 585, and 586.

60 *R v Vézina*, [1986] 1 SCR 2 at para 54 [*Vézina*].

61 *R v Saunders*, [1990] 1 SCR 1020.

62 (1991), 64 CCC (3d) 45 (Que CA).

63 RSC 1985, c N-1 [since repealed].

charged the accused with trafficking in cocaine, the Crown was obliged to prove that the substance actually was cocaine: their failure to do so meant she must be acquitted.

On the other hand, in *R v Crain* the *NC* decision was distinguished on the basis that the accused in *Crain* had not actually given the powdery substance to the purchaser at the time of arrest. "Trafficking" in a substance constitutes either delivering it or offering to sell it. The court in *Crain* held that the Crown, having said that *NC* delivered cocaine, was obliged to prove it. Crain's guilt, on the other hand, depended only on her having *offered* to sell cocaine, which the Crown was able to prove she had done, whatever the substance she actually had might be.[64]

Similarly, in *R v Hanna* the accused was charged with theft of gravel from the Nova Scotia Power Commission and obtained a directed verdict because the only evidence of ownership showed that the gravel was owned by the power corporation. This decision was overturned at trial on the basis that there was no possibility that the accused could fail to identify the event that gave rise to the charge against him.[65]

To the same effect, in *R v Vézina*, the accused was charged with fraud in an information that specified the Bank of Montreal as the victim. In fact, the Crown was unable to prove that the Bank of Montreal would have suffered any loss from the accused's fraud. The Court held that the information would initially have been valid even if it had not specified a victim. Accordingly, it did not matter that the Crown was unable to prove the particular allegation, which was mere surplusage.[66]

Whether a detail will be considered surplusage, or whether the Crown will be held to proof of the fact, often depends on whether the accused's defence will be prejudiced by not taking it into account. In *Saunders*, for example, one accused had taken the stand to testify that he had been involved in one of several conspiracies to import narcotics, but not in the particular conspiracy that was to import heroin. In that case, not holding the Crown to proof of the particular narcotic alleged would have been prejudicial. In *Vézina*, on the other hand, the Court concluded that the accused would not have conducted their defence in any different manner had the allegation that the Bank of Montreal was the victim not been made, and therefore the accused suffered no prejudice. Given the absence of prejudice to the accused, the Crown was not to be held to proof of that fact. Similarly in *R c GL*, one count against the accused alleged that he had touched the complainant "avec

64 *R v Crain*, 2012 SKCA 8.

65 (1991), 109 NSR (2d) 338 (SCAD).

66 *Vézina*, above note 60.

son pénis." The complainant testified to sexual touching by the accused but not to touching with his penis. However, the accused clearly understood the allegation being made against him from the evidence and his defence was a denial of any touching whatsoever, and so there was no prejudice in disregarding that particular aspect of the charge.[67]

Date and location are sometimes essential details, but often not.[68] In *R v Hirsch*, for example, the accused was charged with making a threat on a particular date by means of a Facebook post.[69] The Crown did not prove the threat was made on the date in question, but that did not matter, because the accused was not in any doubt as to which Facebook post was the subject of the charge. On the other hand, in *R v McMillan*, the accused was charged with trafficking in a narcotic in Whitehorse on a particular date. In upholding a finding that the accused was not guilty because the particular date and time were not proven, the Yukon Territory Court of Appeal noted that in this case "specifics as to time and place were necessary to identify the transaction which formed the basis of the charge."[70] In essence, there was evidence that the accused had, at some point somewhere, been involved in trafficking narcotics, and so to mount a defence the accused had to know specifically what the Crown was alleging. Indeed, his defence was based on the fact that there was no proof of him being in Whitehorse and in possession of that narcotic on the date in question.

## 5) Remedies for a Defective Charge

The issue of what to do in the face of a defective charge is intimately bound up with the nature of the defect. We shall first discuss the potential remedies and then turn to the issue of the types of defects leading to a remedy.

---

67 *R c GL*, 2023 ONCA 750.

68 In this regard, note s 601(4.1) of the *Code*, which provides that

> A variance between the indictment or a count therein and the evidence taken is not material with respect to
>
> (a) the time when the offence is alleged to have been committed, if it is proved that the indictment was preferred within the prescribed period of limitation, if any; or
>
> (b) the place where the subject-matter of the proceedings is alleged to have arisen, if it is proved that it arose within the territorial jurisdiction of the court.

69 *R v Hirsch*, 2017 SKCA 14.

70 *R v McMillan*, 2016 YKCA 10 at para 26.

### a) Potential Remedies

The real issue is what to do when a charge is alleged not to be sufficient because it does not comply with the necessary requirements. Historically this was a tortuous area, for reasons no longer relevant. Most of these rules developed in Great Britain under a system in which crimes were defined by the common law, a system that created particular difficulties in ensuring that the accused was genuinely given notice of the charge.[71] More important, at one point the exploitation of technicalities was the only real mechanism open to courts to guard against unfairness, at a time when penalties were very strict.[72] Accordingly, much of the early caselaw dealt with quashing charges against an accused based on defects in form. In Canada, however, there has been "a gradual shift from requiring judges to quash to requiring them to amend in the stead: in fact, there remains little discretion to quash."[73] What we really see in Canada today is a reflection of the fact that the interests of the accused no longer include protection against the death penalty or exile to Australia. Rather, the accused's interests are clarity and sufficient notice in a trial on the merits. Consequently, although breach of these technical requirements can result in an accused avoiding trial occasionally, this is not a common occurrence: almost all the time, the remedy will simply be an amendment to the indictment to make it clearer.

There are three possibilities arising out of an error in an indictment. In the rare event that it is so flawed that it is an absolute nullity, then a trial judge has no jurisdiction to hear the matter, and the charge must be quashed. But in that event, the accused was never in jeopardy, and so the Crown can simply lay a new information without violating the double jeopardy rules (here, the accused's only remedy is the greater clarity of the new charge). Alternatively, the charge might be flawed, but not so flawed that it is a nullity; in that event, the trial judge is to amend the charge. If the accused has been prejudiced by the error, the trial judge is to grant an adjournment in order to remedy that prejudice. The third possibility, that the charge will be quashed, arises only if the prejudice caused by the amendment cannot be remedied by an adjournment.[74]

---

71 David Rose, *Quigley's Criminal Procedure in Canada* (Toronto: Thomson Reuters, 2021) (loose-leaf) [*Quigley*]

72 *Ibid*. See also *R v Sault Ste Marie*, [1978] 2 SCR 1299 [*Sault Ste Marie*], and *Vézina*, above note 60 at para 53: "With the abrogation of the great majority of the capital statutes in the 19th century, however, much of the rationale for the formality and strict adherence to the wording of the indictment disappeared."

73 *R v Moore*, [1988] 1 SCR 1097 at 1128 [*Moore*].

74 See *Moore*, *ibid*, and s 601.

This last possibility is a small subset of the occasions when a charge contains an error, but it is made smaller still by the provisions of section 601 that govern amendments to a defective count. First, that section requires that an objection to an indictment for a defect apparent on its face should be made before an accused has pleaded. At that stage, the likelihood that the accused has already suffered irreparable prejudice is, of course, quite small. Objection can be made after this point, but only with leave of the court. Further, the grounds upon which a judge "shall" simply make an amendment to a count are quite broad: (1) that the charge is laid under the wrong Act; (2) that it fails to state or states defectively an element of the offence, does not negative an exception that should be negatived, or is in any way defective in substance, provided the amendment to be made was disclosed by the evidence; or (3) "that the indictment or a count thereof is in any way defective in form."[75] In addition, the *Code* specifies that errors in the time or place at which the offence occurred are not material, provided limitation periods and territorial jurisdiction are complied with.[76] Finally, a trial judge is specifically authorized to amend an indictment to make it conform to the evidence presented at trial.[77]

As a result, the most likely outcome where there is a flaw in some count, or where some problem arises in proving exactly what is alleged in the count, is that the count itself will be amended. This will occur unless the accused can show that they will be prejudiced if an

---

75 Section 601(3). The Ontario Court of Appeal in *R v McConnell* (2005), 28 CR (6th) 394 (*McConnell*) observed at para 13 that:

> The cases are remarkably unhelpful as to what constitutes a defect in form or substance. An example is found in *R. v. Edgar and Rea* (1962), 1962 CanLII 560 (BC CA), 132 C.C.C. 396, 39 W.W.R. 59 (C.A.), at p. 399 C.C.C.: "if the matter pleaded be in itself insufficient, without reference to the manner of pleading it, the defect is substantial; but that if the fault is in the manner of alleging it, the defect is formal".

76 Section 601(4.1). Note that the amendment power can be used to substitute a summary conviction offence for the offence initially charged, even if the limitation period for instituting that summary conviction charge has passed: *R v Bidawi*, 2018 ONCA 698. Amending a count does not constitute initiating the proceedings, and so the limitation period will have been complied with.

77 Section 601(2). See, for example, *R v EADM*, 2008 MBCA 78, where the accused had been released on an undertaking which included a curfew. He was later charged when police found him violating that curfew, but the information charging him mistakenly referred to him being in violation of a recognizance, not an undertaking. This point was not noticed until after the Crown had closed its case and the accused had unsuccessfully argued a *Charter* application on a separate point. The Court of Appeal concluded that the trial judge had erred in not amending the information to conform to the evidence.

amendment is allowed. Prejudice, in this context, must be something real and substantial and must be irreparable.[78] More specifically, prejudice "speaks to the effect of the amendment on an accused's ability and opportunity to meet the charge,"[79] which requires a court to consider "whether the accused will have a full opportunity to meet all issues raised by the charge and whether the defence would have been conducted differently."[80]

For example, in *KR* the accused was originally charged with obstructing justice in a way which involved a quid pro quo to a witness for a false statement: after the Crown presented its evidence it was permitted to amend the count to remove the quid pro quo aspect and simply leave the fact that the statement had been obtained. It was held that "[t]he fact that the amendment opened up additional routes to liability on the same evidence does not, without more, constitute irreparable prejudice."[81] The Ontario Court of Appeal also took account there of the fact that the defence had not, despite an offer, sought any type of remedy at the time, such as an adjournment or the recalling of witnesses.

Similarly in *Morgan*, the accused was initially charged with break and enter with intent to commit an indictable offence. After the defence had closed its case, the Crown was permitted to amend the charge to one of breaking and entering and committing an assault: that is, from a specific intent offence to a general intent offence. The accused argued that he was prejudiced by this amendment, but the British Columbia Court of Appeal did not accept that argument; they held that the inability to rely on a particular defence did not amount to irreparable prejudice.[82] They were also unpersuaded on the facts that there was any prejudice: the accused's decision as to whether to testify or not would have been no different if the charge had been a general intent one from the start, and in any event the trial judge did not accept the accused's intoxication claim.

On the other hand, in *R v Tremblay*, the Crown's application for an amendment was properly refused.[83] The accused had been charged with keeping a bawdy house for the purpose of practising acts of indecency. The accused called an expert witness and arranged their entire defence around the argument that the acts performed were not indecent. After

---

78 *R v EADM*, 2008 MBCA 78.

79 *R v Irwin* (1998), 123 CCC (3d) 316 (Ont CA).

80 *McConnell*, above note 75 at para 11.

81 *R v KR*, 2025 ONCA 330 at para 20.

82 *R v Morgan*, 2023 BCCA 226 at para 45.

83 *R v Tremblay*, [1993] 2 SCR 932.

all the defence evidence had been presented, the Crown made two applications to amend the charge, first, to delete the words "the practice of indecency" and, when that was refused, to change it to "the practice of prostitution." The Supreme Court held that the trial judge had been correct to refuse the amendment. It might have been allowable much earlier in the trial, but it would have caused irreparable prejudice at the stage it was brought.[84] In that particular case, the Court also held that the acts in question were not indecent, and so the acquittal at trial was upheld.

Beyond these remedies available at the trial stage, note as well section 683(1), setting out the powers of a court of appeal. Among those is the ability, where the court considers it to be in the interests of justice, to "amend the indictment, unless it is of the opinion that the accused has been misled or prejudiced in his defence or appeal."[85] This power can be used, for example, when some fact not proven at trial is found to be surplusage.[86]

Amendment is by far the most likely outcome, so an accused is unlikely to be acquitted based on some technical flaw in a count. An accused is only likely to receive a benefit if the amendment is refused and they are therefore acquitted. That is not the only possibility, however, though in essence the other option depends on further errors being made. For example, in *Moore* the accused was charged on an information that had a flaw in it. The trial judge quashed the information and in response the Crown simply laid a new information, thereafter, obtaining a conviction.

The Supreme Court of Canada overturned that conviction. They concluded that the original quashing was an error and that the charge should have been amended: had the Crown appealed the first trial judge's decision, this would have been the result. However, the Crown

84 To similar effect, see *R v Brownson*, 2013 ONCA 619, where the accused was charged with driving "while disqualified from doing so by reason of an order pursuant to section 259(1) of the *Criminal Code*." In fact, that was not the reason for the disqualification, which was the sole thing the accused attempted to show in questioning the Crown witnesses. The Ontario Court of Appeal held that the Crown's request to amend the indictment, which was not made until the appeal stage, came too late. Similarly in *R v Orubor*, 2024 ABKB 135, an application to amend a s 279.01 charge (human trafficking) to include "or facilitating their exploitation" in addition to the "for the purpose of exploiting them" wording that was in the count laid was not allowed. The accused had arranged their defence around the charge laid, the difference between the two was not minimal, and the application was not made until closing arguments.

85 Section 683(1)(g).

86 See, for example, *GL*, above note 67.

did not appeal that decision, and so the first judge's decision had to stand because the Crown was not entitled to avoid an appeal simply by laying a new information. Therefore, the accused was able to plead *autrefois acquit* at the subsequent trial.[87] A further remedy potentially available when a count is flawed is to order the Crown to provide particulars under section 587 of the *Code*. Particulars are intended to clarify the charge against the accused, in order to provide clear information as to the offence charged, and also to make the pleas of *autrefois acquit* and *autrefois convict* available in the event that further charges are laid.[88] There is no limit on what can be ordered, but particulars include requirements like "further describing the means by which an offence is alleged to have been committed" or "further describing a person, place or thing referred to in an indictment."[89] They cannot be ordered by a judge conducting a preliminary inquiry.[90] They need not be ordered at the start of the trial, however, and in considering whether the particulars are needed for a fair trial, the court is to consider the evidence that has been led.[91] Where particulars are ordered, they are entered into the record and the trial proceeds as though the indictment had been amended in accordance with the particulars.[92]

---

87 *R v Moore*, [1988] 1 SCR 1097. To somewhat similar effect see *McConnell*, above note 75. In that case the count had named the wrong type of car as the one the accused was alleged to have been driving, and at the start the Crown applied to amend it. The trial judge refused, with the result that the Crown led no evidence and the accused was acquitted. The Ontario Court of Appeal upheld the acquittal. The amendment was one which could in principle have been made eventually, to have the count conform to the evidence, except that the Crown did not in fact lead that evidence.

88 *R v JAH* (1998), 105 BCAC 259 [*JAH*]. Justice Dickson (as he then was) held in *Sault Ste Marie*, above note 72, that there was no problem raising a special plea after a trial on a duplicitous charge, because the rule against multiple convictions would prevent another acquittal arising out of the same facts, and acquittal means acquittal on all the offences charged. In either case, even if a charge was duplicitous, an accused could later point to it to justify pleading *autrefois acquit* or *autrefois convict*. The same argument might be made to say that the special plea justification does not arise in the context of particulars either, though it is a weaker argument here. Providing particulars might make clearer factually what actions are alleged to constitute the offence, thus making clear what "cause or matter" was the substance of a previous conviction.

89 Sections 587(1)(f) and (g).

90 *Hynes*, above note 25. Section 551.3 permits a case management judge to exercise the powers that a trial judge has before the stage of the presentation of the evidence on the merits, which would include ordering particulars, though that power is not specifically mentioned in the section.

91 Section 587(2).

92 Section 587(3)(c).

There is no need to lay an amended information.[93] Although the indictment is taken to be amended, the Crown is still not obliged to prove those things that are surplusage, even if they were provided among the particulars.[94]

Once again, the interest being protected for the accused is clarity at trial. An accused cannot use particulars as a way of limiting the options available to the Crown. In *R v Thatcher*, for example, the Crown's theory was that the accused either killed his wife personally or hired another person to do so, but that he was guilty of murder in either case. The Crown's position in this regard was made clear from the start, and the accused's application for particulars was rejected on the grounds that

> the purpose of the application for particulars was not to require the prosecution to provide the accused with additional details with respect to matters referred to in the indictment in order that the accused might be more fully informed of the act or omission charged against them but was to restrict the prosecution to reliance on a part only of the definition of murder contained in the *Criminal Code*.[95]

Still, the most likely result from some defect in a charge is an amendment. The question we turn to next therefore arises: what is considered to be a defect in a charge? In a broad sense, a charge is defective when it departs from the "golden rule," laid down in *R v Côté*, that the accused is entitled "to be reasonably informed of the transaction alleged against him, thus giving him the possibility of a full defence and a fair trial."[96] Consistent with the notion that charges will rarely be quashed for error is the approach to finding error in the first place: generally speaking, the rules allow quite a wide range of forms of charge, with the result that no remedy is available because there is not seen to be any problem.

---

93 *JAH*, above note 88.

94 *Vézina*, above note 60.

95 (1986), 24 CCC (3d) 449 (Sask CA) [*Thatcher*], quoting from *R v Govedarov, Popovic and Askov* (1974), 16 CCC (2d) 238 (Ont CA). The result that the Crown can bring forth alternative theories of liability was upheld in the Supreme Court, though the precise question around particulars was not in issue: *R v Thatcher*, [1987] 1 SCR 652. See also *R v Perdomo-Lopez*, 2020 ABCA 404 at para 57, where the accused sought particulars as to how he was said to have caused the death leading to a manslaughter charge. The trial judge did not err in choosing not to order particulars, on the basis that the pathways to liability were evident given the Crown disclosure and the fourteen-day preliminary inquiry: "the trial judge was correct in concluding it would be wrong to tie the Crown to a specific theory under the guise of needing further particulars."

96 [1978] 1 SCR 8 at 13 [*Côté*].

### b) Insufficient Charges

The most commonly alleged problem with an indictment relates to the requirement in section 581 that a count must contain sufficient detail to give the accused reasonable information and to identify the transaction. In deciding the sufficiency of a count, courts frequently make reference to the test in *R v Brodie* that the indictment must lift the charge "from the general to the particular."[97] Although this standard is frequently cited, caselaw makes it clear that the occasions where it is not attained are infrequent. In part, this is because certain omissions (such as that the count "does not name the person injured or intended or attempted to be injured . . . does not specify the means by which the alleged offence was committed [or] does not name or describe with precision any person, place or thing"[98]) are specifically noted by the *Code* as not creating insufficiency. Beyond that, courts have generally favoured the view that alleged procedural defects should prevent a trial only rarely.

It is worth being clear that the important meaning of "insufficiency" is insufficiency as spoken of in *Moore* — an error egregious enough that the charge must be quashed. It is not uncommon for courts to speak more loosely of degrees of insufficiency,[99] by which it merely means that a charge could have been clearer or that an amendment might be appropriate. However, for insufficiency to have any greater impact, a count must violate the standard in *Moore* or *Côté* and be so badly drawn up that it does not give the accused notice of the charge. This standard is rarely met.

It has been held that "an information will not be held to be a nullity if the information specifies the time, the place, the victim and the offence."[100] Even that statement suggests a higher standard than is insisted upon in practice. A count suggesting that an offence was committed "on or about" a particular date or "at or near" a particular location is likely to be upheld.[101] Counts charging an offence as having

---

97 [1936] SCR 188.

98 Section 583. See also the special rules in ss 584, 585, and 586.

99 See, for example, *R v Webster*, [1993] 1 SCR 3 at para 12: "In my opinion, the learned Provincial Court Judge was correct in his conclusion that while 'some measure of insufficiency exists in each of the charges . . . it is not of such a degree as would vitiate the charges.'"

100 *Re MacLean and the Queen* (1988), 68 CR (3d) 114 (BCCA) [*MacLean*], citing in support *Re Regina and RIC* (1986), 32 CCC (3d) 399 (Ont CA); *R v Dugdale* (1979), 7 CR (3d) 216 (BCCA); *R v Fox* (1986), 50 CR (3d) 370 (BCCA), leave to appeal to SCC refused [1986] 1 SCR ix [*Fox*]; *R v Nadin* (1971), 14 CRNS 201 (BCCA); and *R v Race*, [1988] BCJ No 1819 (CA).

101 *Fox*, above note 100; *R v Ryan* (1985), 12 OAC 172 (CA), leave to appeal to SCC refused [1986] 1 SCR ix.

occurred somewhere within a ten-month period eight years earlier[102] or during a sixty-three-month period[103] have also been upheld. The Court has held that "time is not required to be stated with exact precision unless it is an essential part of the offence charged and the accused is not misled or prejudiced by any variation in time that arises."[104]

Indeed, an indictment can be perfectly valid even if the count is not merely broad in its reference to time, but is incorrect about the time at which the offence is alleged to have occurred. Unless time is of the essence in a charge, the time that the offence occurred is not an essential element. Therefore, the time of an offence normally does not need to be proven, even if it is stated in the count. Accordingly, it does not matter that the wrong time was stated, and it is not even necessary to amend the indictment. This approach is consistent with the surplusage rule discussed above.

Time could be of the essence where an accused was entitled to take items or perform actions (such as fly a plane) during some periods but not others.[105] In those circumstances, an error in the count with regard to time would be significant because the accused's guilt or innocence would depend upon exactly when the actions in question occurred. But, in most cases, time will not be of the essence, as the Court observes in *R v B(G) (No 2)*: "the date of the offence is not generally an essential element of the offence of sexual assault. It is a crime no matter when it is committed."[106] It has been observed that "there are two exceptions to the overarching rule that time is not material to proof of an offence: where the date or date range constitutes an essential element of the offence; and where the date or date range is "crucial to the defence."[107] Alibi evidence led by the accused can sometimes make the exact time more relevant,[108] and whether the Crown has closed its case before seeking the amendment can also be significant.[109] However, an accused cannot, through

102 *MacLean*, above note 100.

103 *R v Colgan* (1986), 43 Man R (2d) 101 (CA), aff'd [1987] 2 SCR 686.

104 *R v Douglas*, [1991] 1 SCR 301 [*Douglas*].

105 See *R v Hamilton-Middleton* (1986), 53 Sask R 80 (CA), and *R v McCrae and Ramsay* (1981), 25 Man R (2d) 32 (Co Ct).

106 [1990] 2 SCR 30 at para 11 [*B(G)*]. See also *R v SD*, 2011 SCC 14.

107 *R v GG*, 2025 ONCA 574 at para 45 [*GG*].

108 See *B(G)* itself, above note 106; *R v Dossi* (1918), 13 Cr App R 158; *R v Parkin (No 1) and (No 2)* (1922), 37 CCC 35 (Man CA); *Wright v Nicholson*, [1970] 1 All ER 12 (QB), all discussed therein.

109 *R v MBP*, [1994] 1 SCR 555 [*MBP*].

cross-examination, artificially "make" the time be more significant than it really is.[110]

It can occur occasionally that a count is struck down on the basis that it does not disclose an offence known to law, though this phrase is not really a term of art.[111] In *R v Fremeau* the Alberta Court of Appeal found that a count in an information did not disclose an offence known to law when it charged that an accused sold "a drug listed or described in Schedule F of the Food and Drug Regulations." The regulation in question did not proscribe selling such drugs; rather, it proscribed selling "*a substance containing* a drug" listed in that Schedule.[112] This somewhat technical approach is uncommon, however, and normally courts will simply look at whether the accused has been reasonably informed of the charge, as required by *Côté*.

Indeed, in *Côté* the charge laid alleged that the accused had refused to provide a breath sample, without explicitly stating that he had done so "without reasonable excuse." Strictly, one could claim that the charge laid, failing to provide a breath sample, was not on its own an offence, but the Court held that the inclusion in the charge of the specific section under which the charge was laid made it impossible for the accused to have been misled.[113] This holding is consistent with section 601(3)(b)(ii) of the *Code*, permitting amendment where a count "does not negative an exception that should be negatived," but goes further. The Court did not find that there would be no prejudice from remedying the defect: they found that there was no defect in the first place. Similarly, in *R v Henyu* an information was quashed at trial for failing to disclose an offence known to law on the basis that it failed to explicitly allege that the accused had caused bodily harm, one of the elements of the offence. Nonetheless, the Court of Appeal held that in

110 See *GG*, above note 107, where the accused was charged with a sexual assault "on or about April 7, 2021." The complainant was asked in cross-examination about the exact time of the assault and the accused then led alibi evidence covering that one-hour period. The trial judge was satisfied that a sexual assault had occurred on April 7 but acquitted the accused on the basis that it had not been proven to have occurred at the time to which the complainant testified. The Ontario Court of Appeal found that to be an error, because there is no such thing as a "partial alibi": "it is only in circumstances where a true alibi is led, one that responds to the entirety of the time period alleged by the Crown, that transforms the time period alleged into something that is 'crucial to the defence'" (para 51).

111 See *Quigley*, note 71 at 17-2.

112 (1984), 34 Alta LR (2d) 1 at para 9 (CA) [emphasis added].

113 *Côté*, above note 96. Note that, in fact, the accused had appealed his conviction at trial on the basis that he did have a reasonable excuse, among other grounds: the error in the charge was raised by the Saskatchewan Court of Appeal.

stating that the accused had stabbed the victim, bodily harm was sufficiently implied.[114]

The Court has created some room for arguments about the sufficiency of charges with its decision in *R v Wis Development Corp.*[115] It is common for charges to be laid by simply repeating the language of the *Code* section that creates the offence, and this approach is specifically permitted by section 581(2). In *Wis Development*, however, the Court accepted that a charge laid in that form was insufficient when it simply said that the accused "operate[d] a commercial air service," without anything more. That phrase could cover a "multitude of activities," ranging from hauling passengers to allowing an aircraft to be photographed for a liquor advertisement, and therefore the information was void for not meeting the sufficiency standard of section 581(3).[116] This vagueness has caused debate at times over whether the wording in particular *Code* sections also covers a multitude of activities and, therefore, would not be sufficient if used when a charge is laid. The fact that an offence can be committed in a number of ways does not make it fall within the *Wis Development* rule, and so charges that an accused had care and control of a vehicle or was keeping a common bawdy house have been found to be unaffected.[117] However, a charge simply asserting that an accused kept a common gaming house was held to violate the rule.[118] Scope for argument regarding when this standard is met remains. However, any problem caused by such a flaw could now be amended (which was not the case for summary offences at the time of *Wis Development*) and so the question has become less important.

### c) Duplicitous Charges

A potential flaw in counts that is conceptually distinct from insufficiency is duplicity. Where insufficiency asks whether an accused has been given too little information, duplicity suggests, in effect, that the accused has been given too much information. A duplicitous count is one that appears to charge the accused with committing two different

114 [1980] 1 WWR 752 (BCCA).

115 [1984] 1 SCR 485 [*Wis Development*].

116 This issue merely laid the groundwork for the central issue in the case, which was the ability to amend the information. Since the case was decided under legislation specific to summary conviction offences and that legislation has since been repealed to allow the general rule to have effect, the case is no longer significant with regard to its main holding. However, that does not affect the initial reasoning concerning whether the information was valid or not.

117 *Fox*, above note 100, and *R v Milberg* (1987), 35 CCC (3d) 45 (Ont CA).

118 *R v Bingo Enterprises Ltd (cob Buffalo Bingo Palace)* (1984), 41 CR (3d) 291 (Man CA).

offences, and it is objectionable because the ambiguity prevents the accused from knowing the case to meet. If any ambiguity does not rise to that level, the charge is not duplicitous.[119] This is a distinct requirement from the "single transaction" rule in section 581(1). That rule limits a count to a single factual situation, while the duplicity rule limits it to a single legal issue.

As with the single transaction rule, courts have not found the duplicity rule to be easily violated. In *R v Sault Ste Marie*, the Court found non-duplicitous a count that said the accused did "discharge or cause to be discharged or permitted to be discharged or deposited" pollutants into a river. This charge tracked the wording of the offence section. The Court held that the section had not created several different offences but only one offence — polluting — which could be committed in a number of ways. The accused would have no doubt about the case to meet, and so no objection should be taken to the charge.[120] Similarly, a charge that did not differentiate between the general theft section and theft by a person required to account, and suggested that the accused was guilty of each, was not duplicitous (again, although two *Code* sections were involved, they were simply identifying two ways of committing theft).[121] This approach is consistent with the idea that a jury must be unanimous *that* the accused is guilty of the offence, but need not be unanimous with regard to *how* the accused committed the offence.[122]

Further, an information that contains two counts separated by the word "alternatively" is not duplicitous, since it would not be a single count charging more than one offence.[123] Particular difficulties can arise in conspiracy cases, and a single count charging an accused with more than one conspiracy would be duplicitous. However, even if more than one conspiracy is proven at trial, the charge is not automatically duplicitous; if it was not, the only issue will be which conspiracy the accused was charged with, and whether any or all of the conspiracies proven to have been committed are covered by the indictment.[124]

---

119 *Sault Ste Marie*, above note 72. See also s 590(1)(a) of the *Code*, providing that a count is not objectionable if it "charges in the alternative several different matters, acts or omissions that are stated in the alternative in an enactment that describes as an indictable offence the matters, acts or omissions charged in the count."

120 *Sault Ste Marie*, above note 72.

121 *R v Fischer* (1987), 53 Sask R 263 (CA) [*Fischer*], dealing with ss 322 and 330. The potential ambiguity was created by the provision of particulars.

122 *Fischer*, *ibid*, and *Thatcher*, above note 95.

123 *R v Brewer* (1988), 8 MVR (2d) 137 (NBCA).

124 See *Douglas*, above note 104, and *R v Papalia*, [1979] 2 SCR 256.

In any event, even if a charge is duplicitous it is not fatally flawed.[125] Section 590(2)(b) allows an accused to apply to have a count that is "double or multifarious" either amended or divided into two or more counts, an application that is to be granted where the ends of justice require it. To divide a count is to make it two or more separate counts (something that is sometimes referred to as "severance," though, more strictly, severance is the process under section 591(3)(a) of sending separate counts to separate trials, discussed above).

Only the trial judge has jurisdiction to divide a count, though the application can be brought on a pre-trial basis.[126] The *Code* allows the count to be divided when it "embarrasses [the accused] in his defence," a criterion broad enough to leave the decision largely in the trial judge's discretion. An appeal court is not to interfere with that discretion unless the judge acted unjudicially or the decision resulted in an injustice. *R v Litchfield*, for example, dealt with a doctor charged with various sexual assaults arising out of examinations performed on a number of patients. Before trial, a judge divided individual counts based on which parts of the complainants' bodies the doctor had been examining, and then severed the counts to be dealt with in different trials. The result, in some cases, was that different parts of a single examination of one patient would be dealt with in separate trials, depending upon which part of the complainant's body was examined. The Court held that this result misapprehended the nature of sexual assault and the order ought not to have been made.[127]

On the other hand, in *R v Lilly* the Court dealt with a real estate broker who was charged with theft based on a series of withdrawals from a trust account into which a number of deposits relating to real property transactions had been made. In the course of the trial it became apparent that the accused was claiming a colour of right defence with regard to some of the withdrawals, while claiming to be unaware of some of the deposits. The Court held that, although it had been acceptable to lay a single count charging the accused with theft, it would have been preferable to divide the count once it became apparent that the accused had two separate defences. Particularly given that it was a jury trial, this approach would have made clearer what was implied in finding the accused guilty.[128] The matter remains in a trial judge's discretion, though, and so, for example, the fact that an accused's employment has

125 Section 590(1) says that a count is not objectionable by reason only that it is double or multifarious.

126 *Litchfield*, above note 27.

127 *Ibid*.

128 *Lilly*, above note 18.

been terminated does not mean that a count of theft must be divided to deal with continuing actions before and after he was fired.[129]

## C. PLEAS

The pleas available to an accused charged with an offence are set out in section 606 of the *Code*. An accused can plead guilty, not guilty, or one of the special pleas provided for in the *Code*. The special pleas, listed in section 607, consist of *autrefois acquit*, *autrefois convict*, pardon,[130] and an expungement order.[131]

The special pleas really amount to the claim that the matter that the accused is called upon to plead is a matter that has already been dealt with — the accused has previously been acquitted, convicted, or pardoned for the offence in question, or has had the conviction expunged. There can be confused issues around whether the matter the accused is charged with at this time is the same matter that was dealt with by previous charges. They are, in effect, all manifestations of the rule against multiple convictions. The discussion here will focus only on the pleas of guilty and not guilty.

A plea of guilty amounts to an admission by the accused of performing the physical actions that make up the offence, accompanied by the necessary mental state. It is a waiver of the right to a trial.[132] This is a significant step, and therefore it is one of the very few decisions which an accused must personally take.[133] But guilty pleas, when they are an aspect of plea negotiations leading to a joint submission on sentence,

---

129 *Fischer*, above note 121.

130 Strictly there is no longer such a thing as a "pardon," since legislation has changed that mechanism to what is now called a "record suspension": *Safe Streets and Communities Act*, SC 2010, c 1. The effect of a record suspension is functionally the same as a pardon and the wording in the *Code* was not changed. See also s 611, allowing the plea of justification to a charge of defamatory libel.

131 Expungement orders were created by the *Expungement of Historically Unjust Convictions Act*, SC 2018, c 11. The *Code* used to contain various offences which dealt with consensual same-sex sexual activity, which are now gone. The *Expungement of Historically Unjust Convictions Act* allows application to have a conviction for one of those offences "expunged," which means that the person "is deemed never to have been convicted of that offence": s 5(1).

132 *R v Adgey*, [1975] 2 SCR 426 [*Adgey*].

133 *R v Wong*, 2018 SCC 25 [*Wong*]. See para 2: "defence counsel are ethically bound to ensure that the ultimate choice is that of the accused." Older caselaw, however, had held that a plea entered by counsel to an indictable offence is, in the normal course of events, binding on an accused who was present at the time: *R*

are seen as a "proper and necessary part of the administration of criminal justice" having benefits to all concerned.[134] Where a joint submission on sentence is made in exchange for a guilty plea, the accused is likely to receive a more lenient sentence, and the Crown avoids any uncertainty about whether there will be a conviction. Because of this importance, and to encourage the parties to make such agreements, a judge is required not to depart from a joint submission on sentence following a guilty plea unless the proposed sentence would bring the administration of justice into disrepute or is otherwise contrary to the public interest.[135]

The Supreme Court has said that "[a]guilty plea may be accepted by a court only if it is voluntary, unequivocal and informed. For it to be informed, the accused must understand the nature of the allegations, the effect of the plea and the consequences of the plea."[136] Beyond that, the *Code* specifies that, for a judge to accept a plea of guilty in the first place, the judge must be satisfied that the accused is making the plea voluntarily and understands three things: (i) that the plea is an admission of the essential elements of the offence, (ii) the nature and consequences of the plea, and (iii) that the court is not bound by any agreement made between the accused and the prosecutor.[137] This final statutory requirement is of course now subject to the stringent standard set by the Court before a judge can depart from such an agreement. Further, for a considerable period of time the rule was that a court had no general obligation to inquire into the plea, but should do so if there was any reason to doubt that the accused understood its effect.[138] However, Bill C-75 amended the *Code* to add the requirement that the court must also be satisfied that the facts support the charge.[139] Nonetheless these requirements could be seen as directory rather than mandatory, since the *Code* also provides that a failure to fully inquire into those conditions does not affect the validity of the plea.[140]

---

*v Dietrich* (1970), 11 CRNS 22 (Ont CA), leave to appeal to SCC refused [1970] SCR xi; *R v Sommerfeldt* (1984), 14 CCC (3d) 445 (BCCA).

134 *R v Anthony-Cook*, 2016 SCC 43 [*Anthony-Cook*] at para 35.

135 *Anthony-Cook*, *ibid* at para 32.

136 *Wong*, above note 133 at para 43.

137 Section 606(1.1)(a) and (b).

138 See *Adgey*, above note 132 and *R v Brousseau*, [1969] SCR 181.

139 Section 606(1.1)(c). Section 36 of the *Youth Criminal Justice Act*, SC 2002, c 1 [*YCJA*], already required a judge to be satisfied that the facts will support a charge before accepting a guilty plea from a young person, and Bill C-75 introduced the same rule for adult accused.

140 Section 606(1.2).

A plea of not guilty is not a claim of innocence but is simply a demand that the Crown proves all the elements of the offence and disproves the existence of any defences. Unless a special plea is required, pleading not guilty puts any defence available in issue, including, for example, whether the accused is not criminally responsible by reason of mental disorder.[141]

Where an accused refuses to plead, the judge is to enter a plea of not guilty.[142] An accused can, with the consent of the Crown, enter a plea of guilty to some other offence arising out of the same transaction, whether it is an included offence or not. If the court accepts the plea, the accused will be found not guilty of the offence originally charged.[143]

An accused can later withdraw a guilty plea if "there are valid grounds for his being permitted to do so," a category the Court has consciously not defined exhaustively.[144] There must be some special circumstance that suggests the guilty plea should not be accepted at face value as a legitimate concession of guilt. So, for example, if the accused has been pressured by counsel into entering a guilty plea, the accused might successfully withdraw the plea.[145] Similarly, a plea might be withdrawn if it is shown that the accused who wished to plead not guilty actually pled guilty in order to obtain an immediate fine rather than spend a week in custody awaiting trial, or to avoid a more serious charge being laid (first-, rather than second-degree murder, for example).[146] In *R v Hanemaayer* an accused who voluntarily entered a guilty plea mid-trial (because he was convinced of the inevitability of his conviction and knew he could receive a lighter sentence by pleading guilty) was allowed to withdraw his guilty plea when evidence proving that another person had committed the offence came to light.[147] However, the mere fact that an accused feels pressure does not mean that the plea was not voluntary: feeling pressure is true of most accused who plead guilty, but is often just the realization that there is no viable alternative.[148]

---

141 Section 613. Although all defences are potentially put in issue by a plea of not guilty, the onus of proof can, in some instances, be on the accused. A plea of not guilty allows an accused to argue entrapment, for example, but the accused will bear the ultimate burden of proof to make out that defence.

142 Section 606(2).

143 Section 606(4).

144 *Adgey*, above note 132, quoted in *R v Taillefer; R v Duguay*, [2003] 3 SCR 307 at para 85 [*Taillefer*].

145 *R v Laperrière*, [1996] 2 SCR 284; *R v Lamoureux* (1984), 40 CR (3d) 369 (Que CA).

146 *R v Cesari* (1986), 50 CR (3d) 93 (Que CA); *R v Hansen* (1977), 37 CCC (2d) 371 (Man CA).

147 2008 ONCA 580 [*Hanemaayer*]. In *Hanemaayer* the withdrawal of the guilty plea came nearly twenty years after the conviction.

148 *R v Carty*, 2010 ONCA 237.

Circumstances other than improper pressure on the accused could lead to the plea being set aside, however. In *R v Taillefer; R v Duguay* an accused received disclosure of significant Crown evidence four years after entering a guilty plea. The Court held that even if a guilty plea was valid — that is, it was voluntary, unequivocal, and based on sufficient information concerning the nature of the charges and the consequences of the plea — it might still be withdrawn if the accused's constitutional rights were violated. The test there asks whether "there was a realistic possibility that the accused would have run the risk of a trial, if he or she had been in possession of that information or those new avenues of investigation": if so, leave must be given to withdraw the plea.[149]

A common ground for seeking to strike a guilty plea is that the requirement that it was an *informed* plea was not met. In *Wong*, the Court set out the framework for setting aside an uninformed guilty plea, saying that it involved two discrete steps: "(1) the accused being misinformed about sufficiently serious information; and (2) that lack of information resulting in prejudice."[150] The first step requires consideration of two distinct components: what did the accused actually know (assessed subjectively), and then whether that knowledge constituted being "sufficiently informed" (assessed objectively).[151]

One relatively common situation is for an accused to lose a pre-trial application over the admissibility of evidence due to a *Charter* violation and then enter a guilty plea, failing to understand that doing so prevents them from appealing the *Charter* ruling. Depending on the facts, that might justify being allowed to withdraw the plea.[152] Other bases for being uninformed can also exist: the issue is very much a factual and case-by-case one.[153]

---

149 *Taillefer*, above note 144 at para 90. See also *R v Aldhelm-White*, 2008 NSCA 86, where twelve separate accused were allowed to withdraw their guilty pleas to drug charges after it was discovered that an investigating officer who had supplied much of the information relevant to the search warrants was himself a drug dealer. The Crown acknowledged that they would not have pursued charges at all had they had that information at the time and supported the applications to withdraw the guilty pleas.

150 *Wong*, above note 133 at para 33.

151 *R v Johnson*, 2024 SKCA 58 at para 24.

152 See, for example, *R v Lam*, 2020 BCCA 276, or *R v Klassen*, 2023 BCCA 103. In the latter case, there was the additional issue that a co-accused had later brought a successful trial within a reasonable time application, which the accused did not realize he was giving up. See also *R v Hunt*, 2021 ABCA 49, though in that case the plea was not found to be uninformed.

153 See, for example, *R v Zaworski*, 2022 BCCA 144, where the accused argued that he was uninformed because he did not understand the exact nature of the

One particular way a plea might be uninformed is if the accused had been unaware of some collateral consequence of the plea, such as its impact on immigration status. In this context, the Court concluded in *R v Wong* that a guilty plea can be withdrawn if the accused shows "(1) that he or she was not aware of a legally relevant collateral consequence and (2) that there is a reasonable possibility he or she would have proceeded differently if properly informed of that consequence."[154]

Various things can count as a legally relevant collateral consequence. In *Wong* itself the accused, a permanent resident of Canada, was unaware that he would be subject to an unappealable removal order upon conviction of the offence to which he pleaded guilty.[155] Unawareness of immigration consequences has arisen as a possible ground in a number of cases.[156] Other cases have found the first step to be satisfied when an accused was unaware of a lifetime (rather than twelve month) ban from receiving disability benefits after a conviction,[157] or was unaware that by pleading guilty they gave up the right to appeal a ruling about the admissibility of evidence.[158]

---

charge against him. In that case, the court of appeal did not allow him to withdraw his plea, pointing out that the accused had received disclosure making clear the nature of the allegations, was represented by counsel, and that evidence had been led at his sentence hearing, all of which suggested that he did in fact understand.

154 *Wong*, above note 133 at para 44. This test is set out in the dissenting judgment of the 4-3 decision, but the majority decision agrees that this is the proper test. *Wong* has an unusual structure. Most of the reasoning in the case is set out in the three-judge dissent, while the four-judge majority is devoted to an explanation of why it disagrees with one aspect of the test set out by the dissent. As the four-judge majority decision was authored by three of those four judges, it appears likely that one judge had a late change of heart, turning what would have been the dissent into the majority.

155 See also *R v Girn*, 2019 ONCA 202, though in that case the Ontario Court of Appeal concluded that the accused in fact *was* aware of that collateral consequence.

156 See, for example, *R v Coffey*, 2017 BCCA 359; *R v Grin*, 2019 ONCA 202; *R v Berhe*, 2022 ONCA 853; or *Johnson*, above note 151. In *Johnson*, the Saskatchewan Court of Appeal concluded at para 26, based on a review of the caselaw, that "the accused need only know that such immigration consequences are a *possibility*. Second, the accused need not know the details of those immigration consequences, but he or she must have a general understanding that they involve '*serious jeopardy*.'"

157 *R v Miller*, 2019 BCCA 78. See also *R v Quick*, 2016 ONCA 26, a pre-*Wong* case in which the accused was allowed to withdraw his guilty plea because he incorrectly thought he would lose his driver's licence for only a year, rather than indefinitely.

158 *R v Del Corro*, 2019 ABCA 156. For pre-*Wong* caselaw to the same effect, see *R v Webster*, 2008 BCCA 458; *R v Duong*, 2006 BCCA 325, or *R v Fegan* (1993), 21

The majority in *Wong* concluded that the second step had to be assessed against a subjective standard. That introduces some ambiguity, since the test in *Taillefer* for a similar situation had seemed to be based on a reasonable person standard.[159] In these cases, an accused is not required to show ineffective assistance of counsel nor the existence of any prejudice beyond that implicit in not having made their plea of choice. Notably, an accused need not show that there was a viable defence had they pleaded not guilty nor, if they would only have pleaded guilty on different conditions, that the Crown would have been willing to accept such conditions. Of course, in assessing such a claim, a court should look to objective circumstantial evidence to test its veracity.

Pre-*Wong* it had been held that an accused cannot withdraw a guilty plea because the judge rejects a joint sentencing submission or because the Crown makes a subsequent application to have the accused declared a dangerous offender.[160] Those decisions might need to be revisited in light of *Wong*. In *R v Espinoza-Ortega*, the Ontario Court of Appeal noted that since *Anthony-Cook*,[161] the circumstances in which a judge does not accept a joint sentence are meant to be rare, and rarer still that the Crown prosecutor would agree that the sentence could not be supported. In those circumstances, the Court of Appeal concluded that the *Wong* test was met and that the guilty plea could be withdrawn.

Guilty and not guilty are, apart from the special pleas, the only pleas available to a person charged with an offence. Experience in the criminal justice system rapidly acquaints counsel with clients who wish to plead "guilty with an explanation," or who want to plead guilty rather than go to trial but wish to maintain their innocence. In the former case, the accused is required to plead not guilty, and a judge receiving a plea of guilty with an explanation should refuse to accept it. The court should inquire into the accused's intention and accept the guilty plea only if it is clear that the accused unequivocally wishes to plead guilty.[162]

In general, although a judge must be satisfied the facts support the charge, they have no obligation to hear evidence after an accused has

---

CR (4th) 65 (Ont CA). See also *R v Newman* (1993), 20 CR (4th) 370 (Ont CA), where the accused argued, though unsuccessfully, that he should be permitted to withdraw his guilty plea for not having been adequately informed of the consequences of pleading guilty due to ineffective representation by counsel.

159 The dissent in *Wong*, above note 133, felt the test there should be objective, as in *Taillefer*, but the majority concluded that *Taillefer* had not in fact created an objective test: see para 35.

160 *R v Rubenstein* (1987), 41 CCC (3d) 91 (Ont CA), leave to appeal to SCC refused (1988), 87 NR 77n; *R v Lyons*, [1987] 2 SCR 309.

161 *Anthony-Cook*, above note 134.

162 *R v McNabb* (1971), 4 CCC (2d) 316 (Sask CA).

pleaded guilty, but they can do so. If in doing so it becomes apparent that the accused did not intend to admit some element of the offence, misapprehended the effect of a guilty plea, or did not intend to plead guilty, the trial judge can allow the accused to withdraw the plea or enter a plea of not guilty.

A judge should not permit an accused to plead guilty simply to "get it over with." The judge should accept a guilty plea only when the accused intends to admit all the elements of the offence, and defence counsel has an ethical obligation in this regard.[163] Equally, an accused cannot enter a "conditional plea." For example, an accused cannot plead guilty to a homicide charge, conditional upon the Crown proving the cause of death.[164] Of course, in a case of theft, it is open to an accused to make factual concessions despite a plea of not guilty, and, for example, admit to having taken items, but advance a claim of colour of right or deny having had the necessary *mens rea*.[165]

Section 650 of the *Code* requires an accused (other than a corporation) to be present in court during the whole trial, and therefore an accused must be present for the plea: this can be done via closed-circuit television or videoconference, provided an accused who is in prison can still consult privately with counsel. Section 800 of the *Code* explicitly permits an accused charged with a summary conviction offence to appear by counsel.

# D. ORDER OF TRIAL

## 1) Trial Procedures

The procedures governing trial are set out in Parts XIX, XX, and XXVII of the *Criminal Code* and cover indictable offences tried by judge alone or judge and jury, and summary conviction trials, respectively.[166] Many

---

163 See, for example, Chapter IX, "The Lawyer as Advocate" in Canadian Bar Association, *Code of Professional Conduct* (Ottawa: Canadian Bar Association, 2006), and the discussion in David Layton & Michel Proulx, *Ethics and Canadian Criminal Law*, 2d ed (Toronto: Irwin Law, 2015), particularly ch 8, s M. See also the discussion there of the plea "*nolo contendere*," which is not permissible in Canada but is, in fact, a way for an accused to decline to contest a charge without conceding its truth.

164 *R v Lucas* (1983), 9 CCC (3d) 71 (Ont CA), leave to appeal to SCC refused (1984), 9 CCC (3d) 71n.

165 See s 655 of the *Code*.

166 Part XIX.1 of the *Code* also sets out the procedures to be used at trials in front of the Nunavut Court of Justice, which is something of a hybrid. Section 573(1) of the *Code* provides that the powers, duties, and function of a provincial court

of the procedures dealing with the actual conduct of trials are common to all three modes.[167]

A trial is to proceed continuously, though the judge can grant adjournments.[168] The primary rule is that anyone who takes part in a proceeding, as an accused or as some other participant, is to do so personally.[169] In the specific case of the trial, the accused is to be present, but a judge is allowed to excuse the accused from attending.[170] In addition, Part XXII.01 was added to the Code in 2019, permitting participation in some circumstances by means of audioconference or videoconference. Separate provisions, but ones with similar requirements for each, allow for the remote appearance of the accused,[171] the judge or justice,[172] or counsel.[173] This is allowed if no other provision prevents it, and it is therefore important to note at the start that the accused must be present in person — that is, cannot attend remotely — for any portion of the trial at which evidence is taken.[174] When appearance by audioconference or videoconference is permissible, the *Code* sets out considerations for the trial judge to take into account in deciding whether to allow it, such as the location and personal circumstances of the accused or participant, the costs of a personal appearance, the accused's right to a fair and public hearing, and other matters.[175]

---

judge may be exercised by the Nunavut Court of Justice, while s 573(2) clarifies that in doing so, the judges of that court are acting as judges of a superior court.

167 Section 572 makes the provisions of Part XX, "Jury Trials," applicable to Part XIX, "Trial without Jury." Section 795 makes those provisions applicable to summary conviction trials. In each case, the provisions apply to the extent that they are not inconsistent with specific provisions in those Parts and with such modifications as the circumstances require.

168 Sections 571 and 645.

169 Section 715.21. This particular provision was added by Bill C-75, above note 6, but that did not change the law. Rather it seems to have been included to affirm that the law around that point has *not* changed, since it is the first section in a newly added Part XXII.01, Remote Attendance by Certain Persons.

170 Section 645. The presumption of attendance works the other way in the case of summary conviction offences, with s 800(2) allowing an accused to appear personally or by counsel, but permitting the judge to require the accused's personal attendance.

171 Section 715.23.

172 Section 715.26.

173 Section 715.25. The section governs remote appearance by a "participant," which is defined as "any person, other than an accused, a witness, a juror, a judge or a justice, who may participate in a proceeding." See also s 650.02 dealing with remote appearance by counsel designated for an accused under s 650.01.

174 Sections 650(1.1), 650(1.2), and 800(2.1).

175 See s 715.23(1) for the complete list of factors relating to an accused, s 715.25(2) for the complete list of factors relating to other participants, and s 715.26(1) for the factors relating to a judge or justice.

If an accused absconds during trial, the court can either issue a warrant for the accused's arrest and adjourn the trial, or continue the trial without the accused. In the latter case, defence counsel can continue acting for the accused, and the accused's right to full answer and defence will not have been violated.[176]

The trial judge has discretion as to where the accused will sit during trial. Typically (but not necessarily) the accused will sit in the prisoner's dock, and the trial judge is not required to permit the accused to sit elsewhere unless the refusal will violate the accused's right to full answer and defence.[177]

The judge can ask questions during the trial, although doing so can raise issues as to whether there is a reasonable apprehension of bias (see the discussion at Section F, below in this chapter). Juries are also entitled to ask questions, though within limits. It must be made clear to the jury that the parties are entitled to present the evidence as they want, and so questioning by jurors should not become another interrogation. Jurors' questions are best left to the end, to be submitted in writing to the trial judge who can discuss with counsel whether the questions should be asked.[178]

## 2) Opening Statements

The Crown presents its case first, and, as a matter of practice, can begin with an opening statement to the jury explaining its theory of the case and the evidence to be called. However, this opening statement does not irrevocably commit the Crown to adopting a particular approach to the trial. The Crown is not obliged to call every witness it indicates will be called and, like any other counsel at trial, is entitled to modify the trial strategy as the case develops. The Crown's theory of the case could change over the course of the trial in response to changing

---

176 See s 475 and *R v Zarubin* (2001), 157 CCC (3d) 115 (Sask CA).

177 *R v Levogiannis*, [1993] 4 SCR 475 [*Levogiannis*], citing *R v Faid*, [1981] 5 WWR 349 (Alta CA), rev'd on other grounds, [1983] 1 SCR 265 [*Faid*]. See also *R v AC*, 2018 ONCA 333 at para 37:

> While the default placement of an accused on trial is in the prisoner's box, there is no presumption in this regard. In every case, the accused's placement must permit him to make full answer and defence, but the issue is to be assessed on a case-by-case basis, having regard to the interests of a fair trial and courtroom security in the particular circumstances of the case.

178 See *R v Nordyne* (1998), 17 CR (5th) 393 (Que CA), and *R v Gagnon* (1992), 47 QAC 232 (CA). See also *R v Lam*, [1998] NWTJ No 79 (CA), where defence counsel's decision to ask some questions of his client, after the jury sent a note with those questions to the judge, was found not to form the basis for an appeal.

circumstances, including defence counsel's closing address.[179] Short of oppressive prosecutorial conduct amounting to an abuse of process, the accused cannot object to a change of plans on the part of the Crown. In choosing not to call a witness who has been announced, of course, the Crown risks the jury drawing some type of adverse inference, and the accused would normally be entitled to point out the change to the jury when making closing submissions.[180]

Normally, the defence is not entitled to make an opening address to the jury immediately following the Crown's opening remarks, but instead makes an opening statement after the close of the Crown's case. However, a trial judge has discretion to let the accused make an opening statement immediately following the Crown's opening. Some authority suggests that making such an opening statement obliges the accused to call evidence, essentially because the purpose of the statement is to outline the evidence that will be called. However, the prevailing view appears to be that, in the special circumstances where the accused is allowed an opening statement immediately following the Crown's, there is no obligation to later call witnesses for direct examination and, indeed, that "counsel acting responsibly cannot be expected to give an undertaking at that stage to call evidence. That decision must be assessed against the concluded Crown case."[181] Nonetheless, the defence might adduce evidence through cross-examination of Crown witnesses, for example, and in appropriate cases should be allowed an opening statement. Cases returned for a new trial that have a measure of predictability might be ones where such an order is appropriate.[182]

## 3) Presentation of the Crown Case

Following the opening statement, Crown counsel is required to present evidence proving the charges against the accused. The procedures

---

179 *R v Pickton*, 2010 SCC 32 at para 19 [*Pickton*], quoting from the dissenting judgment of Binnie J in *R v Rose*, [1998] 3 SCR 262 [*Rose*]. See the discussion of this point specifically in the context of an opening statement in *R v Khawaja*, 2010 ONCA 862.

180 *R v Jolivet*, 2000 SCC 29 [*Jolivet*]; *R v Cook*, [1997] 1 SCR 1113 [*Cook*]. See *R v Biniaris*, 2000 SCC 15, as an example of the Crown changing its theory of the case during the course of trial.

181 *R v Sood* (1997), 58 OTC 115 (Gen Div) [*Sood*]. See also *R v Barrow* (1989), 91 NSR (2d) 176 (SCTD) [*Barrow*], but, in contrast, see *R v Vitale* (1987), 40 CCC (3d) 267 (Ont Dist Ct).

182 *Sood*, above note 181; *Barrow*, above note 181. See *R v Larsen*, 2013 NWTSC 31 for a clear overview of the considerations a judge should take into account in deciding whether to allow an early opening statement.

for taking evidence at trial are generally the same as at a preliminary inquiry; that is, the evidence is to be taken under oath in the presence of the accused, the accused is entitled to cross-examine the Crown witnesses, and the evidence is recorded.[183]

Although in principle it is up to the Crown to prove every essential element of the offence, it is open to the accused to concede various parts of the Crown's case.[184] Often this is done through an agreed-upon statement of facts, but not necessarily. An accused can concede the voluntariness of a statement and waive a *voir dire*, for example, without any particular form of words being necessary (as long as it is clear that the accused understood the issue and made an informed decision regarding waiver). Silence or lack of objection to a statement being admitted is not waiver.[185] Even in cases of silence, however, the trial will not necessarily be fatally flawed by the admission of a statement; a trial judge will have erred only if there was clear evidence objectively showing the need to conduct a *voir dire* despite the failure of defence counsel to request one.[186]

The Crown has considerable discretion in deciding how to present its case, consistent with the adversarial nature of the process. Although judicial case management powers have been increased, particularly with a view to creating efficiencies to protect the right to a trial within a reasonable time,[187] this general proposition has not changed (but see the discussion in Section F(1), Control over the Court Process, below in this chapter). The Crown is not required, for example, to call every witness with relevant information and has no obligation to call a witness it does not consider necessary to the prosecution's case.[188] This rule applies equally even if the witness not called is the complainant. Failing to do so might put the Crown's ability to prove its case at risk, and in some circumstances a trial judge might comment to a jury on

---

183 Sections 557 and 646 adopt, for trials in inferior and superior courts respectively, the preliminary inquiry evidentiary rules in s 540. Note, however, that the amendments to the preliminary inquiry procedures in ss 540(7), (8), and (9) do not carry over to trials.

184 Section 655.

185 *R v Park*, [1981] 2 SCR 64.

186 *R v Hodgson*, [1998] 2 SCR 449.

187 See the discussion of this issue, and of s 551.1, in Chapter 10, Section B(1). See also, for example, the discussion in *R v Dancause*, 2018 QCCS 1565.

188 See *Lemay v The King*, [1952] 1 SCR 232; *R v Yebes*, [1987] 2 SCR 168; *Cook*, above note 180; *Jolivet*, above note 180. See also *R v Roulette*, 2015 MBCA 9, noting that the Crown has no obligation to call particular witnesses and therefore that it is normally improper for counsel to invite the jury to adverse inference from such a failure.

the failure to call the complainant, but the decision is still within the Crown's discretion. The defence is not entitled to have the Crown call all witnesses so it can cross-examine them, but it can call any witness not called by the Crown as part of the defence case. In some circumstances, the defence can apply under the *Canada Evidence Act*[189] to cross-examine the witness.[190] Further, in some cases, the trial judge could choose to call the person as the court's witness, therefore allowing the defence to cross-examine. This might be the right course of action particularly where forcing the defence to call the witness might require the accused to give up the right to speak to the jury last (see the discussion of this issue at Section D(8), below in this chapter).

Although evidence typically takes the form of testimony or documents from witnesses on the stand, other forms of evidence are permitted. Provisions in the *Code* create special rules around proof of ownership and value of property,[191] expert's reports,[192] dates of birth,[193] and previous convictions.[194] Further, other provisions allow for the use of commission evidence for witnesses who, through illness or other "good and sufficient cause," cannot attend the trial.[195] That provision also allows for commission evidence of a witness who is out of Canada, but an amendment to the *Code* in 2019 now provides that if a witness is outside Canada their evidence *shall* be received by way of videoconference unless one of the parties satisfies the court of the very high standard that "the reception of such testimony would be contrary to the principles of fundamental justice."[196] In addition, evidence that was taken at a preliminary inquiry can be used at a trial in some circumstances.[197] Videotaped testimony by a person under eighteen or with a physical or mental disability can sometimes be used at a trial for

189 RSC 1985, c C-5 [*CEA*].

190 *Cook*, above note 180.

191 Section 657.1.

192 Section 657.3.

193 Section 658(3).

194 Section 667.

195 Section 709.

196 Section 714.2. See the discussion of this section in *R v Stevens*, 2019 NSSC 208. A court also *may* receive such evidence by audioconference: s 714.3. Seemingly this option would only be available if videoconferencing would be contrary to the principles of fundamental justice. The standard to be met for using an audioconference is that "it would be appropriate having regard to all the circumstances."

197 Sections 715 and 715.01. Note that the latter section permits the transcript of testimony of a police officer to be used, rather than requiring the officer to appear. See also ss 541 and 657. See generally the discussion of this issue in Chapter 9, Section C(1).

various sexual offences.[198] Further, the use of technology to present evidence is available if it will increase efficiency in any case, not merely in ones with thousands of documents.[199]

Section 652 allows a jury to "have a view," in order to see any place, person, or thing.[200] This ability is open to the jury any time prior to rendering their verdict, including after they have begun their deliberations,[201] and can also be used by a judge conducting a trial without a jury.[202]

A Crown prosecutor will normally have indicated what evidence will be called in the opening address. Failing to call that evidence will not necessarily prove fatal to the prosecution. Thus, for example, if hearsay evidence is admitted in anticipation of direct evidence that is expected to be, but ultimately is not, called, adequate instructions by the trial judge to the jury can cure any problem.[203]

Section 545 of the *Code* allows a trial judge to imprison a witness who refuses to testify for periods of up to eight days at a time.

## 4) Presentation of the Defence Case

### a) Application for a Directed Verdict

At the close of the Crown's case it becomes the defence's turn to present evidence, if it chooses to do so. Before that, however, it is open to an accused to apply for a directed verdict of acquittal. Although a jury, when there is one, reaches a decision in a trial, in limited circumstances the trial judge has the authority to direct that an accused will be acquitted. This power is not created by statute, but arises at common law.[204] The directed verdict (sometimes referred to as a "non-suit" as there is no case to meet) takes its name from the fact that, historically, the trial judge directed the jury to retire and return a verdict of not guilty. The Supreme Court has modified the procedure so that trial judges are instead to withdraw the case from the jury and enter the acquittal personally,[205] but the name has remained. This power applies only to acquittals: a trial judge cannot direct a jury to convict.[206]

---

198 Sections 715.1 and 715.2.

199 *R v Mackay*, 2002 SKQB 316.

200 Section 652.

201 *R v Welsh* (1997), 120 CCC (3d) 68 (BCCA).

202 *R v Prentice* (1965), 47 CR 231 (BCCA), and see s 572.

203 *R v Myers*, [2001] OJ No 4258 (CA).

204 Judges' common law powers in jury trials are preserved by s 672 of the *Code*: *R v Rowbotham*, [1994] 2 SCR 463 [*Rowbotham* 1994].

205 *Ibid*.

206 *R v Krieger*, 2006 SCC 47. See also *R v Singh*, 2025 ONCA 498 where the accused was acquitted by a jury of communicating for the purpose of obtaining the

The test for granting a directed verdict is quite restricted, and is consistent with the differing functions of the judge and jury. The jury is the trier of fact and, therefore, is called upon to assess the credibility of witnesses, decide whether the Crown's evidence has proven the accused's guilt beyond a reasonable doubt, and so on. A trial judge cannot intrude on that function. However, where the Crown has failed to provide evidence on some essential element of the offence, the trial judge can direct the acquittal of the accused. The accused can make such a motion at the close of the Crown's case, and the judge is to rule on it at that time. The accused is entitled to know the result of that motion before deciding whether to call evidence in defence.[207]

The Court has made clear that this is a limited power and is not to intrude on the jury's role. A trial judge cannot direct an acquittal on the basis that the Crown's evidence of identification is manifestly unreliable, for example, because the trial judge is not permitted to weigh the strength of the evidence.[208] The test for a directed verdict is the same as that for a preliminary inquiry judge in deciding whether to send a matter for trial

> whether or not there is any evidence upon which a reasonable jury properly instructed could return a verdict of guilty. The "justice" [is] required to commit an accused person for trial in any case in which there is admissible evidence which could, if it were believed, result in a conviction.[209]

Thus, a directed verdict is not available where the Crown's evidence is merely weak. It is possible only where there is a complete absence of evidence on some point that must be proven. Put affirmatively, the Crown must "adduce some evidence of culpability for every essential definitional element of the crime for which the Crown has the evidential burden," and a motion for a directed verdict will be granted only if it has not done so.[210] This determination must take into account all the bases upon which the accused might be found guilty of the offence, both as the principal or as a party.[211] That absence turns the question

---

sexual services of person under 18 but on his own evidence communicated believing the person was not under 18. The trial judge directed the jury to enter a verdict of guilty on the included offence of communicating for the purpose of obtaining sexual services, but the Ontario Court of Appeal found that to be an error and ordered a new trial on the lesser charge.

207 *R v Boissoneault* (1986), 16 OAC 365 (CA).

208 *R v Mezzo*, [1986] 1 SCR 802 [*Mezzo*].

209 *United States of America v Shephard*, [1977] 2 SCR 1067 at 1080.

210 *R v Charemski*, [1998] 1 SCR 679 at para 3 [*Charemski*].

211 *R v MR*, 2011 ONCA 190.

of the accused's guilt into an issue that can be settled by an exclusively legal, not factual, determination.

The rule also applies when the Crown's case rests on purely circumstantial evidence. In such cases the jury can convict only when there is no rational explanation for the circumstantial evidence other than that the accused committed the crime, and they must be instructed on that basis. Nonetheless, the Court has held that whether that test is met is a question for the jury to decide, not the judge, and so a directed verdict should not be issued.[212] Some ambiguity remains in this context, however. The Court has also held, in assessing the same test in the context of preliminary inquiries, that the judge must engage in a limited weighing of the evidence. Although a judge cannot draw inferences or assess credibility, the judge is to decide whether "if the Crown's evidence is believed it would be reasonable for a properly instructed jury to infer guilt" from that evidence.[213] This formulation of the test seems to create slightly greater scope for a trial judge to decide to grant a directed verdict.[214]

A directed verdict can be granted on the charge laid, but the trial must be allowed to proceed if it is possible that the accused could be guilty of an included offence. In *R v Titus*, for example, the Court agreed that it would be possible to direct an acquittal on a first-degree murder charge, but allow the trial to continue to see whether the accused was found guilty of second-degree murder.[215]

A trial judge's decision whether to grant a motion for a directed verdict is reviewable by an appeal court on a correctness standard, since it is a question of law.[216]

### b) Defence Presentation of Evidence

An accused who does not make, or does not succeed in, an application for a directed verdict is then entitled to call evidence, or otherwise make full answer and defence.[217] Similar to the Crown, the defence is entitled to exercise discretion as to how to present the case. For example, a trial

---

212 *R v Monteleone*, [1987] 2 SCR 154; *Mezzo*, above note 208; *Charemski*, above note 210.

213 *R v Arcuri*, [2001] 2 SCR 828 at para 30. This issue is discussed in Chapter 9.

214 On this point, generally, see David M Tanovich, "Upping the Ante in Directed Verdict Cases Where the Evidence Is Circumstantial" (1998) 15 *Criminal Reports* (5th) 21. See also *R v Beals*, 2011 NSCA 42 and *R v Ponace*, 2019 MBCA 99.

215 [1983] 1 SCR 259 [*Titus*]. In *Titus*, the judge erred by failing to grant the motion for a directed verdict, but instructed the jury at the end of the trial that they could not find the accused guilty of first-degree murder.

216 *R v Barros*, 2011 SCC 51.

217 Sections 541 and 650(3).

judge is not permitted to direct the order in which witnesses are to be called, insisting that the accused testify first.[218] The defence can call witnesses, including witnesses the Crown has decided not to call.[219] The accused is a competent witness at the trial, but is not compellable, and the failure to testify cannot be made the subject of comment by the judge or the prosecutor.[220] This statutory provision is consistent with the accused's right to silence and the presumption of innocence, both now guaranteed by the *Charter*.[221] Normally, the defence cannot cross-examine its own witnesses, though in certain situations doing this is permitted.[222]

## 5) Reopening the Crown's Case

The trial will move to closing arguments once the defence has completed calling all of the evidence it wishes. The Crown is expected to present all of its evidence before the defence is called upon. "Splitting the case" — that is, leading some of the Crown's evidence after the accused's case has been presented — has been prohibited "from the earliest days of our criminal law" for a number of reasons, including that the accused is entitled to know the full case to meet before deciding whether to remain silent or take the stand.[223]

In an exceptional case, however, the Crown can apply to reopen its case and call further evidence, at the discretion of the trial judge. The "keystone principle" in deciding whether to allow the Crown to reopen its case is whether the accused will be prejudiced in making a defence.[224] A trial judge's discretion must be exercised judicially in this regard and in the interests of justice, and the Court has laid down guidelines to assist in this task:

> The ambit of a trial judge's discretion to allow the Crown to reopen its case becomes narrower as the trial proceeds because of the

218 *R v Angelantoni* (1975), 31 CRNS 342 (Ont CA).

219 *Cook*, above note 180.

220 *CEA*, above note 189, s 4(6).

221 See *R v Chambers*, [1990] 2 SCR 1293, and *R v Noble*, [1997] 1 SCR 874. Note that, as discussed at Section B(3), above in this chapter, the situation is somewhat different when a co-accused wishes to make reference to an accused's silence: *Crawford*, above note 40.

222 *CEA*, above note 189, s 9. An accused also has the right to cross-examine a co-accused who testifies, even if they are not adverse in interest: see *R v CI*, 2023 ONCA 576.

223 *John v the Queen*, [1985] 2 SCR 476 at 480–81; *R v Krause*, [1986] 2 SCR 466 [*Krause*].

224 *MBP*, above note 109.

> increasing likelihood of prejudice to the accused's defence as the trial progresses. During the first stage, when the Crown has not yet closed its case, the trial judge's discretion is quite broad. At the second stage, which arises when the Crown has just closed its case but the defence has not yet elected whether or not to call evidence, the discretion is more limited. Finally, in the third phase — where the defence has already begun to answer the Crown's case — the discretion is extremely narrow, and is "far less likely to be exercised in favour of the Crown". The emphasis during the third phase must be on the protection of the accused's interests.[225]

The discretion is most limited in the third stage, of course, because at that point the accused is most likely to be prejudiced by the admission of new evidence on the part of the Crown.

The evidence ought to be new evidence, in the sense that it could not have been foreseen by the Crown and was in the interests of justice. However, that the evidence is new is not sufficient. The Court has held that the type of limited circumstances in which such evidence will be permitted are where the defence directly or indirectly contributed to the Crown's failure to lead the evidence, or where the Crown has made a mistake or omission on a non-controversial issue that was purely formal or technical and that had nothing to do with the substance of the case.[226] Only in those circumstances, or ones closely analogous to them, should the Crown be permitted to reopen its case after the defence has begun to present evidence.[227] It is not relevant that the Crown was not at fault in failing to discover the evidence: the focus is on the prejudice to the accused, which is the same whether the Crown had acted diligently or not.[228] The accused was entitled to know the case to meet before beginning the defence, but that case is at great risk of changing if the Crown is permitted to reopen.[229]

---

225 *R v G(SG)*, [1997] 2 SCR 716 at para 30 [*G(SG)*].

226 *MBP*, above note 109.

227 *G(SG)*, above note 225.

228 *Ibid* at para 30.

229 Note the potential interaction, and slight inconsistency, between this rule and the rule on amending indictments, discussed above. An indictment can be amended to conform to the evidence presented, in some cases, even after the accused has presented evidence, even alibi evidence. In practical terms, an accused might perceive little difference between the Crown leading new evidence to show that an offence occurred at a different time than the accused's alibi covers, and amending a charge so that the offence is alleged to have occurred at a different time than the accused's alibi covers. In theory, they are different issues: in *MBP*, above note 109, for example, the Court noted that without leading the new evidence, the Crown would not be in a position to apply to

Nonetheless, in appropriate circumstances the Crown can reopen its case. In *R v Sylvester*, for example, a police officer received several telephone calls from a person he identified as a witness on a weekend following closing arguments in the case. She told him that she had lied on the stand and then retracted that claim. The Crown was permitted to reopen its case to present this new evidence, and the defence was allowed to cross-examine, to call the witness herself to the stand once again, and to make further submissions. The Ontario Court of Appeal held that no problem arose with this procedure, since the trial judge had adequately instructed the jury on the limited use they could make of the new evidence.[230]

## 6) Rebuttal Evidence

A close cousin to the issue of the Crown reopening its case is the possibility of the Crown leading rebuttal evidence. Rebuttal evidence is permitted

> where the defence has raised some new matter or defence which the Crown has had no opportunity to deal with and which the Crown or the plaintiff could not reasonably have anticipated. But rebuttal will not be permitted regarding matters which merely confirm or reinforce earlier evidence adduced in the Crown's case which could have been brought before the defence was made.[231]

Essentially, rebuttal evidence must concern matters that the Crown is reasonably surprised to find in issue.

This test creates slightly broader scope for admitting rebuttal evidence than for reopening the Crown case. This difference is justified on the basis that, if the test for admitting rebuttal evidence is met, then it cannot be said that the accused did not know the case to meet. If rebuttal evidence deals only with unanticipated matters arising in the defence case, then the evidence led was not part of the original case to meet.[232]

---

amend the information. In that case they held that it was an error to allow the Crown to reopen its case to present new evidence. However, it would not have been an error to amend the charge had the evidence originally presented suggested the offence occurred at a different date than alleged in the indictment. From the accused's perspective, it might appear that the prejudice to an alibi has greater significance in one context than in the other.

230 (1997), 97 OAC 380 (CA).

231 *Krause*, above note 223 at 474.

232 *G(SG)*, above note 225 at para 40.

To preserve that rationale it is important that rebuttal evidence be admitted only when it truly does concern matters the Crown could not have anticipated. In *R v Biddle*, for example, the accused was charged with an assault that occurred somewhere between 10:00 and 10:30 in the evening. The accused took the stand in his own defence, and his testimony included the claim that he had been at a show between 7:30 and 9:15 p.m., then at several bars later on. The Crown then led rebuttal evidence of a witness who testified that the accused had followed her in his car at 8:30 that evening. The Court held that this evidence should not have been allowed in rebuttal and should have been presented as part of the Crown's original case. The Crown knew that Biddle had given a statement to the police about his whereabouts and ought to have anticipated that the defence would challenge the identification evidence. The Crown would have been able to present the witness as part of its case, and its failure to do so prevented the accused from knowing the entire case to meet before testifying.[233]

Rebuttal evidence cannot be led if it will reply only to a collateral issue. However, it need not be determinative of an essential issue either. Rather, the question is whether it relates to an essential issue which might be determinative of the case.[234] If it does and the Crown could not have foreseen that the evidence would be necessary, then it is generally admissible.

The accused's right in section 650(3) to make full answer and defence after the close of the Crown's case applies where the Crown has led rebuttal evidence, permitting the accused to lead surrebuttal evidence.[235] However, this opportunity does not eliminate any prejudice caused by improperly led rebuttal evidence. Indeed, the mere fact of entering the witness box a second time can create the impression that the accused was caught in a lie, and so could leave an adverse impression on the jury.[236]

---

233 [1995] 1 SCR 761 [*Biddle*]. Similarly, see *R v Anderson*, 2009 ABCA 67, leave to appeal to SCC refused [2009] SCCA No 428. The accused had claimed that details of a murder he provided during a "sting" operation had been told to him by two undercover officers. The trial judge permitted the Crown to lead rebuttal evidence from two police officers to say that the undercover officers had not been told those details. The Court of Appeal concluded the rebuttal evidence was improperly admitted: the entire point of having "holdback" evidence was so that an accused could not claim to have learned details from undercover officers, and so the Crown should have led the evidence as part of its case in chief.

234 *R v Aalders*, [1993] 2 SCR 482 at para 37. See also the discussion in *R v Ryan*, 2011 NLCA 53.

235 *R v Ewert* (1989), 52 CCC (3d) 280 (BCCA).

236 *Biddle*, above note 233 at 776.

## 7) Reopening the Defence Case

It is worth noting that it is also open to the defence to apply to reopen its case, though obviously the time in which this could occur is necessarily more restricted because the accused does not present evidence until the Crown's case is done. Whether a trial judge should permit the defence to reopen its case after final argument is a discretionary decision. In considering whether to allow the defence to reopen its case, the trial judge should consider whether the proposed evidence is relevant to an issue in the case, potential prejudice to the other party, and the effect of permitting reopening on the orderly and expeditious conduct of the trial.[237] In *R v Scott*, for example, one co-accused sought a bench warrant for a witness who had not responded to a subpoena. Being unsuccessful in the application, the defence entered no evidence and, along with the Crown, made final submissions. The witness then appeared, and the accused applied to reopen his case. The Court held that the trial judge had not exercised her discretion improperly in refusing to allow the accused to reopen his case and call the witness. The trial judge had an obligation to conduct the trial in an expeditious and orderly manner, had been given no explanation of the way in which the witness's testimony would be relevant, and had to consider the possible prejudice to the co-accused who objected to an adjournment.[238]

It is possible for the defence to apply to reopen its case and admit new evidence not only after argument, but indeed sometimes after a verdict has been reached, though only based on a more rigorous test. The Ontario Court of Appeal has held that a case cannot be reopened if the verdict was reached by a jury or if a judge has acquitted an accused, but that it can be reopened following a judge's guilty verdict in "special circumstances."[239] However, a different standard applies if the application is made after adjudication.[240] It is a discretionary decision on the part of the trial judge, but the prevailing view is that the test for a trial judge to reopen the defence case after a guilty verdict should be based

237 *R v Hayward* (1993), 88 CCC (3d) 193 (Ont CA) [*Hayward*].

238 *R v Scott*, [1990] 3 SCR 979. In contrast, in *Hayward*, above note 237, a similar issue around a missing witness arose, but in that case the witness appeared later in the day, after the Crown had begun submissions. Given that the evidence was relevant to an issue at trial, the Crown was aware of the nature of that evidence, and the witness could be heard immediately; the Ontario Court of Appeal concluded that the trial judge had erred in refusing to allow the defence to reopen its case.

239 *R v Lessard* (1976), 33 CRNS 16 (Ont CA).

240 *R v Arabia*, 2008 ONCA 565 [*Arabia*].

on that for admitting fresh evidence on appeal:[241] "(1) is the evidence admissible under the operative rules of evidence (the admissibility component); (2) is the evidence sufficiently cogent in that it could reasonably be expected to have affected the verdict (the cogency component); and (3) does the party seeking its admission offer a satisfactory explanation for the failure to adduce it at trial (the due diligence component)."[242] Generally courts also include the criterion that the request to reopen is not an attempt to undo a tactical decision made at trial.[243]

When an accused satisfies the test for reopening the trial after verdict, the likely remedy is simply the vacating of the conviction and continuation of the trial. However, it is possible that the appropriate remedy will be to declare a mistrial: for example, where the new evidence is something that had not been disclosed in a timely way. However, a mistrial should only be ordered in the clearest of cases.[244]

## 8) Addresses to the Jury

### a) Closing Arguments by Counsel

In the ordinary course of events all evidence is presented and final submissions are then made. Section 651 of the *Code* sets out the order in which the Crown and the accused are to address the jury. If the defence has not called evidence then the Crown argues first, but if the defence has called evidence then it argues first.[245] Although it has been argued that the right to full answer and defence should entitle the accused to address the jury last in all cases, the Court determined in *R v Rose*, in a closely divided decision, that section 651 of the *Code* does not violate section 7 or section 11(d) of the *Charter*.

Five of the nine members of the Court held that, although there was no question that counsel's address to the jury could be of great persuasive significance, there was not sufficient evidence to show that there was an advantage to speaking last. An accused will be reasonably clear,

---

241 *R v Mysko* (1980), 2 Sask R 342 (CA); *R v Kowall* (1996), 50 CR (4th) 271 (Ont CA) [*Kowall*]; *R v MGT*, 2017 ONCA 736.

242 *R v RG*, 2023 ONCA 343 at para 55 [*RG*].

243 *Kowall*, above note 241 or *R v MacGregor*, 1997 NSCA 88. *RG*, above note 242 did not explicitly list this criterion but allowed the accused to reopen the case because "it is not accurate to say that the application to reopen the trial was an after-the-fact attempt to reverse earlier tactical decisions. This is because there was no strategic reason for why the defence would not have obtained and reviewed the cell phone records to consider whether to adduce them at trial."

244 *Arabia*, above note 240 at para 49 and 52.

245 Where there is more than one accused, all accused are equally affected by the decision of any one of them to call evidence, and the Crown will argue last.

through the Crown's opening arguments and questions to witnesses, as to what argument the Crown will make. In general, therefore, the rule requiring an accused to sometimes speak first did not cause *Charter* problems. In individual cases where irregularities in Crown counsel's address to the jury or other issues threatened an accused's fair trial right, two options are available. The trial judge who, in any event, addresses the jury last in charging them could give curative instructions, instructing the jury to ignore improper aspects of an argument. Further, *Rose* seems to stand for the proposition that a court's inherent jurisdiction would allow it to grant to the defence a limited right of reply following the Crown's address, where not doing so would prejudice the accused's right to a fair trial and to make full answer and defence. This situation might arise where, for example, the accused has been misled by the Crown as to the argument to be advanced, or where the Crown's argument has changed so dramatically that the defence could not reasonably have anticipated and answered it.[246] The right of reply would be confined to addressing the issues improperly dealt with by Crown counsel.

Note that although a majority of the Court found that section 651 was not so unfair that it violated the *Charter*, all nine members of the Court expressed the view that better alternatives could be found. Various proposals have been put forward: these include always allowing the accused to speak last or giving the accused a choice as to when to speak.[247]

It has also been argued section 651 only applies to jury trials. Trials by judge alone are governed by Part XIX of the *Code*, rather than Part XX which governs jury trials. The trial by jury rules are adopted "with such modifications as the circumstances require" for Part XIX,[248] and it

---

246 *Rose*, above note 179. Justice L'Heureux-Dubé, one of the five judges making up the majority in the result, disagreed with the other four judges as to whether a trial judge had inherent jurisdiction to grant a limited right of reply, holding that this jurisdiction had been ousted by s 651. However, the reasons of Binnie J for the four judges who held that s 651 violated the *Charter* (particularly their arguments concerning s 11(d)) suggest that they would agree with the four members of the majority regarding inherent jurisdiction. But see *R v Akpalialuk*, 2021 NUCA 2 [*Akpalialuk*] arguing that the point remains unsettled, on the basis that "If Justice Binnie believed that the trial judge had a discretion to allow reply in exceptional circumstances, he would have said so" (para 64).

247 See, for example, Tim Quigley, "Principled Reform of Criminal Procedure" in Don Stuart, RJ Delisle, & Allan Manson, eds, *Towards a Clear and Just Criminal Law* (Toronto: Carswell, 1999); Law Reform Commission of Canada, *The Jury* (Ottawa: Law Reform Commission, 1982).

248 Section 572.

has been held that in judge-alone trials a right of reply should be given to whomever speaks first.[249]

Counsel must not exceed the appropriate bounds when making submissions to the jury. This rule applies to both Crown and defence, though it applies more strictly to the Crown prosecutor — defence counsel is to be afforded more latitude in the content of a closing argument.[250] Counsel ought not, for example, to offer their personal opinions,[251] use inflammatory language,[252] attack the personal integrity of opposing counsel,[253] misrepresent the evidence,[254] offer an interpretation of the evidence that is inaccurate or unfair,[255] or inject irrelevant issues.[256] Crown counsel should not refer to the accused's failure to testify.[257]

When improper comments are made, a trial judge has a discretion over how to respond and, in some cases, will intervene but in other cases will not.[258] If comments by Crown counsel are sufficiently prejudicial, it will be an error of law for a trial judge to fail to intervene.[259] The fact that improper comments have been made, though an error, will not necessarily render a trial so unfair that an appeal will be granted.[260] Further, although in most cases it will be sufficient for a judge to include a specific corrective comment in the charge to the jury, as noted

---

249 *Akpalialuk*, above note 246 at para 87.

250 *R v Trakas*, 2008 ONCA 410 [*Trakas*].

251 *R v Copp*, 2009 NBCA 16 [*Copp*]; *R v L(L)*, 2009 ONCA 413 [*L(L)*]; *R v S(G)*, 2009 NBCA 82.

252 See the review of cases on this issue in *R v Melanson*, 2007 NBCA 94 [*Melanson*]. See also *R v Horan*, 2008 ONCA 589 [*Horan*].

253 *Horan*, *ibid*.

254 *L(L)*, above note 251.

255 *Shephard v R*, 2019 NBCA 76.

256 See, for example, *Horan*, above note 252, where defence counsel raised the issue of wrongful convictions when it had no particular connection to the case at hand, or *R v Williams*, 2008 ONCA 413 [*Williams*], where the accused raised issues of race that had no evidentiary foundation.

257 *R v Biladeau*, 2008 ONCA 833 [*Biladeau*].

258 Contrast, for example, *Copp*, above note 251, where the trial judge almost immediately intervened, to *Melanson*, above note 252, where the trial judge spoke to the jury about the point as soon as the Crown prosecutor had finished and then also returned to the issue in his charge to the jury, to *Williams*, above note 256, where the trial judge did nothing about the improper remarks.

259 *R v AT*, 2015 ONCA 65.

260 See, for example, *Trakas*, above note 250, or *Copp*, above note 251. In contrast in *Biladeau*, above note 257, where the essence of the improper remarks had been to invite the jury to infer the accused's guilt from his failure to testify, a new trial was ordered.

above in relatively rare situations the judge might grant the prejudiced party a limited opportunity to reply.[261]

### b) Charging the Jury

Once counsel have argued, if there is a jury the judge then gives them instructions, usually referred to as the "charge to the jury." Section 650.1 of the *Code* permits a judge to confer with the Crown and the defence with regard to what matters should be explained to the jury. The purpose of the charge to the jury is to "decant and simplify" the case and leave the jury with a sufficient understanding of the facts as they relate to the relevant legal issues.[262] In general, the trial judge has considerable discretion regarding the content and form of the charge to the jury, though with some limits. An accused has a right to a properly instructed jury, but not to a perfectly instructed jury.[263]

The organization of a jury charge is a matter of common law, and so trial judges do have some latitude in structuring it. The Ontario Court of Appeal has suggested that, despite the broad discretion given trial judge, all jury instructions should ideally incorporate five basic components: i) the legal framework, typically the elements of the offence or offences with which the accused is charged; ii) the factual issues arising out of the legal framework that the jury must resolve; iii) the material evidence relevant to these issues; iv) the position of the Crown and defence on these issues; and v) the evidence supporting each of their positions on these issues.[264] Trial judges are permitted to experiment with new approaches to instructing a jury, provided that at the end the jury understands the nature of their task and has been given the necessary help from the instructions.

In *R v Ménard*, for example, the trial judge gave his instructions in four parts, instructing the jury on substantive law at the start of the trial, giving instructions on two other specific matters during the course of the trial, and reviewing the evidence without reviewing the other instructions (though distributing transcripts of them) at the end of the trial. The Court decided that in the particular circumstances of the case no miscarriage of justice occurred, but did make several comments on the approach taken. They suggested that long and detailed instructions at the start of a trial might be more confusing than helpful

---

261 *Rose*, above note 179 at para 125.

262 *R v Jacquard*, [1997] 1 SCR 314 [*Jacquard*].

263 *Ibid*, reaffirmed in *R v Daley*, 2007 SCC 53 at para 31 [*Daley*]. See also *R v Calnen*, 2019 SCC 6 [*Calnen*] at para 8: "the test is whether the jury was properly, not perfectly, instructed."

264 *R v Newton*, 2017 ONCA 496 at para 11.

and that they increase the risk of a jury being confused by instructions concerning matters that ultimately do not arise in the case. Similarly, where an erroneous statement of law is made at the outset of the trial, the error might have a much greater effect on the trial and be much more difficult to correct, if it can be corrected at all. The Court also held that the principles of reasonable doubt, the presumption of innocence, and the burden of proof were too important to be dealt with by simply, at the end, referring the jury to the transcript of the earlier instructions.[265]

The judge's charge should be fair and dispassionate; it should also be the last thing said to the jury before they commence their deliberations. Judges generally ask counsel, following the charge, whether they felt any portion was unclear or needed clarification, but it is an error to allow counsel to address the jury directly again.[266] Indeed, the instructions drafted by the judge are typically based on extensive pre-charge discussions with counsel, so that it would be rare for counsel to hear the charge for the first time as it is being delivered.[267] A judge should not divide the charge in two, instructing the jury on some matters, then allowing counsel to speak, then finally completing the charge.[268] However, beyond these types of issues, a trial judge's discretion as to how to structure the charge will rarely be interfered with.

A judge cannot leave the jury to their own devices in deciding what evidence must be considered:

> The rule which has been laid down, and consistently followed is that in a jury trial the presiding judge must, except in rare cases where it would be needless to do so, review the substantial parts of the evidence, and give the jury the theory of the defence, so that they may appreciate the value and effect of that evidence, and how the law is to be applied to the facts as they find them.[269]

This does not mean, however, that an exhaustive review of every piece of evidence is required in every case. Rather, the judge must see to it that

---

265 [1998] 2 SCR 109 [*Ménard*].

266 *R v C(JD)* (2003), 186 OAC 234 (CA).

267 *R v Bouchard*, 2013 ONCA 791. Note that counsel giving input to the judge as to the content of the charge constitutes a part of the trial, and so the rule in s 650 that the accused must be present for trial applies to this process. That is, although a judge might use email to provide a copy of the charge to counsel, their submissions to the judge should not be made by email: *R v Hassanzada*, 2016 ONCA 284.

268 *R v Levene* (1983), 36 CR (3d) 386 (Ont CA).

269 *Azoulay v the Queen*, [1952] 2 SCR 495 at 497–98, reaffirmed in *Daley*, above note 263 at para 54.

the jury is able to fully appreciate the issues and the defence presented, which might be best served by omitting reference to some peripheral evidence.[270] Non-direction on a particular piece of evidence is only misdirection if that piece of evidence is the foundation for a defence, justification, or excuse.[271] Otherwise, the judge has considerable latitude in deciding how much or how little evidence should be reviewed.[272] It has been suggested that there are functionally just two important considerations: "would the jury appreciate the potential significance of the evidence to the issues from both the Crown and defence perspective, and was the instruction fair, in the sense that it represented an even-handed treatment of the evidence as it related to the issues the jury had to decide?"[273]

Thus, a judge still has a considerable amount of discretion as to exactly how to review the facts. A judge can decide to review particular facts only once in the charge, for example, even though they might be relevant to more than one issue. Indeed, restating the facts each time they are relevant could make the charge worse, not better.[274] Charges that are very long will not necessarily be an error either. In *R v Fell*, for example, the trial judge gave a four-day charge to the jury. Although the Ontario Court of Appeal suggested that such a length for a charge might be more exhausting and confusing than helpful, they held that there was nothing inaccurate in the charge, and that this exercise of the trial judge's discretion did not make the trial unfair.[275] On the other hand, in *R v Saleh* the trial judge did not "decant and simplify"; instead, he gave the jury a copy of his eighty-seven typewritten pages of notes of the evidence, and this was found to be an error.[276]

Similarly, a trial judge has some discretion over what legal issues to include in the instructions. As long as the jury members are given instructions that allow them to arrive at a just and proper verdict, the trial judge is entitled to narrow the issues for the jury by focusing on what was realistically at issue in the particular case. If the real issue in

---

270 *Ibid* at paras 56–57.

271 *R v Rybak*, 2008 ONCA 354.

272 *R v Royz*, 2009 SCC 13. Courts of Appeal have reached no consistent view as to whether it is advisable for judges to include in the charge a summary of evidence written by counsel: see *R v Minor*, 2013 ONCA 557, criticizing the practice, and *R v Huard*, 2013 ONCA 650 [*Huard*], seeming to approve it.

273 *R v Figliola*, 2018 ONCA 578 at para 11.

274 *Jacquard*, above note 262.

275 (1990), 40 OAC 139. See also *R v Rideout* (1999), 182 Nfld & PEIR 227 (Nfld CA), aff'd on other issues, [2001] 1 SCR 755, reaching a similar conclusion concerning a thirteen-hour jury charge.

276 (2013), 303 CCC (3d) 431 (Ont CA).

a case was whether the accused was liable as a principal, for example, it can be acceptable not to instruct the jury on party liability, even if theoretically that possibility were open.[277] Presenting the jury with a "decision tree," which outlines the questions that the jury should ask itself and the directions their reasoning should go based on those answers, has been found to be helpful, as long as it supplements, rather than replaces, proper instructions.[278]

Much caselaw concerns jury instructions. This is, in part, because appeals generally focus on legal issues, and so whether a judge has accurately described the law to the jury is a potentially fruitful source of argument. A charge should review the facts, the prosecution's theory of the case, the accused's theory of the case, and the defences that arise for the jury. it is generally said that the trial judge should charge on all defences that arise on the facts, whether the accused has raised them or not.[279] However, this must be tempered against the possibility that doing so will undermine defence counsel's strategy at trial.[280] It will also be necessary to charge the jury on whatever particular issues are relevant to the trial, such as the use that can be made of an accused's criminal record, or issues surrounding circumstantial evidence, identification evidence, and alibi evidence. A considerable number of cases have focused on whether trial judges adequately explain the concept of "proof beyond a reasonable doubt" to juries.[281] In reviewing a trial judge's instructions to the jury, the charge must be viewed as a whole, and inadequacies in one portion might be compensated for sufficiently in other parts so that the entire charge is acceptable.[282] In addition, sentences or passages should not be considered in isolation but rather in the context of the entire charge and the trial as a whole: what might initially seem ambiguous might not, on such examination, actually be

---

277 *Pickton*, above note 179 at para 10.

278 *Huard*, above note 272.

279 *Faid*, above note 177.

280 See, for example, *R v Gibb*, 2024 ONCA 255 [*Gibb*], where it was not an error for the trial judge not to have instructed the jury about intoxication, even though there was an air of reality to it. The accused had not wanted intoxication raised, since it would undermine his main defence of provocation.

281 A non-exhaustive list includes *R v Lifchus*, [1997] 3 SCR 320; *R v Starr*, [2000] 2 SCR 144; *R v Beauchamp*, [2000] 2 SCR 720; *R v Russell*, [2000] 2 SCR 731; *R v Avetysan*, [2000] 2 SCR 745, rev'g (1999), 174 Nfld & PEIR 34 (Nfld CA); *R v Rhee*, [2001] 3 SCR 364; *R v Feeley*, 2003 SCC 7; *R v Griffin*, 2009 SCC 28 [*Griffin*].

282 This principle is stated in virtually every case dealing with jury instructions, but see, for example, *Jacquard*, above note 262; *R v W(D)*, [1991] 1 SCR 742 [*W(D)*]; *R v S(WD)*, [1994] 3 SCR 521 [*S(WD)*].

so.[283] If there is some ambiguity, it is not clear that any uncertainty must be resolved in favour of the accused.[284]

The Court has summarized the principles relating to whether a charge to the jury was adequate:

> The cardinal rule is that it is the general sense which the words used must have conveyed, in all probability, to the mind of the jury that matters, and not whether a particular formula was recited by the judge. The particular words used, or the sequence followed, is a matter within the discretion of the trial judge and will depend on the particular circumstances of the case.

In determining the general sense which the words used have likely conveyed to the jury, the appellate tribunal will consider the charge as a whole. The standard that a trial judge's instructions are to be held to is not perfection. "The accused is entitled to a properly instructed jury, not a perfectly instructed jury . . . . It is the overall effect of the charge that matters."[285]

Instructions should also cover the procedural aspects of the jury's deliberation. Confusion in jurors' minds over how long they are expected to deliberate before a "hung jury" could be declared, for example, might improperly affect their deliberations.[286]

Even though the jury is the trier of fact, a trial judge is entitled to offer opinions on matters of fact in the course of the instructions to the jury. A judge should be careful in doing so, however, since to do so could render a trial unfair.[287] Further, the trial judge must not remove the decision from the jury by instructing them to convict. Such an instruction violates an accused's section 11(f) right under the *Charter* to trial by jury.[288] In other words, as noted above, there is no "directed verdict of conviction" that is analogous to a directed verdict of acquittal.

---

283 *R v Jaw*, 2009 SCC 42 [*Jaw*].

284 *Ibid* at para 38. The majority does not settle the point but suggests that uncertainty need not always be resolved in the accused's favour and that attempts to resolve the ambiguity should first be made. The dissenting judgment in *Jaw* points out that the majority relies on principles created in the context of statutory interpretation in reaching their conclusion, which are not applicable in the context of understanding a charge to the jury.

285 *Daley*, above note 263 at para 31.

286 *R v Pan; R v Sawyer*, [2001] 2 SCR 344 at para 98.

287 See, for example, *R v Walker*, 2019 ONCA 806, where the trial judge offered the opinion, in his charge, that the object being held by the accused in a video was a gun, even though both Crown and defence had taken the view that it was not possible to determine what was being held.

288 *Boulet v the Queen*, [1978] 1 SCR 332; *R v Sims*, [1992] 2 SCR 858 [*Sims*]; *R v Krieger*, 2006 SCC 47 [*Krieger*]. In *Krieger*, the trial judge deliberately directed

Following the charge to the jury, judges tell juries not to begin their deliberations immediately. First, the judge consults with counsel to see whether they have any objections or feel that any matters need clarification. Indeed, the practice of a judge providing counsel with a copy of the charge in advance has been favourably commented upon, and the judge ought generally not to deviate from that written charge.[289] It remains within the judge's discretion whether to act on the comments of counsel, and indeed, it can be an error to include an issue in a charge even if both counsel agree it should be there.[290] Failure by counsel to raise an objection at the time does not automatically prevent that matter from later being a basis for appeal, nor does it mean that the error was a harmless one to which the curative provision in section 686(1)(b)(iii) of the *Code* can be applied. However, failure by counsel to object at the time will enter into an appellate court's decision about the overall accuracy of the instructions and the seriousness of the alleged misdirection.[291] This is likely to be especially so where decision at trial is seen as a tactical one, meaning that counsel should not be allowed to reverse it on appeal.[292]

### c) Re-charging the Jury

Where a judge re-charges following submissions from counsel, essentially the same criteria apply to that as to the original charge. In most instances, the re-charge will simply be considered part of the charge, and the question will be whether, taken as a whole, the jury has been properly instructed. A re-charge might rectify an error in the original charge, meaning that, as a whole, the charge is satisfactory.[293] Alterna-

---

the jury to retire and return with a verdict of guilty. See also *R v Gunning*, [2005] 1 SCR 627, where the trial judge directed the jury that one of the elements of the offence in question had been proven by the Crown; this too was an error.

289 *R v Polimac*, 2010 ONCA 346. See also *R v Hungwe*, 2018 ONCA 456 at para 48: "when a trial judge has provided a draft of his jury instructions to counsel, and received their comments on that draft, it is generally a risky step for a trial judge to then add other commentary 'on the fly' as s/he delivers her or his instructions."

290 *Pickton*, above note 179.

291 *Jacquard*, above note 262; *Thériault v the Queen*, [1981] 1 SCR 336. See, for example, *Calnen*, above note 263, where Moldaver J held that no limiting instruction against propensity reasoning had been required, adding that "[e]xperienced defence counsel at trial seemed to be of the same view. Were it otherwise, I would have expected him to seek the kind of limiting instruction which my colleague now says was both obvious and crucial — and to have forcefully objected had the trial judge not capitulated" (para 6).

292 See, for example, *Gibb*, above note 280, or *R v Singh*, 2010 ONCA 808.

293 See, for example, *R v G(RM)*, [1996] 3 SCR 362 [*G(RM)*].

tively, in *R v W(D)*,[294] an error in a re-charge did not form the basis for an appeal, largely because the re-charge was quite short and followed only a few minutes after the original charge, the original charge had instructed the jury correctly, and the trial judge said in the re-charge that the jury should not give special emphasis to the re-charge and should be mindful of the duties he had outlined in the charge.

On the other hand, sometimes it is necessary to re-charge a jury after they have begun their deliberations because the jury has sent a question to the judge. In these circumstances, the re-charge takes on much greater significance. If the jury has asked a question, it will generally relate to an important point in their reasoning, and even if they were correctly instructed on the point earlier, the fact that they have asked a question shows they have forgotten or did not understand the instruction. In this context, the Court has held:

> There can be no doubt about the significance which must be attached to questions from the jury and the fundamental importance of giving correct and comprehensive responses to those questions. With the question the jury has identified the issues upon which it requires direction. It is this issue upon which the jury has focused. No matter how exemplary the original charge may have been, it is essential that the recharge on the issue presented by the question be correct and comprehensive. No less will suffice. The jury has said in effect, on this issue there is confusion, please help us. That help must be provided.[295]

Therefore, when a question is received from a jury it must be considered to be significant. Counsel must be heard as to what response should be made to the question, and the answer must be correct and comprehensive. Since the jury has asked about the issue, instructions must be repeated even if they were given in the original charge, and the need for the re-charge to be correct and comprehensive increases with the greater the delay. Finally, an error in a re-charge following a question from the jury generally cannot be saved by a correct original charge because the fact that a question was asked shows that the jury did not adequately understand the original instructions.[296]

---

294 Above note 282.

295 *S(WD)*, above note 282 at para 18.

296 *Ibid*. See also *R v Shaw*, 2024 ONCA 119 at para 64:

> A question from a jury . . . is an indication of a particular problem the jury is confronting – on which they are focused. Although jury instructions must be read as a whole, courts have recognized that answers to jury questions will be given special emphasis by jurors. As a result, a trial judge has an

It is not necessarily an error for a re-charge simply to repeat the instructions given in the original charge — where the original charge was not given to the jury in writing and the question indicates that the jury has forgotten the instructions, for example. When the jury does have the charge in writing and does not understand it, however, the trial judge ought to try to explain the relevant concepts in different words.[297] Further, even if the trial judge simply repeats the original charge, they must make clear to the jury that they can return to seek further clarification.[298]

Although a trial judge has a duty to assist the jury if they have a question, the judge does not have to answer whatever question the jury has asked right away. It can be appropriate to invite the jury to focus or rephrase their question, provided they are not discouraged from seeking assistance.[299] It is also wise on the judge's part to consult with counsel before answering a question.[300]

Indeed, a jury's question might indicate that it is considering a different route to liability from that proposed by the Crown. Nothing prevents a jury from convicting on such a basis,[301] and so a judge might therefore, in answering a question, be required to charge a jury in a

---

obligation to fully and properly answer a question posed by the jury. A complete and careful response is necessary even if the subject-matter of the question has been reviewed in the main charge.

297 See, for example, *R v Neville*, 2015 SCC 49, where the trial judge replied to a question simply by referring the jury back to the written instructions he had given them, rather than clarifying.

298 *R v Layton*, 2009 SCC 36 [*Layton*]. In *Layton*, the trial judge repeated her initial instructions on reasonable doubt and told the jury that there was little she could do to clarify the concept further. The Supreme Court concluded at para 32 that the re-charge was in error: "A verbatim reiteration of the initial charge would not have been fatal had the judge made it absolutely clear to the jury that it was welcome to return with further questions if jury members were still confused. But the jury was discouraged from doing so by the words the trial judge used."

In contrast, in *R v Miljevic*, 2011 SCC 8, the trial judge specifically encouraged the jury to ask further questions if they were left unclear.

299 See, for example, *R v Couture*, 2007 QCCA 1612, where the jury asked to watch again a videotape of one statement and hear the audiotapes of two others. The trial judge was concerned that doing so (which would take four to five hours) might give undue emphasis to particular parts of the evidence and dilute the arguments of counsel. He invited the jury to consider whether they had a more specific question, which after forty-five minutes they did. As a result, the jury viewed a twelve-second segment of the videotape. The Court of Appeal held that the trial judge had acted correctly.

300 *Griffin*, above note 281.

301 *R v Groot* (1998), 129 CCC (3d) 293 (CA), aff'd [1999] 3 SCR 664.

way that does not accord with either the Crown or defence theory. This possibility gives rise to trial fairness concerns, in that opening up such a possibility for the jury might mean that the accused was not able to present a full and fair defence. Whether the judge can answer the question by instructing on a different route to conviction, or should foreclose that possibility, must be decided on a case-by-case basis.[302]

# E. JURY DELIBERATIONS

## 1) Jury Sequestration

A trial judge can allow the jury to separate at any point before it begins to deliberate, and in this event a publication ban is imposed.[303] Once the jury begins its deliberations, it is sequestered (isolated in a way to keep from it any potential sources of information). At this stage the jury is essentially to be left alone until it has reached a verdict, or until it is apparent that it will not be able to do so. The verdict, whether for conviction or acquittal, must be unanimous. If the jury is ultimately unable to reach unanimity then, as will be pursued below, section 653 of the *Code* permits the trial judge to discharge the jury and order a new trial.

Unanimity, in the case of a conviction, only requires that all members of the jury conclude that the accused is guilty of the offence in *some* fashion: "a jury need not be unanimous on the nature of the accused's participation in the offence."[304] Accordingly, a jury could be instructed on the accused's potential liability both as the principal and as a party, and need not be unanimous as to which route to conviction to take, so long as they all agree the accused is guilty.[305] The rationale for this result is compelling. Even if half the jurors believe the accused was guilty as a principal while half believe the accused guilty as a party, nonetheless they are *all* convinced beyond a reasonable doubt that the accused is not innocent: it would be anomalous, then, if the result of that disagreement was that the accused had to be found not guilty.[306] That approach to unanimity — or more accurately that approach to rejecting the argument that there

302 *R v Grandine*, 2017 ONCA 718.

303 Sections 647 and 648. Note that s 647 allows the judge, before deliberation, to "permit the members of the jury to separate": that language implies that being kept together is the norm, but that is not in fact the case.

304 *Pickton*, above note 179 at para 58.

305 *Thatcher*, above note 95.

306 *Thatcher*, above note 95 at paras 80 and 81.

was not unanimity — has generally been taken to apply equally outside the issue of liability as a party or the principal. Jurors need not all agree on the *facts* leading to conviction as long as they all agree the accused should be convicted.[307] If an information alleges multiple incidents of the same behaviour over a period of time, the jurors need not agree as to *which* incident happened, provided they all are persuaded that at least one did.[308] Where an offence can be committed in more than one way, the jury need not be unanimous as to the manner.[309]

While sequestered, the jury is not literally isolated from all contact with others. Section 647(2) provides that "the jury shall be kept under the charge of an officer of the court as the judge directs, and that officer shall prevent the jurors from communicating with anyone other than himself or another member of the jury without leave of the judge." The purpose of the rule is "to protect jurors from outside influences that might affect their verdict" and so it does not, for example, prevent uncontroversial communications such as telling a server what they want for dinner.[310] Sequestration also does not require that all the jurors be kept together at all times, though they should be instructed not to deliberate unless they are all present.[311]

The jury is also able, though the court officer, to initiate contact with the judge. When a judge receives a non-administrative inquiry from the jury, the judge is to "(a) read the communication in open court in the presence of all parties; (b) give counsel an opportunity to make submissions in open court prior to dealing with the question; (c)

---

307 *R v Morin*, [1988] 2 SCR 345 at para 38, cited to this effect in *Fredette c R*, 2021 QCCA 1844 at para 14 [*Fredette*].

308 In *MRH*, above note 18, the accused was charged with one count of a sexual offence based on two separate incidents. The Supreme Court concluded that it was clear that the jury was in fact unanimous that the first incident had occurred and so left the question of whether such unanimity was required for another day. However, courts of appeal have accepted that no such unanimity is required. See, for example, *Fredette*, above note 307 at para 15, *R v Robinson* (2004), 24 CR (6th) (Ont CA) or *R v GLM*, 1999 BCCA 467. The British Columbia Court of Appeal subsequently declined to strike a five-judge panel to consider overturning *GLM*: see *R v RGS*, 2023 BCCA 52.

309 *Fredette*, above note 307, concerned a first-degree murder charge: murder can become first-degree murder in several different ways.

310 *R v Zvolensky*, 2017 ONCA 273 [*Zvolensky*] at para 234.

311 *Ibid* at para 236. That case also observes that "some casual comment about the case while some of them are in smaller groups does not amount to a miscarriage of justice."

answer the question for the jury in open court in the presence of all parties."[312] Such requests can concern a variety of things.

Juries sometimes request copies of the *Criminal Code*, or portions of it, for example. A trial judge is permitted to give short sections of the *Code* to the jury, but must be careful not to prejudice the outcome of the trial by doing so.[313] It is likely to be a mistake to give the *Code* provisions to the jury and leave them to work out the meaning for themselves, but it could be acceptable to provide photocopies of some sections if they are accompanied by an explanation.[314] However, where giving the jury sections of the *Code* will also involve a complete and lengthy re-charge on the issues relating to those sections, it will usually be better to see whether the jury's concerns can be addressed in some other fashion. A trial judge might be better advised to ask the jury to be more specific about the particular concern that motivates the request, and then try to answer that concern. Similarly, rereading the sections of the *Code* and explaining them to the jury might be a sufficient response to the request.[315]

On some occasions, jurors might take jury aids with them into the jury room — that is, "tools to elucidate the significance of a piece or collection of testimonial, documentary, or real evidence. They include maps, timelines, casts of characters, charts, and slide shows."[316] Jury aids are not evidence themselves, and so their utility depends on whether the evidence upon which they are based is itself accepted. Since they are not evidence, a trial judge has discretion as to whether to allow jury aids to go to the jury room or not.

Where a party seeks to have a jury aid go to the jury room, they should disclose it to the opposing party as soon as reasonably possible and make an application to the court. Where the matter is contested the judge should seek submissions from the parties before deciding. In deciding whether to allow a jury aid to go to the jury room, a judge must balance the value that the aid can provide against its potential to distract or mislead the jury. This question should be assessed by looking at whether the jury aid is reasonably necessary, accurate, and fair.

An aid will be reasonably necessary where it would be unreasonably onerous or time-consuming for the jury to struggle with evidence that is vast, complex, or technical in nature. It need not be impossible

312 *R v Fontaine*, [2003] 1 WWR 634 at para 59 (Man CA), quoting from *R v Dunbar and Logan* (1982), 68 CCC (2d) 13 (Ont CA).

313 *Cathro v the Queen*, [1956] SCR 101.

314 See, for example, *R v Flewwelling* (1984), 63 NSR (2d) 382 (CA); *R v McCormack* (1984), 28 Man R (2d) 29 (CA); *R v Vawryk*, [1979] 3 WWR 50 (Man CA); and *R v Crothers* (1978), 43 CCC (2d) 27 (Sask CA).

315 *R v Keegstra*, [1996] 1 SCR 458.

316 *R v Pan*, 2025 SCC 12 at para 121 [*Pan*].

for the jury to procced without the aid, but where the aid only repackages accessible evidence in a more convenient way, it will not be necessary. The aid must be accurate, in that it cannot distort, misstate, or obscure any evidence, whether intentionally or unintentionally. An aid might be inaccurate if it fails to capture the complexity of the evidence. An aid will be fair where its explanatory value outweighs its prejudicial effect. A judge should consider whether the aid reflects one party's theory of the case: if so, the opposing party can propose alterations or additions or submit its own aid. However, judges should be alive to resource imbalances in assessing this point.

If an aid is allowed in the jury room, it should be formally marked in a manner that distinguishes it from the evidence. The trial judge also must instruct the jury as to the proper and improper uses of the aid.[317]

Similar considerations arise if the jury requests transcripts of the trial judge's instructions or of the argument by counsel. It is not necessarily an error to provide them to the jury, even to provide the argument of only one side if that is all that was requested, although the better choice might be to provide the arguments of both counsel.[318] Distributing transcripts raises the likelihood of error, particularly if the jury receives only part of the judge's instructions.[319] The Court has noted that judges must be sure that the jury receives the entire charge in clear and legible form and that all members of the jury are capable of reading it. It has observed that "it may well be that the dangers associated with such an approach outweigh the potential benefits."[320]

Nonetheless, lower courts have encouraged the careful use of written versions of judges' charges, on the basis that doing so can increase juror comprehension. Some judges provide the entire charge while others, hoping to reduce the volume of material, do not include the summary of the evidence or of counsel's arguments. In some cases, there can be the fear that providing everything will bury the critical part of the instructions and thus mislead the jury. No single approach is suitable for all cases.[321]

---

317 See generally Pan, above note 316 at paras 121–37.

318 *R v Ferguson*, [2001] 1 SCR 281.

319 It has, however, been observed that "what is critical is the nature and extent of any errors, not the form in which they are expressed": *R v Yumnu*, 2010 ONCA 637 at para 355 [*Yumnu*].

320 *Ménard*, above note 265.

321 See the discussion in *Yumnu*, above note 319. See also *R v Poitras* (2002), 57 OR (3d) 538 at para 47 (CA); *R v Henry*, 2003 BCCA 476; and *R v Nieto*, 2007 MBCA 82 at para 47. See also *R v Mathisen*, 2008 ONCA 747 at para 114:

A trial judge is not required to review every aspect of a witness's evidence. A trial judge should, however, adequately and fairly summarize the evidence. A trial

In deciding whether to provide a written version of the entire charge, the Ontario Court of Appeal has suggested that a trial judge should consider many factors:

i. the length of the trial proceedings, including the period between the conclusion of the evidence and the charge;
ii. the volume of evidentiary references contained in the charge, bearing in mind the principles governing evidentiary review;
iii. the danger of diluting the effect of the instructions on the governing legal principles by their submersion in a protracted evidentiary review;
iv. the positions of counsel;
v. the issues to be resolved by the jury in their deliberations;
vi. the danger of simply overburdening the jurors by the volume of the instructions;
vii. whether jurors took notes of the evidence adduced at trial;
viii. the risk that jurors will consider the evidentiary references to be exhaustive of the evidence they should consider in reaching their decision; and
ix. any other relevant circumstances.

It also stressed that jurors should be reminded to consider all of the evidence, not just that to which reference is made in the instructions, and that their recollection of the evidence is the most important criterion, rather than any views the judge may have expressed about factual issues.[322]

The same types of considerations govern when the jury asks to re-hear evidence or asks for clarification of the legal issues during its deliberations. A trial judge has discretion and is not obliged to answer every request from the jury precisely as asked. So, for example, where a jury requests transcripts of the evidence of all the witnesses shortly after commencing deliberations, a trial judge will not err by refusing this request. However, since questions from the jury must be given particular consideration, it is not sufficient to simply refuse (as noted at Section D(8)(b), above in this chapter). A trial judge should consult with counsel on how to respond and propose alternatives or ask the jury to deliberate further to decide more specifically what their concern is, for example.[323] Where the jury's question is unclear, the

---

judge should also instruct the jurors that they ought to consider all the evidence in the case, and that they ought to rely on their own recollection of the evidence rather than the trial judge's recollection.

322 *Yumnu*, above note 319 at paras 367–68.

323 *R v Ostrowski*, [1990] 2 SCR 82; or see, for example, *R v Holden* (2001), 159 CCC (3d) 180 (Ont CA), leave to appeal to SCC refused [2001] SCCA No 574; *R v*

judge should request clarification in order to be able to answer it appropriately.[324]

Other considerations arise when the jury is not seeking a review of the evidence at trial but is seeking additional evidence. The basic rule is that this is not permitted. No information that did not come out at trial can be given to the jury once they have begun deliberating, and it might be necessary to tell the jury that there was no evidence led on the point in question.[325] So, for example, a jury cannot have a demonstration that was conducted at trial repeated for them after the close of both cases.[326] Nor should the jury have material that, although it was used at trial, did not form part of the evidence.[327] However, once again, a refusal of the jury's request might well be an error, and the trial judge should try to determine whether the jury's concern can be satisfied in some other way.

Requests from jurors sometimes do not concern the law or the evidence, but the jury's own deliberations or concerns by one juror about the behaviour of another juror. In *Vézina*, for example, two jurors sent notes to the trial judge that questioned the honesty of two other jurors. The judge consulted with counsel on how to proceed, but without their agreement, and in the absence of the accused, met with the two jurors who had complained and decided that the jury's deliberations could continue. The Court held that the judge erred by meeting with the jurors in the absence of the accused. At any point where the accused's vital interests are at issue the accused is entitled to be present. Had the trial judge received communications that might have concerned

---

*K(BA)* (1998), 19 CR (5th) 400 (BCCA); *R v Perry* (1995), 54 BCAC 275 (CA).

324 *R v H(LI)*, 2003 MBCA 97. See also *R v McLellan*, 2018 ONCA 510, where the jury asked to review the accused's cross-examination, and the trial judge inquired whether it would be helpful for them also to hear the direct examination. Ultimately the jury identified only a small portion of the cross-examination which related to an issue not raised in direct examination. The accused argued on appeal that the trial judge ought to have required the jury also to hear evidence relating to a different point he argued was related, but the Ontario Court of Appeal concluded at para 66 that "It was not the function of the trial judge to speculate as to why they now wanted to rehear the limited portion of McLellan's cross-examination. It was his role to be responsive to the jury's request to rehear certain evidence."

325 *R v Templeman* (1994), 40 BCAC 76.

326 *R v Kluke* (1987), 22 OAC 107 (CA). But see *R v Clair* (1995), 143 NSR (2d) 101 (CA), leave to appeal to SCC refused (1996), 151 NSR (2d) 240n, where it was held that allowing a jury to have a measuring tape did not affect the fairness of the trial, because it merely allowed them to estimate distances (something they could have done without the tape) more accurately.

327 *R v Rowbotham* (1988), 63 CR (3d) 113 (Ont CA).

purely administrative questions, it would have been permissible to meet with the jurors privately. But even in those circumstances, once it became apparent that the integrity of a juror was being questioned, the accused would be entitled to be present and the judge should adjourn the meeting.[328]

Where the issues raised about fellow jurors give rise to legitimate concerns, a trial judge does have a statutory power to remove a juror.[329] The judge is entitled to make inquiries in deciding whether to do so and has discretion over exactly how to do that, but whatever process is used must: 1) be fair to the parties and members of the jury; 2) be open, on the record, and in the presence of the accused and counsel; 3) enable the trial judge to determine the true nature of the internal problem faced by the jury and to resolve it; and 4) preserve the integrity, confidentiality and impartiality of the jury's deliberation process.[330] An accused should not lightly be deprived of the right to have a verdict from a unanimous jury of twelve,[331] and the secrecy of the jury's deliberations must be protected. The power to remove a juror should be used only for serious issues, and so a trial judge ought first to consider whether re-charging all the jurors about the duties of jurors would be the better approach.[332]

---

328 *Vézina*, above note 60. See also *R v Phillips*, 2008 ONCA 726, where the trial judge met briefly with two court officials, knowing only that they wished to raise a concern relating to a juror in a recently completed trial. The judge had the meeting recorded and, having decided that it raised a matter into which he needed to inquire, sent a transcript to the Crown and defence, and convened a meeting with them. The Court of Appeal held that there was no violation of the accused's right to be present at her trial and that in the highly unusual circumstances of the case, the trial judge's actions were entirely appropriate.

329 Section 644(1), allows a judge to discharge a juror for illness "or other reasonable cause."

330 *R v Wise*, 2022 ONCA 586 at para 22 [*Wise*]. See also *R v Giroux* (2006), 207 CCC (3d) 512 (Ont CA) at para 35. In *Wise*, the judge conducted inquiries with most jurors after receiving reports that juror 11 was threatening other jurors and eventually discharged that juror. The inquiries had accidentally disclosed the position that juror 11 was taking, but the judge's subsequent instructions to the remaining jurors made it clear that the discharge was due to juror 11's behaviour, not the position he was taking.

331 An order under s 644 can be made at any point, and if it occurs before the jury has heard evidence, it is possible to replace the juror: s 644(1.1). If it is too late to replace the juror, the jury remains properly constituted as long as the number of members does not fall below ten, unless the judge orders otherwise: s 644(2). If the number of jurors does fall below ten, with consent of the parties the trial can continue on a judge-alone basis: s 644(3).

332 *R v Kum*, 2015 ONCA 36 [*Kum*].

In the absence of these types of requests that necessitate some response, the jury is to be left unhindered to perform its function without communication from others. In *R v Mercier*, for example, a new trial was necessary when a Crown prosecutor entered the jury room in the jury's absence and erased some words from the chalkboard.[333] Not all communication has that result, however. Where there has been contact between the jury and anyone else, the trial judge must conduct an inquiry to determine whether the jury, or perhaps an individual juror, cannot continue. It might be that no prejudice has been caused because the contact was relatively harmless or because it could have no actual impact on the deliberations.[334] On the other hand, where the improprieties are so serious that they affect public confidence in the system, no prejudice needs to be shown. Thus, where a jury, during its deliberations, was taken to dinner with a group of people including a close relative of the murder victim, the absence of actual prejudice was irrelevant.[335]

## 2) Exhorting the Jury

Sometime deliberations continue so long that it appears, or notes are sent from the jury stating, that the jury is deadlocked and will be unable to reach a unanimous verdict. Although the trial judge can discharge the jury under section 653 and order a new trial, normally the first step is to call the jury in and exhort them to reach a verdict. Principles have developed around such exhortations, so that they do not present a threat to the independence of the jury or the interests of the accused. Exhorting a jury properly is a delicate task. A judge should not express an opinion on the facts during an exhortation, even though that is permissible in the original charge.[336] The exhortation also should not suggest that one or another group's opinions on the evidence is preferable. Rather, the exhortation is to focus on the process of deliberation itself and encourage the jury members to

---

333 (1973), 12 CCC (2d) 377 (Que CA) [*Mercier*].

334 In *R v Taillefer* (1995), 40 CR (4th) 287 (Que CA), for example, a juror contacted a witness on the second day of deliberations, but was questioned by the judge and allowed to stay on the jury. The jury did not reach a decision for another eleven days, suggesting that the communication had been of no effect and that the trial judge had not erred in the exercise of his discretion.

335 *R v Cameron* (1991), 2 OR (3d) 633 (CA), leave to appeal to SCC refused [1991] 3 SCR x. See also *R v Hertrich* (1982), 137 DLR (3d) 400 (Ont CA), leave to appeal to SCC refused (1982), 45 NR 629n (SCC).

336 *Sims*, above note 288.

listen to and consider one another's views.[337] No pressure should be placed on the jury, and no factors that are extraneous to the task of reaching a verdict should be introduced.[338] Jurors should not be encouraged to change their minds for the sake of conformity, and no deadline should be imposed.[339] It is an error, therefore, to tell the jury to consider the expense or inconvenience of a new trial, the hardship to participants, or to consider the benefit to the accused of a verdict being reached.[340] It is also an error to direct the minority to reconsider the views of the majority. Rather, it is better to direct all the jurors to reconsider their views.[341]

Nonetheless, it is appropriate for a trial judge to remind the jurors of their oath and encourage them to reach a verdict. In effect, as long as it is clear that the jurors retain the right to disagree, and provided improper pressures and irrelevant considerations are not brought to bear, a trial judge can urge them to try to find a way not to become a hung jury.[342] Further, not every improper exhortation will lead to a new trial. Other factors, such as the length of the deliberations, the question asked by the jury, and the length of the subsequent deliberations following the exhortation, will all help determine whether the exhortation coerced the jury or caused some jurors to accept a verdict that they did not agree with.[343]

---

337 *Ibid.*

338 See, for example, *R v Paul*, 2011 BCCA 46, where the jury specifically asked whether there would be a retrial if they remained deadlocked. The trial judge properly told them that the possibility of a new trial should not influence their deliberations.

339 *G(RM)*, above note 293.

340 See *G(RM)*, above note 293, and *R v Walton*, 2022 ABCA 276 at para 93 [*Walton*].

341 *Ibid*. See also *R v Abreha*, 2023 ABCA 357, where the same error was made. That case notes at para 24 that the latest version of *Watt's Manual of Criminal Jury Instructions* (Third Edition, 2023) suggests wording for an exhortation that makes no reference to the minority or majority.

342 See, for example, *R v Littlejohn* (1978), 41 CCC (2d) 161 (Ont CA).

343 *G(RM)*, above note 293 at para 50. Also "While a short lapse of time between an exhortation and the verdict might well be an indication that a judge has influenced a jury's decision, the reverse is not necessarily true. A large time gap between the exhortation and the verdict may or may not indicate the independence of the jury": *R v Jack* (1996), 113 Man R (2d) 84 at para 91 (CA), Helper J dissenting. Her decision was adopted by the Supreme Court of Canada when the decision was reversed on appeal: [1997] 2 SCR 334. In *G(RM)* the jury reached a verdict only fifteen minutes after the exhortation. In *Walton*, above note 340, where the result was not overturned despite flaws in the exhortation, the jury continued deliberating for a day and half after being exhorted.

## 3) Rendering a Verdict

Once the jury has finished its deliberations and indicated that it is ready to return, the jury announces its verdict in court. The announcement is made by the jury foreman. It is possible to request that the jury be polled — that is, that every juror be asked individually about the verdict. There is no legal requirement for this procedure, however, which is usually allowed where there is some doubt as to whether unanimity exists.[344]

After the jury has been discharged by the trial judge neither it nor the trial judge has any further authority to act. In the vast majority of circumstances that causes no difficulty, but it can do so in the rare situation where an error is alleged to have occurred in recording the verdict but is not discovered until after the jury is discharged. In *R v Head*, for example, the jury foreman announced a verdict of not guilty, and the judge discharged the jury and acquitted the accused. The foreman then indicated that he thought the jury could have found the accused guilty of an included offence. The Court held that the trial judge was *functus officio* and no longer had jurisdiction to inquire into the matter or correct any error, and, therefore, the acquittal had to stand.[345]

Subsequently, in *R v Burke*, while reaffirming the general rule that a trial judge has no jurisdiction to alter a recorded verdict once a jury is discharged, the Court found a rare residual jurisdiction to be used when there has been an irregularity.[346] In that case, the jury had reached a guilty verdict, but the trial judge and many others in the court misheard the foreman, understanding him to say "not guilty." The error was discovered almost immediately after the jury was discharged and was brought to the judge's attention within minutes, but most jurors and the accused had already left. The Court held that there were a number of ways to proceed when such errors occur, but that sometimes the trial judge has a limited jurisdiction to correct errors in the recorded judgment. If the circumstances would require the jury to reconsider its verdict, then the ordinary *functus* rule applies and the trial judge has no jurisdiction to correct. But if no reconsideration of the verdict is involved, then the trial judge must decide whether there is, in the circumstances, a reasonable apprehension of bias. If there is no such apprehension, then the judge can correct the error. But if there is a reasonable apprehension of bias, the trial judge must either allow the verdict that was recorded to stand or declare a mistrial. The incorrect

344 *R v Laforet*, [1980] 1 SCR 869.

345 [1986] 2 SCR 684.

346 [2002] 2 SCR 857 [*Burke*].

verdict must stand unless it is necessary to declare a mistrial to prevent a miscarriage of justice.[347] In *Burke*, no question of the jury reconsidering its verdict arose, and so there was jurisdiction to potentially correct the error. However, since many of the jurors had gone home and had been exposed to media coverage of the case after their discharge, even if there was no actual bias there was a reasonable apprehension of it, and so the verdict could not simply be changed to guilty. Since leaving the incorrect acquittal in place would have led to a miscarriage of justice, a mistrial was declared and a new trial ordered.

## 4) Jury Secrecy

Finally, it is worth observing section 649 of the *Code*, which makes it an offence for anyone present in the jury room to disclose any information about the jury's deliberations, other than in connection with an investigation of obstructing justice, or in the course of obtaining psychiatric treatment or therapy arising out of service at the trial as a juror.[348] This law closely reflects the common law rule on jury secrecy that is to the same effect, though it also prevents anyone who overhears, even accidentally, the jury's deliberations from disclosing any information about them. As a result, it can be difficult, and frequently impossible, for a person who alleges that impropriety occurred during the jury's deliberations to put evidence before a court.[349] The Court has

347 See, for example, *R v Catton*, 2015 ONCA 13, where the accused was charged with dangerous driving causing death in connection with the death of a passenger on a motorcycle, and dangerous driving causing bodily harm in connect with the driver of that same motorcycle. The verdicts announced in court were guilty and not guilty, which were inconsistent verdicts, since they amounted to saying that the accused both was and was not driving dangerously. A written verdict sheet was found in the trial exhibit list indicating that the jury had intended to convict on the included offence of dangerous driving for the second count, which would have removed the inconsistency between the verdicts. Nonetheless, despite saying that that was probably what the jury had intended, rather than to return inconsistent verdicts, the Ontario Court of Appeal found it had no ability to look behind the verdicts recorded in open court.

348 Section 649(2).

349 See, for example, *R v Lewis*, 2017 ONCA 216, where a juror contacted defence counsel after the trial, claiming to have been coerced and bullied into agreement. With the help of counsel, the juror prepared an affidavit: this was found not only to be inadmissible, but unwise. The Ontario Court of Appeal noted that both the juror and her lawyer had put themselves at risk of prosecution by preparing that affidavit and suggested at para 47 that "[t]he better course is to avoid all but publicly available information in the affidavit and leave it to a judge or commissioner to control the questioning of a juror." See also *R v MB*, 2020 ONCA 84.

considered whether these rules violate section 7 of the *Charter*. It concluded that they do not and discussed the policy behind jury secrecy in *R v Pan*.[350]

The facts of *Pan* are complex. Pan was tried for murder three times, the first two trials having been declared mistrials. At the appeal of his conviction at the third trial, Pan objected to the process by which a mistrial was declared at his second trial. Investigations of a possible obstruction charge revealed that one juror at that trial had, among other things, been following media coverage and seeking other information outside of court and reporting the information to the other jurors. The mistrial resulted when that same juror sent a note to the trial judge asking that the jury be polled once it reported its verdict — her intention, it appeared, was to feign agreement in the jury room and then disagree in open court. The trial judge consulted with counsel as to how to respond and ultimately declared a mistrial. Pan's argument hinged on the claim that the mistrial should not have been declared and that he should have been entitled to the acquittal that would have resulted if the second trial continued. To make this argument, it would have been necessary for Pan to lead evidence that section 649 prevented being led.

The Court reviewed the reasons why a guarantee of jury secrecy is valuable: it promotes candour in discussions, and lets the jury consider all possibilities without fear of later recriminations from the public. This rationale is particularly valuable to an unpopular accused or an individual charged with a particularly heinous crime. Related to that rationale was the need to protect jurors from harassment, censure, and reprisals, which would permit them to perform their function more confidently. Finally, jury secrecy promotes finality, though the Court held that this rationale alone would not be sufficient to justify the rule.[351]

The Court held, however, that the common law jury secrecy rule does not prevent every conceivable piece of information relevant to what has gone on in a jury room from being disclosed. The Court drew a distinction between matters extrinsic to the jury's deliberations and those intrinsic to them. An extrinsic matter would be that some third party had contact with the jury or that a juror somehow obtained

350 Above note 286.

351 The jury secrecy rule has been criticized as overly restrictive: see, for example, Sonia R Chopra & James RP Ogloff, "Evaluating Jury Secrecy: Implications for Academic Research and Juror Stress" (2000) 44 *Criminal Law Quarterly* 190; Paul Quinlan, "Secrecy of Jury Deliberations — Is the Cost Too High?" (1993) 22 *Criminal Reports* (4th) 127.

particular information, whereas an intrinsic matter would be the effect that the contact or information had on the jury's deliberations. The common law rule and section 649 prevent only intrinsic matters from being disclosed. As the Court put it:

> statements made, opinions expressed, arguments advanced and votes cast by members of a jury in the course of their deliberations are inadmissible in any legal proceedings. In particular, jurors may not testify about the effect of anything on their or other jurors' minds, emotions or ultimate decision. On the other hand, the common law rule does not render inadmissible evidence of facts, statements or events extrinsic to the deliberation process, whether originating from a juror or from a third party, that may have tainted the verdict.[352]

In *Mercier*,[353] therefore, it was possible to lead evidence that the Crown prosecutor had erased words from the chalkboard in the jury room, since that was an extrinsic matter. However, evidence concerning any effect this action might have had on the jury's reasoning would be intrinsic and therefore not admissible. The Court acknowledged that, in practical terms, it can sometimes be difficult to draw the distinction, but nonetheless held that the jury secrecy rule applies only to intrinsic matters. Understood in this way, the Court held that the common law jury secrecy rule accorded with the goals of jury secrecy and was in accordance with the principles of fundamental justice. Since the statutory rule was consistent with the common law rule, it too passed *Charter* scrutiny.

The jury secrecy rule extends to discussions within the jury room at any stage of the trial, not merely after the trial has concluded and formal deliberations have begun.[354]

Where there has been a breach of jury secrecy, a further issue which arises is what remedy should be given. Although such a breach could lead to a miscarriage of justice and require a mistrial, that is not necessarily the case. Where, for example, there is an inquiry into alleged improper behaviour of jurors in the jury room, the inquiry might despite efforts to the contrary reveal some information about

352 *Pan*, above note 316 at para 77.

353 *Mercier*, above note 333.

354 See, for example, *R v Jojic*, 2010 BCCA 577, where a juror was discharged mid-trial after making a comment to Crown counsel which implied that he had already made up his mind. The trial judge, in questioning the juror, declined to inquire into whether other jurors had privately expressed views suggesting pre-judgment: the Court of Appeal held that this was a proper exercise of discretion.

deliberations, such as the views of some jurors. As long as the honesty of the jury's subsequent deliberations can be maintained (whether the response to the behaviour is to remove a juror or not to do so and to exhort the jury), there will be no miscarriage of justice and no need for a mistrial. Relevant considerations will include how much information was revealed and how important it was, the instructions the trial judge gives afterward, and the length of time the jury continues to deliberate.[355]

## F. POWERS OF THE COURT

A trial judge has a variety of powers to control the process in the courtroom. Many of these powers arise at statute, though some come from the common law. In addition, the *Code* permits courts to make rules of court that can govern, among other things, matters regarding the pleading, practice, procedure at trial, and case management.[356] Such rules, of course, must not be inconsistent with the *Code*.

### 1) Control over the Court Process

Trial judges have a trial management power which allows them to control the process of their court and ensure that trials proceed in an effective and orderly fashion. This power has three interrelated purposes: to ensure that trials proceed fairly, effectively, and efficiently.[357] The power includes the ability to curtail cross examination and to prevent irrelevant or harassing questions.[358] The judge can also ask questions

---

355 See *Kum*, above note 332; *Wise*, above note 330; or *R v Peters*, 1999 BCCA 406.

356 Sections 482 and 482.1. See also Part XVIII.1 of the *Code*, allowing for the appointment of a case management judge for a trial who might or might not be the trial judge. The case management judge has powers at the pre-trial stage aimed at helping the parties streamline the issues (s 551.3), can adjudicate issues referred by the trial judge during trial (s 551.6), and can potentially adjudicate issues that affect related trials at a joint hearing (s 551.7). See the discussion of case management judges and other issues related to "mega-trials" in Christine Mainville, "Report on the CIAJ's Complex Criminal Trials Roundtable" (2015) 62 *Criminal Law Quarterly* 339. See also the discussion of case management judges in Chapter 10, Section B(1).

357 *R v Samaniego*, 2022 SCC 9 at paras 20 and 21 [*Samaniego*].

358 See, for example, *R v John*, 2017 ONCA 622, where the trial judge was found to have properly curtailed questions about a witness' former sex work, which were at the outer bounds of relevance if relevant at all. See also *Samaniego*, above note 357.

of witnesses, decide how to deal with recalcitrant witnesses, and in some circumstances can direct the Crown to call witnesses or can call witnesses on behalf of the court.[359] However, all of these powers must be exercised with caution and can be taken too far. The ability to make decisions about examination and cross-examination of witnesses does not insulate those decisions from the rules of evidence, for example.[360] Further, interventions by a trial judge can violate an accused's right to a fair trial. The test is not whether the accused was actually prejudiced, but "whether a reasonably minded person who had been present throughout the trial would consider that the accused had not had a fair trial."[361]

The trial management power has taken on increased significance in the wake of *R v Jordan*, which imposed presumptive ceilings for the length of trials.[362] An aspect of the trial management power particularly relevant in that context is the power to summarily dismiss a motion brought by one of the parties, rather than conduct a full hearing on the merits.[363] The standard for doing so is meant to balance two sets of underlying values: trial efficiency and trial fairness. Efficient operation of courts is important, especially in the wake of the renewed efforts aimed at reducing trial delay from *Jordan*,[364] and so unmeritorious applications should be dispensed with quickly. In part this means that the application to dismiss itself should not be allowed to take up a disproportionate amount of time,[365] but it also means that summary dismissal applications can contribute to, rather than resolve, inefficiency. Further, summarily dismissing an application can affect an accused's constitutionally protected fair trial rights, and so the standard cannot be set too low. This risk is particularly relevant where an accused raises novel arguments which might have precedential value. Accordingly the standard for dismissing an application summarily, without hearing argument

359 As examples of each see, respectively, *R v Normore* 2018 SCC 42; *R v Hillis*, 2016 ONSC 451; or *R v Owens*, 2018 MBCA 94.

360 *Samaniego*, above note 357 at para 24.

361 *R v Valley* (1986), 26 CCC (3d) 207 at 232 (Ont CA). See also the extended discussion in *R v Potter; R v Colpitts*, 2020 NSCA 9, in the context of an unsuccessful bias application.

362 *Samaniego*, above note 357 at para 23.

363 This power has been acknowledged in courts for decades, variously as a "*Kutynec* application" (from *R v Kutynec* (1992), 70 CCC (3d) 289 (Ont CA)) or a "*Vukelich* application" (from *R v Vukelich* (1996), 78 BCAC 113). The Supreme Court established the rules around and standard for such hearings in *R v Haevsicher*, 2023 SCC 11 [*Haevischer*].

364 See the discussion of Chapter 10, Section B(2)(a)(i).

365 In *Haevischer*, above note 363, itself, the Court observed that the application to summarily dismiss the accuseds' abuse of process motion itself took six days.

on the merits, is high: that the application is "manifestly frivolous."[366] That it is "frivolous" means that it will necessarily fail, and that this is "manifestly" so requires that this is obvious on the face of the record. In applying this standard the judge is to assume the facts alleged by the applicant to be true, take the applicant's arguments at their highest, and generally assume the inferences suggested by the applicant.[367] Examples of manifestly frivolous applications include ones where the judge has no jurisdiction to grant the requested remedy, where evidence is sought to be excluded from a search warrant application which would have been granted even without the excluded evidence, or where some key part of the legal argument is missing.[368] The onus is on the party seeking summary dismissal to show that the application is manifestly frivolous, even if the trial judge raises the issue on their own motion. However, there is a minimal burden on the party bringing the application to provide specifics of the claim, even though the record for the summary dismissal application itself should be of a summary nature.[369]

Another aspect of trial management is the granting or denying of adjournments, which is largely governed by *Code* provisions.[370] At one time the rules concerning adjournments, and particularly the issue of whether a court lost jurisdiction over the accused or the offence by failing to proceed properly, were quite complex. Further, the *Code* formerly contained a provision preventing any adjournment of more than eight days without the accused's consent. Now, however, section 485 specifically preserves the court's jurisdiction over an accused despite a failure to comply with any of the *Code*'s provisions concerning adjournments or remands. Indeed, subsequent to a decision that found the predecessor of section 485 to not preserve a court's jurisdiction where it adjourned a case but failed to proceed on the set date,[371] the provision now more broadly preserves the court's jurisdiction despite a failure "to

366 *Haevischer*, above note 363 at para 62.

367 *Haevischer*, above note 363 at para 84: "The judge should only reject an inference if it is manifestly frivolous, meaning that there is no reasoning path to the proposed inference." Implicit in this is that the judge must at a minimum learn what evidence the applicant intends to rely upon and what argument they intend to make. As the Alberta Court of Appeal put it in the pre-*Haevischer* case *R v Abdulkadir*, 2020 ABCA 214 at para 21, "hear first, decide second."

368 *Haevischer*, above note 363, offers, at para 87, the example of an application for a stay of proceedings where the applicant accepts that an alternative remedy would redress the prejudice.

369 *Haevischer*, above note 363 at paras 93–98.

370 Sections 537 and 645. See also the discussion in *R v JCG* (2004), 189 CCC (3d) 1 (Que CA); and *R v MV* (2004), 189 CCC (3d) 230 (Que CA).

371 *R v Krannenburg*, [1980] 1 SCR 1053.

act in the exercise of that jurisdiction." Where a court does lose jurisdiction over an accused, it can regain it by issuing a summons or warrant for the accused within three months. However, if this is not done, the proceedings are considered dismissed for want of prosecution and the Crown cannot lay new charges without the personal consent in writing of the attorney general or deputy attorney general.[372]

Whether to grant an adjournment in any given case is a discretionary decision which depends on the facts. One common situation is an unrepresented accused seeking an adjournment in order to obtain counsel. Relevant facts in that situation are whether there have been previous adjournments for the same reason, whether the accused was warned that trial would proceed with or without counsel, the accused's degree of familiarity with the legal system, the complexity of the charges and the likelihood that they can receive a fair trial without counsel, the public interest in the orderly and expeditious administration of justice, and whether the accused was refused legal aid. An adjournment should be granted if the accused has been diligent and the lack of counsel is not their fault, but not if the request is an attempt to delay proceedings.[373] More generally, where a party ought to have been able to avoid the need for an adjournment by acting more expeditiously, it is likely not to be granted.[374]

A judge also has the authority to appoint an *amicus curiae*, or "friend of the court." This is an ancient power available to courts with inherent jurisdiction, and is to be used where it is necessary to permit a particular proceeding to be successfully and justly adjudicated. However, this should be done sparingly, only when the assistance of an *amicus* is essential to the judge discharging their judicial functions. In particular, the appointment of *amicus* should not be used simply as a way to have defence counsel act for an unrepresented accused. The roles are not the same, to do so could undermine an accused person's right to choose not to be represented, and there could be a conflict if the *amicus*' obligations to the court required submissions that were not favourable to the accused or were contrary to the accused's wishes.[375] That is not

372 Sections 485(2), 485(3), and 485.1.

373 *R v White*, 2010 ABCA 208. See also *R v Bitternose*, 2009 SKCA 54.

374 See, for example, *R v Cole*, 2010 NSCA 59. The Crown requested an adjournment two weeks before trial because a key witness had to come from China and it would take one month at a minimum to obtain a visa. The trial judge properly refused the adjournment on the basis that the Crown had known for at least four months that it would need a witness from China and should have known that visa requirements would need to be satisfied.

375 See generally *Ontario v Criminal Lawyers' Association of Ontario*, 2013 SCC 43. See also *R v Podolski*, 2017 BCCA 169, holding that a statutory court also has this ability in appropriate circumstances.

to say, however, that in exceptional circumstances an *amicus* could not function similarly to defence counsel.[376] An *amicus* can be appointed to perform adversarial functions, so long as that does not interfere with their duty to the court or with the accused's right to conduct their own defence.[377] Further, the role of *amicus* is likely to at least incidentally provide a benefit to the accused, even if that is not the primary purpose of the role, and that should not be undermined.[378]

Some sections of the *Code* give a judge authority over the manner in which witnesses will testify. Section 486.1 of the *Code* provides for the possibility of a witness having a support person present while testifying. Section 486.2 allows a witness to testify from outside the courtroom or from behind a screen or other device that prevents the witness from seeing the accused. Each of these methods can be ordered for any witness where the trial judge feels it is necessary in order to obtain a full and candid account from the witness.[379] However, in the case of a witness under the age of eighteen, or a witness with a mental or physical disability that interferes with an ability to communicate evidence, the order is presumptively available. In those cases, the

---

376 See *R v Imona-Russel*, 2019 ONCA 252. In that case a lawyer had been appointed as *amicus* and the accused asked that the lawyer be made his counsel. The trial judge refused, which the Ontario Court of Appeal found to be appropriate "where there is a real risk that the accused will discharge counsel as a way of disrupting the trial" (para 94).

377 See *R v Kahsai*, 2023 SCC 20 at para 49:

> In sum, the proper scope of the roles for *amicus* is limited by necessary constraints inherent in the nature of the role. First, the role of *amicus* as a friend of the court means that *amicus* can never discharge functions that would violate their duty of loyalty to the court or undermine the impartiality of the court, such as by advising on key strategic defence choices. Second, the mandate assigned to *amicus* should respect the key strategic decisions asserted by the accused while also respecting what is required for trial fairness. Finally, the appointment of *amicus* cannot be exploited to circumvent the legal aid scheme or judicial decisions to refuse to grant state-funded counsel. While these limits do not preclude *amicus* from performing any adversarial functions, they do restrict the kinds of assistance that *amicus* can provide.

378 See, for example, *R v Walker*, 2019 ONCA 765, where an *amicus* had been appointed for the accused in a dangerous offender application. Ultimately the *amicus* argued in favour of the accused being found a dangerous offender and an indeterminate sentence being imposed, which the Ontario Court of Appeal observed "represents the antithesis of the role that *amicus* was appointed to perform" (para 110).

379 Sections 486.1(2) and 486.2(2). Note that ss 486.2(4) and (5) create a similar ability concerning any witness in the case of terrorism and organized crime offences, which is available in addition when the order is necessary to protect the safety of the witness.

trial judge "shall" grant the application unless the order would interfere with the proper administration of justice.[380]

Where a support person is ordered, the judge can order that that person and the witness not communicate during the witness's testimony.[381] Another witness cannot be the support person unless that is necessary for the proper administration of justice.[382]

The use of a screen is only designed to avoid a face-to-face confrontation between the witness and the accused; the screen allows the witness not to see the accused, but the accused is still able to see the witness.[383] The trial judge has substantial latitude in ordering this procedure, which was found not to violate the *Charter*.[384]

A judge also has a great deal of general discretion in the course of the trial, from intervening to ask questions personally to expressing opinions on the facts. Further, a judge has a trial management power which includes

> the power to place reasonable limits on oral submissions, to direct that submissions be made in writing, to require an offer of proof before embarking on a lengthy *voir dire*, to defer rulings, to direct the manner in which a *voir dire* is conducted, especially whether to do so

---

380 Sections 486.1(1) and 486.2(1). Bill C-16, *An Act to amend certain Acts in relation to criminal and correctional matters (child protection, gender-based violence, delays and other measures)*, first reading December 9 2025 [Bill C-16] has been introduced. If passed in its current form, it will make these steps presumptively available for complainants in respect of certain offences: sexual offences, criminal harassment, trafficking in persons, and violent offences against intimate partners.

381 Sections 486.1(5).

382 Section 486.1(4).

383 *Levogiannis*, above note 177. Similarly, where the witness testifies from outside the courtroom, arrangements must be made to permit the accused to watch the testimony by closed circuit television: s 486.2(7).

384 *Levogiannis*, above note 177, found that a predecessor version of the section did not violate the *Charter*. An order for screens on that version was available only in the case of trials for sexual offences, and there was no presumption that the order would be made for child witnesses. Subsequently the introduction of that presumption was found also not to violate the *Charter*, and to be simply "the next step in the evolution of the rules of evidence" around child and vulnerable witnesses: *R v JZS*, 2008 BCCA 401 at para 43, aff'd 2010 SCC 1.

In general on this subject, see Nicholas Bala & Hilary McCormack, "Accommodating the Criminal Process to Child Witnesses" (1994) 25 *Criminal Reports* (4th) 341. In addition, see Nicholas Bala, RCL Lindsay, & E McNamara, "Testimonial Aids for Children: The Canadian Experience with Closed Circuit Television, Screens and Videotapes" (2001) 44 *Criminal Law Quarterly* 461, for a survey of judges, lawyers, and victim-witness workers on their experience in court with these various devices. The changes to the *Code* provision itself were as a result of work by the Child Witness Project headed by Nicholas Bala.

on the basis of testimony or in some other form, and exceptionally to direct the order in which evidence is called.[385]

An overriding rule, however, is that the trial judge's behaviour must not create a reasonable apprehension of bias. Rudeness on the part of a judge to either the Crown or the defence might or might not cross the threshold, and the fact that the rudeness was equally distributed might or might not help prevent a reasonable apprehension of bias.[386] A judge who expresses an opinion on whether the accused has presented any defence while the Crown decides whether to cross-examine might be seen as making the trial proceed expeditiously.[387] A judge can ask questions of the accused or other witnesses without creating a reasonable apprehension of bias but, in some cases, a judge can carry this too far and a new trial will be necessary.[388] Whether this will be so very much depends on the facts of the individual case.

Finally, note that there is a potentially complicated interplay between a trial judge's inherent power to control the process of the court and a prosecutor's authority to conduct the case. Where a prosecutorial decision is classified as part of "core prosecutorial discretion," a judge can only override it if the decision is shown to be an abuse of process. If the decision is simply a matter of tactics and conduct before the court, on the other hand, then the judge's inherent power to control the process takes priority. However, the Court has recently held that some decisions will be part of prosecutorial discretion but not *core* prosecutorial discretion. In those instances, it will not be necessary to show an abuse of process for a judge to override the decision but something more than the ordinary inherent jurisdiction could be required.[389] This topic is discussed at greater length in Chapter 3, Section B(1)(a).

## 2) Publication Bans

A trial judge has the ability, in various circumstances, to order a publication ban.[390] Such bans should be seen as exceptional, since they prevent public knowledge of court proceedings and, therefore, are in conflict with

385 *R v Felderhof* (2003), 17 CR (6th) 20 at para 57 (Ont CA).

386 See, for example, *R c Hébert*, 2014 QCCA 1441; *R v Pompeo*, 2014 BCCA 317; *R v Switzer*, 2014 ABCA 129; or *R v Gahan*, 2014 NBCA 18. See also Wayne K Gorman, "Judicial Intervention in the Trial Process" (2003) 47 *Criminal Law Quarterly* 481.

387 *R v Currie* (2002), 3 CR (6th) 377 (Ont CA).

388 *R v Brouillard*, [1985] 1 SCR 39. See also *R v Stucky*, 2009 ONCA 151, or *R v Bérubé*, 2007 QCCA 463.

389 See *R v Varennes*, 2025 SCC 22 at para 57.

390 For an explanation of this issue in chart form, see *Anatomy of Criminal Procedure*, above note 19, Chart 2.5(a), "Publication Bans."

the open court principle. The Court has described the open court principle as a "hallmark of a democratic society" and a "cornerstone of the common law."[391] It is protected by freedom of expression because "[r]eporting on court proceedings by a free press is often said to be inseparable from the principle of open justice."[392] Nonetheless, in certain circumstances publication bans are permitted. Most of these bans have a statutory basis, although there is also a common law ability to issue publication bans.

Most noteworthy is the ban outlined in section 486.4, which allows a judge to ban the publication of any information that would identify the complainant or a witness in a trial for a variety of listed sexual offences. A trial judge is required to inform any witness under eighteen and the complainant of the right to make such an application, and where one of those persons or the prosecutor applies, the judge is required to order the ban. An earlier version of this provision was upheld under the *Charter* on the basis that, although the provision violated freedom of the press, it was saved under section 1.[393] It is also of note that at the time, only prosecutors and complainants could make applications under the section. The Court's reasoning focused on the need to encourage victims of sexual assault to report the crime: that consideration entered into both finding that there was a sufficiently important objective and determining that the provision was minimally impairing. Indeed, the Court specifically noted that it was not deciding whether the section would survive a *Charter* challenge if the prosecutor were not applying on the complainant's behalf. Since that time, the section has been expanded to include publication bans on behalf of witnesses under the age of eighteen. It is possible that a *Charter* challenge to the section in this context might succeed.

A similar power to seek a ban on publication of information disclosing the identity of a victim or witness is found in section 486.5. In this case, however, the ban is discretionary, and the trial judge must consider a variety of factors, including the right to a fair and public hearing, the risk of harm to the witness if their identity were disclosed, the impact of the order on freedom of expression, and a number of other matters. In addition, this type of publication ban can sometimes be issued to protect the identity of justice system participants, such as jurors, prosecutors, or police officers. The power is available only in trials for certain offences, such as those dealing with criminal organizations or terrorism offences.[394]

---

391 *Vancouver Sun (Re)*, [2004] 2 SCR 332 [*Vancouver Sun (Re)*] at paras 23–24.

392 *Sherman Estate v Donovan*, 2021 SCC 25 [*Sherman Estate*].

393 *Canadian Newspapers Co v Canada (Attorney General)*, [1988] 2 SCR 122.

394 Sections 486.5(2) and 486.2(5). The section does not apply to appeal courts, but those courts can consider the same issue using the common law power to

There are other specific bans within the *Code* as well. For example, sections 278.9 and 278.95 prevent reporting of information regarding particular applications in the context of trials for sexual offences, and section 648 prevents the publication of evidence from a trial while jurors are separated before beginning deliberations.[395] Section 517 entitles an accused to a mandatory publication ban on all information disclosed at a bail hearing.[396]

The *YCJA* bans the publication of some information too. Subject to exceptions dealing with public safety, no one is to publish information that could identify a young person as one being dealt with under the Act, though this publication ban sometimes does not apply, such as in the case of a young person who receives an adult sentence.[397] Similarly, no one can publish information identifying a young person who was a victim or a witness at proceedings concerning another young person. In the latter case, the young person can apply to be permitted to publish such information personally and is entitled to do so after reaching the age of eighteen.[398]

In addition, the *Victims Bill of Rights* gives victims of an offence the right to request that their identity be protected if they are a complainant or witness in proceedings relating to the offence. However, that Act is to be interpreted in a manner that is reasonable in the circumstances, and in particular one that is not likely to interfere with the proper administration of justice.[399]

Finally, when no statutory provision applies, there is a common law power to impose a publication ban[400] or indeed to depart from the open court principle in other contexts. The Court first set out this power in

---

impose a publication ban, discussed below: *R v Esseghaier*, 2017 ONCA 970 [*Esseghaier*]; *R v Derbyshire*, 2016 NSCA 67.

395 The wording of the section refers to information presented during "any portion of the trial at which the jury is not present." The section has been interpreted to include proceedings prior to jury selection: *La Presse inc v Quebec*, 2023 SCC 22.

396 This publication ban was challenged under the *Charter* but upheld: see *Toronto Star Newspapers Ltd v Canada*, 2010 SCC 21.

397 *YCJA*, above note 139, s 110. Where a young person receives a youth sentence for a presumptive offence (that is, one where the accused will presumptively receive an adult sentence), the *YCJA* creates a reverse onus requiring the young person to justify the publication ban. That reverse onus has been struck down by the Court as violating the *Charter*: see *R v DB*, 2008 SCC 25.

398 *YCJA*, above note 139, s 111.

399 *Canadian Victims Bill of Rights*, SC 2015, c 13, s 2 at ss 12 and 20.

400 See, for example, *R v TWW*, 2024 SCC 19 [*TWW*]. Section 276 of the *Code* creates rules around the use of a complainant's prior sexual history, and s 278.93 creates a procedure to apply for the use of that evidence. In turn s 278.95 imposes a publication ban on that evidence. However, *TWW* concluded that

*Dagenais v Canadian Broadcasting Corp*[401] and then broadened its applicability in *R v Mentuck*.[402] For many years this test was referred to as the "*Dagenais/Mentuck* test." In 2021, however, the test was reformulated in *Sherman Estate*,[403] and cases since variously refer to the "*Dagenais/Mentuck* test," the "*Dagenais/Mentuck/Sherman Estate* test" or just the "*Sherman Estate* test."

*Dagenais* aimed at balancing fair trial rights against freedom of expression, both of them rights protected by the *Charter*.[404] It created a test modelled on section 1 of the *Charter* and the *Oakes* test. In *Mentuck* the Court returned to the subject of publication bans in circumstances where the ban was sought by the Crown and no fair trial right was at issue.[405] The Court recognized that a broader range of interests might need to be contrasted with freedom of expression, and so reformulated the phrasing of the test accordingly. The Court therefore concluded that the real question was one of finding a balance between the many possible interests that made up the proper administration of justice on the one hand and freedom of expression on the other. As a further gloss, in *Sierra Club of Canada* the Court expanded the *Dagenais/Mentuck* analysis to apply to allow protection of interests other than the administration of justice.[406]

*Sherman Estate* did not fundamentally change the test but reformulated it to separate the relevant considerations into three. The Court held:

> In order to succeed, the person asking a court to exercise discretion in a way that limits the open court presumption must establish that:
> (1) court openness poses a serious risk to an important public interest;

---

s 278.95 did not apply at the appeal stage and therefore that the common law governed such applications.

401 [1994] 3 SCR 835 [*Dagenais*].

402 2001 SCC 76 [*Mentuck*].

403 *Sherman Estate*, above note 392.

404 The applicants were members of a Catholic religious order charged with physical and sexual abuse of young boys in their care. They unsuccessfully sought an injunction restraining the CBC from broadcasting a fictional account of sexual and physical abuse of children in a Catholic institution.

405 *Mentuck* involved a "Mr Big" undercover operation. The Crown sought a publication ban on the names of the particular police officers who involved, as well as on the release of information about the technique itself. The Court upheld the former ban but not the latter.

406 In *Sierra Club of Canada v Canada (Minister of Finance)*, 2002 SCC 41, Atomic Energy of Canada Ltd obtained a confidentiality order, keeping the details of contracts for the sale of CANDU reactors confidential in order to protect their commercial interests.

> (2) the order sought is necessary to prevent this serious risk to the identified interest because reasonably alternative measures will not prevent this risk; and,
> (3) as a matter of proportionality, the benefits of the order outweigh its negative effects.
>
> Only where all three of these prerequisites have been met can a discretionary limit on openness — for example, a sealing order, a publication ban, an order excluding the public from a hearing, or a redaction order — properly be ordered. This test applies to all discretionary limits on court openness, subject only to valid legislative enactments.[407]

Courts should be cautious about classifying competing interests as important public ones because of the importance of maintaining the open court principle. Whether something is an important public interest is an abstract policy question, but whether there is a serious risk to it will depend on the facts of the particular case.

In the context of *Sherman Estate* itself, the Court found that "privacy" in general is not an important public interest, but privacy *can* rise to the standard of an important public interest where a violation of it threatens an individual's dignity. Dignity in this context is a social concept that involves presenting core aspects of oneself to others in a considered and controlled manner. Where information will be revealed that consists of intimate or personal details about an individual that go to their biographical core — such as stigmatized medical conditions, sexual orientation, and subjection to sexual assault or harassment — there will be an important public interest.[408] In considering whether there is a serious risk to that public interest, courts should consider the likelihood that the information will in fact be publicly disseminated if revealed in court.

The second step, whether the order sought is necessary, is analogous to the "minimal impairment" branch of *Oakes*. For example, in *TWW* the Crown sought a sealing order and an *in camera* hearing to protect a complainant's privacy interests on appeal when sexual history evidence was in play. The Court concluded that the first step of an important public interest was met but that the risk to the complainant's privacy and dignity did not justify the order the Crown was seeking. The complainant's interest could be addressed by a publication ban on

---

407 *Sherman Estate*, above note 392 at para 38.

408 In *Canadian Broadcasting Corp v Manitoba*, 2023 SCC 27, a publication ban was sought over an affidavit relating to the death of a witness, filed in a wrongful conviction hearing. The Court held that there was "a strong public interest in protecting the privacy of the witness's spouse with respect to the witness's death in order to prevent an affront to the spouse's dignity" (para 9).

any information about the nature of the sexual activity other than that which formed the subjectmatter of the charge.

An application for a publication ban can be made to the trial judge, to another judge of that court if no trial judge has been appointed, or to a judge of the superior court if the level of court for trial cannot yet be established. The application is to be made in the absence of the jury, and the judge has discretion to decide whether to give notice of the application to the media. The trial judge also has discretion as to whether to grant the media standing in the application, whether to permit them to cross-examine or present evidence, and so on.[409]

Where someone has violated a publication ban, the Crown can apply for a mandatory interlocutory injunction to require them to comply, and can also argue for contempt of court (see the discussion of contempt, below). However, obtaining a mandatory interlocutory injunction is not easy:

(1) The applicant must demonstrate a strong *prima facie* case that it will succeed at trial. This entails showing a *strong likelihood* on the law and the evidence presented that, at trial, the applicant will be ultimately successful in proving the allegations set out in the originating notice;
(2) The applicant must demonstrate that irreparable harm will result if the relief is not granted; and
(3) The applicant must show that the balance of convenience favours granting the injunction.[410]

The *Dagenais/Mentuck* (or now, *Sherman Estate*) test applies not only to publication bans but to all discretionary decisions that affect the openness of proceedings and freedom of expression.[411] A decision about whether to release exhibits from a trial (such as a videotaped statement) to the media is therefore also settled by that test.[412] Different considerations might be relevant to the balancing in that context, such as that a person testifying in court is often compelled to do so while a person making an out-of-court statement does so voluntarily.

It is important to remember, however, that this test applies to *discretionary* decisions by a judge. Where a judge has no discretion to exercise — for example, where informer privilege is at stake — a

---

409 *Dagenais*, above note 401.
410 *R v Canadian Broadcasting Corp*, 2018 SCC 5 at para 18.
411 *Vancouver Sun (Re)*, above note 391.
412 *Canadian Broadcasting Corp v the Queen*, 2011 SCC 3. See, for example, *Esseghaier*, above note 394.

publication ban *must* be imposed.[413] Even there, however, steps should be taken to respect the open court principle as much as possible, despite the ban. A two-stage procedure is used. First, the court must verify the existence of the privilege, by holding an *in camera* and potentially *ex parte* hearing at which generally only the police informer and the Crown (the holders of the privilege) will be present. This stage is to satisfy the judge on balance that the person is a confidential informer. At the second stage, the court will determine the appropriate measures to protect informer privilege while accommodating as much as possible the open court principle, the right to be heard, and the adversarial nature of the proceedings. This stage might involve allowing third parties to make submissions on the appropriate confidentiality orders. A judge might issue a public notice inviting interested third parties to make submissions on confidentiality orders and hear their submissions, but this is discretionary.[414]

The open court principle is relevant in other contexts than publication bans. For example, the judge can decide to exclude any or all members of the public from all or part of the trial where it is "in the interest of public morals, the maintenance of order or the proper administration of justice."[415] The *Code* specifically notes that the "proper administration of justice" includes ensuring the interests of witnesses under the age of eighteen in sexual assault trials and of justice system participants.[416] A trial judge who does not grant a request for exclusion in a sexual offence case must give reasons for not having done so.[417]

This power conflicts with the open court principle and can also conflict with freedom of the press since it might prevent journalists from being present for and reporting on some portion of a trial. The Court has held that the provision therefore violates section 2(b) of the *Charter*,

---

413 See *Named Person v Vancouver Sun*, 2007 SCC 43 at para 37:

> *Dagenais/Mentuck*, insofar as that line of cases now represents a "test" for the application of the open court principle in discretionary action by courts, does not apply to the privilege in this case. The informer privilege rule does *not* provide a trial judge with a discretionary power to order a publication ban. Quite the contrary. When a trial judge finds that an informer privilege exists, then, as the Court stated in *Bisaillon v. Keable*, at p. 93, "[i]ts application does not depend on the judge's discretion, as it is a legal rule of public order by which the judge is bound."

414 See *Canadian Broadcasting Corp v Named Person*, 2024 SCC 21. See generally the discussion at paras 71ff for discussion of potential procedures.

415 Section 486(1). The section also permits exclusion of the public "to prevent injury to international relations or national defence or national security."

416 Section 486(2).

417 Section 486(3).

but nonetheless is saved as a reasonable limit, provided the discretion to use the section is exercised properly. Accordingly, the Court held:

(a) the judge must consider the available options and consider whether there are any other reasonable and effective alternatives available;
(b) the judge must consider whether the order is limited as much as possible; and
(c) the judge must weigh the importance of the objectives of the particular order and its probable effects against the importance of openness and the particular expression that will be limited in order to ensure that the positive and negative effects of the order are proportionate.[418]

The burden is on the person seeking the exclusion to provide a sufficient factual foundation, and to show that the particular order is necessary, that it is as limited as possible, and that the salutary effects of the order are proportionate to its deleterious effects.

The Court also relied on the open court principle and an analogy to the *Dagenais/Mentuck* test in considering whether a witness ought to be allowed to wear a niqab in court. The complainant in *R v NS* was a Muslim woman testifying at a preliminary inquiry on sexual assault charges. She wanted to wear her niqab while in court, in accordance with her religious beliefs, while the accused argued that this would interfere with their right to a fair trial, since it made it impossible to see her face as she testified. The Court, in a split decision, concluded that this conflict between the open court principle and trial freedom should be handled by a test which relied heavily on the open court principle as articulated in cases relating to publication bans. They held that when such issues arose, they should be answered on a case-by-case basis by asking four questions:

1. Would requiring the witness to remove the niqab while testifying interfere with her religious freedom?
2. Would permitting the witness to wear the niqab while testifying create a serious risk to trial fairness?
3. Is there a way to accommodate both rights and avoid the conflict between them?
4. If no accommodation is possible, do the salutary effects of requiring the witness to remove the niqab outweigh the deleterious effects of doing so?[419]

418 *Canadian Broadcasting Corp v New Brunswick (Attorney General)*, [1996] 3 SCR 480 at para 69.
419 2012 SCC 72 at para 9 [*NS*].

## 3) Contempt of Court

Judges have the power to find people in contempt of court. This common law power is expressly preserved by section 9 of the *Code*, and appeal procedures from it are set out in section 10. Contempt is divided into contempt committed in the face of the court and contempt not committed in the face of the court, a distinction still reflected in section 10 of the *Code*. Superior courts have jurisdiction over both types of contempt, while inferior courts can punish only the former. The *YCJA* gives youth justice courts very broad jurisdiction, including contempt in the face of and not in the face of either the youth justice court or any other court, when it is committed by a young person.[420] Only contempt in the face of the court will concern us here.

Contempt can cover a variety of behaviours, including insolence to the court or refusal to answer questions while under oath, for example.[421] The accused, a witness, or counsel can be cited in contempt.[422] The power to punish for contempt is intended to maintain the dignity of the court and to ensure a fair trial. A judge can respond to contemptuous behaviour in either of two ways: (1) through the ordinary procedure, which gives the accused the usual procedural guarantees of a criminal trial, or (2) through a more summary procedure.[423] The summary procedure can be used only where it is urgent and imperative to act immediately and, other than in exceptional circumstances, that procedure must comply with the requirements of natural justice. In general terms, this means that "only '[t]he least possible power adequate to the end proposed' should be used."[424] In particular, it means that normally a three-step process is to be followed. First, the person is to be put on notice that they will be required to show cause as to why they should not be found in contempt of court. In other words, the person is being "cited" in contempt. Second, an adjournment should be given, long enough to allow the person an opportunity to consult with counsel and possibly be represented by counsel. Finally, a person who is found in contempt should be allowed to make representations

---

420 *YCJA*, above note 139, s 15.

421 See *R v Arradi*, 2003 SCC 23 [*Arradi*], and *R v K(B)*, [1995] 4 SCR 186 [*K(B)*].

422 See, for example, *R v Wilson*, 2025 ABCA 337, where a Crown prosecutor was cited for contempt by a justice of the peace for his behaviour at a bail hearing, though this was overturned on appeal.

423 *Arradi*, above note 421 at para 29. See *R v Vermette*, [1987] 1 SCR 577, for an example of contempt being dealt with through the ordinary procedure of a separate trial on the charge.

424 *Arradi*, above note 421 at para 33, quoting *K(B)*, above note 421 at para 13, itself quoting *United States v Wilson*, 421 US 309 at 319 (1975).

as to sentence. Although in some cases not all of these steps need to be followed, departure from this model is permitted only in exceptional circumstances. Failure to follow this process is an error of law.[425]

The contempt proceedings can also be conducted in the jury's presence where the contempt has occurred in front of it, since the jury helps make up the court.[426] However, it must be made clear to the jury that the accused's guilt in the contempt proceeding cannot be used to assess guilt in the actual trial.

## 4) Mistrials

One particular judicial power worth discussing separately is the authority to declare a mistrial. A trial judge has the authority to declare a mistrial at virtually any point in the proceedings, from as early as the jury selection stage[427] to as late as the post-conviction but pre-sentence stage.[428] Indeed, a trial judge still has jurisdiction to declare a mistrial after an appeal has been launched, provided a sentence has not yet been handed down.[429] Where there was a jury trial, however, the leading view is that a trial judge is *functus* and no longer has the jurisdiction to declare a mistrial once the jury has rendered its verdict.[430]

A trial judge has discretion about whether to declare a mistrial, and an appeal court should show deference to that decision. The decision is to be based on whether there is a real danger that trial fairness has been compromised, and a wide variety of issues can lead to a mistrial application. Among them are inappropriate publicity or other errors during jury selection, improper comments by the Crown prosecutor during an opening statement or closing submission, or inadmissible evidence accidentally being given to the jury.[431]

However, a mistrial is not automatically granted in the case of such errors and, in fact, is more a remedy of last resort, and a court also must

---

425 *Arradi*, above note 421.

426 Note, similarly, that another judge of the same court is not permitted to hear the contempt proceeding: *R v Doz*, [1987] 2 SCR 463.

427 *R v Williams*, [1998] 1 SCR 1128 [*Williams* 1998], and *R v Bengert (No 13)* (1979), 15 CR (3d) 62 (BCSC), aff'd on other grounds (1980), 15 CR (3d) 114 (BCCA), leave to appeal to SCC refused (1980), 53 CCC (2d) 48n (SCC).

428 *R v McAnespie*, [1993] 4 SCR 501.

429 *R v MacDonald* (1991), 107 NSR (2d) 374 (SCAD) [*MacDonald*].

430 *R v Halcrow*, 2008 ABCA 319, leave to appeal to SCC refused [2008] SCCA No 532. See also *R v Henderson* (2004), 189 CCC (3d) 447; *R v Lawrence*, 2001 NSCA 44.

431 See, for example, *Williams* 1998, above note 427; *R v Dore* (2002), 4 CR (6th) 81 (Ont CA); *Grabowski v the Queen*, [1985] 2 SCR 434; *Pisani v the Queen*, [1971] SCR 738 [*Pisani*]; *R v Khan*, 2001 SCC 86 [*Khan*].

consider whether corrective measures would remedy the irregularity. Other remedies might include making an adjournment, reopening the case, or, quite commonly, clearly instructing the jury that they are to ignore the submissions or information they ought not to have heard. It is only where such other remedies are insufficient that a mistrial should be granted.[432] It might be that a warning to the jury as to what they should or should not consider in reaching their verdict will be sufficient: courts "should not presume that jurors are incapable of following instructions given by the judge."[433]

Although it is typically the accused who applies for a mistrial, it is also open to the Crown to do so.[434] Similarly, although circumstances leading to a mistrial application are more likely to arise in a jury trial, in principle, the power exists in trials held by judge alone as well.[435]

For the most part, the authority to order a mistrial comes from the common law. It is a discretionary decision and although it is subject to appeal, an appeal court is not to interfere with the trial judge's exercise

---

432 See, for example, *R v D(LE)*, [1989] 2 SCR 111 at para 28:

> should inadmissible evidence be adduced, the trial Judge should either instruct the jury immediately to disregard it or, if it is of so prejudicial a nature that the jury would not have the capability of disregarding it, he should discharge the jury and order a new trial . . . . If the trial judge was of the view that an immediate caution to the jury to disregard the evidence was insufficient to ensure a fair trial, then his course was to direct a mistrial rather than admit the evidence of similar acts which had previously been excluded.

(quoting, in part, from *R v Ambrose* (1975), 25 CCC (2d) 90 (NBSCAD), aff'd [1977] 2 SCR 717.)

433 *Khan*, above note 431 at para 82. See also *R v Cawthorne*, 2016 SCC 32. See, for example, *R v Conway*, 2015 QCCA 1389, where the Crown made an incorrect submission to the jury but was interrupted and corrected by the trial judge. The Crown prosecutor then acknowledged to the jury that he had been incorrect, and the judge returned to the point in her instructions to the jury. The Québec Court of Appeal held that the trial judge had been correct to conclude that no mistrial needed to be declared.

434 The Crown applied successfully for a mistrial in *Williams* 1998, above note 427, and unsuccessfully in *Trakas*, above note 251. In *R v CDH*, 2015 ONCA 102 [*CDH*], the Crown obtained an order for a mistrial when the judge, after conviction but before sentencing, had a private meeting with the officer in charge of the case in which they discussed the evidence in the case, the witnesses, and some independent research the judge had done on Match.com.

435 *CDH*, *ibid*, was a judge-alone trial. *MacDonald*, above note 365, was also a judge-alone trial; the judge contacted the Crown and a Crown witness, without the knowledge of the accused, following conviction but before sentencing, and the trial judge granted a subsequent application for a mistrial brought by the Crown and the defence.

of discretion unless clearly satisfied that the judge proceeded on some wrong principle or was wrong.[436] As noted above, there is also a discretion in section 653 of the *Code* for a trial judge to declare a mistrial if satisfied that a jury is unable to agree on a verdict. Although section 653(2) says that this discretion is not reviewable, there are suggestions that the subsection might not withstand *Charter* scrutiny.[437]

As a general rule, a new trial can be held following a mistrial, and the fact of a mistrial does not allow an accused to plead *autrefois acquit* or *autrefois convict*. In particular circumstances, the *Charter* might prevent a new trial from being held after an improper declaration of a mistrial, but only where the principles of fundamental justice are in issue. Where a trial judge declares a mistrial to save a floundering Crown case and give it time to obtain further witnesses, for example, the *Charter* might prevent a new trial, but in ordinary circumstances new proceedings can be commenced.[438]

At any new trial, rulings made at the initial trial with regard to disclosure, admissibility, or the *Charter* will bind the parties at the new trial, if they were or could have been made before evidence was called.[439] However, an exception is made if the court is satisfied that it would not be in the "interests of justice" for the previous rulings to be binding. In determining the interests of justice in the context of section 653.1, relevant factors include:

i. whether any new evidence will be tendered on the proposed rehearing;
ii. whether any new arguments will be advanced on the proposed rehearing and the apparent merit, if any, of those arguments;
iii. the interests of the parties, including any articulable prejudice fostered or perpetuated by the inability to relitigate any issue previously decided;
iv. the public interest in the timely and efficient conduct of criminal trial proceedings and avoidance of unnecessary and duplicative proceedings;
v. any changes in the legal principles governing the ruling on which relitigation is proposed;

---

436 *Bengert*, above note 427. See also *Khan*, above note 431.

437 See *Pan*, above note 316 at para 111. The section was challenged in that case, but the *Charter* issue was not decided since the Crown did not dispute the ability of appeal courts to review the initial decision.

438 *Pan*, *ibid* at para 113.

439 Section 653.1. This provision was added as part of the *Fair and Efficient Criminal Trials Act*, SC 2011, c 16.

vi. the nature of the evidentiary record on the basis of which the prior ruling was made, as for example, *viva voce* testimony; agreed statement of facts; transcripts of testimony given elsewhere and any differences in the record proposed for relitigation;
vii. the nature of the issue(s) involved in the prior ruling and proposed relitigation;
viii. the possibility of inconsistent rulings; and
ix. any other circumstances relating to the balance of the subsequent trial proceedings that may have an impact on the continued applicability of the prior rulings.[440]

The aim of this approach is to avoid the time and expense associated with relitigating issues which have already been decided, and to avoid the possibility of conflicting decisions on the same issue.[441]

## FURTHER READINGS

BALA, NICHOLAS, & HILARY MCCORMACK. "Accommodating the Criminal Process to Child Witnesses" (1994) 25 *Criminal Reports* (4th) 341.

———, RCL LINDSAY, & E MCNAMARA. "Testimonial Aids for Children: The Canadian Experience with Closed Circuit Television, Screens and Videotapes" (2001) 44 *Criminal Law Quarterly* 461.

CHOPRA, SONIA R, & JAMES RP OGLOFF. "Evaluating Jury Secrecy: Implications for Academic Research and Juror Stress" (2000) 44 *Criminal Law Quarterly* 190.

COUGHLAN, STEVE, & ALEX GORLEWSKI. *The Anatomy of Criminal Procedure: A Visual Guide to the Law*, 2nd ed (Toronto: University of Toronto Press, 2026).

GORMAN, WAYNE K. "Judicial Intervention in the Trial Process" (2003) 47 *Criminal Law Quarterly* 481.

LAW REFORM COMMISSION OF CANADA. *The Jury* (Ottawa: Law Reform Commission, 1982).

———. *The Charge Document in Criminal Cases* (Ottawa: Law Reform Commission of Canada, 1987).

———. *Double Jeopardy, Pleas and Verdicts* (Ottawa: Law Reform Commission of Canada, 1991).

440 *R v Victoria*, 2018 ONCA 69 at para 55.
441 *Ibid*.

Layton, David, & Michel Proulx. *Ethics and Canadian Criminal Law*, 2d ed (Toronto: Irwin Law, 2015).

Mainville, Christine. "Report on the CIAJ's Complex Criminal Trials Roundtable" (2015) 62 *Criminal Law Quarterly* 339.

Quigley, Tim. "Principled Reform of Criminal Procedure" in Don Stuart, RJ Delisle, & Allan Manson, eds, *Toward a Clear and Just Criminal Law* (Toronto: Carswell, 1999).

Quinlan, Paul. "Secrecy of Jury Deliberations — Is the Cost Too High?" (1993) 22 *Criminal Reports* (4th) 127.

Rose, David. *Quigley's Criminal Procedure in Canada* (Toronto: Thomson Reuters, 2021) (loose-leaf) ch 17, 18, 20, & 21.

Stuart, Don. *Charter Justice in Canadian Criminal Law*, 7th ed (Toronto: Thomson Carswell, 2018) ch 2 and 6.

Tanovich, David M. "Upping the Ante in Directed Verdict Cases Where the Evidence Is Circumstantial" (1998) 5 *Criminal Reports* (5th) 21.

CHAPTER 12

# APPEALS

## A. INTRODUCTION

Rights of appeal in the Canadian criminal justice system are entirely a creature of statute. Various appeal provisions are set out in the *Criminal Code*, and in addition, the *Code* provides that only appeals authorized in Parts XXI and XXVI can be brought with regard to indictable offences.[1] In fact, however, that has not operated to completely restrict the methods of review for decisions of the lower courts.

First, applications for extraordinary remedies such as *certiorari* can be brought in some cases, though the scope of such applications is more limited than an appeal. Among other things, extraordinary remedies are not available against the decisions of superior courts.[2] Further, in general there are no interlocutory appeals in criminal matters, though jurisdictional errors can be challenged by way of *certiorari*.[3]

1 Section 674. This means that, for example, a judge whose decision is overturned has no ability personally to appeal the order arising out of the appeal (*Alberta (Attorney General) v Malin*, 2016 ABCA 396) and is not a party to any appeal that is launched (*R v Penunsi*, 2016 NLCA 50).

2 *R v Varennes*, 2025 SCC 22 at para 32, citing *Dagenais v Canadian Broadcasting Corp.*, [1994] 3 SCR 835 [*Dagenais*].

3 *R v Awashish*, 2018 SCC 45 at para 20. See also para 10: "Fragmenting criminal proceedings by permitting interlocutory appeals risks having issues decided without the benefit of a full evidentiary record — a significant source of delay and an inefficient use of judicial resources."

The procedures for extraordinary remedies are set out in Part XXVI, and those include provisions for appeals of a decision regarding an application for an extraordinary remedy. Those appeal procedures are separately recognized by section 674 of the Code, and therefore the limits which are set out below relating to appeals from convictions or acquittals do not apply. In particular, if Part XXVI proceedings are commenced relating to a search warrant but charges are subsequently laid based on the evidence obtained through the warrant, the proceedings already commenced do not thereby become interlocutory to the prosecution and governed by the appeal provisions relating to acquittals or convictions.[4]

In addition, in some unusual circumstances an appeal to the Supreme Court might be possible through section 40 of the *Supreme Court Act*.[5] That section permits appeals "from any final or other judgment of . . . the highest court of final resort in a province," provided that the issue is important enough.[6] In *Dagenais v Canadian Broadcasting Corp.*, the Court held that although a literal interpretation of section 674 of the *Code* would exclude relying on section 40 for appeals "in respect of indictable offences," such a literal interpretation could not be adopted.[7] In that case, section 40 was used to allow a third party (the media) to appeal a publication ban, an appeal that would not have been possible under any of the *Code*'s appeal provisions. In *R v Cunningham* the Court concluded that an appeal of a decision whether to allow defence counsel to withdraw should also proceed under section 40, on the basis that defence counsel (like the media in *Dagenais*) is a third party to the main criminal action.[8] See also *R v Laba*, where section 40 permitted the Crown to appeal a ruling that overturned a reverse onus provision in the *Code*, even though they had been successful in the result at the court of appeal: in effect, the Crown was appealing a case that it had won.[9] In *R v Shea* the Court concluded that section 40 permitted appeals of a provincial court of appeal's decision to extend the application for an appeal, though they also observed that it was

---

4 *R v Douglas*, 2016 MBCA 81.

5 RSC 1985, c S-26.

6 The phrase used in s 40 is that the question is "by reason of its public importance or the importance of any issue of law or any issue of mixed law and fact involved in that question, one that ought to be decided by the Supreme Court or is, for any other reason, of such a nature or significance as to warrant decision by it . . . ."

7 *Dagenais*, above note 2 at 858.

8 2010 SCC 10 [*Cunningham*].

9 [1994] 3 SCR 965.

only in very rare circumstances that such a decision could be important enough to warrant granting leave.[10] In *R v Varennes* the Court held that section 40 might be available with regard to a trial judge's order about mode of trial, but that such an appeal could simply be brought as an appeal of the result at trial.[11]

The provision is sometimes used in cases where an appeal of an interlocutory order is in issue, such as when a third party challenges an order for production of privileged communications, as in *R v McClure*[12] or *R v Brown*.[13] In the latter case, the Court noted that such appeals reach it without having been considered by any court of appeal, which denies the Court the benefit of a fuller record and input from that lower court. They suggested that this gap in the *Code*'s appeal provisions was anomalous and an "unnecessary encumbrance" that should be fixed by Parliament.[14]

The focus of this chapter, however, will be on the statutory appeal powers set out in the *Code* itself relating to convictions and acquittals. Although some issues, such as time limits and procedures, are set by rules of court,[15] for the most part, the *Code* determines what can and cannot be done. Although in principle the rules in the *Code* govern "live" disputes between parties, a court of appeal does have the discretion to hear a matter even if it is moot, if the underlying issue continues to have importance. Specifically, the Court has held that a court should pay attention to a number of factors, the strength of which will vary according to the circumstances. Those factors are:

1. whether the appeal will proceed in a proper adversarial context;
2. the strength of the grounds of the appeal,
3. whether there are special circumstances that transcend the death of the individual appellant/respondent, including:
   (a) a legal issue of general public importance, particularly if it is otherwise evasive of appellate review;
   (b) a systemic issue related to the administration of justice;
   (c) collateral consequences to the family of the deceased or to other interested persons or to the public;

10 2010 SCC 26.
11 *Varennes*, above note 2 at para 33.
12 2001 SCC 14.
13 2002 SCC 32 [*Brown*].
14 *Ibid* at para 110.
15 See s 678, requiring an appellant to comply with rules of court and authorizing appeal courts to extend the time for appeals. See, for example, *R v Ansari*, 2015 ONCA 891.

4. whether the nature of the order which could be made by the appellate court justifies the expenditure of limited judicial (or court) resources to resolve a moot appeal;
5. whether continuing the appeal would go beyond the judicial function of resolving concrete disputes and involve the court in free-standing, legislative-type pronouncements more properly left to the legislature itself.[16]

The *Code* creates separate sets of rules for appeals of indictable offences and of summary conviction offences.[17] However, as a matter of convenience it does permit the appeal of a summary conviction matter to be heard along with that of an indictable offence where the two offences were tried together.[18] In the case of indictable offences, different appeal rights are given to an accused and the Crown. For summary conviction offences, however, the appeal rights are essentially parallel. The *Code* provisions deal with appeals of the result in the trial, findings that a person is not criminally responsible or is not fit to stand trial and appeals of sentence. It is the first of these that is of primary interest in this chapter.

## B. APPEALS OF INDICTABLE OFFENCES

### 1) Appeals by the Accused

#### a) Overview of Appeal Provisions

At first glance, it would appear that an accused appealing a conviction has an enormously broad right of appeal.[19] Section 675(1)(a) says that a person can appeal a conviction based on a question of law alone, on a question of fact, on a question of mixed law and fact, or on any ground of appeal "that appears to the court of appeal to be a sufficient

16 *R v Smith*, 2004 SCC 14 at para 50. See also *R v Poulin*, 2019 SCC 47.

17 In addition, s 10 of the *Code* sets out an appeal right in the case of contempt of court convictions.

18 Sections 675(1.1) and 676(1.1).

19 For an explanation of this issue in chart form, see Steve Coughlan and Alex Gorlewski, *The Anatomy of Criminal Procedure: A Visual Guide to the Law*, 2nd ed (Toronto: University of Toronto Press, 2026) [*Anatomy of Criminal Procedure*], Chart 4.1(c), "Appeals by the Accused: Grounds," Chart 4.1(d), "Appeals by the Accused: Narrowing the Bases for Success," and Chart 4.1(e), "Appeals by the Accused: Possible Outcomes."

ground of appeal."[20] In fact, the likelihood of an appeal succeeding is not nearly as great as that section alone suggests. These bases for appeal pass through at least three "filters," each limiting the grounds upon which an appeal might succeed.

The first two filters are found in section 686(1)(a) of the *Code*. Section 675 sets out the bases upon which an appeal can be *made*; the grounds upon which an appeal can be *granted* are considerably narrower. Section 686(1)(a) sets out those grounds:

> (i) the verdict should be set aside on the ground that it is unreasonable or cannot be supported by the evidence,
> (ii) the judgment of the trial court should be set aside on the ground of a wrong decision on a question of law, or
> (iii) on any ground there was a miscarriage of justice.

There is a rough conformity between sections 675 and 686. Section 675(1)(a) permits an appeal to be launched based on a question of law, and section 686(1)(a)(ii) allows an appeal to succeed on the basis of a wrong decision on a question of law. Section 675(1)(b) permits an appeal to be launched based on questions of fact or mixed law and fact, and section 686(1)(a)(i) allows an appeal to succeed on the basis that it cannot be supported by the evidence. Section 675(1)(a)(iii) permits an appeal to be launched based on the catch-all ground that it appears to be a sufficient ground of appeal, and section 686(1)(a)(iii) allows an appeal to succeed on the catch-all basis that there was a miscarriage of justice.[21] It is important, however, to note the differences between section 675 and section 686.

---

20 Section 675(1)(a). Questions of law can be appealed as of right, while the other grounds require leave of the court of appeal. Questions of fact or mixed law and fact can also be appealed "on the certificate of the trial judge that the case is a proper case for appeal." The "sufficient ground" basis of appeal is meant as a kind of residual ground, to allow appeals that should be permitted but do not fit neatly into the other grounds. For example, an application to an appeal court to withdraw a guilty plea based on incompetent representation at trial would be brought under this ground: see, for example, *R v Short*, 2012 SKCA 85.

21 *R v H(E)* (1997), 33 OR (3d) 202 at 210 (CA), observes the connection between these two provisions:

> Section 675(1)(a)(iii) specifically refers to any ground of appeal which does not involve a question of law alone, a question of fact, or a question of mixed law and fact. Sopinka and Gelowitz, in *The Conduct of an Appeal* (Toronto: Butterworths, 1993), note, with respect to this provision, that "[t]his is a residual jurisdiction to relieve against miscarriages of justice that do not strictly raise questions of law or fact."

An appeal can be made under section 675 on the basis of an error relating to a question of fact or mixed fact and law. However, an appeal will not necessarily be granted under section 686(1) simply because such an error is shown. Rather, only such an error that results in an unreasonable verdict or a miscarriage of justice will be sufficient. That is the first filter.

The second filter relates to the primary remaining ground of appeal in section 675: appeals based on a question of law. At face value, section 686(1)(a)(ii) says that demonstrating a wrong decision on such a question will lead to a successful appeal. However, there is some ambiguity in the meaning of the phrase "question of law": it has a broader meaning in section 675 than in section 686(1)(a). Therefore, that an issue is a question of law for the jurisdictional purpose of deciding whether a ground of appeal *exists* does not mean that it is a question of law for the purpose of deciding whether the appeal should be *granted*. For example, whether a verdict is unreasonable is a different issue from whether there was an error on a question of law for purposes of section 686, but whether a verdict is unreasonable is a question of law for purposes of section 675.[22] This change in characterization might cause the first filter to be relevant: despite the error of law the verdict still might not be unreasonable, and so the appeal might not be granted. In addition, since asking about unreasonableness involves greater deference to the trial judge (see the discussion of standard of review at Section B(1)(b)(i), below in this chapter), this further acts to limit the possibility of a successful appeal.[23]

The third filter is found in the fact that even if an appeal meets the conditions of section 686(1)(a), it might not be granted nonetheless. The grounds upon which an appeal might succeed are narrowed even further by section 686(1)(b), which sets out the grounds upon which the court of appeal can dismiss an appeal. Most obviously, a court can

---

22 See, for example, *R v RP*, 2012 SCC 22 at para 5 [*RP*]; *R v Biniaris*, 2000 SCC 15 at para 22 [*Biniaris*], explains why the distinction is not drawn at the early stage:

> The sole purpose of the exercise here, in identifying the reasonableness of a verdict as a question of fact, law or both, is to determine access to appellate review. One can plausibly maintain, on close scrutiny of any decision under review, that the conclusion that a verdict was unreasonable was reached sometimes mostly as a matter of law, in other cases predominantly as a matter of factual assessment. But when that exercise is undertaken as a jurisdictional threshold exercise, little is gained by embarking on such a case-by-case analysis.

23 See *R v Grouse*, 2004 NSCA 108 at paras 33–43, for a detailed explanation of this point.

dismiss an appeal if none of the above grounds for granting it is made out. However, that is not the only basis for dismissing an appeal: even if the accused does succeed in showing that one of the grounds of appeal in section 686(1)(a) is made out, the appeal might still fail.

An appeal can be dismissed on the basis that, although there was an error, the accused "was properly convicted on another count or part of the indictment."[24] In addition, section 686(1)(b) contains two other bases upon which an appeal might be dismissed despite an error:

> (iii) notwithstanding that the court is of the opinion that on any ground mentioned in subparagraph (a)(ii) the appeal might be decided in favour of the appellant, it is of the opinion that no substantial wrong or miscarriage of justice has occurred, or
>
> (iv) notwithstanding any procedural irregularity at trial, the trial court had jurisdiction over the class of offence of which the appellant was convicted and the court of appeal is of the opinion that the appellant suffered no prejudice thereby.

These provisions are referred to as the "curative provisos." Their effect is that not all errors of law will lead to a successful appeal either. Errors in law that cause no substantial wrong, do not create a miscarriage of justice, or are mere procedural irregularities will not lead to a successful appeal by the accused.

These last two provisions are discussed in greater detail at Sections B(1)(b)(iv) and (v), below in this chapter. For the moment, it is sufficient to note that only an error of law under section 686(1)(a)(ii) could be saved by the curative proviso in 686(1)(b)(iii). If the appeal was based on either an unreasonable verdict or a miscarriage of justice then the harmless error exception has no application. In some cases, it can be a matter of dispute as to whether the claim being advanced falls into the "error of law" ground or not, and the existence of the curative proviso makes that decision an important one.[25]

Despite the formal differences between the three grounds for appeal, they are all based on the same underlying theory. In *R v Tayo Tompouba*, the Court held:

> as a general rule, a court of appeal may intervene only if the error was prejudicial to the accused. Unreasonable verdicts (s. 686(1)(a)(i)

24 Section 686(1)(b)(i).

25 See, for example, *R v Calnen*, 2019 SCC 6, where the dissenting judgment held that a trial judge's failure to give a limiting instruction on propensity reasoning made the verdict an unreasonable one, while the majority held that the mistake (if it had been one) would have been an error of law, which would have left the Crown the option of showing that no prejudice was caused.

> *Cr. C.*) and miscarriages of justice (s. 686(1)(a)(iii) *Cr. C.*) are usually, by nature, prejudicial to the accused, while errors of law (s. 686(1)(a)(ii) *Cr. C.*) are *presumed* to be prejudicial.[26]

This view of the relationship between the provisions had previously been articulated by the Ontario Court of Appeal.[27]

Finally, note that appeal courts can deal with issues other than whether the accused was convicted or acquitted. Section 686 also gives the appeal court the ability to hear appeals relating to findings that an accused was unfit to stand trial, that an accused was not criminally responsible by reason of mental disorder, or with regard to special verdicts.[28] In addition, of course, a court of appeal can vary a sentence imposed on an accused.[29]

### b) Appeal Provisions in Depth

#### *i) Standard of Review*

Since the grounds for an appeal by an accused extend beyond errors of law to include unreasonable verdicts and miscarriages of justice, appeal courts must review a variety of findings from lower courts. Specifically, it can be necessary to review questions of law, questions of fact, inferences of fact, and questions of mixed fact and law. The Supreme Court considered the standard of review for each of these issues in *Housen v Nikolaisen*.[30]

---

26 *R v Tayo Tompouba*, 2024 SCC 16 [*Tayo Tompouba*] at para 56. See also *R v Morrissey* (1995), 38 CR (4th) 4 (Ont CA) [*Morrissey*]:

> While s. 686(1)(a) provides three distinct bases upon which this court may quash a conviction, each shares the same underlying rationale. A conviction which is the product of a miscarriage of justice cannot stand. Section 686(1)(a)(i) is concerned with the most obvious example of a miscarriage of justice, a conviction which no reasonable trier of fact properly instructed could have returned on the evidence adduced at trial. Section 686(1)(a)(ii) read along with s. 686(1)(b) (iii) presumes that an error in law produces a miscarriage of justice unless the Crown can demonstrate the contrary with the requisite degree of certainty. Section 686(1)(a)(iii) addresses all other miscarriages of justice not caught by the two preceding subsections. In so far as the operation of s. 686(1)(a) is concerned, the distinction between errors of law and all other types of error has only one significance. Where the error is one of law the Crown bears the burden of demonstrating that the error did not result in a miscarriage of justice. Where the error is not one of law alone the appellant bears that burden.

27 *Morrissey*, above note 26.

28 Sections 686(1)(c) and (d).

29 Section 687.

30 [2002] 2 SCR 235 [*Housen*]. *Housen* is a civil case, but the Court has noted the relevance of its discussion of these issues to criminal matters: see *R v Buhay*, 2003 SCC 30.

With regard to pure questions of law, the standard of review is correctness, and so an appellate court can substitute its opinion for that of the trial judge. It can do this because appellate courts delineate and refine legal rules and ensure their universal application, which requires that they have a broad scope of review with respect to matters of law.[31] Questions of fact, however, are reviewable only on a higher standard. A finding of fact should not be overturned in the absence of a "palpable and overriding error," which amounts to "prohibiting an appellate court from reviewing a trial judge's decision if there was some evidence upon which he or she could have relied to reach that conclusion."[32] The Court has offered three basic rationales for this approach. First, given the number, length, and cost of appeals, there should be limits on how readily available they should be — deferring to a trial judge's findings of fact helps to impose a limit and does so on a principled basis. Second, trial judges are presumed to be competent and able to decide cases justly and fairly — allowing regular appeals would undermine that presumption as well as public confidence in the trial process. Finally, trial judges are better situated to make factual findings because they hear the testimony being given, are exposed to all the evidence, and are familiar with the case as a whole. Their primary role is to weigh and assess evidence, and so their expertise should be respected.

For essentially the same reasons, inferences of fact are held to the same standard of review as findings of fact. The issue is not whether there is evidence that reasonably supports the inference, but rather whether some palpable and overriding error can be shown from drawing the inference.

Questions of mixed law and fact are, in some ways, the most complicated. The Court has noted that these issues fall on a spectrum. Some things that may, at first, appear to be a question of mixed fact and law may be reduced to a question of law, in which case, the correctness standard would apply.[33] However, in other cases the higher standard of review is required, and so the general rule is that where an issue on appeal involves the trial judge's interpretation of the evidence as a whole, it should be overturned only in the case of palpable and overriding error.[34]

---

31 *Housen*, above note 30 at para 9.

32 *Ibid* at para 1.

33 See, for example, *R v Gardner*, 2018 ONCA 584 where the summary conviction appeal judge described the trial judge as making the "finding of fact" that there had been an investigative detention. This was, the Ontario Court of Appeal held, a finding of law, and so the standard of review was correctness rather than unreasonableness.

34 *Ibid* at para 36.

### ii) *Unreasonable Verdicts*

Section 686(1)(a)(i) permits an appeal to be allowed on the basis that the verdict "is unreasonable or cannot be supported by the evidence." This provision applies differently depending on whether the conviction being appealed came from a jury or from a judge alone. In essence, section 686(1)(a)(i) creates a single basis for granting an appeal from the decision of a jury, but two bases for overturning a judge-alone verdict: either that it was "unreasonable" *or* that it "cannot be supported by the evidence." In practice, that means that any verdict can be overturned if it is not one that a properly instructed jury or a judge could reasonably have rendered, and in addition, a judge-alone verdict can be overturned if the trial judge has drawn an inference or made a finding of fact essential to the verdict that (1) is plainly contradicted by the evidence relied on by the trial judge in support of that inference or finding, or (2) is shown to be incompatible with evidence that has not otherwise been contradicted or rejected by the trial judge.[35]

Juries do not give reasons, and, indeed, jurors and everyone else are precluded from revealing anything concerning the deliberations in the jury room.[36] Further, if the jury was charged incorrectly, then there would be an error of law, and the appeal would be based on section 686(1)(a)(ii) rather than (i). Accordingly, the issue of unreasonable verdicts in jury cases arises when the jury has been charged correctly but nonetheless returns with a verdict that seems questionable.

The basic standard for assessing whether a verdict fails on this ground is "whether the verdict is one that a properly instructed jury acting judicially, could reasonably have rendered."[37] For practical purposes this test focuses on the second clause in section 686(1)(a)(i), whether the verdict can be supported by the evidence. This test is framed by two well-established boundaries.[38] On the one hand, the court of appeal should not simply consider the sufficiency of the evidence, and it ought to engage in some weighing of that evidence.[39] On the other hand, the court of appeal cannot merely substitute its view for that of the trier of fact, but rather must ask whether the trier of fact

---

35 *RP*, above note 22 at para 9.

36 See s 649 of the *Code* and the discussion of this issue in Chapter 11, Section E(4).

37 *R v Yebes*, [1987] 2 SCR 168 at para 16 [*Yebes*], reaffirmed in *Biniaris*, above note 22, and *R v Beaudry*, 2007 SCC 5 [*Beaudry*].

38 *R v WH*, 2013 SCC 22.

39 *Biniaris*, above note 22 at para 36. See also *Yebes*, above note 37 at para 25: "While the Court of Appeal must not merely substitute its view for that of the jury, in order to apply the test the Court must re-examine and to some extent reweigh and consider the effect of the evidence."

could reasonably have reached the conclusion it did on the evidence before it.[40]

A general sense of unease or lurking doubt about a jury's decision is not a sufficient basis for a court of appeal to intervene. Such a feeling might trigger a closer inquiry, but cannot be the end of the analysis. The appeal court must proceed further and articulate as precisely as possible what features of the case suggest that the jury's verdict was unreasonable.[41]

Where a jury has been properly instructed but has returned an unreasonable verdict nonetheless, it means that the jury was not acting judicially. It might, for example, have failed to adequately apply advice that it was given about the frailties of eyewitness identification evidence or the limited use of similar fact evidence. To act judicially in this context requires that the jury act dispassionately, apply the law, and adjudicate on the basis of the record and nothing else. It also requires that the jury arrive "at a conclusion that does not conflict with the bulk of judicial experience."[42] This assessment would allow an appeal court to conclude, for example, that no jury could properly have been satisfied that identification was proved given the nature of the evidence led.

The same standard applies to deciding whether a judge has rendered an unreasonable verdict, but the task is different because the trial judge will have issued reasons showing the process by which the verdict was reached. Those reasons have an impact on an appeal court's ability to assess the verdict in two ways.

First, the presence of reasons can help show whether the verdict could be supported on the evidence. As the Court noted in *R v Biniaris:*

> [t]he review for unreasonableness on appeal is different, however, and somewhat easier when the judgment under attack is that of a single judge, at least when reasons for judgment of some substance are provided. In those cases, the reviewing appellate court may be able to identify a flaw in the evaluation of the evidence, or in the analysis, that will serve to explain the unreasonable conclusion reached, and justify the reversal.[43]

In addition, the presence of reasons allows a court of appeal to separately consider (in a way not possible for a jury verdict) whether a result is unreasonable even if it *could* be supported on the evidence. Section

40 *R v Burns*, [1994] 1 SCR 656.

41 *Biniaris*, above note 22 at para 38.

42 *Ibid* at para 40.

43 *Ibid* at para 37.

686(1)(a)(i) refers to verdicts that are "unreasonable *or* cannot be supported on the evidence" and so

> No one should stand convicted on the strength of manifestly bad reasons — reasons that are illogical on their face, or contrary to the evidence — on the ground that another judge (who never did and never will try the case) could *but might not necessarily* have reached the same conclusion for *other reasons*.[44]

Illogical or irrational reasoning could render a verdict unreasonable in various ways. The verdict might be unreasonable because a judge draws an inference or makes a finding of fact essential to it that is plainly contradicted by the evidence. That is, "[f]rom accepted evidence 'X', a court cannot lawfully infer 'not-X'."[45] Alternatively, a verdict could be unreasonable because the judge draws an inference or makes a finding of fact essential to the verdict which is demonstrably incompatible with evidence that was neither contradicted nor rejected.[46] These types of errors are ways of reasoning illogically from the evidence, which make the verdict unreasonable under section 686(1)(a)(i).[47] This issue is distinct from misapprehending the evidence, which would be a basis for appeal as a miscarriage of justice under section 686(1)(a)(iii).[48]

It matters to the remedy that will be given, under this approach to appeals of judge-alone decisions, whether the appeal is granted because the decision is "unreasonable" or because it "cannot be supported by the evidence": see the discussion in Section B(1)(b)(vi), below in this chapter.

One particular circumstance in which a verdict by either judge or jury can be found to be unreasonable is when there are inconsistent verdicts. That is, the same evidence could not reasonably lead both to a conviction and an acquittal, but when more than one charge or accused

---

44 *Beaudry*, above note 37 at para 97 [emphasis in original]. This is from the decision of Fish J, who dissented in the result in *Beaudry*. In *R v Sinclair*, 2011 SCC 40 [*Sinclair*], a majority of seven judges confirmed that Fish J's approach in *Beaudry* was the proper one to appeals under s 686(1)(a)(i) of judge-alone trials.

45 *Sinclair*, *ibid* at para 19.

46 *Ibid* at para 21.

47 These two categories do not exhaust the possibilities. In *R v Wright*, 2013 MBCA 109, for example, the Manitoba Court of Appeal found a judge's verdict to be unreasonable although the error in the case was not precisely either of those identified in *Sinclair*. The judge, in a sexual assault case, had found that the complainant was not to be believed when she said she had not consented, but was to be believed when she said that she revoked her consent: absent an explanation, that was an unreasonable verdict.

48 *Sinclair*, above note 44 at para 15. See the discussion of misapprehension of evidence in Section B(1)(b)(iii), below in this chapter.

is involved, that might in fact occur, which could seem inconsistent. This basis of proving unreasonableness is a difficult one, however. An inconsistency in verdicts will only be unreasonable where "on any realistic view of the evidence, the verdicts cannot be reconciled on any rational or logical basis."[49] Because jury members are not bound by any particular theory of the case, need not all agree with one another on how to reach the same conclusion, and are allowed a wide latitude in accepting some, all, or none of each witness's testimony, it is unusual to be able to say with certainty that the "same evidence" was in play in both cases.[50]

This claim is more likely to succeed when there is only one accused. In *R v JF* the accused was charged with two counts of manslaughter by omission, in one case based on criminal negligence and in the other case based on failure to provide necessaries. In fact, though, the Crown argued that it was exactly the same omission that constituted both the criminal negligence and the failure to provide necessaries. The jury found the accused guilty on the criminal negligence-based charge but not guilty on the failure to provide necessaries charge. The Court held that these verdicts were inconsistent.[51]

In essence, it will be only a rare case, one where the evidence on two different charges is not logically separable, where an inconsistent verdict appeal will succeed. Since the question is whether the verdicts are supportable on any theory of the evidence that is consistent with the law, it is difficult to show that two verdicts are clearly inconsistent with one another.[52] In the case of multiple accused charged with

49 *R v Pittiman*, 2006 SCC 9 [*Pittiman*] at para 7, quoting *R v McShannock* (1980), 55 CCC (2d) 53 (Ont CA) at 56.

50 As noted in *R v Catton*, 2015 ONCA 13 [*Catton*] at para 22, "Verdicts that may at first impression appear inconsistent can often be explained by distinctions in the essential elements of the different offences or in the quality of the evidence relevant to the different offences."

51 *R v JF*, 2008 SCC 60 [*JF*]. The fault requirements for the two offences were not identical, in that one required only a marked departure from the standard of a reasonable person while the other required a marked *and substantial* departure. That did not render the verdicts consistent and, in fact, made the situation worse: the jury had found the higher standard to be met but the lower one not. See also *Catton*, above note 50, where the jury found the accused guilty of dangerous driving causing death in connection with the passenger on a motorcycle involved in an accident, but not guilty of dangerous driving with regard to the driver of that same motorcycle. Those verdicts were inconsistent, because they amounted to the jury saying that they were satisfied that the accused had driven dangerously, but also had a reasonable doubt about that same issue.

52 See, for example, *R v Forcillo*, 2018 ONCA 402, where a police officer shot the victim nine times, causing the victim's death: he was acquitted of murder but

the same offence, it will typically be difficult to prove that verdicts are inconsistent even if some are convicted and some are acquitted, because the jury might have accepted evidence against one accused but not against the other.[53]

Finally, in some limited cases it is open to the Crown to argue that apparently inconsistent verdicts can be reconciled and therefore are not inconsistent, because of a legal error in the jury instructions. In *R v RV*[54] the accused was charged with sexual assault, sexual interference, and invitation to sexual touching. He was acquitted of the sexual assault but convicted of the other two charges: however, exactly the same facts, at the same time and against the same complainant, were the basis of all the charges, which appeared to make the verdicts inconsistent. This is not an uncommon situation,[55] and it is typically thought that the jury has concluded that the accused "touched" the complainant but did not "apply force," not understanding that any touching constitutes an application of force.

The Court concluded that in such cases the Crown could reconcile the verdicts "by showing, to a high degree of certainty, that the acquittal was the product of a legal error in the jury instructions, that the legal error did not impact the conviction, and that the error reconciles the inconsistency by showing that the jury did not find the accused both guilty and not guilty of the same conduct."[56] More specifically, the Court held:

> [33] Where the Crown attempts to rebut an apparent inconsistency on the basis of a legal error, the burden shifts from the accused to the Crown. That burden is heavy. The Crown must satisfy the court to a high degree of certainty that there was a legal error in the jury instructions and that the error:
> (1) had a material bearing on the acquittal;
> (2) was immaterial to the conviction; and
> (3) reconciles the inconsistency by showing that the jury did not find the accused both guilty and not guilty of the same conduct.

---

found guilty of attempted murder. The Ontario Court of Appeal concluded that these verdicts were not inconsistent, because it was possible for the jury to consider the nine shots as two separate volleys, 5.5 seconds apart, and to conclude that the circumstances of the first and second volleys were significantly different.

53 See, for example, *Pittiman*, above note 49.

54 *R v RV*, 2021 SCC 10 [*RV* 2021]

55 See, for example, *R v Tremblay*, 2016 ABCA 30 or *R v LBC*, 2019 ABCA 505.

56 *RV* 2021, above note 54 at para 5.

> [34] If the court can find that these elements are satisfied with a high degree of certainty, the verdicts are not actually inconsistent. Instead, the legal error caused the jury to convict the accused either on different evidence or a different element than it believed was necessary for the charge on which it acquitted the accused. Any apparent inconsistency in the verdicts is thus reconciled, as the jury did not find the accused both guilty and not guilty of the same conduct. It follows that the jury did not act unreasonably in rendering their verdicts.
> [35] In assessing whether the Crown has satisfied its burden, the court must not engage in improper speculation about what the jury did and did not do. The appellate court must be able to retrace the reasoning of the jury with a sufficiently high degree of certainty to exclude all other reasonable explanations for how the jury rendered its verdicts. If it can, any concern about speculation falls away.[57]

The dissenting judgment felt that this approach inquired into the jury's reasoning process, which would be improper, but the majority concluded that it only required considering the impact of jury instructions on a jury's verdict, which is done in a variety of contexts.

*iii) Errors of Law and Miscarriages of Justice*

Section 686(1)(a)(ii) permits an appeal to be granted in the case of "a wrong decision on a question of law," while section 686(1)(a)(iii) permits an appeal based on "a miscarriage of justice." It is convenient to consider these two grounds of appeal together because, although distinct, they share many features in common. Indeed, it has been suggested that the same rationale underlies all three bases of appeal in section 686(1)(a): that of miscarriage of justice. Section 686(1)(a)(i) sets out one basis upon which a verdict would be a miscarriage of justice (that it is unreasonable). Section 686(1)(a)(iii) explicitly includes any other miscarriage of justice as a basis for appeal. It has been suggested that section 686(1)(a)(ii), combined with the curative proviso, is an expression of the idea, mentioned above, that any error of law is presumed to be a miscarriage of justice unless the contrary is shown by the Crown.[58]

One feature that errors of law and miscarriages of justice have in common with one another, but which is distinct from unreasonable verdicts, is that there is no requirement that the verdict was not supportable on the evidence. In other words, even if the court of appeal

---

57 *RV* 2021, above note 54 at paras 33–35

58 *Morrissey*, above note 26. See also *Tayo Tompouba*, above note 26.

concludes that a jury could have convicted despite the legal error or miscarriage, that fact is not a basis for rejecting the appeal.[59]

In *Tayo Tompouba*, the Court elaborated more fully on the requirements for an "error of law" and how to distinguish it from a miscarriage of justice. They defined it as "any error in the application of a legal rule, as long as the error is related to the proceedings leading to the conviction and was made by a judge."[60] Therefore it must involve an error in the application of a legal rule, but that can originate in various ways. It could be a misinterpretation of a legal rule. However, it could equally be an unjustified failure to apply a legal rule. That is, a "wrong decision" on a question of law need not be based on a *decision* but instead could be an improper omission; for example, failing to give an instruction to the jury that ought to have been given. Further, the legal rule erroneously applied need not be substantive in nature but could be a procedural irregularity.

In addition, to constitute an appealable error of law, the legal rule must be related to the proceedings leading to the conviction and must be attributable to a judge. To be related to the proceedings, the error does not have to go directly to the verdict, but it must be related to the proceedings leading to the conviction. Normally it will be the *trial* judge who has made the erroneous decision, but it might be made by a judge who is not the trial judge. The wrong decision might occur prior to trial, for example, if an accused is not properly put to their election or a judge who is not the trial judge makes a wrong decision on an accused's fundamental right to be tried in the official language of their choice.[61]

As a result of this definition of "error of law," failures such as ineffective assistance of counsel or an uninformed guilty plea will usually fall to be assessed as miscarriages of justice. Typically, in such cases there will be no error by a judge in the application of a rule. Similarly, highly discretionary judicial decisions should be assessed as potential miscarriages of justice, because such decisions are so fact-dependent that they cannot be reduced to the simple application of a fixed rule of law.[62]

Most errors that are not based on the unreasonableness of a verdict will relate to an error of law. The primary reason for distinguishing between an error of law and a miscarriage of justice, as noted above, is the availability of the curative proviso — it cannot be resorted to in the

59 *R v Lohrer*, 2004 SCC 80 at para 1 [*Lohrer*].
60 *Tayo Tompouba*, above note 26 at para 60.
61 *Tayo Tompouba*, above note 26 at paras 61–68.
62 *Tayo Tompouba*, above note 26 at para 69.

latter case. However, to a certain extent this distinction is a formal one, rather than one of any real substance. Any mistake at trial that amounts to a miscarriage of justice would, in any case, fail to meet the test for the curative proviso. As a result, the underlying theory of the two subsections is really the same. What differs is the burden and standard of proof. The accused must show that there was an error of law or miscarriage of justice. If they do so, however, the Crown would, in the case of an error of law, be required to show that the curative proviso applied, and would have to meet a very high standard to demonstrate that claim (see the discussion in Section B(1)(b)(iv), below in this chapter).

There is no requirement that an error of law by itself must have led to any unfairness or prejudice; that is only an issue at the curative proviso stage.[63] So, for example, whether there is an air of reality to a defence is a legal question. It is therefore an error of law to instruct a jury on a defence when there is no air of reality to it, or to fail to instruct when there is.[64] The provision of flawed instructions to a jury is an error of law, as is an improper exhortation.[65] Reasoning improperly about circumstantial evidence is an error of law.[66] Applying a stricter standard of scrutiny to the evidence of an accused than to that of the Crown is an error of law (and perhaps even a miscarriage of justice).[67] Using the summary procedure for contempt of court proceedings unnecessarily is an error of law.[68] Failing to give a *Vetrovec* warning, about the danger of relying on the evidence of an unsavoury witness, where one is required is also an error of law.[69] There are also some circumstances in which the way a trial judge deals with facts can constitute an error of law: making a factual finding for which there is no evidence is one example.[70] See the further discussion of this issue

63 *Ibid.*

64 *R v Cinous*, 2002 SCC 29; *R v Pan*, 2025 SCC 12 [*Pan*] at para 86. See, however, *R v Pardy*, 2017 NLCA 49, where the trial judge was found to have been using the phrase "air of reality" in something other than its technical legal sense, and the Court of Appeal concluded at para 17 that "The fact that a phrase has a special legal meaning does not preclude its use as it would commonly be understood."

65 *R v G(RM)*, [1996] 3 SCR 362. See, for example, *R v JB*, 2019 ONCA 591, where failures on the part of the trial judge in exhorting the jury were found to be an error.

66 *R v Villaroman*, 2016 SCC 33. Note that the Supreme Court there decided the court of appeal had wrongly found the trial judge to make such an error.

67 *R v CAM*, 2017 MBCA 70. Courts have observed, however, that this is a "difficult argument to succeed on": *R v Hilton*, 2016 ABCA 397 at para 91, quoting *R v Aird*, 2013 ONCA 447 at para 39.

68 *R v Arradi*, 2003 SCC 23.

69 *R v Bevan*, [1993] 2 SCR 599 [*Bevan*].

70 *R v JMH*, 2011 SCC 45 [*JMH*].

in Section B(2), below in this chapter, in the context of appeals by the Crown.

Miscarriage of justice is a residual category allowing a conviction to be quashed where a trial was unfair or created the appearance of unfairness, regardless of whether the error was procedural or substantive. The standard for showing a miscarriage of justice is a high one, but courts have found them in cases of ineffective assistance of counsel, breach of solicitor-client privilege by defence counsel, or a misapprehension of the evidence that constitutes a denial of justice even though it does not render the verdict unreasonable.[71]

The distinction between an error of law and a miscarriage of justice can be seen to some extent in the facts of *R v Khan*.[72] There, the jury was provided with a transcript that included an exchange between counsel and the judge that had taken place in the jury's absence. This error was discovered a few hours later and the transcript was replaced, and the trial judge rejected a motion for a mistrial application. The Supreme Court held that this appeal was properly brought on the basis of error of law. The issue was whether the trial judge had made a correct legal decision in rejecting the mistrial application. On the other hand, had the error regarding the transcript not been discovered until afterward, so that there was no decision regarding the matter at trial, then the appeal would have been framed in terms of whether there was a miscarriage of justice in providing the jury with the transcript.[73]

A miscarriage of justice can be either substantive or procedural. Any error that deprives an accused of a fair trial is a legal error.[74] For example, a breach of the jury secrecy rule might result in a miscarriage of justice.[75] An allegation of ineffective assistance of counsel that is

---

71 *Tayo Tompouba*, above note 26 at para 72.

72 2001 SCC 86 [*Khan*].

73 To similar effect, see *R v Burgar*, 2018 BCCA 291. The self-represented accused there had introduced medical records to document injuries he said he had suffered, but the jury discovered, during deliberations, that the records related to someone else. Everyone agreed that this was an innocent misunderstanding, and the judge instructed the jury not to draw an adverse inference. The British Columbia Court of Appeal, however, concluded that this was insufficient. On those facts, the medical records mistake adversely affected the fairness of the trial, but the legal basis for the appeal was that the trial judge erred in law in not declaring a mistrial.

74 *Fanjoy v the Queen*, [1985] 2 SR 233 at para 11 [*Fanjoy*].

75 This was the basis of the appeal in *R v Pan*; *R v Sawyer*, 2001 SCC 42, for instance.

raised only on appeal would concern a possible miscarriage.[76] A failure to limit cross-examination would also raise issues of miscarriage.[77]

A miscarriage of justice can also result from a trial judge's misapprehension of the evidence in a trial. However, the fact that the judge has misapprehended the evidence is not on its own enough to show a miscarriage of justice — the standard is more stringent than that. The misapprehension must go to the substance of the evidence, not just to some detail. Further, it must concern a material part of the reasoning of the trial judge. Finally, those errors must play an essential part in the reasoning process resulting in a conviction.[78] For example, in *R v CLY* the trial judge relied, in particular, on the accused's denial of even innocuous tickling and his surprising recall of detail as reasons not to accept the accused's evidence in a sexual touching case; in fact the accused had not denied innocuous tickling and had not shown a particularly strong recall of detail, leading the Supreme Court to overturn the conviction.[79] In cases like this, the misapprehension of evidence means that the accused has not received a fair trial, and so the appeal must be granted even if a conviction could have been supported on the evidence.[80]

A failure to specifically plead miscarriage of justice as a ground of appeal does not deprive the appeal court of jurisdiction to consider the issue. In such a case, however, the grounds should be amended and it might be necessary to grant an adjournment so that there can be a full and fair hearing.[81]

Although the underlying theory of sections 686(1)(a)(ii) and (iii) is the same, they are not identical in application. In some cases the same conclusion would be reached no matter which route was followed. For example, if an error of law causing prejudice is a miscarriage, then the curative proviso does not apply; but if the error causes prejudice, then the curative proviso potentially applies, but would not succeed. So, one

---

76 *R v GDB*, 2000 SCC 22. Note that, to obtain a remedy, it is not sufficient to show that counsel was incompetent. In addition, it must be shown that a miscarriage of justice therefore resulted: *R v Meer*, 2016 SCC 5. That is, "A miscarriage of justice occurs if the ineffective representation sufficiently undermines the reliability of the verdict, or results in an unfair trial. The reliability of a verdict is sufficiently undermined if the appeal court concludes that there is a reasonable probability that the verdict would have been different had the appellant received adequate legal representation:" *R v S(R)*, 2016 ONCA 655 at para 44.

77 *Fanjoy*, above note 74.

78 *Lohrer*, above note 59.

79 2008 SCC 2.

80 *Lohrer*, above note 59.

81 *R v EMW*, 2011 SCC 31.

could say either that the error is a miscarriage not subject to the curative proviso, or that the error is an error of law that was not harmless in the first place.

There are, however, some differences between the two sections. First, as noted, some miscarriages of justice are matters of mixed law and fact. Beyond that, the curative proviso has been interpreted so that it can be satisfied in two different ways, one of which does not amount to suggesting that the error was harmless in itself. It is to that question we now turn.

*iv) The "Curative Proviso"*

Section 686(1)(b)(iii) allows an appeal court to dismiss an appeal despite an error of law provided that "no substantial wrong or miscarriage of justice has occurred." The rationale for such a rule, generally referred to as the curative provision, was explained in *R v Jolivet*: "Where the evidence against an accused is powerful and there is no realistic possibility that a new trial would produce a different verdict, it is manifestly in the public interest to avoid the cost and delay of further proceedings."[82]

The test for whether the curative proviso can be used is well established: it does not apply if there is a "reasonable possibility that the verdict would have been different had the error . . . not been made."[83] The Crown must invoke the proviso in some way to rely on it in an appeal: an appeal court cannot raise the issue on its own.[84] However, the Crown need not cross-appeal in order to put the curative proviso in issue: the question of whether an error of law is serious enough to justify setting aside the verdict will always be intertwined with whether the curative proviso should be applied.[85] Further, the Crown can be found to have raised the proviso implicitly rather than explicitly.[86]

---

82 *R v Jolivet*, 2000 SCC 29 at para 46.

83 *Khan*, above note 72 at para 28, quoting *Bevan*, above note 69 at 617. *Khan* contains a very full summary of the correct approach to s 686(1)(b)(iii).

84 See *Tayo Tompouba*, above note 26 at para 104: "As a general rule, a curative proviso is available on appeal only if raised by the Crown, since a court of appeal may not apply such a proviso of its own motion." See also *R v Pétel*, [1994] 1 SCR 3 at 17: "The Crown has the burden of showing that this provision is applicable...This Court cannot apply it *proprio motu*."

85 *R v Laboucan*, 2009 SCC 18.

86 *R v Samaniego*, 2022 SCC 9 [*Samaniego*] at para 66: "Appellate courts may apply the curative proviso if the Crown has implicitly raised it by arguing, in essence, that no substantial wrong or miscarriage of justice occurred or that the evidence of guilt is so overwhelming such that the verdict would have been the same."

Caselaw has established that there are two entirely different ways of satisfying this test, both of which are quite fact dependent. The first is to show that the error is harmless in itself. If that is so, then the error would not have been capable of causing prejudice to the accused. The other possibility is to show that the evidence against the accused is so overwhelming that if the appeal were granted and a retrial ordered, the result would inevitably be a conviction. In such cases, the error itself might not have been incapable of causing prejudice, but any theoretical prejudice has no genuine impact. In either case, the burden on the Crown to show that the curative proviso applies is meant to be a high one: the standard is to show that the error is *harmless*. That standard will not be met if there is prejudice, even if the court of appeal feels that that prejudice was unlikely to have affected the outcome.[87]

Various types of errors can fall into the first, "harmless error," branch of the curative proviso. Some mistakes could actually be of benefit to the accused. For example, if the trial judge articulates a stricter standard for guilt than is required, there will have been an error of law, but it will certainly not have prejudiced the accused.[88] In other cases, the error might fail to benefit the accused, but be of no real consequence. For example, a failure to permit cross-examination might be in error, but if it is on a point not really in any doubt, then the error is harmless.[89] Similarly, if hearsay evidence is improperly admitted, but on some point that is of no consequence to the accused's guilt, then the curative proviso can be applied.[90] Generally speaking, the harmless error criterion is more likely to be met when only a single error is at issue, rather than the cumulative effect of a number of errors; there is, however, no absolute rule.[91]

There is some ambiguity around the standard for the "harmless error" branch. Some pronouncements by the Court make it seem as though the error must be inherently harmless and one which could not *possibly* affect the result: others, however, seem to imply that it is permissible to "reason back" from a jury's verdict and apply the proviso on the basis that the particular error did not *in fact* affect the result. For example, the Court specifically rejected, in *Sarrazin*, the argument that it ought to be sufficient for the Crown to show that an error was highly unlikely to have affected the result. They held that "there is a significant difference between an error of law that can be confidently dismissed as

87 *R v Sarrazin*, 2011 SCC 54 [*Sarrazin*].

88 See, for example, *R v MacGillivray*, [1995] 1 SCR 890.

89 *United Nurses of Alberta v Alberta (Attorney General)*, [1992] 1 SCR 901.

90 *Gunn v The Queen*, [1974] SCR 273.

91 *R v Jacquard*, [1997] 1 SCR 314.

'harmless', and an assessment that while the error is prejudicial, it is not (in the after-the-fact view of the appellate court) *so* prejudicial as to have affected the outcome."[92] Further, the dissent in that case wanted to apply the curative proviso on the basis of reasoning back, but they were, of course, the dissent. Some lower courts have taken *Sarrazin* to be a rejection of the "reasoning back" approach,[93] and the high standard for the harmless error branch is often cited.[94]

However, the Court had previously said in *Khan* that the harmless error branch included cases "where either the triviality of the error itself, or the lack of prejudice caused by a more serious error of law, justified the application of the curative proviso."[95] Subsequently in *R v RV*, the accused applied to question the complainant about her sexual history under section 276 in order to advance a theory that she was lying to protect her relationship with her boyfriend, but was refused the opportunity to do so. This was found to be an error, but the majority of the Court found that the curative proviso applied: this was so because the error did not prevent the accused from making the argument he wished to make. The dissenting judges, however, argued that the "harmless error" branch did not apply:

> It does not follow that R.V. coming close to what he would have been allowed to ask following a proper s 276 ruling means that the error did not meaningfully impact his *actual* trial. Such an application can only water down the proviso, because it strains common sense for an appellate court to conclude that it knows with certainty what evidence would have been adduced, or what effects such evidence would have had on the trial judge's assessment of the witnesses, had no such errors been made at trial.[96]

In this case, though, it is the judges who reject the reasoning back approach who are in the minority.

Much the same could be said of the subsequent result in *R v Samaniego*, another case where cross-examination was wrongly curtailed. All nine judges agreed that improper curtailment of cross-examination could rarely be saved by the curative proviso, but the majority held

92 *Sarrazin*, above note 87 at para 28.

93 See, for example, *R v MacLeod*, 2014 NSCA 63.

94 See, for example, *R v Mayuran*, 2012 SCC 31 at para 47, applying the provision on the basis that the errors in question "could not possibly have affected the verdict." See also *R v Perkins*, 2016 ONCA 588 at para 30, saying the heavy burden is that "the error was minor and could not possibly have affected the verdict."

95 *Khan*, above note 72 at para 30.

96 *R v RV*, 2019 SCC 41 at para 127.

that in that particular case it was a harmless error. The curtailed cross-examination would have allowed one further opportunity for the accused to put its primary theory forward, but it had done so repeatedly on other occasions and was able to fully do so. Relying on *RV* and the conclusion that any possible prejudice "would have been minimal,"[97] the majority applied the curative proviso. The dissent phrased the test as being whether the error "*could not have had* any impact on the verdict" (emphasis added)[98] and also explicitly relied on *Sarrazin*, noting that it had not been overruled.[99]

The Court's most recent articulation of the first branch is that it applies where "the error or irregularity in question is minor or harmless, such that it had no impact on the verdict."[100] That sounds more like a standard which looks at whether the error in fact had, rather than could have had, an impact, but the Court does not explicitly consider the issue.

Other lower court decisions have analyzed the reasoning in the trial leading to a conviction, whether by the judge or the jury, and then have looked at whether the error would have had an effect on that particular reasoning.[101] Certainly there is a danger in that approach: anything but the most unambiguous of inferences from a judge or jury's reasoning should not be used, or the courts will be watering down the provision in just the way *Sarrazin* said it should not be. In particular there becomes a danger that the accused will effectively be required to explain how the error could have affected the jury's reasoning, which would reverse the proper onus of proof with regard to the curative proviso.[102]

---

97 *Samaniego*, above note 86 at para 72.

98 *Samaniego*, above note 86 at para 161.

99 *Samaniego*, above note 86 at para 165.

100 *Tayo Tompouba*, above note 26 at para 76.

101 See *R v Johnson*, 2017 NSCA 64, where the Nova Scotia Court of Appeal concluded that as the jury must have accepted the evidence of two particular witnesses, and as that evidence was untainted by the error, the harmless error provision applied. See also *R v Trotchie*, 2019 SKCA 43, where the trial judge did not find the accused credible, but the error (improper cross-examination) did not contribute to that conclusion and so the curative provision was applied. See also *R v Heppner*, 2019 BCCA 108, holding at para 86 that "While the error was serious, it is possible in this case to trace the effect of the error and conclude with confidence that [it] could have had no impact on the verdict."

102 See, for example, *R v Nguyen*, 2015 ONCA 278 at para 194: "Unlike in *Sarrazin*, the appellants here have not laid any evidentiary foundation from which to draw a rational inference that if the trial judge erred in law in admitting the evidence of the common-law spouses, his error might possibly have led to bias or prejudice towards the appellants and affected the jury's inference drawing process."

The other basis for applying the curative proviso is that the rest of the evidence is so overwhelming that a conviction on a retrial is inevitable. The most important point to bear in mind is that this branch of the curative proviso imposes a very high standard. It has long been noted that this aspect of the proviso must be used with great circumspection or the accused will be deprived of the right to trial by jury.[103] So, for example, where evidence has been improperly admitted, it is not open to a court of appeal simply to conclude that the remainder of the evidence could or ought to result in a conviction. If that were the case, then there would be no need for section 686(1)(b)(iii).[104] Rather, the appropriate standard is an "onerous" one, and the Supreme Court has restricted use of the proviso on very stringent terms.[105] It has said that the proviso should be applied only if conviction would be "inevitable" or "invariable,"[106] or if the result would "necessarily" have been the same.[107] The proviso can be used only if it is clear that the evidence pointing to the guilt of the accused is so overwhelming that any other verdict but a conviction would be impossible.[108]

> Although there are two branches to the test, the underlying question is the same in each: would the verdict have been the same if the error had not been committed? The "overwhelming evidence" branch asks whether any reasonable judge or jury would inevitably convict given the evidence, while the "harmless error" branch asks whether the error was so minor, irrelevant, or clearly non-prejudicial that any reasonable judge or jury could not possibly have rendered a different verdict if the error had not been made.[109]

---

103 See *R v B(FF)*, [1993] 1 SCR 697 [*B(FF)*]. See also *Colpitts v The Queen*, [1965] SCR 739 at 744, noting the danger that "the judges would in truth be substituted for the jury, the verdict would become theirs and theirs alone, and would be arrived at upon a perusal of the evidence without any opportunity of seeing the demeanour of the witnesses and weighing the evidence with the assistance which this affords."

104 *R v S(PL)*, [1991] 1 SCR 909 [*S(PL)*].

105 *R v Broyles*, [1991] 3 SCR 595.

106 *S(PL)*, above note 104.

107 *B(FF)*, above note 103.

108 *Khan*, above note 72 at para 31. See also *R v Van*, 2009 SCC 22 at para 34 [*Van*], citing *R v Trochym*, 2007 SCC 6. See, for example, *R v Sekhon*, 2014 SCC 15, where an accused was convicted on the basis that he knew of the existence of drugs in a vehicle he was driving. The trial judge had improperly admitted expert evidence with regard to the accused's knowledge, but the other evidence in the case — that he had removed a fob which gave access to the hidden compartment before handing over his keys, that he destroyed a piece of paper while being detained, and many inconsistencies in his story — would inevitably have led to the finding that he knew of the drugs.

109 *Van*, above note 108 at paras 35–36.

Whether the test is made out in any given case will be very much a factual question. In general, courts of appeal should be more cautious in cases involving questions of credibility and should avoid speculating about the bases upon which a jury may have accepted some evidence or rejected other evidence.[110] It has also been observed that the curative proviso will rarely apply when the error in question was to fail to instruct on an included offence. In such cases "withholding a realistic verdict may cause a jury, faced with the choice between a conviction on the principal offence and an acquittal, to convict on the principal offence simply because an acquittal is 'unpalatable.'"[111]

*v) Procedural Irregularities*

Section 686(1)(b)(iv), it will be recalled, allows an appeal court to dismiss an appeal on the basis that "notwithstanding any procedural irregularity at trial, the trial court had jurisdiction over the class of offence of which the appellant was convicted and the court of appeal is of the opinion that the appellant suffered no prejudice thereby." The section is best understood by discussing not what it adds to the analysis of an appeal, but what it takes away from that discussion. The purpose of the subsection is to remove from consideration a wide variety of issues that might technically have been errors though they caused no prejudice to the accused, but that could not have been dealt with under the curative proviso in section 686(1)(b)(iii). Accordingly, it simplifies the appeal process by eliminating those questions from the analysis.

Prior to the enactment of section 686(1)(b)(iv), it was already possible for errors of law to be cured by the harmless error provision in section 686(1)(b)(iii). Most procedural irregularities would be errors of law. However, caselaw concluded that some particular types of errors went to the jurisdiction of the court and that some of these instances could not be classified as "errors of law" and, as a result, the curative proviso could not be applied. Some of these jurisdictional errors were of no real consequence — for example, the exclusion of the accused from a small portion of the trial might be a jurisdictional error but, if nothing of significance occurred during that time, the accused suffered no prejudice. Nonetheless, since the curative proviso did not apply, the appeal had to be granted.

Section 686(1)(b)(iv) now allows appeals based on such technicalities to be dismissed, provided there is no harm to the accused's interests in doing so. In part, this is accomplished by the fact that the section

110 *B(FF)*, above note 103.

111 *Pan*, above note 64 at para 45, and see also para 89.

does not apply if the trial court did not have jurisdiction over the *class* of offence, as opposed to losing jurisdiction over the particular offence or particular offender through some procedural irregularity. The Court has consciously adopted a broad approach to whether a court has jurisdiction: that is to say, an approach that makes it more likely the proviso can apply. There are three classes of offence: indictable offences listed in section 469, all other indictable offences, and summary conviction offences. All that is necessary is that the trial court had jurisdiction in that sense.[112] Accordingly, the proviso would not be available if a section 469 offence somehow were tried in provincial court, for example. They rejected the argument that anything else should constitute not having jurisdiction, such as irregularities in jury selection, on the basis that that "would be to permit the kind of unnecessary complexity that was rife prior to the enactment of the provision."[113]

More important, though, the section applies only if the procedural irregularity caused the accused no prejudice.[114] The Court has noted that the language of section 686(1)(b)(iv) is that the accused "suffered no prejudice," which might set a stricter standard than the "no substantial wrong or miscarriage of justice" standard of section 686(1)(b)(iii), but has not decided the point.[115] The Court has held that it is appropriate to infer that the irregularity *did* cause prejudice and, therefore, that this inference must be rebutted. The analysis of that question is the same as that conducted under the curative proviso in section 686(1)(b)(iii).[116] As a result, section 686(1)(b)(iv) is largely parallel to section 686(1)(b)(iii), but applies only to a narrow range of procedural irregularities which create a jurisdictional error that could not be classified as a pure error of law.[117]

There is a subtle point to note about whether there can be found to be prejudice from the procedural irregularity, which is that it is important to identify what interest of the accused is said to have been

112 *R v Esseghaier*, 2021 SCC 9 [*Esseghaier*] at paras 41–43.

113 *Esseghaier*, above note 112 at para 46.

114 See, for example, *R v Swite*, 2011 BCCA 54, in which there was an error in the manner by which jurors were selected. The British Columbia Court of Appeal found that this was a procedural irregularity rather than an error of law and, therefore, to be dealt with under s 686(1)(b)(iv) rather than s 686(1)(b)(ii). The court concluded that it could not be saved, both because the error deprived the trial court of jurisdiction and alternatively because the error resulted in both actual and presumed prejudice.

115 *Esseghaier*, above note 112 at paras 52–53.

116 *Khan*, above note 72 at para 16.

117 *Tayo Tompouba*, above note 26 at para 76.

prejudiced. In *Tayo Tompouba*, the accused was tried in English and had not been told of his right to have a trial in French. This was a violation of his right to be tried in the language of his choice, and so assessing whether there was prejudice had to look at that right. That is, the question was not whether there was prejudice to his fair trial right. Rather, the kinds of things that might have shown there was no prejudice would have been proof that the accused did not have sufficient proficiency in the official language he was not given the option to choose, that he would have made the same choice even if he had known of the other option, or that he knew of his right to a trial in the language of his choice independently.[118]

The Court has helpfully summarized the correct approach to applying sections 686(1)(b)(iii) and (iv):

> If the procedural irregularity amounts to or is based on an error of law, it falls under ss. 686(1)(*a*)(ii) and 686(1)(*b*)(iii).
>
> If the procedural irregularity was previously (before 1985) classified as an irregularity causing a loss of jurisdiction: s. 686(1)(*b*)(iv) provides that this is no longer fatal to the conviction, and an analysis of prejudice must be undertaken, in accordance with the principles set out in s. 686(1)(*b*)(iii).
>
> If the procedural error did not amount to, or originate in an error of law, which is rare, s. 686(1)(*a*)(iii) applies and the reviewing court must determine whether a miscarriage of justice occurred. If so, there are no remedial provisions in s. 686(1)(*b*) that can cure such a defect, and the appeal must be allowed and either an acquittal entered or a new trial ordered.[119]

### *vi) Consequences of a Successful Appeal*

The *Code* gives a court of appeal some discretion in remedies arising out of an appeal of a conviction, and the caselaw has provided guidance over how that discretion should be exercised. Section 686(2) allows the court of appeal to either enter an acquittal or order a new trial. In addition, section 686(8) (discussed below in Section B(3)(a)) allows a court of appeal to make "any order . . . that justice requires," which includes the possibility of a stay of proceedings.[120] These are the three main

118 *Tayo Tompouba*, above note 26 at para 90. See also *R v Azzi*, 2022 ONCA 366.

119 *Ibid* at para 18.

120 Strictly the section says that when a court of appeal exercises any power "conferred by subsection (2), (4), (6) or (7), it may make any order, *in addition*, that justice requires" [emphasis added]. In *R v Bellusci*, 2012 SCC 44 [*Bellusci*] at para 39, the Court concluded that the power in s 686(8) can be exercised even

options available to a court of appeal when it allows an appeal from a conviction.[121] An appellate court should consider whether an acquittal is the appropriate remedy first and only after that consider the other possibilities.[122]

A new trial places the accused in jeopardy again, but both an acquittal and a stay bring a permanent end to the proceedings. An acquittal is generally seen as preferable for an accused, on the basis that it removes stigma more than a mere stay of proceedings. The Court has cautioned that this difference should not be exaggerated, but that it was true that "a judicial stay says nothing of the court's view of the merits of the case . . . not even that the Crown has failed to prove its case beyond a reasonable doubt."[123] It is for that reason that an acquittal should be the first option considered.

To some extent, the order that should be made depends on the basis upon which the appeal was successful.

For example, in the case of judge-alone trials the Court has distinguished between a verdict which is "unreasonable" and one which "cannot be supported on the evidence": the latter means the verdict could not have been reached at trial by any reasoning, while the former means that the particular reasoning used by the trial judge was flawed. The Court has held that this difference has an effect on the order to be made: a conviction overturned because it cannot be supported on the evidence will result in an acquittal, while one overturned merely for being unreasonable will result in a new trial (since in principle a conviction was possible).[124] In the case of a jury trial this distinction is not drawn, and so the appeal will succeed only if it is shown that the verdict is one that a properly instructed jury acting judicially could not reasonably have rendered.[125] In most cases, that amounts to the equivalent of saying that the verdict could not be supported by the evidence, and so an acquittal is usually the remedy for a successful appeal on this ground.[126] Where the unreasonableness is shown by pointing to

---

without an independent order having been made under one of the previous subsections. See the discussion at Section (3)(a), below in this chapter.

121 *R v Bouvette*, 2025 SCC 18 at para 57 [*Bouvette*].

122 *Bouvette*, above note 121 at para 57.

123 *Bouvette*, above note 121 at para 69.

124 *Sinclair*, above note 44 at para 27.

125 *Biniaris*, above note 22: see the discussion under Section B(10(b)(ii), above in this chapter. See also Fish J in *Beaudry*, above note 37 at para 92, holding that an appeal on this ground in the case of a jury trial could succeed only where the "cannot be supported on the evidence" standard is met, since the particular reasoning of the jury will not be known.

126 *Pittiman*, above note 49 at para 14; *R v Schoenthal*, 2007 SKCA 80 at para 70.

inconsistent verdicts, however, the situation is more complicated. If the inconsistency relates to verdicts against different accused but the evidence against the appellant supported conviction, that would usually mean that there was evidence upon which it would have been possible to convict and so a new trial should be ordered.[127] Although the Court has not made this observation, that distinction is similar to the one drawn with regard to judge-alone trials, namely that something has gone wrong in the reasoning process rather than necessarily with the final conclusion, and so a new trial is required. However, if the inconsistent verdicts both relate to the same accused, an acquittal might be the result.[128] The accused will have been acquitted, on a different charge, on a basis which ought to have applied equally to the conviction: if the Crown has not appealed that acquittal, then arguably an appeal court cannot order a new trial which would deprive the accused of the benefit of that finding.[129] The Court has noted this issue but has not decided it.[130] Alternatively, if the Crown has successfully appealed the acquittal in the case of inconsistent verdicts from a jury trial, then the only remedy is to order a new trial. If the legal error can be isolated to the acquittal, only that charge will be sent for a new trial. However, "[u]nless the appellate court can conclude with a high degree of certainty that the legal error did not taint the conviction, setting aside the acquittal on a charge interconnected with a conviction will require retrial on all charges."[131]

An error of law or miscarriage of justice is more likely to lead to a new trial, and for similar reasons: if this is the only basis upon which the appeal is granted, then although the process was flawed, there was evidence upon which the accused could have been convicted.[132]

---

127 *Pittiman*, above note 49 at para 14.

128 *Pittiman*, above note 49.

129 *JF*, above note 51. See also *R v Brady*, 2017 NSCA 41, where the accused was found guilty of possession for the purpose of trafficking of marijuana, but not guilty of the same offence for the cannabis resin found in the same suitcases. In granting a remedy for the conviction on this inconsistent verdict, the Nova Scotia Court of Appeal held at para 56 that "Although an acquittal might appear to be an unpalatable remedy in light of the strength of the evidence, in my view the law mandates this remedy in these circumstances." See also *Catton*, above note 50.

130 *RV* 2021, above note 54 at para 48.

131 *RV* 2021, above note 54 at para 43.

132 *Morrissey*, above note 26 at para 88, suggests that a court of appeal should therefore first consider whether an appeal succeeds on the basis of an unreasonable verdict, in order to see first whether the accused is entitled to an acquittal.

Other factors could influence whether to order a new trial or give an acquittal. For example, a conviction might have been overturned due to the admission of fresh evidence on the appeal. In that event, the court of appeal has to assess the impact of that evidence: if it persuades the court that the accused is factually innocent or that no jury acting reasonably could convict the accused, then an acquittal can be entered, but failing that a new trial should be ordered.[133] Further, even where there is the possibility of a conviction on the evidence, an acquittal can be ordered if there are special circumstances, for example, that the accused had already served their sentence or some significant time in custody or had been subjected to several trials.[134] In the unusual circumstances of *R v Truscott* — among other things that the accused had served time in custody, the offence had occurred nearly fifty years earlier but the accused had consistently maintained his innocence, and no new trial would, in fact, be possible — an acquittal was ordered on the basis that if there were a new trial it was more likely than not that the accused would be acquitted.[135]

The Court has, in *Bouvette*, expanded on the circumstances in which an acquittal is appropriate on appeal, holding that there are three bases upon which that remedy might be granted. An acquittal can be granted when: 1) there was no evidence upon which a reasonable jury could convict; 2) the Crown undertook to lead no evidence if there were a new trial, or; 3) notwithstanding evidence which could justify a new trial, a "discretionary acquittal" based on the interests of justice should be granted.[136] In the first case, no new trial would be appropriate, even if the basis for saying that no reasonable jury could convict arose from fresh evidence on the appeal: "[i]t would be unjust and pointless to send a matter back for a new trial where the evidence shows that the only reasonable outcome would be an acquittal."[137] In the second case, ordering a new trial where the Crown would lead no evidence "would require *pro forma* proceedings that are at odds with

133 *R v Dhillon*, 2014 BCCA 480 at para 50 [*Dhillon*]; *R v Maciel*, 2007 ONCA 196 at para 46 [*Maciel*].

134 *R v Truscott*, 2007 ONCA 575 at para 249 [*Truscott*]; *Dunlop and Sylvester v The Queen*, [1979] 2 SCR 881 at 900.

135 *Truscott*, above note 134. The Ontario Court of Appeal noted at para 265 that "to order a new trial in these circumstances merely because the remaining evidence clears a relatively low evidentiary threshold, knowing full well that a new trial will never be held, would be unfair to the appellant and does a disservice to the public." See also *R v DRS*, 2013 ABCA 18, applying the same test.

136 *Bouvette*, above note 121 at paras 72–103.

137 *Bouvette*, above note 121 at para 75.

timely and efficient criminal justice"[138] and would impose unnecessary hardship on a successful appellant. The third basis, the discretionary acquittal, was left unsettled. All nine judges agreed that such a basis for granting an acquittal did exist. However, the five-judge majority concluded that *Bouvette* was not a good case in which to try to determine the parameters of that power, as the appellant was already being acquitted on the second basis, and as there had not really been adversarial engagement on the criteria for discretionary acquittals.

Formally, that is where the matter stands, since the majority opted only to say that the power existed without giving it shape. However, the four-judge minority did make concrete suggestions about the criteria that should be used, and the majority do not ever explicitly disagree with them. It seems likely that the view of the dissent will define much of the debate in lower courts until this issue returns to the Supreme Court.

The minority would have held that although a new trial should generally be ordered where there is evidence which could support conviction, special attention should be paid to cases which have the hallmarks of wrongful convictions. In those cases appellate courts should consider whether an acquittal is appropriate even if it cannot conclude that no jury could reasonably convict. More specifically they would have held that "courts of appeal should consider the nature of the miscarriage, the remaining merits of the case, including the likelihood of the trial taking place, and the overall equities of the case."[139]

"The nature of the miscarriage" requires looking at whether features common to wrongful convictions — things like non-disclosure, unreliable expert evidence, eyewitness and cross-racial misidentification, improper police investigations, tunnel vision, false confessions, false guilty pleas, and systemic discrimination — are features of the case. "The remaining merits of case" would look at whether the record establishes clearly that an acquittal at a retrial is more probable than not. The Crown's position — such as the one taken in *Bouvette*, that they would lead no evidence — would be relevant. Finally, the "overall equities of the case" could include many factors, such as that the appellant had already served part or all of their sentence, had undergone multiple trials and appeals, that there had been a significant passage of time, or that the appellant suffered significant personal prejudice.

---

138 *Bouvette*, above note 121 at para 83.

139 *Bouvette*, above note 121 at para 104.

A court of appeal has no more ability to find that an accused is factually innocent than a trial court does, though they are able to express the reasons for acquittal "in clear and strong terms."[140]

Note, as well, that if the appeal would have succeeded except that the accused was properly convicted on some part, then the appeal court can substitute a verdict, affirm the sentence, impose a new sentence, or remit the matter back to the trial court for sentencing.[141] Further, if an accused successfully appeals a conviction on an included offence, a court of appeal cannot order a new trial on the full offence unless there was also a successful Crown appeal from that acquittal.[142]

## 2) Appeals by the Crown

Crown appeals[143] can be brought under section 676 of the *Code*. The first thing to note is that the appeal rights in that section are not parallel to the appeal rights given to an accused in the case of a conviction. The Crown's right of appeal is narrower and, in particular, contains nothing equivalent to the accused's right under section 686(1)(a)(i). That is, the Crown cannot appeal on the basis that an acquittal was unreasonable or could not be supported on the evidence.[144] An acquittal requires only that the trier of fact had reasonable doubt, and there is no need for evidence to support that doubt.[145]

The Crown's more limited right of appeal is a policy decision, primarily rooted in the principle against double jeopardy: that no person should be placed in jeopardy twice for the same matter. Restricting the Crown in that way also respects jury verdicts and helps to guard against wrongful convictions. Historically, the Crown originally only had a right of appeal with leave and for a short period had no right of appeal based on an error of law at all. Indeed, the Court has noted that many countries do not permit acquittals to be appealed or have more limited Crown rights of appeal than Canada. They have therefore stressed the importance of keeping appeals from an acquittal within

140 *R v Mullins-Johnson*, 2007 ONCA 720 at para 24.

141 Sections 686(2) and (3).

142 *R v Guillemette*, [1986] 1 SCR 356.

143 For an explanation of this issue in chart form, see *Anatomy of Criminal Procedure*, above note 19, Chart 4.1(a), "Appeals by the Crown: Grounds" and Chart 4.1(b), "Appeals by the Crown: Possible Outcomes."

144 See *Biniaris*, above note 22 at para 32; and *Sunbeam Corporation (Canada) Ltd v the Queen*, [1969] SCR 221. See also *R v Chung*, 2020 SCC 8 at para 10 [*Chung*].

145 *R v Walker*, 2008 SCC 34 at para 22 [*Walker*]; *JMH*, above note 70 at para 26. See, for example, *R v Barros*, 2011 SCC 51 [*Barros*].

their proper limits.[146] Nonetheless, a right of appeal by the Crown does not violate the *Charter.*[147]

The Crown's right of appeal is primarily set out in section 676(1)(a): "any ground of appeal that involves *a question of law alone.*" This right specifically applies in section 676(1)(a) to verdicts of acquittal or of not criminally responsible on account of mental disorder.[148] Although the language of the section specifically refers to appealing a "verdict of acquittal," an appeal by the Crown can concern jurisdictional errors which are unrelated to the merits of the acquittal.[149] Other portions of section 676 allow appeals of most decisions that could bring an end to a prosecution, such as a finding that the accused is unfit to stand trial,[150] an order of a superior court of criminal jurisdiction that quashes an indictment or fails to exercise jurisdiction on an indictment, and an order of a trial court that stays proceedings or quashes an indictment.[151] These latter powers of appeal would capture situations where the accused has received a *Charter* remedy, such as a stay of proceedings based on entrapment or a violation of the right to a trial within a reasonable time. Similarly, where a trial judge has dismissed charges against an accused on the basis that the offence in question was invalid, or *ultra vires*, this will amount to an acquittal that is appealable,[152] as

146 See generally the discussion in *R v Hodgson*, 2024 SCC 25 at paras 22–31 [*Hodgson*].

147 See *R v Graveline*, 2006 SCC 16 at para 13 [*Graveline*]; and *R v Morgentaler*, [1988] 1 SCR 30.

148 An accused is considered to be "acquitted" even if they were convicted of an included offence, and so the Crown would be entitled to appeal the acquittal on the main offence: s 676(2).

149 *Varennes*, above note 2 at para 34.

150 Section 676(3).

151 Sections 676(1)(b) and (c). Even before these subsections were added, it had been concluded that a judicial decision to quash or stay a charge would fall within the meaning of "acquittal" and, therefore, could be appealed by the Crown: *R v Jewitt*, [1985] 2 SCR 128. It is odd that s 686, setting out the bases upon which Crown appeals can be granted, fails to deal explicitly in any way with appeals launched under ss 676(1)(b) and (c). Courts that have noted this discontinuity have tended, of necessity, to take them as included within the meaning of "acquittal" in s 686(4): see, for example, *R v Fraillon* (1990), 62 CCC (3d) 474 (Que CA); *R v Allen* (1996), 110 CCC (3d) 331 (Ont CA); or *R v Taylor*, 2009 NLCA 43. Section 676 nowhere authorizes an appeal of a discharge at a preliminary inquiry, which therefore can be reviewed only through *certiorari* or overridden through preferring a direct indictment: see the discussion in Chapter 9.

152 See *Cheyenne Realty Ltd v Thompson*, [1975] 1 SCR 87; and *Re Regina and Kripps Pharmacy Ltd* (1981), 60 CCC (2d) 332 (BCCA).

will accepting a plea of *autrefois acquit*.[153] In addition, the Crown can appeal an accused's sentence with leave.[154]

The Court has stressed on a number of occasions that acquittals should not be overturned lightly. The Crown is required to satisfy the court not only that there was an error of law, but that the verdict would not necessarily have been the same had the error not occurred, and the Crown has a heavy onus in doing so.[155] In *R v Graveline*, for example, the accused's defence at trial had been based on non-mental disorder automatism and she did not argue self-defence. The trial judge instructed the jury on self-defence nonetheless and therein erred on a question of law. However, the Supreme Court held on these facts that the Crown did not satisfy its onus to show that the legal error was of any consequence. An abstract or purely hypothetical possibility that the accused would have been convicted was not sufficient; rather, the Crown must show how "in the concrete reality of the case at hand" the error had a material bearing on the acquittal.[156] Something like an error that calls for the wrong standard of proof to be applied, for example, would be needed.[157]

Obviously, a crucial consideration, given the limited nature of the Crown's right of appeal, is exactly what constitutes a question of law.[158] The most straightforward examples are those where an appeal court can render a decision without calling into question any of the trial judge's factual findings.[159] Some straightforward examples include

---

153 *R v Sanver* (1973), 12 CCC (2d) 105 (NBSCAD).

154 Section 676(1)(d).

155 See *R v Sutton*, 2000 SCC 50 at para 2 [*Sutton*], relying on *Vézeau v the Queen*, [1977] 2 SCR 277; and *R v Morin*, [1988] 2 SCR 345.

156 *Graveline*, above note 147 at para 14. See, for example, *R v McRae*, 2013 SCC 68, where the trial judge had a number of factual findings about the accused's state of mind when making several threats, but had never asked the necessary legal question of whether the threats were meant to be taken seriously: since that error might reasonably have affected the result, a new trial was ordered. On the other hand, see *R v Noel*, 2010 NBCA 28, where the trial judge considered information that had not been evidence in the case, but nonetheless reached conclusions that were safely anchored in properly admitted evidence. In that event, the appeal was not granted despite the errors. See also *R v Park*, 2010 ABCA 248, where the trial judge wrongly ordered a directed verdict, but the Court of Appeal dismissed the appeal on the basis that in the absence of the error the trial judge would have acquitted the accused in any event.

157 See *Sutton*, above note 155.

158 It is worth recalling here the discussion above concerning the ambiguity over the meaning of "question of law": see above notes 19 and 20. Here, we are dealing with the broader meaning of a question of law for jurisdictional purposes.

159 *Hodgson*, above note 146 at para 33.

the admissibility of evidence, the interpretation of a statute, the scope of a constitutional right, the definition of the elements of an offence, or whether evidence is capable of being corroborative.[160] A decision concerning the application of a legal standard, such as investigative necessity, is also a question of law.[161] Whether a correct conclusion has been reached on a *Charter* question, such as whether there has been a section 8 violation or whether evidence should be excluded under section 24(2), is also a question of law.[162]

The main point of limiting the Crown to an appeal on a question of law is to prevent re-litigation of the facts.[163] However, matters can sometimes still be classed as questions of law giving rise to a Crown appeal even if they involve consideration of the evidence in some way. An error of law can arise from the way in which a trial judge assesses the evidence. In *JMH*, the Court concluded that this can occur in at least four ways.[164] First, it is an error of law to make a factual finding for which there is no evidence. This basis cannot be used, however, as the equivalent of an "unreasonable acquittal" ground of appeal: an acquittal does not have to be supported by particular factual findings but rather can rest on reasonable doubt.[165]

---

160 *R v B(G)*, [1990] 2 SCR 57 [*B(G)*]; *Hodgson*, above note 146 at para 33.

161 *R v Araujo*, [2000] 2 SCR 992 at para 18. See also *Biniaris*, above note 22, or *Barros*, above note 145.

162 See *R v Chehil*, 2009 NSCA 111, aff'd 2013 SCC 49; and *R v Genest* (1986), 54 CR (3d) 246 (Que CA).

163 See, for example, *R v Boudreault*, 2012 SCC 56, where the trial judge, after applying the correct legal test, concluded that the accused did not satisfy the test for having care and control of a motor vehicle while impaired: the Court held at para 15 that the Crown had no right to appeal because "[t]he judge's conclusion on the facts, however surprising or unreasonable it may appear to another court, did not give rise to a question of law alone." *R v Tortone*, [1993] 2 SCR 973, observes that it is not open to a court of appeal even to draw different inferences from the facts than the trial judge has drawn simply because it would have drawn different inferences. However, a court of appeal can overturn a verdict where the trial judge has not directed his or her mind to issues that require determination in order to reach the verdict.

164 *JMH*, above note 70 at para 24, describes these as ways in which treatment of facts can amount to an error of law "giving rise to a Crown appeal of an acquittal." That is correct in the sense that Crown appeals must be based on an error of law, but that is also a basis upon which an accused can appeal, and some of the issues discussed seem more suited to that context. See also *Hodgson*, above note 146 at para 35.

165 *JMH*, above note 70 at paras 25–27. See, for example, *R v Powell*, 2010 ONCA 105. See also *R v Clark*, 2015 BCCA 488 at para 43: "It is well established that it is an error of law for a trial judge to engage in speculation or conjecture in finding facts."

Second, a question of law could concern the legal effect of undisputed facts. The facts might be agreed, or the trial judge might have made all necessary findings of fact, but a court of appeal might disagree with the trial judge's conclusion without engaging in fact finding itself. In such a case, the nature of the disagreement would really concern the law rather than the facts. Third, assessment of the evidence based on a wrong legal principle is an error of law; for example, the failure of a trial judge to consider all the evidence is a question of law if it is based on a misapprehension of some legal principle. The Court has described these two bases as "two sides of the same coin": "they both address errors where the trial judge's application of the legal principles to the evidence demonstrates an erroneous understanding of the law, either because the trial judge finds all the facts necessary to meet the test but errs in law in its application, or assesses the evidence in a way that otherwise indicates a misapprehension of the law."[166] There is a significant body of caselaw finding that, particularly in sexual assault cases, it is an error to rely on myths and stereotypes about the expected behaviour of victims.[167] Where a trial judge relies on such stereotypes in decision-making, this is an error of law of the third type, assessing evidence based on a wrong legal principle.[168]

Finally, it is an error of law for a trial judge to consider (or to instruct a jury to consider) individual pieces of evidence separately to decide whether they constitute proof beyond a reasonable doubt. The proper approach is to consider the whole of the evidence and determine on that basis whether the guilt of the accused had been established beyond a reasonable doubt. This rule does not mean, however, that a trial judge must refer to every item of evidence considered or detail the

---

166 *Chung*, above note 144 at paras 11 and 18.

167 See, for example, *R v Shearing*, 2002 SCC 58 at para 121:

> While in most instances the adversarial process allows wide latitude to cross-examiners to resort to unproven assumptions and innuendo in an effort to crack the untruthful witness, sexual assault cases pose particular dangers. *Seaboyer*, *Osolin* and *Mills* all make the point that these cases should be decided without resort to folk tales about how abuse victims are expected by people who have never suffered abuse to react to the trauma.

168 See the concurring reasons of Rowe J in *R v Kruk*, 2024 SCC 7 at para 197. The issue in *Kruk* was whether to recognize a rule parallel to that about myths and stereotypes, finding it an error to rely on "ungrounded common-sense assumptions." The Court declined to create such a rule, holding at para 96 that "[t]he list of errors of law is not closed — but the rule against ungrounded common-sense assumptions is not on it."

way each item of evidence was assessed (see the discussion of duty to give reasons, at Section B(3)(d), below in this chapter).[169]

Although these bases for an appeal allow for some delving into factual matters, the Court has stressed that the limited nature of a Crown appeal means that the nature of the alleged legal error must be identified with precision:

> A failure to precisely identify the error of law risks expanding Crown appeals beyond the scope of s. 676. This risk is especially high when the error pertains to an alleged shortcoming in the trial judge's handling of the evidence. Such expansion would undermine important principles, including that against double jeopardy. Thus, it is not enough to simply assert or state that a trial judge has committed a legal error with respect to their assessment of the evidence. Appellate courts should articulate with precision how the trial judge erred in law.[170]

Where the court of appeal grants an appeal from an acquittal in a trial by judge alone, it has two main choices: to order a new trial or to enter a conviction. In the latter case, the court can either impose sentence or remit the matter to the trial court for sentencing. A court of appeal should choose to enter a conviction only where the trial judge has already made all the findings necessary to support a guilty verdict, or where those facts are not in dispute.[171] This conviction need not be on the main charge: it could, for example, be on an included offence.[172] However, the court of appeal is not permitted to enter a conviction where the trial was by judge and jury; in that case, the only option is to order a new trial.[173] The new trial does not necessarily have to duplicate the issues in the previous trial. A court of appeal can limit the issues and so, for example, direct that the new trial will be held only to determine whether an entrapment defence should succeed or whether the accused is guilty of an included offence.[174] Indeed, the findings at

---

169 See *JMH*, above note 70; *R v Morin*, [1992] 3 SCR 286; and *B(G)*, above note 160.

170 *Hodgson*, above note 146 at para 40.

171 *R v Cassidy*, [1989] 2 SCR 345.

172 Section 686(4)(b)(ii) allows the court of appeal to enter a conviction "with respect to the offence of which, in its opinion, the accused should have been found guilty but for the error in law."

173 Section 686(4). Giving this greater protection in the case of trial by jury does not violate the *Charter*: *R v Skalbania*, [1997] 3 SCR 995.

174 See, respectively, *R v Pearson*, [1998] 3 SCR 620; and *R v Cook* (1979), 9 CR (3d) 85 (Ont CA). This is allowed under s 686(8). The combined effect of ss 676(2), 686(4), and 686(8) is that a person could, for example, be convicted of only an included offence at trial but ordered to face a new trial on the main charge, or

a previous trial might require that any new trial can only be on some included offence.[175]

## 3) Other Appeal-Related Issues

### a) Powers of a Court of Appeal

Various *Code* provisions create particular powers relating to appeals. Section 686(8) permits a court of appeal to "make any order, in addition, that justice requires." In *R v Bellusci* the Quebec Court of Appeal had overturned a stay entered by the trial judge and had ordered that the judge continue with the trial. Although the Court found that the Court of Appeal had erred in overturning the stay, they concluded that in an appropriate case, a court of appeal could simply order a trial judge to continue a trial, rather than order a new trial. Specifically, they concluded that the words "in addition" in section 686(8) did not mean that a court granting the appeal from acquittal must have already made an order for a new trial or conviction under section 686(4) before being able to make a further order under section 686(8). Rather, setting aside the acquittal or stay would be enough of an exercise of section 686(4) to trigger the remedial power in section 686(8).[176] A court of appeal cannot order the continuation of a trial on an amended indictment, however.[177] Nor can an appeal court order a new trial limited to a particular theory of liability on a single criminal charge.[178]

Under section 683, a court of appeal can order exhibits or other items produced, hear witnesses or admit an examination of a witness, and refer questions to a special commissioner.[179] That section also permits an appeal court to amend the indictment where the accused has not been misled or prejudiced.

A court of appeal is also entitled to raise new issues beyond those brought forward by the parties, although they should do so only in rare circumstances.[180] A new issue is one that cannot reasonably be said to stem from the issues as framed by the parties, and so it does not include

be convicted of the main offence at trial but be convicted or ordered to face a new trial on an included offence.

175 See, for example, *R v Barton*, 2019 SCC 33 [*Barton*], where errors led to an accused's retrial on unlawful act manslaughter, but not on first degree murder, because the nature of the errors identified could not have had an effect on the latter acquittal.

176 *Bellusci*, above note 120 at para 39.

177 *R v Gunn*, [1982] 1 SCR 522.

178 *R v Cowan*, 2021 SCC 45 at para 7.

179 See the discussion at Section B(3)(b), below in this chapter.

180 *R v Mian*, 2014 SCC 54 [*Mian*].

questioning about things which are components of issues already before the court.[181] Because the judge's role in an adversary system is to both be and seem to be independent and impartial, a court of appeal should raise a new issue only when failing to do so would risk an injustice, such as there being good reason to believe that the result would have differed had the error not been made.[182] It must also be the case that there is a sufficient record on which to raise the issue, and that raising the issue would not result in procedural prejudice to any party.[183] If a court of appeal does raise a new issue, all parties must be given advance notice of the issue in order to make informed submissions.[184]

In addition, a court of appeal can assign counsel for an accused or order an accused released pending an appeal.[185] In the case of an appeal from conviction, to be released the accused must demonstrate that the appeal is not frivolous, that he will surrender himself into custody in accordance with the terms of the order, and that his detention is not necessary in the public interest.[186] Note that although the "public interest" criterion was found to be unconstitutionally vague in the pretrial context (see the discussion in Chapter 6), it has been upheld with regard to bail pending an appeal.[187]

Note, as well, that an accused has the right to be present at the appeal. However, that right may not apply if the appeal is based on a question of law alone and the accused is both in custody and represented by counsel. In addition, the appeal court can order that an accused in custody appear only by electronic means.[188] In some circumstances, it is also possible for an appeal to be brought even though the accused is deceased. A court of appeal has the jurisdiction to do so, but should choose to exercise that jurisdiction only where it is in the interests of justice.[189]

181 *Ibid* at paras 31–35. See, for example, *R v St. John's (City)*, 2017 NLCA 71, concluding that deciding a case based on the *actus reus* not being proven, although that point had been conceded by counsel, did not constitute deciding based on a new issue.

182 *Mian*, above note 180 at para 45. See *R v Bourgeois*, 2017 ABCA 32 at para 49: "*Mian* does not permit a judge to say: 'I would have come to a different conclusion on the facts, so failing to raise this new issue will create an injustice'."

183 *Mian*, above note 180 at para 41.

184 *Ibid* at para 35. See also *Barton*, above note 175 at paras 50–51 and *R v Suter*, 2018 SCC 34 at paras 29–34.

185 Sections 684 and 679.

186 See the discussion of these criteria in *R v Mapara* (2004), 186 CCC (3d) 273 (BCCA).

187 *R v Farinacci* (1993), 25 CR (4th) 350 (Ont CA).

188 Section 688.

189 *R v Smith*, 2004 SCC 14.

### b) Bail Pending Appeal

A person who has been convicted of an offence can apply for bail pending the appeal. An application can be made to a single judge of the court of appeal, but that decision can be reviewed by a panel.[190] The onus is on the appellant (because the presumption of innocence does not apply post-conviction) to establish that "(a) the appeal . . . is not frivolous; (b) he will surrender himself into custody in accordance with the terms of the order; and (c) his detention is not necessary in the public interest."[191] Of those three criteria, it is the "public interest" criterion that is the most difficult to assess, though it is also rarely the controlling factor.[192]

Broadly, the approach to bail pending appeal looks at the same considerations as the grounds for detention in a pre-trial application for bail. The public interest criterion consists of two components: public safety and public confidence in the administration of justice. "Public safety" tracks the secondary ground for detention in section 515(10)(b), that the detention is necessary for the protection or safety of the public.[193] "Public confidence" involves weighing two competing interests: enforceability and reviewability. "Enforceability" reflects the need to respect the general rule of the immediate enforceability of judgments, while "reviewability" acknowledges that the justice system is not infallible and that persons should be entitled to a meaningful review process which did not require them to serve all or a significant part of a custodial sentence before having their conviction overturned.[194]

The Court has concluded that the public confidence criterion should largely be governed by the requirements in section 515(10)(c) of the *Code*, which deals with detention based on maintaining confidence in the administration of justice. That section mentions the gravity of the offence, the circumstances surrounding the commission of the offence, and the potential length of imprisonment as relevant factors, all of which go to the seriousness of the offence. Those factors should therefore be considered when assessing the enforceability aspect of public confidence: "[t]he more serious the crime, the greater the risk that public confidence in the administration of justice will be undermined if the accused is released on bail pending trial."[195] The reviewability criterion is analogous to the last factor mentioned in

---

190 See ss 679 and 680.

191 Section 679.

192 *R v Oland*, 2017 SCC 17 [*Oland*] at para 29.

193 See the discussion in Chapter 6, Section D.

194 *Oland*, above note 192 at para 25.

195 *Oland*, above note 192 para 47.

section 515(1)(c), the strength of the prosecution's case or in the context of bail pending appeal, the strength of the grounds of appeal. It was independently necessary for the accused to show that the appeal was "not frivolous," which is a very low bar.[196] Beyond that initial threshold consideration, however, judges should make a preliminary assessment of the strength of an appeal, based on the material provided and the relevant authorities.

Ultimately a judge will balance all the factors, keeping in mind that public confidence is to be measured through the eyes of a reasonable member of the public who is thoughtful, dispassionate, informed of the circumstances of the case, and respectful of society's fundamental values. Judges should also consider the anticipated delay in deciding an appeal and whether all or a significant portion of a sentence will be served before the appeal can be decided: if so the reviewability interest takes on a greater significance.

### c) Fresh Evidence on Appeal

It is possible for evidence to be introduced on appeal that was not before the trial court; however, this cannot be done in an unconstrained way. In *R v Palmer*, the Court laid down guidelines for the introduction of fresh evidence on appeal:

1) The evidence should generally not be admitted if it could have been adduced at trial by due diligence (but this principle is not to be applied as strictly in a criminal case as in civil cases).
2) The evidence must be relevant in the sense that it bears upon a decisive or potentially decisive issue in the trial.
3) The evidence must be credible in the sense that it is reasonably capable of belief.
4) It must be such that, if believed, it could reasonably, when taken with the other evidence adduced at trial, be expected to have affected the result.[197]

Note that the evidence sought to be introduced must have been capable of admission at the initial trial; hearsay or opinion evidence that would not have been admissible at trial is no more admissible on appeal.[198]

---

196 *Oland*, above note 192 at para 20.

197 [1980] 1 SCR 759 at 775 [*Palmer*].

198 See, for example, *R v Arabia*, 2008 ONCA 565; *R v Assoun*, 2006 NSCA 47, leave to appeal to SCC refused [2006] SCCA No 233; or *R v Archer* (2005), 34 CR (6th) 271 (Ont CA) [*Archer*].

The due diligence requirement is, in large measure, intended to prevent the reassessment in hindsight of a strategic decision made at trial.[199] Accordingly, this criterion is not always an absolute one and should not be determinative. Courts retain a discretion to allow fresh evidence in when a strong case is made out on the other criteria, even if the evidence could in principle have been led at trial.[200] This is particularly so when the decision by the accused not to have led the evidence was a reasonable one given Crown counsel's strategy at trial.[201]

The requirement that the evidence must bear upon a potentially decisive issue does not mean that it must relate directly to guilt or innocence in the sense that it is a new witness that can offer the accused an alibi — the evidence could also give reason to doubt other evidence that had been relied on at trial. In *R v Trotta*, for example, fresh evidence was admitted and a new trial was ordered in light of evidence that the testimony of a pathologist called by the Crown was unreliable.[202] In *R v Hurley* fresh evidence that the accused's DNA had been found in various places in a hotel room was admitted, on his application, because it could help counter the Crown's argument that he had cleaned up the scene in an effort to hide his presence there.[203] In *R v JAA* the evidence went to whether a mark on the accused's finger was a bite mark, which had been an important factor in the trial judge's decision in the face of conflicting testimony.[204] However, evidence that could bear only on a peripheral issue will not, due to the fourth criterion above, be admitted.[205]

---

199 See, for example, *R v Falkner*, 2008 BCCA 277; *Archer*, above note 198; or *R v Perlett* (2006), 212 CCC (3d) 11 (Ont CA) [*Perlett*].

200 See the discussion of this issue in *Maciel*, above note 133, and, in particular, the observations that "[i]t can never be in the interests of justice to maintain a verdict where the court is satisfied that the verdict is factually incorrect" (para 47) and that "[i]t is not in the interests of justice to maintain a conviction where, on the totality of the evidence available to the appellate court, that court is satisfied that no reasonable jury could convict the appellant" (para 48).

201 *R v JAA*, 2011 SCC 17 [*JAA*]. In *JAA* the accused sought to lead expert evidence to show that a mark on his finger was not a bite mark. The Crown had not led expert evidence on the point at trial, though a police officer had testified (possibly impermissibly) that the mark appeared to him to be a bite. The particular point turned out to be significant in the trial judge's reasons, though the accused had not expected that to be the case, and that expectation was not unreasonable.

202 2007 SCC 49.

203 2010 SCC 18.

204 *JAA*, above note 201.

205 See *Perlett*, above note 199; or *R v Flis* (2006), 205 CCC (3d) 384 (Ont CA).

The Court has also commented on the procedure to be used in fresh evidence applications. It has directed that, unless the application is dismissed immediately, judgment should be reserved on whether to admit the evidence until after the appeal is heard. In that way, the appeal court will be better able to decide whether the evidence could reasonably have been expected to affect the result of the case. If it could, the appeal court can also consider how great an impact it might have had in order to decide whether to order a new trial or, relying on the fresh evidence, decide the matter itself.[206]

Note, as well, that the *Palmer* criteria do not create the only test by which new evidence can be introduced on appeal, though it is the most common one. However, in some cases, evidence showing that the validity of the trial is in issue, rather than evidence relating to guilt or innocence. In such cases, the *Palmer* criteria do not apply. In *R v Taillefer; R v Duguay* (discussed more fully in Chapter 8) the fresh evidence was evidence that had, wrongly, not been disclosed to the accused earlier. In those circumstances, the Court held that the less strict test from *R v Dixon*, relating to disclosure, was more appropriately applied.[207] More generally, when the trial process itself is in issue the strict *Palmer* criteria do not apply.[208] Equally, if a matter is first arising in the appeal court, so that there is no evidence on the issue below, an appeal court can choose to receive evidence.[209]

### d) Duty to Give Reasons

A judge in a criminal trial has a duty to give reasons; however, this has not always been taken to be the case. For more than one hundred years the stated rule was that a trial judge had no general duty to give reasons, and it is still not the case that every adjudicator in every context has such a duty. In 2002, however, with its decision in *R v Sheppard*[210] the Court concluded that the failure to give sufficient reasons will be an error of law giving rise to a ground of appeal, in certain circumstances. Subsequently in its 2008 decision in *R v REM*, the Court concluded that

---

206 *R v Stolar*, [1988] 1 SCR 480.

207 2003 SCC 70 [*Taillefer*]. See also *R v Dixon*, [1998] 1 SCR 244.

208 See, for example, *R v Schneider* (2004), 192 CCC (3d) 1 (NSCA); *R v Wolf* (2005), 197 CCC (3d) 481 (Ont CA); and *R v MacInnis* (2006), 212 CCC (3d) 103 (NSCA).

209 See, for example, *R v KRJ*, 2016 SCC 31, where the issue of whether the alleged s 11 *Charter* violation in the case could be saved under s 1 had not been considered in the courts below, and so the Supreme Court received evidence on the point (though with consent in that case).

210 2002 SCC 26 [*Sheppard*].

a criminal trial, where the accused's innocence is at stake, is always one of those circumstances.[211]

Reasons serve three main functions. First, they tell the parties why the decision was made, demonstrating that the judge has heard and considered the evidence on both sides and has not taken any extraneous considerations into account. Second, reasons make the decision publicly accountable, so that justice is not only done but is seen to be done. Third, reasons permit effective appellate review. When a trial judge has clearly laid out the factual findings and legal principles, parties are in a better position to decide whether to appeal, and appellate courts are in a better position to assess whether there has been an error.

In addition, the process of writing reasons directs the judge's attention and reduces the likelihood of over- or under-emphasizing some point. Finally, reasons help the law to develop uniformly. Accordingly, a criminal trial judge now has a duty to give sufficient reasons for the decision. The real question today, therefore, is "[w]hat, in the context of a particular case, constitutes *sufficient* reasons?"[212]

A trial judge's reasons do not need to be the equivalent of a jury instruction, and should not be held up against some abstract standard.[213] They are to be assessed as a whole, in the context of the evidence, the arguments, and the trial, and a misstatement will not necessarily be fatal.[214] Further, an appeal court is not to intervene "simply because it thinks the trial court did a poor job of expressing itself."[215] Trial judges are only required to give reasons that the parties can understand and that permit appellate review.[216]

The Court has said that "[w]hat is required is a logical connection between the 'what' — the verdict — and the 'why' — the basis for the verdict," but that this does not require the judge to explain exactly *how* the decision was reached in a watch-me-think fashion.[217] A trial judge need not set out every finding or conclusion and need not expound

---

211 2008 SCC 51 at para 10 [*REM*]. See generally the discussion in Judge Wayne Gorman, "'Ours Is to Reason Why': The Law of Rendering Judgment" (2015) 62 *Criminal Law Quarterly* 301.

212 *REM*, above note 211 at para 14.

213 *Ibid*; *R v Rhyason*, 2007 SCC 39; *R v Gagnon*, [2006] 1 SCR 621 at para 19.

214 See, for example, *R v Laboucan*, 2010 SCC 12, where the trial judge made reference to the accused's motive to lie in assessing credibility. The Court held that such a consideration was problematic and unhelpful, and that triers of fact would be well advised to avoid that path altogether. Nonetheless, in the context of the decision as a whole, the statement did not constitute an error.

215 *Sheppard*, above note 210 at para 26.

216 *Ibid*, and *R v Boucher*, 2005 SCC 72.

217 *REM*, above note 211 at para 17.

on points of law or pieces of evidence that are not, in the context of the case, in dispute.[218] Reasons are particularly important when the relevant law is unsettled law or where there is confused and contradictory evidence on a key issue. Even then, however, the basis of the trial judge's conclusion might be apparent from the record even without being articulated.[219] In general, what is necessary is that the trial judge makes clear the path taken through confused or conflicting evidence, so that the parties can understand the basis for the decision.

In *Sheppard*, for example, there were significant inconsistencies and conflicts in the evidence, as well as issues of credibility. The trial judge delivered "boiler plate" reasons that indicated, in a single sentence, that he had considered the testimony and the burden on the Crown in finding the accused guilty. The Court held that these reasons were insufficient for the accused, or an appeal court, to know the basis for the conviction, and upheld the order for a new trial.

On the other hand, in *REM* the trial judge had given much more expansive reasons, though the court of appeal had found them to be insufficient for various reasons. Specifically, the trial judge did not explain which of the offences were proved by which of the eleven incidents on which evidence had been led, failed to mention some of the accused's evidence, failed to make general comments about the accused's evidence, failed to reconcile his generally positive findings on the complainant's evidence with the rejection of some of her evidence, and failed to explain why he rejected the accused's plausible denial of the charges. The Supreme Court overturned the court of appeal's decision, holding that they had, in effect, substituted their own views about credibility for that of the trial judge under the guise of finding the reasons insufficient. The central issue at trial had been credibility. The trial judge's reasons made it clear that he had accepted a great deal of the complainant's evidence, that he was not left with a reasonable doubt on the whole of the evidence or from the contradictory evidence of the accused, and therefore that the accused's guilt had been established

---

218 See, for example, *R v O'Brien*, 2011 SCC 29, where the trial judge had improperly allowed character evidence to be admitted, though no party had relied on that evidence in argument. The only issue in the case was identity, and the trial judge indicated that he relied solely on the DNA evidence in reaching his conclusion on that issue. The Nova Scotia Court of Appeal had ordered a new trial because the reasons did not demonstrate that the trial judge had not been unconsciously influenced by the character evidence. The Supreme Court overturned this result, holding at para 17 that "[t]rial judges are entitled to have their reasons reviewed based on what they say, not on the speculative imagination of reviewing courts."

219 *Sheppard*, above note 210 at para 55.

beyond a reasonable doubt. While some aspects of the reasons could have been explained more fully, the Court said, when the record was considered as a whole, the basis for the verdict was evident, and so the reasons were not insufficient.[220]

That is not to say, however, that any reasons that go beyond "boiler plate" will be sufficient. In *R v Dinardo* the issue was also credibility in a sexual assault case and the trial judge again convicted. Although the trial judge was not required to explicitly lay out the proper test for determining whether there was reasonable doubt, the trial judge's reasons did not make clear that he had actually applied that test. Critical evidence, such as that the complainant was mentally challenged, had a history of making up stories to get attention, and had wavered about whether the accused had committed the assault in question, was not averted to in the reasons. The trial judge's failure to avert to these critical matters left the Court in doubt that he had directed his mind to the central issue of credibility and meant the reasons were insufficient.[221]

The Court has summarized the proper approach to assessing reasons for sufficiency:

> (1) Appellate courts are to take a functional, substantive approach to sufficiency of reasons, reading them as a whole, in the context of the evidence, the arguments and the trial, with an appreciation of the purposes or functions for which they are delivered (see *Sheppard*, at paras. 46 and 50; *Morrissey*, at p. 524).
> (2) The basis for the trial judge's verdict must be "intelligible," or capable of being made out. In other words, a logical connection between the verdict and the basis for the verdict must be apparent. A detailed description of the judge's process in arriving at the verdict is unnecessary.
> (3) In determining whether the logical connection between the verdict and the basis for the verdict is established, one looks to the evidence, the submissions of counsel and the history of the trial to determine the "live" issues as they emerged during the trial.[222]

When reasons are found not to be sufficient, that can be the basis for granting an appeal. In the case of an appeal from conviction, the insufficient reasons might be an unreasonable verdict, an error of law,

---

220 *REM*, above note 211 at para 67. To similar effect, see *R v HSB*, 2008 SCC 52.
221 2008 SCC 24.
222 *REM*, above note 211 at para 35. See also *R v Vuradin*, 2013 SCC 38 and *R v Wolynec*, 2015 ONCA 656 at paras 51–60.

or a miscarriage of justice, depending on the circumstances of the case and the nature and importance of the trial decision being rendered.[223]

The duty to give reasons also applies to acquittals, but in a different fashion. There is no "unreasonable acquittal" ground of appeal, and the Crown and the accused have different tasks at trial. A conviction requires proof of every element beyond a reasonable doubt, but an acquittal requires only that there be reasonable doubt. Reasonable doubt need not be based on factual findings supporting it and can arise simply because an inadequate foundation for guilt has been laid. In that event, it takes less for reasons to be adequate in the case of an acquittal.[224]

Note, in addition, that issues can arise because of the timing with which reasons are released. Reasons need not always be given contemporaneously with the decision, and so there is normally no difficulty with the routine practice of a judge issuing a decision with reasons to follow. However, when there is delay the possibility of problems increases. Judges benefit from the presumption of integrity, which includes the presumption that they are setting aside personal biases and deciding impartially. In some cases, when other factors are present along with delay, it might seem that the reasons were no longer drafted with an open mind, but rather to justify the conclusion of guilt that had already been reached.[225]

This possibility is a danger particularly where reasons are not issued until after the accused has launched an appeal. In such a case, there could be cause to think that the reasons were designed to justify the verdict, rather than to reflect the decision-making process that was used. This reasoning can apply not only when the entire reasons are not released until later, but also when an amendment is made to those reasons, and the amendment seems like a justification for conviction rather than the operation of an open mind.[226] Delay itself is not the

223 *Sheppard*, above note 210 at para 55.

224 *Walker*, above note 145; *Sinclair*, above note 44.

225 *R v Teskey*, 2007 SCC 25.

226 In *R v Arnaout*, 2015 ONCA 655, the accused was convicted of attempted murder on the basis that he had put ricin into water bottles. Seventeen months later and after an appeal had been launched, the judge at a dangerous offender hearing amended those reasons to include the possibility that the accused had tried and failed to put the ricin in. The Ontario Court of Appeal concluded that to a reasonable observer this would look like shoring up the weakest part of the reasoning. The change did not rebut the presumption of integrity for the original reasons, though, and so the remedy was to excise the later amendments (though as a matter of fact the convictions based on the unamended reasons were then found to be unreasonable).

deciding factor, but it increases the possibility that reasons will not be seen to have been impartial.[227]

## C. APPEALS OF SUMMARY CONVICTION OFFENCES

Part XXVII of the *Code* contains the rules governing summary conviction offences, which include appeal provisions. Which set of appeal provisions are to be used depends on the nature of the proceedings below, rather than the nature of the offence. As a result, even if an indictable offence wrongly is dealt with through the summary conviction procedures, it is the summary conviction appeal provisions which will apply.[228]

Appeals from summary conviction proceedings share many qualities with appeals from indictable offences, though there are some differences worth noting. The most notable difference is the court to which the appeal is brought. Indictable offences are appealed to the court of appeal for the province. Generally speaking, summary conviction appeals are taken to the province's superior court of criminal jurisdiction that is *not* the court of appeal.[229] There are also differences in the grounds upon which an appeal can be brought, which are broader for both accused (called the "defendant" in the case of summary conviction offences) and the Crown, and are essentially parallel to one another. Under section 813 of the *Code*, a defendant can appeal a conviction or order made against them, and the Crown can appeal "an order that stays proceedings on an information or dismisses an information." One result of this is that, unlike with indictable offences, the Crown can appeal a summary conviction matter not just on questions of law but also on questions of fact or mixed law and fact.[230] In addition, section 813 lets both parties appeal sentences, verdicts of not criminally responsible, and fitness to stand trial decisions. No explicit limits are attached to any of these grounds.

As with indictable offences, though, the bases for granting appeals are narrower than the grounds for launching them. Indeed, they are narrower in precisely the same way. Section 822(1) incorporates most

227 See also *R v Wang*, 2010 ONCA 435, cautioning against making substantive changes when issuing a written version of reasons delivered orally.

228 *R v Branscombe*, 2017 SKCA 71.

229 See the definitions in ss 2, 673, and 812. See, however, the discussion of appeals under s 830, below in this section.

230 See *R v Abramoff*, 2018 SKCA 21, and the cases listed at para 18.

of sections 683 to 689 by reference. As a result, all of the rules in section 686(1) that concern appeals from convictions or acquittals are equally applicable to summary conviction offences. Recall, as well, that when a summary conviction offence is appealed along with an indictable offence, the appeals can, with leave, be combined.[231]

As a result of this incorporation, other provisions applicable to indictable offences, such as the powers of the court in section 683, also apply. In addition, bail pending a summary conviction appeal can be granted, though under the specific provisions in section 816 rather than those governing indictable offences.

There are, however, other notable differences between summary conviction and indictable appeals, which include the possibility of other methods of appeal.

First, under section 822(4), it is possible for an appeal of a summary conviction matter to take place by trial *de novo*. Proceeding in this way can be justified if there is a problem with the condition of the record — a grounds of decreasing relevance given the methods of recording proceedings in common use today — or if "for any other reason" the interests of justice would be better served by doing so. As a practical matter trials *de novo* are a rarity.

In addition, sections 829 to 838 create an alternative method of appeal, though again these provisions are little used. They incorporate many of the provisions regarding other summary conviction appeals, but the grounds upon which they can be brought are more limited. Either party can appeal a decision in this way on the basis that it is erroneous in point of law, it is in excess of jurisdiction, or it constitutes a refusal or failure to exercise jurisdiction. All of these are grounds upon which an appeal could have been launched under section 813.[232] A defendant is permitted to opt for only one of the two methods of appeal.[233] Appeals under Section 830 can be brought either on a transcript or an agreed-upon statement of facts.[234] In such cases, the appeal could, in some provinces, go directly to the provincial court of appeal.[235]

---

231 Sections 675(1.1) and 676(1.1).

232 David Rose, *Quigley's Criminal Procedure in Canada* (Toronto: Thomson Reuters, 2021) (loose-leaf) [*Quigley*] notes at 24–39 the possibility that the quashing of an information prior to plea might be appealable only under s 830, though he also observes that a new information could simply be laid in such circumstances.

233 Section 836.

234 Section 830(2).

235 This result follows because s 829 defines "appeal court" for s 830 appeals as the superior court of criminal jurisdiction for the province, but the definition of that term in s 2, for some provinces, includes the court of appeal.

Finally, whichever method of appeal is brought at the first level, the *Code* permits a potential second level of appeal from summary conviction matters to the court of appeal. Such appeals depend on leave of the court and can be brought only on a question of law.[236] The rules in sections 673 to 689, which govern appeals of indictable offences, are incorporated by reference to these appeals.[237]

Provincial courts of appeal have tended to the view that a second level of appeal ought not to be routinely granted, in part, on the basis that it would be anomalous to have more expansive rights of appeal in the case of less serious offences. Accordingly, most have set down guidelines that are intended to make a second level of appeal the exception rather than the rule.[238]

All courts that have considered the issue hold that the two key considerations are the significance of the legal issues raised to the administration of criminal justice generally and the merits of the particular argument in the case. Not all courts have established exactly the same rules around these criteria.

The Ontario Court of Appeal in *R v RR* treats those two criteria as creating two alternative bases for granting leave to appeal. That case held:

> Leave to appeal may be granted where the merits of the proposed question of law are arguable, even if not strong, and the proposed question of law has significance to the administration of justice beyond the four corners of the case. Leave to appeal may also be granted where there appears to be a "clear" error even if it cannot be said that the error has significance to the administration of justice beyond the specific case.[239]

---

236 Section 839. Once again, it is a question of law for jurisdictional purposes that is in issue.

237 Section 839(2).

238 There is some disagreement over exactly how stringent the leave standard should be. In *R v RR*, 2008 ONCA 497 [*RR*], the Ontario Court of Appeal held that leave to appeal should be only "granted sparingly" (para 37), and in the later case of *R v Ul-Rashid*, 2013 ONCA 782 at para 3, they held that the Court of Appeal "must be satisfied that it is essential that leave be granted." In contrast, in *Newfoundland Recycling Ltd v R*, 2009 NLCA 28 at para 7 [*Newfoundland Recycling*], the Newfoundland and Labrador Court of Appeal disagreed with this point and held that the test "should not be unduly stringent." See also *R v Gavin*, 2009 PECA 23 [*Gavin*], concurring with both *RR* and *Newfoundland Recycling*, suggesting that some courts do not perceive the tests as very different.

239 *RR*, above note 238 at para 32.

An appeal is more likely to be allowed when the issues have no general importance if the appellant is facing a significant deprivation of liberty: where even a short custodial sentence will be imposed, it would be "rare and remarkable" for leave to be refused.[240] The *RR* approach has been adopted by many other courts of appeal.[241]

An alternative approach, however, requires that both criteria be met, but relaxes the strictness of the test in other ways. The Court of Appeal for Yukon held that the test required that "(a) the ground of appeal involves a question of law alone, (b) the issue is one of importance, *and* (c) there is sufficient merit in the proposed appeal that it has a reasonable possibility of success."[242] "Reasonable possibility of success" seems like a lower standard than the "clear error" requirement in *RR* and so would be easier to meet. However, it would need to be met in addition to the "significance" criterion. On this test it seems that even a clear error which was not significant outside the confines of the case would not justify leave to appeal. The British Columbia Court of Appeal has also supported this approach.[243]

A third standard is applied by the Newfoundland and Labrador Court of Appeal. In their view, the "reasonable possibility of success" and "significance to the administration of justice" grounds are two alternative routes, as in *RR*.[244] However, they reject the notion that either of these routes sets a stringent standard such as a requirement for a

---

240 *R v Brownson*, 2013 ONCA 619 at para 17.

241 See *R v Evans*, 2014 ABCA 339; *R v Kirk*, 2014 ABCA 373; *R v Petrin*, 2013 NWTCA 1; *R v RWM*, 2011 MBCA 74; *R v Culligan*, 2018 MBCA 60; *R v Lindsay*, 2011 BCCA 99; *R c Cloutier*, 2010 QCCA 350; *Gavin*, above note 238; *R v MacNeil*, 2009 NSCA 46; or *R v Pottie*, 2013 NSCA 68.

242 *R v Winfield*, 2009 YKCA 9 at para 13 [*Winfield*] [emphasis added], reaff'd in *R v Reeves*, 2024 YKCA 3.

243 *R v Lord*, 2011 BCCA 295. See also *R v Nikal*, 2025 BCCA 361, and *R v Sue*, 2025 BCCA 363.

244 See *R v Burry*, 2022 NLCA 11 at para 6:

> In this jurisdiction, the test for leave pursuant to section 839 is well settled. As the appellant, Mr. Burry must establish (*R. v. Newfoundland Recycling Limited*, 2009 NLCA 28, 284 Nfld. & P.E.I.R. 153 ("*NL Recycling*"), at para. 9):
> (a) the appeal must "be taken on a ground that involves a question of law alone", and
> (b) the ground(s) of appeal must be such that:
> (i) either the ground of appeal has a "reasonable possibility of success", or
> (ii) "the proposed question of law [has significance] to the administration of justice".

"clear error." Rather "the intended appellant must meet the appropriate test for leave to be granted. That test should not be unduly stringent."[245]

In any event, it is important to recall that the second level of appeal is to consider whether the summary conviction appeal court judge committed any legal error — it is not a second review of the trial judge's decision.[246]

## D. APPEALS TO THE SUPREME COURT OF CANADA

As noted in Section A, above in this chapter, in unusual circumstances matters other than a conviction or acquittal can be appealed to the Supreme Court under section 40 of the *Supreme Court Act*. The more important issue, however, is the actual appeal of the result at trial beyond a provincial court of appeal. Sections 691 to 695 create a right to appeal decisions of a court of appeal regarding indictable offences to the Supreme Court of Canada.[247]

Some appeals are allowed as of right, such as where there is a dissent in the court of appeal, while others require leave of the Court. The principal object of an appeal as of right is to rectify legal error, and the existence of a dissent is evidence that there might be such an error. Allowing an appeal to the Supreme Court is therefore meant to be a safeguard against wrongful convictions.[248]

Section 693 sets out the Crown's right of appeal, which is limited to a question of law on which a judge of the court of appeal dissents or any question of law with leave. The accused's right of appeal is more complicated. Under section 691(1) an accused who is convicted at both trial and appeal has the same right of appeal as the Crown: on a question of law where there was a dissent or on any question of law with

245 *R v Newfoundland Recycling Ltd*, 2009 NLCA 28 at para 7.

246 See *R v Van Zyl*, 2025 SKCA 104 at para 30, and the cases cited therein: "[a]n appeal to this Court under s. 839 is an appeal against the decision of the summary conviction appeal judge, not the trial judge's decision." See also *Winfield*, above note 242 at para 12.

247 In an appropriate case, presumably the appeal power under s 40 of the *Supreme Court Act*, above note 5, could be used to appeal a decision of a court of appeal concerning a summary conviction matter: see *Quigley*, above note 232 at 24–40.

248 *R v CP*, 2021 SCC 19 at paras 59–62, per Abella J. The issue in *CP* was whether s 37(10) of the *Youth Criminal Justice Act*, which denied these same rights of appeal to young persons, violated the *Charter*. Abella J was in the dissent finding that it did, while the majority found no *Charter* violation.

leave. Where the accused was acquitted at trial and that was overturned on appeal, those same two options exist, but there is a third ground: the accused can appeal as of right if the court of appeal entered a conviction.[249] This ground exists to ensure that an accused person has one level of appeal after conviction to raise a question of law.[250]

All of those grounds for an appeal require that they are based on a question of law; no other ground of appeal is permitted. Whether an issue constitutes a question of law, as opposed to a question of mixed law and fact, has already been discussed in the context of appeals to the court of appeal, and that analysis is equally applicable here.[251] For example, the application of a legal standard to the facts is a question of law, and "[i]t is of no moment that the issue may be characterized as not being a 'question of law alone.'"[252] There are, however, some considerations that are unique to the Supreme Court context.

A court of appeal can, under section 686(1)(a)(i), allow an appeal based on a finding that it was unreasonable or cannot be supported by the evidence. This question obviously could involve some consideration of facts, and the unreasonableness of a particular verdict might raise questions of mixed law and fact. However, as a class, the question of whether a court of appeal has properly applied section 686(1)(a)(i) is a question of law. It is therefore possible to bring an appeal to the Supreme Court based on whether the court of appeal ought to have allowed the appeal.[253]

Similarly, under section 686(1)(b)(iii) a court of appeal can use the curative proviso and dismiss an appeal based on the finding that there was no substantial wrong or miscarriage of justice. Once again, whether the court of appeal has made a correct decision in applying the curative proviso is a question of law and so is appealable to the Supreme Court.[254] Presumably, the same rationale should apply to the "procedural irregularity" saving provision in section 686(1)(b)(iv).

---

249 Section 691(2)(b) also gives a right of appeal where the accused enters a guilty plea but the trial judge enters a stay of proceedings and the court of appeal then lifts the stay: *R v Li*, 2020 SCC 12.

250 *R v Magoon*, 2018 SCC 14 [*Magoon*] at para 38.

251 See *R v Sanichar*, 2013 SCC 4, for a split in the Supreme Court over whether the basis for disagreement in the court of appeal had been over a question of law or not and, therefore, whether there was jurisdiction for them to hear the appeal. See on this point Gerard J Kennedy, "Persisting Uncertainties in Appellate Jurisdiction at the Supreme Court" (2013) 100 *Criminal Reports* (6th) 97.

252 *Samaniego*, above note 86 at para 122.

253 See *Yebes*, above note 37; and *Biniaris*, above note 22.

254 See *R v Mahoney*, [1982] 1 SCR 834; and *R v Jolivet*, 2000 SCC 29.

Apart from the fact that the only ground of appeal is on a question of law, there is also the issue of when the accused or the Crown will be permitted to appeal. Any appeal to the Supreme Court must be based on a question of law. Within that, an appeal will only be allowed if the Supreme Court gives leave, where a judge of the court of appeal dissented on a question of law, or where the court of appeal entered a conviction.[255] The Court has noted that a "dissent" in this context means "a disagreement which affects the result." So, for example, if the majority find that there was no *Charter* violation while the minority finds there was a violation but the evidence should not be excluded, that minority opinion does not constitute a dissent but rather an opinion concurring in the result.[256]

Note as well that the right to appeal is not simply on a question of law but "specifically to those questions of law on which a judge of the court of appeal dissents."[257] Where a dissent is based, for example, on whether a trial judge erred in a pre-trial ruling, the Supreme Court cannot consider the separate issue of whether the trial judge ought to have reconsidered that ruling.[258]

These are the only circumstances in which the Crown can appeal or in which an accused who was convicted both at trial and on appeal can appeal: that is, on the particular question of law over which there was a dissent or for which leave was given. However, if an accused was acquitted at trial but that acquittal was replaced with a conviction on appeal, then a further basis for appeal is allowed. In that case, the accused can also appeal on *any* question of law, whether there was a dissent in the court of appeal or not.[259] However, it must be a question of law relating to the substituted conviction. That is, if an accused were convicted of second degree murder and the court of appeal substituted a conviction for first degree murder, only questions of law relating to the first degree murder substitution could be appealed as of right under section 691(2). If the accused wished to argue issues relating to the second degree murder conviction, they would need to qualify to do so under section 691(1).[260]

---

255 Sections 691 and 693.

256 *R v D'Amico*, 2019 SCC 23. The Court says that this is the interpretation for s 691, dealing with appeals by the accused, but there is no obvious reason it should not apply equally to appeals by the Crown under s 693.

257 *R v TWW*, 2024 SCC 19 [*TWW*] at para 46.

258 *TWW*, above note 257.

259 Section 691(2).

260 *Magoon*, above note 250.

Sections 691(1) and (2) exhaust an accused's appeal rights (other than those relating to a not criminally responsible finding in section 692). That is to say, an accused can appeal if: they were convicted at trial and that conviction was upheld on appeal or they were acquitted at trial but that acquittal was overturned on appeal. The result is that an accused who was convicted at trial but has that conviction overturned on appeal has no basis to appeal the *order* made based on the conviction being overturned. An accused who wants to argue that they should have been acquitted as a remedy rather than given a new trial cannot appeal that issue to the Supreme Court.[261]

Note that one option for a court of appeal is to overturn the actual conviction at trial, but substitute a conviction on some other count. In such a case, both the Crown and the accused will have a right of appeal.[262] Note, as well, that, even if the Supreme Court grants leave to appeal on a question of law, that does not preclude it from ultimately concluding that the issue raised is not one of law after all, and dismissing the appeal on that basis.[263] Like a court of appeal, the Supreme Court has the power to appoint counsel for an accused.[264] In addition, the Supreme Court has the power to make any order that the court of appeal could have made.[265] If the Supreme Court orders a new trial which would be held before a judge and jury, the accused has the right to re-elect another mode of trial.[266]

## FURTHER READINGS

Coughlan, Steve, & Alex Gorlewski. *The Anatomy of Criminal Procedure: A Visual Guide to the Law*, 2nd ed (Toronto: University of Toronto Press, 2026).

Gorman, Wayne. "'Ours Is to Reason Why': The Law of Rendering Judgment" (2015) 62 *Criminal Law Quarterly* 301.

Rose, David. *Quigley's Criminal Procedure in Canada* (Toronto: Thomson Reuters, 2021) (loose-leaf) ch 24.

Sopinka, John, & Mark Gelowitz. *The Conduct of an Appeal*, 3d ed (Markham, ON: LexisNexis Canada, 2012).

261 *R v Sullivan*, 2022 SCC 19 at para 89.
262 *Biniaris*, above note 22 at para 18.
263 *R v Demeter*, [1978] 1 SCR 538.
264 Section 694.1.
265 Section 695(1).
266 Section 695(2).

# GLOSSARY

**absolute jurisdiction offence.** An offence listed in section 553 of the *Criminal Code*. An accused has no election for these offences, which can be tried only by a provincial court judge.

**administration of justice offence.** An offence committed against the integrity of the criminal justice system, such as failing to comply with bail conditions, failing to appear in court, or breach of probation.

**ancillary powers doctrine.** The process through which new police powers can be created at common law. The test for the creation of ancillary powers is drawn from the British case *R v Waterfield*, which is applied in Canada today in a way quite distinct from the approach in its country of origin.

**appearance notice.** A written demand given to a person in lieu of arresting, or continuing to detain after having arrested, that person, requiring the person to appear in court to answer to charges at a particular place and time. The contents of an appearance notice are set out in section 500 of the *Code*.

**arrest.** An arrest consists of words of arrest accompanied either by the touching of the person with a view to detention or by the person submitting to the arrest. The word "arrest" need not be used, provided the accused can be reasonably supposed to have understood that they are under arrest. Arrest powers are given in the *Criminal Code* to everyone, including private citizens, and additional arrest powers are given to property owners and peace officers.

**attorney general.** A member of cabinet and the chief law officer for a jurisdiction. The attorney general has jurisdiction over all or most matters of criminal law, including law-making and prosecutions. In most jurisdictions, the attorney general is also responsible for policing, although this role is sometimes taken on by the solicitor general or some other minister. The attorney general is given various discretionary powers in the *Criminal Code*, some of which must be exercised personally and some of which can be exercised on their behalf by a Crown prosecutor.

**authorization.** A warrant allowing for the interception of private communications.

**autrefois acquit.** A plea by an accused under section 607 of the *Code* claiming that they were previously charged with the same offence and acquitted.

**autrefois convict.** A plea by an accused under section 607 of the *Code* claiming that they were previously charged with the same offence and convicted.

**bail.** The name in common usage for the process by which a justice can release a person who has been accused of an offence until the trial is held. Bail can be granted either unconditionally or on various conditions. It is properly referred to as "judicial interim release."

**boilerplate.** Generic or standardized wording used with little or no attention to the particular context. The term can be attached to language used in many circumstances, including judges' instructions to a jury or reasons for judgment, or in an application for a warrant.

**carding.** A common term for the practice on the part of police of stopping individuals on the street to ask questions or seek identification, in the absence of any basis to conduct an **investigative detention** or arrest. See **street check** and **racial profiling**.

**challenge for cause.** The process by which the Crown or the accused can challenge a potential juror in order to suggest that the person should not serve on the jury. The most common basis for challenge for cause is that the juror "is not indifferent between the Queen and the accused": that language in the *Criminal Code* has now been amended to say that the juror "is not impartial."

**change of venue.** Moving the location of a trial from one territorial jurisdiction to another.

**charge document.** The document setting out the charges based upon which an accused will stand trial. See **information** and **indictment**.

***Charter of Rights and Freedoms*****.** Sections 1–34 of the *Constitution Act, 1982*, setting out various guaranteed rights which, subject to the justification clause in section 1 of the *Charter*, take priority over any other legislation. The most important sections for criminal law purposes include the fundamental freedoms guaranteed in section 2 (such as freedom of expression), the legal rights provisions in sections 7–14 (such as freedom from unreasonable search and seizure, and the right to counsel), and the remedies provisions in sections 24 and 52.

**common law.** Judge-made law, as distinct from laws set out in statutes or regulations.

***Constitution Act, 1867*****.** The Act of the British Parliament that is the first of Canada's constitutional documents and that initially created Canada as a separate country from Great Britain. It is the source of the division of powers between the federal and provincial governments.

**count.** An individual charge within a single information or indictment.

**court of appeal.** The highest court in a jurisdiction for indictable offences, but designated differently in various provinces and territories. For summary conviction matters, the court of appeal is the jurisdiction's superior court of criminal jurisdiction that is not the highest court in the jurisdiction. See the definitions in sections 2, 673, and 812 of the *Criminal Code.*

**court of criminal jurisdiction.** A trial-level court hearing criminal matters, but designated differently in various provinces and territories. See the definition in section 2 of the *Criminal Code.*

**criminal offence.** A violation of any non-regulatory offence, whether summary conviction or indictable, which is found in the *Criminal Code* or in other federal legislation, and which is constitutionally justified under section 91(27) of the *Constitution Act, 1867.*

**Crown election.** Hybrid offences can be tried either by indictment or on summary conviction. The Crown elects which mode of trial will be used.

**Crown prosecutor.** A lawyer responsible for the carriage of public prosecutions on behalf of the Crown. Most public prosecutions are conducted by provincially appointed Crown prosecutors, but federal Crown prosecutors also conduct some prosecutions, particularly with regard to narcotics offences.

**curative proviso.** A portion of the rules governing appeals that permits an appeal to be dismissed despite the presence of a legal error at trial, if it is found that the error is harmless and does not cause a miscarriage of justice. See section 686(i)(b)(iii) of the *Criminal Code.*

**curtilage.** The area surrounding and associated with a dwelling house.

***Dagenais/Mentuck* test.** The test governing whether a discretionary publication ban should be issued. More recently sometimes referred to as the *Dagenais/Mentuck/Sherman Estate* test or the *Sherman Estate* test.

**detention.** A restraint of liberty other than arrest in which a person may reasonably require the assistance of counsel, but might be prevented or impeded from retaining and instructing counsel without delay. The restraint of liberty might arise because of physical constraint, or because a police officer or other agent of the state assumes control over the movement of a person by a demand or direction, whether with or without legal authority to do so. See also **psychological detention.** In section 9 of the *Charter* jurisprudence, dealing with arbitrary detention, the word "detention" includes arrests.

**direct indictment.** A Crown prosecutor has the ability, under section 577 of the *Criminal Code*, to prefer a "direct indictment," which has the effect of requiring an accused to be placed on trial for the indictable offence charged therein, either without a preliminary inquiry having been held or completed, or despite a discharge at the preliminary inquiry. This power can be used only with the personal consent in writing of the attorney general or deputy attorney general. Also referred to as a "**preferred indictment**."

**disclosure.** The right of a person charged with an offence to be informed of all relevant evidence, whether incriminatory or exculpatory, in the hands of the Crown.

**division.** The process of dividing a count that is duplicitous into two or more separate counts.

**division of powers.** The manner in which legislative jurisdiction is divided between the federal and provincial governments in accordance with sections 91 and 92 of the *Constitution Act, 1867.*

**DNA warrant.** A warrant issued under section 487.05 of the *Criminal Code* authorizing the taking of bodily samples from a person for the purpose of DNA analysis.

**double.** See **duplicitous.**

**duplicitous.** A single count in an indictment that is ambiguous as to which offence an accused is being charged with. Referred to in section 590(1) of the *Criminal Code* as being "**double** or multifarious." See also **division.**

**election.** An accused who is charged with an indictable offence is, in most cases, offered a choice as to mode of trial: superior court judge with a jury, superior court judge alone, or provincial court judge. In such cases, the accused is said to have an election as to mode of trial. See **absolute jurisdiction offence** and **exclusive jurisdiction offence**.

**exclusive jurisdiction offence.** An offence listed in section 469 of the *Criminal Code*. These offences (barring prosecutorial consent) can be tried only through a jury trial in a superior court of criminal jurisdiction, and so the accused has no election.

**exigent circumstances.** An urgent situation generally involving imminent harm to a person or the destruction of evidence, but the precise definition can vary with the context. When police could satisfy the conditions for obtaining a warrant but exigent circumstances make it not practicable to obtain that warrant, they are sometimes authorized to act without the warrant.

**expungement order.** An order under the *Expungement of Historically Unjust Convictions Act*, relating to various previously existing offences that dealt with consensual same-sex sexual activity. A person who receives an expungement order in relation to an offence covered by that statute "is deemed never to have been convicted of that offence."

**general warrant.** A warrant issued under section 487.01 of the *Criminal Code* that authorizes the bearer to use any device, investigative technique, or procedure, or do any thing described in the warrant that would constitute an unreasonable search and seizure if it were not authorized by warrant.

**hybrid offence.** An offence that may be prosecuted either as an indictable offence or as a summary conviction offence. See **Crown election**.

**implementational duties.** The obligation imposed on the police to act towards a person who has been arrested or detained and has asserted the right to counsel in particular ways, including facilitating that person's contact with counsel and holding off from attempting to elicit incriminating information until the person has had a reasonable opportunity to make contact.

**indictable offence.** The more serious category of offences, which generally have no minimum penalty but can carry sentences as severe as life imprisonment without possibility of parole for twenty-five years. Indictable offences are tried on an indictment and might have a preliminary inquiry. In most cases, an accused has an election as to mode of trial, though this is not the case for **absolute jurisdiction offences** or **exclusive jurisdiction offences**.

**indictment.** A document nominally prepared once an accused has been committed for trial after a preliminary inquiry, though it will usually be laid without a preliminary inquiry having been conducted (see **direct indictment** or **preferred indictment**). This document specifies the particular offence or offences with which the accused is charged and is the document based upon which the trial for an indictable offence will occur.

**information.** A document sworn in front of a justice of the peace, alleging that a person has committed an offence. An information is required for the issuance of some process, such as an arrest warrant, and is the document based upon which the trial for a summary conviction offence will occur.

**information to obtain.** Generally referred to as an ITO, an information to obtain is the affidavit sworn by a person seeking a warrant.

**informational duties.** The obligation imposed on police to inform a person who is arrested or detained of particular pieces of information, such as the right to counsel, the existence of legal aid, and the telephone numbers for duty counsel.

**informer privilege.** A form of privilege protecting the identity of those who provide information confidentially to the police with regard to an offence. Informer privilege overrides the Crown's obligation of **disclosure** to an accused, but is subject to the **innocence at stake exception**.

**innocence at stake exception.** An exception to **solicitor–client privilege** and **informer privilege**. The innocence at stake exception allows privilege to be breached where an accused establishes that a communication exists that could raise a reasonable doubt as to their guilt, that the information sought from the communication is not available from any other source, and that they are otherwise unable to raise a reasonable doubt.

**investigative detention.** The common law police power to briefly detain an individual where, on an objective view of the totality of the circumstances, there is a clear nexus between the individual to be detained and a recent or ongoing criminal offence, and the decision to detain is reasonable based on all the circumstances, including the extent to which the interference with individual liberty is necessary to perform the officer's duty, the liberty interfered with, and the nature and extent of that interference.

**joinder.** Joining more than one count, or more than one accused, on a single information.

**judgment.** See **verdict**.

**judicial interim release.** See **bail**.

**judicial referral hearing.** A hearing under section 523.1 of the *Criminal Code* allowing a judge or justice to respond to an **administration of justice offence** without additional criminal charges being laid. If a judge or justice is satisfied that the accused failed to comply with some order but did not thereby cause harm, they can cancel the previous document and make a new release order, leave the order in place, or order the accused detained in custody pending trial. No matter which option is chosen, no separate and additional charge can be laid against the accused for the initial violation of conditions.

**jurisdiction.** The legal authority to act in certain manners. Parliament must have jurisdiction to legislate over particular criminal matters, and courts and judges must have jurisdiction in various ways (for example, territorially) to conduct a trial.

**jury.** The triers of fact in some criminal trials. Juries normally consist of twelve individuals drawn from the community where the trial takes place, selected from a **jury array** after a process involving **challenge for cause**. The jury is sometimes referred to as the **petit jury**.

**jury array.** A large number of potential jurors summoned to court from whom the actual jurors for a particular trial will be chosen. An array is also called a **jury panel**.

**jury panel.** See **jury array**.

**jury roll.** A list that as far as possible contains the names of all people eligible to be jury members in the region; from this, a jury array is summoned for jury selection.

**justice.** As used in the *Criminal Code*, a justice of the peace or a provincial court judge.

**ladder approach.** The concept, in the bail provisions, that an accused is entitled to be released without conditions, and that the onus is on the Crown to justify not only the imposition of conditions at all, but also each additional more-restrictive condition.

**Libman test.** The rule that if an offence has a real and substantial connection to Canada, then Canadian courts have territorial jurisdiction over that offence, even if significant portions of the offence occurred extraterritorially.

**miscarriage of justice.** An unfairness in a criminal trial that justifies an appellate court in overturning an accused's conviction. Section 686(1) of the *Criminal Code* sets out three bases upon which an appeal from conviction can be granted: an unreasonable verdict, an error of law that is not harmless (see **curative proviso**), and a miscarriage of justice. Miscarriage of justice is the underlying principle of all three bases: the first two are specific examples.

**peace bond.** Common term applied to a **recognizance** under section 810 of the *Criminal Code*, whereby a person who reasonably fears personal injury from another person can apply to have that other person promise to keep the peace and be of good behaviour, and potentially be bound by other conditions. Other similar provisions have been added to the *Code*, though for the most part they are designed to be used by the state rather than by an individual: see, for example, section 810.01, dealing with the fear that the person will commit a criminal organization offence.

**peace officer.** A person exercising authority under the *Criminal Code* to investigate criminal offences and exercise powers such as arrest. In most instances, a peace officer will be a police officer, but the definition also encompasses others, including, for example, some customs officers, correctional officers, and pilots while an aircraft is in flight. See the definition in section 2 of the *Code*.

**peremptory challenge.** Formerly, the right of the accused or the Crown to object to a member of the jury array being chosen to serve on the jury, without being required to offer any explanation for the objection. The Crown and the accused each had a limited number of peremptory challenges, which varied with the offence charged. As of 2019, peremptory challenges were removed from the *Criminal Code*.

**petit jury.** See **jury**.

**pre-enquete.** An *ex parte* hearing at which a **justice** considers an **information** and decides whether to issue either a **summons** or arrest **warrant**, or not to allow the matter to proceed further.

**prefer.** To lay an indictment in front of a superior court in order to prosecute the accused under it.

**preferred indictment.** Another term for a direct indictment.

**preliminary inquiry.** A hearing conducted in accordance with Part XVIII of the *Criminal Code*, before an accused is placed on trial for an indictable offence. An accused will either be committed for trial or discharged at the end of the preliminary inquiry. Originally, a preliminary inquiry was presumptively required in the case of all indictable offences (although it could be waived), but in its current form, the preliminary inquiry is held on request, will usually be restricted to particular issues, and is only available for offences punishable by fourteen years imprisonment or more.

***prima facie* case.** The presentation of evidence which, if believed, would establish each of the elements necessary for the prosecution to succeed. In assessing whether a *prima facie* case is made out, a judge does not ask whether the evidence is likely to be believed; merely whether, if it were, would it establish the necessary things.

**private prosecution.** A criminal charge laid and pursued by a private individual.

**production.** The right of a person accused of a criminal offence to be provided, in some cases, with information in the hands of third parties but not in the hands of the Crown.

**promise to appear.** Formerly, a written promise to attend court at a particular place and time, and a potential basis upon which **bail** could be granted. As of 2019, promises to appear were removed from the *Criminal Code*, though the same goals are still achieved through either an **appearance notice** or a **release order**.

**prosecutor.** The person who carries forward criminal proceedings. In public prosecutions, the prosecutor will be the **attorney general**, and in private prosecutions, the prosecutor will be the person laying the charge. In either case, the term includes counsel acting on behalf of the prosecutor, and in the case of a private prosecution for a summary conviction offence, it will also include an agent acting for the person who laid the charge.

**prosecutorial discretion.** The constitutional principle that the attorney general and Crown prosecutors are entitled to act independently in making prosecutorial decisions and that decisions made as part of that discretion are not reviewable by courts, short of an **abuse of process**. Core elements of prosecutorial discretion include the discretion to continue or stay a prosecution, to accept a guilty plea to a lesser charge, and to take control of a **private prosecution**.

**psychological detention.** The term used to describe forms of detention other than physically taking control of the person. Originally the Supreme Court restricted this term to situations where a person was not required by law to comply with the demands of a peace officer, but reasonably believes they have no choice but to comply. Subsequently, the Court has used the phrase to include that situation, but also to include situations where the person is in fact required to comply with the demand, such as a breathalyzer stop.

**public prosecution.** A criminal charge laid and pursued on behalf of the state by a Crown prosecutor.

**publication ban.** A court order requiring that evidence from a preliminary inquiry, trial, or other proceeding not be reported publicly. Publication bans can be either mandatory or discretionary.

**quash.** To set aside a decision (such as discharging an accused at a preliminary inquiry or issuing a search warrant) so that it no longer has effect.

**racial profiling.** Any action taken by one or more person in authority with respect to a person or group of persons, for reasons of safety, security, or public order, that is based on actual or presumed membership in a group defined by race, colour, ethnic or national origin, or religion, without factual grounds or reasonable suspicion, that results in the person or group being exposed to differential treatment or scrutiny. Racial profiling also includes any action by a person in a situation of authority who applies a measure in a disproportionate way to certain segments of the population on the basis, in particular, of their racial, ethnic, national, or religious background, whether actual or presumed. (See *Quebec (Commission des droits de la personne et des droits de la jeunesse) v Bombardier Inc (Bombardier Aerospace Training Center)*, 2015 SCC 39.)

**reasonable belief (reasonable grounds to believe).** The standard required to authorize many police powers, such as obtaining a **search warrant** or **arresting** a person without a warrant. Reasonable belief as a standard to arrest requires that the arresting officer *subjectively* believe that the suspect has committed the offence and that *objectively* a reasonable person would reach the same conclusion. Reasonable grounds do not require as much evidence as a ***prima facie* case**, but set a higher standard than reasonable suspicion.

**reasonable expectation of privacy.** The amount of privacy that a person is entitled to expect in a free and democratic society. Privacy consists of at least personal, territorial, and informational privacy.

**reasonable suspicion (reasonable grounds to suspect).** A standard authorizing some police investigative techniques, such as an **investigative detention**. Reasonable suspicion is a lower standard than **reasonable belief**, but must be more than a mere hunch and must exist both subjectively and objectively. It deals with the possibility, rather than the probability, of crime.

**recognizance.** A written acknowledgment under the *Criminal Code* of the responsibility for a debt, to be forfeited upon failure to comply with the terms of the recognizance. A recognizance is used in connection with a **peace bond** or in similar situations where a person is undertaking to comply with conditions in order to be released: see, for example, section 83.3 dealing with the prevention of terrorist activity. Recognizances were formerly a basis upon which **bail** could be granted, but the term now used in that context is **release order**.

**release order.** An order under section 515 of the *Criminal Code* allowing a person to be released from custody pending trial, either with or without conditions.

**reverse onus.** A statutory provision requiring that the accused be responsible for providing evidence on some relevant point, either to raise a doubt about whether the point is true or to show on balance of probabilities that it is not true.

**search.** Any investigative technique that infringes on a person's reasonable expectation of privacy. A search conducted without a warrant is *prima facie* a violation of the right in section 8 of the *Charter* to be free from unreasonable search and seizure.

**search incident to arrest.** The power of a police officer to **search** a person who has been **arrested**. The arrest must have been lawful; the search must be for some purpose related to that arrest and must be conducted reasonably. No separate reasonable grounds are necessary to conduct the search, which is justified if the arrest itself was lawful.

**search incident to investigative detention.** The power of a police officer to search a person who is subject to an **investigative detention**. The power arises only when there are separate reasonable grounds to believe that the safety of the police officer or others is at risk. The search power is initially limited to a pat-down search.

**search warrant.** A warrant issued under section 487 of the *Criminal Code* authorizing the bearer to search a building, receptacle, or place and seize evidence or other specified items.

**severance.** A judicial decision not to try more than one accused, or more than one count, on the same information.

**show cause hearing.** A term sometimes used to describe a **bail** hearing, on the basis that the **prosecutor** is required to "show cause" why the accused should not be released.

**solicitor–client privilege.** The rule that communications made in confidence between a solicitor and client cannot be compelled to be disclosed. The privilege rests with the accused, and a lawyer is not allowed to reveal the content of the communications without the consent of the client. An exception to solicitor–client privilege arises with the **innocence at stake exception**.

**stand aside**. See **stand by**.

**stand by**. Under section 633 of the *Code*, if a member of a jury array requests an exemption from serving on the jury, rather than granting the exemption the judge can instead require that juror to "stand by." The effect is that, although names for jury selection are generally selected randomly, the name of the juror who was instructed to stand by will be left until all other members of the jury array have been called. As a result, the juror's name might never be considered. If the juror's name is reached, the judge will decide at that point whether to grant the exemption. Also often referred to as the power to "**stand aside**."

**stay of proceedings**. An order preventing, either temporarily or permanently, any further action on a prosecution. Crown prosecutors have a power under the *Criminal Code* to temporarily stay proceedings for a period not exceeding one year (see sections 579 and 579.1(2) of the *Code*), and judges can permanently stay proceedings as a remedy for a *Charter* breach.

**street check**. Common term covering a number of activities on the part of the police, ranging from noting down observations they make about individuals on the street and retaining the information in a central database, to **carding**. See **racial profiling**.

**strip search**. The removal or rearrangement of the clothing of a person to permit a visual inspection of a person's private areas, namely genitals, buttocks, and breasts (in the case of a woman), or undergarments. Additional requirements must be met before a strip search is allowed as a **search incident to arrest**.

**summary conviction offence**. A generally less serious category of offences that carry less severe penalties (by default, a maximum of two years less a day imprisonment) and that cannot be prosecuted more than twelve months after the date of the offence. Summary conviction offences are tried on an **information** and the trial necessarily takes place in front of a provincial court judge.

**summons**. A written notice issued by a judge or justice in accordance with Form 6 of the *Criminal Code*, requiring the person to whom it is given to appear in court at the stated place and time.

**superior court of criminal jurisdiction**. A trial-level court hearing criminal matters, sometimes with a jury, and designated differently in various provinces and territories. See the definition in section 2 of the *Criminal Code*.

**surety.** A third party who agrees to forfeit a sum of money if the person for whom they stand surety fails to appear in court in accordance with the terms of a **release order**.

**talesman.** A person immediately summoned from the surrounding neighbourhood of a court for jury selection purposes by a sheriff, after a **jury array** has been exhausted without a complete **jury** having been selected.

**telewarrant.** A procedure authorized under section 487.1 of the *Criminal Code* allowing certain types of warrants to be obtained by means of telecommunication where it is impracticable for the peace officer to appear personally to make application.

**undertaking.** A written promise given by an accused person to appear in court at a stated place and time and to comply with other conditions. The contents of an undertaking are set out in section 501 of the *Code*.

**unreasonable verdict.** A **verdict** that a properly instructed **jury**, acting judicially, could not have rendered. This standard will be met in the case of a jury when the verdict cannot be supported on the evidence, and also in the case of a trial by judge alone, when the reasons are illogical or irrational even if the verdict could be supported on the evidence.

**verdict.** Strictly, a decision rendered by a **jury**, as opposed to a decision rendered by a judge, which is a **judgment**: see, for example, section 676(1)(a), dealing with an appeal against "a judgment or verdict of acquittal." The distinction is not always made in the *Code*: see, for example, section 672.27.

**warrant.** A judicial authorization given to peace officers, empowering them to perform particular actions, such as to search a location or arrest a person.

***Waterfield* test.** See **ancillary powers doctrine**.

# TABLE OF CASES

# INDEX

# ABOUT THE AUTHOR

**Steve Coughlan** is a professor of law at the Schulich School of Law, Dalhousie University in Halifax, where he has taught since 1991. His areas of teaching have included criminal law and procedure, constitutional law, health law, and appellate advocacy. Professor Coughlan has received teaching awards at the faculty, university, and regional levels, including the Dalhousie Law School Teaching Excellence Award, the Hannah and Harold Barnett Award for Excellence in Teaching First Year Law, the Dalhousie University Alumni Association Award of Excellence for Teaching, and the Association of Atlantic Universities Distinguished Teacher Award.

Professor Coughlan is the editor-in-chief of the *Criminal Reports* and the lead editor of the National Judicial Institute Criminal Law e-Letter. He is one of the authors of the Carswell *Annual Review of Criminal Law* (2004 to present), of *Learning Canadian Criminal Law* (10th through 16th editions), of *Learning Canadian Criminal Procedure* (15th edition), of *Law Beyond Borders*, and of *Detention and Arrest*, among other books. In 2019 he was named by *Canadian Lawyer* magazine as one of the Top 25 Most Influential Lawyers in Canada.